KENNY-COLWELL

History of an Early Texas Family

Written by Mary Jo Kenny

Inspired Forever Books

Dallas, Texas

Inspired Forever Books
Dallas, Texas
(888) 403-2727
https://inspiredforeverbooks.com
Words with Lasting Impact

Library of Congress Control Number: 2024903115

ISBN 13: 978-1-948903-80-6

Printed in the United States of America

TABLE OF CONTENTS

Acknowledgments..1

Introduction..3

Chapter 1: Eliza Jane Colwell and William Curry Kenny 5

    The Colwells Come to Texas...5

    Dr. William Curry Kenny Comes to Tennessee Colony 10

Chapter 2: Descendants of Eliza Jane and William Curry Kenny 19

    James Polk Kenny..19

    Mary Ophelia Kenny 24

    Descendants of Mary Ophelia Kenny and Jeff Kersey 26

        Berta (Mary) Kersey 26

        Lawrence Kersey...27

        Adelia Rowena Kersey..27

        Sam H. Kersey 29

        William Duncan Kersey 30

        Clarence Ray Kersey 32

    Martha Adelia Kenny 40

    Descendants of Martha Adelia Kenny and Pinckney Scarborough..............41

        Verna Florence Scarborough 41

        Katherine Judson "Katie" Scarborough...............................44

Descendants of Martha Adelia Kenny and John Irvin Wofford.....................................50

   Eula May Wofford 50

   Ocie Melinda Wofford 52

   Jettie Belle Wofford 54

   Hattie Lou Wofford..55

   Edna Earl Wofford...56

   William Bryan Wofford 57

Stepchildren of Martha Adelia Kenny..59

   Maude Levonia Wofford 59

   Jessie Lafayette Wofford 60

   Irvin Larkin Wofford 60

   William Alexander Wofford 60

Ocie Anna Kenny...70

Descendants of Ocie Anna Kenny and Edward Harper Seagler......................................72

   Edward Harper Seagler Jr. 72

Descendants of Ocie Anna Kenny and William Towers Collins.....................................72

   Ruby Towers Collins..72

   Henry Lucien Collins 78

   Jackie Mae Collins..81

   Odie Warren Collins...85

   Robert Bruce Collins 86

Stepchildren of Ocie Anna Kenny..89

   Mary Ethna Collins..89

   Willie Laverne Collins..89

   Lola Helen Collins..89

William Colwell Kenny 105

Descendants of William Colwell Kenny and Fannie Kenny..114

   Meta Empress Kenny 114

   Roy Clifton Kenny 122

   Eunice Lucille Kenny 128

   Lalla Rookh Kenny 146

Billie (or Willi) Leona Kenny 149

Jack Kenny 155

Mary Maurine Kenny 187

Florence Belle Kenny 203

Descendants of Florence Belle Kenny and Henry Thornton 204

Clytie C. Thornton 204

Odie Thurman Thornton 204

Henry Clayton Thornton 209

Annah Allyne Thornton 218

Robert Thomas Thornton 220

Minnie Lee Thornton 222

Vera Fern Thornton 223

Wylie Garland Thornton 223

Kathryn Judson "Kate" Kenny 235

Stepchildren of Kathryn Judson "Kate" Kenny 236

Claude James Clark 236

Elvis Lee Clark 237

Rybert (Rupert) Kyle Clark 237

Jackie May Kenny 239

Descendants of Jackie May and William Thornton 240

Minnie Orena Thornton 240

Clive Thornton 240

Daniel Raymond Thornton 241

Chapter 3: Kenny Family Background 247

Alexander Kenny 249

Descendants of James and Mary Kenny 253

Margaret Ann "Peggy" Kenny 253

Elizabeth "Eliza" Morehouse Kenny 258

William Curry Kenny 268

Isabella Kenny 268

Jane Kenny 271

Descendants of Mary and George Wade 277

    Lawrence Thompson Wade 277

    Henry R. Wade 279

    James Taylor Wade 280

    Mary Fleming Wade 282

Chapter 4: The Colwell Family 307

    Wiley F. Colwell 309

    Lemuel Colwell 332

    William Colwell 323

    Allie Colwell 323

    Matthew Colwell 329

    Andrew Jackson Colwell 339

    Susan Colwell 343

    Martha Colwell 347

    Caroline Elizabeth Colwell 347

    George Colwell 354

Appendix A 365

Appendix B 367

Appendix C 369

Appendix D 371

    Family Background of William Colwell of Oglethorpe County, Georgia 371

    Children and Grandchildren of William Barnes Colwell and Mary Cartwright 372

ACKNOWLEDGMENTS

Many people contributed to the information in this book. My sister, Sue Weathers, helped develop the first draft into a manuscript with increased clarity and reduced errors. Many family members provided family stories. These include Sue Weathers, Raymond Kenny, Robert Kenny, Betty Russell Thompson, Irene Crow Rampley, Greg and Marilyn Rampley, R. C. Kenny, Jeanette Kenny Lorenz, Louise Russell Stallings, Ron Richards, Leona Kenny Davis, Patrick Kneer, Dan Kenny, Jon Kenny, and Maurine Kenny Davis.

My efforts to find distant family members whom I did not know personally resulted in many valuable contacts. These include Bonnie Wolverton, Mary Jane Kersey Granum, Sandra McGeorge, Louise Collins Massey, Charles and Mary P. Edwards, Joy Collins Edwards, Alban Bridges, Garland Thornton, Ruth Ann Thornton Rosenthal, Stacy McAdams, Maude Ann Gilmore, Carol J. Hull, and Ruth Morris Canterbury.

My computer-use problems were solved by my friend Clark Easter.

My sincere thanks to all those who provided information and to the many others who provided encouragement.

INTRODUCTION

From childhood, I was interested in stories about the past and present as told at family gatherings. Three of my grandparents had died by the time I was seven years old, and I often wondered about the family stories they could have told. The fourth grandparent, Frances Leona Clark Kenny, was a good source for family stories. While I was in high school, I would sometimes spend the night with her so I could attend after-school events. On these occasions, as well as other times, she would talk about events of her childhood, events from her children's adolescence, and family stories she had been told. This helped me develop an interest in the people and events that made up my family background.

As an adult, I had access to a local branch of the LDS FamilySearch Library. My friend Shirley Larson was also interested in her family background, and we developed a pattern of going to the library on Friday evenings. We also spent some vacation time at the main LDS FamilySearch Library in Salt Lake City and traveled to areas where our ancestors had lived to research data in local cemeteries, libraries, and courthouses. We also attended regional and national genealogy society meetings to improve our research skills.

By the year 2000, I had collected considerable data. I decided I should put it in a form that could be shared by others curious about the family history. I decided to do a family history, which would include family stories as well as genealogical data. Concentrating first on the paternal side of the family, I began by requesting stories from distant family I had never known through identifying and contacting contributors to local history publications and members of local genealogy groups. I was able to find several people willing to share information, as shown in the list of contributors.

CHAPTER 1:
Eliza Jane Colwell and William Curry Kenny

The Colwells Come to Texas

Eliza Jane was not a native Texan, but she came to the area as a child too young to have much memory of having lived elsewhere. She was born August 1, 1830, in Hardeman County, Tennessee, the second child of Wiley Colwell and Elizabeth Keziah "Kizzie" Hanks. Her parents had gotten married in Hardeman County on May 11, 1827. She had an older brother, William Thomas. Prior to the trip to Texas, two younger sisters, Mary Ann and Cynthia C., were added to the family.

Hardeman County, Tennessee, was a frontier area. It had been opened to white settlers around 1820, after a treaty with the Chickasaw Indians was signed in 1818. Settlement had been rapid, with courts being established by 1823. At about the same time, roads had been built, towns had been created, and stage connections had been established to neighboring areas. By the 1830 census, the county population had reached 11,655.

Eliza Jane was about four years old when the Colwell family made the trip from the increasingly civilized Hardeman County to the wilderness of the Mexican state of Tejas. It is not known what prompted them to make the move, but the opportunity for inexpensive land was likely an important consideration. Immigration to Texas was actively promoted by several *empresarios* citing the availability of rich farmland and abundance of water. Anglo-Americans had been moving into Mexican territory, including Texas, for several decades. The rate of such immigration dramatically increased after Moses Austin was granted land for a colony in 1820. This was followed by other grants for Anglo colonies and an influx of Anglo colonists, as well as others who settled on land without bothering with formal acquisition. By 1835 there was much dissatisfaction among the Anglo colonists with the Mexican government and an increasing desire to break away from Mexico and join the United States. It is not known whether the Colwell family was aware of this unrest when they decided to make the journey.

The trip to Texas was probably undertaken early in the year 1835 as a part of a wagon train. They arrived in the area that was to become Angelina County by late spring or early summer. By 1835 a number of roads had been cut through the wilderness, largely replacing the Natchez Trace, which had been the only overland route available from Tennessee to Mississippi and Louisiana earlier in the century. These new roads carried a considerable number of travelers from Tennessee to Louisiana and Texas. Since Hardeman County is west of the Natchez Trace, it is likely that the Colwells used one of the more recently constructed roads. From the Texas border, the Old Spanish Road took them to the town of Nacogdoches, where applications could be made for land. It is not known how many families made the trip with the Colwell family, but there were likely several since such a trip was considered too dangerous for a small number of travelers. Probably among those making the trip with Eliza Jane's family were her grandparents, William and Mary Colwell, and their other children, William, Lemuel, Allie, Matthew, Jackson, Susan, Martha, Caroline, and George.

The trip was long, probably about three months. It may have seemed endless to a four-year-old, but it was good to have the older aunts and uncles to share the childcare with her parents, and the younger ones to be playmates. Even children as young as four would have walked a considerable portion of the distance, though they were not expected to walk as much as older children.

Their destination was in the Mexican Department of Nacogdoches, a vast area of East Texas extending from a few miles east of the Brazos River to the Sabine River, and from the Gulf Coast to the Red River. There were few towns in the entire department. The historic Mexican town of Nacogdoches was the site of most of the legal activities, including applications for land grants. Nacogdoches was built on the site of a Hasinai Caddo Indian village. The Indians had cleared land for garden plots and had planted orchards of peaches, plums, and chestnut trees. A Spanish mission and fort near the Indian village had been established in 1716, abandoned, and reestablished in 1721. A single priest and a small contingent of soldiers had maintained a Spanish presence at the location until 1772, when the Spanish king ordered the dismantling of the fort and mission and commanded the settlers be removed to San Antonio. A few settlers had defied the orders and remained in the area. They had provided a nucleus for later settlement. Few Spanish settlers had come to the area prior to 1779, at which time a twenty-year growth period began. By 1835, the Spanish, now Mexicans, who had settled the town had become a minority due to an influx of settlers from the United States; however, Mexican officials were still in control of legal activities.

The primary official of the district was the alcalde, who processed land applications and had the charge of maintaining order in the municipality. Eliza Jane's grandfather, William Colwell, applied for land in July 1835, and her father, Wiley, and her uncle William applied in September 1835. Those receiving Mexican land grants were expected to take an oath of citizenship to Mexico and declare themselves adherents of the Catholic Church. The latter was a formality for the Colwells since the only Catholic church in Nacogdoches was abandoned in 1835. No Catholic services were held again until 1847.

The senior William Colwell family was enumerated in the 1835 Mexican census for Texas. The Wiley Colwell family has not been found on that census. The reason for this discrepancy is not known.

The area where the Colwells settled, near the current town of Zavalla, had a gently rolling terrain and was heavily forested with longleaf, shortleaf, loblolly, and slash pine as well as gum, magnolia, elm, hickory, and oak trees. There were a few log cabins, whose occupants opened their homes to the newcomers. There was some open land, where it was said the Indians had grown crops. The Hasinai Indians, who had occupied the area since about the fourteenth century, had been greatly reduced in numbers by 1835. Many had died of disease during the Spanish and French periods, and others had moved westward in response to the intrusion of white settlers.

Although most of the Indians native to the area had moved westward by 1835, fear of Indian attack was constant on the Texas frontier. Stories of Indian encounters were handed down in family lore. According to one story, Kizzie Hanks Colwell was awakened early one morning by one of the younger children giggling. The child was interacting with an Indian by reaching a hand through the spaces between the unchinked logs of the cabin. A more frightening experience occurred when an apparently drunk Indian grabbed Kizzie's infant and threatened to bash it against a tree. Kizzie did not panic but calmly approached the Indian, smiling encouragingly. Eventually, he released the baby and disappeared into the woods. Family lore did not reveal which of Eliza Jane's younger siblings was the baby involved.

One of the first tasks the new settlers faced was to build cabins. The dwellings were constructed of logs; many were one room with a dirt floor. Some had two rooms under the same roof, with an open space between the rooms. The door to each room opened into the space between. The covered area provided a cool workplace during the summer, as well as a space to store items and a place for the dogs—thus the name, dogtrot house. All cabins contained a large fireplace made of mud or stone, which served for both heating and cooking. Cooking utensils were mostly cast-iron pots and Dutch ovens. Most of the furniture was homemade and usually crude unless someone in the family was skilled in woodworking. Simple tables, chairs, benches, and storage shelves were found in most homes. Rope was stretched across simple bed frames to hold mattresses filled with cotton, feathers, or sometimes straw. No description of the Colwells' first cabin has been handed down, but it was likely similar to those described here.

The settlers were dependent on the local ecosystem for food. Deer and wild turkey were abundant and were important sources of meat. Corn was grown on most farms and was ground into meal for corn bread, the most common bread. Potatoes, sweet potatoes, beans, and garden vegetables were important food sources after gardens were established. Some settlers brought dairy cattle and chickens, which provided additional food.

Eliza Jane told her grandchildren about a time when the cabins were under construction. Their cabin had finished walls, a roof, and a partially completed loft, but it had no doors or windows. Until the cabin was completed, the Colwell family shared the cabin of a family of earlier settlers. Several of the children fell sick, but Eliza Jane and her brother had not contracted the illness. Her mother had Eliza Jane and her brother sleep in the loft of the partially completed cabin to protect them from contracting the illness. During the night, she and her brother heard a large animal moving around in the cabin below them. Convinced that it was a panther, they were very quiet and still until it went away. They were relieved when their father put up temporary door and window coverings for them the next night.

Eliza Jane also told the story of her mother's encounter with a panther while riding a horse to a neighboring cabin. Suddenly a panther leaped from a tree. The horse saw the panther before Kizzie did, and leaped forward so that the panther's claws just grazed the rump of the horse. Fortunately, Kizzie was able to hang on as the horse ran from the danger.

The Colwells had scarcely gotten their cabins built and were settling in when there began to be talk about the Mexican Army heading toward Texas. Soon it became more than a rumor. Families passing through on their way back toward Louisiana related that the Mexicans had killed all the defenders of the Alamo. Many local families packed their belongings and joined the exodus to the safety of Louisiana; others organized the men into militias to repel the Mexicans. The women and children who did not flee felt vulnerable to Indian attacks if they remained in the settlements, so they followed the developing army. The Colwells were among those who followed the army. How many of the Colwell men fought as unofficial militia members with the Texas Army has not been established, but it is known that Lemuel Colwell was in that number. It was a hectic spring, filled with constant movement and fear of attack. When it was evident that victory was theirs at San Jacinto, Eliza Jane saw the defeated Santa Anna sitting under a tree—a story she relayed to her grandchildren.

Living in the independent Republic of Texas rather than in a part of Mexico had little effect on the everyday lives of the settlers. Governments were organized along lines familiar to the Anglo population; the Nacogdoches Department became Nacogdoches County, with a sheriff rather than an alcalde. Officials were elected, roads were established, and a judicial system was set up. While the elected officials negotiated to have Texas annexed to the United States, the settlers were busy with more immediate activities. Land was cleared; cabins were built or improved; crops were planted, cultivated, and harvested; gardens were planted; and communities were established. Fear of Indians persisted; reports of Indian attacks were not uncommon. Most of these attacks occurred near or west of the Brazos River. Under the presidency of Mirabeau B. Lamar, 1838–1842, an active campaign was established against the Indians to push all tribes, peaceful as well as hostile, to the west. The campaign was successful in opening most of East Texas to settlement.

Angelina County, a part of the old Nacogdoches Department, was organized on April 22, 1846, by an act of the Texas legislature. The county was named for an Indian girl who had befriended the early Spanish and French explorers in the area. It is the only Texas county named for a woman. The legislative act named John Bowman, Wiley Colwell, James A. Ewing, William Glang, Henry Massengill, and James McAnally to a commission charged with selecting a site for the county seat. The commission selected two sites, Moses Bluff and Dunagan. An election was held on February 3, 1847, for the voters in the county to make the final selection. The initial vote was disputed, and a second vote on April 3 selected Moses Bluff by a vote of thirty-seven to two. Moses Bluff was renamed Marion and became the first county seat. The first criminal trial, which occurred before the courthouse was built, was held under a tree. An individual was accused of stealing and butchering a hog. The ears of the hog were produced as evidence. By the time the jurors were approved and the trial got underway, it was discovered that dogs had eaten the evidence. A mistrial was declared.

Building roads and establishing ferry crossings were predominant concerns of early county officials. Eliza Jane's father, uncles, uncles-in-law, and neighbors were ordered to oversee or be participants in roadbuilding in areas near their farms. Her father, Wiley, along with others, was commissioned to develop a road from Dunagan and Dollarhide Cross to Thompson's Bluff under the oversight of John Stovall, husband of Eliza Jane's aunt Caroline.

On January 11, 1847, Wiley Colwell posted a bond of $500 as security for the position of justice of the peace. The records did not indicate how long he held that office.

Among the first marriages in the new Angelina County were those of Eliza Jane's uncle Mathew Colwell to Caroline Worden on September 11, 1846; her sister Mary Ann to John Anderson on April 10, 1848; and her uncle A. J. Colwell to Nancy H. Hughes on Feb 18, 1850.

Although the early Texas settlers were interested in education, few schools were available. In 1830 the legislature for the Mexican state of Coahuila y Tejas provided for the creation of elementary schools, but the law had not been implemented in the Nacogdoches District. Once Texas was established as a nation, the Texas Congress granted 17,712 acres of public land for the creation of public schools in each county. Despite the grant, the only public schools established in the tenure of the republic were in the town of Houston. Schools were not available during the early years of Angelina County. Eliza Jane and her siblings had little formal education. Wealthy families sent their children to boarding schools in the United States. Some of the towns had small private schools, but most education was left to the mothers.

Eliza Jane's mother tried to teach her children some reading and writing skills, but books were scarce, and there were many demands on Kizzie's time. However, Eliza Jane learned useful information about the plants and animals in the area—those to avoid and those that could be beneficial. She learned how to prepare the land for a garden, when and how to plant seeds, how to care for the garden, when plants should be harvested, how to store the harvest for winter, and how to select, prepare, and store seeds for next year's crop. She learned when to butcher hogs, how to cure the meat and render the lard, how to leach lye from wood ashes, and how to use lye with lard to make soap. Lessons included how to spin cotton and wool into thread; weave, knit, and sew it into clothing; piece quilt tops; cord cotton for batting; and make quilts for the beds. Candle making was among the skills she learned. Candles and fireplaces were the only sources of light for most homes. How to bank coals in the fireplace with ashes so they would be ready to use to build a fire the next morning and how to cook a variety of foods over the resulting fire were among her lessons. She learned to care for chickens, ducks, and geese and how to select the soft down feathers, clean them, and make them into pillows and feather beds. By helping care for her younger brothers and sisters and cousins, she became knowledgeable of the needs of children. Her education was made up of those things a woman needed to know to help her family survive on the frontier.

Little is known about how the Colwell family was affected by the annexation of Texas by the United States and the war with Mexico. A personal history by Maurine Kenny, written in 1924 as part of an assignment for a class at Tarleton College, indicated that William Curry Kenny first entered Texas as a captain in the US Army during the Mexican War and that he became acquainted with the Colwell family at that time. No confirmation of that story has been found.

In 1849 or early 1850, the Colwell family moved from Angelina County to Anderson County, where Eliza Jane's maternal grandparents, aunts, and uncles had settled. The Wiley Colwell family is shown on the 1850 census on a farm in Anderson County, with Eliza Jane's sister Mary Ann and her husband, John Anderson, on the adjoining farm.

Dr. William Curry Kenny Comes to Tennessee Colony

William Kenny was the first doctor in the community of Tennessee Colony. He arrived sometime after the 1850 census—no census data has been found for him for 1850. A widower, he had traveled from Louisiana with his young son and two female slaves. It is not known whether they arrived overland or by the relatively newly established boat traffic on the Trinity River.

William Curry Kenny was born on April 2, 1809, in South Carolina. Within two years of his birth, his family moved to Williamson County, Tennessee. His father, James Kenny, died soon after participating in the Battle of New Orleans in 1815. His mother, Mary, was executor of his father's estate. Mary Kenny married George Wade in 1817. The Wade family moved to Mississippi around 1831. It is assumed that William C. Kenny remained in Williamson County, Tennessee. There he married Elizabeth Oldham on September 4, 1838. The young couple moved to Caldwell Parish, Louisiana, where Elizabeth died in 1840. The 1840 census shows the William C. Kenny household with William, who was listed as a farmer, and a young male between the ages of sixteen and twenty. The younger male was probably one of William's young half brothers who came to be with him after the death of his wife.

It is not known when or how William Curry Kenny became a doctor. Since he was listed as a farmer in the 1840 census, he likely obtained his training to become a doctor between 1840 and 1850, when he made his appearance in Texas. Medical education in the mid-nineteenth century varied greatly in both nature and quality. A few universities had established academic-based medical curricula and included an association with large hospitals patterned after European medical schools. Other universities offered a series of lectures from highly qualified doctors but did not have a working relationship with a hospital. A growing number of proprietary schools offered medical training of much less rigorous quality. Few of the European models but a larger number of the other two forms of medical education existed in the states of Louisiana, Tennessee, and Mississippi before 1850. These are the probable sites for William's medical education.

In the early nineteenth century, there were no established and recognized standards for the practice of medicine. Many pioneer-area doctors gained their medical experience by working with an established physician in an apprentice relationship. The apprentices were usually young boys, but adult men were not excluded. Both William's brother-in-law Edward M. Long, in Mississippi, and his half brother James Taylor Wade, in Louisiana, were doctors. It is possible that William worked with one or both to gain or expand his medical knowledge.

A second marriage for William, probably in Louisiana, was to Sarah Colvin. They had one son, James Polk Kenny. Records of their marriage, Sarah's death, or James Polk's birth have not been found.

The dates on which William arrived in Tennessee Colony and established his medical practice have not been established. In May 1853, William purchased 320 acres of land on the waters of Spring Creek, near Tennessee Colony, from John Nix for $400. Though William was close to Eliza Jane's father in age, the new doctor was successful in courting her. They were married on July 12, 1853, in Anderson County. They made their home on the recently purchased land. Apparently, the title of the land was disputed. In 1856, William paid $320 to Charles Stewart for the same 320 acres, the land on which his family resided.

WILLIAM CURRY KENNY AND HIS WIFE ELIZA JANE COLWELL.

Not only was William the first doctor in Tennessee Colony, but the first cookstove and sewing machine in the community were owned by his family. Cooking was normally done over the fireplace, and sewing was done by hand.

William's medical office was located one and a half miles northeast of Tennessee Colony. By 1858, a second doctor, Dr. Cade, had also established a practice in Tennessee Colony.

On March 3, 1856, William was part of a group of Masons who met at James Hanks's store to draft an application for the charter of a Masonic lodge in Tennessee Colony. The Tyre Lodge 198 at Tennessee Colony was chartered in January 1857. Members of the lodge joined with other community members to build a two-story building. The lodge used the second floor; the first floor was used as a church and school. The building was completed in 1860 and was the school attended by the Kenny children.

As shown in the 1860 census, the Kenny family consisted of William, Eliza Jane, and their children, James P., Ophelia, and Adelia. They lived adjacent to the family of Eliza Jane's sister Mary Ann; her husband, John Anderson; and their children. William is listed as a doctor and John Anderson as a farmer.

Anderson County was not immune to the political turmoil surrounding the issues of slavery and states' rights. During the spring of 1860, a well-publicized event in Palestine, the county seat of Anderson County, was a public book burning. Books promoting abolition, or even mildly critical of the institution of slavery, were collected and burned. Some people in Tennessee Colony participated in the burning, and others who did not participate condoned the action. Still others considered the burning of books to be a disgraceful act, an affront to educated people and a suppression of ideas and thought. Books had little interest to Eliza Jane, a result of the lack of school facilities during her childhood; therefore, she probably had little concern that books were burned. William had grown up with books and had more education than most people of his generation. He was likely among those who condemned the book burning.

The summer of 1860 was very hot, as well as politically unsettled. When a series of fires consumed parts of some northeastern Texas towns, rumors began to fly. Primary among the rumors was that the fires were started by slaves as a part of a slave uprising. Many feared a general slave revolt. This fear led to the killing of several innocent slaves in parts of the state. A split in the party during the Democratic Party Convention resulted in two nominees for president and produced much political interest and discussion. The autumn of 1860 was filled with more political talk than usual in Anderson County. The candidacy of Abraham Lincoln for president was stirring up more than a little controversy. A frequently expressed opinion was that the election of Lincoln would result in intolerable changes in the country.

Kizzie Hanks Colwell had another story to tell her daughter. She was convinced that the candidate, Lincoln, was the son of her father's cousin Nancy Hanks. Nancy had been dead for many years, but she had married a person named Lincoln. Kizzie was sure Nancy's son was named Abraham. Other Hanks family members concurred, but discussion of this relationship to Lincoln remained entirely within the family. Children of that decade and several following decades were cautioned not to mention the relationship outside the family. Local sympathies were so strongly against Lincoln that even a distant cousinship would not have been well received.

When Lincoln was elected in November, without votes from Texas and other Southern states where he did not appear on the ballot, the political discussion accelerated to dominate almost all public discourse. As various Southern states called conventions to consider secession from the union, a strong movement developed to request such a convention for Texas. Governor Sam Houston was a strong opponent of secession and refused to cooperate with the call for a secession convention. Under intense political pressure, he did call a special session of the Texas legislature, which determined there should be a referendum vote on secession.

On February 23, 1861, Anderson County joined most Texas counties in voting for secession, with 870 votes in favor and fifteen against. There was much speculation on the identity of the fifteen who were against, but their identities were never revealed. William C. Kenny was reported to have high regard for Sam Houston, but it is not known whether this regard was extended to agreement on the issue of secession. Eliza Jane learned from her Colwell relatives that Angelina County had opposed secession, with 184 votes against and 139 for secession.

There were many slaves in Anderson County prior to the Civil War. The book *History of Anderson County* states that the value of the slaves exceeded the combined value of land, horses, and cattle in the county. Among the slaveholders was the Kenny family. The 1860 census slave schedule shows two adult women, both age thirty-two, two teenage boys, and twelve children ranging in age from one to eleven. The slave owner is listed as W. C. Kenny, but probably some or all of the slaves actually belonged to his son, James Polk Kenny. The thirteen-year-old is listed as owning property valued at $5,000, while W. C. Kenny is listed as owning real estate valued at $1,200 and personal property valued at $5,169. The slaves may have been James's inheritance from his mother.

War fever ran high in the county after the vote for secession. The Anderson County newspaper, the *Trinity Advocate*, carried articles on how to go to war but none on how to prevent war. Soon military units were organized and dispatched to fight for the Confederacy. Among those enlisting was Eliza Jane's brother, Wiley Colwell Jr. A rousing send-off was given to the units as they left for the war. Word of what was happening to the units as the war progressed was slow in arriving. It was months before they learned that Wiley Colwell Jr. had been captured during his unit's first encounter with enemy forces in the Battle of Little Rock and that he had died not long after being taken prisoner.

The war years were years of anxiety and hardship, though Texas experienced fewer hardships than other Confederate states. The battles were not within Texas, and crops were good. There were no food shortages. Both his age and the need for a doctor in the community kept William C. Kenny at home during the conflict as the war progressed and a draft was initiated applying to all males between the ages of seventeen and fifty. Travel restrictions were put in place. William, as well as all local lawyers and merchants, required a permit from the presiding military officer to leave the county for any purpose.

The Reconstruction years of 1865 through 1874 were described as chaotic. About one-fourth of those who went to war did not return, and those who did return were often bitter and disheartened. Some were disabled. They returned to economic disaster. State and county officials were removed from office and were barred from holding office, voting, or being active in many civic areas. Martial law was established, and military tribunals replaced civil courts. The military rule lasted seven years. Many officials coming to Texas to implement the US Congress's mandates on Reconstruction, especially those seeking positions of power, appeared to be more interested in punishing former Confederates than aiding former slaves to make the transition to freedom. The Reconstruction officials seeking implementation of Lincoln's guidelines for transition often met rejection from the local population. Prior to the Civil War, most people in Anderson County felt contempt for anyone who mistreated his or her slaves. Conditions of the war and Reconstruction caused widespread anger, and that anger became directed toward black people. The former slaves, not the institution of slavery, were considered the cause of economic instability. By the mid-1870s, people condoned or ignored the emergence of the Ku Klux Klan and its practice of intimidation, abuse, and murder. The Klan became strong in Anderson County.

By 1870, the Kenny family had expanded to include Ocie, Will, Florence, and Kate. William is still listed as a physician, but with a personal property value of only $1,266. By census time, the older daughter, Ophelia, had married and had her own home. Mary Ann and John Anderson were no longer enumerated adjacent to William and Eliza Jane. William and Eliza Jane's youngest daughter, Jackie, was born in December 1971.

The 1870s were a time of both economic turmoil and economic growth for Anderson County. In 1871, William joined J. W. Stafford and James Hoyle in purchasing ten lots in Tennessee Colony, most from the estate of the late John Wolverton Jr. Their intended use of the lots is not known. The railroad was big news for the county. In 1872 a bond election approved the issuance of $150,000 in bonds to secure railroad expansion into the county. Shortly thereafter, the railroad began construction through the county.

New problems began to plague the Kenny family. Son-in-law Jeff Kersey, married to Ophelia, was charged with selling liquor without a license and other liquor law violations. A subsequent group of lawsuits involved not only the Kerseys but also William and Eliza Jane. The property on which they resided was listed as guarantee in a suit, and when the suit was decided against them, William signed over his property to the sheriff of Anderson County. Shortly afterward, the family moved to Erath County. The Kenny family was one of many moving westward during the 1870s. Census data shows the population of Erath County as 1,801 in 1870 and 11,796 in 1880.

The 1880 census shows W. C. Kenny operating a farm adjacent to James Polk Kenny. W. C.'s occupation is listed as farmer, not physician, so it is assumed that he was no longer practicing medicine as his primary occupation. The five younger children—Ocie, Will, Florence, Kate, and Jackie—are listed in the family; both Ophelia and Adelia had married and established their own homes.

Erath County remained home to William and Eliza Jane until their deaths. The size of the family expanded temporarily in the fall of 1883, when the deaths of Adelia's and Ocie's husbands brought the two daughters and their children to the family home for a period. Gradually, all the children left to establish their own homes, except for Kate, who left home to become a teacher.

William Curry Kenny died on December 22, 1894. According to family oral history, as told by Leona Kenny Davis, he and Eliza Jane had walked to the nearby Thornton farm to visit with their daughter and her family. While walking home near dusk, William stumbled over a cultivator wheel lying in the grass, fell, and broke his leg. During his recuperation from the broken leg, a blood clot formed, causing instant death. He was buried in Hannibal Cemetery, Erath County.

After her husband's death, Eliza Jane closed her home and turned the operation of the farm over to her children living nearby. During her remaining years, she lived with her children, staying a few months at a time with each. She has not been located on the 1900 census. Eliza Jane died in February of 1910. The place and cause of her death are not known. A photograph of Eliza Jane and her children, taken in 1909 or early 1910, shows her looking very frail. She was buried in Hannibal Cemetery by her husband.

SOURCES

1850 US Census, Anderson County, Texas. FHLC #0024887, LDS FamilySearch Library, Salt Lake City, UT.

A Memorial and Biographical History of Navarro, Henderson, Anderson, Limestone, Freestone and Leon Counties, Texas. Chicago, IL: The Lewis Publishing Company, 1893. FHLC #0982474, item 8, FamilySearch Library, Salt Lake City, UT.

Advertisement. *Trinity Advocate*, July 7, 1858. Microfilm at Palestine Public Library. Transcript provided by Bonnie Wolverton.

Biesele, Megan. "Angelina County." Texas State Historical Association. Updated September 29, 2020.

Bowman, Bob, ed. *Land of the Little Angel: A History of Angelina County, Texas.* Lufkin, TX: Lufkin Printing Company, 1976. Angelina County Historical Survey Committee.

Buenger, Walter L. "Secession." *Handbook of Texas.* Texas State Historical Association. Updated February 24, 2021.

Ericson, Joe E. *Early East Texas: A History from Indian Settlements to Statehood.* Bowie, MD: Heritage Books Inc., 2002.

Ericson, Joe E. *The Nacogdoches Story: An Informal History.* Bowie, MD: Heritage Books Inc., 2000.

Fehrenbach, T. R. *Lone Star: A History of Texas and the Texans.* NY: American Legacy Press, 1968.

Fehrenbach, T. R., A. Ray Stephens, and William M. Holmes. *Historical Atlas of Texas.* Norman, OK: University of Oklahoma Press, 1984.

Goodspeed, Edgar J. *The Goodspeed Histories of Fayette and Hardeman Counties of Tennessee.* 1887. Reprint, Columbia, TN: Woodward and Stinson Printing Co., 1973. FHLC #0924074, item 2, LDS FamilySearch Library, Salt Lake City, UT.

Hannibal Cemetery (2312 County Rd. 111, Erath County, TX). E. J. Kenny headstone.

Hannibal Cemetery (2312 County Rd. 111, Erath County, TX). W. C. Kenny headstone.

Hardeman County, Tennessee, Marriage Records. LDS FamilySearch Library, Salt Lake City, UT.

History Book Committee of Lufkin Genealogical and Historical Society, comps. *The History of Angelina County, Texas, 1846–1991.* Curtis Media Corporation, 1992. LDS FamilySearch Library, Salt Lake City, UT.

Hohes, Pauline Buck. *A Centennial History of Anderson County, Texas.* Tucson, AZ: Americana Unlimited, 1976. First published 1936 by Naylor Company (San Antonio, Texas).

"John C. Anderson." 1860 US Census, Anderson County, Texas, beat 10, Tennessee Colony PO, p. 78, dwelling 683, family 680. FHLC #0024881, LDS FamilySearch Library, Salt Lake City, UT.

"John Nix to William C. Kenny." *Anderson County, Texas, Deed Book D*, p. 671. Anderson County, Texas, Courthouse.

Johnson, Gladys Hanks. *Our Hanks Family.* Monograph, privately printed, 1965. Copy in possession of Mary Jo Kenny.

Jordan, L. T., and Kathryn Hooper Davis, Eds. *Ordered by the Court: Angelina County, Texas, County Commissioners Court Minutes 1846–1855.* FamilySearch Library, Salt Lake City, UT.

"Kenney, W." 1870 US Census, Anderson County, Texas, p. 47, dwelling 346, family 346. FHLC #002487, LDS FamilySearch Library, Salt Lake City, UT.

Kenny, Maurine. "My Life Story." Paper presented in partial completion of a course at Tarleton College. In possession of Mary Jo Kenny.

"Kenny, W. C." 1880 US Census, Erath County, Texas, Precinct 1, ED 149, p. 13, dwelling 196, family 196. LDS FamilySearch Library, Salt Lake City, UT.

Minutes of the Angelina County, Texas, County Commissioners Court 1846–1855. Copied exactly from original, including spellings, spacings, punctuation, and blanks, by Mrs. L. T. Jordan. Typed and indexed by Kathryn Hooper Davis. FamilySearch Library, Salt Lake City, UT.

Morgan, Ramona B. Harrison, comp. Angelina County, Texas, Marriage Records, 1846–1899. Lufkin, TX: Angelina County Genealogical Society, 1996.

Ransom, Robert G. "An Essay on Medical Education" in *The History of Medicine in Rutherford County, Tennessee*. Monograph. Rutherford County Historical Society. LDS FamilySearch Library, Salt Lake City, UT.

"The Tennessee Colony Story." *Palestine Herald Press*, October 2, 1970. Accessed at the Palestine Public Library, Palestine, TX.

Tolbert, Frank. *An Informal History of Texas*. NY: Harper & Brothers, 1961.

Wolverton, Bonnie. "A Brief History of Tennessee Colony Community" in *Tennessee Colony Cemetery, Tennessee Colony, Texas*. Second printing, February 1991. FamilySearch Library, Brookings, OR.

Wolverton, Bonnie. Letter to Mary Jo Kenny. September 9, 1996.

"W. C. Kenny." 1850 US Census, Anderson County, Texas, beat 10, Tennessee Colony PO, p. 78, dwelling 684, family 680. FHLC #0024881, LDS FamilySearch Library, Salt Lake City, UT.

"Wolverton, J. A. to W. C. Kinney, J. W. Stafford and James Hoyle." *Anderson County, Texas, Deed Book O*, p. 440. Anderson County Courthouse, Palestine, TX.

CHAPTER 2:

Descendants of Eliza Jane and William Curry Kenny

James Polk Kenny
(24 May 1847–21 Sep 1914)

SONS OF WILLIAM CURRY KENNY: WILLIAM C. (LEFT) JAMES POLK (RIGHT)

James Polk Kenny—son of Dr. William Curry Kenny and his second wife, Sarah Colvin—was born in Louisiana. Little is known about his mother. Records for the marriage of William Curry Kenny and Sarah Colvin or for the death of Sarah Colvin Kenny have not been located at the time of this writing. At the age of four or five, James relocated from Louisiana to Texas with his father, and he grew up in Anderson County, Texas. At the age of thirteen, he was living with the family in Tennessee Colony. He evidently had inherited property, possibly slaves, from his mother, since the 1860 census lists James as owning property worth $5,000, only $700 less than his father's personal property.

In March 1864, shortly before his seventeenth birthday, James enlisted in Company I, Seventh Texas Cavalry Regiment. He served with this unit until the end of the Civil War.

The only James Kenny found on the 1870 Texas census was twenty-four, living in Marion County, listed as a bookkeeper, and sharing a dwelling with Lewis Berry. Berry was listed as a twenty-eight-year-old male laborer born in Arkansas.

On December 14, 1875, James Polk Kenny purchased, from H. K. Zimmerman, an exemption claim to 160 acres of land on Barton Creek in Erath County, Texas. The patent to the 160 acres was granted to James by O. M. Roberts, governor of Texas, on May 13, 1879.

James's wife was Adella Belle (1857–1911). Her family name, the names of her parents, and where James and Adella were married are not known. Searches of marriage records from Anderson, Marion, and Erath Counties did not reveal their marriage.

James and Adella established a farm on the Barton Creek property, where they were joined by his father's family in 1879. The 1880 census shows the two families in adjacent dwellings, both engaged in farming. The agricultural schedule of 1880 shows J. P. Kenny owning 260 acres of land, with 40 acres being tilled and 220 acres in woodland. The farm was valued at $800, machinery and implements at $75, and livestock at $440. The livestock included thirteen dairy cows, eighteen other cows, seven calves, and seven horses. During 1880, crops worth $250, twenty-one swine, twenty-four poultry, and ninety-six dozen eggs had been sold.

The Erath County holdings of James were expanded with the purchase of an additional 99.5 acres on February 11, 1882, for the sum of $100, paid with two promissory notes to J. H. Hyman and W. R. Gordon for $50 each at 10 percent interest. On February 21, 1884, James bought a one-third interest in the undivided Drury Oldham survey from A. M. Bowers for $225. Ownership of one-third of total tract meant that he had one-third ownership of the entire property, but no specific portion.

In 1884, James sold holdings on Barton Creek and purchased land in Stephenville. The purchase included Lots 3 and 4 of Block 6. Lot 3 fronted both Washington and Columbia Streets and contained a livery stable. Included with the livery stable were six horses, three buggies with harnesses, and one hack (a horse rented out for a variety of uses) with a harness. The deed dated June 14, 1884, and recorded July 29, 1884, specified a purchase price of $2,418.75, with $1,618.75 paid in cash and three promissory notes of $266.66 each, due June 1, 1885; July 1, 1885; and January 1, 1886. The notes were payable to J. R. Long, seller of the property.

James and Adella were in the livery stable business for slightly over a year. They sold the lot containing the livery stable, two buggies with harnesses, and one hack with a harness for $1,500. The additional lot, the horses, and the remaining buggy with a harness were not included in this sale.

Activities of James and Adella from 1884 to 1901 are not known. In 1901, they moved to Dallas, Texas. James applied for a Confederate pension on February 13, 1906. In his application, he detailed his service in the Confederacy and stated that he had no property and that he was in ill health because of kidney problems, which limited his ability to work. Jeff Wood and O. D. Pace supplied supporting documentation for his military service. His application was approved on September 25, 1906.

The 1910 census shows James and Adella living on Kaufman Road in Dallas County, where James was a peddler of vegetables. Since all the other household heads on the same census page were truck farmers, it seems probable that James took some of his neighbors' produce into Dallas and sold it to grocery stores or door to door.

Adella died on July 31, 1911, at the age of fifty-four. At the time of her death, she had been a resident of Dallas for ten years and was residing on Second Avenue, the place of her death.

Dallas City Directories of 1912, 1913, and 1914 show James living on the northwest corner of Calvin Street and Second Avenue. His occupation during these years was listed as *huckster*. To contemporary minds, the term *huckster* conjures images of a snake oil salesman, or other less-than-honorable activities, but in the late nineteenth and early twentieth centuries, a huckster was a seller of small items. James died on September 21, 1914, at Parkland Hospital in Dallas at the age of sixty-seven. The cause of death was heart failure. He was buried in Lagow Cemetery adjacent to Adella. James and Adella had no children.

Lagow Cemetery has an interesting history. In 1883, Richard Lagow donated one acre of land to the people of School Precinct No. 62 for "burying ground" purposes. Over the next several years, several people were buried there. In 1889, this land became the object of a lawsuit by Sarah Milligan and others against Sidney Evans and others, in which it was charged:

> That the defendants, moved by a mercenary and avaricious desire to speculate over the graves of the buried dead, and to oppress and outrage the people of the community, determined by unhallowed means to oust them from the use of the graveyard. That they importuned the heirs to deed them the land and after repeated and unsuccessful efforts, finally induced a lady heir of the estate under false threats of subjecting her to the pains and penalties of the civil and criminal law, to give them a deed to the property for the paltry sum of $60.

The petition further recites:

> Since procuring the deed aforesaid, the defendants have, by use of threats and arms, attempted to eject the people who would visit the graves of their dead. The Plaintiff, Mrs. Sarah Milligan, whose husband lies buried there, attempted to visit his grave for the purpose of cleaning off and decorating it, and she was violently set upon by defendants and threatened and commanded not to go there and was prevented from doing so; that defendants are now desecrating said graveyard and are attempting to use same for worldly purposes, and are fencing and partitioning the same into smaller lots and that they are about to use a portion of it for a calf lot.

The suit was settled by Judge Burke in favor of the plaintiffs, and the land was restored to use as a cemetery.

Lagow Cemetery was not shown on any of several Dallas city maps consulted, but it can be found on Carpenter Street, separated from Second Street by a two-story brick building. Lagow Park occupies a site at the corner of Second and Carpenter Streets and is shown on Dallas city maps. A visit to the cemetery in July 2001 by me, Sue Weathers, and Dale Weathers revealed a plot generously shaded by mature post oak trees. It had been recently mowed, apparently with a tractor mower, and the metal gate had been recently removed, according to a nearby shopkeeper, leaving the cemetery open. Relatively few stones remained standing, but some that had fallen were still readable. The marker for Adella Belle Kenny was standing and gave her birth date as July 31, 1857, and her death date as July 31, 1911. The adjacent stone for James Polk Kenny had fallen but was still readable. It gave only the name J. P. Kenny and the dates 1847–1914.

SOURCES

"Erath County, Texas." *Deed Book F*, p. 62. County Courthouse, Stephenville, TX.

"Erath County, Texas." *Deed Book J*, p. 424. County Courthouse, Stephenville, TX.

"Erath County, Texas." *Deed Book O*, p. 359. County Courthouse, Stephenville, TX.

"Erath County, Texas." *Deed Book Q*, p. 517. County Courthouse, Stephenville, TX.

"Erath County, Texas." *Deed Book R*, p. 185. County Courthouse, Stephenville, TX.

"Erath County, Texas." *Deed Book W*, p. 24. County Courthouse, Stephenville, TX.

"Jim Wheat's Dallas County Texas Archives." http:freepages.history.rootsweb.com/~jwheat/index.html. Citing *Dallas Daily Times Herald*, August 17, 1889, p. 8, col. 1. Updated August 16, 2016.

"Kenny, James P." 1910 US Census, Dallas County, Texas, ED 19, Justice Precinct 27, enumerated April 23, 1910, dwelling 120, family 120. Ancestry.com, 2006.

"Kenny, James P." Confederate Pension Applications, 1899–1975. Application #11876. Ancestry.com, digital image from Texas State Library and Archives Commission, Austin, TX. Collection #CPA11868, roll #29, pension files #11868 to #11887.

"Kenny, James P." Dallas City Directories for 1912, 1913, and 1914. Genealogy Department, Dallas Public Library (1515 Young St., Dallas, TX).

"Kenny, James P." Dallas County Death Records. Genealogy Department, Dallas Public Library (1515 Young St., Dallas, TX).

"Kenny, J. P." 1880 US Census, Erath County, Texas, Agricultural Schedule. FamilySearch Library, Salt Lake City, UT.

"Kenny, J. P." 1880 US Census, Erath County, Texas, Precinct 1, ED 49, p. 13, dwelling 195, family 195. FamilySearch Library, Salt Lake City, UT.

"Kenny, J. P." Standard Certificate of Death. Texas State Board of Health, #18195. September 21, 1914.

"Kenny, J. P." Texas Death Certificates, 1903–1982. Ancestry.com, 2013.

"Kenny, Mrs. Belle." Texas Death Certificates, 1903–1982. Ancestry.com, 2013.

"Kenny, W. C." 1860 US Census, Anderson County, Texas, beat 10, Tennessee Colony PO, p. 24, dwelling 684, family 680. FHLC #0024881, FamilySearch Library, Salt Lake City, UT.

Lagow Cemetery (Carpenter St., Dallas, TX). Belle Kenny gravestone.

"Lewis, Benjamin." 1870 US Census, Marion County, Texas, ward 3, city of Jefferson, enumerated July 30, 1879, p. 32, dwelling 257, family 291. FamilySearch Library, Salt Lake City, UT.

TOP ROW FROM LEFT: OCIE ANNA KENNY COLLINS, DELIA KENNY WOFFORD,
WILLIAM COLWELL KENNY, JACKIE KENNY THORNTON, FLORENCE KENNY THORNTON.
BOTTOM ROW FROM LEFT: KATE KENNY CLARK, ELIZA JANE COLWELL KENNY, OPHELIA KENNY KERSEY.

Mary Ophelia Kenny
(1 Aug 1855–5 Sep 1928)

Mary Ophelia Kenny, called Ophelia by her family, was born in Tennessee Colony, Anderson County, Texas. The oldest child of William Curry Kenny and Eliza Jane Colwell, she grew up in Tennessee Colony and attended school there. Ophelia was very short of stature and had feet so tiny that her granddaughter Mary Jane could wear Ophelia's shoes as a preschooler.

On May 2, 1870, three months before her fifteenth birthday, Ophelia married Thomas Jefferson Kersey (11 Sep 1842–10 Mar 1913) of Tennessee Colony. Jeff Kersey was born in Alabama. He had lived in Nacogdoches and Navarro Counties before coming to Anderson County. He was a veteran of the Civil War, having served in the Twentieth Texas Infantry. Jeff and Ophelia made their home in Tennessee Colony and are shown on the 1870 census as operating a grocery store. Also in the household was Jane Alston, a black woman, age thirty, who was listed as a domestic servant.

Problems developed for Jeff within the first year of their marriage. In December 1870, Jeff was brought before the district court on six charges of selling liquor without a license.

When the cases came to trial, the court found in favor of Jeff on five of the charges but found him guilty on one charge. A fine of fifty dollars was assessed.

One can imagine a scenario in which the local grocers had always provided whiskey to their customers, and they didn't think the restrictive liquor laws applied (or should apply) to them. The whiskey may have been made by one of the locals, and perhaps Jeff felt he was doing everyone a favor by making it available in his grocery store. Both he and his customers may have felt that the license law infringed on their rights as veterans and frontiersmen. For whatever reason, the pattern of illegal selling of liquor persisted. In 1871, Jeff was charged with eleven additional bills of indictment, including selling liquor without a license, selling whiskey by the drink, and selling whiskey on Sunday. After numerous court appearances, the cases were settled on December 21, 1871, with five of the charges being dropped and Jeff pleading guilty to six charges. He was fined fifty dollars for each of the guilty charges.

A lawsuit, the nature of which was not revealed in the minutes, was filed against Jeff by E. P. Jameson, resulting in a finding for the plaintiff and the awarding of damages of $245.19 plus court costs on January 5, 1872. Jeff was named, along with W. C. Kenny and E. J. Kenny, in a lawsuit of unspecified nature brought by James Herald on December 8, 1875, and it continued beyond April 30, 1876. It is not known whether Jeff made a personal appearance at these hearings.

Ophelia and Jeff's first child, Berta, was born on September 20, 1873, probably in Anderson County but possibly after they moved away.

On August 30, 1872, Jeff and Ophelia sold ten acres of land in Anderson County to John R. Kendrick. With assets severely depleted by fines and lawsuits, Jeff and Ophelia left Anderson

County—probably in 1875, though it is not certain. Family tradition holds that Jeff worked on railroad construction as the lines progressed westward through Texas and that the family moved west with its progression. At times they, as did other families of workers, lived in modified boxcars on sidings near the construction sites. It was during this period that their next three children—Lawrence, Adelia, and Sam—were born. Berta, their firstborn, died at the age of five.

Jeff's first railroad job was probably with the International–Great Northern Railroad, since that was being built in Anderson County and nearby areas in 1873 and 1874. He later worked for the Fort Worth and Denver Railway, which was first chartered in 1873 and constructed from Fort Worth to Amarillo between 1881 and 1888, reaching Wichita Falls, Texas, in 1882 and the Texas–New Mexico border in 1888.

The family settled in Potter County, Texas, in 1887, where Jeff and Ophelia's third son, William Duncan, became the first child born in the newly established county. Six years later, in 1893, their youngest child, Clarence Ray, was born in Potter County. At the time they settled near Amarillo, Jeff was a construction foreman on the Fort Worth and Denver Railway. He later became road-master on the Amarillo District of that line. He also tried his hand at farming. In an *Amarillo Globe-News* interview in 1935, William Duncan indicated the following:

> "My father filed on four sections of land out there. He tried to farm—probably the first farm established in the county. Dissatisfied with drainage and drought conditions, he tackled the problem of water control. He built dam after dam on those four sections—and he never gave up until at last he had no farm but a wide expanse of dams."

Jeff Kersey purchased a Potter County retail liquor license on November 5, 1891, for $450. On February 3, 1892, he purchased a billiard table license at a cost of $30. Even with proper licenses, he did not entirely avoid clashes with the law. Records show that he was confined in the Potter County Jail on June 28, 1894. His description was given as fifty-one years old; five feet, ten inches tall; brown hair; gray eyes; and dark complexion. The nature of the offense was not specified.

In 1894, disaster was narrowly averted for the family when frightened horses ran away with the wagon carrying the family into town. The wagon overturned, and family members were strewed over the roadside. All family members sustained injuries, but Lawrence, despite his injuries, was able to go for help; fortunately, everyone recovered.

On September 18, 1902, Jeff and Ophelia purchased a lot in Llano Cemetery, presumably for the burial of their son Lawrence. Documentation of Lawrence Kersey's death has not been found, but Leona Kenny Davis indicated that Lawrence was killed in a railroad accident at about age twenty-three.

By 1903, the family had moved from the farm and were living in Amarillo at 206 Pierce Street, where they resided until leaving the area around 1918 or 1919. Jeff Kersey died on March 10, 1913, from "complications la grippe" and bronchitis. He was buried with Masonic rites; his funeral was held in the family residence with Rev. W. P. Jennings of the First Christian Church officiating.

At age sixty-nine, the reverend was described as "one of the oldest and most widely known residents of the Panhandle."

Ophelia continued to live in the home with her sons. In 1913, Lena, Duncan's wife, was listed in the home, but Clarence Ray was not. By 1915, Duncan and Lena had moved to 405 North Fillmore, and Clarence Ray was sharing the home with his mother. On June 15, 1914, Ophelia and her children sold a strip of land forty feet wide facing Pierce Street and running the entire length of Lot 2 in Amarillo to Mrs. Matilda Smith of Potter County.

In 1918 or 1919, Ophelia and Clarence Ray moved to Denver, Colorado, where they joined Ophelia's daughter Adelia. The 1920 census shows the family living at 2234 Julian Street, Denver, Colorado, with Ophelia as head of a household consisting of her son Clarence Ray, her daughter Adelia Williamson, and her grandchildren Frank L. and Verna O. Williamson.

In the spring of 1928, Ophelia traveled to Breckenridge, Texas, to visit with her sisters Florence and Jackie. While there she stayed in the home of Florence. Ophelia had been in poor health for some time, and her health deteriorated while in Texas. She died on the fifth of September in Florence's home. Her funeral was held at 4:30 p.m. on the tenth of September in the chapel of the Melton Funeral Home; interment was in the Oak Lawn section of Breckenridge Cemetery. Funeral costs of $267.50—$200 for the casket, $35 for embalming, $15 for the hearse, $10 for opening the grave, and $7.50 for lining the grave—were paid in full by Ray Kersey. Her sisters, brother, and children were expected to attend the funeral. Her grave is unmarked.

Descendants of Mary Ophelia Kenny and Jeff Kersey

Berta (Mary) Kersey
(20 Sep 1873–20 Nov 1878)

The firstborn of Ophelia and Jeff Kersey was called Berta, but her name was probably Mary Roberta or Mary Alberta. Records of Sandra McGeorge and Helen Kersey Cooke have only the name Berta, but Mary Jane Kersey Granum indicated in a telephone conversation that she remembered being told that the name of Ophelia's first child was Mary. Family records list Berta's birth year as 1873, at which point the family probably was residing in Anderson County. If she was born while they were still in Anderson County, she was probably doted upon by her grandparents and young aunts, the youngest of whom were only a few years older than her. As a young child, she made the trip westward with the building of the railroad. Family records indicate she died on November 20, 1878, but do not indicate the cause of death, whether from accident or disease. Bryan, Texas, is listed as place of death, but burial place is not indicated. She may have been buried in Bryan Cemetery, a nearby small-town cemetery, a country graveyard, a ranch burial plot, or an open pasture near the railroad construction site of the day.

Lawrence Kersey
(4 Feb 1876–13 Sep 1902)

Lawrence Kersey was born either in Ennis or Ellis County, presumably along the westward route of the railroad. Few records of Lawrence Kersey have been found. The book *In Cattle Country: A History of Potter County* lists Lawrence Kersey as one of the students attending the school established by W. D. Twitchell in his home at 710 Pierce Street for the 1895–1896 term and the following year. An article on Amarillo and Potter County schools in the golden-anniversary edition of the *Amarillo Globe-News* lists the teachers in a new District 3 school in 1898 as Donald McDonald, Mary Burrows, and L. C. Kersey. It is not known whether L. C. Kersey is Lawrence Kersey, but it seems likely. High school diplomas were sufficient for teaching in many Texas schools until well into the twentieth century.

Mary Jane Kersey Granum remembered that older family members described Lawrence as being very bright, with aspirations of becoming a minister.

Leona Kenny Davis indicated that Lawrence Kersey died in a railroad accident around age twenty-three. He was unmarried. Mary Jane Kersey Granum indicated that he was hit by a train while walking on the railroad. The cause of the accident is unknown. The family assumed that the scholarly Lawrence was so deep in thought that he was unaware of the approaching train. The book *Early Records of Potter and Oldham Counties* indicates that Lawrence Kersey is buried in Block 28, Lot 46 of Llano Cemetery, a lot purchased by Jeff and Ophelia Kersey on September 16, 1902. Jeff Kersey is buried in the lot adjacent to Lawrence.

Adelia Rowena Kersey
(2 Nov 1877–1 Apr 1953)

Adelia "Delia" Kersey was the third child and only daughter of Jeff and Ophelia Kersey to survive to adulthood. She was probably named after Ophelia's sister Adelia. It is notable that Ophelia, Adelia, and Ocie all named their daughters after their younger sisters. The precise location of Adelia's birth is not known, but it was probably along the railroad track approaching Amarillo. Adelia settled in Amarillo with her family and probably attended school there. On July 16, 1896,

Adelia married Charles W. Williamson (June 1865–1905) in Amarillo. Adelia and Charles had two children, Frank L. and Verna Ophelia. Charles died from cancer, leaving Adelia with two small children to raise.

Adelia was a charter member of the Bonita Chapter of the Order of the Eastern Star in Amarillo, Texas. She loved music and had a lovely voice in addition to being an accomplished pianist. She played piano for silent movies in an Amarillo movie theater. She taught her children to sing harmony. They frequently performed at Amarillo community events.

Her second marriage was to Robert Tucker. The 1910 census of Potter County shows them living in Amarillo with Adelia's two children. According to Jeff Kersey's obituary, Adelia Tucker was living in McMurry, Washington, in 1913. The marriage was not long lasting, since a June 1914 sale of a parcel of land belonging to Jeff Kersey by his heirs lists Adelia Williamson, "femme sole" (single), of Erath County. The 1920 census shows Adelia R. Williamson, age forty-two, and her children—Frank L., age twenty-two, and Verna O., age nineteen—living with Adelia's mother and brother Clarence Ray at 2234 Julian Street, Denver, Colorado. She was listed as a widow who was employed as a nurse.

Adelia married Fred H. Sprague on August 24, 1922, in Littleton, Colorado. The 1925 City Directory for Denver, Colorado, shows Fred H. and Delia W. Sprague living at 2234 Julian Street. Fred Sprague's occupation is listed as real estate. The 1930 census shows the Spragues living at the Julian Street home and working in real estate and nursing, respectively. Also in the household were Adelia's sister-in-law Laura Jean Kersey and niece Mary Kersey.

After the death of Fred in 1951, Adelia moved to Kernville, California, to be near her son, Frank. She died on April 1, 1953, in the Kern General Hospital. She had been hospitalized after breaking her hip in a fall in her home in Kernville on February 11. Her sister-in-law and very close friend Laura Kersey was with her when she died. Funeral services were held on April 4, 1953, at the Greenlawn Chapel in Bakersfield, California, with Rev. C. M. Ward officiating. Interment was in the Oak Hill section of the Greenlawn Memorial Park, Bakersfield.

- **Frank L. Williamson (1898–1960):** Born in Amarillo, Texas, Frank spent his early years there. Frank did not get along with Robert Tucker, his stepfather, and he did not like his stepfather's treatment of his mother. At age fourteen or fifteen, he ran away from home, lied about his age, and joined the US Navy. He served in the navy during World War I, as indicated by the 1930 census. After World War I, Frank left the navy for years. The 1920 census lists him in the Denver, Colorado, household headed by Ophelia Kersey, his grandmother. His occupation is listed as fireman. By 1930, Frank had returned to the navy and made it his career.

  Frank and his wife, Anna, both born in Texas, are listed on the 1930 census of San Diego, California. With them is Martin B. Williamson, age twenty-eight, listed as a brother. Not a son of Adelia, Martin may have been Anna's brother. During World War

II, Frank was a chief petty officer working in the administrative offices of the headquarters of the Eleventh Naval District in San Diego, California. Upon retiring from the navy, he moved to Kernville, California, where he enjoyed boating and fishing on Lake Isabella. He and Anna had no children.

- **Verna Ophelia Williamson (1901–23 Sep 1927):** Verna's birth and early years were in Amarillo, Texas. She moved to Colorado with her mother and was enumerated in the 1920 census in the Denver household headed by Ophelia Kersey, her grandmother. At that time, she was working as a clerk in a mercantile company. On February 28, 1920, Verna married Eugene Thompson in Denver, Colorado. Verna contracted an illness, probably tuberculosis, which led to prolonged sickness and eventual death. Mary Jane Kersey Granum remembered Verna only as a very beautiful woman who was extremely ill. Verna had no children.

Sam H. Kersey
(5 Jun 1879–24 Jul 1955)

Sam H. Kersey, the fourth child of Jeff and Ophelia Kersey, was probably born along the westward progression of the railroad. No census records have been found for him as a child or as an adult. He was not listed in the early Amarillo City Directories. Sam married Sarah Nelson around 1900 to 1905, probably in Texas or New Mexico. Their daughter Leona was born in New Mexico around 1907. A second daughter, Ethel, was born in Arizona in 1909. By 1913, Sam was living in or near Phoenix, Arizona. The Phoenix City Directory of 1915 lists a Sam Kersey residing at 1017 Lincoln whose occupation was dairyman. Sam and Sarah were divorced around 1915 to 1918. Leona and Ethel lived for a while with their grandmother Ophelia but later went to live with their mother. The 1920 census shows Sarah and her second husband, Owen Pittman, living in Kansas City, Missouri, with Leona Kersey, age twelve, and Ethel Kersey, age ten.

An examination of Phoenix City Directories, including surrounding communities, from 1918 through 1929 does not reveal a listing for Sam Kersey. The 1930 directory shows Samuel H. Kersey, occupation cook, residing at 3806 N. Tenth Street in Phoenix. Sam Kersey is not listed again in the city directories until 1945, when he is shown as a laborer for the city parks, residing on Route 5, Box 555, Phoenix. He is not listed in the 1946–1947 directories, but from 1948 through 1952, he is listed as an employee of the Phoenix Parks Department. His 1949–1950 residence is listed as 2130 W. Indian School Road; the Householder Index section shows that address as the home of William. E. Gill and wife Sara. Other directories show Sam as residing at 333 W. Washington, the address of the administrative offices of the Phoenix Parks Department. By 1955, Sam was listed without an occupation but again in the home of William E. and Sarah J. Gill on 2130 W. Indian

School Road. Sam Kersey is listed as living in Phoenix, Arizona, in 1928 at the time of his mother's death and again in 1942 upon the death of his aunt Kate Kenny Clark.

Mary Jane Kersey Granum remembered her uncle Sam as having a wry sense of humor and as being in demand as a caller for square dances. She indicated that he had worked in a variety of occupations, including mining and driving a Wells Fargo coach. Sam was buried in Prescott, Arizona.

- **Leona Elizabeth Kersey (ca. 1907–unknown):** Leona was born in New Mexico but spent most of her early childhood in Arizona. After her parents' divorce, she and her sister stayed with their grandmother Ophelia for several months before joining their mother and stepfather, Owen Pittman, in Kansas City, Missouri. Around 1927, Leona married Hugh A. Miller (ca. 1903–unknown). In 1930, Hugh worked as an abstract clerk for a title and trust company in Kansas City. Leona and her husband had no children at the time of the 1930 and 1940 censuses.

- **Ethel Fay Kersey (5 Aug 1909–unknown):** Ethel was born in Yavapai County, Arizona, and grew up in Arizona and Kansas City, Missouri. She was living in her mother's home at the time of the 1920 census. Ethel married Gene Raymond Rowland on November 19, 1925. They had one daughter, Barbara, shown as two years old on the 1930 census. Mary Jane Kersey Granum remembered that she and her mother visited Ethel in her home after Ethel was married, but she did not remember the year. No record for Ethel has been found beyond the 1930 census. Gene Rowland remarried in 1938.

William Duncan Kersey
(2 Apr 1888–Dec 1969)

William Duncan Kersey was the first child born after the establishment of Potter County. His birthplace was just north of the Fort Worth and Denver Railway track, near the Ridgemere Addition of Amarillo. In an interview for the centennial edition of the *Amarillo Globe-News*, Duncan described the events of his birth:

> "I have been told that my parents summoned Dr. J. W. Cartwright, the only physician in this part of the panhandle. My arrival apparently wasn't such a blessed event in his life. He failed to show up until 12 hours afterward. Neglect in my early hours evidently contributed to a very sturdy constitution—I've got along without doctors just as well ever since."

Duncan attended Amarillo public schools. In 1902, he left school and started working for the Santa Fe Railway as a callboy, subsequently moving to telegraph operator, relief agent, and then agent at several stations, including Texico-Belen and Vaughn, New Mexico. He returned to Amarillo in 1907 to work for the Fort Worth and Denver Railway as operator and dispatcher. He lived in Potter County at the time of his father's death. He married Lena Smith, and the Amarillo City Directories of 1913 and 1914 show them living with Ophelia at 206 Pierce. Their only child, a son, was stillborn in November 1913. The 1915 directory lists Duncan living at 405 N. Fillmore. Both Duncan and Lena signed the papers for the sale of property inherited from his father. The marriage ended in divorce.

In 1915, Duncan moved to El Paso, where he was assistant paymaster and then assistant agent for the El Paso Southern Railway. He entered the US Army in 1918 and was enrolled in the Infantry Central Officers Training School in Arkansas when the war ended. He was discharged without having completed his training.

On February 10, 1920, Duncan married Laura Jean Black (1893–21 May 1960), daughter of William and Minnie Black, in Little Rock, Arkansas. Over the next several years, he worked as a dispatcher for various railroads, including the Burlington, the Denver and Rio Grande, the Missouri Pacific, and the Rock Island. They were living in Amarillo at 409 N. Taylor in 1927 and San Angelo in 1928. In 1930, Duncan was in Reno, Nevada, while his wife and daughter, Mary Jane, were with his sister in Denver, Colorado. Mary Jane indicated that her father was seeking work in 1930. In 1936, he, his wife, and his daughter were living in Portland, Oregon, where he worked as a dispatcher for the Spokane, Portland and Seattle Railway, a position he held until his retirement. He continued to reside in Portland until his death.

- **Mary Jane Kersey (1921–5 May 2013):** Mary Jane, daughter and only child of Duncan Kersey and Laura Jean Black, was born in Denver, Colorado. Her first home was that of her grandmother Ophelia in Denver. Her father named her Minnie Ophelia after her two grandmothers and sent telegrams to family members announcing her arrival under that name. Her mother, however, thought Minnie Ophelia was old fashioned and preferred Mary Jane. That was the name registered with her birth. Mary Jane attended schools in Texas, Colorado, and Oregon. She studied dance at William Christensen's ballet company in Portland and taught dance lessons while still in high school. As a tap dancer, she was in demand as an entertainer at local civic organizations. After graduation from Lincoln High School, she obtained a job in the kick line at the Casino da Urca in Rio de Janeiro, Brazil.

  From Brazil, Mary Jane went to New York and changed her focus from dancing to acting. Her first residence in New York was the Rehearsal Club, the rooming house that inspired Edna Ferber and George S. Kaufman's play *Stage Door*. Adopting the stage name Billie Dee (from her mother's pet name for her father), she had roles in a number of Broadway and off-Broadway shows, including *Crazy with the Heat, Let's Face It!,* and *Cyrano*. In these plays she shared the stage with many actors, including Raymond Burr, Victor Borge, Danny Kaye, Eve Arden, and José Ferrer.

In 1948, Mary Jane went to Germany to entertain the troops. She was given the temporary rank of major to qualify her for lodging on base during her tour.

After returning to New York, she acted in theaters in New York, New Jersey, Connecticut, New Hampshire, Pennsylvania, Washington, DC, Illinois, and Texas. She also had appearances on several television shows.

In 1960, Mary Jane returned to Portland to help care for her widowed father. In Portland she had major roles in productions by the North End Players and Slocum House Theater. At this time she acted under the name Mary Jane Manchester after a brief marriage to Mel Manchester. She and Ethan Granum were married in 1970. As founding members of the Irving Street Players, she and Ethan participated in many aspects of its productions, including acting, set designing, and lighting designing. Mary Jane had the leading role in productions of *On Golden Pond, Love Letters, Trip to Bountiful*, and many other plays.

Mary Jane and Ethan lived in the house her parents purchased in 1936 in the Willamette Heights section of Portland. Mary Jane died on May 5, 2013, at the age of ninety-two. She was survived by her husband, Ethan; stepsons, David, Ted, and Michael Granum; six grandchildren; and three great-grandchildren.

Clarence Ray Kersey
(16 Aug 1893–24 Dec 1976)

The youngest child of Ophelia and Jeff Kersey—Clarence Ray, called Ray by his family—was born in Potter County, Texas. During his early years, the family lived on a ranch several miles from town. When it came time for him to start school, his mother decided to teach him at home for two years. She apparently did a very good job, since he was able to begin the fourth grade when he entered the Amarillo schools.

Soon after graduating from Amarillo High School, Ray began working for the railroad and moved around extensively during his early years of railroad work. He lived in Amarillo at the time of his father's death in 1913 and in Post, Texas, in 1914.

When the United States entered World War I, Ray joined the army, where he became a motorcycle mechanic and attained the rank of corporal. He served a tour of duty in Europe as a motorcycle mechanic and continued to own and ride motorcycles after his return to civilian life.

He moved to Denver, Colorado, and is shown on the 1920 census in his mother's household. His occupation is given as teller for the Tramway Company. On October 21, 1922, Ray married Helen Hutchison Mate (9 Aug 1889–10 Jan 1979) in Denver, Colorado. Helen, the daughter of James Mate and Harriet Lee Hutchison, was born in Ripley, West Virginia. Ray and Helen made their home in Denver for several years; the 1928 Denver City Directory shows Clarence R. Kersey and wife Helen H. living at 4544 Quitman. He is listed as deputy chief clerk for the C&S Railroad. Ray, Helen, and their two young children, Bob and Ruth, moved to El Paso, Texas, on a hot July day in 1929. Ray worked for the Southern Pacific Railroad in El Paso, in a variety of job roles. The 1940 census shows the family living in a home they owned at 4015 Hastings Street in El Paso. They were living in the same place in 1935. Ray was working as head rate clerk for a steam railroad. After retiring from the railroad, he worked for R. T. Hoover and Son, Cotton Merchants, for three years.

Ray died in El Paso, Texas, from a heart attack. His wife, Helen, survived him by just over two years. Both were buried in Fort Bliss National Cemetery.

- **Robert Lee "Bob" Kersey (15 Dec 1923–26 Jan 2014):** Born in Denver, Colorado, Bob grew up and attended school in El Paso, Texas. He served as a navy pilot during World War II. His plane was shot down, and his cousin Frank Williams was able to keep the family apprised of the search efforts from his navy position. Bob was safely rescued.

  Bob married Sally Morrison, and they had two children: Kenneth Foster Kersey and Linda Suzanne Kersey. The marriage ended in divorce. Bob then married Virginia Ryan, who had two children by a previous marriage: Kelly Michael Rick and Cynthia Ellen Rick. Bob adopted Kelly and Cynthia, and their last name was changed to Kersey. Bob and Virginia had one child, Lee Craig Kersey.

  Bob served as assistant director of the student union at the University of California and director of the student union at the University of New Mexico. He was appointed director of the student union at the University of Nevada at Reno, effective February 1958. He later became director of student affairs for the university. He and Virginia continued to live in Reno until Bob's death.

  - **Kenneth Foster Kersey (1 Jul 1954–):** Kenneth was born in Alameda County, California. He married B. Christine Weems in Storey County, Nevada, on May 2, 1981. The marriage ended in divorce. His second marriage was to Lisa Marie Cochran on July 26, 1998, in Reno, Nevada. They have one son, Brian.

  - **Linda Suzanne Kersey (30 Apr 1957–):** Linda married Ronald Thurman Spezia in July 1977. At the time of their marriage, she was a playground leader for the city of Reno, and Ronald was a receiving clerk for Warehouse Market. They have two children, Christopher and Katie. Linda and Ronald were divorced.

  - **Kelly Michael (Rick) Kersey (13 Sep 1960–):** Kelly married Susan K. Hunerlach on May 28, 1983, in Reno, Nevada. They have two children, Ryan and Lauren.

  - **Cynthia Ellen (Rick) Kersey (31 Oct 1960–):** Cynthia has two daughters, Megan Ceccarelli and Natalie Ceccarelli.

- **Lee Craig Kersey (17 Jul 1970–2009).**

- **Ruth Virginia Kersey (1 Nov 1925–25 Nov 2014):** Ruth was born in Denver, Colorado, but grew up and attended school in El Paso, Texas. She married Ernest Wilson McGeorge (4 May 1921–21 Apr 2007), who was a first lieutenant in the US Army during World War II. Ernest was born in Ohio to William and Florence McGeorge. Ruth and Ernest lived in El Paso, Texas, where Ernest worked as accountant and assistant secretary-treasurer for the E. T. Olds Plumbing and Heating Corporation. In 1962, they moved to New Orleans. They later moved to Albuquerque, New Mexico, and finally to Phoenix, Arizona. Ernest obtained a degree from the University of Arizona and worked as a stockbroker and financial manager. Their retirement home was in Mesa, Arizona. Ernest died at age eighty-six. He was buried with a military ceremony in Arlington Cemetery. Ruth survived him and lived to the age of eighty-nine. She was also buried in Arlington Cemetery.

  - **Robert Lloyd "Bob" McGeorge (22 May 1945–):** Born in El Paso, Texas, Bob has lived in Lincoln, Nebraska; Rockville and Potomac, Maryland; and Sunland Park, New Mexico. Bob and his wife have two daughters, Lauren and Annie.

  - **Douglas Ernest "Doug" McGeorge (30 Oct 1947–):** Doug was born in Ohio. His marriages to Sue Reynolds and to Rose M. Sobie both ended in divorce. He and Rose Lanello were married on November 23, 1977, in El Paso, Texas. He has lived in Chandler, Gilbert, Mesa, Phoenix, and Tempe, Arizona. He and Rose Lanello lived in Albuquerque, New Mexico. They have two children, Michael Edward and Jennifer Jill.

  - **Sandra Lee "Sandy" McGeorge (23 Jun 1950–):** Sandy received a bachelor's degree from Arizona State University with an emphasis on history and English. She also has an associate of arts in international business from Mesa Community College and an associate of arts in legal assistant/paralegal studies from Scottsdale Community College. She lives in Queen Creek, Arizona. Sandy was a management assistant and grants coordinator for the town of Queen Creek, Arizona, until her retirement. She has one son, Ryan McGeorge Rogers.

  - **Ronald Craig McGeorge (1 Dec 1951–14 Nov 1972):** Craig was born in El Paso, Texas, and he was murdered in Phoenix, Arizona. He was shot by an irate individual who objected to Craig leaving his disabled car in front of the individual's house.

- **Helen Louise Kersey (30 Dec 1929–Dec 2018):** Helen was born in El Paso, Texas. She attended El Paso public schools. Helen married Jack Lee Cooke (5 May 1920–25 Jul 1991). Jack was born in El Paso, Texas, to Daniel Jay Cooke and Julia Belle Duden. Jack was a glider pilot in the US Air Corps during World War II. After his return to El Paso, Jack worked for the Rocky Mountain Banking Company, and Helen was a full-time homemaker and mother.

  - **Julia Ruth Cooke (17 Feb 1950–):** Julia was born in El Paso. She married Donald Rain Adams on May 13, 1972, in El Paso. Julia taught first grade in Sugar Land, Texas. Julia and Donald have three children—Craig Spencer, Grant Shindler, and Katie Louise—all of whom were born in El Paso.

  - **Jeffrey Ray Cooke (30 Mar 1951–):** Native of El Paso, Texas, Jeffrey resides in California. He and his ex-wife have two daughters, Hayley Louise and Julie Nance.

SOURCES

Amarillo City Directories, 1903 through 1919. Amarillo Public Library, Amarillo, Texas.

Amarillo Sunday News and Globe, Golden Anniversary Edition, 1938, section B, p. 18. Photocopy provided by Amarillo Public Library, Amarillo, TX.

Anderson County, Texas, Deed Book P, p. 89. Anderson County Courthouse, Palestine, TX.

"Black, William." 1910 US Census, Pulaski County, Arkansas. Ancestry.com, 2006.

City Directories of the United States 1902–1935. Denver, Colorado, reel 24, 1928. Microfilmed by Research Publications, Woodbridge, Connecticut, 1985. FHLC #1611490.

"Clark, Kate Judson." Obituary. *Phoenix Globe*, January 12, 1945, p. 6, column 1. Microfilm, Arizona State Library, Phoenix, Arizona.

Cooke, Helen Kersey. Letter to Mary Jo Kenny. July 31, 2004.

Cooke, Helen Kersey. Telephone conversation with Mary Jo Kenny. June 2004.

Davis, Leona Kenny. Paper prepared around 1976 giving information about her grandparents, aunts, and their families. Only known copy in possession of Mary Jo Kenny.

"First White Child Born in County Revisits Scenes of Boyhood After 20 Years." *Amarillo Globe-News*, August 1, 1935. Photocopy provided by Amarillo Public Library.

Funeral home records on file at the Swenson Memorial Museum, Breckenridge, Texas.

Granum, Mary Jane Kersey. Letter to Mary Jo Kenny. October 20, 2004.

Granum, Mary Jane Kersey. Letter to Mary Jo Kenny. December 1, 2003.

Granum, Mary Jane Kersey. Telephone conversation with Mary Jo Kenny. February 2004.

"Granum, Mary J." Social Security Death Index. Ancestry.com, 2008.

"Granum, Mary Jane." United States Obituary Collection, Portland, Oregon, web edition, July 15, 2013.

"Granum, Mary Jane." US, Find A Grave Index, 1600s–Current. Ancestry.com, 2012.

"Kersey, Adelia, to Charles W. Williamson." Texas Marriage Collection, 1814–1909 and 1966–2002. Ancestry.com, 2005.

"Kersey, C. Ray." 1940 US Census, El Paso County, Texas, p. 11B, ED 256–272. Ancestry.com.

"Kersey, Clarence R., to Helen H. Mate." Colorado County Marriages and State Indexes, 1862–2006. Ancestry.com, 2016.

"Kersey, Clarence R." 1930 US Census, El Paso County, Texas, p. 11B, ED 43, house 3209, number 278, family 278.

"Kersey, Clarence R." US Veterans Gravesites ca. 1776–2006. Ancestry.com.

"Kersey, Clarence R." Texas, Find A Grave Index, 1836–2011. Ancestry.com, 2012.

"Kersey, Clarence Ray." Texas Death Certificates, 1903–1982, No. 101724. Ancestry.com, 2013.

"Kersey, Clarence Ray." World War I Draft Registration Cards, 1917–1918. Ancestry.com.

"Kersey, Clarence." Social Security Death Index. Ancestry.com.

"Kersey, Duncan." 1930 US Census, Reno, Washoe County, Nevada, p. 3B, ED 13, house 106, family 54. Ancestry. com.

"Kersey, Duncan." 1940 US Census, Portland, Multnomah County, Oregon, sheet 6A, house 3320, family 149. Ancestry.com.

"Kersey, Duncan." Oregon Death Index, 1903–1998, certificate 18812. Ancestry.com, 2000.

"Kersey, Duncan." US, Social Security Applications and Claims Index, 1936–2007. Ancestry.com, 2015.

"Kersey, Duncan." US Veterans Gravesites, ca.1775–2006. Ancestry.com, 2006.

"Kersey, Duncan." US World War I Draft Registration Cards, 1917–1918. Ancestry.com.

"Kersey, Ethel Fay." Arizona Genealogy Birth and Death Certificates. Ancestry.com.

"Kersey, Ethel Faye." Missouri Marriage Records, 1805–2002. Ancestry.com, 2007.

"Kersey, Ethel Faye." Missouri, Jackson County Marriage Records, 1840–1985. Ancestry.com, 2015.

"Kersey, Helen Louise." Texas Birth Certificates, 1903–1932. Ancestry.com, 2013.

"Kersey, infant son of Duncan Kersey." Texas Death Certificates, 1903–1982. Ancestry.com, 2013.

"Kersey, Jeff." 1870 US Census, Anderson County, Texas, p. 21, line 17, dwelling 304, Palestine PO. FHLC #0553072, LDS FamilySearch Library, Salt Lake City, UT.

"Kersey, Jefferson." 1910 US Census, Potter County, Texas, sheet 19A, enumeration date May 22, 1910, ED 199, dwelling 204, family 353. Ancestry.com.

"Kersey, Jefferson." Obituary. *Amarillo Sunday Globe-News*, March 11, 1913. Photocopy provided by Amarillo Public Library.

"Kersey, Jefferson." Texas Death Index, 1903–2000. Ancestry.com.

"Kersey, Jefferson." US, Find A Grave Index, 1600s–Current. Ancestry.com, 2012.

"Kersey, Jefferson." Texas, Find A Grave Index, 1836–2011. Ancestry.com, 2012.

"Kersey, Laura J." Oregon Death Index, 1903–1998, certificate 6596. Ancestry.com, 2000.

"Kersey, Lawrence." US, Find A Grave Index, 1600s–Current. Ancestry.com, 2012.

"Kersey, Leona Elizabeth." Missouri Marriage Records, 1805–2002. Ancestry.com, 2007.

"Kersey, Leona Elizabeth." Missouri, Jackson County Marriage Records, 1840–1985. Ancestry.com, 2015.

"Kersey, Mary Jane." Rio de Janeiro, Brazil, Immigration Cards, 1900–1965. Ancestry.com.

"Kersey, Mary O." 1920 US Census, Denver, Colorado, p. 211, sheet 6, ED 24, enumeration date January 7, 1920, dwelling 127, family 143. Microfilm, FHLC #182015, LDS FamilySearch Library, Salt Lake City, UT.

"Kersey, Mary Ophelia Kinney." Texas, Find A Grave Index, 1836–2011. Ancestry.com, 2012.

"Kersey, Mary Ophelia." US, Find A Grave Index, 1600s–Current. Ancestry.com, 2012.

"Kersey, Mrs. Mary Ophelia." Texas State Department of Health, Bureau of Vital Statistics, Standard Certificate of Death, Registered District 41222.

"Kersey, Ophelia." Obituary. *The Breckenridge American*, September 6, 1928. Swenson Memorial Museum, Breckenridge, TX. Transcript supplied by Frieda Mitchell.

Kersey, Robert Lee. Telephone conversation with Mary Jo Kenny on July 25, 2004.

"Kersey, Robert Lee." US Navy Casualties Books, 1776–1941. Ancestry.com, 2012.

"Kersey, Robert." United States Obituary Collection. Ancestry.com, 2006.

"Kersey, S. H." Arizona Voter Registrations, 1866–1955. Ancestry.com, 2016.

"Kersey, Sam H." 1940 US Census, Yavapai County, Arizona. Ancestry.com, 2012.

"Kersey, Sam H." Arizona Death Records, 1887–1960. Ancestry.com, 2016.

"Kersey, Sam Houston." US, Social Security Applications and Claims Index, 1936–2007. Ancestry.com, 2015.

"Kerzey, Ethel Fay." Arizona Birth Records, 1880–1935. Ancestry.com, 2015.

Key, Della Tyler, et. al. *Early Records of Potter County.* Daughters of the American Revolution, Llano Estacado Chapter. Photocopy of selected pages from the Amarillo Public Library.

Key, Della Tyler. *In the Cattle Country: A History of Potter County.* Quanah, TX: Nortex Offset Publications, 1972, p. 51. Amarillo Public Library.

"Kinney, M. O., to Jefferson Kersey." Texas, US, Select County Marriage Index, 1837–1977. Ancestry.com, 2014.

"Kirsey, Jefferson." Texas State Board of Health, Standard Certificate of Death, Registered No. 568.

"McGeorge, Ernest W." Social Security Death Index. Ancestry.com, 2008.

"McGeorge, Ernest Wilson." Obituary. Ancestry.com.

"McGeorge, Ernest." US Department of Veterans Affairs BIRLS Death File, 1850–2010. Ancestry.com, 2011.

"McGeorge, Ruth Virginia." US, Find A Grave Index, 1600s–Current. Ancestry.com, 2012.

McGeorge, Sandra. Letter to Mary Jo Kenny. October 2003.

McGeorge, Sandra. Letter to Mary Jo Kenny. September 17, 2003.

"Miller, Hugh A." 1930 US Census, Jackson County, Missouri. Ancestry.com, 2002.

Minutes of District Court, Anderson County, Texas. Book K, Cases 910, 911, 912, 913, 914, and 915. FHLC #0987157, LDS FamilySearch Library, Salt Lake City, UT.

Minutes of District Court, Anderson County, Texas. Book L, Cases 1167, 1168, 1167, 1179, 1171, and 1172. Disposition Book L, pp. 194–197. FHLC #0987157, LDS FamilySearch Library, Salt Lake City, UT.

Minutes of District Court, Anderson County, Texas. Book O, pp. 2, 13, 57, 261. FHLC #0987159, LDS FamilySearch Library, Salt Lake City, UT.

Mitchell, Frieda (from the Swenson Memorial Museum, Breckenridge). Letter to Mary Jo Kenny. August 13, 1998.

"Newly Appointed Student Union Building Director Arrives At Campus and Tells of His Plans." *Nevada State Journal*, February 15, 1958. Ancestry.com.

"Ozar, Simon." 1940 US Census, Jackson County, Missouri. Ancestry.com, 2012.

"Pittman, Owen." 1920 US Census, Kansas City, Missouri. Ancestry.com.

Phoenix City Directories, 1930 through 1955. Phoenix City Library.

"Sam Kersey." Phoenix, Arizona, City Directory 1915. Phoenix City Directories for 1912, 1913, and 1916 were consulted but did not have a listing for Sam Kersey.

Program for the play *Love Letters*, by A. R. Gurney, presented by the Irving Street Players, November 2003, featuring Mary Jane Granum.

"Robert Lee Kersey." University of Nevada, Minutes of the Board of Regents, 1950.

"Register of Prisoners Confined in the Potter County Jail 1889–1905." Archives of the Panhandle Plains Historical Museum, Canyon, Texas. Abstracted by Lois Nix. Photocopy of selected pages from the Amarillo Public Library.

"Rowland, Gene." 1930 US Census, Jackson County, Missouri. Ancestry.com, 2002.

"Sprague, Adelia Rowena." Funeral notice. Photocopy of original in possession of Mary Jane Granum.

"Sprague, Adelia Rowena." Obituary. Photocopy of a newspaper clipping, original in possession of Mary Jane Granum. Name of newspaper and date were not included in the clipping.

"Sprague, Adelia Rowena." US, Social Security Applications and Claims Index, 1936–2007. Ancestry.com, 2015.

"Sprague, Fred H." 1930 US Census, Denver County, Colorado, ED 225, family 229. Ancestry.com.

"Sprague, Fred H." 1940 US Census, Denver County, Colorado, p. 9B, ED 16–40, house no. 2234. Ancestry.com.

"Tucker, Robert." 1910 US Census, Potter County, Texas, p. 13A, ED 199, family 219. Ancestry.com.

Werner, George C. "Fort Worth and Denver Railway." *Handbook of Texas*. Texas State Historical Association. https://www.tshaonline.org/handbook/entries/international-great-northern-railroad.

Werner, George C. "International-Great Northern Railroad." *Handbook of Texas*. Texas State Historical Association. https://www.tshaonline.org/handbook/entries/international-great-northern-railroad.

"Williamson, Adelia R., to Fred H. Sprague." Colorado County Marriages and State Indexes, 1862–2006. Ancestry.com, 2016.

"Williamson, Frank L." 1930 US Census, San Diego, California. Ancestry.com.

"Williamson, Frank L." California Death Index, 1940–1997. Ancestry.com, 2000.

"Williamson, Frank L." US, Social Security Applications and Claims Index, 1936–2007. Ancestry.com, 2015.

Martha Adelia Kenny
(28 Oct 1858–31 Jan 1942)

Martha Adelia Kenny, known as Delia, was born in Tennessee Colony, Texas. She attended school in Tennessee Colony and may have taken music lessons there. Leona Kenny Davis indicated that Delia played the guitar skillfully.

Delia did not make the move to Erath County with her family but instead married Pinckney L. Scarborough (1852–1882) on September 26, 1878, in Anderson County. P. L. was the son of James Ransom Scarborough and Caroline Holley. The 1880 census of Anderson County lists P. L., Adelia, and infant Verna living on a farm near Tennessee Colony. A second daughter, Katie, was added to the family in the summer of 1881.

In the fall of 1880, Delia's younger sister Ocie married Ed Seagler and became Delia's close neighbor. The 1880 census enumerated Ed Seagler as head of household on the farm adjoining the Scarborough farm. The household included Ed's mother, his nine-year-old niece Suzie Good, and three farmworkers. P. L. and Ed had apparently been long-term friends.

According to family stories, P. L. and Ed went on a fishing trip in the fall of 1882. Both contracted what was identified as "swamp fever"—probably malaria. P. L. died on December 3 and Ed on December 14. Both were buried in Tennessee Colony Cemetery. William Kenny brought a wagon from Erath County and moved his two widowed sisters and their children to their parents' home near Berlin Hall, now Hannibal. It was undoubtedly a very sad Christmas for the family.

It is not known how long Delia and Ocie remained at their parents' home in Erath County, but both eventually returned to Anderson County. According to Leona Kenny Davis, Delia supported herself and her young daughters through sewing and giving sewing lessons during her widowhood.

Adelia Kenny Scarborough and John Irvin Wofford (20 Jan 1856–15 Nov 1932) were married on May 29, 1889, in Henderson County, Texas. As Jettie Wofford reported to her cousin Leona, Delia met John Irvin Wofford of neighboring Henderson County at a dance. This meeting may have been several years before their marriage, since a newspaper article about John I. Wofford indicated that Delia had been his first boyhood sweetheart. John was born in Fincastle, Texas, to Pennington Wofford and Rebecca Alvira Anderson. His first wife was Martha Lavonia Mullins (1850–1887). John was a widower with four children: Maude, Jessie, Larkin, and Willie. The combined family at the time of their marriage included Maude, eleven; Jessie, nine; Verna, nine; Katie, eight; Larkin, four; and Willie, two.

Soon after John and Delia married, they purchased a four-hundred-acre farm in the Pine Grove community, five miles southeast of Athens, Texas. They built a home on this land and later built a second larger home for their growing family. The farm, with the larger house, has remained in the Wofford family through Willie Wofford and his son William Avant Wofford. The Wofford farm was accepted in the Family Land Heritage Program of the Texas Department of Agriculture.

This program denotes continuous operation of a farm or ranch by the same family for one hundred years or more in the state of Texas.

The Wofford family attended the Pine Grove Missionary Church near Athens. delia and John were accepted into the church by letter in 1890. Baptismal records of the church show memberships for Maude Wofford, Verna Scarborough, Katie Scarborough, Eula Wofford, and Willie Wofford.

By the 1900 census, six more children—Eula May, Ocie Melinda, Jettie Belle, Hattie Lou, Edna Earl, and William Bryan—had been added to the family. Maude, Verna, and Katie were no longer living at home, making a household of eleven members.

The 1910 census reveals a household of eight, with Jessie, Larkin, and Eula May no longer in the household. Nearby, Delia's daughter Katie was enumerated with her husband, Walton Deupree, and daughters, Maude, Addie, and Florence.

John and Delia's daughter Jettie; her husband, Bruce Hodge; and their son, James C. Hodge, shared the home with John and Delia in 1920. Willie Wofford and his wife, Alma, lived adjacent to John and Delia and shared in the operation of the farm. Katie and Verna lived nearby with their families.

Prior to 1930, John turned over the management of the farm to his son Willie, though he probably retained an advisory role. The 1930 census shows him with no occupation. He and Delia resided on South Palestine Road, Athens; Jettie and Bruce Hodge and son James continued to live with John and Delia. Bruce operated a gasoline service station, and Jettie was a stenographer for the Office of the County Judge. After retirement, John and Delia enjoyed traveling, which included visits with their dispersing extended family. John died in 1932 and was buried in Athens City Cemetery. Delia continued to make her home with Jettie and Bruce Hodge. She died nine years after her husband and was also buried in Athens City Cemetery.

Descendants of Martha Adelia Kenny and Pinckney Scarborough

Verna Florence Scarborough
(18 May 1880–12 Oct 1928)

Verna was born in Tennessee Colony, Anderson County, Texas. She was very young when her father died and was seven years old when her mother remarried. At age thirteen, Verna left the Wofford home to live with her father's sister, Mollie Scarborough Hodge, in Anderson County. The 1900 census shows Verna in the Anderson County home of Adolphus and Mollie Hodges. She was not listed as employed.

On April 7, 1904, Verna married Joseph Collins Owen (12 Jul 1875–20 Jan 1930). Joe was the son of David Allen Owen and Lucinda Woodward. Joe was born in Henderson County, Texas, and attended Pine Grove School. After studying at Teachers' Normal School, conducted by Judge William F. Freeman in Athens, Joe taught school for three years. He then worked as a topographical engineer for Southern Pacific Railroad. After Verna and Joe married, they bought and operated a farm in the Mill-Run community, near Athens. The 1920 census shows them and their four children—Rufus, Louella, Margaret, and Roy—in Justice Precinct 2 of Henderson County. Also in the household was Joe's mother, Lucy Owen, and his nephew Alvin Tomason. Verna's death in 1928 was followed by Joe's death less than two years later.

- **Rufus Hodge Owen (11 Dec 1904–17 Apr 1964):** Rufus was born in Anderson County, Texas. The 1930 census shows him working on the Owens' Henderson County farm. Rufus attended Mill Run School, Athens High School, and Brantley Draughon Business College of Fort Worth, Texas. He never married. He entered the US Army on October 4, 1942, and served in the 754th Regiment, stationed in Tehran, Iran. He left the army on June 2, 1945, and worked in a variety of positions, including as a guard at the atomic plant in Los Alamos and science inspector in the University of California Laboratories in Los Alamos. He was a member of the Christian Church, a masonic lodge, Shriners, Veterans of Foreign Wars, and the American Legion. He died in New Mexico and was buried in Santa Fe National Cemetery.

- **Louella Owen (14 May 1906–19 Nov 1988):** Louella was born in Henderson County, Texas, and attended Mill Run School, Athens High School, and North Texas State College in Denton, Texas. She taught school for six years before attending graduate business school in Dallas, Texas. She worked for two years as a planning agent with the Resettlement Administration in Texarkana, Texas. Changing her career direction, she graduated from the Baylor School of Nursing in Dallas, Texas, and did graduate work in nursing administration at the University of Indiana and the University of Minnesota. Louella entered the US Army Nursing Corps and served in North Africa, Italy, and France during World War II. After the war, she was assigned to Walter Reed Army Hospital, Washington, DC; Tripler Army Hospital, Hawaii; and Fort Belvoir, Virginia. She retired from the army on June 1, 1959, with the rank of major. After retiring, Louella worked with a research team on hospital supplies at Emory University in Atlanta, Georgia, and served as director for the Texas League of Nursing, headquartered in Austin, Texas. She was a member of the Episcopalian Church. Louella never married; she died in Houston, Harris County, Texas.

- **Margaret Owen (4 Jun 1908–Jun 1984):** Margaret was born in Henderson County, Texas. After attending Mill Run School and graduating from Athens High School, she was employed by J. C. Penney Company until her marriage to John Montgomery on April 29, 1927. The 1930 census shows John Montgomery as head of a household that included Margaret and her brothers and sister. They were apparently living on the family farm only a few months after their father's death. John was working in a music store, probably in Athens. John and Margaret did not remain in Henderson County long; their son, Roy Brian Montgomery, was born in October of 1930 in Van Zandt County. At that time, John was working as a clerk in a furniture store. Divorce or death records for John have not been found, but it is assumed that John died around 1931 or 1932. Margaret married Harry Gaston Sylvan Dossey (17 Feb 1903–27 Apr 1947) in December 1932. Gaston was the son of Kinchen Dudley Dossey and Ida Kate Williams. He attended high school and law school in Dallas, was a veteran of World War I, and was a member of a Masonic lodge and the Baptist Church. Gaston and Margaret are shown on the 1940 census in McLennan County, Texas. Gaston died in Austin, Texas, from a heart attack. Margaret moved to Harris County, where she worked in the Hermann Hospital in Houston, Texas, and in the Veterans Hospital. She was a member of the Christian Church. Margaret died in Houston, Texas.

- **Roy Brian Montgomery (24 Oct 1930–22 Feb 2006):** Roy was born in Van Zandt County, Texas. The 1940 census shows him living with his mother and stepfather in McLennan County, Texas. He was employed by an air freight company. City directories show him living in Genoa, Houston, Cleveland, and Cold Springs, Texas. He was a member of the Baptist Church. Roy married Bobbie Sue McCoy. They lived in Houston, Harris County, Texas, where both of their children were born. Roy and Bobbie Sue were divorced in September 1971 in Harris County, Texas. Roy died in Katy, Harris County, Texas. Their children were Linda Sue (11 Jan 1954–) and Roy Brian Jr. (27 Oct 1955–).

- **Gaston Joe Dossey (18 Jun 1936–):** Gaston was born in Tarrant County, Texas. He graduated from San Jacinto High School in Houston, Texas. He spent two years in Germany as a soldier in the US Army and achieved the rank of sergeant in the active US Army Reserve. Gaston was employed with the O&M Manufacturing Company of Houston, Texas. He married Betty Marie Batterson, daughter of Walter William Batterson and Sallie Mae Ransom. Betty worked for First City National Bank in Houston. Both were members of the Baptist Church.

  - **Tina Marie Dossey (12 Nov 1955–):** Tina was born in Harris County, Texas. She married Keith W. Wood on September 20, 1980. They were divorced in 1989.

- Infant male Dossey was born prematurely and died on October 23, 1938.

- **Roy Owen (3 Nov 1916–13 Jan 1979):** By the time Roy was fourteen, he had lost both parents. He stayed with his sister for a while, then lived with his aunt Jettie, who was reported to have thought of him as her own son. Roy graduated from Texas A&M with a major in agronomy. He served in the US Army and became a lieutenant colonel in the US Army Reserve. He was a maintenance engineer at the University of California plant in Los Alamos, New Mexico. Roy married Theresa Marie Slavazza (7 Mar 1913–24 Mar 2001), who was born in Los Alamos to Batista and Gioconda Slavazza. Theresa was a registered nurse and active in the Catholic Church, the Parent-Teacher Association, the American Heart Association, and polio drives. Roy died in New Mexico and was interred at Santa Fe National Cemetery. Theresa died in Los Alamos, New Mexico.

- **Karen Lou Owen (9 Apr 1945–Nov 1967):** Karen died in Los Alamos, New Mexico, of kidney disease.

- **Michael Joseph Owen (14 Feb 1948–):** Michael was living in Los Alamos at the time of his sister's death. He also lived in Albuquerque and Santa Fe, New Mexico.

Katherine Judson "Katie" Scarborough (7 Aug 1881–26 Mar 1971)

Katie Scarborough was born in Tennessee Colony, Anderson County, Texas. Katie spent most of her childhood in Henderson County. She was only sixteen months old when her father died. She married Walton Porter Deupree (17 Jul 1880–21 Jun 1936), son of Porter Deupree and Mollie Powell, on October 16, 1901, in Henderson County, Texas. They made their home in the Pine Grove community of Henderson County, where all their children were born. Census data shows them living near Delia and John Wofford.

In 1910, Walton and Katie were listed with three daughters, Mary ("Maude"), Addie, and Florence. Also in the home were Walton's aunt, Lizzie Powell, and James Spencer, a farmworker. By the 1920 census, Walton and Katie's children Tom, Lois, Walton, and Byron had been added to the family. In 1930, all of Walton and Katie's children except Addie were living at home. Both Maude and Florence were teaching in the local public schools. Tom was helping his father with the farm, while the other children were enrolled in school.

On April 17, 1931, Walton suffered a paralyzing stroke from which he never fully recovered. His semi-invalid status continued for several years; he died in June of 1936. Rev. D. R. Cartledge of Athens Baptist Church conducted the funeral, and interment was in Athens Cemetery.

Katie's oldest son, Tom, assumed major responsibility for the farm, and he and Katie continued operating the farm and maintaining the home. Katie was devoted to her family and maintained close ties with them. She maintained a garden and took pride in her home-canned goods.

She enjoyed piecing quilts and quilting and taught her granddaughters to quilt. Katie died in Henderson County at age eighty-nine.

- **Mary Adelia "Maude" Deupree (27 Sep 1905–5 May 1944):** Maude married Albert Simpson Avant (2 Feb 1906–6 Feb 1947) on November 21, 1930, in Henderson County. Maude died at the birth of their only child, Mary Margaret Avant, who also died.

- **Addie Lou Deupree (30 May 1907–-19 Oct 1991):** Addie Lou married French Beard "Nince" Williams (8 Jul 1909–25 Dec 1975) on March 31, 1929, in Henderson County. His parents were French Beard Williams and Bessie May Owen. Nince and Addie Lou lived in Fort Worth, Texas. The 1940 census of Fort Worth shows Nince, Addie Lou, and their son, French, sharing a home with Nince's sister, Mary; her husband, Curtis Dumas; and their son, Curtis Dumas. Nince was working as a machinist, and Addie Lou was a bookkeeper for a shoe store. Addie Lou survived her husband for sixteen years. She was buried in Athens, Henderson County.

  - **French Byron Williams (8 Nov 1930–):** French Byron and Patricia Ann Winnett (14 Nov 1932–) were married on January 9, 1951. They lived in Fort Worth and in Marathon, Texas.

    - **Byron David Williams (5 Oct 1951–):** Byron married Patricia Lynn Gibbs (19 Apr 1957–) on June 24, 1980. Their children were Daniel Caleb (10 Oct 1981–) and Paul David (1 Apr 1984–).

    - **French Lane Williams (29 Oct 1954–):** French Lane married Shirley O. Glover (20 Sep 1959–) on May 23, 1974. A second wedding, to Jutanah Lynn Lukor (1 Apr 1962–), was on September 21, 1981. The children of French Lane and Shirley are Sherry Lynn (14 Dec 1974–) and Jeremiah Lane (9 Jan 1977–). The children of French Lane and Jutanah are Brittany Michelle (4 Aug 1983–) and Ashley Lanae (15 Nov 1988–).

    - **Mark Owen Williams (25 Oct 1956–):** Mark married Shirley Ann Mitchell (21 Jun 1966–) on November 4, 1984. Their daughter is Shatiel Amanda (2 Jul 1989–).

    - **Matthew Vince Williams (9 Dec 1957–):** Matthew married Deanne Gail Meadows (8 Jan 1960–) on November 14, 1987.

    - **Daniel Jay Williams (29 Nov 1959–).**

- **Florence Belle Deupree (13 Jan 1909–17 Feb 1992):** Florence was born in Henderson County, Texas, the third child of Walton and Katie Deupree. She attended the local schools and obtained a teaching credential from what was then North Texas State Normal School (later North Texas State University). At the time of the 1930 census, she was living at home and teaching at a local school. On September 20, 1930, Florence married George Ernest McElhany, and the couple made their home in Athens, Texas, where George worked for the local ice company. Prior to 1936, he was transferred to the company's plant in Corsicana, Texas, and the family moved there. A later move took the family to Houston and George to employment for the Houston Oil Company. The 1940 census shows the family in Houston.

On September 2, 1941, George McElhany ended his life, leaving Florence with three small children to raise. She moved her young family back to Henderson County to be near her family and resumed her teaching career. At first, she taught in the local rural schools and spent summers at North Texas State to complete her bachelor's degree and permanent teaching credential. She then taught third grade at Athens Public School, a position she kept until her retirement.

- **Barbara Jean McElhany (4 Apr 1931–15 Jun 2014):** Barbara Jean attended school in Henderson County and North Texas State College. She married Luther Doyle Martin (15 Sep 1930–) on January 24, 1950. His career as a minister in the Church of Christ took them to various parts of the country, including Upstate New York, Montana, Oklahoma, and Texas. Upon retirement from an active ministry, they settled in Linden, Texas.

  - **Barbara Carol Martin (7 Feb 1951–):** Barbara met her husband, Jonathan Snow Haywood, while attending college in Oklahoma City. They reside in Clancy, Montana, where Barbara is a computer operator for the state corrections system and Jonathan is a carpenter and handyman. They have one son, Terry Martin (12 Jun 1972–).

  - **Dianna Lynn Martin (28 Mar 1952–):** Dianna also met her husband, Kenneth Randall McMaster, at college in Oklahoma City. After their wedding, they lived in Seattle, Washington, until Kenneth's employer, Boeing Aircraft, transferred them to Virginia. They live in Sterling, Virginia, where Dianna is a full-time homemaker and has homeschooled their children: Ryan Andrew (14 Jul 1979–), Sean Alan (5 May 1981–), and Wade Cameron (2 Nov 1983–).

  - **George Elliot Martin (2 Jan 1955–):** George is a registered nurse in Tuscaloosa, Alabama, where he specializes in surgical nursing for eye surgery. He and Barbara Beth Hodges (16 Sep 1955–) were married on May 23, 1975. Barbara taught school while George was in college but then was a full-time homemaker until their children were in school. She then became a secretary at their church. George and Barbara have three children: Victoria Rachelle (20 Mar 1981–), Cynthia Renee (1 Sep 1982–), and Christina Laynette (10 Dec 1986–).

- **Jerry Ann McElhany (6 Sep 1932–20 Oct 2015):** Jerry Ann attended school in Henderson County, Texas, and North Texas State Teachers College. She married Bryan Neal Bishop (18 Sep 1924–27 Apr 2003) on August 15, 1953. His parents were Joe B. Bishop and Lorene Reid. Bryan served in the US Army Air Force during World War II. They made their home in Argyle, Denton County, Texas. They had four children.

  - **Wayne Bryan Bishop (9 Oct 1954–):** Wayne married Emory Ann Parrish on June 19, 1982. Their children are Michael Ann (15 May 1984–), Brett Randall (11 Sep 1985–), and Reid Allen (16 Nov 1988–).

  - **Samuel Ernest Bishop (22 May 1956–):** Samuel married Sharon Louise Brown (9 Jan 1965–) on October 24, 1983. Their children are Matthew Donovan (11 Aug 1985–), Christopher Daniel (15 Mar 1987–), and Keri Michelle (31 Jul 1989–).

  - **Karen Gail Bishop (19 Dec 1958–):** Karen married Thomas Robert Smith (3 Sep 1958–) on June 3, 1978. Their children are Bryan Thomas (6 Nov 1978–), Fletcher Scott (11 Aug 1981–), Katie Elizabeth (9 Aug 1990–), and Amy Marie (9 Aug 1990–).

  - **Craig Randall Bishop (21 Apr 1962–).**

- **George Walton McElhany (8 Aug 1934–):** George married Violet Summers on November 7, 1981. Her children from an earlier marriage are Charles Edward Donovan and Anne Marie Donovan.

- **Thomas Powell "Tom" Deupree (14 Aug 1910–25 May 1980):** Tom took over the management of the family farm when his father had a stroke, and he continued in that role after his father's death. Tom never married, and he operated the farm for his mother during her lifetime. He died in Henderson County.

- **Lois Elizabeth Deupree (7 May 1912–17 Jul 2010):** Lois married William Edward "Bill" Philips (1 Nov 1908–1977) on October 21, 1933, in Henderson County. The 1940 census shows Lois and her son, Mickey Philips, in her mother's home in Henderson County. Bill was not in the household. Lois died in Nederland, Jefferson County, Texas, at the age of ninety-eight.

  - **Walton Evans "Mickey" Philips (12 May 1934–):** Walton married Katherine Convers (22 Apr 1939–) on June 3, 1960. Katherine's son by a previous marriage, Gary Wayne, carries the Philips name.

- **Walton Porter Deupree Jr. (25 May 1916–23 Sep 1989):** Walton and Mattie Jo Bell (18 Mar 1917–19 Sep 1991) were married on June 24, 1939; the marriage lasted over fifty years. A fifty-year wedding anniversary celebration was hosted by their son Joe Hugh and his wife on June 21, 1989. Walton Porter died later the same year in Athens, Henderson County.

- **Walton Porter Deupree III (9 Feb 1940–):** Walton married Carolyn Ann Alford (28 Sep 1941–) on October 4, 1963.

    - **Joel Scott Deupree (14 Jan 1966–):** Joel married Sonja Michelle Snow (18 Mar 1964–) on December 7, 1985.

    - **Walton Kevin Deupree (22 Aug 1967–):** Walton Kevin married Donna Ann Golden (13 Sep 1967–) on April 4, 1987.

    - **Kelli Stephanie Deupree (23 Mar 1970–):** Kelli married Kenneth Wayne Piketon on November 11, 1989.

    - **Christina Ann Deupree (2 Apr 1974–).**

- **Joe Hugh Deupree (31 Oct 1954–):** Joe Hugh married Darlene Jones (4 Jul 1952–) on June 20, 1977. Their children are Amy Elizabeth (25 May 1978–) and Jenniver Renee (8 Dec 1979–).

- **Byron Scarborough Deupree (7 Apr 1919–19 Aug 2008):** In Athens High School, Byron was a member of the football squad and the Future Farmers of America club. In 1942, he entered the US Army Air Corps and trained at Shepherd Field. He was stationed at Love Field in Dallas, Texas. On May 13, 1950, he married Dorothy Evelyn Broome (28 Dec 1919–16 Apr 1989) in Fort Worth, Texas. They were living in Fort Worth, Texas, in 1958, but later returned to Henderson County, where they established a ranch. In addition to ranching, Byron worked for General Dynamics and Athens Lumber.

    - **Richard Byron Deupree (10 May 1952–):** Richard married Kathleen Mary Psencik (25 Oct 1957–). In 2008, they lived in Athens, Texas. Their children are Susan Mary (30 Apr 1981–), Andrew Byron (22 Mar 1983–), and Erin Michelle (22 Aug 1990–).

    - **Thomas Powell Deupree (16 Nov 1956–):** Thomas married Josie Torres (25 Jul 1957–) on May 20, 1988. They lived in Palestine, Texas, in 2008.

- **James Joseph "Joe" Deupree (5 Dec 1921–Jun 1991):** In June 1941, Joe enlisted in the US Army Air Corps. Training at Shepherd Field was followed by a tour of duty in Hawaii. Joe and Margie Bell Hatton (15 Nov 1921–) got married on August 3, 1946. Joe died in Tarrant County, Texas.

- **Tommie Ellen Sterling (3 Oct 1943–):** Tommie, Margie's daughter from a previous marriage, was a part of the Joe Deupree household. She married Pat Pittman, and they had one son, James Marion Pittman. A second marriage to Authur G. Hawkins produced a daughter, Chaffin Michele Hawkins.

- **Mary Jo Deupree (19 Jun 1947–):** Mary Jo married James Kidwell (29 Aug 1945–) on January 25, 1965. Mary Jo and James's children are Tammy Rochelle (7 Sep 1965–) and Victor James (3 Mar 1971–21 Dec 1985). Mary Jo married Norman Virgil (26 Jan 1941–) on March 4, 1974. Amy Lee Virgil (16 Feb 1977–) is Mary Jo and Norman's daughter.

- **James Michael Deupree (18 Jul 1950–):** James married Lou Beth Hokit on July 1, 1969. A second marriage to Deborah Lynn Brown (4 Aug 1951–) took place on February 21, 1981. James and Lou Beth's children are Jamie Beth (3 Jun 1970–), Kristin Denise (25 Jul 1975–), and Darcy Parish (16 Jul 1984–).

- **Verna Katharine Deupree (19 Jun 1923–26 May 1975):** Verna married Douglas Clifford Evans (6 Sep 1925–6 Sep 2003) on October 14, 1943. They lived in Athens, Henderson County, Texas.

  - **Katie Lucille Evans (5 Jun 1944–):** Katie married Fred Kenneth Miller (19 Jan 1944–) on January 24, 1964. Her second marriage was to Toney Royceston Knox (11 Nov 1936–) on January 20, 1984. The children of Katie and Fred are Mark Kenneth (24 Mar 1965–), Lorilyn (10 Mar 1968–), and Keri Jolyn (14 Mar 1972–).

  - **Douglas Clifford Evans Jr. (22 Dec 1945–):** Douglas married Karen Jean Schindewolf (16 Dec 1945–) on February 6, 1965. Their children are Lisa Kay (3 Apr 1965–) and Paul James (3 Apr 1969–).

  - **Anita Elaine Evans (20 Mar 1949–):** Anita married Billy Milton Hood (25 Jul 1945–) on June 1, 1968. Their children are Alton Bradley (5 Sep 1969–), Penny Lee (18 Jan 1971–29 Jan 1971), Amy Lynn (24 Jul 1972–), and Kathryn Elaine (26 Jun 1977–).

Descendants of Martha Adelia Kenny and John Irvin Wofford

Eula May Wofford
(5 Feb 1890–26 Oct 1979)

Born in Henderson County, Eula May entered a large family of half siblings. On October 20, 1909, she married James Albert DuPuy (14 Oct 1883–25 Mar 1925) of Anderson County, Texas. James was born in Anderson County to Albert Gallatin Dupuy and Mamie Emily Hamlett. James and Eula May made their home in Anderson County. After the death of James's parents—his father in 1910 and his mother in 1914—his younger brother lived with James and Eula until maturity. The 1920 census shows James and Eula operating a farm near Tennessee Colony. Five years later, James was riding his horse through a pasture when he failed to see a telephone wire someone had stretched across the area the day before. The wire caught him under the chin, knocking him off his horse and breaking his neck, a fatal injury. He was buried in Tennessee Colony Cemetery with a headstone carrying a Masonic lodge symbol.

After James's death, Eula May moved her family to Denton, where she obtained a teaching credential. After returning to Anderson County, Eula taught in several Anderson County schools, including schools in Tennessee Colony and Palestine. She was a highly respected teacher and taught until retirement. Eula May died in Anderson County at age eighty-nine and was buried in Tennessee Colony Cemetery.

- **Jonibel Dupuy (15 Oct 1910–Sep 1989):** Jonibel married Guy Nolen Tomkins (14 Jun 1910–15 Feb 1993). Guy's parents were Reed Tomkins and Laura Collier. The 1940 census of Anderson County shows Jonibel, Guy, and their daughter Sylvia in the Palestine home of Eula DuPuy. Guy's occupation was listed as timekeeper for a team contract. Guy enlisted in the US Army on March 14, 1941, and was released on October 16, 1945. They continued to live in Palestine, Jonibel's residence at the time of her death. She was buried in Tennessee Colony Cemetery. Guy survived her for almost six years. His last residence was listed as Bullard, Smith County.

  - **Sylvia Tomkins (25 Dec 1935–):** Sylvia married Starley Mac McKay (1 Nov 1932–4 Jul 2015). They lived near Bullard, Smith County, Texas.

    - **Starla Diann McKay (10 Nov 1959–14 Aug 1979):** Starla was born in Smith County, Texas. She died in Dallas, Texas.

    - **Douglas McKay (6 Feb 1962–):** Douglas has lived in Bullard, Arlington, and Grand Prairie, Texas.

- **Mary Elizabeth Tomkins (ca. 1940–):** Mary married Foy Vinyard (21 Oct 1940–) on April 4, 1959. They were divorced on March 5, 1974, in Jefferson County, Texas. Her second marriage was to James Hullen.

  - **Leslie Eden Vinyard (29 Oct 1959–):** Leslie was born in Anderson County.

  - **Christopher Dean Vinyard (16 Nov 1963–):** Christopher was born in Anderson County and has lived in San Antonio and Boerne, Texas.

- **Mary Lucile Dupuy (4 Dec 1911–14 Dec 2001):** Lucile was born in Anderson County. She married Guy William Keeling (22 Feb 1910–24 Feb 1995) in 1930 in Anderson County. Guy was a rancher, and Lucile taught in the Palestine schools. She was a member of the First Christian Church of Palestine, the Eastern Star, and the Daughters of the American Revolution. She was buried in Tennessee Colony Cemetery.

  - **Carol Joyce Keeling (1 Oct 1931–):** Carol married Robert Eugene Pierce (11 Feb 1927–6 Jan 1972). His parents were Earl Pierce and Clara Lumen of Palestine, Texas. Robert enlisted in the US Air Force on November 19, 1950, and was released on April 30, 1971. While in the air force, they were stationed in Sacramento, California; Austin, Texas; Florida; and Alabama. After he retired from the air force, they returned to Palestine, Anderson County, Texas. In 1972, Robert and their daughter Lee Ann were killed in an automobile accident in Tyler, Smith County, Texas. Both were buried in Roselawn Park Cemetery in Palestine. Carol married Prescott Carson on March 6, 1976, in Dallas, Texas. They were living in Tyler, Texas, in 2001.

    - **Vickie Lynn Pierce (1955–):** Vickie married Thomas C. Smith on July 27, 1975, in Anderson County. They were divorced on May 16, 1990, in Anderson County. Their children are Christopher Brandon (17 Oct 1977–), Lee Michael (18 Apr 1980–6 Aug 1998), and Matthew Robert (27 Jun 1984–).

    - **Lee Ann Pierce (13 Jun 1957–26 Jan 1972):** Lee Ann was born in Sacramento, California. She was in ninth grade at Davy Crockett Junior High School in Palestine, Texas, when she died.

    - **Robert Earl Pierce (5 Apr 1961–4 Jan 1995):** Robert was born at Bergstrom Air Force Base in Austin, Texas, and died in Tyler, Smith County, Texas.

  - **Eula Marilyn Keeling (2 Mar 1933–11 Feb 2004):** Marilyn married Edwin Hunter Dietz (30 Sep 1928–4 Feb 1991). Edwin was born in Palestine, Texas, to Harold Hugh Dietz and Cora Ethyl Lister. Edwin and Marilyn lived in

Palestine, Anderson County, Texas, where Marilyn was a secretary for the East Texas Diagnostic Center. In 1997, Marilyn married Roy Dean Landers (4 Jul 1930–2023) and moved to Tyler, Texas. Marilyn Landers is buried in Tyler Memorial Park.

- **Edwin Hunter Dietz Jr. (24 Aug 1955–):** Edwin married Brenda C. Griffin (23 Nov 1955–19 Feb 2010) in Tarrant County on November 5, 1984. They were divorced on April 9, 1987. His second marriage, to Mary Knuffke (17 May 1960–), took place on February 20, 1993. They lived in Arlington, Tarrant County, Texas.

- **Bryan Eugene Dietz (17 Nov 1959–):** Bryan Eugene was named for Edwin's twin brother, Eugene Milton Dietz. Bryan lives in Irving, Dallas County, Texas.

- **Denise Michell Dietz (29 Oct 1961–):** Denise married David Starcher (30 Jan 1962–) on August 25, 1984. They live in Irving, Dallas County, Texas. Their son is Jared Alan (24 Feb 1990–).

- **Guy William Keeling Jr. (12 Dec 1939–):** Guy married Sally Francis Barnes (4 Mar 1942–), daughter of Ray Jackson Barnes and Reba McNeal of Palestine.

  - **David William Keeling (12 Mar 1969–):** David was born in Bexar County, Texas.

  - **Katharine Elizabeth Keeling (19 Dec 1972–):** Katharine was born in Dallas, Texas.

- **James Albert Dupuy (5 Sep 1914–9 Nov 1937):** James Albert was born in Anderson County. He attended school in Tennessee Colony and obtained a position as assistant superintendent at the Carnation Milk Plant in Falfurrias, Texas. He died as the result of an auto accident near Falfurrias. He was unmarried.

Ocie Melinda Wofford
(7 Jul 1891–Dec 1955)

Called "Link" by the family, Ocie Melinda was born in Henderson County, Texas. She attended school in the county and was listed in the home of her parents in the 1910 census. At age eighteen, she had not attended school in the past year. Link married Edgar Lynn Watson (13 Dec 1883–21 Jun 1955) on June 21, 1913, in Henderson County. They made their home in Athens, Texas. In

1920, they were renting a home on Corsicana Street. Edgar was working as a mail clerk in the post office, and Link was caring for their two children. By 1930 they owned their home on Owen Street in Athens. Edgar was still working as a mail clerk in the post office, but he was later appointed postmaster for Athens. He continued in that position until retirement. Link lived to see her son become a decorated war hero and her daughter married to a US congressman. She died in 1955 from acute leukemia and was buried in the old section of Athens Cemetery. After Link's death, Edgar married Link's sister Edna, who had lost her husband. Edgar died in 1959 and was buried by Link in Athens Cemetery.

- **John Lynn Watson (13 Aug 1914–Feb 1971):** Born in Henderson County, Texas, John Lynn attended schools in Athens, Texas. The 1940 census shows him living with his parents in Athens, Texas, working as a clerk in a drugstore. On January 24, 1941, he enlisted in the US Armed Forces in Dallas, Texas. He listed his civilian occupation as motion-picture actor and motion-picture director. He noted that he had one year of college, was single, was without dependents, was sixty-nine inches tall, and weighed 151 pounds. His acting career seems to have been brief, since little record of it has been found. He was assigned to the paratroopers and trained at Camp Bowie, Fort Benning, Fort Mitchell, and Fort Bragg. Serving in Africa, Italy, and Sicily, he rose to the rank of captain. He earned two Purple Hearts (one for life-threatening wounds), an OLC, a Bronze Star, an ETO Ribbon, and a Pre-Pearl Harbor Ribbon. After the war, John Lynn obtained a law degree and practiced law in Austin and Houston, Texas. He and his first wife, Harriet, were divorced. His second marriage was to Jo Ann Whitmire (13 Nov 1920–9 Aug 2005). John Lynn died from a heart attack while recuperating from injuries sustained in a Jeep accident while on a New Mexico hunting trip.

  - **John Joseph Watson (22 Aug 1952–28 Dec 1958).**

- **Alice Louise Watson (14 Jan 1918–2 Sep 1996):** Born in Henderson County, Texas, Louise attended school in Athens. On August 30, 1938, in Athens, Henderson County, Louise married Thomas August Pickett (14 Aug 1906–7 Jun 1980) of Anderson County. Tom was born in Travis, Falls County, Texas. His family moved to Anderson County when he was a child, and he attended Palestine public schools. He graduated from the University of Texas at Austin, studied law, and was admitted to the Texas bar in 1929. At the time of their marriage, he was district attorney for the Third Judicial District of Texas.

  In 1944, Tom was elected as congressman for the Seventh Texas District and served in the Seventy-Ninth through Eighty-Second Congress. He resigned from Congress effective June 30, 1952, to become vice president of the National Coal Association, a position he held until March 31, 1961. He served as vice president of the Association of American Railroads from April 2, 1961, to November 30, 1967. He and Louise retired to Leesburg, Florida. tom died in Leesburg. Louise continued living in Florida until her death in Orange County, Florida.

- **Helen Louise Pickett (16 Sep 1942–):** Helen was born in Anderson County, Texas, and married Robert N. Larsh in Alexandria County, Virginia, on September 5, 1964. The marriage ended in divorce in 1988. Helen taught high school for twenty-five years before her retirement in 2007.

  - **Heather Louise Larsh (1967–):** Louise married Frank A. Barclay on June 2, 1990, in Hardin County, Texas. They had two children, Andy and Frank Jr. Louise and Frank were divorced, effective March 2002. Louise married Patrick L. Albro in Harris County, Texas, on May 24, 2002.

  - **Thomas Nash Larsh (31 May 1970–):** Thomas was born in Harris County, Texas, and worked as a pilot for Continental Airlines.

- **Alice Melinda Pickett (10 Oct 1945–):** Alice was born in Washington, DC.

Jettie Belle Wofford
(26 Mar 1893–5 Aug 1983)

Jettie Wofford was reported to have been a strikingly beautiful woman. She married Bruce Hodge (1 Jan 1893–30 Dec 1962) in Henderson County on June 24, 1914. Bruce was the son of James Clarence Hodge and Mary Beth "Bethany" Burns. During the early years of their marriage, Bruce and Jettie lived with Delia and John Wofford. Bruce operated a gasoline service station during the 1920s but sold it to become a farmer, an occupation he continued for the rest of his life. He also drove a school bus for the Athens School District. Jettie worked as a secretary at a wholesale company and as a billing agent for a wholesale grocery company. In 1960, Bruce was admitted to Terrell State Hospital, where he died from pneumonia two years later. After his death and her retirement, Jettie made her home with her twin sister, Hattie, and Hattie's husband, Lonnie Carroll, in Anderson County, Texas. After her sister's death in 1973, Jettie moved into a nursing home for her last years. There she developed mild dementia. Jettie died in Anderson County and was buried in Athens Cemetery.

- **James Clarence Hodge (21 Apr 1917–23 Sep 1999):** James was born in Henderson County and married Mae Leopard around 1938. A graduate of Texas A&M University, he worked for the Texas Agricultural Department. James served in the US Army during World War II and was stationed in various locations within the United States, with his last assignment in Washington State. After the war, he returned to the Athens, Texas, area. James died in Henderson County. Mae was living in Athens in 2004.

- **James Clarence Hodge Jr. (21 Jun 1939–):** James attended the University of Texas at Austin. His wife's name is Margaret.

- **Stephen Lee Hodge (2 Jul 1947–):** Stephen Lee married Ann Stanford on November 24, 1965; the marriage ended in divorce in 1974. Subsequent marriages to Marianne Pool in 1974 and to Michelle "Shelly" Fisher in 1985 also ended in divorce.

  - **Laura Ann Hodge (2 Jan 1966–):** Laura was born in Smith County, Texas.

  - **Mae Cathleen Hodge (29 Apr 1968–):** Mae was born in Travis County, Texas.

- **Jon Marc Hodge (9 Jan 1959–):** Jon Marc married Mary Krupala on March 20, 1982, in Henderson County, Texas.

  - **Joshua Brian Hodge (20 Nov 1985–):** Joshua was born in Henderson County, Texas.

Hattie Lou Wofford
(26 Mar 1893–26 Aug 1978)

Twin to Jettie, Hattie Wofford was born in Henderson County, Texas. She attended Athens public schools and took classes at Metropolitan Business School. She worked in Dallas for several years. The 1920 census shows her living in a Dallas rooming house.

Hattie married T. A. "Lonnie" Carroll (30 Aug 1893–29 Aug 1980) in 1921. Lonnie was born in Anderson County, Texas, to Addie and J. L. Carroll. Hattie and Lonnie made their home near Tennessee Colony, Texas, where Lonnie worked for the post office. The 1930 census shows him as a rural mail carrier. Hattie's sister Jettie lived with them for several years after her retirement. Hattie died in 1978 and was buried in Tennessee Colony Cemetery. Lonnie survived her two years. Hattie and Lonnie had no children.

Edna Earl Wofford
(22 Aug 1894–May 1986)

Edna Earl Wofford was born and attended school in Henderson County. The 1920 census shows her in her parents' household. Edna married Guy Elmer Wallace (25 May 1893–27 Mar 1953). Guy was born in Richmond, Texas, to William Watson and Betty Dunagan. His 1917 World War I draft registration shows him working as a public stenographer in Athens, Texas. He indicated that he was medium height and medium build with brown eyes and black hair. Edna and Guy established a home in Athens, where Guy opened a music store.

On the morning of August 18, 1927, two individuals observed a boy "sleeping" under an automobile in the alley behind the music store. After securing their team of horses, they returned to check on the boy. Finding the boy unresponsive, they alerted the authorities, who made an unsuccessful effort at resuscitation. The boy was identified as eight-year-old Spencer Daniel. His friend Gene Johnson related that he and Spencer had been playing behind the music store when Spencer had climbed onto a platform by an automobile and placed his hands on the automobile. When he'd done so, he'd cried out, and Gene had grabbed him, receiving an electrical shock. Frightened, Gene had then run home to tell his mother what had happened.

Guy Wallace had attached an electrical line from inside the music store to the automobile battery in order to charge the battery. It was determined that the boy died from electrical shock, and Guy was charged with negligent homicide. A jury trial on September 29, 1927, gave a not-guilty verdict, but Guy and Edna moved from Athens to Dallas soon after this incident. The 1930 census shows them living on Fitzhugh Street in Dallas in a home they owned with their two children, Guy Jr. and Betty. Guy was proprietor of a radio shop. He later expanded to an appliance store, noted in Dallas City Directories as the AAA Automatic Appliance Company.

The 1940 census shows the family living on Homer Street in Dallas, Texas, with Guy working as a salesman for a retail refrigeration company. They were living at the same address at the time of Guy's death in 1953. Having both lost their spouses, Edna and Edgar Watson—the widower of Edna's sister Link—were married on July 16, 1956. Edgar's death in 1959 left Edna a widow again. Little has been found on Edna's activities from 1959 until her death in 1986.

- **Betty Jane Wallace (8 Jun 1925–11 Mar 1980):** Betty was born in Dallas County. She married Sam Eisenberg (1909–1995). Betty died in Los Angeles, California.

- **Guy Elmer Wallace Jr. (7 Mar 1929–7 Oct 1997):** Guy Elmer was born in Dallas County, Texas, and attended Texas A&M University, lettering in football in 1951. He married Theadora "Teddy" Marie Hubert (11 Nov 1928–15 Nov 2000). Her parents were Laverne Anthony Hubert and Blanche M. Sullivan. Guy and Teddy lived in Refugio and Kleberg Counties, Texas. Guy died in Dallas, Texas.

- **Guy Anthony Wallace (3 Aug 1953–):** Guy was born in Refugio, Texas, and married Joanne Teresa Collins on January 5, 1974, in Harris County, Texas. They were divorced on May 7, 1997, in Kleberg County, Texas. Their daughter is Kara Trista (12 Jun 1976–).

- **Rebecca Lynn Wallace (6 Jan 1957–):** Rebecca was born in Kleberg County. She married David M. Pavelke on August 25, 1977, in Kleberg. They lived in Bexar County, Texas, where both their children were born. Their children are Phillip Daniel (30 Aug 1982–) and Lauren Emily (11 Sep 1984–).

- **John William Wallace (3 May 1958–):** John was born in Kleberg County. He married Deborah A. Sheffey on March 27, 1982. Their children are Susannah Michelle (20 Oct 1982–), Robert (30 Mar 1984–), and John Andrew (23 Mar 1986–).

- **Samuel Thomas Wallace (18 Nov 1959–):** Samuel was born in Kleberg County and married Julia Pinkerton on January 11, 1986, also in Kleberg County. Their children are Katherine Lavaughn (25 Jun 1986–) and Alyssa Marie (22 Feb 1989–).

William Bryan Wofford
(8 Jan 1897–15 Dec 1984)

Bryan was the youngest child and only son of Martha Adelia Kenny and John Irvin Wofford. He attended Pine Grove School in Henderson County. His World War I registration card shows him as tall, with a medium build, gray eyes, and dark-brown hair. He was doing farmwork and was married. He and Bertie Browning (15 Jun 1896–5 Dec 1974) were married on January 8, 1918, in Henderson County. Bertie was born to James Presley Browning and Mary Emily Wilson. Bryan was inducted in the army and participated in combat operations in Europe. On completion of his military service, Bryan returned to Henderson County, where he and Bertie operated a farm. Except for a period of time during World War II where they are found on the 1942 city directory for Fort Worth, Texas, they continued operating the farm until about 1970. At that time, they sold the farm and moved to Athens, Texas. A few years later, Bertie's health began to deteriorate, leading to her death. Bryan continued living in Athens until his own health prompted a move to Bell County. He was admitted to the Tutor Nursing Home in Temple, Texas, and died there three months later.

- **Nedra Jane Wofford (21 Apr 1919–3 Feb 1991):** Born in Henderson County, Nedra attended Mill Run Elementary School. Nedra married Leon Fontenot, born around 1915 in St. Tammany, Louisiana. The couple is shown on the 1940 census in Crowley, Acadia Parish, Louisiana. Leon was working as a civil engineer. Leon and Nedra's son was born in Tarrant County, Texas. After World War II, they moved to Midland, Texas. Nedra died in Alameda, California.

  - **Jane Ann Fontenot:** Jane was born around 1940, probably in Louisiana. She grew up and attended school in Midland, Texas. Among her school friends was Laura Welch. Though a Democrat and supporter of liberal policies, Jane Ann was on the White House guest list when Laura Welch Bush became the First Lady of the United States. Jane Ann studied nursing, earned a master's degree, and became a certified nurse midwife in Berkeley, California. Living in Oakland, California, she was active in organizations endorsing the Mother-Friendly Childbirth Initiative. Jane Ann was married and divorced. She has two daughters, Kasiah and Geneveive.

  - **Michael Leon Fontenot (9 Jan 1943–):** Michael was born in Tarrant County, Texas. He and his wife, Ann, live in Boulder, Colorado. They have two children, Mark and Amy.

- **Linda Florine "Doll" Wofford (22 Dec 1920–14 Mar 1998):** Linda was born in Henderson County, and she married Lait, a member of the US Navy at the time of their marriage. They lived in California until the marriage ended in divorce. Linda and her son, Bryan, returned to Henderson County. They lived with Bryan and Bertie Wofford for a time, then moved to Temple, Texas. Linda died in Temple. She was buried in Pine Grove Cemetery, Henderson County.

  - **Bryan Lait:** Bryan and his wife, Sherry, live in Mobile, Alabama.

- **Jo Ann Wofford (11 Oct 1922–4 Jul 1992):** Jo Ann attended Pine Grove Elementary School and graduated from Athens High School. She married John William Lehr (3 Jul 1916–26 Oct 2011) on December 21, 1941. John was born in Henderson County, Texas, to John Reilly Lehr and Ona Bell Davis. The Lehr family operated the Lehr-Carroll Funeral Home in Athens until the death of John Reilly Lehr in 1945. John William Lehr was a member of the US Army at the time of their marriage, having enlisted on April 3, 1941. After being discharged from the army, John studied at Waco Dental School. He established a dental practice in Shamrock, Texas. They moved to Temple in 1960. Jo Ann died in Temple, Texas, and is buried in Bellwood Memorial Park in Temple. John retired from his dental practice in 2001 at the age of eighty-four.

- **Linda Jane Lehr (5 Jun 1946–):** Linda was born in Waco, Texas, and graduated from Temple High School and Mary Hardin–Baylor University. She taught special education courses in Temple, Texas. Linda married Robert Wayne Bethke. The marriage ended in divorce. Their children are Robert Wade (14 Oct 1968–) and Jessica Lynn (22 Feb 1972–).

- **Lisa Ann Lehr (9 Dec 1951–):** Lisa was born in Shamrock, Texas, and graduated from Temple High School and Southwest Texas State University in San Marcos, Texas. She works for the Texas Department of Disability and Aging Services in Temple, Texas. After working as a caseworker for a number of years, she became a regional case reader in 2000. She reviews cases to determine whether they follow policy and procedures. Lisa Ann married Charles Douglas Millsap on April 7, 1984.

- **Mary Lynn Lehr (7 Feb 1955–1984):** Mary Lynn was born in Wellington, Texas, and attended Temple public schools and graduated from Temple High School and Texas A&M University. She obtained a teaching credential but chose a career as a wife and mother. She married Lanny Blacklock. Mary Lynn died from breast cancer at age twenty-nine. Their children are Cory Lynn (1 Apr 1978–) and Sean Thomas (5 Mar 1981–).

Stepchildren of Martha Adelia Kenny

Maude Levonia Wofford (21 Feb 1878–6 Jun 1946)

On July 10, 1897, Maude married Burrel Thomas Walters (29 Apr 1875–21 Sep 1946), son of Altamus Temples Walters and Sarah Shirley. They operated a farm in Henderson County, in the same community where John and Delia Wofford lived.

- **Orena Madie Walters (1899–1937).**

- **Margaret Adelia Walters (1901–unknown).**

- **Helen Lavonia Walters (1902–1936).**

- **Burrel Wofford Walters (1904–1962).**

- **Eula Wilson Walters (1906–unknown).**

- **Johnnie Victoria Walters (1909–unknown).**

- **Jessie Will Walters (1919–1978).**

Jessie Lafayette Wofford
(13 Dec 1880–6 Mar 1955)

A resident of Henderson County his entire lifetime, Jessie married Lula T. Stone (15 Nov 1882–16 Jan 1963). They operated a farm in the Pine Grove community. Jessie was a member of the Baptist Church.

- **Gilmer Wofford (1903–unknown).**

- **Blanche Wofford (1907–1919).**

Irvin Larkin Wofford
(3 Jul 1884–8 Apr 1961)

Larkin left Henderson County as a young man. When he registered for the World War I draft in 1918, he was living in Kern County, California, working as a forest ranger. The 1920 Kern County census shows Larkin as a farmer with his wife, Naomi, and children, John and Naomi. The 1940 census indicates they owned the farm, valued at $2,500. His wife is listed as Margaret, but burial records give her name as Margaret Naomi.

- **John Irvin Wofford (1915–unknown).**

- **Naomi Lucylle Wofford, married name Nichols (1917–unknown).**

William Alexander Wofford
(15 Nov 1886–1 May 1957)

Willie remained in the family home until his marriage to Mary Alma Avant (10 Oct 1893–unknown) of Tennessee Colony in 1919. They then moved into the smaller house originally built by John and Delia. Willie worked with his father on the farm with gradually increasing responsibilities until assuming full operation when his father retired. Eventually Willie's son, William Avant, operated the farm, which was recognized by the state of Texas as being under continuous operation by one family for one hundred years.

- **William Avant "Bill" Wofford (1920–unknown):** Bill married Nell England Robinson, and they lived in the home built by his grandfather. Their children are Cindy Lynn, William Alexander, and Leslie Sue.

- **Mary Tyrone Wofford (1822–unknown):** Mary married Maynard Massengale, a fishing guide. Mary taught school in Henderson County, including the Athens Independent School District.

- **Jettie Martha Wofford (3 Dec 1925–27 Jul 1993):** Martha married Malachy Francis Byrne Jr. Their children are Malachy, William Timothy, Cynthia Therese, Mary Ann, and Thomas Francis.

- **Hattie Sue Wofford (3 Dec 1925–unknown):** Sue was a civilian employee of the US Army at Fort Sam Houston in San Antonio, Texas. She retired in San Antonio.

SOURCES

"Avant, Albert S." 1940 US Census, Henderson County, Texas, p. 7B, ED 1-9. Ancestry.com, 2012.

"Avant, Albert Simpson." Texas, Find A Grave Index, 1836–2011. Ancestry.com, 2012.

"Avant, Mary Dupree." Texas Death Certificates, 1903–1982. Ancestry.com, 2013.

"Avant, Mary." US, Find A Grave Index, 1600s–Current. Ancestry.com, 2012.

"Bishop, Bryan Neal." US Veterans Gravesites, ca. 1775–2006. Ancestry.com, 2006.

"Bishop, Bryan." US Department of Veterans Affairs BIRLS Death File, 1850–2010. Ancestry.com, 2011.

"Bishop, Jerry Ann McElhaney." United States Obituary Collection. Ancestry.com, 2006.

Bishop, Samuel. *Family of Katie Judson Scarborough Deupree*. Argyle, Texas, 1990. Unpublished family record. Copy provided by Barbara Martin, July 2000.

"Broom, Dorothy Evelyn." US, Social Security Applications and Claims Index, 1936–2007. Ancestry.com, 2015.

"Carroll, Hattie." US, Find A Grave Index, 1600s–Current. Ancestry.com, 2012.

"Carroll, Mrs. Hattie Louise." Texas Death Certificates, 1903–1982. Ancestry.com, 2013.

"Carroll, Thomas A." 1930 US Census, Anderson County, Texas, Tennessee Colony, ED 1-20, sheet 14B, lines 79–81, April 25, 1930. FamilySearch Library, Salt Lake City, UT.

"Carroll, Thomas A." 1930 US Census, Anderson County, Texas, Tennessee Colony, Precinct 5, ED 1-20, sheet 14B, lines 79–81, dwelling 300, family 312. LDS FamilySearch Library, Salt Lake City, UT.

"Carroll, Thomas A." 1940 US Census, Anderson County, Texas, p. 4A, ED 1-29. Ancestry.com, 2012.

"Carroll, Thomas A." US, Find A Grave Index, 1600s–Current. Ancestry.com, 2012.

"Carroll, Thomas." Social Security Death Index. Ancestry.com, 2008.

"Carson, Carol Joyce." US, Find A Grave Index, 1600s–Current. Ancestry.com, 2002.

"Cemetery Records for Henderson County, Texas." Compiled in 1977 by Henderson County Historical Commission. FHLC #1398560, item 8, LDS FamilySearch Library, Salt Lake City, UT.

"Couple Observes 50th Anniversary." The TxGenWeb Project. Henderson County, October 31, 2003.

Davis, Leona Kenny. Conversation with Mary Jo Kenny. Summer 1981.

Davis, Leona Kenny. Paper on family history, untitled and undated. Only known copy in Mary Jo Kenny's possession since 1981.

"Deupree, Addie Lou, to F. B. Williams." Texas Select County Marriage Records, 1937–2015, Anderson County. Ancestry.com, 2014.

"Deupree, Byron Scarborough, to Dorothy Evelyn Clift." Texas, Select County Marriage Records, 1837–2015. Ancestry.com, 2014.

"Deupree, Byron Scarborough." Social Security Death Index. Ancestry.com, 2008.

"Deupree, Byron Scarborough." US, Find A Grave Index, 1600s–Current. Ancestry.com, 2012.

"Deupree, Byron." US Department of Veterans Affairs BIRLS Death File, 1850–2010. Ancestry.com, 2011.

"Deupree, Dorothy Evelyn." US, Find A Grave Index, 1600s–Current. Ancestry.com, 2012.

"Deupree, female." Texas Birth Certificates, 1903–1932. Ancestry.com, 2013.

"Deupree, Florence, to G. E. McElhaney." Texas County Marriages, 1817–1965. Ancestry.com, 2016.

"Deupree, James J." US, World War II Army Enlistment Records, 1938–1946. Ancestry.com, 2005.

"Deupree, James Joseph." US, Find A Grave Index, 1600s–Current. Ancestry.com, 2012.

"Deupree, James Joseph." US, Social Security Applications and Claims Index, 1936–2007. Ancestry.com, 2015.

"Deupree, Katie J. Scarborough." Texas, Find A Grave Index, 1836–2011. Ancestry.com, 2012.

"Deupree, Katie J." Social Security Death Index. Ancestry.com, 2008.

"Deupree, Katie Judson." Texas Death Certificates, 1903–1982. Ancestry.com, 2013.

"Deupree, Katie." 1940 US Census, Henderson County, Texas, p. 2B, ED 107-7, line 64. Ancestry.com, 2012.

"Deupree, Margie B." US, Find A Grave Index, 1600s–Current. Ancestry.com, 2012.

"Deupree, Mary, to A. S. Avant." Texas Select County Marriage Records, Harris County, Houston, Texas, 1937–2015. Ancestry.com, 2014.

"Deupree, Mattie Jo." US, Find A Grave Index, 1600s–Current. Ancestry.com, 2012.

"Deupree, Thomas Powell." Texas Death Certificates, 1903–1982. Ancestry.com, 2013.

"Deupree, Thomas Powell." US, Find A Grave Index, 1600s–Current. Ancestry.com, 2012.

"Deupree, Walter P." 1930 US Census, Henderson County, Texas, Justice Precinct 1, ED 107-6, sheet 10A, lines 13–23, dwelling 192, family 199. LDS FamilySearch Library, Salt Lake City, UT.

"Deupree, Walton Porter III." US, Find A Grave Index, 1600s–Current. Ancestry.com, 2012.

"Deupree, Walton Porter, to Mattie Joe Bell." Texas County Marriages, 1817–1965. Ancestry.com, 2016.

"Deupree, Walton Porter." US, Social Security Applications and Claims Index, 1936–2007. Ancestry.com, 2015.

"Deupree, Walton, Obituary." Henderson County TxGenWeb. *Athens Daily Review*, June 25, 1936.

"Deupree, Walton." 1940 US Census, Henderson County, Texas, p. 2B, ED 107-7. Ancestry.com, 2012.

"Dietz, Eula Marilyn." US, Social Security Applications and Claims Index, 1936–2007. Ancestry.com, 2015.

"Dossey, Gaston Joe." Texas Birth Index, 1903–1997. Ancestry.com, 2005.

"Dossey, Gaston S." 1940 US Census, Tarrant County, Texas, p. 5A, ED 155-72. Ancestry.com, 2012.

"Dossey, Gaston Sylvin." Texas Death Certificates, 1903–1982. Ancestry.com, 2013.

"Dossey, infant male." Texas Death Certificates, 1903–1982. Ancestry.com, 2013.

"Dossey, Margaret." Social Security Death Index. Ancestry.com, 2008.

"Dossey, Margaret." US City Directories (Beta), 1951. Ancestry.com, 2011.

"Dossey, Margaret." US, Find A Grave Index, 1600s–Current. Ancestry.com, 2012.

"Dossey, Margaret." Texas, Find A Grave Index, 1836–2011. Ancestry.com, 2012.

"Dupree, Lois, to Willie E. Phillips." Texas County Marriages, 1817–1965. Ancestry.com, 2016.

"Dupree, W. P." 1920 US Census, Henderson County, Texas, Sup. Dist. 3, ED 13, p. 11, dwelling 162, family 169. LDS FamilySearch Library, Salt Lake City, UT.

"Dupree, Walton Porter." Henderson County Death Records, vol 4, p. 315. FHLC #1481016, LDS FamilySearch Library, Salt Lake City, UT.

"Dupree, Walton." 1910 US Census, Henderson County, Texas, Sup. Dist. 3, ED 11, sheet 15, dwelling 8. LDS FamilySearch Library, Salt Lake City, UT.

"Dupuy, Eula M." 1930 US Census, Denton County, Texas, dwelling 249, family 255, ED 5. Ancestry.com, 2002.

"DuPuy, Eula M." 1940 US Census, Anderson County, Texas, p. 4A, ED 1-29. Ancestry.com, 2012.

"Dupuy, Eula May Wofford." Texas, Find A Grave Index, 1836–2011. Ancestry.com, 2012.

"DuPuy, Eula May." Texas Death Certificates, 1903–1982, #81535. Ancestry.com, 2013.

"Dupuy, Eula." Social Security Death Index. Ancestry.com, 2008.

"Dupuy, James A." 1920 US Census, Anderson County, Texas, Justice Precinct 5, p. 2A, ED 21, image 632. Ancestry.com, 2006.

"DuPuy, Mary Lucile, to Guy Keeling." Texas, Select County Marriage Index, 1837–1965. Ancestry.com.

"DuPuy, Mary Lucile." Texas Birth Certificates, 1903–1932. Ancestry.com, 2013.

East Texas Family Records 7, no. 4 (Winter 1983): 29–33. FHLC #1321125, LDS FamilySearch Library, Salt Lake City, UT.

"Eisenberg, Betty J." US, Find A Grave Index, 1600s–Current. Ancestry.com, 2012.

"Eisenberg, Betty Jane." California Death Index, 1940–1997. Ancestry.com, 2000.

"Eisenberg, Betty." Social Security Death Index. Ancestry.com, 2008.

"Evans, Kathryn." Texas, Find A Grave Index, 1836–2011. Ancestry.com, 2012.

"Evans, Verna Kathryn." Texas Death Certificates, 1903–1982, #36037. Ancestry.com, 2013.

Frozzell, Bonner. *History of the Family of Judge David Allen Owen: Family of Joseph Collins Owen*, pp. 80–81. Palestine, TX: unknown, 1962. Henderson County Clint W. Murchison Memorial Library.

Henderson County Historical Commission. "Cemetery Records of Henderson County, Texas." Compiled 1977. Microfilm, FHLC #1398560, item 8, LDS FamilySearch Library, Salt Lake City, UT.

Henderson County, Texas, Marriage Book 9, p. 632. Henderson County Courthouse, Athens, Texas.

"Hodge, Bruce C." 1940 US Census, Henderson County, Texas, p. 8B, ED 107-3. Ancestry.com, 2012.

"Hodge, Bruce." 1930 US Census, Henderson County, Texas, Precinct 1, ED 107-2, sheet 10B, lines 73–77, dwelling 211, family 239, April 9, 1930. FamilySearch Library, Salt Lake City, UT.

"Hodge, James C., to Mae Pearl Leopard." Texas County Marriages, 1817–1965. Ancestry.com, 2016.

"Hodge, James Clarence." Texas Birth Certificates, 1903–1932. Ancestry.com, 2013.

"Hodge, James Clarence." US, Find A Grave Index, 1600s–Current. Ancestry.com, 2012.

"Hodge, James." 1940 US Census, Henderson County, Texas, p. 4B, ED107-4. Ancestry.com, 2012.

"Hodge, Jettie B. Wofford." US, Social Security Applications and Claims Index, 1936–2007. Ancestry.com, 2015.

"Hodge, Jettie Belle." US, Find A Grave Index, 1600s–Current. Ancestry.com, 2012.

"Hodge, Jettie." Social Security Death Index. Ancestry.com, 2008.

Hodge, Mae Leopard. Telephone conversation with Mary Jo Kenny. November 11, 2004.

"Hodges, Adelphe." 1900 US Census, Anderson County, Texas. LDS FamilySearch Library, Salt Lake City, UT.

"Keeling, Carol J., to Prescott L. Carson." Texas Marriage Index, 1824–2014. Ancestry.com, 2018.

"Keeling, Carol Joyce, to Robert Eugene Pierce." Texas, Select County Marriage Records, 1837–2015. Ancestry.com, 2014.

"Keeling, Carol Joyce." Texas Birth Certificates, 1903–1932. Ancestry.com, 2013.

"Keeling, Eula M., to Roy D. Landers." Texas Marriage Collection, 1814–1909 and 1966–2002. Ancestry.com, 2005.

"Keeling, Eula Marilyn, to Edwin Hunter Dietz." Texas, Select County Marriage Records, 1837–2015. Ancestry.com, 2014.

"Keeling, Guy William, Jr., to Sally Frances Barnes." Texas, Select County Marriage Records, 1837–2015, #24364. Ancestry.com.

"Keeling, Guy William, Sr." US, Find A Grave Index, 1600s–Current. Ancestry.com, 2002.

"Keeling, Guy William." Texas Birth Index, 1903–1997. Ancestry.com, 2005.

"Keeling, Guy." 1940 US Census, Anderson County, Texas, p. 7B, ED 1-18, line 75. Ancestry.com, 2012.

"Keeling, Lucile DuPuy, James Albert DuPuy Sr." In *Pioneer Families of Anderson County Prior to 1900*, 103. Anderson County Genealogical Society, 1983.

Keeling, Lucile DuPuy. Letter to Mary Jo Kenny. October 26, 1987.

Keeling, Lucile. Letter to Mary Jo Kenny. October 1987.

"Keeling, Mary L." US, Social Security Applications and Claims Index, 1936–2007. Ancestry.com, 2015.

"Keeling, Mary Lucile DuPuy." Obituary. *Palestine Herald Press*, December 15, 2001. Find A Grave Memorial 321353540. Ancestry.com, 2007.

"Keeling, Mary Lucile." US, Find A Grave Index, 1600s–Current. Ancestry.com, 2002.

"Kenny, Delia, to P. L. Scarborough." *Anderson County, Texas, Marriage Book*. Palestine, TX: Anderson County Courthouse.

"Landers, Eula Marilyn." US, Find A Grave Index, 1600s–Current. Ancestry.com, 2012.

Larsh, Helen. Email to Mary Jo Kenny. November 9, 2007. Subject: Re: Ocie Melinda Wofford.

Martin, Barbara Jean. Letter to Mary Jo Kenny. July 20, 2000.

Martin, Barbara Jean. Letter to Mary Jo Kenny. July 7, 2000.

Martin, Barbara Jean. Telephone conversation with Mary Jo Kenny. October 30, 2004.

"Martin, Barbara." United States Obituary Collection. Ancestry.com, 2006.

"McElhaney, Barbara Jean." Texas Birth Certificates, 1903–1932. Ancestry.com, 2013.

"McElhaney, Barbara, to Luther Doyle Martin." Texas, Select County Marriage Records, 1837–2015. Ancestry.com, 2014.

"McElhaney, female." Texas Birth Certificates, 1903–1932. Ancestry.com, 2013.

"McElhaney, Florence Belle Deupree." Texas, Find A Grave Index, 1836–2011. Ancestry.com, 2012.

"McElhaney, Florence, Local School Faculty." *Athens Daily Review*, September 29, 1950. Henderson County TX Gen Web, October 31, 2003.

"McElhaney, Florence." Social Security Death Index. Ancestry.com, 2008.

"McElhaney, George E." 1940 US Census, Harris County, Texas, Houston, p. 9B, ED 286-67. Ancestry.com, 2012.

"McElhaney, George Ernest." Texas Death Certificates, 1903–1982. Ancestry.com, 2013.

"McElhaney, George Ernest." US, Find A Grave Index, 1600s–Current. Ancestry.com, 2012.

"McElhany, George W., to Violet M. Summers." Texas Marriage Index, 1824–2014. Ancestry.com, 2005.

"Montgomery, John D." 1940 US Census, Henderson County, Texas, Precinct 1, OFW 9A, ED 0006, image 1040. Ancestry.com, 2002.

"Montgomery, John." 1930 US Census, Henderson County, Texas, Justice Precinct 1, ED 107-6, p. 258, sheet 9A, lines 18–22, dwelling 173, family 179. Ancestry.com, 2006.

"Montgomery, Roy B." Texas Divorce Index, 1968–2011. Ancestry.com, 2005.

"Montgomery, Roy B." US Public Records Index, vol. 2. Ancestry.com, 2011.

"Montgomery, Roy Bryan, to Bobbie Sue Montgomery." Texas Select County Marriage Records, 1837–2015. Ancestry.com, 2014.

"Montgomery, Roy Bryan." Texas Birth Certificates, 1903–1932. Ancestry.com, 2013.

"Montgomery, Roy." US Department of Veterans Affairs BIRLS Death File, 1850–2010. Ancestry.com, 2011.

"Owen, Joe C." 1920 US Census, Henderson County, Texas, Voting Precinct 2, Sup. Dist. 3, ED 13, p. 20, dwelling 333, family 342. Ancestry.com, 2006.

"Owen, Louelia." Social Security Death Index. Ancestry.com, 2008.

"Owen, Louelia." US Department of Veterans Affairs BIRLS Death File, 1850–2010. Ancestry.com, 2011.

"Owen, Louelia." US, Social Security Applications and Claims Index, 1936–2007. Ancestry.com, 2015.

"Owen, Louelia." Texas, Find A Grave Index, 1836–2011. Ancestry.com, 2012.

"Owen, Mrs. Verna." Texas Death Certificates, 1903–1982. Ancestry.com, 2013.

"Owen, Roy." US, Social Security Applications and Claims Index, 1936–2007. Ancestry.com.

"Owen, Rufus H." US, World War II Army Enlistment Records, 1938–1946. National Archives and Records Administration. Ancestry.com.

"Owen, Rufus Hodges." US Veterans Gravesites, ca. 1775–2006. National Cemetery Association. Ancestry.com.

"Owen, Rufus Hodges." New Mexico, Find A Grave Index, 1850–2011. Ancestry.com.

Owen, Teresa M., Social Security Death Index. Ancestry.com, 2008.

"Owen, Verna F." Texas, Find A Grave Index, 1863–2011. Ancestry.com.

"Owens, Joseph." 1910 US Census, Henderson County, Texas, Justice Precinct 1, sheet 10A, ED 11, family 9. Ancestry.com, 2006.

"Phillips, Lois D." Social Security Death Index. Ancestry.com, 2008.

"Phillips, William Edward." Texas Death Certificates, 1903–1982, #21926. Ancestry.com, 2013.

"Pickett, Helen L., to Robert N. Larsh." Virginia Marriage Records, 1936–2014. Ancestry.com, 2015.

"Pickett, Louise W." US, Find A Grave Index, 1600s–Current. Ancestry.com, 2012.

"Pickett, Thomas Augustus." *Biographical Directory of the United States Congress, 1774–2005*. The Continental Congress, 2005.

"Pickett, Thomas Augustus." US, Find A Grave Index, 1600s–Current. Ancestry.com, 2012.

"Pickett, Tom." 1940 US Census, Anderson County, Texas, house 1003, sheet 14A, ED 1-8. Ancestry.com, 2012.

"Pierce, Lee Ann." Texas Death Certificates, 1903–1982, #06048. Ancestry.com, 2013.

"Pierce, Robert Eugene." Texas Death Certificates, 1903–1982, #06046. Ancestry.com, 2013.

"Scarborough, Delia, to John Irvin Wofford." *Henderson County, Texas, Marriage Book 3*, p. 523.

"Scarborough, Katherine, to Walter Deupree." *Henderson County, Texas, Marriage Book 5*, p. 440.

"Scarborough, P. L." 1880 US Census, Anderson County, Texas, subdivision 6, Sup. Dist. 1, ED 6, p. 24, dwelling 194. LDS FamilySearch Library, Salt Lake City, UT.

"Scarborough, Vera, to Joe Owen." Texas County Marriages, 1817–1965. Ancestry.com, 2016.

"Scarborough, Vera, to Joe Owen." Texas, Select County Marriage Index, 1837–1965. Ancestry.com.

"Scarborough, Wm." 1870 US Census, Anderson County, Texas, p. 20, dwelling 295. FHLC #0295672, LDS FamilySearch Library, Salt Lake City, UT.

"Spencer Daniel Death." *Athens Weekly Review*, August 18, 1927. Old Newspaper Articles of Henderson County. Submitted by Bunny Freeman. Henderson County TXGenWeb.

"Sterling, Margie Hattan." US, Social Security Applications and Claims Index, 1936–2007. Ancestry.com, 2015.

"The Men and Women in World War II from Henderson County." Transcribed by Laura Gregory Calvin. Accessed on roots-web.com.

"Thomas A. Pickett Biographical Sketch." Baylor Collection of Political Papers. *Biographical Directory of the United States Congress 1774–1989*, p. 1,646. Bicentennial Edition. The Continental Congress, 1989.

"Tomkins, Guy N." Social Security Death Index. Ancestry.com, 2008.

"Tomkins, Guy N." US, Find A Grave Index, 1600s–Current. Ancestry.com, 2002.

"Tomkins, Jonibel D." Social Security Death Index. Ancestry.com, 2008.

"Tomkins, Jonibel DuPuy." Obituary. *Palestine Herald Press*, September 14, 1989. Posted online by Pam Gregory Hall.

"Tomkins, Jonibel." US, Find A Grave Index, 1600s–Current. Ancestry.com, 2002.

"Wallace (Wofford), Linkie, to Edgar L. Watson." Texas, Select County Marriage Index, 1837–1965. FamilySearch Library Film #1018624. Ancestry.com.

"Wallace, Bettie Jane." Texas Birth Certificates, 1903–1932. Ancestry.com, 2013.

"Wallace, Betty Jane." US, Social Security Applications and Claims Index, 1936–2007. Ancestry.com, 2015.

"Wallace, Edna Earl, to Edgar Lynn Watson." Texas, Select County Marriage Records, 1837–2015. Ancestry.com, 2014.

"Wallace, Guy E." 1930 US Census, Dallas County, Texas, Dallas Block 1106, ED 57-45, p. 221, sheet 2A, lines 98–101, dwelling 62, family 79, April 2, 1930. LDS FamilySearch Library, Salt Lake City, UT.

"Wallace, Guy E." 1940 US Census, Henderson County, Texas, p. 5A, ED 255-36. Ancestry.com, 2012.

"Wallace, Guy E." US, Social Security Applications and Claims Index, 1936–2007. Ancestry.com, 2015.

"Wallace, Guy Elmer." Texas Birth Certificates, 1903–1932. Ancestry.com, 2005.

"Wallace, Guy Elmer." Texas Death Certificates, 1903–1982. Ancestry.com, 2013.

"Wallace, Guy Elmer." US, Find A Grave Index, 1600s–Current. Ancestry.com, 2012.

"Wallace, Guy." 1930 US Census, Dallas County, Texas, Dallas, block 1106, ED 57-45, lines 98–101, April 2, 1930. LDS FamilySearch Library, Salt Lake City, UT.

"Wallace, Guy." Texas Death Index, 1903–2000. Ancestry.com, 2006.

"Watson, Alice Louise, to Thomas Augustus Pickett." Texas, Select County Marriage Records, 1837–2015. Ancestry. com, 2014.

"Watson, Alice Louise." US, Social Security Applications and Claims Index, 1936–2007. Ancestry.com, 2015.

"Watson, Edgar L." 1930 US Census, Henderson County, Texas, Athens, Justice Precinct 1, ED 107-2, p. 214, sheet 16A, line 18-23, dwelling 314, family 360. FamilySearch Library, Salt Lake City, UT.

"Watson, Edgar." 1920 US Census, Henderson County, Texas, Athens, Sup. Dist. 3, ED 16, sheet 2B, p. 68, dwelling 42, family 50, January 3, 1920. FamilySearch Library, Salt Lake City, UT.

"Watson, Edgar." 1940 US Census, Henderson County, Texas, sheet 16B, house 301, line 58. Ancestry.com, 2012.

"Watson, Edna." US, Social Security Death Index, 1935–2014. Ancestry.com, 2008.

"Watson, John L." US, World War II Army Enlistment Records, 1938–1946. Ancestry.com, 2005.

"Watson, John." Social Security Death Index. Ancestry.com, 2008.

"Watson, Melinda Linkie." Texas Death Certificates, 1903–1982. Ancestry.com, 2013.

"Watson, Melinda." US, Find A Grave Index, 1600s–Current. Ancestry.com, 2002.

"Williams, Addie L." Social Security Death Index. Ancestry.com, 2008.

"Williams, Addie Lou." Texas, Find A Grave Index, 1836–2011. Ancestry.com, 2012.

"Williams, French B., Sr." 1940 US Census, Tarrant County, Texas, p. 24B, ED 257-124, line 84. Ancestry.com, 2012.

"Williams, French Beard 'Nince.'" Texas, Find A Grave Index, 1836–2011. Ancestry.com, 2012.

"Williams, French." Social Security Death Index. Ancestry.com, 2008.

"Williams, Frenche Byron." Texas Birth Index, 1903–1997. Ancestry.com, 2005.

"Wofford, Adelia." Henderson County Historical Commission. "Cemetery Records of Henderson County, Texas." Compiled 1977. Athens City Cemetery. FHLC #1398560, #8, p. 49, LDS FamilySearch Library, Salt Lake City, UT.

"Wofford, Bryan, to Bertie Browning." Texas County Marriages, 1817–1965. Ancestry.com, 2016.

"Wofford, Bryan W." 1940 US Census, Henderson County, Texas, p. 3B, ED 107-8. Ancestry.com, 2012.

"Wofford, Edna E." US, Social Security Applications and Claims Index, 1936–2007. Ancestry.com, 2015.

"Wofford, Eula Mae, to James Albert Dupuy." Texas, Select County Marriage Records, 1837–2015. Ancestry.com, 2014.

"Wofford, Hattie, to T. A. Carroll." Texas, Select County Marriage Index, 1837–1965. Ancestry.com, 2014.

"Wofford, J. I." 1900 US Census, Henderson County, Texas, Justice Precinct 1, Sup. Dist. 7, ED 54, p. 33B, dwelling 151. LDS FamilySearch Library, Salt Lake City, UT.

"Wofford, Jettie B., to Bruce C. Hodge." Texas, Select County Marriage Index, 1837–1977. Ancestry.com, 2014.

"Wofford, John I." 1910 US Census, Henderson County, Texas, Sup. Dist. 3, ED 11, sheet 14, dwelling 8. LDS FamilySearch Library, Salt Lake City, UT.

"Wofford, John I." 1920 US Census, Henderson County, Texas, Voting Precinct 2, Sup. Dist. 3, ED 13, sheet 11, p. 11, dwelling 174, family 181. LDS FamilySearch Library, Salt Lake City, UT.

"Wofford, John I." 1930 US Census, Henderson County, Texas, Precinct 1, ED 107-2, sheet 10B, lines 73–77, dwelling 211, family 239. LDS FamilySearch Library, Salt Lake City, UT.

"Wofford, John Irvin." Henderson County Historical Commission. "Cemetery Records of Henderson County, Texas." Compiled 1977. Athens City Cemetery. FHLC #1398560, #8, p. 49, LDS FamilySearch Library, Salt Lake City, UT.

"Wofford, Mary Alma." Henderson County Historical Commission. "Cemetery Records of Henderson County, Texas." Compiled 1977. Athens City Cemetery. FHLC #1398560, #8, p. 49, LDS FamilySearch Library, Salt Lake City, UT.

"Wofford, Mrs. John I." Texas Death Certificates, 1903–1982. Ancestry.com, 2013.

"Wofford, Nell Robinson." *Family Histories of Henderson County*, vol. 2, p. 191. LDS FamilySearch Library, Salt Lake City, UT.

"Wofford, Ocie M." US, Social Security Applications and Claims Index, 1936–2007. Ancestry.com.

"Wofford, W. B." 1920 US Census, Henderson County, Texas, Justice Precinct 1, p. 9B, ED 13. Ancestry.com, 2005.

"Wofford, W. B." 1930 US Census, Henderson County, Texas, Justice Precinct 1, ED 107-7, sheet 4A, p. 267, April 9, 1930. FamilySearch Library, Salt Lake City, UT.

"Wofford, William A." Henderson County Historical Commission. "Cemetery Records of Henderson County, Texas." Compiled 1977. Athens City Cemetery. FHLC #1398560, #8, p. 49, LDS FamilySearch Library, Salt Lake City, UT.

"Wofford, William B," 1930 US Census, Henderson County, Texas, p. 4A, ED 7, image 1058. Ancestry.com, 2002.

"Wofford, William B." US, Social Security Applications and Claims Index, 1936–2007. Ancestry.com, 2015.

"Wofford, William Bryan." Texas Death Certificates, 1903–1982. Ancestry.com, 2013.

"Wofford, William Bryant." World War I Draft Registration Cards, 1917–1918. Ancestry.com, 2005.

Wolverton, Bonnie. *Tennessee Colony Cemetery*, 2nd printing, 1951. Brookings FamilySearch Library, Brookings, Oregon.

Ocie Anna Kenny
(4 Aug 1860–31 Mar 1937)

Ocie, the third daughter of William Curry and Eliza Jane (Colwell) Kenny, was born during a hot and turbulent summer in Tennessee Colony. Her early years were those of the Civil War, though she was too young to remember much of that era. The years of change after the Civil War would have been during her early school years in the Tennessee Colony schools.

She was eighteen when she moved with the family to Erath County. She is shown with the family on the 1880 Erath County census. In the fall of 1880, Ocie returned to Anderson County, where, on November 17, 1880, she married Edward Harper Seagler (10 Mar 1859–14 Dec 1882), probably at the home of her sister Delia. Delia and her husband, P. L. Scarborough, lived near the Seaglers. Ed was only a year older than Ocie, and they had probably known one another since childhood. Ed was the youngest of nine children of George Seagler and Anna Jane Holly. Family tradition indicated that Ed was named for Dr. Edward Harper, who treated the oldest Seagler child, who became very ill on the trip from Alabama to Texas.

The Seaglers and the Scarboroughs had been neighbors for several years. The 1870 census shows the Scarborough and Seagler families as families 295 and 297. The 1880 census shows P. L. Scarborough with Delia and infant Verna as family 205; family 204, headed by Ed Seagler, included his mother, his niece Suzie Good, and three boarders.

Ed and Ocie settled on the Seagler farm, and the two sisters undoubtedly enjoyed being close neighbors. Little is known about the Seaglers' first child, who probably was born and died in the first years of their marriage, though he or she may have lived beyond Ed Seagler's death. The only references to this child that have been found were a reference in the 1910 census to a child who was not living and a statement by Leona Kenny Davis that there were two children of this marriage. Tennessee Cemetery records show an infant Seagler who was born May 10, 1881, and died on July 21, 1881. This could be their child, but the identities of the infant's parents are not recorded.

In the fall of 1882, according to family stories related by Leona Kenny Davis, Ed Seagler and P. L. Scarborough went on a fishing trip, where both caught what was called swamp fever—probably malaria. Both died within a few weeks. Ed died eleven days before Christmas and was buried in Tennessee Colony Cemetery.

Ocie and her sister Delia returned to their parents' home in Erath County, where they stayed for a period of time. Ocie's son, Edward Harper Seagler Jr., was born September 6, 1883; it is not known whether he was born in Erath County or Anderson County, since it is not known when Ocie returned to Anderson County. How she supported herself and her son during her widowhood is also unknown.

Ocie Kenny Seagler and William Towers Collins (26 Dec 1855–28 Aug 1911) obtained a marriage license in Anderson County on December 27, 1889, and were married on January 1, 1890, by G. W. Hudson, justice of the peace.

Will was born in Dooly County, Alabama, to William Judson Collins and Matilda F. Pedan. The family moved to Texas around 1870–1871. Will first married Sarah Helen Hudson, who died on January 1, 1887, leaving Will with three young daughters. At the time of Will and Ocie's marriage, Mary Ethna was eleven, Willie Laverne was eight, and Lola Helen was six.

The family lived on a farm near Tennessee Colony. Five children were born to this couple: Ruby Towers, Henry Lucien, Jackie May, Odie Warren, and Robert Bruce. The first four were born in Anderson County, but the youngest, Robert Bruce, was born in Kemp, Kaufman County. Will had lived in Kemp and had family and friends there. The Collins family had gone to a church meeting in Kemp, and Robert Bruce chose that time to make his appearance.

By April of 1910, when the 1910 census was taken, only the four younger children were living at home. The family owned their farm without a mortgage, and the four children were in school.

After Will's death in 1911, Ocie and her sons continued to operate the farm for the next several years. The major responsibility lay with nineteen-year-old Henry Lucien, since the other two sons were only twelve and ten, respectively.

When Lucien and Ara Bella Shelton were married in 1914, they lived with Ocie and the younger children for their first year of marriage before moving into a home nearby. The 1920 census shows Ocie and Eva Hudsen, a family friend, with Eva's son Tamini living adjacent to Lucien and Ara Bella. Farming was the occupation of all except Tamini, who is listed as in the army.

In 1922, Lucien, Odie Warren, Jackie May, Robert Bruce, and their respective families moved to California. Ocie moved with them. Most of the time, she resided with Lucien's family, but she spent some time with each of the other children. The 1930 census enumerates her with the family of her daughter, Jackie May Shelton, in Kern County, California.

In 1931, the Lucien Collins family returned to Anderson County, Texas, and Ocie returned with them. She resided with them for the remainder of her life. Her granddaughter Louise said of her grandmother, "She was a dear sweet grandmother—very patient; we loved having her with us. She and my mother got along beautifully." Ocie died in Anderson County, Texas, and was buried in Tennessee Colony Cemetery.

Descendants of Ocie Anna Kenny and Edward Harper Seagler

Edward Harper Seagler Jr.
(6 Sep 1883–9 Jan 1957)

It is not known whether Edward Seagler Jr. was born in Erath County or Anderson County. He grew up and married Minnie Scarborough (29 May 1889–23 Nov 1957) in Anderson County. Minnie was the daughter of Robert Scarborough and Lizzie Bell Farris. Edward and Minnie operated a farm in Anderson County. They had one biological child, Virginia, who was born and died on November 23, 1919, in Anderson County. At the time of the 1920 census, Minnie's father was with them. Marvin Richard Batten was a foster child raised by Ed and Minnie. Seven-year-old Richard was with them in the 1930 census and again in the 1940 census at seventeen. The children of Richard—David, Nancy, and Nedra—are listed as grandchildren in Edward's obituary. Edward died in Rusk State Hospital in Cherokee County, Texas. Minnie died later the same year in Houston. Edward, Minnie, and their infant, Virginia, are buried in Tennessee Colony Cemetery.

Descendants of Ocie Anna Kenny and William Towers Collins

Ruby Towers Collins
(13 Oct 1890–16 May 1966)

Ruby, the oldest child of Ocie Anna Kenny and William Towers Collins, never experienced being an oldest child. The family already consisted of four children, Edward H. Seagler, Mary Ethna, Willie Laverne, and Helen Lou Collins. Ruby married Robert Rufo Edwards (17 Jul 1882–6 Apr 1961) on July 4, 1906, in Holly Springs, Texas. Rufo was the son of James Robert Edwards and Mattie Lyles Calcote. Ruby and Rufo lived in the Tennessee Colony area, where they had a farm and operated a cotton gin and a gristmill on the western edge of the town. Ruby and Rufo were very sensitive to those around them who needed help, and on at least two occasions, they took into their home, for extended periods of time, families who were down on their luck. Ruby and Rufo had eight children, all of whom were born in Tennessee Colony. A story related by their son Bedford involved the operation of the gristmill. In the fall they ground freshly harvested corn into cornmeal for the local farmers. This created fine corn dust particles in the air. Rufo and the older boys who did the grinding would come home covered in this dust. Bedford and the younger children would pretend they thought ghosts were entering the house.

Rufo was a member of a Masonic lodge. He died in Tennessee Colony, Texas. Ruby died in Holly Springs, Texas, five years later. Both were buried in Tennessee Colony Cemetery.

- **Robert William Edwards (26 Aug 1908–29 Jun 1992):** Robert married Velma Erlene Hall (1918–2000). In 1930 they were living in Grayson County, Texas. The 1940 census shows Robert and Velma living with his parents in Anderson County, Texas. He was engaged in farming. Both of their children were born in Houston, Texas, which was the location of Robert's death.

  - **Mason Roylen Edwards (16 Jul 1941–):** Mason was born in Wichita County, Texas, and married Janice R. Waters on December 31, 1986, in Harris County, Texas. They lived in Houston and Brazoria, Texas.

  - **Georgia Romelle Edwards (11 Sep 1948–):** Georgia was born in Harris County, Texas.

- **Clyde Clay Edwards (8 Feb 1911–5 Apr 1992):** Clyde married Ruby Lynn Weems (20 Sep 1916–1 Aug 1977) on December 5, 1936. In 1940, Clyde and Ruby were living in Mesilla, Doña Ana County, New Mexico. Clyde was working as a truck driver for a construction project. Clyde's sister Pauline was living with them. Clyde died in Rockport, Texas. Both Clyde and Ruby are buried in Tennessee Colony Cemetery.

  - **Bobby Lynn Edwards (1938–):** In the 1940 census of Mesilla, Doña Ana County, New Mexico, Bobby is shown as a two-year-old who was born in New Mexico. Bobby married Jack Eugene Sargent on April 2, 1957. The marriage ended in divorce effective September 12, 1979, in Bexar County, Texas. Bobby married Wilbur C. Westmoreland on November 7, 1987, in Tarrant County, Texas.

    - **William Clyde Sargent (19 Feb 1958–13 Jun 1958):** William Clyde was born in Live Oak County, Texas, but died in San Antonio, Texas.

    - **Sherrye Lynn Sargent (13 Nov 1959–):** Sherrye was born in Bexar County, Texas, and married Jon C. VanDam on June 22, 1985, in Nueces County, Texas. They were divorced on December 6, 1988. Sherrye lived in Corpus Christi and Houston, Texas, and in Greenwood Village, Colorado.

- **Betty Glynn Edwards (ca. 1939–):** Betty was born in New Mexico and married Samuel Faidley Mapes around 1960.

  - **Samuel Dewayne Mapes (27 Sep 1963–):** Samuel was born in Live Oak County, Texas, and married Melanie K. Motley on July 21, 1990, in Harris County, Texas. A second marriage to Christy M. Steffek occurred on January 31, 2004. Samuel and Melanie's children are Morgan Marie (23 Nov 1993–) and Bridget Ann (3 Oct 1997–).

  - **Ricky C. Mapes (15 Dec 1964–):** Ricky lived in Houston, Texas. On January 19, 1991, he and Morgan A. Sharifi were married in Harris County, Texas. Their daughter is Morgan Marie (30 Jun 1996–).

  - **Micky Felix Mapes (15 Dec 1964–):** Micky married Lori T. Myers on December 18, 1992, in Harris County, Texas. He has lived in Magnolia, Humble, and Longview, Texas, and in Arkadelphia, Arkansas.

  - **Matthew Douglas Mapes (6 Aug 1969–):** Born in Gregg County, Texas, Matthew has lived in Dallas and Arlington, Texas, as well as Jacksonville, Arkansas. Matthew married Julie Wieland on July 8, 1995, in Dallas, Texas. They were divorced on February 1, 2005. At the time of their divorce, they had two children.

- **Donald C. Edwards (ca. 1942–).**

- **Jessie R. Edwards (ca. 1944–).**

- **Jesse Russell Edwards (3 Apr 1912–21 Jun 1975):** On December 5, 1936, Jesse married Claire Odell Taylor (24 Jul 1912–6 Jun 1988), daughter of William J. Taylor and Lula Galloway. Together they raised Odell's daughter, Billie Dell. Jesse died in Houston, Texas, and Odell died thirteen years later in Woodville, Texas. Both were buried in Tennessee Colony Cemetery.

  - **Billie Dell Hanks (11 Mar 1934–):** Billie was born in Anderson County, Texas, to Claire Odell Taylor and St. Elmo Hanks, and she married Robert Leroy Collins around 1950. Their children are Robert Leroy (24 Aug 1952–), Stephen Delroy (24 Aug 1952–), and Keith Dewaine (30 Apr 1961–).

- **Charles Rainey Edwards (2 Nov 1915–4 May 2011):** Charles married Mary Rowland Peter (13 Oct 1919–13 Jul 2006), daughter of James Russell Peter and Mary Rowland Bigelow, on August 21, 1943, in Oakland, California. Mary was born in Taylorsville, California, and died in Paso Robles, California. Charles died in San Luis Obispo, California, at age ninety-six.

- **Mary Karen Edwards (2 May 1949–):** Mary was born in Oakland, California, and married Robert Lee Manning on June 5, 1970.

  - **Tracey Lynn Manning (25 Mar 1972–):** Tracey was born in Oakland, California, and married Mark Maurice Miles on November 6, 1990. Their children, both born in Harrison, Arkansas, are Daniel Scott (26 Aug 1991–) and Matthew Allen (18 Jun 1993–).

  - **James Robert Manning (12 Apr 1978–):** James was born in Groton, Connecticut.

- **Kathleen Ann Edwards (6 May 1950–11 Jun 1950).**

- **Bedford Duncan Edwards (14 May 1917–5 Nov 2006):** Bedford was born in Tennessee Colony, Texas, and enrolled in Baylor Law School. While studying at the Baylor University library, he met Joyce Harlan (20 Jan 1924–29 Sep 2013), a library science student who worked part time in the library. Joyce was born in Waco, Texas, to Aaron Oscar Harlan and Sue Eva Goodgion. Bedford and Joyce were planning a Waco wedding for December 21, 1941, but Pearl Harbor changed that. Instead, they were married in San Diego, California, on January 17, 1942, where Bedford was in training for the navy. Joyce worked at Consolidated Aircraft Corporation in San Diego while Bedford completed his training. Bedford was sent to the Navy Supply Corps School in Boston, and Joyce worked at the Harvard Law Library. Bedford received an overseas assignment, and Joyce returned to Waco, where she worked for Cox's Department Store. After the war, Bedford established a law practice in Waco. Bedford remained in the navy reserve for many years, attaining the rank of lieutenant commander. Joyce was a full-time homemaker and mother until her children were older; then she returned to work at the Baylor University library. Both were involved in community activities. Joyce was a Sunday school teacher, and Bedford was a deacon, member of the board of directors, finance committee member, and Sunday school teacher for the Seventh and James Baptist Church. Bedford was a member of a Masonic lodge and the Scottish Rite and York Rite bodies. A member of several civic and charitable organizations, he was president of the Lions Club. Joyce was active in the Parent-Teacher Association and the Waco-McLennan County Bar Auxiliary. She served as a volunteer for the Waco Symphony and the Waco Historical Society. A very special event for them was when their son, daughter, and son-in-law all received law degrees in 1978. Both Bedford and Joyce died in Waco, Texas.

  - **Joy Elaine Edwards (16 Sep 1947–):** Elaine received a BA degree from Baylor University in 1969. On April 12, 1969, she married David Arthur Nelson (20 Jan 1948–), who was also completing a bachelor's degree at Baylor University. David was born in Corpus Christi, Texas, the son of Arthur E. Nelson and Bertie Mae Dunlap. David completed a master's degree at Texas A&M, and both Elaine and David completed law degrees at Baylor University Law School in 1978. Elaine's degree was cum laude, and she won the Constitutional Law Award and won first place in the Moot Court Competition. Both established law practices in Dallas, Texas. Elaine was head legal counsel for Austin Industries in Dallas.

- **Carol Christine Nelson (11 Nov 1973–23 Sep 1996):** Carol was born in Dallas, Texas. At Highland Park High School, she was a member of the National Honor Society, a cheerleader, editor of the yearbook, and an officer of the Hi-Lites Service Club. She graduated with an art history major from the University of Texas at Austin. A member of the Kappa Gamma sorority, she served as chapter president in 1995. She died at LaGuardia Airport in New York. A collision of buses and a taxi caused the vehicles to lurch onto the sidewalk where she was walking. Her sorority created a scholarship in her name. A memorial garden was established in her name at Camp Mystic, near Hunt, Texas, which she had attended for nine years.

- **Harlan Claire Nelson (8 Feb 1981–).**

- **Galen Bedford Edwards (10 Aug 1952–):** Galen was born in Waco, Texas, and married Cathy Sue Murphy (12 Aug 1953–) on May 19, 1973, in Waco. Cathy was the daughter of Nolan Murphy and Dorothy Louise Lester of Waco. Galen completed a bachelor of business administration degree and Cathy a bachelor of science degree in 1975 from Baylor University. Galen completed his law degree in 1978 from Baylor University Law School. He served as president of the Waco Junior Bar Association and was chosen as Outstanding Young Lawyer of the Year for 1986–1987. He entered his father's law practice in Waco. Cathy is court coordinator for the District Court of McLennan County. Their children are Ryan Bedford (23 May 1980–), Cameron Nolan (8 Feb 1985–), and Austin Sawyer (25 Apr 1989–).

- **Clara Pauline Edwards (24 Mar 1919–11 Jan 1982):** Born in Tennessee Colony, Texas, Clara is shown on the 1940 census in the home of her brother Clyde Clay in Mesilla, Doña Ana County, New Mexico. Clara married Ervin A. Ketchum (25 Feb 1909–7 Nov 1988). They lived in El Paso and Grand Saline, Van Zandt County, Texas. Clara died in Van, Texas, from a heart attack, complicated by diabetes. Ervin died in Van six years later.

- **Russell Lee Ketchum (7 Sep 1942–17 Dec 1989):** Born in Dallas, Texas, Russell died in Van, Texas, and was buried in Tennessee Colony Cemetery.

- **Mattie Ocie Edwards (4 Aug 1924–27 Jun 1982):** Mattie was born in Tennessee Colony, Texas. Family records indicate a marriage to Jake Smith around 1943. No public records have been found for this marriage or for its dissolution. A second marriage was to Roy Marvin Linderman (7 Oct 1913–7 Oct 1975), son of Andrew Jackson Linderman and Vernie F. Murphree. Roy worked in the construction, upholstery, and manufacturing industries. They lived in Anderson and Dallas Counties. After Roy's death in Dallas, Texas, Mattie returned to Anderson County. She married Randal Letroy Bowman (25 Nov 1920–26 Jun 1990), also from Anderson County, on November 19, 1966, in Cherokee County, Texas. Mattie died in Tennessee Colony and was buried in Tennessee Colony Cemetery. On the Find A Grave Index, she is listed as Mattie Ocie Smith.

- **Roy Eugene Linderman (7 May 1947–26 Jan 2002):** Gene was born in Anderson County, Texas. He married Peggy Louise Henry (15 Mar 1951–) around 1965. Peggy was born in Anderson County to James Dudley Henry and Pawnee Ophelia Hawthorne. Gene and Peggy were divorced. Gene married Nancy Jeanell Hooper around 1973. A third marriage to Pamela A. Wilson on May 7, 1986, in Anderson County ended in divorce effective on January 7, 1993. Records show Gene living in Palestine, Kerrville, and Montalba, Texas. His last address was Montalba, Anderson County, Texas.

  - **Jeanna Louise Linderman (18 Oct 1966–):** Jeanna was born in Anderson County and married Gregory B. Lloyd on November 16, 1987, in Anderson County.

  - **Jamie Renee Linderman (22 Aug 1969–):** Jamie was born in Anderson County and married John F. Hinds on March 12, 1984, in Angelina County, Texas. The marriage ended in divorce effective March 9, 2004. The couple had four children.

  - **Russell Eugene Linderman (22 Jul 1972–18 Jan 2008):** Russell was born in Anderson County. He and Mindy M. Bissey were married on February 17, 1999, in Anderson County. A second marriage to Tammy E. Vanden took place on September 19, 2005, in Burnet County, Texas. Russell died in Kerrville, Texas.

  - **Janna Anell Linderman (21 Sep 1974–):** Janna was born in Anderson County, Texas.

- **Ruby Ladell Linderman (11 Jun 1958–):** Ruby was born in Anderson County, Texas, and married David L. Conaway on September 22, 1978, in Anderson County. A second marriage to Kirby D. Rhodes in Anderson County ended in divorce effective May 22, 1995, in McLennan County, Texas. The children of Ruby and Kirby are Roy Wayne (27 Jun 1982–) and Rusty Dean (9 Dec 1984–).

- **Melba Nadine Edwards (6 Sep 1929–9 Aug 1979):** Melba Nadine married Oscar Vernon DeBose (14 Dec 1920–5 Jul 1969) around 1948. Oscar was born in Victoria, Texas, and he was a veteran of World War II. He and Melba Nadine lived in Dallas, Texas, during the early years of their marriage. Each of their children was born in Dallas. Later, Oscar worked as a road equipment operator in Henderson County, Texas. Oscar died in Henderson County in a boating accident. Melba Nadine married Heril Linderman (22 Jun 1922–11 Mar 1995) of Dallas, Texas. Heril was a brother of Roy Linderman, husband of Melba's sister Mattie Ocie. Melba Nadine died in Dallas from streptococcal sepsis. She was buried in Tennessee Colony Cemetery.

  - **James Robert Dubose (1 Jan 1950–4 May 2012):** James married Irma Carolyn Cheshier. They lived in Dallas, Texas. The marriage ended in divorce. His second marriage was to Elizabeth Kay Brown.

    - **Sherry Lynn DuBose (20 Sep 1971–8 Jul 1973).**

  - **John Ervin DuBose (15 Nov 1952–):** John married Debra Kay Weaver on August 15, 1970, in Dallas, Texas. They lived in Dallas, where each of their children was born. They were divorced on November 8, 1990. Their children are Jennifer Elaine (11 Jan 1972–), John Ervin Jr. (14 Jan 1976–), and Justin Oscar (27 Apr 1990–).

  - **Jackie Marvin DuBose (12 Dec 1953–):** Jackie Marvin and Laura Hammond were married on May 10, 1976, but were divorced a year later. Jackie and Michele Frazier were married on September 2, 1977, in Dallas, Texas.

Henry Lucien Collins
(29 Feb 1892–23 Dec 1958)

Henry Lucien Collins was born in Tennessee Colony, Anderson County, Texas, and was only nineteen years old when his father died. He assumed the role of "man of the family" and took major responsibility for the operation of the farm. As a child, Lucien felt a closeness to his half sister Lola, who frequently took care of him. This close relationship continued through adulthood. Lucien's World War I draft registration card shows him as medium height and medium build with brown eyes and black hair.

On December 27, 1914, Lucien married Ara Bella Shelton (17 Jun 1889–12 Oct 1972), the daughter of E. T. Shelton and Guida Hanks. Since both Lucien and Ara Bella were descendants of Rev. Thomas Hanks, they were second cousins, once removed. During the first year of their marriage, Lucien and Ara Bella lived with Ocie, then moved into their own home nearby. The 1920 census shows the young family, consisting of one son and three daughters, living adjacent to Ocie.

In 1922, the family relocated to California, where Lucien's brother Bob was living. They made the trip by train to Taft, California, where they made their home for the next nine years. Not long after they arrived in California, their fifth child, Jackye Delores, was born, but she was destined to live only a short time. She died of double pneumonia on January 16, 1923. In 1923, the family lived in Ford City, Taft County, California, where Lucien worked as a clerk. The 1930 census shows the family living outside of Taft, California. Lucien was a storekeeper associated with the petroleum industry. All the children except two-year-old Bobbie were attending school.

The family returned to Anderson County, Texas, in 1931. Lucien farmed for several years, then operated a grocery store in Tennessee Colony. Ara Bella was postmistress for Tennessee Colony. Lucien and Ara Bella died in Tennessee Colony and were buried in Tennessee Colony Cemetery.

- **William Royal Collins (23 Aug 1915–24 Sep 1944):** William Royal was born in Tennessee Colony, Texas. He joined the army in 1942. He was a member of the 322nd Infantry, Eighty-First Division. He received training at Camp Rucker and San Luis Obispo, California. Attaining the rank of private first class, William served in the Pacific. He received a fatal wound at Auguer Island and was awarded the Purple Heart and Silver Star posthumously.

- **Una Velma Collins (1 Dec 1917–13 Feb 2006):** In 1940, Una was working as a secretary in a Fort Worth hotel and living with the family of Clarence F. Hurt on Willing Street. Her sister Naomi shared the lodging. Una married Paul Larenzo Stewart (14 Apr 1918–Jul 1984) on March 1, 1941. Paul was born in Ewell, Upshur County, Texas. They lived in Fort Worth, Texas, and both died there.

  - **Paul Larenzo Stewart Jr. (21 Dec 1946–Jan 1987):** Born in Fort Worth, Paul lived in Argyle and Arlington, Texas.

  - **William Gregg Stewart (29 Jan 1954–):** William was born in Fort Worth. He married Karen A. Morris in 1973. They were divorced three years later. A second marriage to Tina Michelle Brunson occurred on May 8, 1981, in Tarrant County. Their son is Loren Paul (23 Jul 1985–).

- **Mary Louise Collins (13 Jan 1919–31 Jan 2004):** Born in Tennessee Colony, Texas, Louise was three years old when the family moved to California and nine when they returned to Tennessee Colony. This was her home for the rest of her life. On November 5, 1939, Louise married Charles Lloyd Carroll (19 Apr 1912–14 Dec 1971), the son of Stanley and Hattie Carroll. Louise's second marriage was to Edward Higdon Massey, who died in 1997. Louise lived on a farm south of Tennessee Colony. She was interested in family history and custodian of many family records as well as a contributor to local history publications. An active community member, Louise was a longtime member of the Tennessee Colony church, where she taught the women's Sunday school class. She was a member and an officer of the Tennessee Colony Cemetery Association, the Tennessee Colony Chapter of the Order of the Eastern Star, the Yaupon Garden Club, and the Fort Houston Chapter of the Daughters of the Republic of Texas. In 1993, she was named to the Wall of Honor in the local community-improvement association. Louise died from injuries suffered in an automobile accident in Palestine, Texas.

- **Gary Lynn Carroll (24 Sep 1941–8 May 1984):** Gary married Linda Gayle Wood. He is buried in Tennessee Colony Cemetery. Gayle moved to Beaufort, South Carolina.

- **Janet Carroll (5 Mar 1945–):** Janet married Edward Hubert Massey (23 Oct 1942–), who was born in Anderson County to Edward Higdon Massey and Gladys Wolverton. They made their home in Plano, Texas.

  - **Tammy Lynne Massey (9 Aug 1963–):** Tammy married Scott Sanders. They live in Easton, Maryland.

  - **Edward Hubert Massey (12 May 1971–):** Edward and Kimberly G. Secretario were married on March 8, 2003, in Collin County, Texas. Edward and Kim live in Plano, Texas.

- **Charles Collins Carroll (4 Apr 1953–30 Dec 2011):** Collins lived in Tennessee Colony, Texas.

- **Naomi Jean Collins (23 Oct 1920–28 Dec 2015):** In 1940, Naomi was living in Fort Worth and working as a stenographer for an insurance company. On May 25, 1942, Naomi married Eugene Clinton Owen (17 Feb 1921–24 Jul 2001). Eugene was born in Athens, Henderson County, Texas, to Hoy Owen and Freddie Beatrice Montgomery. Naomi and Eugene lived in Houston, Texas, where both died.

  - **Cynthia Jean Owen (9 Aug 1947–):** Cynthia was born in Harris County, Texas, and married Michael J. Koch on July 13, 1947, in Harris County. Both of their children, Elizabeth Owen (22 Feb 1979–) and Amy Owen (15 Jul 1982–), were born in Harris County. Cynthia and Michael were divorced on March 16, 1987.

  - **Stephen Collins Owen (December 20, 1949–):** Stephen married Laura Goodson on April 12, 1975, in Dallas, Texas. They lived in Dallas, where their children were born. Stephen and Laura were divorced on March 19, 1996. Stephen married Susan Bohl on April 16, 1999, in Dallas.

    - **Stephen Collins Jr. (22 Sep 1977–).**

    - **Molly (8 May 1981–).**

- **Samuel Clinton (20 Dec 1985–).**

- **Charlotte Louise Owen (15 Aug 1952–15 Aug 1952).**

- **David Michael Owen (21 Jun 1955–):** David married Dinorah Vasquez on September 1, 1986, in El Paso, Texas. Their son, Roger Clinton, was born in El Paso.

- **Mark Douglas Owen (8 Sep 1957–):** Mark married Sonia Guerra in Travis County, Texas, on April 23, 1983. They lived in Harris County, where their children—Emily Anne, Sara Elizabeth, and William Collins—were born.

- **Jackye Delores Collins (30 Nov 1922–16 Jan 1923):** Jackye was born and died in Taft, California.

- **Bobbie Ruth Collins (3 Jul 1927–18 Mar 1985):** Bobbie was born in Taft, California, but returned to Tennessee Colony, Texas, as a preschooler. She married George Milner Wright (1919–1985) on June 22, 1947. They were divorced. Bobbie died in Dallas, Texas, and was buried in Tennessee Colony Cemetery.

  - **George Randal Wright (25 Mar 1950–30 Aug 1972):** George was born in Rusk County, Texas. The California death record for Randal G. Wright—who was born on March 25, 1950, and died on August 30, 1972, in Ventura, California—is assumed to be for George Randal Wright.

  - **Sheryl Ruth Wright (20 Apr 1953–):** Sheryl was born in Dallas, Texas. She married Billy M. Farmer on October 19, 1973, in Dallas. They had two children. They were divorced in 1990.

Jackie Mae Collins
(11 Apr 1896–15 Aug 1983)

Jackie was born in Tennessee Colony, Texas, and married Clifton Thomas Shelton (10 Mar 1895– 10 Apr 1973) on July 4, 1916. Clifton was the son of Elbridge Shelton and Guita Hanks and a brother of Ara Bella, the wife of Jackie's brother Lucien. The family moved to Taft, Kern County, California, around 1920. They traveled by automobile rather than by train, as did Lucien's family. Clifton's mother, Guita, traveled with them. The 1930 census shows them living in Township 4 of Kern County, California. Their four children were in school, and Ocie Collins was with the family. Clifton was working as a mechanic in a garage. By 1940, they were living in a home they owned on Fillmore Street in Kern, California. Clifton's occupation was listed as truck driver. Two sons,

Clifford and Elbridge, were still at home. Clifton died in Taft, California, and Jackie died there ten years later. Both were buried in Taft.

- **Eva Louise Shelton (11 Feb 1917–30 Jun 2000):** Eva was born in Palestine, Anderson County, Texas, but moved to California as a young child. She met Howard Uda Hogan (15 Dec 1916–16 Dec 2013) when they were classmates in the seventh grade in Taft, California. They were married on July 29, 1935, in Kern County. Howard was born in Visalia, California, to Uda Douglas and Audrey Hogan. Soon after their marriage, Eva and Howard moved to Fresno, California, where Howard attended barber school. Upon returning to Taft, Howard worked with his father before he and his brother established a barbershop. The 1940 census shows Howard, Eva, and their two children living with his mother in Taft, Kern County, California. During World War II, Howard served three years in the US Navy, where he was involved in a number of operations in the Pacific. A case of mumps caused him to be in a Pearl Harbor Base infirmary on the date of the Japanese attack. After the war, the family moved to Visalia, where Howard and his brother Harold purchased the Sportsman Barbershop. Howard and Eva also had a citrus farm, on which they made their home. Eva was a homemaker and the manager of the ladies' ready-to-wear department in a department store. Eva died in Visalia, Tulare County, California. Howard continued to live in their home in Visalia to the age of ninety-seven.

  - **Peggy Louise Hogan (19 Feb 1937–12 Sep 2012):** Born in Bakersfield, California, Peggy enjoyed her childhood on the farm with its chickens, cows, and horses. She participated in rodeo events and 4-H activities. After graduating from Visalia High School, Peggy attended business college and worked for Southern California Edison Company. She married C. Dewayne Milford on October 11, 1958. They lived in Porterville, California. After Dewayne's death, Peggy married Gordon T. Woods on October 4, 1983, in Carson City, Nevada. She enjoyed spending time with her children and grandchildren and also with Gordon's children and grandchildren. Peggy died from pancreatic cancer.

    - **Leighann L. Milford (12 Sep 1960–):** Leighann was born in Tulare County, California. She married Richard A. McCue in that county on November 19, 1983. They lived in Clovis, Porterville, and Fresno, California. Their son is Dewayne Brandon (23 May 1984–).

    - **Leisa Milford (29 Dec 1961–3 Sep 2004):** Native of Tulare County, California, Leisa married Jeffrey Noble. They lived in Clovis, Fresno County, California. Leisa died and was buried in Clovis.

- **Kenneth Howard Hogan (20 Dec 1939–):** Kenneth was born in Taft, California, and married Vivian Jeanette Turner on August 9, 1961, in Tulare County. They lived in Visalia, California.

  - **Steven K. Hogan (24 Apr 1962–):** Steven was born in Tulare County, California, and married Kathy A. Moreno on August 1, 1983, in El Dorado County, California. They lived in Tulare and Kings Counties, California. Their children were Justin Steven (12 Feb 1985–), Nathan Michael (26 May 1987–), and Vanessa Ada (9 May 1988–).

  - **Janet E. Hogan (28 May 1965–):** Born in Tulare County, California, Janet married Greg Gayner. Their children are Alyssa Ashley and Ali Gayner.

- **Mary Helen Shelton (19 May 1918–13 Apr 2005):** Helen was born in Anderson County, Texas, and married John Frank James (21 Jun 1916–14 Aug 1987) on July 24, 1937, in Oak View, California. John was the son of Jack James and Lora Gibson. He worked as an electrician and a salesman. Helen was a seamstress. She also enjoyed quilting and participating in quilting clubs. They made their home in Taft and Oildale, Kern County, and in Ventura, California. The 1940 census shows them living in Kern County with their infant son. John died in Oak View, California. Helen continued living in Ventura for several years until she moved to Globe, Arizona, where her oldest son lived. She died at the Copper Mountain Inn Nursing Home in Globe, Arizona. She was buried in Ventura, California, where her husband had been buried.

  - **John Frank James Jr. (1 Jun 1938–):** John was born in Taft, California, and married Flora A. Garrison on February 6, 1960. They lived in Globe, Arizona. Their children are Kimberly A. (17 Jan 1963–), Erin (13 May 1969–), and Cynthia M. (1 May 1973–).

  - **Gary L. James (14 Dec 1944–):** Born in Oildale, Kern County, California, Gary was living in Loveland, Colorado, in 2005.

- **Clifford Thomas Shelton (26 Jan 1921–7 Jan 1976):** Born in Tennessee Colony, Texas, Clifford was an infant when the family made the move to California. He and Delores Simms (27 Oct 1921–9 Jan 1999) were married on October 30, 1942, in Taft, California. Delores was born in Kern County, California, daughter of Clifford Simms and Henrietta Schindle. Clifford enlisted in the US Army on December 3, 1942, and served in the US Army Air Corps during World War II. After the war, they lived in the Los Angeles area, where Clifford was an accountant and a café owner. Delores worked as a bookkeeper. Clifford died in Canoga Park, California. His body was cremated, and the ashes were placed in the Pacific Ocean. Delores lived in Los Angeles until her death.

- **Clifford Thomas Shelton Jr. (7 Aug 1943–):** Clifford was born in Long Beach, California. Clifford and Lynne O'Brien were married on October 24, 1964, in Kern County, California. They lived in Alameda and Orange Counties, California. Their children are Clifford T. (9 Feb 1966–) and Todd W. (8 Aug 1967–).

- **Christa Shelton (16 Dec 1947–):** Native of Kern County, California, Christa married Clinton E. Deerdorf on June 10, 1967, in Los Angeles. Their children are Clinton E. (19 Jun 1968–) and Courtney D. (18 Mar 1975–).

- **Craig Cecil Shelton (3 Sep 1949–):** Craig was born in Kern County, California, and married Sandie M. Fazalare on December 27, 1969, in Los Angeles. They have lived in Mission Hills and Simi Valley, California. Both of their children, Deanna M. (13 Apr 1973–) and Chantel J. (18 Sep 1976–), were born in Los Angeles County.

- **Clark David Shelton (12 Aug 1953–28 Feb 1956):** Clark's birth and short life were in Kern County, California. His ashes were scattered into the Pacific Ocean.

- **Elbridge William Shelton (27 Sep 1922–):** Listed as William Elbridge in the birth records for Tennessee Colony, Texas, he used the name Elbridge W. He married Bessie Lucille Foust (14 Sep 1922–9 Jan 2013), daughter of Elya Foust and Dorothy Edsell, on August 10, 1941, in Las Vegas, Nevada. Bessie was born in Fellows, California. Elbridge worked as a barber and a plant manager for a high school in New Cuyama, California. Bessie worked as an agricultural bookkeeper. Bessie was a member of the Eastern Star. She played the organ and enjoyed traveling and reading. After retirement, Elbridge and Bessie moved to Dunsmuir, California, where their youngest daughter and her family lived. Elbridge died in Dunsmuir. Bessie died at Golden Living Care Center in Redding, California. Both she and Elbridge were buried in Dunsmuir Cemetery.

  - **Donna Lynne Shelton (23 Jun 1943–):** Donna was born in Long Beach, California, and married James Grimmett on January 16, 1964. James enlisted in the US Air Force and served in a variety of deployments. After returning to civilian life, the family moved to Lubbock, Texas.

    - **Janet Shellene Grimmett (26 Dec 1964–):** Janet was born while her parents were stationed in Japan. She married George McNair. Their daughter is Rebecca Shellene (Feb 1996–).

    - **James Shelton Grimmett (23 Oct 1966–):** James was born in Riverside County, California. He married Dawn M. McGraw on December 18,

1990, in Lubbock, Texas. Their children are Elizabeth (Aug 1992–) and James Morgan (Dec 1998–).

- **JoDee Suzanne Grimmett (April 2, 1970–).**

- **Johnny Raymond Shelton (23 Sep 1944–):** Johnny was born in Long Beach, California. He and Betty June Westbrook (17 Nov 1940–) were married on December 12, 1970, in Kern County, California. Both of their children, John Michael (12 Dec 1970–) and Jeffrey Todd (22 Feb 1973–), were born in Kern County. The family later moved to Albany, Oregon.

- **Patricia Lee Shelton (21 May 1951–):** Patricia was born in Bakersfield, California. She married Jamie Devereau on April 6, 1974, in Santa Barbara, California. They lived in Sacramento and Placer County, California—the birth-places of their two children, Ramsey Knight (18 May 1978–) and Brittany Dee (25 Jun 1985–)—before moving to Dunsmuir, California.

Odie Warren Collins
(1 Jan 1899–15 Mar 1962)

Odie joined the US Army on March 22, 1919. He was deployed overseas and was exposed to poison gas. This left him with lung problems, which lasted his lifetime and required several visits to veterans' hospitals. He was discharged from the army on July 13, 1920. On April 2, 1920, he married Lola Sandlin. Lola is thought to be the unnamed infant daughter born to William and Ada (Liles) Sandlin on July 25, 1903, in Tarrant County, Texas. This family moved to Anderson County, where they are found on the 1910, 1920, and 1930 censuses. The daughter's name is spelled Lorna on the censuses, suggesting a spelling error or a different person. A Lola A. Sandlin of approximately the same age is found on the 1910 census of McLennan County, the daughter of William and Mary A. Sandlin. No daughter is listed with the family in the 1920 census.

Lola Collins, age seventeen, is found in San Antonio, Texas, in the 1920 census. She is listed as married, but Odie, who had not yet been discharged from the army, was not with her. Soon after his discharge, Odie and Lola moved to California. They are shown on the 1930 census in Los Angeles County, living adjacent to Odie's brother Robert Bruce and his family. Odie was working as an inspector of oil well equipment. Records show Odie and Lola living in Burbank as well as several locations within Los Angeles County. On June 23, 1932, Odie was admitted to the National Home for Disabled Veterans in Sawtelle, California. He was discharged on August 9, 1932, but readmitted on September 12, 1932. The record does not indicate when he was discharged. The 1940 census of Los Angeles County lists Odie, identified as married, but does not show Lola. Odie was listed as a laborer for a building contractor. Odie and Lola are listed in the 1953 city directory for Burbank, California. Both are associated with a drugstore on Cornell Drive. Odie died in Los Angeles. He was buried in Fort Rosecrans National Cemetery in San Diego, California. Several death records have been found for persons named Lola Collins, but none can be identified as the Lola married to Odie Collins. The only child of Odie and Lola was stillborn.

Robert Bruce Collins
(5 Feb 1901–28 Feb 1961)

The only child of Ocie Anna Kenny and William Towers Collins not born in Tennessee Colony, Robert Bruce was born in Kemp, Kaufman County, Texas. Family stories indicate that the family had gone to a special church function in Kemp when Bob made his appearance. He grew up and attended school in Tennessee Colony. Bob married Beulah Wilson (22 Aug 1903–19 Jul 1981), daughter of Luke Matthew Wilson and Martha Angeline Shipp, on December 24, 1921, in Fort Worth, Texas. Not long after their wedding, Bob and Beulah moved to Kern County, California. They are shown there on the 1930 census living adjacent to Bob's brother Odie. Bob was working as a mechanic.

During the Depression years, the family made several moves as Bob sought work in a time of high unemployment. In late 1930, Bob left the family in California and became a scout for the military in the Huachuca Mountains. He moved the family to Ruby, Arizona, where their second daughter was born. While in Arizona, Bob worked in a gold mine and with the Civilian Conservation Corps. A move back to Kern County brought them near Bob's sister Jackie. Additional moves transported them to Texas; to Carlsbad, New Mexico; and back to Texas. The 1940 census shows the family in a rented home in Tom Green County, Texas. Bob was working as a mechanic in his own shop. After Pearl Harbor, Bob volunteered to help with the salvage operation. The family moved to San Diego while Bob was in Pearl Harbor.

Upon returning to Texas, they lived in San Angelo and Fort Worth. Bob worked as a mechanic, a carpenter, and a bartender, the latter despite an active role in the Baptist Church. Beulah was a homemaker, a clerk, and a seamstress. She was a member of the Methodist Church. Bob died in Fort Worth, Texas. He was buried in Caddo Peak Cemetery in Joshua, Texas. Beulah died in San Angelo, Texas, and was buried in Lawnhaven Memorial Gardens in San Angelo.

- **Joy Lee Collins (24 Apr 1928–2 Jan 2010):** Born in Ford City, Taft County, California, Joy attended school in a variety of locations as the family moved during the Depression and wartime years. Joy married Charles Creach (21 Nov 1927–26 Mar 1981) on February 2, 1945, in Paint Rock, Texas. Charles was born in Rowena, Texas, to Charles Clarence Creach and Pearl Lillian Doss. He worked as a truck driver and as a partner in a trucking company. They lived in San Angelo, Fort Worth, Cleburne, and Joshua, Texas. Joy did general office work and was a homemaker. Both Joy and Charles were members of the Methodist Church. Charles died in Crowley, Texas, and was buried in Caddo Peak Cemetery in Joshua, Texas. Joy's second marriage was to William Harrison Edwards on May 7, 1985, in Anadarko, Oklahoma. They lived in Crowley, Texas. William died on February 25, 1999. Joy died in Fort Worth, Tarrant County, Texas.

- **Curtis Dale Creach (23 Mar 1946–):** Curtis was born in San Angelo, Texas. He and Carolyn Bea Shipman were married on July 31, 1965, at her home in Joshua, Texas. They were living in Tarrant County, Texas, in 1966. Their daughter was Charlette Lawreen (16 Mar 1966–).

- **Cheryl Kay Creach (28 Sep 1947–):** Cheryl was born in San Angelo, Texas. She married Freddie Dale Duke on October 16, 1966, at Joshua Methodist Church. They made their home in Joshua, Johnson County, Texas.

- **Sonny Jay Creach (26 Oct 1954–):** Sonny was born in Fort Worth, Texas. He and Teresa Faye Woods were married on April 4, 1980, in the Methodist church in Burleson, Texas. Teresa was the daughter of Ray Woods and Fay Jackson. Sonny and Teresa lived in Cleburne, Johnson County, Texas. Their children are Charles Roy and Stephen J.

- **Denice Darnell Creach (23 Jan 1964–):** Denice was born in Cleburne, Texas, and married Brian Paul Bewley on June 24, 1984, in Johnson County, Texas. They lived in Alvarado, Johnson County, Texas. Both of their children, Nicholas Paul (14 Jul 1994–) and Jacob Brian (18 Mar 1997–), were born in Tarrant County, Texas.

- **Shirley Jean Collins (27 Sep 1932–6 Jun 2002):** Shirley was born in Ruby, Santa Cruz County, Arizona. She married Calvin Barton Collins (16 Oct 1929–2 Apr 1967) on November 20, 1947, in Mertzon, Texas. Calvin was born in Comanche, Texas, son of Calvin Barton Collins and Birdie May Finley. He worked as a truck driver. Shirley was a homemaker, a waitress, and a driver for a test fleet. Shirley was a member of the Methodist Church. Calvin died in San Angelo, Texas, and was buried in Lawn Haven Memorial Gardens, San Angelo. Shirley married Earnest Edward Bell of Dallas, Texas, on May 4, 1967. They were divorced on June 15, 1981, in Coleman County, Texas. Shirley died in Waco, McLennan County, Texas.

- **Kathy Ann Collins (4 Aug 1949–):** Kathy was born in San Angelo, Texas. She married Jimmie Dale Rodgers on October 22, 1977, in San Angelo, Texas.

- **Judy Lynn Collins (25 Jul 1951–):** Judy was born in San Angelo, Texas. She married Bobby Gerald Coleman on July 30, 1972, in Lawton, Oklahoma. Their son, Steven Dewayne (17 Apr 1978–), was born in Hays County, Texas. Judy and Bobby were divorced in Williamson County, Texas, effective May 16, 1995. Judy lived in Bartlett, Bell County, Texas, in 2006.

- **Gary Lewis Collins (29 Oct 1953–):** Gary was born in San Angelo, Texas. He married Delores Patricia Little on May 5, 1984, in Brownwood, Texas. They were divorced on August 29, 1990, in Brown County, Texas.

- **Janet Lea Collins (24 Dec 1955–):** Janet was born in Fort Worth, Texas. She married Robert James McDonald on February 4, 1982, in San Angelo, Texas.

- **Calvin Bruce Collins (30 Jun 1958–):** Calvin was born in Tarrant County, Texas. He married Janice Charletta Quinney on February 4, 1988, in Big Lake, Texas. They resided in Waco, Texas, in 2007.

- **Reba Jean Collins (4 Oct 1960–):** Reba was born in San Angelo, Texas. She married Virgil Brown on September 22, 1997, in Williamson County, Texas.

- **Janet Beth Collins (27 Dec 1935–):** Janet was born in Taft, Kern County, California. She married John Charles McKenzie (15 Jun 1931–27 Dec 1994) on August 26, 1951, in San Angelo, Texas. John was born in Abilene, Texas, to John Nixon McKenzie and Edith Dodson. John and Janet lived in Fort Worth, Waco, Temple, and Austin, Texas. John was a carpenter, and Janet did general office work. John and Janet were divorced in 1973. Janet married John Mathias Edward Reutebuch of Hamilton County, Texas, on May 22, 1981. They lived in Hamilton and Austin, Texas. John Reutebuch died on April 29, 2000, in Hamilton.

  - **Deborah Kay McKinzie (12 Jun 1952–):** Deborah was born in Fort Worth, Texas. She married Charles E. Johns.

  - **Cynthia Lou McKenzie (2 May 1953–):** Cynthia was born in Fort Worth, Texas. She married Billy R. Stapleton.

  - **Nancy Jan McKenzie (22 Sep 1955–):** Nancy was born in Waco, Texas. She married Randy Young in December 1980.

  - **Jeanie Marie McKenzie (9 Oct 1957–):** Jeanie was born in Temple, Texas. She married Patrick Ranglan.

  - **Thomas Dee Newton McKenzie (May 23, 1961–):** Thomas was born in Austin, Texas. He married Karen Storm.

- **Jeryl Rae McKinzie (29 Apr 1962–):** Jeryl married Jennifer V. Barnett on July 2, 1983, in Upshur County, Texas. They lived in Hamilton, Texas.

  - **Kaitlyn Ann (30 Jun 1989–).**

  - **Kimberly Rae (25 Jul 1997–).**

Stepchildren of Ocie Anna Kenny

Mary Ethna Collins
(8 Sep 1878–26 Oct 1911)

Mary Ethna married James A. Wolverton (12 Oct 1871–8 Aug 1950) on May 15, 1898, in Anderson County, Texas. They lived in Tennessee Colony, Texas. Their children were Allen R. (1901–1961), Alva H. (1901–1996), Mattie G. (1904–1983), and James C. (1905–1967).

Willie Laverne Collins
(8 Jun 1880–6 Nov 1967)

Willie Laverne married William Martin Genett (May 1875–24 Oct 1928) on July 17, 1902. They lived on a farm near Valliant, McCurtain County, Oklahoma. After her husband died, Willie made her home with her daughter and son-in-law, Ethna and Cletus Hovey, in Electra, Wichita County, Texas. She died in Wichita County, Texas. Willie and William's children were Fred Sears (1903–1999), Elmer Lee (1905–1975), Bessie Mae (1907–1988), Frank Vernon (1909–1987), and Ethna Lola (1914–2003).

Lola Helen Collins
(8 Mar 1883–31 Mar 1965)

Lola married Clarence Graham Seagler (19 Jan 1879–22 Sep 1932). They lived in Tennessee Colony during the early years of their marriage but moved to Idalou, Texas, when their children were young. They operated a farm near Idalou. Their children were Graham C. (1901–1988), Brookell (1904–1934), C. Reagan (1906–1988), Grady Williams (1912–1968), Luneta Betty (1915–2003), George Gaston (1917–1994), Lola Oleta (1920–2001), and Nedra (1925–).

SOURCES

"Barton, Helen." US, Find A Grave Index, 1600s–Current. Ancestry.com, 2012.

"Bell, Shirley J." Texas Divorce Index, 1968–2011. Ancestry.com, 2005.

"Bowman, Randal L." US, Find A Grave Index, 1600s–Current. Ancestry.com, 2012.

"Boyd, Lola Olita." US, Social Security Applications and Claims Index, 1936–2007. Ancestry.com, 2015.

"Boyd, Olita." US, Find A Grave Index, 1600s–Current. Ancestry.com, 2012.

"Carroll, Charles L." US, Social Security Applications and Claims, 1936–2007. Ancestry.com, 2015.

"Carroll, Charles Lloyd." Texas Death Certificates, 1903–1982. Ancestry.com, 2013.

"Carroll, Charles Lloyd." US, Find A Grave Index, 1600s–Current. Ancestry.com, 2012.

"Carroll, Gary Lynn." Texas Birth Index, 1903–1997. Ancestry.com, 2013.

"Carroll, Gary Lynn." US, Select Military Registers, 1862–1985. Ancestry.com, 2013.

"Carroll, Gary Lynn." US, Find A Grave Index, 1600s–Current. Ancestry.com, 2012.

"Carroll, Gary." Social Security Death Index. Ancestry.com, 2008.

"Carroll, Janet." Texas Birth Index, 1903–1997. Ancestry.com, 2014.

"Carroll, Louise." US, Find A Grave Index, 1600s–Current. Ancestry.com, 2012.

"Collins, Ara." Social Security Death Index. Ancestry.com, 2008.

"Collins, Ara." US, Find A Grave Index, 1600s–Current. Ancestry.com, 2012.

"Collins, Beulah Wilson." Texas Death Certificates, 1903–1982. Ancestry.com, 2013.

"Collins, Beulah." US, Find A Grave Index, 1600s–Current. Ancestry.com, 2012.

"Collins, Bobbie Ruth." California Birth Index, 1905–1995. Ancestry.com, 2005.

"Collins, Bobbie Ruth." US, Social Security Applications and Claims Index, 1936–2007. Ancestry.com, 2015.

"Collins, Henry L." 1920 US Population Census, Anderson County, Texas, Tennessee Colony, ED 23, sheet 2A, line 24, image 643. Ancestry.com, 2005.

"Collins, Henry, to Ara Shelton." Texas, Select County Marriage Index, 1837–1977. Ancestry.com, 2014.

"Collins, Jackie, to Clifton Shelton." Texas, Select County Marriage Records, 1837–2015. Ancestry.com, 2014.

"Collins, Jackye D." California, Find A Grave Index, 1775–2012. Ancestry.com, 2012.

"Collins, Jackye Delores." California Birth Index, 1905–1995. Ancestry.com, 2005.

"Collins, Janet B., to John M. Reutebuch." Texas Marriage Collection, 1814–1909 and 1966–2002. Ancestry.com, 2005.

"Collins, Janet Beth, to John Charles McKinzie." Texas Marriage Collection, 1814–1909 and 1966–2002. Ancestry.com, 2005.

"Collins, Janet Beth." California Birth Index, 1905–1995. Ancestry.com, 2005.

"Collins, Joy Lee, to C. J. Creach." Texas County Marriages, 1817–1965. Ancestry.com, 2016.

"Collins, Joy Lee." California Birth Index, 1905–1995. Ancestry.com, 2005.

"Collins, Keith Dewaine." Texas Birth Index, 1903–1997. Ancestry.com.

"Collins, Keith Dewaine." Texas Marriage Collection, 1966–2011. Ancestry.com.

"Collins, L. H." 1940 US Census, Anderson County, Texas, sheet 11B, ED 1-29. Ancestry.com, 2012.

"Collins, L. Henry." Texas Death Certificates, 1903–1982. Ancestry.com, 2013.

"Collins, Lola, to C. G. Seagler." Texas County Marriages, 1817–1965. Ancestry.com, 2016.

"Collins, Lola." 1920 US Census, Bexar County, Texas, San Antonio. Ancestry.com, 2005.

"Collins, Louise, to Charles L. Carroll." US and International Marriage Records. Ancestry.com, 2004.

"Collins, Louise, to Edward H. Massey." Texas Marriage Collection, 1814–1901 and 1966–2002. Ancestry.com, 2005.

"Collins, Lucian H." 1930 US Census, Kern County, California, p. 7A, ED 42, dwelling 158, family 199. Ancestry.com, 2002.

"Collins, Lucian H." 1930 US Population Census, Kern County, California, Township 7, ED 42, line 7. LDS FamilySearch Library, Salt Lake City, UT.

"Collins, Lucian Henry." US, Find A Grave Index, 1600s–Current. Ancestry.com, 2012.

"Collins, Lucian Henry." World War I Draft Registration Cards, 1917–1918. Ancestry.com, 2005.

"Collins, Mary E., to J. A. Wolverton." Texas, Select County Marriage Records, 1837–2015. Ancestry.com, 2014.

"Collins, Mary L." US, Social Security Applications and Claims Index, 1936–2007. Ancestry.com, 2015.

"Collins, Mrs. Ara B." Texas Death Certificates. Ancestry.com, 2008.

"Collins, Mrs. Beulah Wilson." US, Social Security Applications and Claims Index, 1936–2007. Ancestry.com, 2015.

"Collins, Mrs." Obituary. *Palestine Herald Press*, Anderson County, Texas, 1955–1983. Compiled by Bonnie Wolverton, Palestine Library.

"Collins, Ocie." US, Find A Grave Index, 1600s–Current. Ancestry.com, 2012.

"Collins, Odie W., to Lola Sandlin." Texas, Select County Marriage Records, 1837–2015. Ancestry.com, 2014.

"Collins, Odie W." 1930 US Census, Los Angeles County, California, p. 12A, ED 1355, image 542.0. Ancestry.com, 2002.

"Collins, Odie W." 1940 US Census, Los Angeles County, California, p. 3B, ED 60–775. Ancestry.com, 2012.

"Collins, Odie W." 1952 Burbank, California, City Directory. US City Directories. Ancestry.com, 2011.

"Collins, Odie W." California Death Index, 1940–1997. Ancestry.com, 2000.

"Collins, Odie W." US National Homes for Disabled Volunteer Soldiers, 1866–1938. Ancestry.com, 2007.

"Collins, Odie W." US Veterans Gravesites, ca. 1775–2006. Ancestry.com, 2006.

"Collins, Odie W." California, Find A Grave Index, 1775–2012. Ancestry.com, 2012.

"Collins, R. B., to Beulah Wilson." Texas, Select County Marriage Records, 1837–2015. Ancestry.com, 2014.

"Collins, R. B." Texas, Find A Grave Index, 1836–2011. Ancestry.com, 2012.

"Collins, Robert B." 1930 US Census, Los Angeles County, California, p. 12A, ED 1355, image 542. Ancestry.com, 2002.

"Collins, Robert B." 1940 US Census, Tom Green County, Texas, sheet 3B, ED 226-21, household 74. Ancestry.com, 2012.

"Collins, Robert B." US City Directories (Beta). Ancestry.com, 2011.

"Collins, Robert B." US, Social Security Applications and Claims Index, 1936–2007. Ancestry.com, 2015.

"Collins, Robert Bruce." Texas Death Certificates, 1903–1982. Ancestry.com, 2013.

"Collins, Robert Bruce." US Public Records Index, vol. 1. Ancestry.com, 2010.

"Collins, Robert Leroy." Texas Birth Index, 1903–1997. Ancestry.com, 2013.

"Collins, Shirley J." Social Security Death Index. Ancestry.com, 2008.

"Collins, Shirley Jean, to Calvin B. Collins." Texas County Marriages, 1817–1965. Ancestry.com, 2016.

"Collins, Shirley Jean." Arizona Birth Records, 1880–1935. Ancestry.com, 2015.

"Collins, Shirley Jean." US, Social Security Applications and Claims Index, 1936–2007. Ancestry.com, 2015.

"Collins, Shirley Jean." US, Find A Grave Index, 1600s–Current. Ancestry.com, 2012.

"Collins, Stephen Delroy." Texas Birth Index, 1903–1997. Ancestry.com, 2013.

"Collins, Stephen Delroy." Texas Marriage Collection, 1966–2011. Ancestry.com.

"Collins, William R." US, Headstone Applications for Military Veterans, 1925–1963. Ancestry.com, 2012.

"Collins, William R." US, World War II Army Enlistment Records, 1938–1946. Ancestry.com.

"Collins, William R." Texas, Find A Grave Index, 1836–2011. Ancestry.com, 2012.

"Collins, Williams." 1900 US Census, Anderson County, Texas, Justice Precinct 5, Sup. Dist. 7, ED 13, sheet 2A, line 24, family 124. FHLC #1241607, LDS FamilySearch Library, Salt Lake City, UT.

"Collins, Willie T." 1910 US Census, Anderson County, Texas, Precinct 6, p. 7B, ED 13, family 17. Ancestry.com, 2004.

"Collins, Willie, to W. M. Genett." Texas, Select County Marriage Index, 1837–1977. Ancestry.com, 2014.

"Creach, Charles J." Texas Birth Certificates, 1903–1932. Ancestry.com, 2013.

"Creach, Charles Jay." Texas Death Certificates, 1903–1982. Ancestry.com, 2013.

"Creach, Charles." US, Department of Veterans Affairs BIRLS Death File, 1850–2010. Ancestry.com, 2011.

"Creach, Joy Lee." US, Find A Grave Index, 1600s–Current. Ancestry.com, 2012.

Davis, Leona Kenny. Family record paper prepared around 1960. Copy in possession of Mary Jo Kenny.

"Deardorff, Clinton E." California Birth Index, 1905–1995. Ancestry.com, 2005.

"Deardorff, Courtney D." California Birth Index, 1905–1995. Ancestry.com, 2005.

"Devereaux, Brittany Dee." California Birth Index, 1905–1995. Ancestry.com, 2005.

"Devereaux, Ramsey Knight." California Birth Index, 1905–1995. Ancestry.com, 2005.

"DuBose, Jackie M., to Laura Hammond." Texas Marriage Collection, 1966–2011. Ancestry.com, 2014.

"DuBose, Jackie M." Texas Divorce Index, 1968–2011. Ancestry.com, 2005.

"DuBose, Jackie Marvin." Texas Birth Index, 1903–1997. Ancestry.com, 2005.

"DuBose, James Robert, to Elizabeth K. Brown." Texas, Select County Marriage Records, 1837–2015. Ancestry.com, 2014.

"DuBose, James Robert." Texas Birth Index, 1903–1997. Ancestry.com, 2005.

"DuBose, James Robert." Texas Death Index, 1903–2011. Ancestry.com, 2008.

"DuBose, James Robert." Texas Divorce Index, 1968–2011. Ancestry.com, 2005.

"DuBose, Jennifer Elaine." Texas Birth Index, 1903–1997. Ancestry.com, 2005.

"DuBose, John Ervin, to Debie Kay Weaver." Texas Marriage Collection, 1966–2011. Ancestry.com, 2014.

"DuBose, John Ervin, Jr." Texas Birth Index, 1903–1997. Ancestry.com, 2005.

"DuBose, John Ervin." Texas Birth Index, 1903–1997. Ancestry.com, 2005.

"Dubose, John Ervin." Texas Divorce Index, 1968–2011. Ancestry.com, 2005.

"DuBose, Justin Oscar." Texas Birth Index, 1903–1997. Ancestry.com, 2005.

"DuBose, Oscar Vernon." Texas Death Certificates, 1903–1982. Ancestry.com, 2003.

"Edwards, Bedford D." US City Directories (Beta). Ancestry.com, 2011.

"Edwards, Bedford D." US Public Records Index, vol 1. Ancestry.com, 2010.

"Edwards, Bedford D." US Select Military Registers, 1862–1985. Ancestry.com, 2013.

"Edwards, Bedford Duncan." Social Security Death Index. Ancestry.com, 2008.

"Edwards, Bedford Duncan." US, Find A Grave Index, 1600s–Current. Ancestry.com, 2012.

"Edwards, Bobbie." Texas Marriage Collection, 1966–2011. Ancestry.com.

Edwards, Charles. Letter to Mary Jo Kenny. March 25, 1998.

"Edwards, Charles Rainey." Social Security Death Index. Ancestry.com, 2008.

"Edwards, Charles." Obituary Daily Times Index, 1995–2011. Ancestry.com, 2012.

"Edwards, Clara P." US, Social Security Applications and Claims Index, 1936–2007. Ancestry.com, 2008.

"Edwards, Clyde Clay." US Public Records Index, vol. 2. Ancestry.com, 2010.

"Edwards, Clyde Clay." US World War II Draft Cards Young Men, 1940–1945. Ancestry.com, 2011.

"Edwards, Clyde Clay." Texas, Find A Grave Index, 1836–2011. Ancestry.com, 2012.

"Edwards, Clyde." Texas Death Index, 1903–2000. Ancestry.com, 2006.

"Edwards, Clyde." US 1940 Census, Doña Ana County, New Mexico, p. 8A, ED 7-13. Ancestry.com, 2012.

"Edwards, Clyde." US Social Security Death Index, 1935–2014. Ancestry.com, 2008.

"Edwards, Georgia Romelle." Texas Birth Index, 1903–1997. Ancestry.com.

"Edwards, Irma Joyce." US, Find A Grave Index, 1600s–Current. Ancestry.com, 2012.

"Edwards, Jesse R., to Odell Hanks." Texas, Select County Marriage Records, 1837–2015. Ancestry.com, 2014.

"Edwards, Jesse R." US, Social Security Death Index, 1935–2014. Ancestry.com, 2008.

"Edwards, Jesse R." Texas Death Index, 1903–2000. Ancestry.com, 2008.

"Edwards, Jesse Russell." Texas Death Certificates, 1903–1982. Ancestry.com, 2013.

"Edwards, Jesse." Texas, Find A Grave Index, 1836–2011. Ancestry.com, 2012.

Edwards, Joy Collins. Family Group Sheets. Sent to Mary Jo Kenny. September 17, 1999.

Edwards, Joy Collins. Letter to Mary Jo Kenny. September 17, 1999.

Edwards, Joyce and Bedford. Family Group Sheets. March 1998.

Edwards, Joyce. Letter to Mary Jo Kenny. March 17, 1998.

Edwards, Joyce. Letter to Mary Jo Kenny. March 25, 1998.

"Edwards, Joy Lee." Social Security Death Index. Ancestry.com, 2008.

"Edwards, Joyce Harlan." Obituary. Wilkirson-Hatch-Bailey Funeral Home, Waco, Texas.

Edwards, Mary P. Family Group Sheets. March 22, 1998. Compiled by Charles and Mary Edwards.

"Edwards, Mary P." Social Security Death Index. Ancestry.com, 2008.

"Edwards, Mason R." Texas Marriage Collection, 1966–2011. Ancestry.com.

"Edwards, Mason Roylen." Texas Birth Index, 1903–1997. Ancestry.com.

"Edwards, Mattie Ocie, to Randal Latroy Bowman." Texas Marriage Collection, 1966–2011. Ancestry.com, 2005.

"Edwards, Mattie Ocie." Texas Birth Certificates, 1903–1932. Ancestry.com, 2013.

"Edwards, Mattie Ocie." Texas Birth Index, 1903–1997. Ancestry.com, 2005.

"Edwards, Melba Modine." Texas Birth Certificates, 1903–1932. Ancestry.com, 2013.

"Edwards, Melba Modine." Texas Birth Index, 1903–1997. Ancestry.com, 2005.

"Edwards, Melba Nadine, to Oscar Vernon DuBose." Texas, Select County Marriage Records, 1837–2015. Ancestry.com, 2014.

"Edwards, Odel." Obituary. *Palestine Herald Press*, June 6, 1988.

"Edwards, Odell Taylor." Texas, Find A Grave Index, 1836–2011. Ancestry.com, 2012.

"Edwards, Odell." Texas Death Certificates, 1903–1982. Ancestry.com, 2013.

"Edwards, R. R." 1930 US Census, Anderson County, Texas, Precinct 5, ED 1-25, p. 14A, line 13. LDS FamilySearch Library, Salt Lake City, UT.

"Edwards, R. R." 1940 US Census, Anderson County, Texas, sheet 11A, ED 1-29. Ancestry.com, 2012.

"Edwards, R. R." 1940 US Population Census, Swisher County, Texas, p. 7B, ED 219-4. Ancestry.com.

"Edwards, R.W." 1930 US Census, Grayson County, Texas, Precinct 1, p. 3B, ED 16. FHLC #2342071. Ancestry.com, 2002.

"Edwards, Robert R." 1910 US Census, Anderson County, Texas, p. 35, Justice Precinct 5. Ancestry.com, 2006.

"Edwards, Robert R." 1920 US Census, Anderson County, Texas, Justice Precinct 5, p. 4B, ED 23. LDS FamilySearch Library, Salt Lake City, UT.

"Edwards, Robert Rufo." Texas Death Certificates, 1903–1982. Ancestry.com, 2013.

"Edwards, Robert Rufo." US, Social Security Applications and Claims Index, 1936–2007. Ancestry.com, 2015.

"Edwards, Robert W." 1940 US Census, Anderson County, Texas, p. 11A, ED 1-29. Ancestry.com, 2012.

"Edwards, Robert W." Texas Death Index, 1903–2000. Ancestry.com, 2006.

"Edwards, Robert W." US Public Records Index, vol. 1. Ancestry.com, 2010.

"Edwards, Robert W." US, Social Security Death Index, 1935–2014. Ancestry.com, 2008.

"Edwards, Robert W." US, Find A Grave Index, 1600s–Current. Ancestry.com, 2012.

"Edwards, Rubie Lynn." Texas Death Certificates, 1903–1982. Ancestry.com, 2013.

"Edwards, Rubie Lynn." US, Social Security Applications and Claims Index, 1936–2007. Ancestry.com, 2015.

"Edwards, Ruby Towers." Texas Death Certificates, 1903–1982, file #33329. Ancestry.com, 2013.

"Edwards, Ruby." US, Find A Grave Index, 1600s–Current. Ancestry.com, 2012.

"Edwards, Rufo R." US, Find A Grave Index, 1600s–Current. Ancestry.com, 2012.

"Edwards, Velma E." Social Security Death Index. Ancestry.com, 2008.

"Edwards, Velma E." US, Find A Grave Index, 1600s–Current. Ancestry.com, 2012.

"Edwards. Bedford D." Obituary. Wilkirson-Hatch-Bailey Funeral Home, Waco, Texas.

"Farmer, Sheryl W." Texas Divorce Index, 1968–2011. Ancestry.com, 2014.

"Foust, E. B." 1930 US Census, Kern County, California, Santa Fe, p. 11A, ED 0060, image 1183.0. Ancestry.com, 2002.

"Gaynor, Alyssa Ashley." California Birth Index, 1905–1995. Ancestry.com, 2005.

"Genett, Bessie M." US, Social Security Applications and Claims Index, 1936–2007. Ancestry.com, 2015.

"Genett, Elmer Lee." US, Find A Grave Index, 1600s–Current. Ancestry.com, 2012.

"Genett, Frank V." Social Security Death Index. Ancestry.com, 2008.

"Genett, Frank Vernon." US, Find A Grave Index, 1600s–Current. Ancestry.com, 2012.

"Genett, Frank." US Department of Veterans Affairs BIRLS Death File, 1850–2010. Ancestry.com, 2011.

"Genett, Fred S." US, Social Security Applications and Claims Index, 1936–2007. Ancestry.com, 2015.

"Genett, Fred Sears." US, Find A Grave Index, 1600s–Current. Ancestry.com, 2012.

"Genett, William M." US, Find A Grave Index, 1600s–Current. Ancestry.com, 2012.

"Genett, Willie Laverne." Texas Death Certificates, 1903–1982. Ancestry.com, 2013.

"Genett, Willie M." US, Social Security Applications and Claims Index, 1936–2007. Ancestry.com, 2015.

"Genett, Willie." 1910 US Census, Pottawatomie County, Oklahoma, p. 2B, ED 0223. Ancestry.com, 2006.

"Genett, Willie." US, Find A Grave Index, 1600s–Current. Ancestry.com, 2012.

"Grimmett, Elizabeth Lucille." Texas Birth Index, 1903–1997. Ancestry.com, 2005.

"Grimmett, James S." California Birth Index, 1905–1995. Ancestry.com, 2005.

"Grimmett, James S." Texas Marriage Collection, 1966–2011. Ancestry.com, 2014.

"Grimmett, Jodee S." US Public Records Index, vol. 1. Ancestry.com, 2010.

"Hanks, Billy Dell." Texas Birth Index, 1903–1997. Ancestry.com.

"Harlan, Aaron Oscar." 1940 US Census, McLennan County, Texas, p. 8A, ED 155-19. Ancestry.com, 2012.

"Harvey, Ethna Genett." US, Find A Grave Index, 1600s–Current. Ancestry.com, 2012.

"Harvey, Ethna Lola." US, Social Security Applications and Claims Index, 1936–2007. Ancestry.com, 2015.

"Henry, Peggy Louise." Texas Birth Index, 1903–1997. Ancestry.com, 2005.

"Hinds, Jamie R." Texas Divorce Index, 1968–2011. Ancestry.com, 2005.

"Hogan, Audrey." 1940 US Census, Kern County, California, sheet 2B, ED 15-54. Ancestry.com, 2012.

"Hogan, Eva Louise." Social Security Death Index. Ancestry.com, 2008.

"Hogan, Eva Louise." US, Social Security Applications and Claims Index, 1936–2007. Ancestry.com, 2015.

"Hogan, Eva." US City Directories (Beta). Ancestry.com, 2011.

"Hogan, Eva." US Social Security Death Index. Ancestry.com.

Hogan, Eva Shelton. Letter to Mary Jo Kenny. December 1998.

Hogan, Eva. Family Group Sheets. Sent to Mary Jo Kenny. December 1998.

"Hogan, Howard U." California Birth Index, 1905–1995. Ancestry.com, 2005.

"Hogan, Howard Uda." Obituary. *Visalia Times-Delta/Tulare Advance-Register*, December 20, 2013.

"Hogan, Janet E." California Birth Index, 1905–1995. Ancestry.com, 2005.

"Hogan, Justin Steven." California Birth Index, 1905–1995. Ancestry.com, 2005.

"Hogan, Kenneth H." California Marriage Index, 1960–1985. Ancestry.com, 2013.

"Hogan, Kenneth H." US Public Records Index, vol. 1. Ancestry.com, 2010.

"Hogan, Kenneth Howard." California Birth Index, 1905–1995. Ancestry.com, 2005.

"Hogan, Nathan Michael." California Birth Index, 1905–1995. Ancestry.com, 2005.

"Hogan, Peggy L." California Marriage Index, 1949–1959. Ancestry.com, 2013.

"Hogan, Peggy Louise." California Birth Index, 1905–1995. Ancestry.com, 2005.

"Hogan, Steven K." California Birth Index, 1905–1995. Ancestry.com, 2005.

"Hogan, Uda D." 1930 US Population Census, Kern County, California, ED 15-37, Sup. Dist. 4, sheet 10A. Ancestry. com.

"Hogan, Vanessa Ada." California Birth Index, 1905–1995. Ancestry.com, 2005.

"Horvey, Cletus O." 1940 US Census, Wichita County, Texas, p. 21A, ED 243-59. Ancestry.com, 2012.

"Hudsen, Eva." 1920 US Population Census, Anderson County, Texas, Justice Precinct 5, ED 13, sheet 2A, line 21. FHLC #1241607, LDS FamilySearch Library, Salt Lake City, UT.

"Hurt, Clarence F." 1940 US Population Census, Tarrant County, Texas, p. 2A, ED 257-68. Ancestry.com, 2012.

"James, Cynthia M." California Birth Index, 1905–1995. Ancestry.com, 2005.

"James, Erin." California Birth Index, 1905–1995. Ancestry.com, 2005.

James, Helen. Family Group Sheets. Mailed to Mary Jo Kenny. January 1999.

"James, John F." 1940 US Census, Kern County, California, Taft Heights, Township 7, ED 15-57, sheet 21A, line 37, April 20, 1940. Ancestry.com, 2012.

"James, John Frank." California Birth Index, 1905–1995. Ancestry.com, 2005.

"James, John Frank." California Death Index, 1940–1997. Ancestry.com, 2000.

"James, John." US Department of Veterans Affairs BIRLS Death File, 1850–2010. Ancestry.com, 2011.

"James, John." US, Social Security Death Index, 1935–2014. Ancestry.com, 2008.

"James, Kimberly A." California Birth Index, 1905–1995. Ancestry.com, 2005.

"James, Kimberly A." California Marriage Index, 1960–1985. Ancestry.com, 2013.

"James, Mary H." US, Social Security Death Index, 1935–2014. Ancestry.com, 2008.

"James, Mary Helen (Shelton)." Obituary Daily Times Index, 1995–Current. Ancestry.com, 2012.

"James, Mary Helen." Obituary. *Ventura County Star*, April 17, 2005.

"James, Mary Helen." US Public Records Index, vol. I. Ancestry.com, 2010.

"James, Mary Helen." US, Find A Grave Index, 1600s–Current. Ancestry.com, 2012.

"Ketchum, Clara P." US City Directories, 1821–1982. Ancestry.com, 2011.

"Ketchum, Clara Pauline." Texas Death Certificates, 1903–1982. Ancestry.com, 2013.

"Ketchum, Clara Pauline." US, Find A Grave Index, 1600s–Current. Ancestry.com, 2012.

"Ketchum, Clara." US, Social Security Death Index, 1935–2014. Ancestry.com, 2008.

"Ketchum, Clara." Texas Death Index, 1903–2000. Ancestry.com, 2006.

"Ketchum, Ervin A." US, Social Security Applications and Claims Index, 1936–2007. Ancestry.com, 2015.

"Ketchum, Ervin A." US, Find A Grave Index, 1600s–Current. Ancestry.com, 2012.

"Ketchum, Ervin." US Department of Veterans Affairs BIRLS Death File, 1850–2010. Ancestry.com, 2011.

"Ketchum, Russell L." US, Social Security Death Index, 1935–2014. Ancestry.com, 2008.

"Ketchum, Russell Lee." Texas Birth Index, 1903–1997. Ancestry.com, 2005.

"Ketchum, Russell Lee." US, Social Security Applications and Claims Index, 1936–2007. Ancestry.com, 2015.

"Ketchum, Russell Lee." US, Find A Grave Index, 1600s–Current. Ancestry.com, 2012.

"Kinney, O. A., and E. A. Seagler." Texas, Select County Marriage Records, 1837–2005. Anderson County Marriage Records, Book 8, p. 447A. Ancestry.com, 2014.

"Koch, Michael J." Texas Divorce Index, 1968–2011. Ancestry.com, 2014.

"Law Students Graduate." *Waco Tribune Herald* (August 1978): 7A. Photocopy provided by Joyce Edwards.

"Linderman, Heril L." US, Social Security Death Index, 1935–2014. Ancestry.com, 2008.

"Linderman, Jamie R., to John F. Hinds." Texas Marriage Collection, 1966–2011. Ancestry.com, 2014.

"Linderman, Jamie Renee." Texas Birth Index, 1903–1997. Ancestry.com, 2005.

"Linderman, Janna Anell." Texas Birth Index, 1903–1997. Ancestry.com, 2005.

"Linderman, Jeanna L., to Gregory B. Lloyd." Texas Marriage Collection, 1966–2011. Ancestry.com, 2014.

"Linderman, Jeanna Louise." Texas Birth Index, 1903–1997. Ancestry.com, 2005.

"Linderman, Melba Nadine." Texas Death Certificates, 1903–1982. Ancestry.com, 2013.

"Linderman, Melba." Texas Death Index, 1903–2000. Ancestry.com, 2008.

"Linderman, Nadine Edwards." Texas, Find A Grave Index, 1836–2011. Ancestry.com, 2012.

"Linderman, Roy E., to Peggy Louise Henry" Texas Marriage Collection, 1966–2011. Ancestry.com, 2014.

"Linderman, Roy E." Texas Divorce Index, 1968–2011. Ancestry.com, 2005.

"Linderman, Roy E." US, Social Security Death Index, 1935–2014. Ancestry.com.

"Linderman, Roy Eugene." Texas Birth Index, 1903–1997. Ancestry.com, 2005.

"Linderman, Roy Eugene." US Public Records Index, vol. 1. Ancestry.com, 2010.

"Linderman, Roy Marvin." Texas Death Certificates, 1903–1982. Ancestry.com, 2013.

"Linderman, Roy Marvin." US, Find A Grave Index, 1600s–Current. Ancestry.com, 2012.

"Linderman, Ruby L., to David L. Conaway." Texas Marriage Collection, 1966–2011. Ancestry.com, 2014.

"Linderman, Ruby Ladell." Texas Birth Index, 1903–1997. Ancestry.com, 2005.

"Linderman, Russell E., to Mindy M. Bissey." Texas Marriage Collection, 1966–2011. Ancestry.com, 2014.

"Linderman, Russell E., to Tammy E. Vanden." Texas Marriage Collection, 1966–2011. Ancestry.com, 2014.

"Linderman, Russell E." *Kerrville Daily Times*. United States Obituary Collection. Ancestry.com, 2006.

"Linderman, Russell E." US, Social Security Death Index, 1935–2014. Ancestry.com, 2008.

"Linderman, Russell Eugene." Texas Birth Index, 1903–1997. Ancestry.com, 2013.

"MacNair, George C." US Phone and Address Directories, 1993–2002. Ancestry.com.

"Mapes, Jacob Garrett." Texas Birth Index, 1903–1997. Ancestry.com.

"Mapes, Matthew D." Texas Divorce Index, 1968–2011. Ancestry.com.

"Mapes, Matthew D." Texas Marriage Collection, 1966–2011. Ancestry.com.

"Mapes, Matthew D." US Public Records Index, vol. 1. Ancestry.com.

"Mapes, Matthew Douglas." Texas Birth Index, 1903–1997. Ancestry.com.

"Mapes, Micky F." Texas Marriage Collection, 1966–2011. Ancestry.com.

"Mapes, Micky F." US Public Records Index, vol. 1. Ancestry.com.

"Mapes, Micky Felix." Texas Birth Index, 1903–1997. Ancestry.com.

"Mapes, Ricky C." Texas Marriage Collection, 1966–2011. Ancestry.com.

"Mapes, Ricky C." US Public Records Index, vol. 1. Ancestry.com.

"Mapes, Ricky Clyde." Texas Birth Index, 1903–1997. Ancestry.com.

"Mapes, Samuel D." Texas Marriage Collection, 1966–2011. Ancestry.com.

"Mapes, Samuel Dewayne." Texas Birth Index, 1903–1997. Ancestry.com.

"Massey, E." Social Security Death Index. Ancestry.com, 2008.

"Massey, Edward H., Jr." Texas Marriage Collection, 1814–1909 and 1966–2011. Ancestry.com, 2012.

"Massey, Edward Higdon." Texas Death Certificates, 1903–1982. Ancestry.com, 2013.

"Massey, Edward Hubert." Texas Birth Index, 1903–1997. Ancestry.com, 2014.

"Massey, Louise Collins Carroll." Obituary. *Palestine Herald-Press*, February 3, 2004.

Massey, Louise. Family Group Sheets. May 30, 1996.

Massey, Louise Collins. Letter to Mary Jo Kenny. January 23, 1996.

Massey, Louise Collins. Personal records, copied at her home in Tennessee Colony by Mary Jo Kenny on May 30, 1996.

"Massey, Louise Collins." Texas Death Certificates, 1903–1982. Ancestry.com, 2013.

"Massey, Tammy Lynne." Texas Birth Index, 1903–1997. Ancestry.com, 2014.

"McCue, Dewayne Brandon." California Birth Index, 1905–1995. Ancestry.com, 2005.

"McCue, Leighann M." US Public Records Index, vol. 1. Ancestry.com.

"McKinzie, Janet B." Texas Divorce Index, 1968–2011. Ancestry.com, 2005.

"McKinzie, John." US, Social Security Applications and Claims Index, 1936–2007. Ancestry.com, 2015.

Men and Women in the Armed Forces from Anderson County, Palestine, Texas. Dallas, TX: Universal Publishing Company (1945).

"Milford, Coy." US Department of Veterans Affairs BIRLS Death File. Ancestry.com, 2011.

"Milford, Leighann L." California Birth Index, 1905–1995. Ancestry.com, 2005.

"Milford, Leighann L." California Marriage Index, 1960–1985. Ancestry.com, 2013.

"Milford, Lisa Marie." California Birth Index, 1905–1995. Ancestry.com, 2005.

"Milford, Peggy L." US Public Records Index, vol. 1. Ancestry.com, 2010.

"Milford, Peggy Louise." Nevada Marriage Index, 1956–2005. Ancestry.com, 2007.

"Noble, Lisa Marie." US, Social Security Death Index, 1935–Current. Ancestry.com.

"Owen, Charlotte Louise." Texas Death Certificates, 1903–1982. Ancestry.com, 2013.

"Owen, Cynthia Jean, to Michael J. Koch." Texas Marriage Collection, 1814–1909 and 1966–2011. Ancestry.com, 2014.

"Owen, Cynthia Jean." Texas Birth Index. Ancestry.com, 2013.

"Owen, David M., to Dinorah Valquez." Texas Marriage Collection, 1814–1909 and 1966–2011. Ancestry.com, 2015.

"Owen, David M." Texas Divorce Index, 1968–2011. Ancestry.com, 2014.

"Owen, David Michael." Texas Birth Index. Ancestry.com, 2013.

"Owen, Eugene C." US, World War II Army Enlistment Records, 1938–1946. Ancestry.com, 2005.

"Owen, Eugene C." US, Find A Grave Index, 1600s–Current. Ancestry.com, 2012.

"Owen, Eugene Clinton." Texas Birth Certificates, 1903–1932. Ancestry.com, 2013.

"Owen, Eugene Clinton." US, Social Security Applications and Claims Index, 1936–2007. Ancestry.com, 2015.

"Owen, Mark D." Texas Marriage Collection, 1814–1909 and 1966–2011. Ancestry.com, 2015.

"Owen, Mark Douglas." Texas Birth Index. Ancestry.com, 2013.

"Owen, Naomi C." US Public Records Index, vol. 1. Ancestry.com, 2010.

"Owen, Naomi Collins." United States Obituary Collection. Ancestry.com, 2006.

"Owen, Naomi." US, Find A Grave Index, 1600s–Current. Ancestry.com, 2012.

"Owen, Stephen C., to Laura Goodson." Texas Marriage Collection, 1814–1909 and 1966–2011. Ancestry.com, 2015.

"Owen, Stephen C." Texas Divorce Index, 1968–2011. Ancestry.com, 2014.

"Owen, Stephen Collins." Texas Birth Index. Ancestry.com, 2013.

"Owen, Stephen, to Susan Bohl." Texas Marriage Collection, 1814–1909 and 1966–2011. Ancestry.com, 2015.

Pederson, Nancy, ed. "Joyce Edwards Staff Member of the Month." *P-Slips* 2, no. 8 (April 1997). Copy supplied by Joyce Edwards.

"Peter, Mary R." California Birth Index, 1905–1995. Ancestry.com, 2005.

"Peter, Mary Rolland." US, Social Security Applications and Claims Index, 1936–2007. Ancestry.com, 2015.

"Reutebuch, Janet Beth." United States Obituary Collection. Ancestry.com, 2006.

"Reutebuch, Janet Beth." US, Find A Grave Index, 1600s–Current. Ancestry.com, 2012.

"Reutebuch, John Mathis." US, Social Security Applications and Claims Index, 1936–2007. Ancestry.com, 2015.

"Rhodes, Ruby L." Texas Divorce Index, 1968–2011. Ancestry.com, 2005.

"Rutebach, John Mathis." US, Find A Grave Index, 1600s–Current. Ancestry.com, 2012.

"Sandlin, W. P." 1910 US Census, Anderson County, Texas, Palestine Ward 2, p. 10B. ED 0005. Ancestry.com.

"Sandlin, William A." 1910 US Census, McLennan County, Texas, Justice Precinct 3, p. 17B, ED 0097. Ancestry.com.

"Sandlin." Texas Birth Certificates, 1903–1932. Ancestry.com, 2005.

"Sargent, Bobbie L." Texas Divorce Index, 1968–2011. Ancestry.com.

"Sargent, Sherrye L." Texas Marriage Collection, 1966–2011. Ancestry.com.

"Sargent, Sherrye Lynn." Texas Birth Index, 1903–1997. Ancestry.com.

"Sargent, William Clyde." Texas Birth Index, 1903–1997. Ancestry.com.

"Sargent, William Clyde." Texas Death Certificates, 1903–1982. Ancestry.com, 2013.

"Seagler, Brookell." Texas Death Certificates, 1903–1982. Ancestry.com, 2013.

"Seagler, C. Regan." US, Find A Grave Index, 1600s–Current. Ancestry.com, 2012.

"Seagler, Charles R." Social Security Death Index. Ancestry.com, 2008.

"Seagler, Clarence G." US, Find A Grave Index, 1600s–Current. Ancestry.com, 2012.

"Seagler, Clarence Graham." US, World War I Draft Registration Cards, 1917–1918. Ancestry.com, 2005.

"Seagler, Clarence." 1910 US Census, Anderson County, Texas, p. 16B, ED 0021. Ancestry.com, 2006.

"Seagler, Edward Harper, Sr." Texas, Find A Grave Index, 1836–2011. Ancestry.com, 2012.

"Seagler, G. W. 'Joe.'" US, Find A Grave Index, 1600s–Current. Ancestry.com, 2012.

"Seagler, G. W." Lubbock County, Texas, p. 6A, ED 152-33. Ancestry.com, 2012.

"Seagler, George Gaston." US, Social Security Applications and Claims Index, 1936–2007. Ancestry.com, 2015.

"Seagler, George." US Department of Veterans Affairs BIRLS Death File, 1850–2010. Ancestry.com, 2011.

"Seagler, Grady Williams." Texas Death Certificates, 1903–1982. Ancestry.com, 2013.

"Seagler, Graham C." Social Security Death Index. Ancestry.com, 2008.

"Seagler, Graham Collins." US, Find A Grave Index, 1600s–Current. Ancestry.com, 2012.

"Seagler, Lola H." US, Find A Grave Index, 1600s–Current. Ancestry.com, 2012.

"Seagler, Lola." Texas Death Certificates, 1903–1982. Ancestry.com, 2013.

"Seagler, Luneta Betty." US, Social Security Applications and Claims Index, 1936–2007. Ancestry.com, 2015.

"Seagler, Ocie, to William T. Collins." *Anderson County Marriage Book 11*, p. 220. Palestine, TX: Anderson County Courthouse.

"Seagler, Clarence G." 1920 US Census, Anderson County, Texas, p. 2B, ED 23. Ancestry.com, 2005.

"Seigler, Ann." 1870 US Census, Anderson County, Texas, p. 20B, image 44. FHLC #553072, LDS FamilySearch Library, Salt Lake City, UT.

"Seigler, E. H." 1880 US Census, Anderson County, Texas, Precinct 6, p. 175, ED 6. FHLC# 1255288, LDS FamilySearch Library, Salt Lake, UT.

Shelton, Bessie and William. Family Group Sheets. Sent to Mary Jo Kenny. December 1998.

"Shelton, Bessie Lucille." Obituary. *Siskiyou Daily News*, Yreka, CA, January 15, 2013.

"Shelton, Celef T." 1920 US Census, Anderson County, Texas, Justice Precinct 5, p. 11A, ED 23, image 661. Ancestry.com, 2005.

"Shelton, Chantel J." California Birth Index, 1905–1995. Ancestry.com, 2005.

"Shelton, Christa M." California Marriage Index, 1960–1985. Ancestry.com, 2013.

"Shelton, Christa Marie." California Birth Index, 1905–1995. Ancestry.com, 2005.

"Shelton, Clark David." California Birth Index, 1905–1995. Ancestry.com, 2005.

"Shelton, Clark David." California Death Index, 1940–1997. Ancestry.com, 2000.

"Shelton, Clifford T." California Birth Index, 1905–1995. Ancestry.com, 2005.

"Shelton, Clifford T." California Death Index, 1940–1997. Ancestry.com, 2000.

"Shelton, Clifford T." California Marriage Index, 1960–1985. Ancestry.com, 2013.

"Shelton, Clifford T." US, Social Security Death Index, 1935–2014. Ancestry.com, 2008.

"Shelton, Clifford T." US, World War II Army Enlistment Records, 1938–1946. Ancestry.com, 2005.

"Shelton, Clifford Thomas." Texas Birth Certificates, 1903–1932. Ancestry.com, 2013.

"Shelton, Clifford Thomas." Texas Birth Index, 1903–1997. Ancestry.com, 2005.

"Shelton, Clifford." US Department of Veterans Affairs BIRLS Death File, 1850–2010. Ancestry.com, 2011.

"Shelton, Clifton T." 1926 Ford City, California, City Directory. US City Directories, 1821–1989. Ancestry.com.

"Shelton, Clifton T." 1930 US Census, Kern County, California, ED 32, image 190.0. FHLC #2339856, LDS FamilySearch Library, Salt Lake City, UT.

"Shelton, Clifton T." 1930 US Census, Kern County, California, Township 4, ED 32, image 190, April 9, 1930. Ancestry.com, 2002.

"Shelton, Clifton T." California Death Index, 1940–1997. Ancestry.com, 2000.

"Shelton, Clifton Thomas." US, Find A Grave Index, 1600s–Current. Ancestry.com, 2012.

"Shelton, Clifton Thomas." World War I Draft Registration Cards, 1917–1918. Ancestry.com, 2005.

"Shelton, Clifton." 1940 US Census, Kern County, California, p. 5A, ED 15-58. Ancestry.com, 2012.

"Shelton, Clifton." US Social Security Death Index. Ancestry.com.

"Shelton, Craig C." California Marriage Index, 1960–1985. Ancestry.com, 2013.

"Shelton, Craig C." US Public Records Index, vol. 1. Ancestry.com, 2010.

"Shelton, Craig Cecil." California Birth Index, 1905–1995. Ancestry.com, 2005.

"Shelton, Deanna M." California Birth Index, 1905–1995. Ancestry.com, 2005.

"Shelton, Delores Celeste." US, Social Security Applications and Claims Index, 1936–2007. Ancestry.com, 2015.

"Shelton, Donna Lynne." California Birth Index, 1905–1995. Ancestry.com, 2005.

"Shelton, E. T." 1900 US Census, Anderson County, Texas, Justice Precinct 5, ED 13, sheet 5, p. 230, June 6, 1900. FHLC #1241607.

"Shelton, Elbert William." Social Security Death Index. Ancestry.com, 2008.

"Shelton, Elbert William." United States Obituary Collection. Ancestry.com, 2006.

"Shelton, Elbert William." California, Find A Grave Index, 1775–2012. Ancestry.com.

"Shelton, Jackie May." California Death Index, 1940–1997. Ancestry.com, 2000.

"Shelton, Jackie May." US, Find A Grave Index, 1600s–Current. Ancestry.com, 2012.

"Shelton, Jackie." Social Security Death Index. Ancestry.com, 2008.

"Shelton, Jeffrey T." California Birth Index, 1905–1995. Ancestry.com, 2005.

"Shelton, John M." California Birth Index, 1905–1995. Ancestry.com, 2005.

"Shelton, John R." California Marriage Index, 1960–1985. Ancestry.com, 2013.

"Shelton, Johnny Raymond." California Birth Index, 1905–1995. Ancestry.com, 2005.

"Shelton, Mary Helen." Texas Birth Certificates, 1903–1932. Ancestry.com, 2013.

"Shelton, Patricia L." California Marriage Index, 1960–1985. Ancestry.com, 2013.

"Shelton, Patricia Lee." California Birth Index, 1905–1995. Ancestry.com, 2005.

"Shelton, Todd W." California Birth Index, 1905–1995. Ancestry.com, 2005.

"Shelton, William Elbridge." Texas Birth Certificates, 1903–1932. Ancestry.com, 2013.

"Simms, Clifford." 1930 US Census, Kern County, California, Township 7, p. 5B, ED 0038, image 313. FamilySearch Library, Salt Lake City, UT.

"Simms, Delores C." California Birth Index, 1905–1995. Ancestry.com, 2005.

"Smith, Mattie Ocie." US, Find A Grave Index, 1600s–Current. Ancestry.com, 2012.

"Stewart, Loren Paul." Texas Birth Index, 1903–1997. Ancestry.com, 2005.

"Stewart, Paul L., Jr." US Public Records Index, vol. 1. Ancestry.com, 2010.

"Stewart, Paul L., Jr." US, Find A Grave Index, 1600s–Current. Ancestry.com, 2012.

"Stewart, Paul L." US, Find A Grave Index, 1600s–Current. Ancestry.com, 2012.

"Stewart, Paul Lorenzo." Texas Birth Certificates, 1903–1932. Ancestry.com, 2013.

"Stewart, Paul Lorenzo." Texas Birth Index, 1903–1997. Ancestry.com, 2005.

"Stewart, Paul." US Department of Veterans Affairs BIRLS Death File, 1850–2010. Ancestry.com, 2011.

"Stewart, Paul." US, Social Security Death Index, 1935–2014. Ancestry.com, 2007.

"Stewart, Una C." US Public Records Index, vol. 1. Ancestry.com, 2010.

"Stewart, Una C." US, Find A Grave Index, 1600s–Current. Ancestry.com, 2012.

"Stewart, Una Velma." US Social Security Death Index, 1903–1932. Ancestry.com, 2008.

"Stewart, William G., to Karen A. Morris." Texas Marriage Collection, 1966–2011. Ancestry.com, 2014.

"Stewart, William G., to Tina M. Brunson." Texas Marriage Collection, 1814–1909 and 1966–2011. Ancestry.com, 2014.

"Stewart, William G." Texas Divorce Index, 1968–2011. Ancestry.com, 2014.

"Stewart, William Gregg." Texas Birth Index, 1903–1997. Ancestry.com, 2005.

"Stiles, LuNeta Betty." US, Find A Grave Index, 1600s–Current. Ancestry.com, 2012.

"Taylor, Clara Odell." Texas Birth Certificates, 1903–1932. Ancestry.com, 2013.

Tennessee Colony Cemetery (Co Rd 2230, Tennessee Colony, TX). Ocie Collins headstone. Data copied by Mary Jo Kenny on May 30, 1996.

"Vandam, Sherrye L." Texas Divorce Index, 1968–2011. Ancestry.com.

"Weems, female." Texas Birth Certificates, 1903–1932. Ancestry.com, 2013.

"Westbrooks, Betty June." California Birth Index, 1905–1995. Ancestry.com, 2005.

"Wolverton, Allen R." Texas Death Certificates, 1903–1982. Ancestry.com, 2013.

"Woods, Mrs. Peggy Milford (Hogan)." Obituary. *The Porterville Recorder*, September 22, 2012. Ancestry.com, 2014.

"Woolverton, Alan R." US, Find A Grave Index, 1600s–Current. Ancestry.com, 2012.

"Woolverton, Alva H." US, Find A Grave Index, 1600s–Current. Ancestry.com, 2012.

"Woolverton, Alva Herman." Texas Death Certificates, 1903–1983. Ancestry.com, 2013.

"Woolverton, Helen M." US, Social Security Applications and Claims Index, 1936–2007. Ancestry.com.

"Woolverton, James A." 1910 US Census, Anderson County, Texas. Ancestry.com, 2006.

"Woolverton, James A." US, Find A Grave Index, 1600s–Current. Ancestry.com, 2012.

"Woolverton, James Allen." Texas Death Certificates, 1903–1982. Ancestry.com, 2013.

"Woolverton, James Carlton." Texas Death Certificates, 1903–1982. Ancestry.com, 2013.

"Woolverton, Mary Ethna." US, Find A Grave Index, 1600s–Current. Ancestry.com, 2012.

Wolverton, Bonnie. *Tennessee Colony Cemetery*. FamilySearch International, 1991. Revised and updated edition, March 15, 1994.

"Wright, Bobbie." US, Social Security Death Index, 1935–Current. Ancestry.com, 2008.

"Wright, Bobbie." US, Find A Grave Index, 1600s–Current. Ancestry.com, 2012.

"Wright, George M., Jr." US World War Army Enlistment Records, 1938–1946. Ancestry.com, 2005.

"Wright, George M., Jr." US, Find A Grave Index, 1600s–Current. Ancestry.com, 2012.

"Wright, George Milner." Texas Birth Certificates, 1903–1932. Ancestry.com, 2013.

"Wright, George Randal." Texas Birth Index, 1903–1997. Ancestry.com, 2005.

"Wright, George." US Department of Veterans Affairs BIRLS Death File, 1850–2010. Ancestry.com, 2011.

"Wright, Sheryl R., to Billy M. Farmer." Texas Marriage Collection, 1814–1909 and 1966–2011. Ancestry.com, 2015.

"Wright, Sheryl Ruth." Texas Birth Index, 1903–1997. Ancestry.com, 2005.

William Colwell Kenny
(6 Nov 1862–17 Aug 1936)

William Colwell Kenny, the middle child and only son of William Curry Kenny and Eliza Jane Colwell, was born in Tennessee Colony, Anderson County, Texas. Known as Will to the family, he attended school in Anderson County and moved with the family to Erath County in 1879. It is not known whether he finished high school in Anderson County, but the schools in the Berlin Hall (later renamed Hannibal) community went through only the elementary school years. The 1880 census shows seventeen-year-old Will living with the family and working on the farm.

Around 1885, Will spent a year, or possibly longer, as a cowboy for a ranch in the Davis Mountains. He probably made the trip with his sister Florence and her husband, Henry Thornton, who moved to Reeves County about that time. It was a time of expansion of ranching and farming in this area, newly opened to settlers after the removal of the Apache Indians. After his experience as a cowboy, Will returned to Erath County, where he continued to work on the family farm.

PICTURE OF WILLIAM COLWELL KENNY TAKEN AS A YOUNG MAN.

Soon after returning to Erath County, Will began courting Fannie Clark, a neighbor girl who was as tall as Will, with blue eyes and red hair that tended to curl. Since her mother's death when she was fifteen, Fannie had assumed responsibility for her household and the care of her nine younger brothers and sisters. Will and Frances Leona "Fannie" Clark (12 Jul 1869–5 Aug 1966) were married at the Methodist church at Berlin Hall on August 28, 1889. The ceremony was after the regular Sunday-morning service and was attended by most of the congregation. Fannie's father, J. O. A. Clark, opposed the marriage, probably because Fannie had been the housekeeper for the family for the past four years and because Will was less pious than the Clarks in his religious practices. J. O. A. would not allow Fannie's younger sisters to attend the ceremony.

Will was a skillful musician and frequently played the fiddle for local dances. When he fell in love with Fannie and the two began talking about marriage, his playing for dances became a problem. The Clarks considered dancing sinful and dance music unacceptable. Will promised Fannie that if they were married, he would never again play dance music. According to their children, he kept strictly to his word. From the strings of his fiddle came patriotic songs, marches, religious hymns, and folk ballads, but never polkas, waltzes, or other dance tunes. Although dance tunes were not acceptable, music was a very important part of the family activities. Family-singing evenings accompanied by the violin and later the piano were common. Francis Russell Richards, Will and Fannie's granddaughter, indicated that during the summers when she stayed with her grandparents, Will singing "Stars in my Crown" as he came in from the morning chores delighted her so much that the hymn became one of her all-time favorites.

During the early years of their marriage, Will and Fannie owned and operated a farm in the Oak Dale community, near Huckabay. It was at this location that all their children were born and the older children grew to adulthood. The 1900 census shows the family living on the farm located north of the Santa Fe Railroad, outside of Stephenville. They owned the farm, but it was still

WILLIAM COLWELL KENNY AND FRANCES CLARK KENNY

mortgaged. Sixteen-year-old Aaron Hill was living with the family and doing farmwork. The farm was located on the Bosque River, which would occasionally overflow its banks and flood some of the fields.

From the early days of their marriage, Fannie maintained a flock of chickens to provide eggs and chicken for family meals. She took pride in her chickens, and her usual wedding gift to community couples was two hens and a rooster, to help them start their own flock.

Laundry day was a very busy day for the family. A horse was hitched to a sled, which had been loaded with the iron washpot, firewood, buckets, washtubs, a washboard, homemade lye soap, and the dirty clothes sorted by color. This was all carried to the river, where the washpot was filled with water dipped from the river and heated. Clothes would be scrubbed on the washboard in one of the tubs, then rinsed in two others. Each item was wrung out by hand and spread on a nearby fence or bushes to dry. It was usually a full-day operation.

The major cash crop for the farm was cotton, but they also raised corn, oats, and hay for animal food. They had horses for work and riding, cattle and pigs for food, and dairy cattle as well as Fannie's chickens. An extensive garden provided vegetables. Will took pride in his straight, even rows in his fields.

Will was of medium height and slender build, and he had brown eyes. As a young man, he had brown hair, but his children remembered him as a balding man with a fringe of hair. He was full of fun and good humor, loved good-natured teasing, and told funny stories. Fannie was as tall, or perhaps even slightly taller, than her husband, with a large bone structure, despite a slender build. Presenting a serious demeanor in public was important to her. She found it embarrassing when ringlets of curls from her fiery-red hair would slip out of the bun at the back of her head and wreath her face in curls. This tended to happen on hot summer days when the hair would become damp with perspiration.

Will and Fannie had seven children: Meta, Roy, Eunice, Rookh, Leona, Jack, and Maurine. Fannie was the disciplinarian with their children as they were growing up; Will was more likely to tease them about minor transgressions than punish them. Jack reported that a frequent wake-up call from his father was "A little while back, there was a boy called Jack," followed by a rhyme about some mischief Jack and his friends had gotten into—frequently something Jack thought had been concealed from his parents' knowledge. As the girls grew up to dating age, Will would call to them in the mornings with a combination of their name and their current boyfriend's name, such as Meta-Luther. This was true for all except Rookh, who tended to date a number of people and no one consistently. After Rookh's name, he would begin a recital of every young man of her approximate age in the community.

Will apparently had the ability to make each of his children feel that they were very special to him. Years after his death, Jack, Eunice, Maurine, and Rookh were talking about their father and his activities during their childhood. Jack indicated that he thought his father showed him some slight partiality, probably because he was the youngest boy. Eunice, Rookh, and Maurine each indicated they felt they were given slight partial treatment. Each had been made to feel very special.

WILLIAM COLWELL FAMILY. TOP ROW: EUNICE, LEONA, ROY, META, ROOKH.
BOTTOM ROW: JACK, FANNIE, MAURINE, WILL.

In addition to Will and Fannie's own children, the household frequently had additional members. Children of Will's and Fannie's siblings often came for extended stays, especially during the summer. With five of Fannie's brothers being preachers, each summer presented many religious revival meetings needing preachers—and preachers wanting to conduct revival meetings. One can assume that the preachers' children found farm life preferable to going from one revival meeting to another.

When Annah Thornton, wife of Fannie's brother Pierce, died at the birth of their third child, Fannie and Will took Annah and Pierce's three children into their home until Pierce remarried a few years later. Faye, the oldest of the three, indicated that it was Fannie who, more than anyone or anything else, helped her adjust to her devastating loss. She said that she resented anyone describing Fannie as stern and lacking in compassion, for she saw Fannie very differently.

On one occasion Eunice accompanied Will on a trip to Stephenville to get supplies. There they saw a little boy crying at the window of the jail. Will said no child should be in jail; he went to talk to the deputy sheriff in charge of the jail to investigate. Will was granted custody of the child. Thus, Gene Zanella came to live with them. His mother had died, and his father, who worked in the Thurber Coal Mine, could not adequately care for him. Gene had been jailed for stealing food from a grocery store. He lived with the Kenny family for some time before moving to the home of a neighbor whose own son had died and who took a special interest in Gene. One thing that impressed Gene while he lived with the Kenny family was that Fannie made both Gene and Jack new suits to wear to Eunice's wedding. In his teen years, Gene left the area, and the family lost contact with him, but he reestablished contact as an adult and eventually moved back to Erath County.

In later years, Will and Fannie's grandchildren, Bill and Isa Lee Rampley and Frances and Louise Russell, spent several summers with their grandparents as Meta and Eunice attended summer school, working toward their respective degrees and updating teaching credentials.

Soon after Henry Ford's assembly line made the automobile affordable to the moderate-income farmer, Will bought an automobile. One of the children rode into Stephenville with him and brought the horse home while Will made the purchase and received instructions on how to operate the car. Purchase of an automobile was still a major event in the community, so news of the purchase spread. Not only his own family but most of the neighborhood children and some adults were there to witness the arrival of the new car. Will proudly drove by the house and toward the shed adjacent to the barn, where the car was to be stored. He was closely followed by the children and the dogs, amid much shouting, laughter, and barking. As he approached the shed, Will pulled back on the steering wheel and shouted, "Whoa." The car sailed through the back of the shed, scattering boards to and fro. Around and around the field it went, followed by the children and the dogs and accompanied by shouts of "Whoa." Will did eventually get the car stopped; he learned about brakes, and this was the first of several cars he owned and drove during his lifetime.

Will was one of the first farmers in the Oak Dale community to establish a dairy herd. Some forty years later, the community was largely made up of dairy farms. The dairy did not prove successful for Will. The Bosque River flooded, washing away many of the dairy cows. The farm had been mortgaged to pay for the cows, so the farm had to be sold. In 1916, the family moved back to Hannibal, where Will operated the Hannibal general merchandise store for a few years. On one of his buying trips for the store, Will bought a dark-green fabric for Fannie to make a "Sunday" dress. Leona remembered that green dress and its contrast with Fannie's red hair as one of the prettiest dresses her mother ever owned.

The family occasionally had groups, usually relatives, for dinner. The children of the family waited until the guests had eaten before they could eat. As adults, they complained that they had only chicken wings, necks, and backs. As a result, when they were in charge of large family meals, the children were served first at a separate table.

The largest social event hosted by Will and Fannie was the wedding of Fannie's sister Bessie to John Hicks. Fannie made all the dresses for herself, Bessie, and the Kenny daughters. She made so many dresses that she forgot how many, and the day before the wedding she apologized to Rookh for not having made her a dress. Rookh's dress had been one of the first dresses made. Providing food for the entire Clark and Hicks clan was also a large undertaking. The planned menu was expanded when a mule kicked and killed a young pig, and roasted suckling pig was added. John Hicks's father refused to attend the wedding. As a Union veteran of the Civil War, he was unwilling to witness the marriage of his son to the daughter of a Confederate veteran.

Farming, not merchandising, was Will's real love, so when they had saved enough money, they purchased another farm in the Hannibal community. The 1920 census shows the family on the farm, near the town of Thurber. Early in the 1920s, Will and Fannie retired from farming, moved to Stephenville, and bought the house at 741 West Long Street. Jack was left to run the farm alone until it could be sold. In 1924, Will ran for tax assessor, won, and served two terms in that office. One story he told of his reelection campaign concerned going to a thresher crew in a district that had not supported him in his first contest. While passing out cards and speaking to the workers, he stepped up on the platform where a man was feeding bundles of grain into the thresher. The man handed him a bundle and stepped off the platform. While the man got a drink of water and had a smoke, Will fed the thresher with the skill of one who had done it many times. On election day, Will carried the voting precinct with a strong majority.

The 1930 census shows Will, Fannie, and their daughter Maurine living in their Long Street home in Stephenville. Though Will was no longer actively farming, he listed his occupation as farmer. During the early years of the Depression, money became very scarce. Will and Fannie had the opportunity to rent their house in Stephenville, so they moved to a house on a farm their son, Jack, and his wife, Ava, had bought in the Acrea community. They helped get the house ready for the family to move in and remained there for about a year. At this point, Will's health was beginning to fail, and he was limited in his activities. Among the things he could do was entertain the children by telling stories or reading to them. Occasionally when Will wanted to read the newspaper, he would read it to the children. Both were satisfied with that arrangement.

Will and Fannie moved back into their house in Stephenville in 1934, and Will died there of heart failure two years later. His coffin was placed in the living room of the home as the family gathered and friends came to pay their respects. He was buried in West End Cemetery in Stephenville. The gravestone was installed on January 19, 1937. Fannie wrote in her diary:

> Today the monument to W. C. K.'s grave was erected. I like it. It is modest and retiring—a lot like his life was to me. When death claims me I shall be laid close by his side. I like that, too.

Fannie felt very alone and lacking in purpose after Will's death. She opened her diary entry on January 1, 1937, with the following:

> Today finds me alone. Husband died Aug 17th, 1936, and children all married and scattered, living their lives in their own way.

> This is a cold, cloudy, misty day. I feel empty-handed and orphaned, but I must strive on. I have always wanted with my own hands to hold the sheckels of life for the defense of my family, and now they are gone. But I must try to enrich the world by my life—I shall do what I can. I can be a devout Christian and I will.

Fannie survived Will by thirty years. Her home was her major financial asset. In 1937 she rented her house to give her a cash income. She spent some time with her children, brothers, and sisters, but her primary objective was to return to her own home. She did not want to spend her time drifting from place to place as her mother-in-law had done in her final years. Returning home, she continued to rent a portion of her home for income. After Fannie's grandson Bill married Irene Crow, the couple rented rooms for a few years. In the spring of 1939, Fannie and her daughter Rookh worked out a plan by which she could use the property for income and still be in her home. The lot, a double lot, extended to McNeil Street. When they had first acquired the place, the back section had been used for a vegetable garden, but Fannie was no longer gardening. Fannie deeded the McNeil Street lot to Rookh, who built a small house on the lot. The arrangement was that Fannie would receive all rent from the McNeil Street house, which would revert to Rookh on Fannie's death. The 1940 census shows Fannie living in her home on Long Street.

Fannie never learned to drive an automobile, but she lived close enough to the center of town that she could walk to town until the last few years of her life. If she became tired while downtown, she would find a nearby automobile and sit in it until she felt rested. She may or may not have known the automobile owner, but in either case, they seemed to find her explanation very plausible if they returned before she completed her rest. If she did know the owner, they would chat for a while before both moved on.

Not one to be shy about expressing her opinions, Fannie sometimes surprised people with her candor. One time when a candidate for the state legislature handed her his card and introduced himself, Fannie's response was "I know who you are; I put the first clothes on you that you ever had on." After an initial startled reaction, the candidate quickly reestablished connection with his parents' former neighbor. Fannie was interested in politics and considered voting a very important right. She occasionally reminded her granddaughters that she had not been able to vote as a young woman and that she would not miss voting on election day. In a letter to her daughter Maurine, she mentioned that it was election day, and she was going to vote, ending the note with "I always do."

Communication with her family was important to Fannie, and she usually forwarded letters from one child or sibling to another, with her own note written on the back if there was a blank space. She could put more information on a one-cent postcard than anyone else I have known. She used the telephone more sparingly and had the somewhat disconcerting habit of hanging up as soon as she finished talking, without saying goodbye. The other telephone party may not have finished talking or did not know whether they were accidentally disconnected.

Although she had reared seven children and cared for other children and grandchildren for extended periods of time, in her later years Fannie was somewhat impatient with young children. She usually felt that they should behave in a more mature manner than they did. However, by the time those children became teenagers, she treated them as adults and expressed the thought that they were more mature and should be given more responsibilities, often more than their parents felt was appropriate.

Education was highly valued by Fannie, who expressed pride in the educational accomplishments of her family. She sometimes stated that if she had extra money, she would use it to help young people get an education. Yet when told her granddaughter was going to pursue an advanced degree, her response was "But you already have your degree."

Fannie tended to make a strong impression on those who knew her. Her granddaughter Louise Russell Stallings included the following comments about Fannie in a letter:

> My memories of Grandmother from the time I was an infant, when I was totally awed by her strength (physical and moral) and her matter-of-factness, and—as we both grew older—of her unbounded grace, generosity, and love of humanity, and, yes, her matter-of-factness. I still see that beautiful, plain, honest, but almost saintly face every time I think of her.

Fannie enjoyed going places and doing things away from home. When invited to go somewhere, Fannie could be counted on to be on her front porch with her hat on and ready to go at least half an hour before the appointed time to be picked up. She was a lifelong Methodist; her faith and the church were very important to her. She was able to be active in the Methodist church, occasionally singing a solo hymn and attending church services each Sunday except when ill or out of town, until she was well past ninety.

Although she had several bouts of pneumonia requiring hospitalization, Fannie's health was generally good. She was able to visit family, piece quilts, and do jigsaw puzzles and many other activities until she was approaching ninety. As her ability to maintain her house and other activities diminished, accentuated by several hospital stays, her children arranged for a companion to stay with her. After a couple of companions stayed for only a few months each, Dolly Laughlin became her long-term companion. The two made a good combination; Dolly seemed to like all Fannie's family and friends, and her positive attitude and humor helped keep Fannie from getting depressed over her failing abilities. Together they discovered television soap operas and variety shows and had these to discuss and criticize when there was nothing of family, neighborhood, or world news to talk about. They found a lot to criticize about dress and behavior in the variety shows but watched them regularly. The time came, however, when Dolly could no longer provide the care needed, and Fannie spent her last two years in a care facility. Fannie died in the nursing home at the age of ninety-seven. She was buried beside Will in West End Cemetery in Stephenville, under the double stone that had awaited her for thirty years.

FANNIE KENNY'S 90TH BIRTHDAY. FROM LEFT TO RIGHT THEY ARE LEONA K. DAVIS, MAURINE K, DAVIS, AVA H. KENNY, FANNY C. KENNY, META K. PETSICK, EUNICE K. RUSSELL, AND ROOKH K. RICHARDS.

Descendants of William Colwell Kenny and Fannie Kenny

Meta Empress Kenny
(10 Sep 1890–12 Jan 1966)

Meta, the oldest child of Will and Fannie Kenny, was born at the family home in the Oak Dale community in Erath County, Texas. As an infant, she contracted polio and was very ill. Will and Fannie spent many hours massaging and exercising her paralyzed limbs, though this method of treatment for polio was not recognized by the medical community for several decades. Either the massage and exercise treatments worked or the disease itself spared her the crippling effects; she recovered from polio with only a slight limp, which she carried throughout her life.

Because her bout with polio left her with some reduced mobility, Meta was not expected to help with the farmwork as were other members of the family. Instead, her responsibilities were in the house. By the time she was a teenager, she did much of the cooking for the family. She became an excellent cook and baker, and her dishes were always favorites at family gatherings. Her peach cobblers were family favorites, and some thought her chocolate fudge cake was the best.

As the oldest of seven children, Meta always had some responsibility for the younger children. She was always "Sister" to her siblings and was often sought out by them for advice when they were growing up. Each of the three older girls in the family took special responsibility for one of the younger siblings. Leona was Meta's special charge, and the two developed a closeness that lasted until Meta's death and carried over with their children. Bruce Rampley and Ann Davis were among the closest of the cousins. Leona became Meta's helper in the kitchen. In her later years, Leona related that the Saturdays when she and Meta did the baking while the rest of the family were doing other work were among the happiest memories of her childhood.

Meta was a large woman, tall and large-boned like her mother's family. She was never obese but did carry a weight that was consistent with her large-boned structure. She had brown eyes and dark-brown hair that never developed much gray as she aged.

According to her sister Leona and cousin Faye Clark Goosetree, Meta's first serious romance was with Willie Wofford, stepson of Martha Adelia Kenny. The families thought they were too young to marry; the romance waned, and each eventually married someone else.

Meta married Luther Rampley (26 Jul 1887–12 Oct 1937) on December 29, 1912. Luther, born in Carnesville, Georgia, was the son of John S. Rampley and Cora Wyly. The 1920 census shows them operating a farm in the north part of Erath County, with Thurber as the closest town. By 1930, they were living on a farm a few miles west of the village of Bluff Dale, Texas. Their two-story farmhouse was a few hundred yards from the Paluxy River. Because it was near the headwaters, the Paluxy was little more than a creek, but it had running water through most summers, good swimming and wading places, and excellent picnic spots on the banks. It was a favorite gathering spot for the Kenny family.

During the early decades of the twentieth century, a person could qualify to teach in the rural schools of Texas by completing high school and passing a teachers' qualifying examination. After Huckabay High School, Meta passed the teaching examination and began teaching in the Huckabay school where Jack and Maurine were among the students. Meta loved teaching, was a very good teacher, and spent much of her life in the classroom. From the time she started teaching just out of high school until she was disabled by a stroke in 1964, the only times she was not teaching were soon after her marriage and during the time her children were young. Though neither the 1920 census nor the 1930 census show her as a teacher, family oral history indicates that she did teach during some of those years. She regularly updated her teaching credential and eventually earned her bachelor's degree by attending college during the summers. Her children, Bill and Isa Lee, were often left with her parents while she was in school.

Meta brought to her teaching a breadth of knowledge, wisdom, imagination, and compassion as well as a vast store of anecdotes to illustrate points. She expected a lot of her students, but these expectations were attainable and were usually attained. She expected her students to place among the top scores on the countywide scholastic achievement tests, and, at least when she was teaching at Acrea, they consistently did so. She emphasized to her students that even though they attended a small rural school, they could learn as much as anyone in any school.

While she was teaching at Acrea, my brothers and I attended the one-room school. Meta emphasized reading for fun as well as for knowledge. The library at Acrea consisted of a closet at the end of the entrance hallway, with dimensions of about four feet by four feet. It housed unissued textbooks as well as a small number of books for recreational reading. Meta encouraged students to read, and it was not difficult for avid readers to read all the books available, some more than once.

Because my brothers and I had always called Meta "Aunt Meta," we had difficulty consistently calling her Mrs. Rampley at school. Soon the other students requested permission to call her Aunt Meta, and she became Aunt Meta to all students in the Acrea school. She must have liked the title, because after she moved to Gustine, she told the story to her new students, and she became Aunt Meta in that school as well.

Perhaps because she was my teacher for four years, I always felt a great admiration for and some degree of awe of Meta. She did much to influence my desire to become a teacher and helped model the quality of teaching I aspired to. I even patterned my handwriting to look like hers, which I considered distinctive.

Luther Rampley died of cancer in the fall of 1937. Meta was teaching at the Acrea school and was scheduled for the 1937–1938 school year. Her sister, Eunice, assumed Meta's teaching responsibilities while Luther was in the final stages of his illness, and she continued until Meta got the affairs settled after his death.

On August 30, 1941, Meta married J. Frank Petsick, who also had been widowed. The Petsick and Kenny families had been friends for many years and were neighbors in Hannibal. The younger Kenny children were about the same age as the older Petsick children, and they had been good friends while growing up. Of the marriage, Meta's mother said that she had always expected one of her children to marry a Petsick; she just hadn't expected it to be the "old man."

After their marriage, Meta and Mr. Petsick moved to Gustine, Texas, where Meta taught in the Gustine schools. Mr. Petsick was a trader in both cattle and land, and they moved several times as he bought and sold ranches. Over the years, Meta taught in Gustine, Goldthwaite, Pettit, and Jonesboro schools.

Meta was very organized and efficient in managing her household. Each morning she would get up early, do some household tasks or a load of laundry, and prepare a full meal to leave for Mr. Petsick's noon meal before going to school. She continued to organize and host family gatherings. The Petsick ranches always had good picnic spots, usually near a river or creek. The weekend closest to July 12, which was Fannie Kenny's birthday, was frequently a time for a family gathering at Meta's.

Meta was teaching at Jonesboro when she had the first of a series of strokes that finally took her life. She reported to the principal that she was not feeling well and drove herself to the hospital, where she received the diagnosis of a stroke. She lived several more years but was never able to teach again. She died in Hico, Texas, and was buried beside Luther Rampley at Wesley Chapel Cemetery near Bluff Dale.

- **Bill Kenny Rampley (3 Sep 1913–12 Jun 1993):** Bill, the oldest child of Meta and Luther Rampley, was born in Stephenville, Texas. His early years were spent on the family farm near the town of Thurber in Erath County. He and his sister, Isa Lee, often spent summers with their grandparents, Will and Fannie Kenny, while his mother attended college classes to update her teaching credential and complete her bachelor's degree. During these summers, he developed a close bond with the three younger Kenny children, Leona, Jack, and Maurine. Jack would take Bill with him on his various activities, play with him, and tease him. Bill adored him.

  The family moved near Bluff Dale before 1930, where Bill finished public school. After graduating from high school, Bill attended North Texas Agricultural College (later Arlington State University), but he dropped out of college when his father became ill with cancer. At that time, he assumed responsibility for running the family farm.

  On February 26, 1939, Bill and Irene Crow (8 Feb 1916–24 Oct 2005) were married in Fort Worth, Texas. Irene was the daughter of J. M. Crow and Vitha Braden of Bluff Dale, Texas. Bill and Irene rented space in Fannie's home in Stephenville, and Irene continued working as a nurse at the Stephenville hospital while Bill managed the farm. In 1940, Bill accepted a job with Douglas Aircraft, and he spent the World War II years working in their plants in Tulsa, Oklahoma, and in California. While in California, Irene took painting lessons and did several lovely paintings that were later framed by her daughter-in-law, Marilyn, and hung in Irene's retirement apartment.

  After the war, Bill began working for Conoco Oil Company, an employment he continued until his retirement in 1978. He and Irene first lived in Hobbs, New Mexico, where Bill built a house for them. When Bill was transferred to Oil Center, close to Eunice, New Mexico, they lived in a house provided by the company, which they were later able to purchase. They lived in this house until their son, Greg, left home to go to college. During this time, Bill was a field supervisor, working from Eunice, New Mexico, a position requiring long hours. Camping was a favorite vacation activity for the family, and Colorado a favorite camping destination. Bill enjoyed hunting, and both Bill and Greg enjoyed riding horses. Irene concentrated her efforts on her home and family. A talented seamstress, she enjoyed making carefully tailored clothes. She did some painting and was an active member of the Methodist church, where she taught fourth-grade Sunday school. One member of her class was Marilyn McCulloch, who later became Greg's wife.

Living in the desert meant occasional encounters with rattlesnakes. Irene shot one snake coiled under their porch, severing the snake. Though dying, it still bit their favorite corgi dog, Bitsy. Fortunately, Bitsy did survive the bite.

In the early 1970s, Bill and Irene moved into the town of Eunice, where they bought and renovated a home with a large yard. Bill planted a garden and fruit trees and enjoyed maintaining his garden and lawn. This home was on the road to Carlsbad, and occasionally they gave aid to travelers whose cars broke down.

After the move to Eunice, Conoco assigned Bill to work as a consultant conducting inventory in a large area ranging from South Texas to Indiana and Kansas. Irene went with him on these trips. They enjoyed seeing the countryside and experiencing the different regional foods, customs, dialects, and lifestyles.

In 1977, Bill was sent to Libya to do inventory work for Conoco. Irene met him in London for a Christmas holiday they described as magical. Upon returning to Libya, Bill began having heart problems in January 1978. He returned home and retired. He and Irene bought a home in Glendale, Arizona, near their son. For the next few years, they were able to enjoy retirement. They made several trips throughout the West in their travel trailer and became closer to their grandchildren. After triple heart bypass surgery, Bill did less traveling and more gardening and furniture refinishing. Both he and Irene attended Shadow Rock Congregational Church and were active with the Older Boulders. They took a number of trips with this group, including trips to Branson, Missouri, and Washington, DC.

Bill's health gradually deteriorated; he developed kidney disease in addition to his heart problems and underwent dialysis for five years. Irene revived her dormant nursing skills to care for him in their home. Bill died in Glendale three months before his eightieth birthday. He was buried in Wesley Chapel Cemetery in Erath County, Texas, where his parents were buried.

Irene continued in their home in Glendale for several years and enjoyed working with an investment planner, making some successful stock market ventures. Declining health and cognition status, and harassment from neighbor boys, made an apartment for seniors a more reasonable option for her. For about a year she enjoyed the convenience and companionship offered by the apartment. In December 2001, Irene suffered two compression fractures of the spine and, after hospitalization, was moved to an assisted-living facility. Another fall and broken hip required a move to a nursing home. From there, she moved into a care facility for people with dementia, where she died at the age of eighty-nine. In the spring of 2006, her son, Greg, and daughter-in-law, Marilyn, made a trip to Texas, where they placed her ashes in Wesley Chapel Cemetery.

- **Gregory Paul Rampley (12 Dec 1945–):** Greg, the only child of Bill and Irene, was five years old when they moved first to Hobbs, then to Oil Center, New Mexico. The house they moved into in Oil Center was his home until he entered college. He enjoyed desert living: horseback riding and hunting rabbits with his father and riding his motor scooter over the sand dunes. When he was a teenager, Irene bought him a Model A Ford on one of her trips to Hico. Irene helped him re-cover the seats. Bill supervised and advised him on the mechanical work but insisted that Greg do all the actual work on getting the car in running condition.

  Greg attended public schools in Eunice. It was through youth activities at their Methodist church that he got to know Marilyn McCulloch, who also attended Eunice public schools but was two years behind Greg. Marilyn was the daughter of Ray and Wilma Horton McCulloch of Eunice, New Mexico. The two began dating in high school. Upon completing high school, Greg enrolled in the electrical engineering program at New Mexico State University, and Marilyn followed him there two years later, working toward a math teaching credential. Greg and Marilyn were married on September 14, 1968. The building they chose for their wedding reception was scheduled for demolition, and Greg credited Irene with getting the demolition delayed until the week after the wedding.

  After completing his degree in electrical engineering, Greg began a twenty-two-year employment with the Arizona Public Service Electrical Company in Phoenix, Arizona. Marilyn taught high school math until she had children, at which time she moved to preschool teaching. She was a preschool teacher for ten years, then preschool director for thirty years.

  Greg became engineer adviser to salesmen with an electrical-supply-and-manufacturing company of Missouri. Although his headquarters were still in Phoenix, the position required appreciable travel. For five years he enjoyed this job and seeing much of the western part of the country, but he did not like being away from his family. A subsequent position with the Salt River Project in the Maintenance Engineering Department allowed him to spend less time on the road.

  In 2010, Greg was diagnosed with rheumatoid arthritis, which somewhat limits his activities. In 2011, Greg and Marilyn retired from their jobs, which allows them more time for family, travel, and volunteer work. Greg and Marilyn are members of the Shadow Rock United Church of Christ, where Greg is an usher and Marilyn is the preschool director and sings in the choir. They are supporters of the nonprofit Steppingstone Foundation, which is designed to help the working poor of Arizona. Greg has increased his church responsibilities, and Marilyn has taken training and works as a hospice volunteer as well as with Life Cycle Celebrations. She also directs the Phoenix West Threshold Choir. Greg and Marilyn have two children.

- **Sonia Rachelle Rampley (29 Mar 1971–):** Born in Phoenix, Arizona, Sonia attended Greenway High School in Phoenix. She graduated from Arizona State University with a major in special education. While in college, she was a member of the varsity badminton team. Music and drama are special interests of Sonia's. Sonia married Mark Feldtkeller in 1997, and together they raised his sons by a previous marriage, Justin and Josh. Mark builds artistic custom doors and rock walls, and Sonia teaches special education and drama at Big Park Elementary School in Sedona, Arizona. Sonia and Mark have two children together, Masan Elizabeth (5 Apr 1998–) and Braedan Kari (16 Jul 2001–).

- **Colby Greg Rampley (5 Feb 1973–):** Born in Phoenix, Arizona, Colby attended Greenway High School, where he was active in various sports. He obtained bachelor's and master's degrees in chemical engineering from the University of Arizona. In 1997, Colby married Amy Robbins, who was a medical student in Phoenix at the time of their marriage. Amy completed her medical training and is a practicing pediatrician in north Phoenix. They have two children, Cameron Alexander (1 Apr 2003–) and Aidan Riley (1 Jul 2005–).

- **Isa Lee Rampley (7 Jul 1915–30 Aug 1989):** The only daughter of Meta and Luther, Isa Lee was born in Erath County, Texas. With her brother Bill, she spent several summers of her childhood with her grandparents, Will and Fannie Kenny, while her mother attended school. The year after she graduated from high school, she spent the summer in Texon with her uncle and his wife, Jack and Ava Kenny. She helped Ava with the children, two-year-old Mary Jo and the eight-month-old twins, Robert and Raymond. There she met and fell in love with an oil field coworker of Jack's, Tommie Terry "Ted" Henry. Isa Lee and Ted Henry were married on November 11, 1933, in Fort Worth, Texas. Ted, son of E. Lee and Jennie Henry, had grown up in Rising Star (called Twinkle by Ted). His parents continued to reside in Rising Star. Isa Lee and Ted made their home in Texon, Forsan, and Big Springs, where Ted worked for Conoco Oil Company until his retirement.

Isa Lee was a quiet, reserved person; Ted assumed the role of family clown. He was always teasing and joking and greatly enlivened family gatherings. He especially liked to tease Fannie Kenny, whom he called his "best girl" and invited to sit in his lap.

Fannie appeared to be both pleased and embarrassed by this attention.

Isa Lee and Ted had two children, Tommie Wayne and Danny Lee. When Danny was less than a year old, Isa Lee contracted polio. Because she was unable to care for the children and protect them from contagion, they were sent to live elsewhere. Tommie stayed with Meta, and Danny stayed with Rookh and Dan Richards. As had been true with her mother, Isa Lee recovered from polio with only a slight limp. It was more than a year before she recovered sufficiently to resume care of her children.

Isa Lee and Ted continued to live in Big Springs after his retirement from the oil company. Ted's health deteriorated after retirement, and he spent extended time in a nursing home. He died on January 3, 1989; Isa Lee survived him only a few months.

- **Tommie Wayne Henry (14 Jul 1937–1 Dec 1997):** Born in San Angelo, Tom Green County, Texas, Tommie grew up in Forsan and Big Springs, Texas. During the time he lived with Meta, he developed a close bond with his grandmother as well as a good relationship with the Petsick family, especially Wade, the youngest Petsick son.

  Tommie obtained a degree and teaching credential from North Texas State University. While in Denton, he frequently visited Maurine and Byron Davis in nearby Sherman. They enjoyed him and his visits very much. Tommie returned to Big Springs, where he taught math and history in the high school and served as an elementary school principal. He married Jackie Sue Hancock in Big Springs; they had no children. Tommie was well respected in the school district and in the community, but signs of early onset of Alzheimer's disease prompted him to take early retirement. Tommie died at the age of sixty. Jackie continued to live in Big Springs for a period of time before moving closer to her family.

- **Danny Lee Henry (20 Jun 1944–10 Apr 1994):** As an infant, Danny lived with Rookh and Dan Richards while his mother recovered from polio. He became a substitute for the child they never had. After returning to his family, Danny's relationship with Dan and Rookh was more that of a grandchild than a great-nephew. Danny received a business administration degree in marketing from Texas Tech University in Lubbock, Texas. In 1968, Danny inherited the Richards home and some ranch property from Dan and Rookh. He lived in Paducah and operated the ranch. Danny married Margaret Suzanne Lindsay (29 Aug 1945–19 Apr 2012). Her parents were Vernon Lindsay and Margaret Wade. She taught third grade and was active in Paducah civic organizations. Danny developed throat cancer and died in Paducah, Texas, at age forty-nine. Suzanne spent her last years in Gainesville, Texas, the site of her death. Both danny and Suzanne were buried in Paducah.

- **Danny Lee Henry Jr. (5 Oct 1968–):** Born in Tarrant County, Texas, Danny Lee attended Paducah schools. On July 16, 2005, he married Amy R. Tomlinson in Cooke County, Texas.

- **Patrick Wade Henry (10 Oct 1971–):** Born in Cottle County, Texas, Patrick attended Paducah High School. On September 7, 1993, Patrick married Christy D. Hodge in Harris County, Texas. They made their home in Gainesville, Texas. After their divorce, Patrick returned to Paducah. Their son is Hunter Henry.

- **Gary Wayne Henry (24 Apr 1978–):** Born in Childress, Texas, Gary grew up in the Paducah, Texas, area. Gary Wayne Henry married Deborah Kubler in April 1996 in Bernalillo, New Mexico. They live near Gainesville, Texas.

- **Bruce Wyly Rampley (6 Feb 1925–1 Jul 1966):** Bruce, youngest child of Meta and Luther Rampley, was born in Stephenville, Texas. He attended schools in Bluff Dale and Stephenville and graduated from Gustine High School. Shortly after high school graduation, he entered the US Army Air Corps and served through World War II. After being discharged from the army, he attended Tarleton State College and obtained bachelor's and master's degrees in secondary education from North Texas State University. He taught at Weatherford High School from 1950 through 1952. In the summer of 1952, he was employed by the engineering department of General Dynamics in Fort Worth, where he worked until 1965. On June 9, 1951, Bruce married Virginia Ann Ball, daughter of D. S. and Ina Frances Fowler Ball of Decatur, Texas. Bruce and Virginia had two children, Cynthia Ann and David Scott. Bruce developed melanoma and, with treatment, experienced a remission, but the cancer returned. His brother, Bill, came to Fort Worth to be with Bruce during his final few weeks. Bruce died in Fort Worth at age forty-one. He is buried at Rose Hill Cemetery of Fort Worth. Virginia Ann Ball Rampley lived in Granbury, Texas, after her retirement from teaching but later moved to Fort Worth. She enjoys quilting and gardening, as exhibited by her own beautiful yard.

  - **Cynthia Ann Rampley (5 Sep 1952–):** Cynthia was born and educated in Fort Worth, Texas. She married Robin Wilson in Fort Worth on September 19, 1982. Cynthia works as a hairstylist in Fort Worth.

  - **David Scott Rampley (23 Jan 1959–):** Scott earned a bachelor's degree in architecture from the University of Texas at Arlington. He has been active in architectural and design projects in the Fort Worth–Dallas area. Scott lives in Dallas, and he shares his mother's interest in gardening. He married Chris Robinson on March 13, 1993. They divorced in 1998.

Roy Clifton Kenny
(27 May 1892–Sep 1939)

Roy, oldest son of Will and Fannie, was born in Oak Dale, Erath County, Texas. He attended schools in Huckabay and helped with work on the farm. He was a talented artist and could draw very well, a skill that impressed his sisters. His sister Leona related that when they were working in the fields as children, Roy would keep them entertained with continuing stories, relating some each day. It was many years later that she learned that his stories were from the books he read each night, ready to relay the contents to his siblings the next day.

After finishing at the Huckabay school, Roy announced that he wanted to join the navy. Fannie indicated that she could not stand to have him do that; it would kill her if he joined the navy. He did not join the navy. On October 4, 1913, at the age of twenty-one, Roy married eighteen-year-old Mabel Claire Roberts, the daughter of Charles and Lizzie Wright Roberts of Erath County. The 1920 census shows them living in Stephenville adjacent to the Roberts family. Roy's occupation was indicated as a contractor. They had two children, listed as Roy and Wright.

Around 1924, Roy, Mabel, and their children moved to Cameron County in the Rio Grande Valley. There Roy engaged in farming and other occupations. According to family reports, Roy was a gambler. He had an attraction to risky ventures, thinking each was going to be his big break. None ever were. Whether his gambling also extended to games of chance was never discussed in the family. With his growing family and the economic depression of the 1930s, money was always a problem. He borrowed money from his parents, brother, and sisters. He was very grateful for their help and sure he could pay them back when his next deal came through. These deals never came through. In early September of 1939 he told his family that he was going to Stephenville to see relatives. About ten days later, he was found dead in Cameron County. The cause of death was unknown. His brother, Jack, suspected that Roy had taken his own life. Roy's son Huck thought his father's death might have been homicide or from natural causes. No obvious sign of trauma was seen on the body, but the indication was that he had been dead several days before the body was found. His death certificate indicates death from unknown cause. He was buried in Stephenville's West End Cemetery in the plot with his father.

After Roy's death, Mabel moved to Stephenville. She rented an apartment on Long Street, not far from her brother and sisters and mother-in-law. Mabel died on February 10, 1943, and was buried next to Roy in Stephenville's West End Cemetery.

- **Roy Charles Kenny (25 Sep 1914–14 May 2001):** Roy was known to the family as R. C. He was born and spent his early school years in Stephenville, Texas. When he was about ten years old, the family moved to Cameron County, Texas. His remaining schooling was done in the San Benito schools. He married Nell Jean Tarwater, daughter of Louis Scott and Bessie Tarwater, of Raymondville, Texas, on October 31, 1937. Their son, Scott, was born a year later.

On July 8, 1942, R. C. enlisted in the US Army Air Corps. His enlistment record shows him to be five feet, eight inches tall and weighing 137 pounds. He had completed two years of college. Before joining the air corps, he had worked as an embalmer and as a boiler inspector. At Randolph Field and in Okmulgee, Oklahoma, he trained as a glider pilot and flew missions in North Africa and in Europe. In a letter to Maurine and Byron Davis, dated October 7 and postmarked October 12, 1944, R. C. said of his glider experience:

Well, we are all about over our little ordeal in Holland now and sweating out another. Had a few close ones but got out ok with nothing serious. Lost several good buddies, though, but of course that's to be expected. This glider guiding gets to where it's not so funny at times. If there was some way of evasive action or protection or if you could even fight back it wouldn't be so bad but this going over enemy territory at 500 ft. (we crossed over 45 miles of it in Holland) gets to be a little touchy.

After the war, R. C. returned to college and completed his degree. He and his family moved to Tullahoma, Coffee County, Tennessee, where they bought a home. Nell Jean died in Tullahoma on September 18, 1981. R. C. continued to live in their home for another twenty years. His sister, Jeanette, and his niece Karen Kenny were frequently with him during his last illness.

- **Roy Scott Kenny (29 Oct 1938–25 May 1989):** Scott spent his early years in the city of his birth, Harlingen, Texas. His later school years were in Tennessee. As an adult, he lived in a number of areas and was involved in several occupations, including flying crop-dusting planes and dealing in Nevada casinos. He was married twice, first to Rosland Evans in 1959 and then to Pam Lynn on July 9, 1973, in Las Vegas, Nevada. In addition to the two marriages, there was a long-term relationship with Vivianne Reno, which produced a child whom he recognized as his. He was working as a dealer in Las Vegas at the time of his death, which occurred under suspicious circumstances.

  - **Gary S. Kenny:** Gary was the son of Scott and Rosland. He married Dawn Elaine Holbert on December 11, 1978, in Las Vegas, Nevada. The US Public Records Index shows him living in Las Vegas and in Nashville, Arrington, College Grove, and Lynchburg, Tennessee. He married Tammie Spray on September 12, 1986, in Lynchburg, Tennessee. Upon his grandfather's death, Gary inherited R. C. Kenny's home in Tullahoma.

  - **Dominique Riggs Reno:** Dominique was the daughter of Scott and Vivianne. The family had lost contact with her at the time of her grandfather's death.

- **Katrina J. Kenny (7 Dec 1973–15 Nov 1998):** Katrina was the daughter of Scott and Pam. She was a troubled person who had problems with drug addiction. In her late teens, she came to live with her grandfather, who hoped to be a positive influence in her life. While there she committed suicide.

- **Earl Wright Kenny (21 Jan 1918–10 May 1943):** The second son of Roy and Mabel, Earl Wright was born in the Oak Dale community, near Stephenville, Texas. His early years were spent in the Stephenville area. He was six years old when the family moved to the Rio Grande Valley, so all his school years were in that area. His sister, Jeanette, indicated that Earl Wright was the kindest and most considerate of her brothers. He was the one who always considered the needs and interests of his little sister. His cousin Betty Russell Thompson also remembers him as being kind, patient, and very handsome.

  As a youth, Earl Wright was an active member of the Baptist church in Rio Hondo. He later moved his membership to San Benito, then to Stephenville. After finishing high school, he worked in a gasoline station and as a parking lot attendant. He joined the National Guard and rose to the rank of sergeant. On November 25, 1940, Earl Wright enlisted in the infantry branch of the army. His enlistment record describes him as single, seventy-three inches tall, and weighing 152 pounds. He did army training at Camp Bowie, Texas, and Camp Blanding, Florida. He volunteered for the US Army Air Corps and took flight training at Ballinger and Perrin Field, Texas, in 1942. He was in advanced training at Lubbock Field, Texas, when a crash took his life. His unit was practicing low-altitude close-formation flight when one pilot either turned wrong or failed to make an indicated turn; two planes collided, killing him and three other cadet pilots.

  Rookh and Dan Richards went to Lubbock after the crash and took charge of the body. Earl Wright's friend and fellow cadet N. H. Kelly accompanied them to Stephenville. Several family members gathered at the depot to see the night train bearing his casket, and many tears were shed as the casket was unloaded. The funeral at the First Baptist Church in Stephenville had a military honor guard of cadets from John Tarleton College, who also served as pallbearers. Dr. H. L. Spencer, pastor of the First Baptist Church, was assisted by Rev. E. C. Carter of the First Methodist Church in the service. Earl Wright was buried in East End Cemetery in Stephenville.

- **Edward Colwell Kenny (9 Oct 1920–8 May 1988):** Huck, as Edward was known in the family, was born in Stephenville, Texas. With red hair and freckles, Huck was described by his sister, Jeanette, as full of fun and mischief. He also had an air of self-confidence from an early age. He was about four when the family moved from Erath County to the Rio Grande Valley. In the move, Roy drove a truck with household goods, and Mabel drove the car. At one rest stop, Huck was left behind, with each parent thinking he was with the other. As soon as they realized he was missing, they left the truck parked and hurried back to locate what they expected to be a frantic child. Instead, they found him calmly playing by the curb of the gasoline station, confident that they would come back for him.

His mischief sometimes got him in trouble at school. During that period of time, many schools used a paddle as a disciplinary tool. The paddle would hit the seat of the pants with a resounding whack that could be heard throughout the school. Huck's response to the paddle when he was the recipient was to call loudly "Strike one" and "Strike two" and continue as if umpiring a baseball game. Soon many in the school were trying to suppress giggles.

Huck attended school in San Benito, including San Benito High School. After high school, he joined the National Guard and later enlisted in the US Army. His enlistment record, dated November 25, 1940, indicates he had three years of high school education, was employed as a salesperson, was seventy-two inches tall, and weighed 156 pounds.

On June 5, 1942, Huck married Marian Emma Goodwin (5 Aug 1922–Jun 1978), daughter of Henry "Blue" and Bertie Marie Goodwin. Marian was born in Erath County, Texas.

In the military, Huck rose to the rank of lieutenant before he was deployed to the Pacific theater in the early spring of 1943. He had been in Hawaii only a few weeks when he learned of his brother Earl Wright's death. This was very hard for him, as he explained to his uncle Jack in a letter—Earl Wright was not only his brother but also his best friend. Huck spent the remainder of the war in the Pacific.

After the war, Huck took advantage of the G. I. Bill to attend college and get his degree. While at Tarleton, he, Marion, and their son, Don, lived in Fannie Kenny's little house on McNeil Street.

After the completion of his degree, Huck and Marion moved to Artesia, New Mexico, where he worked for Dow Chemical Company. When they first moved to Artesia, they stayed in an apartment until they could find a house. The apartment did not allow dogs, so Don had to leave his dog, Cindy, with Uncle Jack until they were able to move into a house. From Artesia, the family moved to Liberal, Kansas, where Huck and Marion continued to live the rest of their lives. Marion died in Liberal, Seward County, Kansas. Huck survived her by ten years; he also died in Liberal, Kansas.

- **Don Goodwin Kenny (7 Aug 1943–29 Sep 1974):** A delightful and imaginative child, Don won the hearts of all the relatives in the Stephenville area while his father was enrolled in Tarleton. He and his cocker spaniel dog, Cindy, had many imaginary adventures. Some of these adventures included his imaginary horses, Red Cedar and White Pine. When he climbed to the top of a small tree in Fannie Kenny's yard, breaking some tree limbs, he explained that he had to get away from that big bear. We all enjoyed having Don visit our farm, and he seemed to love being there. He apparently adored Jack, and he would follow

Robert and Raymond every step they took. Don attended school in Artesia. He served a term with the US military. Don married Mary F. Powajba on March 16, 1968, in Solano County, California, where the couple made their home. While on a scuba diving venture on the Sonoma, California, coast, Don drowned.

- **Karen Marie Kenny (4 Mar 1948–):** Don called Karen Fuzzy. She was born in Mitchell County, Texas, but spent her early days in Stephenville. She was still quite young when the family left Erath County for Huck to complete his degree and then move to Artesia. She attended school in New Mexico and in Kansas. Karyn Kenny, assumed to be the same as Karen, attended Wichita State University, where she lived in the Grace Wilkie Residence Hall and participated in the Pep Council. Karen married Bill Maas, and they make their home in Minnesota. When her uncle R. C. Kenny was battling his final illness, Karen and Jeanette Lorenz both spent appreciable time with him. Jeanette expressed high regard for Karen. Karen and Bill have two children.

- **Anyce Jeanette Kenny (22 Oct 1923–11 May 2010):** The youngest child and only daughter of Roy and Mabel, Jeanette was also called Jenny by her family. Her obituary indicates she was born in Cameron County, Texas, but if the move to the valley occurred in 1924, she would have been an infant at the time of the move. She attended school in San Benito and joined the Women's Army Auxiliary Corps after completion of high school. At the time she joined her brothers in military service, the *Fort Worth Star-Telegram* paper carried an article about the four military siblings. She met Ed Lorenz, a native of Ohio, while in the military. They were married in January 1943. Her mother, Mabel, was able to attend Jeanette's wedding, but she died shortly after the wedding.

Jeanette and Ed made their home in Cincinnati, Ohio. Jeanette felt that Ed's family did not fully accept her because she did not share their Catholic religion. She rarely attended Lorenz family gatherings because she did not feel accepted, and this fact may have contributed to friction between her and Ed over the years. Her marriage to a Catholic also caused a rift between Jeanette and her grandmother, Fannie Kenny. Though lonely at first, Jeanette soon found her time fully occupied with her own family. While Ed worked for Procter & Gamble, Jeanette devoted her time to being a homemaker and raising her children. Their daughter Terri described her parents' marriage as being "rocky." They did divorce in 1978. Jeanette entered into a second marriage, which lasted only three years. She and Ed remarried in 1982 and apparently established a comfortable companionship. Jeanette enjoyed going to garage sales and finding special items for her grandchildren. She enjoyed animals and was concerned about animal welfare. At her death, memorial gifts were requested to be sent to Save the Animals Foundation in Cincinnati. In their later years, Jeanette and Ed moved from their home in Cincinnati to Montgomery, Ohio. It was there that she died at the age of eighty-six. Ed survived Jeanette by less than two years, dying on January 13, 2012, in Montgomery, Ohio, at age ninety-six. Jeanette and Ed had four children.

- **Susan Lorenz (9 May 1947–):** Susan was born in Cincinnati, Ohio. She married Jim Procopio. They had one daughter. After the marriage ended in divorce, Susan married Robert J. "Bob" West. They resided in Cincinnati, Ohio. On August 12, 1993, she and Bob West were divorced, and she later married Scott Rekers of Deer Park, Ohio.

  - **Laura Procopio (1967–):** Laura married Joe Gheling of Cincinnati, Ohio. Their son, Ryan, was born in 2008. She and Joe were divorced, and she continues to live in Cincinnati.

- **Kenny Charles Lorenz (25 Aug 1950–13 Oct 2010):** Kenny was born in Cincinnati, Ohio. He married Donna R. Bohle on May 29, 1974, in Hamilton County, Ohio. They were divorced on November 5, 1975. His second marriage was to Mary Lear on April 30, 1983, in Hamilton County, Ohio. They were divorced on August 6, 1993. Kenny Lorenz died in Blue Ash, Hamilton County, Ohio. He had heart and liver disease, complicated by years of heavy alcohol consumption.

  - **Kelly Lorenz:** Kelly, whose married name is Anderson, was born in 1974 to Ken Lorenz and Donna Bohle. She lives in Colorado with her daughter, Keanna.

  - **Marie Lorenz:** Marie, whose married name is Rensing, was born in 1979 to Ken Lorenz and Mary Lear. Her marriage ended in divorce. She lives in Cincinnati, Ohio, and has no children.

  - **Rita Lorenz:** Rita was born in 1982 to Ken Lorenz and Mary Lear. She is single and lives in Cincinnati, Ohio.

- **James Russell Lorenz (1 Mar 1953–):** James and his wife, Mary, lived in Aurora, Colorado, at the time of his parents' deaths.

- **Teresa Ann "Terri" Lorenz (12 Jul 1957–):** Terri married James Everhart on August 4, 1984, in Hamilton County, Ohio. They moved from Ohio to Denver, Colorado, in 1987; it was there that both of their children were born. Later they moved to Morrison, Colorado. Terri works as a physical therapist, and Jim is a business owner. They enjoy living in the foothills of the Rocky Mountains. Their daughters are Erin (1990–) and Kate (1993–).

Eunice Lucille Kenny
(3 Jan 1894–6 Dec 1979)

On January 3, 1937, Fannie Kenny wrote the following in her diary:

> This is Eunice's birthday. She was a pretty, fat little baby—we were so proud of her. Dr. Stanloe was our physician. When she was a few days old, I developed blood poison and was sick a long time. Mrs. Sarah Holt was my nurse and housekeeper during that time.

The year of the birth was 1894, and the place was the Oak Dale community, near Huckabay, in Erath County, Texas.

Eunice attended Huckabay schools and completed Huckabay Academy at age sixteen. She began teaching in New Hope, a community northwest of Stephenville, the following fall.

On December 22, 1912, shortly before her nineteenth birthday, Eunice married D. M. Russell at twilight in the Kenny home in Oakdale. At the time D. M. was teaching at the Rocky Point school on the east side of Stephenville. Dink Mander Russell (29 Apr 1889–5 Jan 1977), the son of Eli W. and Martha (Laden) Russell, was born in Swallow Bluff, Hardin County, Tennessee. The Russell family moved from Tennessee to Erath County, Texas, in 1904. D. M. graduated from McIlhaney Academy and John Tarleton Agricultural College.

During the summer of 1915, Eunice and D. M. joined her brother Roy and his wife, Mabel, on a trip to New Mexico to explore land and work opportunities advertised as existing there. The trip was by horse and wagon while West Texas was still relatively unsettled. There were long distances of open space, and camping was the usual overnight experience. Two young children, R. C. Kenny and Lucille Russell, added to the challenge. When they arrived in New Mexico, the opportunities were not what they had expected, and they decided to return home. Roy and Mabel decided to sell their wagon and horses and return to Stephenville by train. D. M. and Eunice did not consider such a sale to be a prudent choice, so they made the challenging trip across West Texas alone. They stopped to visit friends in Hamlin, Texas, and D. M. secured a teaching position there for the fall. Shortly after securing the teaching position, they bought their first automobile. After one year in Hamlin, they moved back to Erath County, where D. M. taught in Harbin.

In the spring of 1917, their daughter Lucille died of pneumonia. D. M. and Eunice were living in Bunyan, Texas, according to D. M.'s 1917 World War I draft registration. D. M. had just completed the year teaching in the Bunyan school, and Eunice was caring for their young child Martha Frances. In 1918, they purchased a lot on Jones Street in Stephenville and built a home. The 1920 census shows them living on Jones Street in Stephenville with daughters Martha F. and Louise. D. M was teaching in the public schools. They lived in the Jones Street home until 1921, when D. M. was named principal of Dublin High School. During the school year 1923–1924, they lived in Bryan, Texas, while D. M. completed his degree at the A&M College of Texas (now Texas A&M University) and Eunice homeschooled Frances.

In 1928, D. M. and Eunice sold the house in Stephenville and purchased a farm one mile west of Stephenville from Tom M. Bridges and his siblings. The Russell family had leased this property for several years. D. M. operated the farm with the help of his father and brother until it was sold in 1944. Part of that property was bought by the city of Stephenville for the municipal airport.

Eunice loved teaching, and from all reports she was an outstanding teacher with the ability to adapt teaching techniques to student learning styles and to recognize unique talents and interests of students. She expected and received high levels of performance from her students. During her years of teaching in the Bunyan, Dublin, and De Leon schools, she primarily taught elementary grades but sometimes taught English and history in the upper grades.

Both Eunice and D. M. were serious about expanding their knowledge and improving their teaching skills. To that purpose, they frequently took extension courses and attended college during the summer. During those summer studies, their young daughters, Frances and Louise, frequently stayed with their grandparents, Will and Fannie Kenny, or their Russell grandparents. Eunice's transcript shows credits from John Tarleton College, Texas Wesleyan College, the University of Texas, Abilene Christian College, North Texas State Teachers College, Austin College, and McMurry College. She received her bachelor's degree from McMurry College in August of 1944.

The high level of unemployment during the Depression of the 1930s resulted in a policy that schools would hire only one individual in a family. Eunice was unable to teach during this decade but devoted her time to her family and community activities. Her daughter Louise talked about Eunice preparing food and caring for sick people in the community of Millsap, where they lived for much of that time.

Even when teaching, Eunice was active in community organizations. Over the years she was a participant and often an officer in study clubs, garden clubs, the American Association of University Women, the Daughters of the American Revolution, and Methodist church organizations. She often volunteered at community libraries, taught Sunday school, and could be depended upon to help with costumes and sets for school plays.

D. M. went into school administration and was superintendent of several school districts where he was known for consolidating rural schools and developing central schools with a complete curriculum. The 1930 census shows D. M. as superintendent of De Leon schools, with the family living in a rented house on Labadie Street in De Leon. This was their home when their youngest child, Betty, was born in 1931. After leaving De Leon, D. M. was superintendent in Azle and Saint Jo. Saint Jo was their home at the time of the 1940 census. In 1941, D. M. experienced a cerebral hemorrhage, from which he recovered, but he decided to retire from administration and spend the remainder of his career as a vocational agriculture teacher. He received one of the early Smith–Hughes certificates as a vocational agriculture teacher. With the lifting of restrictions of two teachers from a family in a school district, Eunice was able to return to teaching. During and after World War II, she taught in Rochester, Lipan, Gordon, and Morgan Mill schools.

Eunice was a very caring person and assumed the role of "big sister" caretaker to her siblings. Maurine lived with the Russells in Dublin so she could go to high school, as did several other young people over the years. When Leona went to the tuberculosis sanatorium, Eunice and D. M. took Peggy Ann, Leona's daughter, into their Millsap home for the duration of Leona's stay. Eunice made funeral and burial arrangements for Jack and Ava's infant who died at birth. She took Meta's teaching job at the Acrea school when Meta's husband was in the final weeks of cancer. Eunice was involved when Rookh and Ava had major surgery and during Jack's final illness. She assumed major responsibility for her mother during Fannie's final years. She was always a caring presence in times of family crisis.

While teaching in a variety of schools, Eunice and D. M. frequently rented a house in the community. They usually improved the house, typically with paint and wallpaper. Eunice told of one time their landlord indicated he was increasing the rent because the house was in a much better condition. Their biggest remodeling job came in 1944, when they bought a farm near Lipan with a careworn farmhouse and converted the house into a beautiful country home. This became a favorite gathering place for family and friends. Both Eunice and D. M. enjoyed people and welcomed friends and family. They took great pride in this home and the registered Hereford cattle they raised on the land.

In 1972, when country life became more difficult, Eunice and D. M. bought a home on Washington Street in Stephenville. They remained active with family events and in the First Methodist Church. Over the years, the health of both gradually declined. D. M. died in the Stephenville hospital. Their granddaughter, Rev. Barbara Stallings McKnight, assisted Rev. Bob Weathers in the funeral services at the First Methodist Church. Unable to maintain her home alone, Eunice moved to a skilled nursing facility, first in Stephenville, then in Conroe, where her youngest daughter, Betty, lived. In October of 1979 she suffered a massive stroke and died in Conroe at age eighty-five. Again, Rev. Barbara Stallings McKnight officiated at the funeral service at the First Methodist Church in Stephenville. Eunice's grandsons were pallbearers and interment was at West End Cemetery in Stephenville.

- **Eunice Lucille Russell (22 Dec 1914–15 Apr 1917):** Lucille was born on her parents' second wedding anniversary. Her life was very short, only two years, three months, and twenty-six days. She died from pneumonia, a complication of whooping cough. She was buried in West End Cemetery in Stephenville. A small stained-glass window in the First Methodist Church in Stephenville was endowed in her memory.

- **Martha Frances Russell (26 Nov 1916–11 Feb 1993):** Frances, the second child of Eunice and D. M. Russell, was born in Stephenville, Texas. She attended public schools in Dublin, De Leon, and Millsap and graduated as valedictorian from Millsap High School in May 1933. During the summers when her parents were attending college to complete their degrees and update and improve teaching credentials, Frances and her sister Louise often stayed with their grandparents, Will and Fannie Kenny. Over the summer of 1925, Frances stayed with her mother's sister, Rookh Kenny Richards, in Paducah, Texas. There she became acquainted with Dan Richards's extended family, whom she began to regard as additional aunts, uncles, and cousins. This began a pattern of yearly summer visits to Paducah by Frances, Frances and Louise, or the whole Russell family.

Frances obtained a bachelor's degree in music and primary education from North Texas State University in Denton in August 1936. She taught public school music in Azle and Dublin, Texas, for two years. By then she and T. J. Richards (26 Feb 1914–10 Sep 1990), a nephew of her uncle Dan Richards, had decided that they were much more than "cousins." They were married on December 22, 1938, in the Russell home in Saint Jo, and they made their home on the Richards ranch near Paducah. The home they built was near the original home of T. J.'s grandfather, the original T. J. Richards, for whom he was named.

T. J., the only son of Wilson Q. Richards and Mineola Westmoreland, was born on the Richards ranch south of Paducah. He attended Paducah public schools and graduated from Paducah High School in 1931. He tied as valedictorian with his friend and future brother-in-law, Horace Stallings. After three years at Texas A&M, he returned to Paducah without completing his degree. The Depression and the need for his help managing the family ranch after his father's death prompted this action. His interest in progressive agriculture and ranch management resulted in a lifelong commitment to improving conditions for ranchers and farmers. He was active in the Texas Farm Bureau, for which he served as a trustee; the Southwest Animal Health Research Foundation; the Texas and Southwestern Cattle Raisers Association; and other groups. He was also active in politics.

As an accomplished musician, Frances taught music to many youngsters in Cottle and surrounding counties. She served as organist and choir director for the Paducah First Methodist Church. After additional study of religious music at Southern Methodist University, Frances was awarded the title of diaconal minister of music in the Methodist Church. In this capacity she trained musicians in the Northwest Conference of the United Methodist Church. A member and an officer of the National Fellowship of United Methodists in Music and Worship Arts, Frances was a leader in developing the worship service and the United Methodist Hymnal.

In addition to raising two sons and being in demand for musical programs both in Paducah and throughout the state, Frances was active in a number of civic and community organizations. These included the Paducah Parent-Teacher Association, the Study Club, the Texas Federation of Women's Clubs, the American Guild of Organists, the Hymn Society, the Choristers Guild, the Daughters of the American Revolution, and the Order of the Eastern Star. She held a variety of offices in many of these organizations.

T. J. Richards died in Paducah, Texas. Frances related that after T. J.'s death, she was deciding what to do with the satellite TV dish. She had considered it strictly T. J.'s toy. When she began looking through the material on programming, to her surprise, she learned that it actually covered much more than sports and news programs.

Frances developed pulmonary fibrosis and, after a short illness, died in the hospital in Lubbock, Texas, at age seventy-six. She was buried in the Paducah cemetery beside T. J.

- **William Q. Richards (29 Sep 1939–3 Feb 2016):** William Q. Richards was born at the Richardses' homeplace three miles south of Paducah. As a child, he was called Billy Q., but later he went primarily by the name of Q. He attended public schools in Paducah and was valedictorian of his Paducah High School graduating class. While in high school, he was active in student government and music activities and was president of the National Honor Society.

  Q attended Texas A&M University and earned a degree in range management. While a student at Texas A&M, he not only was active in student government but also was part of a group that persuaded the university to recognize student chapters of major political parties. After a year at Baylor Law School, he returned to Paducah to enter the family ranching and farming business.

  In addition to working with the family ranching and farming business, Q taught science at Paducah High School. Regina Ferguson had planned to teach in Paducah for one year while awaiting another position, but instead of going to the other position, she married Q the following summer. The daughter of Thomas William and Laura Jean Mock Ferguson, Regina was active in music and drama as well as other school activities. She earned a BS in elementary education from North Texas State University, where she was on the Dean's Honor Roll while being active in student government, athletics, and sorority activities.

  Both Q and Regina have been active members of the Paducah First Methodist Church and the Cottle-King Livestock and Rodeo Association. Q has served on the board of trustees of Paducah Independent School District as well as in the role of director of Cottle County Soil and Water Conservation District for six years. He was active with County Extension programs, the county Republican Party organization, and other community activities. Regina has been active in the Euterpean Club and the Study Club in addition to being a homemaker and caring for her growing family. Q and Regina have six daughters. A stroke initiated a decline in Q's health, which led to his death at age seventy-five.

  - **Lara Katherine Richards (21 Aug 1973–):** Lara was born in Lubbock, Texas. She graduated from the University of Notre Dame. She received a law degree from Tulane University and established a law practice in New Orleans.

- **Martha Belinda Richards (24 Oct 1975–):** Martha was born in Lubbock, Texas. She graduated from Midwestern University in Wichita Falls, Texas. She works for a newspaper in Colorado.

- **Rachel Regina Alyson Richards (25 Jan 1980–):** Rachel entered this world at Childress Hospital in Childress, Texas. After obtaining a bachelor's degree from the University of Texas, Rachel worked for the federal government in Washington, DC. She received a law degree from the University of Michigan and moved to Anchorage, Alaska, and established a law practice there. On October 10, 2015, Rachel married John Colder. John conducts guided tours of the Alaska wilderness. With few ties beyond her parents in Paducah, Rachel chose Saint Jo, Texas, for her wedding. It had been the location of the wedding of her grandparents, Frances and T. J. Richards.

- **Lydia Blair Elizabeth Richards (31 May 1982–):** Lydia was born in Childress, Texas. She graduated from the University of the South and obtained a medical degree from Baylor Medical School in Houston, Texas. She completed medical residency in New Orleans. On October 18, 2014, Lydia married Randolph Starr in New Orleans.

- **Emily Abigail Richards (2 Dec 1985–):** Emily was born with spina bifida, which has limited her activities. She attended public school in Henrietta, Texas, and lives in Paducah with her mother.

- **Bethany Rebecca Richards (2 Dec 1985–):** Twin to Emily Abigail, Bethany was born in Childress, Texas. She graduated from Henrietta High School in the class of 2004. She attended Texas A&M University and graduated from the College of Santa Fe in 2009 with degrees in art therapy and psychology. Bethany lived in New Orleans, Louisiana, and worked in the Biological Sciences Department of Loyola University. She attended Southwest Medical School in Dallas, Texas.

- **Ronald Russell Richards (19 Jul 1942–):** Ronald was born in Paducah, Texas. He was called Ronnie as a child and Ron as an adult. Ron attended Paducah public schools, where he was active in school bands and Boy Scouts. He was a member of the All-Regional Band for three years during high school and graduated as valedictorian from Paducah High School.

Ron attended Texas A&M University, where he was a member of the Fightin' Texas Aggie Band for four years and a member of the Corps of Cadets, where he attained the rank of cadet major. He earned a degree in range management from Texas A&M University. Graduate studies at Oklahoma State University resulted in a master's degree in animal science and a PhD in animal breeding.

Ron married Alyson Ann Hall, daughter of Sue G. and Alvin E. Hall of Oklahoma City, Oklahoma. Born in Pawhuska, Oklahoma, Alyson graduated from Northwest Classen High School in Oklahoma City, where she was active in music activities and student government. Two summers were spent in Mexico under the sponsorship of a Presbyterian church. She obtained a degree in elementary education from Oklahoma State University and taught fifth grade in Stillwater, Oklahoma.

After completing his PhD, Ron took a position as beef production specialist at the University of New Mexico, from which he had the opportunity to spend two years in Asunción, Paraguay. On returning from Paraguay, Ron and Alyson moved to Matador, Texas, where they spent several years farming and ranching in Cottle and Motley Counties. Their next move was to Wimberley, Texas, where Ron was employed as a science teacher in Wimberley High School. He taught physics, biology, and chemistry and was selected as one of the high school science teachers to participate in a statewide experiment studying biomolecular factors affecting the functioning of the immune system. Ron, now retired from teaching, and Alyson live in Wimberley, Texas.

- **Will Russell Richards (11 Feb 1971–):** Will was born in Asunción, Paraguay, while his parents were there on a University of New Mexico project. He attended school in Matador, Texas, and graduated from Motley High School in Matador. Will graduated from Texas A&M University with a degree in engineering technology. Will married Jennifer Nixon in Georgetown, Williamson County, Texas. Initially they lived in Jarrell, Texas, where Will worked for Design and Assembly Concepts, but they later moved to Georgetown, Texas. Their daughter, Annelise Clare, was named for Bonnie Clare Richards, Will's sister.

- **Bonnie Clare Richards (21 Sep 1972–12 Apr 1996):** Bonnie was born in Paducah, Texas. She graduated from Wimberley High School. She entered Texas A&M University with a major in education and plans for a career in bilingual education. Weeks before her scheduled graduation from Texas A&M University, Bonnie was killed when the car she was driving was struck by a dump truck that had run a red light. She was awarded her degree posthumously in May of 1996.

- **Lucas Dan Richards (31 May 1978–):** Luke began playing the drums at age eleven and was provided a quality set of drums by his parents. Active in the Wimberley Methodist Church, he played timpani and sang in the church choir. He graduated from Wimberley High School and obtained a degree from Texas State University, San Marcos. In 2003, he joined the Paul Eason Band as a drummer and did considerable traveling with the band. In 2004, he and two other members of the band formed the Taylor Davis Trio. After several years of travel with the band, he left the band and worked for a time with his brother at Design and Assembly Concepts in Georgetown, Texas. Later, he was employed by Schlumberger. Lucas and Laura D'Amore were married in the First Methodist Church in Wimberley, Texas. He and Laura live in Kyle, Texas. Their children are Thomas Joseph and Patrick Lucas.

- **Louise Russell (1 Dec 1919–6 Apr 2000):** Named Treasure Louise, she was always known as Louise. An imaginative and creative child, Louise was sometimes a puzzle to her grandmother, Fannie Kenny, who once stated that she never knew what to expect from Louise when she was staying with them.

Louise attended public school in De Leon and Millsap, Texas. She graduated from North Texas State Teachers College, now the University of North Texas, in January 1938, with a major in English and a teaching credential. She and Horace Leslie Stallings (11 Jun 1915–21 Apr 1961) were married on April 13, 1941, in the Russell home in Saint Jo. Horace, the son of Reuben Irvin Stallings and Lily Mae Parks, was born in Clyde, Texas, but grew up and graduated from high school in Paducah, Texas. After the death of Horace's father, he and Louise moved to Paducah, where Louise taught English and Horace operated his father's grocery store. On January 20, 1942, Horace enlisted in the US Army Air Corps, but he then transferred to military police. He served in England, France, and Germany. According to their daughter, Barbara, neither the grocery store operation nor the military life had been in their plans when they had first gotten married. After his discharge in 1945, Horace and Louise moved to a farm near Paducah to pursue his dream of farming. Within a few years he was persuaded to become county judge of Cottle County. After one term as county judge, Horace and the family moved to Waco, where he completed a law degree at Baylor Law School. He set up a law office in Paducah before accepting a legal position with Stewart Title Company in Fort Worth. His last position was with the legal division of Gulf Oil Corporation in Midland, Texas.

Louise taught in Paducah, Hughes Springs, Chillicothe, Keller, Amarillo, Fort Worth, and Midland public schools. She served as head of the English department in Midland. She apparently followed in her mother's footsteps not only in enjoying teaching but also in doing an outstanding job. In a letter to her sister Maurine, Rookh Richards quoted the superintendent of the Paducah schools as saying Louise was the best English teacher he had ever had in his schools. Louise Stallings was one Midland teacher mentioned by Laura Bush in her book *Spoken from the Heart*, in which she also mentioned English honors classes.

On April 21, 1961, Horace took his own life while in Paducah, Texas. Louise was left a single mother and sole supporter of the four children. After her children graduated from Midland High School, Louise moved to Stephenville and obtained a faculty position in the English Department of Tarleton State University.

After several years at Tarleton, Louise took a leave of absence to complete a doctoral program. Texas A&M University, the alma mater of her father, D. M., was the school chosen for her doctoral study. Her research resulted in the book *The Unpolished Altar: The Place of the Bay Psalm Book in American Culture*. After completion of her PhD in 1977, Louise returned to the English Department at Tarleton State University. Louise enjoyed her students and frequently had groups of students in her home for study groups or social interaction. She was especially interested in international students and helping them adapt to college life.

Louise read widely. She related to her sister Betty that her idea of a perfect winter evening included a fire in the fireplace, a glass of wine, and a good book.

Retirement in 1983 brought a move to Austin, Texas, where she could be closer to family. For several years, she enjoyed retirement and all the opportunities offered by the Austin community. In 1992 she said of her retirement, "I thought I'd be like the old firehorse and leap into harness when I heard the school bell ring, but that has never been so." When ill health made it necessary for Louise to go to a care facility, she felt very restricted and described it as being "in jail." Louise died in Austin, Texas.

- **Barbara Jane Stallings (1 May 1942–):** Born at home in Paducah, Texas, Barbara attended schools in Paducah and Midland and graduated from Midland High School. Barbara was in college at the time of her father's death. She graduated from North Texas State University with a major in secondary education and a teaching credential. Barbara and Kenneth Alan McKnight (4 Jul 1942–23 Apr 2003) were married on September 5, 1964, in Midland, Texas. They made their home in Victoria and Placedo, Texas. Kenneth, the son of Carl McKnight and Mabel Reynolds, was born in Beaumont, Texas. While in Victoria, Barbara was active in the Junior Woman's Club and the Book Review Club. Barbara taught in the Victoria and Bloomington schools and studied for the ministry. She became an ordained Methodist minister and conducted funeral services for her grandparents, D. M. and Eunice Russell, and other relatives. Kenneth worked for Carbide Pipeline Company, eventually becoming safety director in a territory covering the Gulf Coast from Lafayette, Louisiana, to Brownsville, Texas.

Barbara and Kenneth enjoyed horses and horse trail riding and were active in trail-riding groups. They purchased a horse trailer with a compact living space to facilitate participation in trail riding in various locations. Kenneth developed colon cancer and died about the time he had planned to retire. Barbara remained in the Placedo area for a while, then moved from the hurricane-prone area to Morgan Mill, Texas, where she was able to pursue her interest in horses and trail riding. She enjoys jazz and classical music and historical novels. Interested in maintaining family contacts, Barbara organized annual family reunions at Morgan Mill.

- **Mary Kathryn "Katy" McKnight (6 Dec 1966–):** Katy was born in Victoria, Texas. She lived in Houston for several years. Katy and her daughter moved to the Morgan Mill area, and Katy earned a BS degree in animal industries from Tarleton State University. Following her mother's interest in horses and trail riding, Kate served as executive director of the Texas Horse Council. She is an active supporter of her daughter's sports activities.

  - **Rebecca Louise Burney (3 Jun 2004–):** Rebecca was born in Sugar Land, Texas. She is active in sports, with an emphasis on softball.

- **William Alan McKnight (24 Mar 1968–):** Born in Victoria, Texas, William graduated from Bloomington High School, in Bloomington, Texas. Crystal S. Seaman (24 Jul 1970–) and William were married on August 14, 1993, in Victoria, Texas. Crystal was born in Port Lavaca, Texas. William graduated from Texas A&M University with a degree in mechanical engineering. He works at Invista in Victoria, Texas. Crystal graduated from the University of Houston–Clear Lake and has taught in Pearland and Victoria public schools. Both of their children were born in Victoria, Texas. Their children are Andrew Alan and Zachary Aaron.

- **Robert David Stallings (15 Mar 1944–):** David was born in Knox City, Texas. He graduated from the University of Texas with majors in business and geology. David married Sheila Ann Birden (14 Oct 1945–) on June 14, 1968, in Austin, Texas. Sheila's parents are Charles Birden and Doris Turner. David became certified in hospital administration and served as director of nursing homes in Pennsylvania. On returning to Texas, David and Sheila lived in Austin, Texas. David obtained a degree in petroleum engineering and worked for an oil company until a downturn in the oil economy resulted in workforce reduction. He and Sheila operate a restaurant and an antique business in Santa Anna, Texas.

- **David Charles Stallings (14 Jul 1971–):** David was born in Austin, Texas. He graduated from Texas Tech University and works in computer services at Dell Computers. David married Nikki Lane Manuel on November 7, 1996, in Austin. Their children are Parker David and Lauren Louise.

- **Robert Christopher "Chris" Stallings (23 Dec 1975–):** Chris was born in Austin, Texas. As a member of the US Army Intelligence, Chris specializes in intercepted signals intelligence. He serves as an instructor in the Korean language.

- **Michael Patrick Stallings (22 Oct 1982–):** Patrick was born in Austin, Texas. He graduated from the US Military Academy at West Point and received a bachelor's degree in mathematics. He served in Iraq and Afghanistan. Patrick has also worked in the US Senate and at Fort Hood, Fort Bliss, and Fort Benning. Patrick married Tiffany Lynn Williams on July 3, 2006. Their children are Ryan Russell "Russ" and Franklin Phillip "Phil."

- **John Russell "Rusty" Stallings (17 Apr 1948–13 Mar 2005):** Rusty was born in Paducah, Texas. He attended Texas A&M University, where he played football, including the Southwest Conference and Cotton Bowl Championship teams. He was also a member of the Texas A&M Corps of Cadets and the Ross Volunteers. He served as company commander of Cadet Company H-1 in the 1969–1970 academic year. Rusty graduated from Texas A&M in 1970 and entered veterinary medicine graduate school that fall. As a graduate student, he continued his football interest by serving as graduate assistant coach to the freshman team.

  Rusty married Kerry A. Fisher (24 Sep 1949–), daughter of Flake Fisher and Marjorie Ham of Bryan, Texas, on December 19, 1970, in College Station, Texas.

  Rusty and Kerry moved to Plano, Texas, where they became active members of Prestonwood Baptist Church. Rusty established the Prairie Creek Pet Care Center in Plano. Over the years the practice expanded, and in 2004 he built a new clinic to become his "dream" practice. One Sunday morning, Rusty reported having chest pains. When they did not subside, he decided to go to the hospital. While driving to the hospital, he experienced a massive, fatal heart attack. The car went out of control, and in the subsequent crash, Kerry was thrown from the vehicle and sustained major injuries, recovery from which required several months. Rusty was buried in Plano.

Kerry married Dusty David Butler on October 17, 2007. They live on Eagle Mountain Lake, northwest of Fort Worth, Texas.

- **Timothy Andrew "Tank" Stallings (11 Jun 1977–):** Tank was born in Dallas, Texas. He graduated from Plano Senior High School. He attended Blinn College in Bryan, Texas. He and Kelly Robertson were married on July 27, 2012. They live in Plano, where he has a landscaping business and Kelly teaches in high school and coaches girls' basketball. Their children are Jay Russell and Elene Irene.

- **Sarah Kathryn Stallings (30 Aug 1978–):** Kathryn was born in Dallas, Texas. She married William Robert Parr on September 28, 2001. The marriage ended in divorce. Their daughter is Rachel Alev "Allie." Kathryn married Brian Creveling (31 Dec 1976–) on November 3, 2007. A native of Ridgewood, New Jersey, Brian was a 1999 graduate of the University of Texas. Kathryn is a 2000 graduate of Texas A&M with a bachelor's in marketing. In 2012, she received a master's degree in Christian education from Southwestern Seminary. Kathryn and Bryan adopted two girls from Ethiopia on May 30, 2013, "Tess" Belaynesh Tesfaye Shumetie and "Bela" Beletu Tesfaye Shumetie.

- **Thomas Leslie "Tommy" Stallings (9 May 1949–):** Born in Paducah, Texas, Tommy lived in several cities as his father completed his law degree and established a practice. Tommy attended public schools in Amarillo, Fort Worth, and Midland. He played football in Fort Worth and Midland. At Midland High School, he was in the National Honor Society and participated in Junior Achievement. He attended a National Science Foundation–sponsored summer program for students interested in engineering at Texas A&M University in the summer of 1966. One summer while in high school, he worked for the Gulf Oil Corporation in their reproduction department and assisted a surveyor with survey work in West Texas. Tommy graduated from Midland Lee High School in 1967. As a National Merit Scholarship finalist, he received a scholarship from Gulf Oil Corporation to attend Texas A&M University. While at Texas A&M, he participated in the engineering college's Cooperative Education program, working two semesters for the Monsanto Company in Texas City and one semester for Thiokol Corporation. Thiokol was the operating contractor for the US Army's Longhorn Army Ammunition Plant in Karnack, Texas. Tommy received a BS degree in chemical engineering in 1971.

Tommy's first employment after graduation was with Baroid Division of NL Industries, where he worked on several offshore oil rigs off the Louisiana coast. Accepting a job offer from the Silas Mason Company in 1972 brought a move to Amarillo, Texas. Silas Mason Company is the operating contractor for the Pantex Department of Energy plant in Amarillo. Much of the work he does requires a classified document clearance, so he is unable to discuss his work. A chronic ailment unresponsive to medical treatment from 2006 through 2008 resulted in use of his accrued sick leave. He retired from his job in 2008.

Tommy has always been an avid reader, and for many years he kept a horse for pleasure riding. He has enjoyed traveling to New Mexico and Florida, since he owns a time-share in Kissimmee, Florida. He grew up in the Methodist Church but has attended nondenominational churches in Amarillo. Tommy has never married and has no children but has enjoyed watching his five nephews and two nieces grow up.

- **Elizabeth Rookh "Betty" Russell (28 Jun 1931–):** Betty was born at the Blackwell Clinic in Gorman, Texas. Betty's story as she wrote it:

She was named for her great-aunt Elizabeth Martin Clark Hicks and her aunt Lalla Rookh Kenny Richards, but she never used the full name, being called Betty Rookh by family and later just Betty.

Betty attended public schools in Saint Jo, Rochester, and Lipan, Texas, where she graduated as valedictorian of her class. She participated in UIL activities, played basketball, and was active in the Future Homemakers of America. Her favorite "out-of-school" activity was horseback riding, and she participated in several rodeos. An important part of her teen years was helping her parents in the development of the ranch at Lipan.

Betty graduated from Texas State College for Women (now Texas Woman's University) with a degree in speech and from the University of Houston with an MEd in special education. She was a speech therapist in the Bryan, Houston, and Conroe public schools. While serving as a speech therapist in Conroe, she was charged with developing and supervising the program to serve children with special needs. She spent several years at the Region VI Education Service Center developing a Special Education Instructional Materials Center, supervising educational diagnosticians, and assisting school districts in developing their special education services. Her last assignment was as director of the Montgomery County Special Education Cooperative. During these professional years, she served on the board of the Montgomery County Mental Health/Mental Retardation Commission, a president of the Region VI Chapter of the Texas Council of Administrators of Special Education, and as a member of the Texas State Commission on Professional Competencies.

On February 24, 1951, she married her high school sweetheart, Robert Edwin Thompson, son of Monroe Dwalt and Mary Thelma Winn Thompson. Robert was born on August 1, 1932, in Paluxy, Texas, and attended school there and in Lipan.

He was a good student and athlete and was especially interested in his vocational agriculture and FFA projects. He attended John Tarleton Agricultural College for two years and spent four years as an aviation electrician in the US Navy. Most of this time he was stationed at Hickam Air Force Base in Honolulu. Betty and the family joined him there. Upon his discharge, he obtained a degree in agriculture economics/rural sociology from Texas A&M and went to work for the Boy Scouts of America as a district executive in southwest Houston and later in Montgomery County. He was offered a teaching position in the Conroe ISD and obtained his MEd in educational administration from Sam Houston State University. He spent twenty years in Conroe, most of it as principal of two elementary schools. He moved to the Willis ISD as principal of Willis High School and later became business manager and interim superintendent. During his professional years, he served as a member of the advisory board of the Texas State Teachers Association (TSTA) and president of the District VI TSTA, the Montgomery County TSTA, and the Conroe chapter of the TSTA. He was also active in the Elementary Principals Association and Association of School Business Managers.

Both Betty and Robert were involved in activities involving their sons, Steve and Rusty, from Cub Scouts through Explorer levels; summer baseball leagues; junior high and high school basketball, football, and track; and family camping trips. Betty was a Den Mother, and Robert was Explorer Scout Master and, in the summer, directed Camp Strake for the Houston Area Council, BSA. Both were active in their Methodist church as board members and teachers.

Upon retirement, they spent some happy years on Lake Conroe, where they enjoyed entertaining children, grandchildren, and extended family. Both of them were involved in community service groups and the Montgomery County A&M Club, where they were active on fundraising and scholarship-selection committees. Their second retirement home was in Bryan, where they continue their work as members on the Development Council for the TAMU College of Education, commissioners for the Methodist Children's Home, teachers of Sunday school, and board members of several community service organizations.

- **Robert Stephen "Steve" Thompson (18 Dec 1951–):** Born in Lipan, Texas, Steve attended school in Houston and Conroe and graduated from Conroe High School. In high school he lettered in football and track, sang in the choir, and was president of the National Honor Society and the Fellowship of Christian Athletes. Steve obtained a bachelor's degree from Texas A&M University in 1974 and began his teaching career in the Conroe public schools. After completing a master's of education from Sam Houston University, Huntsville, Texas, he taught social studies in Conroe, Willis, and Hays County schools. Steve was active in the Association of Texas Professional Educators (ATPE) and served as president of the Hays ATPE for many years. During his tenure as president, the

Hays ATPE was chosen as Texas's outstanding local unit. He became director of the Content Mastery Center at Lehman High School, where he taught for twelve years until retiring in 2016.

On November 17, 1972, Steve and Verna Larue Dana (10 Mar 1954–) were married in Huntsville, Walker County, Texas. Verna was born in Houston, Harris County, Texas, to Don Loran Dana and Elna Ruth Porter. Verna was a graduate of Sam Houston State University and an elementary school teacher. Steve and Verna are both active members of the Church of Jesus Christ of Latter-day Saints. Verna volunteers in the local LDS FamilySearch Library and is an excellent genealogy researcher.

- **Jonathan Stephen Thompson (28 Aug 1973–):** Born in Bryan, Brazos County, Texas, Jonathan attended public school in Willis and Hays Consolidated and graduated from Bowie High School in Austin. He attended Texas A&M University and served terms in the US Army and the US Navy.

  Jonathan lived in Morgantown, West Virginia, with his wife, Monica LeAnn Gilliland (9 Jan 1979–), and worked as a field service and sales technician for Pason Systems USA Corp. Monica was born in McKinney, Collin County, Texas, to Wesley Burk Gilliland and Betty Lee Patterson. With the downturn in the oil industry, Jonathan lost his position, and the family returned to Aubrey, Texas. At the time of this writing, Jonathan is working in temporary jobs until a long-term position becomes available.

  Their children are Elizabeth Nicole, Xavier Robert, and Ian Wesley.

- **Jason Robert Thompson (16 Aug 1974–):** Born in Bryan, Brazos County, Texas, Jason attended public schools in Willis and Hays Consolidated. He graduated from Jack C. Hays High School in Buda, Texas. He served in the Persian Gulf War as a member of the US Navy. He later served as a navy recruiter in California, Texas, Oklahoma, and New Hampshire/Vermont, attaining the rank of senior chief petty officer in 2013. In California, Jason married Socorro Imelda Juarez (13 May 1966–), who was born in Hermosillo, Sonora, Mexico. They lived in Bow, New Hampshire. Jason retired from the navy in the summer of 2016 and now lives in Oklahoma City. Their children are Amanda Maria, Karina Nicole, and Ryan Stephen.

- **Suzanne Alayne Thompson (23 Mar 1976–):** Suzanne was born in Conroe, Texas. She attended public schools in Willis and Austin. A 1994 graduate of Jack C. Hays High School in Buda, Texas, she completed a bachelor's degree in 2003 at Texas Woman's University in Denton, Texas. Suzanne and Thomas Gregory Hillin were married on June 22, 2002, in Kaufman County, Texas. Suzanne obtained an MA degree in library science in the spring of 2005. They lived in Texas, California, and Pennsylvania during Thomas's employment as an engineer for Raytheon. Suzanne and Thomas divorced in 2013. She resides in Austin, Texas, where she is owner of Suzy's Book Stop.

- **Mary Elizabeth Thompson (8 Jul 1978–):** Born in Stephenville, Erath County, Texas, Mary Elizabeth attended public schools in Willis and Austin, graduating from Jack C. Hays High School in Buda, Texas. She obtained a bachelor's degree in financial planning from the University of North Texas and credentials as a Certified Financial Planner from the state of Texas. She has worked as a financial adviser in Los Angeles, California, and Little Rock, Arkansas. Mary married Kyle Andrew McCraw in 2003. Kyle, an electrical engineering graduate of the University of Arkansas, works for the city of Little Rock. Their twin daughters were born in Burbank, Los Angeles County, California. They are Catherine Elise and Dana Elizabeth.

- **Seth Russell Thompson (23 Mar 1981–):** Born in Conroe, Texas, Seth attended public schools in Austin and graduated from Jack C. Hays High School in Buda, Texas. He entered the US Navy and served as an air traffic controller on the USS *Tarawa* during the Iraq War. He resigned from the navy and joined the US Army, where he was commissioned as warrant officer and became a Black Hawk helicopter pilot. He served in South Korea, Germany, and Afghanistan. National news reported the rescue of personnel in a downed Apache helicopter in April 2013; his family learned that Seth piloted the first helicopter to reach the scene for the rescue. His home base is Fort Hood, Texas, where he is a pilot instructor. Seth married Sandra Rosalina Valadez-Chavez (7 Nov 1980–), who was born in Tijuana, Baja California, Mexico. They have two children, Sophia Renee and Ethan Russell.

- **Sara Emily Thompson (19 Oct 1995–):** Born in Austin, Travis County, Texas, Sara attended elementary school in Buda, Texas, but was home-schooled by her parents for high school so she could devote more time to music. She is an accomplished pianist and a National Merit Scholar. With dual enrollment in Austin Community College and the University of Texas at Austin, she was named Collaborative Pianist at the University of Texas. At the university, she accompanied choirs and opera workshop students. The university position came with a campus parking permit, though at the time she obtained the position, she was too young to have a driver's license. She is organist for her church and attends Brigham Young University. Fluent in German, she spent the summer of 2016 in Germany.

- **Russell Winn "Rusty" Thompson (28 Oct 1963–12 Mar 2016):** Rusty was born in Conroe, Montgomery County, Texas. He attended Conroe public schools and graduated from Conroe High School in 1981. He played basketball in Conroe High School until a routine physical examination revealed the early stages of Hodgkin's disease. After extensive treatment, he went into remission. He was a member of the National Honor Society and was president of the Industrial Arts Club. Having grown up in an Aggie family, Rusty's only choice for college was Texas A&M University. At A&M, with a major in industrial education, he was commanding officer of Squadron 5 of the Corps of Cadets. After graduating from Texas A&M in 1985, he entered A&M's graduate school. While in graduate school, he had another bout with Hodgkin's but was able to return to remission and complete his master's degree in 1987. After three years of employment at Texas Tech University, Rusty returned to Texas A&M in the Department of Student Activities. He was adviser to several student organizations, including Bonfire, Yell Leaders, Class Councils, Aggie Wranglers, Muster, and Fish Camp. In 2013, Rusty was named director of student affairs for Texas A&M University, his dream job. Awards he received included Advisor of the Year, President's Meritorious Service Award, the Randy Matson Award, and the John J. Koldus Award.

  Rusty and Tina Marie Kozelsky were married on July 18, 1987, in Walker County, Texas. Tina, a fellow Aggie, shared with Rusty a devotion to A&M University, and they enjoyed participating in many campus activities together. Rusty suffered a massive heart attack while participating in a recognition event on the A&M campus. He was airlifted to Houston, where he died a few days later. The fact that the large church where his funeral services were held was filled to capacity indicated the high regard students and staff of the university felt for him. He was buried in the Aggie Field of Honor.

  - **Blayne Russell Thompson (1 Aug 1988–):** Blayne was born in Lubbock, Texas, but was a young child when the family moved to Bryan.

    He attended Bryan, Texas, public schools, where he played football, was a member of the National Honor Society, participated in several clubs, and graduated with honors in 2006. As a Boy Scout, he attained the rank of Eagle Scout. He received scholarships to attend Texas A&M University, where he was in the Corps of Cadets, a scholastic officer for his squadron, and a three-year member of Class Councils. He was president of Class Councils in his senior year. He was class president during his sophomore, junior, and senior years.

In 2008 he spent six weeks in Fiji and Australia as a part of the study-abroad program at Texas A&M University. There he did research on the Great Barrier Reef, tropical rainforests, and the outback. He was one of twenty-six American student ambassadors to the United States–China Relations Conference in 2009. When he graduated in 2010, Blayne received the Robert Gates Award as Outstanding Senior.

In June 2010, Blayne married Janie Womac. Janie was a 2008 graduate of Texas A&M and completed a master's degree there in 2010. She is employed at the University of Houston.

Blayne graduated from Baylor Law School, magna cum laude, in May 2013. He accepted a position in the law firm of Nelson, Rose and Fulbright in Houston, Texas.

- **Brenna Anne Thompson (6 Feb 1994–):** Brenna was born in College Station, Texas. She attended Bryan public schools and graduated from Bryan High School. She was active in the student council and the National Honor Society and was a varsity cheerleader for three years. An active Girl Scout, she rose to the rank of Star Scout. She graduated from Bryan High School with honors in 2012. Following family tradition, she enrolled in Texas A&M University, where she has been a member of Lohman Learners, a Fish Camp counselor, and Muster hostess. During her sophomore year, she participated in a three-month study program in Italy and England. She served as president of the student chapter of the Texas State Teachers Association. She graduated from A&M University in May 2016 and began a career as an elementary school teacher. Brenna married J. Lawton Chain Lander on July 15, 2017.

Lalla Rookh Kenny
(13 Sep 1896–7 Mar 1967)

The 1891 publication of the illustrated New American Edition by Thomas Y. Crowell and Company created a renewed interest in Thomas Moore's 1817 romantic poem, *Lalla Rookh*. Among those impressed by the book was Fannie Clark Kenny. When her third daughter was born, Fannie named her Lalla Rookh. Rookh, as she was always called, had brown hair and brown eyes, was medium height, and had a slender build. She was always fun loving and adventurous. She and her older sister Eunice were especially close growing up, and this closeness continued through adulthood.

When Rookh reached the age to begin dating, she dated many young men but for a number of years did not become serious about anyone. Her mother became impatient with Rookh playing the field. She is reported to have said, "Rookh, you are just like a butterfly. You flit from flower to flower, but if you are not careful, you will end up on a cow dab." After her marriage, Dan, her husband, would sometimes introduce himself at family gatherings as "Rookie's cow dab."

Rookh attended school at Oak Dale and Huckabay. After graduating from high school, she followed the example of her two older sisters in obtaining a teaching position in a local school. During the summers, Rookh would sometimes go to school to improve her teaching skills and sometimes would visit friends around the state. One such visit was probably made with her cousin Edna Wofford Watson. They visited Edna's sister-in-law, Starlie Watson, wife of Merrill Richards of Paducah, Texas. There Rookh met Merrill's younger brother, Dan. She and Dan found that they had many interests in common; both worked hard when there was work to be done, but they liked to dance, take trips, and enjoy life.

The Richards family was a prominent ranching family in Cottle County. Dan (31 Aug 1889–14 Oct 1968), the youngest child of T. J. and Frances Jenkins Richards, was born in Blue Ridge, Collin County, Texas. The family moved to Cottle County when he was a young child. As a youngster he was the prankster of the family. He attended Paducah public schools, Goodnight College in Amarillo, and Texas Christian University in Fort Worth. During World War I, Dan served in the US Navy. In addition to working on the family's extensive ranch holdings, he managed the "River Place," jointly owned by Dan and his brother Merrill.

Rookh was teaching in Bluff Dale when she accepted a proposal of marriage from Dan Richards. As Dan told the story of their marriage to Ron Richards, the plan was for Dan to come by train to Stephenville, where they would be married. However, Dan drank too much, fell asleep, and failed to get off the train at Stephenville. When he awoke in Fort Worth and sobered up, he hired a car and a uniformed chauffeur to take him back to Stephenville. Rookh had been crushed when Dan did not get off the train as planned, and her parents objected to her marrying him after that incident. They were not impressed with the big black car and the uniformed chauffeur. Rookh, though, knew that she wanted to marry Dan; they obtained a marriage license in Stephenville and were married on October 10, 1922, at the home of Rookh's sister Leona Davis, in Thurber. From there they were driven back to Fort Worth, where they caught the train to Quanah and from there drove to the ranch near Paducah.

Rookh soon learned the skills of being a ranch wife in West Texas. She learned to deal with hard water, conserve the limited water from the cistern, raise a garden under arid conditions, feed ranch hands when branding and roundup brought in twenty to thirty extra workers, and fill the lonely hours when Dan needed to be away checking the remote areas of the ranch. On one such trip, Dan came home with a bad cut on his leg. Because he was a long distance from home, he had put stock salt on the wound to discourage infection and completed his tasks before coming in.

Around 1929, Dan and Rookh built a brick home in Paducah, and both became increasingly involved in the community. They were interested in school activities and were avid supporters of many school activities, including the school sports teams. They frequently attended both home and out-of-town games. Their home was always open to young people, and they were "Aunt Rookh and Uncle Dan" to three generations of Paducah students.

The decade of the 1930s brought severe drought. Ranchers had to reduce their cattle herds to conserve the grass and to have enough water to supply the needs of the remaining cattle. As the drought became more severe, great black clouds of dust would roll off the South Plains, only a few miles away. The dust would darken the day as if it were night and cover everything with dirt. The fact that this was ranching country with relatively little farming meant that little of the dust bowl clouds originated in Cottle County, but it was among the first areas for dropping the load of dust.

The family car was always Rookh's car. During the 1930s, it was a Buick, but after World War II, the car was a Cadillac. Dan drove the pickup around the ranch and around town, but only Rookh drove the car.

During World War II, most people, including Rookh and Dan, would pick up servicemen who were hitchhiking. Rookh and Dan would do more than take them to the nearest intersection. If the serviceman's destination was not too far out of their way and they had sufficient gasoline ration stamps, they would take him to his home. When the destination was too far or they had insufficient ration stamps, they would take him to a major bus terminal and buy him a ticket home. These tickets were sometimes for out of state, even to distant states.

Since they had no children of their own, Rookh and Dan took special interest in nieces and nephews. They always remembered birthdays, Christmases, graduations, and other special occasions with a nice gift. Rookh always expressed interest in the activities of nieces and nephews and was affectionate and fun to be around. She would play board games and do puzzles with them and sometimes engaged in contests as to who could do the most unusual wrap of a Christmas gift. Sue Kenny Weathers remembers one winter when Rookh offered to let Sue wear her mink coat to a special school event, and Rookh gave her a very special dress for graduation. The offer of the coat loan was declined, but the dress was treasured and has been kept.

At family gatherings, Dan always gave each child "treat" or movie money. During the Depression years, the "treat" money was at least a dime and usually a quarter, enough for a special treat when a double-dip ice cream cone was a dime. After World War II, the "treat" money was a dollar. In Paducah, Dan carried candy in his pickup truck, which he shared liberally. Many local children called him "Uncle Dan, the Candy Man."

When Isa Lee Rampley Henry contracted polio, Rookh and Dan took her infant, Danny, and cared for him for over a year until his mother had recovered sufficiently to resume his care. This experience developed a special bond between Rookh, Dan, and Danny.

The Paducah area has very unreliable rainfall levels, and Dan's parents had installed an underground cistern on a screened back porch to store rainwater. By this time, Dan's mother was living alone in the home, had become rather frail, and was in the early stages of dementia. Dan took Danny with him to take his mother a lunch that Rookh had prepared. Rookh had another commitment in town and did not accompany them. While Dan and his mother were in the kitchen, Danny wandered onto the back porch. Workers had left the cistern cover ajar, and somehow Danny managed to push it aside enough to fall in. Dan secured a water hose to let himself down into the cistern, heeding his mother's instructions to take off his boots first, and told her to call the fire department. Danny had gone under and was coughing when Dan reached him. The water was chest deep to Dan and very cold. Dan held the frightened child until the unit from the fire department arrived to rescue them.

After the rescue, Rookh was notified and took Danny to the hospital. Dan went home to get dry clothes. It was there that Betty Russell—who, with her parents, was visiting with her sister Frances—learned about what had happened. While at a friend's home in Paducah, Betty learned that a fire truck and police car had been seen at Mrs. Richards's home. After rushing to Rookh and Dan's home, she knocked, then opened the door and called to them. A tearful Dan came out of the bedroom wearing pale-blue silk underwear, cowboy boots, and a Stetson hat and carrying a bottle of whiskey. Betty, only a teenager, tried to comfort and reassure him before going back to Frances's home (which had no telephone) to tell her family they were needed in town. Danny recovered quickly from his ordeal, but everyone was amazed that he was able to survive for the time required for Dan to get to him—and that Mrs. Richards was able to give a coherent account of the event to the fire department. Dan felt a great sense of relief in being able to save the child, but the close call haunted him for many years. The telling of the story often brought tears to his eyes.

Dan wore cowboy boots in almost all situations. The few times he attempted to wear dress shoes, such as at a formal wedding, he reported finding them extremely uncomfortable, to the point of making it difficult to walk.

Rookh was an active member of the Paducah Methodist Church, where she sang in the choir and participated in many other church activities and outreach programs. She was a volunteer in many community activities, including the 23 Study Club, for which she served as president and in which she had a near-perfect attendance record.

Rookh and Dan were both generous and loving people. They were active in helping people in need and in helping their community. Both the Veterans of Foreign Wars building and the educational building of the Methodist Church of Paducah received generous donations from Rookh and Dan.

Dan donated land for building an airport east of Paducah, which became known as Dan E. Richards airport.

Dan did have the problem of heavy drinking. When drunk, he became very sentimental but never belligerent or abusive. He was careful not to drive while drinking and not to drink in places where alcohol was not accepted. Even with that care, his drinking did get him into trouble at a

Clark reunion. The reunion was one of several that had been held at a Methodist camp in Glen Rose. One afternoon Dan wanted a beer, and he asked Bruce Rampley to drive Rookh's car to an area away from the camp so he could have a beer from the cooler in the trunk. Bruce agreed, and Ann Davis, Louise Stallings, Gloria Griggs, and Betty Russell went along for the ride. Away from the camp, Dan had his beer, and the group enjoyed chatting. They were parked just outside the camp while Dan stowed the empty bottle in the trunk. As he was doing so, one of the Clark preachers happened by. At the general meeting that night, the preacher denounced Dan as corrupting the youth of the family. By the end of the session, Rookh was in tears, and her siblings were furious. Neither Rookh nor her brother or sisters attended another Clark reunion at Glen Rose.

Rookh's German chocolate cakes and Aunt Bill's Brown Candy, renamed Aunt Rookh's Brown Candy by the family, were special treats at Christmas. The candy was a joint project for Dan and Rookh, and they made many batches each Christmas. Although other family members tried to follow the recipe, none were able to make a candy as good as Rookh and Dan's.

Rookh died at the Richards Memorial Hospital in Paducah at the age of seventy. Dan donated a set of Maas chimes to the Paducah Methodist Church in her memory. Dan survived Rookh slightly over one year; he died at the Richards Memorial Hospital in 1968.

Billie (or Willi) Leona Kenny
(27 Nov 1896–Apr 1986)

It is not clear whether Leona's full name was Billie Leona or Willi Leona. In the family Bible she is listed as Willi Leona in the birth section and Billie Leona in the marriage section. Always called Leona, the fifth child of W. C. and Fannie Kenny was born in Oak Dale, Erath County, Texas. Although she was named for both of her parents, in her later years she felt the circumstances of her birth did not give her a privileged status in the family. As she told the story, during the summer before her birth, her father injured his back and was unable to do much physical activity for a couple of months. The corn was ready for harvest during that time, so Fannie, though visibly pregnant, worked with a neighbor boy to bring in the harvest. Leona felt that at her birth her parents had wanted a male child who would grow up to do more of the farmwork.

Leona and Meta developed an especially close relationship during Leona's childhood. Meta was old enough to assume some of the care for Leona as a young child. Later, Leona became Meta's helper when Meta was in charge of the Saturday baking while other family members attended to different chores. This early experience helped both Meta and Leona become excellent cooks. Leona described these Saturday sessions as being among her happiest memories of childhood.

Leona attended Oak Dale and Huckabay schools. After graduating from Huckabay High School, she attended Tarleton College (then John Tarleton Agricultural College) and obtained her teaching credential. She taught in some of the rural schools in Erath County, including Clabber Hill. The 1920 census shows her living in her parents' home and engaging in teaching as an occupation.

Her first year of teaching provided an interesting family story that she related many years later. During the first few days of the school year, she was having trouble establishing discipline with a group of unruly boys only a few years younger than her. At the end of a school day, she was approached by a woman who looked to be tough and hardened by backwoods pioneer life. The shotgun she carried under her arm did not lessen Leona's apprehension that she was to be accused of dealing too harshly with those she had disciplined. The woman asked if she was the new teacher, then if her name was Kenny. The next question asked if she was related to Dr. Kenny. Leona answered that he was her grandfather, but he had died before she had been born.

The woman then explained that when her oldest two children were small, they had become very sick. Dr. Kenny treated them and stayed with them until they were on their way to recovery. At the time she had not been able to pay him anything, and he'd died before she was able to do so. She felt she had a debt, and one way she could pay it was to see that his granddaughter was treated well. Her boys would see to it. The mother had a strong influence over her boys; they became Leona's enforcers of discipline, and she had no more trouble with unruly boys.

Leona grew to be the tallest of the sisters. She had a slender but well-proportioned build, and her dark-brown (almost black) hair developed streaks of gray at the temples, giving her a distinguished appearance. She had a flair for choosing clothes with a classic elegance, and her carriage displayed them to an advantage.

James Clarence Davis (Clarence or J. C.) (3 Jul 1899–Jan 1979) first dated Leona's sister Rookh, but his attentions soon turned to Leona. According to her sister Maurine, Leona and Clarence's union was very much a love match. They were married on June 1, 1921, in Erath County, probably at the Kenny home. They made their home in Thurber, the largest town in the county at the time they moved there. It was a company town totally owned by the Texas Pacific Coal Company. Every house, church, and business building was owned by the company and rented to the respective occupants. In addition to a coal-mining operation, which supplied coal for the Texas Pacific Railroad as well as other railroads, the company had the largest brick factory west of the Mississippi River and the Ranger Oil Field. Thurber bricks were used for numerous buildings and for paving many streets and roads in the area, including many of the buildings and streets of Fort Worth.

Peggy Ann, the only child of Leona and Clarence, was born while they were living in Thurber. The 1930 census shows them in Thurber, where Clarence worked as a purchasing agent.

In May 1930, Leona made a trip to Carlsbad, New Mexico, for evaluation of a persistent respiratory problem. She was diagnosed with tuberculosis and entered a sanatorium for a cure. Peggy Ann was sent to stay with Eunice and D. M. Russell for the period Leona was in the sanatorium.

Soon after Leona returned from the sanatorium, the Texas Pacific Coal Company changed its name to the Texas Pacific Oil Company and moved its headquarters to Fort Worth. The coal mines and brick factory were closed. Thurber was abandoned, and the buildings, all of which belonged to the company, were sold or demolished, leaving only a large smokestack to show where the town had been. Most employees related to the oil business, including Clarence, moved to Fort Worth. Clarence and Leona bought a home at 2212 Sixth Avenue in Fort Worth and resided there for the rest of their lives.

Around the time of the move to Fort Worth, Leona and Clarence's marriage began to deteriorate. Their relationship became increasingly distant, with occasional hostile overtones. On at least one occasion the hostility grew into violence. Domestic abuse was not to be tolerated by the family, and Jack Kenny and D. M. Russell visited Clarence with an ultimatum. The violence apparently stopped, but the distance in their lives increased. Many family members assumed that Leona and Clarence stayed together only for Peggy Ann's sake, but they remained together after Peggy Ann left home, married, and eventually died. At that point, the only things they apparently shared were a domicile and adoration of the grandchildren.

Leona decided to pursue a career path to become financially independent. She first worked with the Welcome Wagon for Fort Worth, then as a salesperson for Stanley Home Products, a company for which she eventually became a district manager. Later she studied real estate and established a real estate business, which she ran from her home. She was a very capable person with an outgoing personality and an ability to express herself effectively and forcefully. She not only became financially independent, but she also became a very successful businesswoman. She found helping people obtain homes that met their needs more satisfying than making a lot of money. Beyond providing herself with nice clothes and a good car, both necessities for her business, her primary concern in making money was to help provide for Peggy Ann and, later, to help the grandchildren. She did, however, resent the fact that under Texas law at the time, she could not buy land for speculation without the signature of Clarence, an action she would not request—nor would he have complied. Her real estate activities were during a period of rapid growth of the Fort Worth area, and she was aware of many possibilities for profitable investment.

Peggy Ann was the primary focus of Leona's life. Leona was pleased that her career helped provide extras for Peggy Ann while growing up and helped her go to college. It helped provide the wedding Peggy Ann wanted, helped Peggy Ann and Bill set up their home, and provided extras for the grandchildren. In the fall of 1964, Peggy Ann was diagnosed with Hodgkin's disease, and Leona helped finance treatments to fight the disease. The treatments were unsuccessful, and Peggy Ann died in February 1965. Peggy Ann's death left Leona devastated, and sadly within the next two years, she experienced the death of Meta, the sister with whom she had the closest bond; her nephew Bruce; her sister Rookh; and her mother. Despite her overwhelming sense of loss, Leona did not give in to despair. Instead, she concentrated her energies and efforts on making things better for her grandchildren. They became the new focus of her life. Her grandson Pat described Leona as "the kindest and most trusting person I have ever met, and her trustworthiness was often to her detriment, as people would take advantage of her, but she never seemed to mind too much."

Both Leona and Clarence spent considerable time with the grandchildren. Leona usually had them over for supper once a week and, as they reached college age and adulthood, helped them financially. Clarence took the boys fishing and hunting, activities that they enjoyed but that held little interest for their father.

Leona's determination extended to her physical well-being; she recovered full mobility after suffering a severe break in her leg and later a broken vertebra. Her main concern with her broken leg was that it limited her ability to drive her car. She resisted the physical limitations of growing older and did not like to admit her age, even when revealing her age would mean a reduced entry fee to state parks and other events.

Her close relationship to her sister Eunice became even more important to Leona after Meta's death. Soon, though, Eunice's deteriorating health and move out of the area deprived her of that association. At that point, Leona and her sister Maurine, both unable to travel for visits in person, established a pattern of calling one another each Sunday. Both would watch a specific televised church service, then have a telephone conversation discussing the service, news about family members, or current events.

Clarence died in 1978, at eighty years of age. Leona lived alone, except for a longtime renter upstairs, until her granddaughter Julie and Julie's two young boys moved to Fort Worth to be with Leona. Leona was able to reestablish a close relationship with Julie, and she appeared to adore the boys. Leona died at age eighty-seven.

- **Peggy Ann Davis (13 Nov 1928–15 Feb 1965):** Born in Palo Pinto County, Texas, Peggy Ann was a good-natured and affectionate child. Defying the stereotypes of an only child, she was generous and considerate and always kind to younger cousins. She was also a beautiful child who grew into a beautiful woman. As children, Betty and Mary Jo, cousins almost three years younger, considered her a paragon of perfection. She always seemed to enjoy doing things with these cousins, whether it was exploring her neighborhood in Fort Worth, riding horses on the farm, playing in the creek at Aunt Meta's, going to a movie, picking wild grapes, or going to see her Davis cousins. She had an especially close relationship with her mother, her cousin Bruce Rampley, and her aunts Meta and Eunice.

  Ann, as she was called as she grew older, attended public schools in Fort Worth and graduated from Paschal High School. She attended the University of Texas at Austin, graduating with a major in psychology. It was at the university that she got to know William Clark Kneer, who was completing his degree in architecture. They were married in Fort Worth the summer after they graduated.

Ann and Bill made their home in Fort Worth, first at 4014 Merida Avenue and later at 5320 Wooten Drive. Bill was first employed by a large architectural firm, but after several years, he and his friend T. Z. Hamm decided to establish their own architectural firm, Kneer and Hamm Architects, with an initial investment of $500 each. They did commercial and residential buildings in Fort Worth as well as other Texas cities, including Dallas and Austin.

Ann concentrated her efforts on her home and children. Ann developed Hodgkin's disease, and despite many efforts to overcome the cancer, she died in Fort Worth, Texas, at the age of thirty-seven.

On April 29, 1967, Bill married Jo Ann Stetle, a receptionist in his architectural firm. Bill continued to live and work in the Fort Worth area until his death on February 28, 1986.

- **William Clark Kneer III (15 Apr 1951–):** Born in Fort Worth, Tarrant County, Texas, Bill attended public schools in Fort Worth. Bill married Lisa Kerr Armstrong on August 20, 1977.

    - **William Clark Kneer IV (9 Mar 1987–):** William was born in Fort Worth, Tarrant County, Texas.

- **John David Kneer (17 Feb 1953–):** Born in Fort Worth, Tarrant County, Texas, David graduated from Southwest High School in Fort Worth in the class of 1971. He and Nancy A. Wilson (1958–) were married on November 1, 1990. Nancy graduated from Warren Western Reserve, Warren, Ohio, and from Kent State University in the class of 1980 with a major in English. She has worked for Citicorp, first in the mortgage department and more recently with the methods automation and engineering team.

    - **Connor Wilson Kneer (31 Aug 1993–):** Connor was born in Dallas, Texas. He graduated from R. L. Turner High School in Dallas, Texas, with the class of 2012.

- **Julia Ann Kneer (26 Aug 1954–):** Julia was born in Fort Worth, Tarrant County, Texas. Julia married Edward Robinson Jr. on August 30, 1974. They lived in Brownwood, Texas, until their divorce, at which time Julia and her boys moved back to Fort Worth. They moved into the upstairs apartment in Leona's home and were with her as Leona's health declined. Julia works for the *Fort Worth Star-Telegram* newspaper.

    - **Edward Damian Robinson (21 Apr 1977–):** Born in Brown County, Texas, Edward moved to Fort Worth as a child.

- **Michael Ryan Robinson (10 Mar 1982–):** Born in Brown County, Texas, Michael attended public schools in Fort Worth and graduated from Paschal High School in the class of 2000.

- **James Patrick Kneer (6 Feb 1958–):** Patrick was only seven when his mother died, too young to have many memories of her. The chaotic time after his mother's death was a vivid memory for him. His father experienced depression and was overwhelmed with the responsibilities of caring for four bewildered, confused, and frightened children. His work became his life. The two grandmothers provided as much stability for the children as they could. Pat and Julia spent several summers with their father's sister, Sally Flatley, in Kansas City, Missouri.

  Pat attended Fort Worth Country Day School, graduating in 1976. A degree in business administration with a specialization in accounting from North Texas State University was followed by a position as an accountant for Atlantic Richfield in Dallas. He married Sandra Sue Crow (1957–) on August 4, 1979.

  The year 1986 was a very traumatic year for Pat and Sandy. Within a three-month period, they experienced the death of Pat's grandmother, Leona; his father, Bill Kneer; and their four-month-old daughter, Allison. Allison, their first child, died from sudden infant death syndrome.

  After a few years working as an accountant, Pat decided to pursue his primary interest in computer programming and computer support. A move to Midland made this possible. Pat and Sandy had a son and a daughter who grew up in Midland, Texas. Pat and Sandy are active members of the First Methodist Church of Midland and participate in outreach programs providing food for those in need.

  - **Allison Suzanne Kneer (30 Jan 1986–May 1986):** Allison died of sudden infant death syndrome at four and a half months old.

  - **Alexander Patrick Kneer (6 Jun 1987–):** Born in Denton County, Texas, Alexander attended schools in Midland, Texas. He obtained a degree in mechanical engineering at Texas Tech University.

  - **Sarah Ann Kneer (31 May 1989–):** Born in Denton County, Texas, Sarah Ann attended public schools in Midland and Dallas Baptist University.

Jack Kenny
(27 May 1901–4 Oct 1958)

Jack and his brother Roy shared May 27 birthdays. The nine-year difference in age meant that they shared few activities while growing up.

Jack was originally named William Clark (according to the 1920 census) or Curry Clark (as some family members reported). He was called Clark or "Clarkie," a name he thoroughly disliked. He soon began insisting that his name was Jack. Before long, everyone (except his mother) was calling him Jack. Eventually, even his mother accepted his adopted name. The only official documents showing the name Clark are the 1910 and 1920 censuses. The family Bible had tape over the original name, Clark, and Jack was written on the tape.

Jack's early years were spent at the Oak Dale home, and his early school experiences were at Oak Dale and Huckabay. He was fifteen when the family moved to Hannibal. There was no high school in Hannibal, and it was too far to commute to Stephenville as his sisters had done from Oak Dale. Instead of going to high school, he did farmwork and other odd jobs, hunted, fished, and roamed the countryside with his friends. He became friends with Otis and Otho Petsick and other local boys. This group of boys set out to kill off the wolves in the area and were successful in their extermination. At the time, this was considered by the local farmer to be very beneficial. The role of predators in an ecosystem had not yet been identified.

The group of boys also had time to get into appreciable mischief. The local Masonic lodge—with wide membership in the community, including Will Kenny—met in a room above the Hannibal general merchandise store. One night when the lodge members were meeting upstairs, the boys noticed the padlock to the stairway door was hanging unlocked by the latch. They locked the stairway door, leaving the Masons locked in the upstairs room.

Summertime was a time for swimming in Barton Creek or other nearby creeks. Swimming was done in the nude. If one group of boys came upon others swimming, it was considered great fun to take all the clothes and tie them on the top of a nearby windmill. Someone then had to climb in the nude to the top of the windmill to retrieve the clothes. To maximize embarrassment for the windmill climber, the chosen windmill was usually in full view of a house inhabited by one or more teenage girls.

After his parents moved to Stephenville, Jack stayed on the family farm and operated it for a couple of years until it was sold. It was at that time that he learned to cook and maintain the house to meet his basic needs. He called those years his "baching years."

Jack met Ava Henry through his sister Maurine. Both Ava and Maurine were living with their sisters and attending high school in Dublin. They became friends and visited one another's homes during summers and vacations. Jack and Ava began a correspondence lasting several years.

After leaving the farm, Jack worked for the highway department for a while. One of his duties was to help lay out the streets for some of the developing towns of West Texas. He took pride in the fact that his team took pains to make the streets run true north and south.

The 1920s were a time of an oil boom in Texas. Large oil deposits were discovered in West Texas. Jack decided he wanted to work in the oil field, where the pay was reported to be very good. His mother disapproved. She said that it would kill her if he went to the oil field, where he was likely to encounter all kinds of wickedness. Jack promised to avoid wickedness, to write frequently, and to come home on holidays when he could. Jack set off for the oil field, and Fannie took to her bed, telling Will to let people know that she was dying. When she had not died after a week, she got out of bed and went about her usual activities.

Jack did return to Stephenville at every opportunity, but much of his time was spent with Ava Henry. They were married on September 11, 1927, at the Henry home in Acrea with close family members in attendance. Ava's dress was a golden-brown silk with a drop waist, a pleated skirt, and a V-shaped yoke with gold-colored metallic embroidery. Absent from the wedding ceremony was Ava's father, Larkin. Although he did not disapprove of Jack and he gave them a quality young mare as a wedding present, Larkin rode off on his horse shortly before the ceremony and stayed away all day.

Jack and Ava moved into one of the family units in the Santa Rita Oil Well. Among their neighbors were the Robinsons, who became their close friends. Because of the isolation of the oil field, the families in the housing group developed a close-knit community.

Jack and Ava's first baby was born on June 3, 1929. Ava's sister Lula came out a few weeks ahead of the anticipated birth date to be with Ava at the delivery. Jack and Ava had chosen the name Carl Lynn for a boy. Although little Carl Lynn seemed to be perfect in all aspects, he never took a first breath. Both Jack and Ava felt that the lack of competence of the company doctor may have contributed to his death. The doctor was much more experienced in setting bones and stitching cuts resulting from oil field accidents and brawls than in delivering babies or caring for newborns.

It was also in 1929 that Jack and Ava purchased the 160-acre farm just north of the Henry place. The farm had been greatly neglected and the cultivated land abandoned and overgrown with weeds. The grassland was heavily covered by brush and had been overgrazed. They thought they could restore it to productivity, and with a few years of their oil field salary, they would be in a position to start the restoration.

When time came near for the birth of a second baby, they arranged for Ava to take a room in a boardinghouse across the street from the Blackwell Clinic in Gorman, Texas. Upon informing Eunice and D. M. in nearby De Leon of their plans, Jack and Ava learned that Eunice was also scheduled to give birth in late June and planned on using the same clinic. Betty Russell was born on June 28, 1931, and Mary Jo Kenny was born two days later on June 30. Jack learned of her arrival when a fellow oil field worker came roaring in in a truck from the oil field office, where telegrams were received, to the workstation, yelling with a strong Norwegian accent from quarter of a mile away, "Jack has a girl baby!"

Additional reason to feel skeptical of the company doctor came when the baby developed pneumonia during her first winter. At that time pneumonia was frequently fatal. As an anticipated crisis approached, the doctor told Jack and Ava not to call him if the baby got worse, because he had done what he could. To make matters worse, a severe sandstorm occurred that night. Windows and doors were covered with wet sheets to keep out some of the sand. An older Norwegian woman, possibly the wife of the man who had announced the baby's arrival, stayed through the night, applied onion poultices, and helped in many other ways. Ava credited her with the child's survival.

By 1932, a new hospital had been established in San Angelo, so that was the site of Ava's next labor and delivery. Robert and Raymond were the first twins to be delivered at the hospital. In the excitement of delivering twins, no one remembered to identify which twin arrived first.

Both Jack and Ava enjoyed farm life, and they did not feel that the oil fields were a good place to raise children. They also wanted to be closer to both sets of aging parents. As the Depression became more severe, the security of the land was a draw to them. With three young children, they left the oil field and moved to the farm in 1933. They joined Will and Fannie, who had rented out their house in Stephenville and were staying in the house on Jack and Ava's land. Will and Fannie had worked to get the house in a more livable condition because it had been abandoned for several years.

The move to the farm took Jack and Ava back to a lifestyle very similar to that of their childhoods. There was no electricity and no running water. The house was made of wood-frame construction and had never been painted. The interior walls were wallpapered, and there was no insulation between the walls, creating drafty conditions. As originally built, the house was three rooms with a fireplace at each end and porches running the full length of the north and south exposures. An open dogtrot separated two rooms from the third. At some time, the east ends of both porches had been enclosed for rooms, a small bedroom in the north room and a kitchen in the south. The original house probably had a kitchen detached from the main house, as was customary at that time. A screened porch was established on the south end of the dogtrot, and the north end was enclosed with double doors that could be opened in warmer weather. Heat was supplied primarily by the east room fireplace. The fireplace in the west room was mostly used for special occasions. On winter nights, the live coals in the fireplace were covered with ashes to keep them from being depleted. By uncovering the coals and adding kindling, a fire could be started quickly in the morning. The wood-burning kitchen range also supplied heat.

Water was supplied by a windmill down the hill. A rock tower held a cypress storage tank, and a concrete stock watering tank stood on the east side of the storage tank. Within the first few months of living in the house, Jack laid a water pipe from the storage tank to the kitchen. Theirs became the first house in the Acrea community to have indoor running water—a single cold-water spigot over a kitchen sink with one outdoor spigot to which a hose could be attached. The typical arrangement for water supply in the community was an open well with two buckets on a pulley.

There were some amenities that had not been available when Jack and Ava were children. A wind charger on the roof provided electricity for a radio. Three small autotype batteries sat on a shelf below the radio, one powering the radio, one being charged by the wind charger, and one in reserve. Ava had a gasoline-powered Maytag wringer-type washing machine, which was started by a rope pull similar to gasoline-powered lawn mowers. It tended to be difficult to start, making starting the washing machine motor often the most difficult task of washday. Transportation was primarily by automobile, though horses were sometimes ridden for short trips.

Reclamation of the abandoned cultivated land started in 1934 with the first terrace system in the area. This job involved two horses, which Ava drove, and a slip and ten-inch turning plow operated by Jack. The grandparents took care of the children. Jack ran the terrace lines with advice from the county agricultural agent and the use of a level borrowed from the bank. The farming operation was a joint operation with Jack and Ava, with decisions made jointly, though Ava usually did more of the recordkeeping and little of the actual fieldwork after this initial terrace building.

The farm was a diversified operation. During the first several years, cotton was planted for a cash crop, but this practice was discontinued by World War II when demand for meat made cattle a predominant source of income. Hereford cattle were dominant, but pigs and later goats and sheep were raised for home use and for sale. The wool and mohair from the sheep and goats were good sources of income in good market years but not always reliable. A flock of hens provided eggs to be used, with extras sold with the expectation that the egg money would cover the cost of groceries purchased. After cotton growing was discontinued, cultivated land raised primarily corn, oats, and hay for animal feed. Power for the farmwork was provided by draft horses. Two early horses were named Dan and Kate. Around 1940, Dan and Kate were sold, and a tractor was purchased. It was sad to see them go, for they had been gentle and dependable, but the tractor was more efficient. One draft horse named Jim was kept several years longer. He was very gentle and would stand at the water trough and allow the children to climb on his back and slide down.

An extensive garden supplied most of the vegetables used. These would be used fresh during season and canned for later use. Corn was at the right stage for canning for only a short time. The corn canning was a total family activity, sometimes assisted by other family members, usually Maurine or the Russell family. The children would help shuck and silk the corn, and the adults would cut it off the cob, place it in cans, and seal and process the cans. A flanging-and-sealing machine was required for the sealing and a pressure canner for the processing. When the cans came out of the pressure canner, the children got to carry the bucket with cans down to the water trough, dump them in to cool, and go into the water to retrieve them when they were cool. A red wagon was used to transport the cans up and down the hill.

Ava did the canning of fruit and vegetables, with some assistance from the children when they were old enough. The garden was below the hill, and the red wagon was used to transport the vegetables up the hill. Ava had a specific number of quarts of each item to be canned each year.

In addition to corn, green peas, black-eyed peas, beans, tomatoes, and okra were canned as well as vegetable-soup mix. Peaches, pears, and grape juice were also canned and made into jams and jellies. All except the corn were canned in glass mason jars. Since the woodstove was the source of heat, canning was a very hot job on a hot summer day. The canned goods were stored in the cellar, along with potatoes and onions, which were also raised in the garden. Some of the beans were allowed to mature and were stored as dried beans. Caution was needed in taking items into the cellar or retrieving them since snakes, including venomous rattlesnakes, sometimes found their way into the cellar.

Summers were hot in Texas, and without air conditioning or electric fans, the house did not always cool off at night. By midsummer, beds were often moved to the backyard for outdoor sleeping. The canopy of stars made enjoyable viewing when awake, and dry summers reduced mosquito problems. Metal bedsteads were chosen so that only the bedding needed to be moved onto the porch if a sudden rain shower occurred. The showers were infrequent but always welcome.

A special day was pecan-gathering day. It was always done on a pleasantly cool fall day, with a picnic lunch to make it a full-day activity. Jack would climb the tree and, with a long thin pole, rap the branches to make the pecans fall. Ava and the children would rake through the fallen leaves to gather the pecans. The trick was to stay away from the branch being hit because that caused a rain of pecans. When Raymond and Robert became old enough to take turns doing the thrashing, they appeared to take glee in raining pecans down on the pickers. The girls thought they were deliberately targeted, and they probably were.

Before electricity came to the area in the summer of 1941, food was kept cool by blocks of ice delivered twice a week. The ice was placed in an icebox, and milk, butter, and other perishable items were kept cool on the shelves. A supplemental cooling method consisted of a flat shallow pan with about two inches of water. Crocks of buttermilk cottage cheese or other items were placed in the pan and covered with a cloth that extended down into the water. The wicking effect and evaporative cooling helped keep the items cool.

The centerpiece of summer meals was whatever was ripe from the garden, along with eggs or chicken. Eggs were abundant in the summer, but meats were those that could be consumed in one or two meals, making chicken the major meat. Fish fries were for special occasions when the family would spend the day at the creek, seine a fishing hole, and have fish with other picnic supplies brought along. Beef and pork were not used in the hottest part of the summer because the cured pork tended to become rancid in hot weather, and fresh beef or pork could not be stored safely or consumed in one day.

The first cold snap in the fall was hog-killing time. One or two hogs would be shot and dipped in hot water, the hair would be scraped off, and the carcass would be hung and eviscerated. The carcass had to hang a couple of days before being ready to eat, but supper the first night was liver, which was enjoyed because it was the first red meat anyone had eaten in several months. For the next few weeks, fresh pork was on the menu, while most of the pig was cured with a special sugar-and-salt mixture into hams and bacon or converted into sausage. Jack had a special spice mix to add to the ground pork, and the resulting sausage was cooked, packed into jars, and covered with lard, which had been rendered through heating the pork fat. The hams and bacon were also packed in lard as a preservative.

A longer cold spell was required for killing a beef because it needed a longer hanging time. Sometimes two neighbors would go together, with one neighbor killing the first beef, and each taking half. A few months later, the process would be repeated, with the second neighbor supplying the beef. The fresh beef was eaten while it lasted, and what could not be eaten fresh was canned. The canned beef was not as tasty as the fresh, but it was acceptable in soups and stews and, with the addition of onion, pickle relish, mustard, and mayonnaise, could be made into a palatable sandwich spread. When the ice plant in Stephenville established a cold storage unit and slaughtering service, a whole beef could be packaged, frozen, and stored in a lockbox in the frozen storage room. This service was more useful after electrical refrigeration made it possible to keep the meat frozen until it was to be used.

Before 1941, light was provided by kerosene lamps. On most of the lamps, a lighted wick provided the light, but one lamp had a mantle that produced a brighter, more steady light. It was this lamp, on the dining table, that provided light for reading and doing homework assignments on winter evenings. The clear glass chimneys on all the lamps would become sooty and needed frequent cleaning. Old newspapers were usually used to clean the chimneys. Because they were made of thin glass, the chimneys broke easily and were often replaced.

Two babies were born into the family during the pre-electricity days. William Colwell was born on June 6, 1934, at home. He was born with a cleft lip and cleft palate. The disability was severe enough that he could not suckle; Maurine and Jack took the infant to a hospital in Fort Worth where he could be appropriately treated. Leona regularly checked on his condition and reported back to Jack and Ava. He spent most of his short life in the hospital, with only brief periods at home. He died in the hospital on October 9, 1934. His death certificate indicated that he died of pneumonia, complicated by a cleft palate. This occurred during the Depression, and the increased medical bills created the greatest financial strain Jack and Ava experienced during their marriage. They had to sell their workhorses to pay the bills and use borrowed horses until they could afford replacements. Ava said that at Christmas she had only one dollar to buy gifts for the three children. A small, undressed doll and two small toy cars were purchased. Doll clothes were made from fabric scraps, as were three fabric animals stuffed with cotton. A doll bed and two stick horses were made from wood scraps. The children thought they had great gifts.

The second baby, a beautiful little girl, was born on September 29, 1938. She was named Norma Sue, the name influenced in part by a book the three older children had read aloud to one another over the summer. The title was *Bunny Brown and His Sister Sue*, and they thought Sue was a wonderful name for a perfect little girl.

The first few years at the farm saw not only the death of a child but also the deaths of Ava's father, Larkin Henry, in 1935 and Jack's father, Will Kenny, in 1936. Ava's mother, Parolee, died a few months after Sue was born in 1938.

After Parolee's death, Jack and Ava purchased the Henry property from the other heirs, thus significantly increasing the size of their farm. Larkin had maintained his cultivated land in good condition, so it did not need the extensive restoration of the original property. Brush was a problem on grazing land, and brush clearing and the introduction of goats to control the brush was initiated.

Electricity came to the farm in the summer of 1941. Jack had been influential in getting enough families in the neighborhood to sign up as members of the rural electrical cooperative to qualify for the service. He was also active in governing the organization over the next several years.

Jack and Ava participated in community activities. Ava was a leader in the local and county-wide Home Demonstration Club. Jack was a member of the local school board and was frequently called for jury service. He was also a member of the local Masonic lodge and was active in soil-conservation projects and in bringing electricity to the area. His soil-conservation projects included terracing the fields and contour plowing. He sometimes remarked that his contoured fields were a sharp contrast to the straight furrows in which his father took pride. He introduced the use of vetch and other legumes to enhance soil quality and harvested vetch seed to sell to other farmers. Land improvement included brush removal and planting of grass seed adapted to the area. In the early years, brush removal was assisted by Booker Bunch, who had spent winters assisting Larkin with winter chores. After Larkin's death, Booker came to Jack and Ava's home and helped with chores in return for a place to sleep and food. In the spring he would leave for migrant farmwork.

Robert, Raymond, and Mary Jo attended the Acrea school in grades one through six. The school was located on a hill above the dirt country road as it curved from a northward direction from Highway 377 to a westward direction past the Henry home. The land for the school had been donated by Larkin Henry with the stipulation that the land would return to the estate if it ceased to be used for a school. The school building was rectangular, with an entryway porch and a mansard-type roof. The interior space was equipped with folding panels that could be closed to make two rooms or opened to create one large room. A hallway at the entrance held hooks for coats and was enclosed at one end and fitted with shelves to form the library and storage for unissued textbooks. A roll-down canvas curtain, with a painted mountain scene, at the east end could transform that section into a stage. Windows provided light, and a large woodstove provided heat. In front of the building was a flagpole and a swing set. Down the hill to the east of the building was a more elaborate swing-and-climbing-bar set and a ball field. A well with a hand pump fitted to a pipe with holes in a concrete trough served as a drinking fountain. The girls' toilet was about fifty yards behind the school, and the boys' toilet was behind the playing field.

The school building also served as a church, with a Methodist minister officiating two Sundays a month and a Baptist minister two Sundays. A fifth Sunday in a month resulted in Sunday school meeting but no church service. During the summer, the churches would hold a weeklong "revival" meeting. Services would be held each evening and twice on Sunday, but not in the school building. A brush arbor was erected on the end of the playing field. The brush arbor was made of a framework of poles with sides open. Branches from shrubs and trees placed over the top created a shady place much cooler than an enclosed building.

World War II affected the family more indirectly than directly. Students in the Acrea school were reading stories about children in European countries, frequently followed by hearing over the radio that Hitler had invaded that country. Pearl Harbor Day remained vivid in the memories of those old enough to realize its significance. The Kenny family had gone to Stephenville and stopped by the home of Uncle Lee and Aunt Bessie Driskill on the way home. Greeted with the news of Pearl Harbor, they listened to the radio news reports for some time before continuing home.

During the war, demand for farm products was high; therefore, prices were good. On the farm Jack had hired help, Jack and Annabelle Rodgers. Many things were rationed, including gasoline, tires, shoes, sugar, and meat. Though the beef cattle were raised on the farm, Jack felt that they should not consume more beef than was allowed in rationing. On the other hand, he liked to have meat at most meals, so he learned from a Mexican neighbor how to dress and barbecue young goat. They had meat at most meals, with the rationed beef and pork supplemented with non-rationed goat, lamb, and chicken. They were careful with tires and shoes and, during the summers, applied for extra sugar for canning.

The farm was scoured for scrap metal for use in the war effort. Sue was home when uniformed men, probably Tarleton cadets, collected an old automobile that had been abandoned below the windmill. The children had spent many hours in that old car, converting it in their imagination into an automobile, bus, train, airplane, or ship for travel to familiar or unknown places.

Because all the male cousins except Bill Rampley, who worked in a defense plant, entered the armed services, concern for their safety was ever present. Photographs of them in uniform lined the mantle, and the radio news reports were filtered with concern about them and soldiers from the community. The war felt closer to the Kenny children when cousins John L. Gordon and Bruce Rampley, who were closer to their age, went into the army. When John L. was stationed at Camp Walters near Mineral Wells, he frequently came to the Kenny home on a short-term pass. When Jack's friend Ab Davis volunteered for the navy, Jack helped the elder Mr. Davis run their farm. Ava helped Bessie Davis by caring for their children when Bessie needed to attend to farm business.

The end of the war, and the resulting availability of material, made it possible to consider a new house. Ava wanted to be on the road and the mail route, so the location was near the Henry house. Consideration was made to remodel the Henry house, but Jack indicated that he had never lived in a new house, and he did not like the idea of just remodeling. The Henry house and parts of the house they had been using were torn down, and some materials were reused in building the new house. Arrangements were made for the family to "camp out" in the unused Acrea school building during the construction. Ava spent most of her days working at the construction site. The older children were in charge of preparing the evening meal.

In 1956, Jack was named Outstanding Farmer by the Bosque Soil Conservation District. His efforts in conservation on his own land and his work to educate others on soil conservation were noted in an article in the *Stephenville Empire-Tribune* of May 11, 1956.

The postwar years were busy and fairly prosperous for the country, but a severe drought beginning in 1950 and ending in 1957 meant that rural Texas experienced less economic prosperity. The three older children completed high school and left home for college and to begin careers. Because the drought resulted in a reduction in the cattle herd and removal of sheep from the property, Jack and Ava decided to expand the chicken business sufficiently to make it a major source of income as a semi-retirement plan. They built a larger chicken house and increased the size of their spring order for baby chickens.

They also invested in a television set, since transmission now reached the area. They learned to enjoy the televised sports programs, especially college football and professional baseball. Ava became quite an expert on professional baseball and continued her interest by following the teams, especially the Texas Rangers, for the rest of her life.

In the summer of 1958, Jack's health began to decline. By the fall, he was seriously ill and hospitalized. Blood supply to the brain had been gradually restricted by constriction of the carotid artery. He died at the age of fifty-seven in the Stephenville hospital. Although he had not been able to finish high school, Jack was very well read and self-educated on a wide range of topics. He had always read his children's high school and college textbooks—as well as a variety of newspapers, magazines, and other books. He had the ability to talk to people in almost any field and learn a lot about their specialty. This was a very loving and caring father and concerned and active community member. He was more directly involved in his children's upbringing than were many men of his generation.

While working as preschool director at Chapel Hills Methodist Church, Sue Kenny Weathers wrote a column for the church newsletter in honor of Father's Day, 1994.

My Father's Values

By Sue Kenny Weathers

1. Complete the tasks you start; don't be a quitter.
2. Do every job better than you are expected to.
3. You are never too good or too important to do a job that is to be done.
4. Treat everyone with equal respect.
5. Keep your word, and don't back down on a commitment you make.
6. Don't brag on yourself; if you are capable, people will know.
7. Always take time to help those who need help.
8. Worship is a private commitment, not a public display.
9. Don't spend money you don't have.
10. Learning is important. Take time to read some every day.

11. Observe and enjoy the world of nature.
12. Find joy in everyday experiences.
13. Take care of your reputation. It is a valuable asset.
14. Don't gossip.

To this list one could add one more that was also a strong value by which Jack and Ava lived and that they emphasized for their children.

15. Participate in activities that will improve your community.

Ava remained on the farm and operated the egg-production business for several years after Jack's death. Raymond, who had determined not to continue a career in the air force after the end of his enlistment period, returned to the farm to maintain its operation and to help Ava with the chickens. During Sue's final year at the University of Texas, her friend Dale Weathers, who was back in Stephenville after completing his degree, frequently came to the farm to help Ava with chores, eat her corn bread, and watch ball games with her. Thus, Ava became much better acquainted with and appreciative of the qualities of her future son-in-law.

Since Ava did not drive, operating the egg business and maintaining her life at the farm became increasingly difficult, especially after Raymond and his family moved to Fort Worth. She decided to sell the chickens and move into Stephenville. At first, she rented a house not far from Fannie Kenny's home, but when the opportunity arose, she bought a house on Green Street, not far from Tarleton College. She rented a front bedroom to a series of Tarleton students and enjoyed their company. She became involved in the senior citizens organization and was a major force in their fundraising activities. Financial management was not new to her since she had always been the bookkeeper and financial manager of the farm. In this capacity she was very resourceful and able to get maximum value for the funds available.

Ava's first heart attack was in 1963. She went to Sue's home in Killeen, Texas, to recuperate. After several weeks, she was able to return home and resume her activities with the senior center.

Ava enjoyed traveling, and a daughter in California and a son in Virginia gave her a good opportunity to travel. She did not like to fly—until train travel was restricted sufficiently that flying was the only way to get to places she wanted to go. She was a good travel companion and especially liked automobile trips.

After John Gordon died, Ava's sister Lula stayed with Ava for a period of time. During this time Ava taught her sister about financial management, a task in which Lula had not been involved during her marriage. Ava and Lula looked enough alike that some people occasionally got them confused. Ava and Lula enjoyed sharing activities at the senior center and continued these activities when Lula moved to a small house near the center. Lula especially enjoyed the games of Forty-Two at the center and was an expert player. Their close association ended when Lula broke a hip and moved to Gatesville, Texas, where her daughter lived. Although Stephenville and

Gatesville were only about one hundred miles apart, the lack of public transportation and the fact that neither drove an automobile made visits with one another infrequent.

Among the activities of the senior center was a quilting group. Ava participated in the quilting but also in piecing of quilts, trying a variety of patterns. She enjoyed crocheting and crocheted a variety of items, including place mats and potholders. One item she designed was a throw made from old jeans with a Western-style appliqué on each square and the squares crocheted together with red yarn. This throw was donated to a fundraising activity at the Virginia school where the Robert Kenny children attended, and it was purchased by Lynda Johnson Robb, daughter of President Lyndon Johnson.

Ava's final heart attack came after Mother's Day, 1979. Sue, Dale, Raymond, and Peggy had spent a very pleasant Mother's Day with her. Dale did notice that she had some difficulty with movements in her left shoulder. On Monday morning, Dale realized he had left his wallet in Stephenville. When he called to check on the wallet, Ava reported that she was not feeling well. Sue called Louise Stallings with a request she check on Ava. Louise reported that there did not seem to be immediate danger and that Ava did not want Louise to take her to the hospital. The next day Ava's friend Lucille McCleskey insisted that Ava see a doctor. The doctor admitted her to the hospital for observation but initially considered her shoulder pain to be a flare-up of an old injury in which she had dislocated that shoulder. At that time, symptoms of heart attack in women were not as readily identified by the medical community, although Ava had had a previous heart attack. Sue returned to Stephenville as soon as she learned Ava was hospitalized. The doctor eventually recognized the problem as a heart attack and began treating it as such. Ava seemed to be responding and was cheerful and looking forward to watching the Rangers baseball game. The doctor recommended to Sue that she return to Dallas to complete the school year. She did so with the thought of returning in a few days to take Ava home with her for recuperation. About 4:00 a.m. the next morning, on Wednesday, May 17, 1979, Sue got the call that Ava had died. Sue notified the rest of the family, and necessary arrangements were made. Barbara Stallings McKnight agreed to the family's request to participate in the funeral service. Ava was buried beside Jack in Acrea Cemetery.

Ava was always a caring person, but she was also independent, courageous, wise, and resourceful. Her wisdom probably exerted the greatest influence on her children.

- **Carl Lynn Kenny (13 Jun 1929–13 Jun 1929):** Carl Lynn was born in the oil field camp of Santa Rita, Texas. Although he appeared to be a perfectly formed, full-term baby, he never took his first breath. Maurine borrowed her father's automobile to drive to Santa Rita and bring the baby back to Stephenville for burial. Funeral services, organized by Eunice, were held in Will and Fannie's living room. Burial was in West Side Cemetery in Stephenville. Maurine gave the details of the service in a letter to Jack and Ava, including who attended, songs sung, scriptures read, and a synopsis of the minister's remarks.

- **Mary Jo Kenny (30 Jun 1931–):** Ava and Jack determined that their second baby should be born where good medical attention was available. Learning that the Blackwell Clinic in Gorman, Texas, had a good reputation, they arranged for Ava to stay in a boardinghouse across the street from the hospital before the due date. Mary Jo was born two days after her cousin Betty Russell was born at the same clinic.

  Mary Jo attended the school in Acrea, one of six students entering the first grade in 1937. She usually walked to school, accompanied by their collie dog in her first year and by her brothers after that. The transfer to the Stephenville school in the seventh grade was a big change from the Acrea school. A persistent bronchial infection following whooping cough caused her to drop out of school and repeat the seventh grade. As a result, she and her brothers were in the same class through the rest of her public-school years.

  Upon entering Stephenville High School, one of her objectives was to read every book of interest in the high school library. She came close to meeting that goal. High school graduation was followed by enrollment in Tarleton State College. Here she discovered an interest in and aptitude for science. Her chosen field of home economics provided extensive study of science as well as a variety of career opportunities for women. The two-year program at Tarleton was followed by completion of a BS degree at the University of Texas at Austin.

  Her first teaching experience was at Burnet High School. The assignment included some summer programs and visits to students' homes. This was a time of one of Texas's severe droughts and considerable hardships for many rural residents. Some of the homes visited revealed a lack of resources and a need for the practical side of home economics.

  After teaching at Burnet for two years, she returned to the University of Texas to complete a master's degree in food and nutrition. Realizing an interest in teaching at the college level, she accepted a position at Sacramento State College. It was a new institution, founded only a few years earlier and on a permanent campus only two years. She became one of a three-member home economics faculty along with Catharine Starr and Earl Andrews. Female faculty were in the minority, with only about a dozen in the entire college. She found it interesting to be a part of the growth of the campus from its early days with five small permanent buildings to a state university with over twenty thousand students.

  After several years teaching, Mary Jo entered Cornell University to study for a doctoral degree in nutrition. Upon completion of the doctorate, she returned to California State University, Sacramento, where she taught a variety of courses regarding food and nutrition. After serving a three-year term as department chair, she realized that her interests and abilities were more suited to classroom teaching than administration. Her friend Doris Beard replaced her as department chair. An active member of the California Home Economics Association and the California Nutrition Council, Mary Jo served terms as secretary and president of the latter organization. University activities included participation in several department and school committees and membership in the faculty senate.

Summers provided opportunities to attend professional conferences and for travel within the United States and to other countries.

Age sixty seemed a good age to retire and spend time on genealogy research and on travel. Her friend Shirley Larson retired the same year. After some searching, they found a retirement place in Crescent City, California. The house overlooked the ocean. While structurally sound, it needed numerous cosmetic changes. Renovation resulted in a home they enjoyed for twenty-two years.

Community activities included work with a literacy program, an unsuccessful attempt to start a League of Women Voters chapter, a successful effort to establish a local Habitat for Humanity, and membership in the Community Concert board of directors.

Postretirement travel included auto trips within the United States, three trips to Alaska, and trips to China, Thailand, Cambodia, Malaysia, Baja California, Costa Rica, the Panama Canal, Iceland, Norway, and Ireland.

When Shirley developed health problems, it seemed wise to move to an area closer to family. Sugar Land, Texas, was chosen because Shirley's sister had located there, and Mary Jo's family was close enough to see more frequently. When Shirley's sister and brother-in-law decided to move to South Carolina, Sue helped find assisted living and independent living for Shirley and Mary Jo at Briarview Senior Living in Carrollton, near Dallas and near Sue, Dale, and Rachel.

- **Raymond Lee Kenny (4 Oct 1932–):** Raymond and Robert were the first twins born in the relatively new San Angelo hospital, and the staff were so excited that no record was made of which twin was born first. The move to the Erath County farm was made when the twins were about a year old, which made life on the farm Raymond's earliest memory. Early activities included creating roads and towns for toy cars in the yard, climbing chinaberry trees, and riding down the hill in their little red wagon. The Texas horned toads were a fascination and would obligingly pull miniature wagons made from matchboxes before being released unharmed. Later, climbing to the top of the barn and sliding down the tin roof to the shed below became a fun activity.

  When the twins were about three, Mr. Garrett, the rural mail carrier, delivered to the boys a collie puppy. On his first night, the puppy was placed in a box in the bedroom. When the puppy would cry, Raymond or Robert would get up to console him. The puppy was named Major, after a favorite dog Jack had had as a boy, but he was usually called Puppy. He was a close companion to the family for many years, until he was accidentally poisoned.

  Starting school did not provide many new experiences. Raymond and Robert had already gone over most of the first-grade work with their sister and could read quite well and do simple math before they started school. By the time they entered the Acrea school, the enrollment was declining. When they were ready to transfer to Stephenville Junior High School, the Acrea school was closed through consolidation with the Stephenville school.

One spring Jack injured his back and was unable to drive a vehicle for a period of time. It was necessary to have another driver in the family. Raymond, not yet fourteen, had driven the pickup and tractor around the farm for some time. He was allowed to take the driving test and obtain a driving license.

Farm chores were part of Raymond's daily routine from an early age. The type of chores evolved with maturity. By the time he was in high school, most summers were spent with farmwork. High school Future Farmers of America projects included raising a Jersey cow and a pig named Queenie.

After graduating from Stephenville High School, Raymond entered Tarleton State College with a major in agriculture. Raymond enjoyed drawing, and some of his college notebooks were decorated with caricatures of his professors and class members. While in Tarleton, he was a member of the special drill company Wainwright Rifles. This drill team performed at home football games and other special events.

After being part of twin team throughout their school years, including Tarleton, Raymond and Robert decided to go to different four-year universities. Each went to a school with strength in his area of professional interest. Raymond transferred to Texas A&M University for his last two years of college. He graduated in 1953 with a major in range management and a commission in the US Air Force.

Raymond and Darlene Brooks (19 Oct 1934–27 Mar 2001) were married in the summer of 1953. Darlene was the daughter of Syble Nadine Knox and George Lewis Brooks and the stepdaughter of Leck Pack of Stephenville. She was a 1953 graduate of Stephenville High School.

Raymond's call to active duty in the air force came in August 1953. He received his primary pilot training at Spence Air Base in Moultrie, Georgia, and basic training at Goodfellow Air Force Base in San Angelo, Texas. He was assigned to Harlingen Air Force Base in Harlingen, Texas, where his first assignment was as a pilot for navigation-training missions. Later he served as a maintenance flight test pilot. In early 1958 he was transferred to Mountain Home Air Force Base, Idaho, where he served as tanker pilot for air-to-air refueling. By fall of 1958, his four-year enlistment period had been completed, and he had determined that he did not want a permanent career in the air force. He requested and was granted a release from active duty in November 1958.

Raymond moved his family, now including three-year-old Mark and infant Sara, to the farm in Acrea, where he built a home and purchased the title to the farm from his sisters and brother. Raymond maintained the farm and cattle operation and helped Ava with the chickens. A third child, Martha, was born while they were living on the farm.

In 1963, Raymond joined the staff of the Ranch Management Program at Texas Christian University, and the family moved to Fort Worth. In addition to classroom teaching, he accompanied students on field trips to working ranches around the state. John "Chip" Merrill, Raymond's friend from Tarleton and Texas A&M, was his associate in the Ranch Management Program. Raymond worked in the Ranch Management Program until 1976. Raymond and Darlene were divorced at that time. Raymond took a position with Alta Verde Industries, an integrated agricultural corporation in Quemado, Maverick County, Texas. With Alta Verde, he worked in a number of positions, including farm manager and feedlot manager.

Raymond and Peggy Cadenhead (21 Sep 1933–) were married in 1978 in San Antonio, Texas. Peggy had grown up in the Quemada area, and her parents still lived there. She was born in Wheeler County, Texas, to Bill and Rachel (Alred) Cadenhead. Peggy attended Eagle Pass High School, where she was active in a number of organizations, including the National Honor Society, Cap and Gown, Square Dance Club, and International Relations Club. She graduated as salutatorian of her 1952 class. Peggy was a civilian employee of the air force; her duties included organizing moves for air force personnel when they were transferred. She had been working in San Antonio but was able to transfer to Del Rio after their marriage. Raymond and Peggy met through the church both he and her parents attended. Her parents reminded Peggy that they knew Raymond first.

When Raymond left Alta Verde Industries, he and Peggy built a home overlooking the Rio Grande River on land adjacent to the home of Peggy's mother. Peggy's father had died a few years earlier. Raymond did much of the carpentry and cabinetwork for the house. A metal roof was chosen for the home because occasional vega (a native cane) fires along the river produced showers of embers.

From 1984 to 1989, Raymond served as general manager of the Maverick County Water District. This position required him to work with a variety of local political entities as well as represent the county's interests in hearings and meetings in Austin. After he resigned from the water district, Raymond and Peggy became interested in developing an apple-production operation on the farm in Acrea. In spite of much effort in establishing an irrigation system and putting in the trees, the apple trees would not flourish in soil still holding cotton root-knot nematodes, residual pests from having cotton once grown there.

During this period of time, Peggy had increasing responsibility in the care of her mother. Mrs. Cadenhead's health declined, eventually requiring a move to a nursing home, where she lived a couple of years before her death.

Raymond's employment by the San Angelo Feed Yard as supervisor of animal health and pasture cattle resulted in a move to San Angelo in 1989. He and Peggy became active in the San Angelo Saint Paul Presbyterian Church and participated in a number of church projects, including building homes for Habitat for Humanity and repairing homes for low-income people with the Christmas in April project. Peggy helped organize the Christmas in April projects while Raymond participated in the construction work. Raymond went to Nicaragua on a church-sponsored trip to help build Habitat for Humanity homes in a Nicaraguan village.

Raymond enjoys working with wood and has done a variety of practical and decorative items. For his sister Sue, he designed and made a base for a glass-top table. He did wood carving, mostly of animals and birds, before becoming interested in wood turning. He reproduced spindles for the restoration of a cradle that had been in the Henry family for over one hundred years. Lathe-turned bowls and decorative items were made from a variety of woods, and many had intricately patterned laminated wood. When the cypress water-storage unit on the farm dried and fell apart, Raymond collected the pieces and reassembled it. He and Mark replaced it on its rock-tower base by the windmill.

Retirement in 1996 made it possible to spend more time with Habitat for Humanity and on other projects for nonprofit organizations as well as his woodworking. In 1999, Raymond and Peggy moved back to the Acrea farm and built a house on a hill overlooking the South Paluxy valley. Their son, Mark, works with Raymond on the operation of the farm. Raymond delivers Meals on Wheels, and both Raymond and Peggy continue to be active in church activities. Peggy has been a member of the pastoral search committee and has been a delegate to regional, state, and national church conferences. They enjoy being close enough to see the children and grandchildren frequently.

- **Mark Wayne Kenny (29 Nov 1955–):** Born in Harlingen, Texas, Mark was three years old when the family moved to the Acrea farm. He enjoyed the freedom the farm provided him, playing with his grandmother's collie dog, and riding horses. He started school in the Stephenville school system but moved to Fort Worth schools after the second grade.

  Mark graduated from Paschal High School in Fort Worth. While in high school, he decided to let his hair grow until it became shoulder length. It was not yet common for males to wear their hair long. He received numerous critical remarks about this choice. On one occasion Clarence Davis was giving Mark a hard time about his hair; Clarence asked Ava what she thought about it. Ava's response was "I like the boy, and the boy likes the hair, so I am okay with it."

  Mark completed the Ranch Management Program at Texas Christian University and moved into the house his parents had built on the farm. He had some cattle and established a deer-hunting lease on the farm. Both deer and wild turkey had become sufficiently abundant in the area to allow hunting.

On June 30, 1984, Mark and Christina "Tina" Riley were married in Bluff Dale, where she had grown up. Mark continued to operate the farm, and Tina worked in Stephenville. They were divorced in 1989. After the divorce, Mark began doing long-distance hauling, first with a trailer behind his pickup, then with a large truck. He became a major hauler for a Fort Worth firm. Now he no longer does hauling, but he continues to work with his father to operate the farm.

- **Sara Diane Kenny (25 Apr 1958–):** Born in Stephenville, Texas, Sara spent her earliest months in Mountain Home, Idaho. She was less than a year old when the family moved to the farm in Acrea. She attended public school in Fort Worth and graduated from Paschal High School, Fort Worth, Texas, class of 1976.

The summer after high school graduation, Sara participated in a six-week student travel program in Europe. The program took her to several countries, but most of the time was spent in Rome and Athens.

Sara obtained a job at John Peter Smith Hospital in Fort Worth. There she met Bill Willis (29 Apr 1951–), who also worked at the hospital. Sara and Bill were married on December 29, 1979, at a Methodist church in Fort Worth, Texas. Bill was born in Arkansas. He graduated from Warren High School, Warren, Arkansas, and the University of Arkansas at Monticello. He came to Texas and John Peter Smith Hospital in 1978. Sara and Bill lived in Fort Worth; Waxahachie; Russellville, Arkansas; and Waco, Texas—all places where Bill worked as a hospital administrator. Sara was a homemaker and did volunteer work. They lived in Waxahachie through their children's school years. In Waxahachie, Sara was a founding member of the Newcomers Club, active in the Parent-Teacher Organization, and a sustaining member of the Waxahachie Junior Service League. Sarah enjoys renovating older homes, especially her own. She renovated two such homes in Waxahachie and one in Waco. The Waxahachie home on Brown Street was selected to be on the Annual Gingerbread Trail Tour of Historic Homes, and the kitchen of the other home was featured in a national magazine.

Sara enjoys reading and collecting fossils, petrified wood, and vintage costume jewelry. Bill's hobbies include tennis, motorcycle riding, and reading. After Bill retired, they rented "Ava's house" in order to spend more time at the farm, where fossil hunting is good and quiet time for reading is available. Later they purchased a home in Stephenville, which will provide another renovation project for Sarah. She has also become active in researching Erath County history for the local history museum.

- **Jordan Wesley Willis (2 Jun 1982–):** Jordan was born in Bryan, Texas, but most of his early years were in Waxahachie. Before his sister was born, the importance of being the big brother had made an impression on him. The day she was born, he made a sign to wear to his first-grade class declaring "I am Leigh's big brother." He attended school in Waxahachie and graduated from Waxahachie High School. He received a bachelor's degree summa cum laude, from Arkansas Technical University, with a major in sociology. Further study in sociology at the University of Buffalo, State University of New York, with a Presidential Scholarship earned him a master's degree and enabled him to work toward a PhD.

  On August 11, 2012, Jordan married Alissa Corby in Buffalo, New York. Last-minute airline cancellations meant that neither his parents nor his sister was able to make the trip to attend the wedding, much to their disappointment.

  The marriage ended in a divorce in 2015, and Jordan left the Buffalo area for Waco, Texas, where his parents lived. When they moved to Stephenville, he relocated to the house on the farm. He has been renewing an interest in music while exploring possibilities for utilizing his professional training. He and his cousin Curry Marks organized a band for the summer of 2016. In the fall of 2017, he was bitten by a rattlesnake that had somehow gotten into his house. Recovery required a hospital stay and many units of antiserum.

- **Leigh Willis (16 Nov 1987–):** Leigh was seven weeks early and weighed less than five pounds when she was born at Baylor Medical Center, Waxahachie, Texas. She was otherwise healthy and thriving and soon reached a normal weight. As a toddler, Leigh had beautiful naturally curly hair that fell in a cascade of ringlets. Her mother reported that on almost all outings, Leigh would attract a lot of attention, and people would comment on her beautiful blonde curls. Leigh's memories were that the curls tangled easily and were difficult and painful to comb.

  Leigh attended school in Waxahachie; Russellville, Arkansas; and Waco. She obtained a degree in nursing from McLennan County College of Nursing in Waco, Texas. Leigh obtained a position as a registered nurse at Hillcrest Baptist Medical Center in Waco, working in the neonatal intensive care unit.

  On January 15, 2011, Leigh married Cap Mericle in Waco. Cap had spent time as a child and youth in Alaska and Hawaii. In 2012, they purchased a house in Waco. In 2013, Leigh left her nursing position to spend more time on her house and to work with her mother on buying and selling jewelry online. After a move to Stephenville, Leigh decided on a career change and completed courses leading to a laboratory technician degree. She works as a laboratory technician in Glen Rose, Texas.

- **Martha Jean Kenny (22 Apr 1960–):** Born in Stephenville, Erath County, Texas, Martha attended public schools in Fort Worth and graduated from Paschal High School in Fort Worth. As a child, Martha was adventurous and willing to try new things. She drove to California with her aunt Mary Jo, then returned alone on her first airline trip. A few years later, Martha was able to go to Colombia, South America, to visit friends she had met in Fort Worth while the friends' father was attending the Ranch Management Program at Texas Christian University. Fortunately, this was before Colombia became embroiled in drug trafficking.

  From an early age, Martha was concerned about the environment and animal rights. She pointed out the animal cruelty that occurred with many rodeo practices before many others had made this observation. Her interest in the environment resulted in Martha describing herself as a tree hugger. She continues to enjoy animals, especially cats.

  Martha's sense of security was shattered when a close friend was murdered in Fort Worth. It took some time to rebuild a feeling of security.

  Martha attended the University of Texas at Austin and graduated in 1989 from the University of Texas at Dallas with a psychology major.

  On June 3, 1989, Martha and James Marks were married at the home of her sister, Sara, in Waxahachie, Texas. Martha and James lived in Dallas, Stephenville, Fort Worth, Arlington, and McKinney, Texas. Both worked in a variety of positions; Martha's work often involved bookkeeping and financial records. Martha and James were divorced in 2011. Both remained in McKinney for a few years. After her children finished high school, Martha purchased a home in Fort Worth, which enabled her to avoid a long drive to her Fort Worth–based job.

  - **James Curry Marks (20 Sep 1995–):** Born in Dallas, Texas, Curry attended schools in Arlington and McKinney. Interested in music, Curry played trumpet in a McKinney High School jazz band and also in the high school marching band. After his parents' divorce, Curry lived with his father until the age of eighteen. He then moved to his mother's home. Curry graduated in the 2014 class of McKinney High School. After one year at McKinney Community College, Curry transferred to Texas Tech University, where he graduated in 2022 with a major in computer science.

- **Hannah Nicole Marks (17 Jan 1998–):** Born in Fort Worth, Tarrant County, Texas, Hannah attended school in Arlington and McKinney. At McKinney High School, she learned to play the bassoon but changed to the trombone to be in marching band. She enjoyed being the only female trombone player in the band. She also enjoyed sharing band events with her brother. After her brother finished high school, Hannah chose to do home study and complete a GED rather than complete high school. She moved to Fort Worth with her mother but later moved to Lubbock, Texas.

- **Robert Wayne Kenny (4 Oct 1932–):** Born in San Angelo, Texas, Robert attended Acrea and Stephenville schools. As identical twins, Robert and Raymond were so much alike that only members of the immediate family could consistently tell them apart. Leona spoke of a time when she identified a three- or four-year-old twin as Bob but later called him Ray. His response was "I am still Bob." Reading and drawing were his early interests. Although he did his share of farmwork, he considered it more of a necessity than a desirable activity.

While attending Stephenville High School, Robert was art editor of the 1949 yearbook. In Tarleton, he declared a journalism major and was editor of the *JTAC*, Tarleton school paper. Tarleton was a military school, and all male students were part of the ROTC and wore uniforms to class. Robert and Raymond looked enough alike that professors and other students would sometime stop Raymond with information for the student newspaper. Raymond would relay the information to Robert without revealing to the individual that they were not talking to the editor.

As a journalism major at the University of Texas at Austin, he worked on the *Daily Texan* newspaper and became its editor for the 1953–1954 year.

Robert worked briefly for the *Corpus Christi Caller-Times* in Corpus Christi, Texas, before receiving his draft notice for the US Army. He did his basic training at Fort Ord in California, after which he received training for the Counterintelligence Corps at Fort Holabird, Maryland. He was stationed at Fort Hood, Texas, and Fort Polk, Louisiana. He was assigned to military intelligence, and he jokingly said the designation qualified him to drive the colonel's jeep. On maneuvers, however, he was assigned to interrogation.

On July 22, 1956, he and Shirley Elise Strum were married in the Strum home in Tyler, Texas. The daughter of Marcus and Florence (Golenternek) Strum, Shirley had grown up in Tyler and graduated from Tyler High School. Marcus owned Leon's shoe stores in Tyler and Waco and the Bootery in Austin. In the summers and on holidays, Shirley sometimes helped in the Tyler store and developed a high degree of skill in gift wrapping. At the University of Texas at Austin, Shirley had a double major in English and journalism, was a member of the Texas Stars baton team, worked on the *Daily Texan*, and served as editor of the *Daily Texan* for the 1954–1955 year.

Robert and Shirley lived in Leesville, Louisiana, where Shirley worked as secretary in a law office until Robert could obtain an early discharge from the army. Both began advanced degree programs in the fall term at the University of Minnesota, financed through the GI Bill of Rights and a Woodrow Wilson Scholarship. Master's degree studies in English for Shirley and history for Robert proved both interesting and challenging, but the cold winters of Minnesota made for a difficult adjustment.

Upon completion of their master's degrees, Robert and Shirley applied for several advanced study opportunities and were exploring possibilities when the application they most wanted, Shirley's Fulbright Fellowship for study in England, was approved.

While in London, they adjusted to the informal schedule of classes, lectures called when the professor was ready rather than on a rigid schedule, and the seminar style of most classes. Robert had to learn to read sixteenth-century texts before he could do much research, a task he described as learning both a new alphabet and a new language. They were able to see a lot of English countryside, indulge in low-cost theater and concerts, attend an audience with the queen mother, hear a speech by Winston Churchill, and go to a hunt ball. The first few months in London, they lived in the apartment of Shirley's cousin, who was touring the United States. After that they had a more typical London apartment with paraffin heat, no refrigerator, and a shared bathroom.

At the Christmas break and during the summer, Robert and Shirley were able to visit the rest of the continent. They were enchanted by Paris and had a very enjoyable visit with Shirley's relatives in Brussels. They were somewhat frustrated that their skill in speaking French did not allow much depth in conversation. The following summer, they were able to visit a wider range of locales within the European continent.

Upon returning to the United States, they obtained temporary employment at the University of Texas while applying for doctoral study programs. They were accepted at the University of Chicago, where both completed doctoral degrees.

Robert's first teaching position after completion of his doctorate was at Washington and Lee University in Virginia. When the opportunity arose to teach at George Washington University, he accepted the position, and Shirley obtained a position at Gallaudet College, a school for the hearing impaired. Although most of her students were skilled at lipreading, Shirley had to learn sign language for more-effective communication with her students.

After twenty-six years at George Washington University, Robert became chairman of the History Department, then dean of the Columbian College of Arts and Science. Later he served two years as dean of the Graduate School of Arts and Sciences, a position he held until his retirement. Shirley moved from Gallaudet to the Catholic University of America (1966–1970), then to the University of Maryland, where she became chair of the English Department. She then was at Provost from 1979 to 1985. She was named Outstanding Woman at the University of Maryland in 1983 and received the Distinguished Alumnus Award for Professional Excellence in 1980 from the University of Chicago Club of Washington, DC.

On a trip to New Mexico, Robert and Shirley became enchanted with the New Mexico area and purchased a second home in Santa Fe. This became a favorite retreat for them and a favorite ski destination for their sons.

In 1986, Shirley became the seventh president of Queens College in New York. She was also the first female president of the college. Robert remained as dean at George Washington University, so they had a commuter marriage for seven years until Robert retired in 1992 and moved to New York. He completed a master's degree in fine arts in 1984 with an emphasis on painting. Upon retirement, he was able to continue his passion for painting, develop skills as a gourmet cook, and do some writing. His paintings have been shown in New York, New Mexico, Virginia, and Washington. He has generously provided a large number of paintings as gifts for family members.

Shirley became president of Stony Brook University in 1994. Her inauguration ceremony held two family-related events. Her son Rabbi Joel Kenny gave the benediction, and four-year-old Chava left her front-row seat to join her grandmother in the recessional. As president of Stony Brook University, Shirley had the opportunity to travel to many countries where Stony Brook had interests, and Robert accompanied her on these trips. They were guests of the Leakey family at the fiftieth anniversary of Mary Leakey's hominid discoveries at Olduvai Gorge in Tanzania.

In the summer of 1997, Robert and Shirley learned that their son Joel had contracted acute leukemia. Much of Robert's time over the next two years was spent working with Joel to fight the disease, including serving as bone marrow donor for a transplant. It was also during this time that Robert required cardiac bypass surgery. When Joel was transferred to MD Anderson Hospital in Houston, Robert rented an apartment to be near Joel in the hospital. It was also a place for both Robert and Joel to stay when Joel received treatment as an outpatient. Shirley spent as much time as she could with Joel, as did his brothers and sister. Joel's death was a very difficult time for the entire family.

Shirley retired in 2009, and they moved back to their home in McLean, Virginia. They divide their time between McLean and Santa Fe, with time for travel, writing, and Robert's painting. Shirley served as interim president for Augusta University in the 2011–2012 year, enabling them to experience a different part of the country.

- **David Jack Kenny (25 Oct 1959–):** David was born in Chicago, Illinois, while his parents were graduate students. David's parents arranged their class schedules so one would be free to care for the baby. They often exchanged childcare responsibilities on campus. Long before he was old enough for school, David began teaching himself to read by identifying words on billboards.

David entered school in Virginia, first in a private elementary school, then a public high school. In contrast to the experiences of some, David enjoyed the large public high school, with its diversity of academic offerings and students.

David and Anne Rocini, a native of West Virginia, met at West Virginia University, though neither attended that school. A friend of David's had a major role in the university spring production. A group of Virginia friends, including David, attended the production. Anne's sister Mary and other West Virginia University friends gave a party for the cast after the production and included the Virginia visitors. Anne had been recruited to provide her skills and her car for the party preparation. David and Anne began a friendship and by May of that year had decided to share an apartment in Arlington, Virginia.

Over the next ten years, Arlington was home to both, though David spent two and a half of those years at Stanford University, working on completing his bachelor's and master's degrees. David and Anne were married on March 9, 1988, the tenth anniversary of the day they met at the party. The ceremony was at the home of David's parents, with dinner following in a private room at the couple's favorite restaurant.

David and Anne purchased a home in Falls Church, Virginia, where they lived for approximately twenty years. During most of this time, David worked as a statistician for a national diabetes study with George Washington University. Anne worked at Inova Fairfax Hospital's administrative office. David did advanced study at George Washington University, resulting in a second master's degree. A dissertation proposal for a PhD degree was accepted but never completed. During this time, they purchased a lot on Hatteras Island, North Carolina, and had a house built. They used this as a vacation home and a vacation rental. It became their full-time home for over two years when both were employed by the Coastal Studies Institute of the University of North Carolina's research campus in Dare County, North Carolina.

David became interested in competing in marathons and participated in a number of marathons, including the Marine Corps, Boston, Big Sur, and Outer Banks marathons. He always finished within the top 10 percent of his age group. After hurting his feet in 2002, he began doing half marathons rather than full marathons. The races selected were frequently in areas David and Anne wanted to explore.

In 2001, David took flying lessons, obtained his pilot's license, and bought an airplane. He became certified in instrument flight conditions and came to love flying. He volunteered for Mercy Medical Angel flights, but his schedule did not give him the flexibility to get many human patients to scheduled appointments, so he gradually changed to Pilots N Paws, since animal transports did not require as rigid a time schedule.

In the spring of 2008, David became a statistician for the Airplane Owners and Pilots Association, headquartered in Frederick, Maryland. David and Anne bought a house near the Frederick airport, and Anne secured a position in the Admissions Department of Hood College.

Both David and Anne enjoy dogs, and they have had one or more dogs during much of their marriage. Their first dog, Winston, an English setter, was originally bought by a colleague of Anne's for his father, an avid hunter. When the father had a heart attack, the bouncy, energetic eight-month-old puppy did not work well in the friend's home. David met Winston and immediately fell in love with him; conditions were right for them to acquire their first dog. Winston was with them for thirteen years. He was followed by two retired greyhounds. The greyhounds often made trips to the beach house but, surprisingly, did not like to run on the beach. The greyhounds were followed by Miss B from a Dare County, North Carolina, shelter, then Gershwin a few months later from Friends of Homeless Animals in Northern Virginia. After they moved to Frederick, David participated in Great Escape II, where over twenty-five dogs were moved from southern shelters to northern shelters, with a stopover in Frederick. Anne fell in love with a tiny black-and-white puppy and was in tears as it was sent on the final leg of the journey. A week later David flew to Connecticut to pick up the puppy, Bubbles, for Anne.

- **Joel Strum Kenny (1 Feb 1962–23 Dec 1999):** Born in Lexington, Virginia, Joel grew up in Northern Virginia and graduated from Langley High School in McLean. As a child, he was a skilled model builder, and he and his brothers built model airplanes, enough to cover the ceiling of the family room of their home. When Joel was a teen, his interest turned to building model rockets, an activity in which he earned two national championships in competition, thirty trophies, and many additional awards, resulting in a feature article in *Science World* magazine.

Joel became interested in theology. While attending the University of Texas at Austin, he became a member of an Orthodox Jewish organization. He moved to New York, where he met Deborah Ann Kuker, a member of the same religious organization. They were married on December 13, 1987, in New York.

Joel continued his religious studies and became proficient in reading archaic Hebrew and Greek documents. He completed a PhD at New York University. As a rabbi, he had a congregation in New York where he was highly respected and was especially effective in working with young people.

In 1997, Joel contracted acute leukemia. Although he received the best treatment available in two noted cancer-treatment-and-research facilities, he died in MD Anderson Hospital in Houston, Texas. His parents and brothers Dan and Jon were with him at the end.

- **Avraham Noah Kenny (4 Nov 1988–):** Avi was born in New York, New York. He developed an early interest in photography and took outstanding nature-related photographs, which he posted online. After graduating from Ardsley High School, Avi attended Brown University in Providence, Rhode Island. On completion of his degree, he spent a year as evaluations officer of Tiyatien Health, an organization founded by survivors of Liberia's civil war. It is an innovative social justice organization, partnering with rural communities and the Liberian government to advance health care and fundamental rights of the poor. Avi worked with data processing for Teach America, headquartered in New York, and with Last Mile Health in Liberia. He is near completion of a PhD in biostatistics at the University of Washington.

- **Chava Esther Kenny (28 Jun 1990–):** Chava, born in New York, was named in honor of her great-grandmother Ava. She attended Ardsley High School in Ardsley, New York, and graduated from Harvard University with an English major. While at Harvard, she worked as an intern at Harvard College Women's Center and did peer advising for the Harvard College Advising Program. She spent two years teaching English in Spain. After returning to Boston, she married Tony Bator in 2022. Their original wedding date was delayed by the COVID-19 pandemic of 2020. Chava is product manager for a custom jewelry firm, and Tony teaches history at a high school.

- **Rachel Leah Kenny (13 Nov 1992–):** Born in New York, Rachel graduated from West Simsbury High School in Connecticut in 2009. While studying at George Washington University, she worked as a survey research assistant, and during the summer of 2011, she tutored elementary students as a research assistant with Teachers College, Columbia University. A 2013 graduate of George Washington University with majors in psychology and fine arts, Rachel took advantage of an opportunity to work with children in Ghana through Global Leadership Adventures.

On returning from Ghana, she took a position as executive assistant at KIPP in Washington, DC. In 2013 Rachel was employed by National Geographic. She completed a master's degree in environmental management at the University of California at Santa Barbara and is employed at the World Resource Institute in Washington, DC.

- **Daniel Clark Kenny (22 Jan 1964–):** After Dan's Washington, DC, birth, his mother learned that her students had a lottery on who could best guess the date and time of the birth. She did not indicate whether she learned the identity of the lottery winner. The family moved from Arlington to McLean, Fairfax County, Virginia, when Dan was six months old. He attended private elementary school, where everyone knew his parents, "thwarting any attempts at mischief." At Langley High School in McLean, Virginia, he was impressed that the closeness to the CIA headquarters resulted in frequent testing of air-raid sirens. In high school he joined the wrestling team but was more interested in the camaraderie than becoming a serious competitor.

Dan enjoyed his experiences at the University of Colorado, where he was able to develop his individualized curriculum and to explore the Boulder area. He graduated in 1986 with majors in biology and environmental conservation. After a couple of years in jobs involving running antiquated printing presses for a small printing company and managing apartment complexes, he obtained a position with the Environmental Protection Agency, where he was able to utilize his background in biology and environmental studies. His work in the Office of Pesticide Programs has included reviewing applications for new pesticides, new pesticide uses, and changes to pesticide labels, all of which must be evaluated for safety before they can be registered. After ten years he was promoted to team leader in insecticides and later to branch chief in the herbicide field. In this position, he must balance what is right against pressures from the pesticide industry, which wants everything registered; the environmentalists, who want nothing registered; the growers, who want maximum flexibility; and the public, who want affordable food safe from dangerous and destructive pests. His area of responsibility covers all herbicides used within the entire country. In 2013 he was awarded a gold medal for outstanding work in herbicide control.

Always interested in architecture, Dan and his brother Jon decided to try their hand at house renovation before Dan joined the EPA. The first house they bought for renovation was described by their mother as the ugliest house she had ever seen. They found the work enjoyable, and their finished product implemented a better design and was quite attractive. Unfortunately, the housing market crashed about that time, so they had to rent the house until the market improved enough for a sale in 2014. It was not a good time to begin a career in real estate. However, Dan and Jon have continued their interest in renovating houses, now fitting in renovations alongside their full-time jobs. One of the several houses they renovated was for themselves in the Mount Vernon area.

Dan is interested in antique cars and has worked on restoring cars, especially vintage Mustangs. He has begun to sell some of his restored cars but intends to keep his favorite 1964 Mustang convertible. He also completed the restoration work on three vintage cars that his brother Joel had begun but had been unable to finish. These three cars were designated for Joel's three children.

Dan is attracted to water—oceans, lakes, rivers. He has purchased land on Lake Anna in Virginia, where he built a boathouse and a residence. Scuba diving trips with Jon and friends to the Caribbean and other locales are much-anticipated vacations. Between the scuba trips, his daily interest in water is satisfied with maintaining several aquariums at home and one at work.

Dan describes his philosophy as "Plan for tomorrow, but definitely live for today." He enjoys family and had always thought he would have his own family, but he has been an important part of the growing years of Joel's children. He enjoys travel, scuba trips, working on houses, experimenting with indoor and outdoor plants, and activities with his friends. After experiencing a heart attack, Dan took early retirement to spend more time on his nonprofessional interests.

- **Jonathan Matthew Kenny (6 Mar 1965–):** Born in Washington, DC, Jon attended Langley School, a private cooperative school, from kindergarten through eighth grade. There he developed a lifelong interest in natural science and sports. The summer after completing the eighth grade, he helped the school maintenance staff with the painting and general repair of the schoolrooms. He enjoyed the experience. He found Langley High School very large and less challenging than he expected. Of his high school experience, he said, "My freshman year, I played football and soccer and managed to dislocate both shoulders—one in each sport. I would dislocate my shoulders again at various intervals my freshman and sophomore years. Eventually I would have surgery on each [during] my junior/senior years. As a result I spent much of high school in a sling in pain and bored."

His 1987 bachelor's degree in cellular biology and physiology was from the University of California, Santa Barbara, chosen in part for its distance from McLean but mostly for its location on the Pacific coast. He began his studies in marine biology and obtained scuba certification before changing his major to cellular biology and physiology. His college studies were much more rewarding than high school. One summer job enabled him to work as a security guard for the 1984 Olympics. He said, "I was paid to defend Russian and German female rowers twice my size from outside marauders with a cup of coffee."

After completing his degree, Jon returned to Northern Virginia, where he obtained a position with Lens Crafters. He started as a laboratory technician and became laboratory manager after about one year. As manager for Lens Crafters in Springfield, Virginia, Jon supervised the busiest laboratory in the country, with an average of forty-five employees. He won recognition for the outstanding unit in the chain. Seeking expanded opportunities, Jon obtained a master of business administration from the Darden School of Business at the University of Virginia. One summer job during his studies was with Madoff Securities in New York, around the time Madoff was starting his investment scheme that later landed him in jail. Disinclination to live in New York City kept Jon from accepting a job offer with Madoff Securities. On completing his MBA, Jon interviewed for a position with Enron. His disappointment over not getting a job he wanted changed to gloating when the company's fraud was exposed.

In 1996, Jon purchased a franchise of Sir Speedy, a national printing company. He has expanded the company by acquiring other printing companies and developing web design and signage as well as diversifying functions to meet the challenges of digital printing. Over the years he has worked with over one hundred employees in three different locations. He now has an independent shop.

While their parents were living in New York, Jon and his brother Dan lived in their parents' McLean home and maintained it for them. At this time, they became interested in microbrewing and, for a while, made their own beer.

Jon shares an interest in real estate with his brother Dan. In addition to the houses they have bought together and renovated for resale or rental, Jon has developed additional properties in Northern Virginia and Baltimore, Maryland. He has also acquired land in Cozumel, Mexico, and Los Cerrillos, New Mexico, for future development and a condominium in Cozumel for use in scuba diving trips and as a rental property. Jon enjoys working with real estate and hopes to spend more time on real estate development in the future.

- **Sarah Elizabeth Kenny (30 Jul 1970–):** Born in Fairfax, Virginia, Sarah graduated from Langley High School, McLean, Virginia. She attended Arizona State University and obtained a bachelor's degree in fine arts with minors in creative writing and art history from George Washington University. Additional study includes a master's degree in art therapy from George Washington University and a master's degree in creative writing from Stony Brook University.

Sarah is interested in music, has written a number of songs, has recorded as a vocalist, and plays guitar. Her interest in music was shared by Ben Azzara, whom she married on July 1, 2001. Their home in Washington, DC, was often a stopover for musicians they knew.

Sarah and Ben were divorced in 2011, and Sarah moved to New York City. She later moved to Hampton Bays, New York. She worked in a variety of areas, including physical training, retail, and as theater administrative assistant at Guild Hall of East Hampton. She was assistant stage manager and assistant wardrobe manager for Guild Hall. Since Guild Hall attracts a number of well-known actors and directors, Sarah has had the opportunity to work with many very talented people. She currently teaches English composition and creative writing at Stony Brook University.

- **Madeline Azzara (8 Jul 2006–):** An outgoing and vivacious child, Madeline was chosen to model children's clothes in advertisements for JCPenney stores at age four. This led to other modeling opportunities over the next several years. Madeline was a good traveler and enjoyed being the only young child on trips with her extended family. In 2019 she had her long hair shaved off to provide hair for wigs for cancer patients.

- **William Colwell Kenny (6 Jun 1934–9 Oct 1934):** William was born at the Kenny home in Acrea. It was evident early that his cleft lip and a cleft palate made it impossible for him to suckle. Jack and his sister Maurine took the baby to a hospital in Fort Worth, the nearest place where he could receive appropriate care to save his life and eventual surgery to correct the problem. Leona, who lived in Fort Worth, kept the family informed of his status in the hospital. Over the next few months, he spent a little time at home and most in the hospital. It was there that he died from pneumonia, complicated by cleft palate and hydrocephalus. He was buried in Acrea Cemetery, adjacent to his Henry grandparents and great-grandparents and Ava's sister Ora.

- **Norma Sue Kenny (29 Sep 1938–):** Sue was born at the Kenny home in the Acrea community. Her grandmother, Fannie Kenny, made note of Sue's birth in her diary, but much to Sue's disappointment, Fannie spent more diary space on the splinter she got in her side that day than she did on the arrival of her youngest grandchild.

Not yet three years old when electricity came to the Acrea area, she had to be reminded that although standing in front of the open door of the new refrigerator was an effective way to cool off on a hot day, it was not an acceptable action. A few serious reprimands soon convinced her to discontinue the practice. Her efforts to wander away from the yard as a preschooler were always thwarted by the collie dog, who barked to alert Ava if Sue wandered. Although adored by her brothers and sister, who considered themselves indulgent toward her, she remembers being often told that she was too little to do what they were doing.

Sue sometimes visited the Acrea school in its last year of existence and was included in its last school photograph. She entered first grade in the Stephenville public school. She continued with this class through elementary school, junior high, and high school. In high school she engaged in a number of extracurricular activities, her favorite of which was yearbook publication. In her junior year, she was coeditor of the yearbook with Dale Weathers, and in her senior year, she was sole editor. She was selected as class favorite and graduated as salutatorian from Stephenville High School in the class of 1957.

During her two years at Tarleton State College, sad lessons of life were learned. Her father, Jack, became ill and died in October of 1958. Lessons on sickness, grief, and responsibility occupied her time and mind, with college courses in English, history, chemistry, etc. becoming secondary. Editing the 1958–1959 Tarleton yearbook did more to add to her stress than to provide enjoyment.

In 1961 Sue graduated from the University of Texas at Austin with a major in English.

Sue and Raymond Dale Weathers were married on July 21, 1961, in the Methodist church in Bluff Dale, Texas. Dale, born on August 31, 1936, in Stephenville, Erath County, Texas, was the son of Earl Weathers and Nell Drake. Earl Weathers owned and operated a sandwich shop, first on the square in downtown Stephenville and later near his home on Graham Street. Dale grew up in Stephenville and attended Stephenville public schools. Active in Boy Scouts, he achieved the status of Eagle Scout. He was well known in the Stephenville area from his six years of bicycle delivery of the daily *Fort Worth Star-Telegram* to many of the homes. He also worked in the Stephenville icehouse during the summers of 1953 through 1959, sometimes working eleven-hour days at the rate of 66.5 cents an hour. Dale attended Tarleton State College and graduated from the University of Texas at Austin with a degree in history and a commission in the US Army.

Sue taught English at Pflugerville High School, and she and Dale lived in Pflugerville the first year of their marriage. Dale was called into service in the military police, a unit that many family members thought an unlikely fit for mild-mannered, quiet-spoken Dale, but he was successful in that role. While in the army, they were stationed in Augusta, Georgia, and Killeen, Texas. The houses they rented usually had relatively bare yards, and Sue learned that coleus was a quick-growing source of color and texture, and castor beans could rapidly provide a privacy screen. This was before she learned of the poisonous nature of castor beans.

On completion of military service, Dale obtained a position with State Farm Insurance Company in Dallas, Texas. Sue worked for Mobil Oil Company as a seismic migration clerk. They first rented a home in Farmers Branch before purchasing the first of two homes they owned in Dallas. Dale joined the US Army Reserve after leaving active duty and spent time each summer at army reserve camps around the country. Sue teased him that this was like going to Boy Scout camp.

Both Sue and Dale learned careful money-management techniques from their parents and practiced them during the early years of their marriage. Their living within their means and avoiding debt meant they had no credit rating when they were ready to buy their first home. They were able to assume the loan of the previous owner and eventually found a credit card company that recognized lack of debt as a good credit risk.

When their daughter, Rachel, reached preschool age, Sue took classes to qualify to teach preschool. She later became a preschool director, first at Chapel Hill Presbyterian and then at Chapel Hill Methodist preschool. She had a very good rapport with the preschool children. On one occasion one of the preschoolers told his mother that he wanted to get Mrs. Weathers something really special for Christmas, something breakable. The resulting coffee mug was a favorite.

Sue and Dale invested in a series of rental houses, and both became skilled in renovations and repairs necessary to maintain rental properties in good condition.

In the fall of 1988, a routine physical examination revealed that Dale had a serious heart condition, and in March of 1995 he underwent triple bypass surgery. Recovery was gradual, with a few frightening episodes of fibrillation, but he did recover strength and heart function. He became a self-taught expert on selecting and preparing heart-healthy food.

After retirement in 1996, they gradually sold their rental houses and spent their time on fun activities. Sue taught English as a second language for several years. Dale devotes time to his hobbies of photography and writing. He has compiled his scenic photos and family photos into several self-published books. These books give an excuse for travel and more photos. The books include family-oriented books for both the Weathers and Kenny families, books chronicling their travels, and books on historic and other interesting areas in the Dallas area. Sue served as consultant and proofreader for each of the books. Sue also wrote and published three short books, with fewer photographs. These books focused on the family and preserved stories and memories important to her and her siblings.

Trips to New Orleans to visit Rachel and her family were high on the travel priority list for a number of years. Rachel's hundred-year-old house had no end of projects that kept Sue and Dale from completely forgetting their house-maintenance skills. Sue spends time on her own creative-writing projects and on maintaining the landscaping in their yard. After Rachel and her family moved to Dallas, Sue and Dale assumed the role of after-school care of the grandchildren.

- **Rachel Katherine Weathers (11 Feb 1969–):** Born in Dallas, Texas, Rachel attended Dallas public schools and graduated from Dallas Arts Magnet High

School. While attending the University of Dallas, she was able to spend a semester at their facility in Italy. Though much of the time was organized around planned experiences, she was able to do some traveling on her own in Italy, and the planned activities included visits to many of Italy's art treasures.

Rachel graduated from the University of Texas at Austin with a major in English and a background and interest in art. She worked in an art gallery in Austin, Texas, before enrolling in Tulane University for advanced study in art history.

Rachel and Scott Farrin met while attending the University of Texas. They were married on July 1, 1995, in Dallas, Texas. They made their home in New Orleans, where Rachel first worked for an art gallery before joining Neal Auction Company. Scott taught English at the University of New Orleans. After taking a series of classes in Washington, DC, Rachel became a furniture and painting appraiser for the Neal Auction Company. Her work frequently took her into historic and more recent estates to catalog and appraise materials for auction.

When Hurricane Katrina inundated the city of New Orleans in 2005, Rachel was in Dallas in honor of her father's birthday. What had been planned as a long weekend turned out to be a six-week stay. Scott heeded the warning to evacuate, took the dog, and drove to his aunt's home in Memphis, Tennessee. When they were able to return to New Orleans, they found their home undamaged because it was located on higher ground in the historic district. The homes of many of their friends and coworkers had been damaged or destroyed. The campus of the University of New Orleans had been flooded, making it necessary for Scott to teach some of his courses on the internet.

Rachel and Scott sold their home in the historic district of New Orleans and bought a one-hundred-year-old house in Algiers Point, on the west bank of the Mississippi River. The Algiers Point Ferry was an important commute vehicle for them.

Rachel became a painting and furniture appraiser for Heritage Auctions after a move to Dallas in 2016. Sue and Dale helped her renovate a house near their home. Scott completed his commitment for the 1916–1917 year at the University of New Orleans before moving to Dallas in the summer of 1917. He obtained a teaching position with Collin County Community College. When the COVID-19 pandemic resulted in schools closing, Rachel found it necessary to quit her job at Heritage Auctions and seek some part-time work to provide adequate childcare. This need was heightened by the fact that the virus was especially fatal to people over sixty-five years old, meaning it was important for Sue and Dale to avoid exposure.

- **Evangeline Farrin (17 Mar 2007–):** Evie was born in New Orleans, Louisiana. She attended an international school, where she became proficient in Spanish. Evie enjoys art and drawing and exhibits talent as well as an interest in art. Evie found the move from New Orleans difficult, but a new kitten and new friends made it easier. Her thirteenth birthday occurred at the beginning of the isolation for the pandemic, and she named it her "panteenth" birthday. When it came time for high school, both she and her mother were pleased that she was accepted by the Dallas Arts Magnet School.

- **William Reason Farrin (1 Jul 2010–):** William was born in New Orleans, Louisiana. He has severe autism and needs special care and education.

Mary Maurine Kenny
(9 Dec 1905–9 Dec 1985)

The youngest of Will and Fannie's children, Maurine was born at their Oak Dale home. She described herself as being a frail infant, given to frequent illness. As a one-year-old, she fell into the fireplace, causing a severe burn on her right hand. This injury may have contributed to her tendency to use her left hand in most activities. As a result of her frequent illnesses and her problems in restoring the use of her right hand, she did not start school until eight years of age. Because she had learned to read as well as other skills from her older siblings, she started in the second grade. Within the year she was promoted to the third grade. The school she attended was a rural school flanked by two churches and adjacent to the rural cemetery, all surrounded by the stately oak trees that gave the community its name.

She was eleven and in the sixth grade when the family moved to the Hannibal community. She found the hills around Barton Creek to be quite beautiful, especially in the springtime. Maurine and Jack developed a close relationship and enjoyed doing many things together. Most of the joint adventures they talked about were in the Hannibal area. One such adventure involved each crawling under the porch of a vacant house from different sides to check on a noise, only to find a very large rattlesnake coiled and ready to strike. Both made a hasty retreat.

This close relationship continued into adulthood, and Jack felt closer to Maurine than any other sibling. Maurine was always a participant in the happy and sad times for Jack and Ava's family. She was there at Christmas, graduations, and weddings and helped celebrate birthdays. She was the one to take the body of Jack and Ava's first baby from the oil field camp to Stephenville for burial, and she accompanied Jack to take the infant William to Fort Worth for treatment.

Hannibal school went only through the seventh grade, so she completed that school at the age of twelve. The next year, she and one other student were given first-year high school work at the Hannibal school as an extra assignment. For her sophomore high school year, Maurine went to Bunyan to live with her sister Eunice and Eunice's husband, D. M. Russell, and attended school there. She shared a room with Thelma Bowden, a young orphan girl whom the Russell family was helping attend school. The two became very good friends, working together and going to school together.

The following summer, the Russell family moved to Dublin, where D. M. was hired as principal of Dublin High School. Both Maurine and Thelma Bowden returned to the Russell home to continue their schooling. Maurine made a new set of friends, one of whom was Ava Henry. During the summer between her junior and senior years, she spent most of her time with her parents in Hannibal but also visited some of her new friends who lived in areas other than Dublin.

Only two weeks into her senior year, Maurine had an attack of appendicitis. At first it did not seem very serious, but within a few days it was apparent that the appendix had ruptured and that she was seriously ill. Her father took her by train to Harris Sanatorium in Fort Worth for emergency surgery. She remained in the hospital for seventeen days and was unable to go back to school for six weeks. She then had the challenge of catching up with the missed schoolwork. In spite of this start, she described her senior year in high school as a very happy time.

In the fall of 1923, Maurine borrowed $100 to enable her to attend Tarleton College. She found college work more difficult than high school but soon adapted to the challenge. She completed her work at Tarleton, receiving her associate in science on May 27, 1925. She obtained a teaching credential and was hired to teach home economics at Huckabay High School.

Maurine saved her money and was able to attend North Texas State Teachers College, where she obtained a bachelor of science in home economics and a permanent teaching credential on May 31, 1929.

Maurine probably met Byron Davis at North Texas State Teachers College. The 1929–1930 school year saw numerous letters exchanged between Maurine—in Stephenville, probably having returned to her teaching position at Huckabay—and Byron in Albany, Texas. He was then in his second year as principal of Albany High School. He had taught English and coached athletics there for three years.

Byron (21 Jul 1903–1 Apr 1984) was the son of James Lafayette Davis (1867–1943) and Emily Veronica Osburn (1867–1944). Byron grew up in McKinney, Texas, where he graduated from McKinney High School. He attended Austin College and the University of Texas and obtained a bachelor of arts degree from North Texas State University and a master of arts degree from the University of Colorado. One summer while attending the University of Colorado, he took the train to Kansas City, where he joined with a friend to drive to Colorado. He reported that on that drive, they encountered paved roads in only some towns.

Maurine and Byron were married on May 24, 1930, in the Stephenville home of her parents. They lived in Albany the first year of their marriage. In 1931, they moved to Sherman, Texas, where Byron served as chairman of the English Department, coached debate, and sponsored the senior class. Maurine became involved in community activities and began doing some painting. She was a skilled artist and did paintings for her brother and sisters, with each painting uniquely designed to go well with the style of the recipient's home. She also did a number of paintings for her own home and for special friends.

In 1937, Byron was named principal of Sherman High School. In 1942, Byron entered the US Army, and he and Maurine were assigned to a military base in Enid, Oklahoma. Prior to the war, Maurine and Byron had built a home, which they had occupied only a few months before Byron had entered the army. In the service, Byron rose to the rank of captain, but both he and Maurine were glad to return to civilian life in 1945. Byron resumed his position as principal of Sherman High School. Because they were unable to find a suitable candidate for the position on short notice, Maurine began working as the high school secretary on a temporary basis. She excelled in the position, where she remained after Byron was named school superintendent. She was later named office manager.

Their home, which they had rented out during the war, had not been well maintained during their absence; they sold it and built a new home on McKown Avenue. The new home had a large yard with trees, which attracted backyard birds. There was space to build a small separate building for Byron to use as an office after his retirement.

Maurine and Byron always took an interest in neighborhood children. One neighbor, Barbara Wellmaker, developed a special affection for them and often visited their home. On occasion, she would take trips with them, including trips to visit relatives.

Byron was appointed superintendent of the Sherman public schools in 1953, a position he held until his retirement. As soon as the Supreme Court agreed to hear the Brown v. Board of Education case, Byron called a meeting of all the school principals in the district. He explained to them that he thought the ruling would be against segregation, and he wanted that district to have a plan in case that was the ruling. He asked the principals to identify community members who would serve with them on a panel to draft a plan, and he began a series of integrated in-service workshops for the teachers. By the time the Supreme Court issued its ruling, the Sherman School District had a plan ready to implement, which was to start with the first grade and integrate each subsequent first grade. Byron expressed some disappointment that it was a twelve-year plan. While many Texas schools were resisting the order, resulting in disorder and discord, the Sherman area was spared discord. Community member Dana A. Blocker, in a letter to Maurine after Byron's death, expressed appreciation for his efforts. It was written on April 10, 1984, and reads:

> Dear Mrs. Davis: It must be a source of strength to you to hear so many people speak with love and respect about Mr. Davis, relating personal memories of his many acts of kindness and compassion. I remember those things, too, but I think I shall remember longer

what was perhaps the greatest act of courage and wisdom ever shown in this community by one person. That was his singular service in the engineering of a quiet, peaceful and orderly integration of the races in Sherman Schools in the early 1960's. That's how I'll remember him; and I know, also, that he got a lot of help from you in making decisions that served us all. May God continue to bless you, Dana A. Blocker

In many respects, Byron was an innovator in education. As the integration plan was being implemented, some of the teachers pointed out that many of the black children had not had the opportunities of other first graders and would not be starting on the same level. Byron initiated a summer preschool for these students, well before the national Head Start program began.

Both Maurine and Byron were active in community organizations. Byron was an active member of the Sherman Rotary Club and regularly taught a men's Sunday school class at the First Baptist Church. Maurine was a knowledgeable birder and enjoyed participating in local bird walks and in out-of-the-area trips with the local Audubon group. She grew prize-winning African violets and was active in the Red River African Violet Society, serving a term as president of the association.

Maurine maintained a close relationship with the Kenny family and always attended graduations, weddings, and other special family events, even when Byron could not go with her. Fannie's birthday and Christmas with the Kennys were rarely missed. During World War II years, she regularly sent packages to her nephews in service. A letter from R. C. Kenny expresses his appreciation for the many packages she sent while he was overseas. During her mother's declining years, Maurine was always there when Fannie was ill or otherwise needed her help. In a letter to Maurine, Fannie wrote, "You have always been my stand-by."

In February 1963, Maurine and Byron were driving by the Woodlawn Country Club when they had to stop quickly to avoid hitting a puppy in the road. The puppy ran under the car and had to be coaxed out. Maurine picked up the puppy and determined she would take it home, not follow Byron's suggestion to leave it there. When an effort to find the puppy's owners was fruitless, Tippy, named for the white tip of her tail, became a very important member of the family. She remained so for sixteen years, twelve of which she had the full attention of both Byron and Maurine. She usually stayed as close to Byron as possible, sleeping at the foot of his bed and staying by his side when he was home. Byron even made a trip home from work during a storm to be sure Tippy was safe—an action that caused his staff to tease him about risking his life to take care of the dog.

A second puppy, Becky, was on the golf course when Byron and his brother, Osborn, were playing. She made an effort to gain the attention of golfers. She finally jumped into Byron's golf cart, so, of course, he took her home. Tippy did not quickly accept the intruder, but eventually they came to tolerate one another. Becky established a stronger attachment to Maurine and helped ease the pain for both Maurine and Byron when Tippy died.

After retirement, Byron was able to pursue his passion for golf, a game he played well and in which he helped several young people get involved, including at least one who became a golf professional. He took pride in the fact that he was able to score a seventy-five on his seventy-fifth birthday.

In the late 1970s, Maurine's activities became considerably restricted by severe back pain caused by osteoporosis. At that point she could no longer drive to attend family events. It was at this time that her weekly telephone conversations with her sister Leona and the visits from her nieces and nephews became especially important to her.

In April 1984, Byron collapsed at the breakfast table and was dead by the time the paramedics arrived a few minutes later. The year following Byron's death, Becky was more than a companion to Maurine. As Sue Weathers expressed it, "In that time of grief and confusion, Becky got her up in the morning, demanded they eat regular meals and stay awake during the day. Becky was a spoiled, demanding dog who Maurine loved unashamedly. She was a watchdog in the truest sense—she watched over Maurine every day."

Byron had left a will leaving all their assets to Maurine. If she predeceased him, their Baptist church and the Sherman Rotary Club's scholarship fund would be the major recipients. Many assumed she would follow Byron's ideas for the estate, but now that Maurine was in charge, she had her own ideas. She made a will providing a generous donation in Byron's name to the Sherman Rotary Club for a scholarship. She also made bequests to nieces and nephews, both Davis and Kenny; to Byron's brother; and to Barbara Wellmaker. The Baptist church was completely left out since she had heard nothing from them after Byron's funeral, and she felt they had supported the church generously over the years.

Soon after Byron's death, it became apparent that Maurine was not able to take care of herself and her home alone. Sue Weathers and Byron's nephew, Osborn Davis, took turns going to Sherman on alternate weekends to do food shopping and attend to other needs. After several months, it became apparent that more help was needed. A live-in caregiver, Renata, was hired. After a couple of unsatisfactory hires, Renata proved to be a capable and concerned caregiver who remained with Maurine until her death. Maurine died on her eightieth birthday, December 9, 1985. She announced that she would have ice cream for breakfast since it was her birthday. She collapsed soon thereafter, was taken to the hospital, and died without regaining consciousness.

Maurine may have made the arrangements before her death; Renata took Becky home with her.

Maurine and Byron devoted their lives to helping and educating children and gave special help to a number of young people. They had no children of their own.

SOURCES

Will Kenny and Fannie Clark

Stories told at family gatherings are included. The stories were remembered by one or more individuals, but the identity of the tellers and the occasion of the storytelling have been forgotten. Contributors include Raymond Kenny, Robert Kenny, Sue Kenny Weathers, and Betty Thompson.

Bible records. W. C. Kenny family Bible. Photocopy of original family data pages, 1964. In the possession of Mary Jo Kenny.

"Clark, J. O. A." 1880 US Census, Erath County, Texas, p. 30, ED 154, family 245. Ancestry.com, 2005.

Davis, Leona Kenny. Stories told to Mary Jo Kenny during visits from 1975 through 1985.

Kenny, Fannie Clark. Personal diary. Copy in possession of Mary Jo Kenny.

Kenny, Fannie Clark. Stories of her childhood or her children told to Mary Jo Kenny during visits. 1945–1964.

"Kenny, Frances L." Texas Death Certificates, 1903–1982. Ancestry.com, 2013.

"Kenny, Frances L." Texas, Find A Grave Index, 1836–2011. Ancestry.com, 2012.

"Kenny, Frances." 1940 US Census, Erath County, Texas, p. 4A, ED 72-2. Ancestry.com, 2012.

Kenny, Raymond. Stories remembered from family gatherings and visits with Fannie Clark Kenny.

"Kenny, W. C., grantee, George D. Gibson, grantor." *Erath County Deed Book 52*, p. 21, May 24, 1894.

"Kenny, W. C." 1880 US Census, Erath County, Texas, p. 13.1, ED 149, line 3. FHLC #1255302, FamilySearch Library, Salt Lake City, UT.

"Kenny, W. C." 1920 US Population Census, Erath County, Texas. FamilySearch Library, Salt Lake City, UT.

"Kenny, W. C." Funeral Notice. Stephenville, Texas. August 19, 1936.

"Kenny, Will C." 1930 US Census, Erath County, Texas, Stephenville, Precinct 1, ED 72-2, 751 Long Street, dwelling 58, family 67, April 26, 1930. FamilySearch Library, Salt Lake City, UT.

"Kenny, William C." 1900 US Census, Erath County, Texas, ED 6X, sheet 20, line 56, dwelling 343, family 344. FHLC #1241631, FamilySearch Library, Salt Lake City, UT.

"Kenny, William C." 1910 US Population Census, Erath County, Texas, District 1, ED 19, dwelling 12, family 12, August 16, 1910. FamilySearch Library, Salt Lake City, UT.

"Kenny, William C." Texas, Find A Grave Index, 1836–2011. Ancestry.com, 2012.

Rampley, Irene Crow. Correspondence. March 10, 1994.

Rampley, Irene Crow. Interview with Mary Jo Kenny. Glendale, Arizona. Summer 1994.

Stallings, Louise. Letter to Mary Jo Kenny. January 17, 1992.

Thompson, Betty Russell. Email to Mary Jo Kenny. March 8, 2013.

"W. C. Kenny, Well Known Resident of Erath County, Dies Here Monday Night." *Tribune* 38, no. 30. Stephenville, TX.

"William Colwell Kenny." Standard Certificate of Death. Texas Department of Health, Bureau of Vital Statistics, 40393.

Meta Kenny and Luther Rampley

"Crow, Irene." Texas Birth Certificates, 1903–1932. Ancestry.com.

"Crow, Irene." US, Social Security Applications and Claims Index, 1936–2007. Ancestry.com, 2015.

"Henry, Danny L., Jr. to Amy R. Tomlinson." Texas Marriage Index, 1824–2014. Ancestry.com.

"Henry, Danny Lee, to Margaret Suzanne Lindsay." Texas, Select County Marriage Records, 1837–2015. Ancestry.com, 2014.

"Henry, Danny Lee, Jr." Texas Birth Index, 1903–1997. Ancestry.com, 2005.

"Henry, Danny Lee." *1964 La Ventana Yearbook*. Texas Tech University. US School Yearbooks. Ancestry.com.

"Henry, Danny Lee." *1967 Yearbook*. Texas Tech University. US School Yearbooks. Ancestry.com.

"Henry, Danny Lee." Texas Birth Index, 1903–1997. Ancestry.com, 2005.

"Henry, Danny Lee." US, Find A Grave Index, 1600s–Current. Ancestry.com, 2012.

"Henry, Danny Lee." US, Social Security Applications and Claims Index, 1936–2007. Ancestry.com, 2015.

"Henry, Danny." Texas Death Index, 1903–2000. Ancestry.com, 2005.

"Henry, E. Lee." 1920 US Census, Eastland County, Texas, Precinct 7, roll T625-1797, ED 120, image 507. Ancestry.com, 2005.

"Henry, E. Lee." 1930 US Census, Eastland County, Texas, roll 2325, p. 5B, ED 32, image 883. Ancestry.com, 2002.

"Henry, Gary Wayne." Texas Birth Index, 1903–1997. Ancestry.com, 2005.

"Henry, Isa L." Social Security Death Index. Ancestry.com, 2008.

"Henry, Isa Lee." US, Social Security Applications and Claims Index, 1938–2007. Ancestry.com, 2015.

"Henry, Isa Lee." Texas, Find A Grave Index, 1836–2011. Ancestry.com, 2012.

"Henry, Margaret Suzanne." US, Find A Grave Index, 1600s–Current. Ancestry.com, 2012.

"Henry, Patrick Wade." Texas Birth Index, 1903–1997. Ancestry.com, 2005.

"Henry, T. T. 'Ted.'" Texas, Find A Grave Index, 1836–2011. Ancestry.com, 2012.

Henry, Tom. Letter to Mary Jo Kenny. Undated, around 1992.

"Henry, Tom." US Phone and Address Directories, 1993–2002. Ancestry.com.

"Henry, Tommie T." Social Security Death Index. Ancestry.com, 2008.

"Henry, Tommie T." US, Social Security Applications and Claims Index, 1936–2007. Ancestry.com, 2015.

"Henry, Tommie Terry." US WWII Draft Cards Young Men, 1940–1947. Ancestry.com, 2011.

"Henry, Tommie Wayne." Texas Birth Index, 1903–1997. Ancestry.com, 2005.

"Henry, Tommie." Texas Death Index, 1903–2000. Ancestry.com, 2006.

"Henry, Tommy Wayne." US, Find A Grave Index, 1600s–Current. Ancestry.com, 2012.

"Kenney, Meta, to L. L. Rampley." Texas, Select County Marriage Records, 1837–2015. Ancestry.com, 2014.

Petsick, Meta Kenny Rampley. Story told at family gathering around 1948.

"Petsick, Meta Rampley." Texas Death Certificates, 1903–1982. Ancestry.com, 2013.

"Petsick, Meta." Texas Death Index, 1903–2000. Ancestry.com.

"Petsick, Mrs. J. F." Obituary. *Hico News Review*. Ancestry.com, 2014.

Rampley, Anne Ball. Letter to Mary Jo Kenny. November 9, 1998.

"Rampley, Bill Kenny." Texas Birth Certificates, 1903–1932. Ancestry.com.

"Rampley, Bill Kenny." Texas Birth Index, 1903–1997. Ancestry.com.

"Rampley, Bill, to Irene Crow." Texas, Select County Marriage Records, 1837–2015. Ancestry.com, 2014.

"Rampley, Bill." 1940 US Census, Erath County, Texas. Ancestry.com.

"Rampley, Bill." US City Directories, 1921–1989. Ancestry.com.

"Rampley, Bill." US Public Records Index, vol. 1. Ancestry.com.

"Rampley, Bill." US, Social Security Death Index, 1935–Current. Ancestry.com.

"Rampley, Bill." Texas, Find A Grave Index, 1761–2012. Ancestry.com.

"Rampley, Bruce W., to Virginia Anne Ball." Texas, Select County Marriage Records, 1837–2015. Ancestry.com, 2014.

"Rampley, Bruce W." US, Social Security Applications and Claims Index, 1936–2007. Ancestry.com, 2015.

"Rampley, Bruce Wyly." Texas Birth Certificates, 1903–1932. Ancestry.com, 2013.

"Rampley, Bruce Wyly." Texas Death Certificates, 1903–1982. Ancestry.com, 2013.

"Rampley, Bruce Wyly." US WWII Draft Cards Young Men, 1940–1947. Ancestry.com, 2011.

"Rampley, Bruce." US, Find A Grave Index, 1600s–Current. Ancestry.com, 2012.

"Rampley, Bruce." *Yucca North Texas State College Yearbook 1949*. US School Yearbooks. Ancestry.com, 2010.

"Rampley, Cynthia Ann, to Robert Elder Wilson." Texas, Select County Marriage Records, 1837–2015. Ancestry.com, 2014.

"Rampley, Cynthia Ann." Texas Birth Index, 1903–1997. Ancestry.com, 2013.

"Rampley, David Scott, and Cris Noel Rampley." Texas Divorce Index, 1968–2014. Ancestry.com, 2015.

"Rampley, David Scott, to Cris Noel Robinson." Texas, Select County Marriage Records, 1837–2015. Ancestry.com, 2014.

"Rampley, David Scott." Texas Birth Index, 1903–1997. Ancestry.com, 2013.

"Rampley, female." Texas Birth Certificates, 1903–1932. Ancestry.com, 2013.

Rampley, Greg and Marilyn. Christmas letter. 2010.

Rampley, Greg and Marilyn. Email to Mary Jo Kenny. March 27, 2013.

"Rampley, Gregory Paul." Texas Birth Index, 1903–1997. Ancestry.com, 2013.

Rampley, Irene Crow. Letter to Mary Jo Kenny. December 1993.

Rampley, Irene. Letter to Mary Jo Kenny. December 17, 1991.

"Rampley, Irene V." US, Find A Grave Index, 1600s–Current. Ancestry.com,

"Rampley, Irene." US, Social Security Death Index, 1935–Current. Ancestry.com.

"Rampley, John S." 1910 US Census, Erath County, Texas, Precinct 4, dwelling 51, family 51. FamilySearch Library, Salt Lake City, UT.

"Rampley, L. L." 1920 US Census, Erath County, Texas, Thurber, Precinct 7, p. 267, dwelling 61, family 64. FamilySearch Library, Salt Lake City, UT.

"Rampley, Luther." 1930 US Census, Erath County, Texas, Precinct 5, p. 203, line 43, dwelling 122, April 1930. FamilySearch Library, Salt Lake City, UT.

"Rampley, Luther." Texas Death Certificates, 1903–1982. Ancestry.com.

"Rampley, Luther." Texas Death Index, 1903–2000. Ancestry.com.

"Rampley, Luther." Texas, Find A Grave Index, 1761–2012. Ancestry.com.

"Rampley, Luther." World War I Draft Registration Cards, 1917–1918. Ancestry.com.

Rampley, Marilyn. Letter to Mary Jo Kenny. Undated, around 2000.

"Rampley, Meta Empress, to J. F. Petsick." Texas, Select County Marriage Records, 1837–2015. Ancestry.com.

"Rampley, Meta Kenny." Texas, Find A Grave Index, 1936–2011. Ancestry.com, 2012.

"Rampley, Meta." 1940 US Census, Erath County, Texas. Ancestry.com.

"Rampley, Meta." Texas, Find A Grave Index, 1751–2012. Ancestry.com.

"Rampley." Texas Birth Certificates, 1903–1932. Ancestry.com, 2013.

Roy Kenny and Mabel Roberts

"Airplane Crash Fatal to Cadet." *Stephenville Empire Tribune.* May 1943.

Davis, Leona Kenny. Conversations with Mary Jo Kenny. 1980–1984.

Everhart, Teresa Lorenz. Email to Mary Jo Kenny. June 23, 2013.

"Goodwin, Emma." Texas Birth Certificates, 1903–1932. Ancestry.com, 2013.

"Goodwin, Henry C." 1930 US Census, Brown County, Texas, roll 2302, p. 11A, ED 8, image 831. Ancestry.com, 2002.

"Goodwin, Marion." US, Social Security Applications and Claims Index, 1936–2007, Ancestry.com, 2015.

"Kenney, Jeanette, to Edward J. Lorenz." Oklahoma County, Oklahoma, Marriage Index, 1889–1951. Ancestry.com, 2013.

"Kenny, Don G., to Mary F. Powajba." California Marriage Index, 1960–1985. Ancestry.com, 2007.

"Kenny, Don G." California Death Index. Ancestry.com, 2000.

"Kenny, Don Goodwin." Texas Birth Index. Ancestry.com, 2005.

"Kenny, Don." US, Department of Veterans Affairs BIRLS Death File, 1850–2010. Ancestry.com, 2011.

"Kenny, Don." Social Security Death Index. Ancestry.com, 2008.

"Kenny, Earl W." Texas Death Certificates, 1903–1982. Ancestry.com, 2013.

"Kenny, Earl W." US, World War II Army Enlistment Records, 1938–1946. Ancestry.com, 2005.

"Kenny, Earl W." US, Find A Grave Index, 1600s–Current. Ancestry.com, 2012.

"Kenny, Edward C." US, World War II Army Enlistment Records, 1938–1946. Ancestry.com.

"Kenny, Edward Caldwell." US, Social Security Applications and Claims Index, 1936–2007. Ancestry.com, 2015.

"Kenny, Edward, to Marion Goodwin." Texas, Select County Marriage Records, 1837–2015. Ancestry.com, 2014.

"Kenny, Edward." US Department of Veterans Affairs BIRLS Death File, 1850–2010. Ancestry.com, 2011.

"Kenny, Gary S., to Tammy Spray." Tennessee State Marriages, 1780–2002. Ancestry.com.

"Kenny, Karen Marie." Texas Birth Index. Ancestry.com, 2005.

"Kenny, Mabel C." Texas, Find A Grave Index, 1836–2011. Ancestry.com, 2012.

"Kenny, Mabel Clair." Texas Death Certificates, 1903–1982. Ancestry.com, 2013.

"Kenny, Mabel W." 1940 US Census, Cameron County, Texas, Precinct 8, line 30, May 15, 1940. Ancestry.com.

"Kenny, Marion G." Texas, Find A Grave Index, 1836–2011. Ancestry.com, 2012.

"Kenny, Marion." Social Security Death Index. Ancestry.com, 2008.

"Kenny, Nell Jean." Social Security Death Index. Ancestry.com, 2008.

"Kenny, Nell Jean." Texas, Find A Grave Index, 1836–2011. Ancestry.com, 2012.

Kenny, R. C. Letter to Mary Jo Kenny. 1995.

"Kenny, R. S." Social Security Death Index. Ancestry.com, 2008.

"Kenny, Roy and Pamela Lynn." Oregon Divorce Records, 1961–1985. Ancestry.com, 2015.

Kenny, Roy C. Letter to Captain and Mrs. Byron Davis. October 7, 1944.

"Kenny, Roy C., to Nell Jean Tarwater." Texas County Marriages, 1817–1965. Ancestry.com, 2016.

"Kenny, Roy C." 1920 US Census, Erath County, Texas, Stephenville Precinct 1, roll T625-1801, p. 4B, ED 5, image 101, January 7, 1920. Ancestry.com, 2005.

"Kenny, Roy C." 1940 US Census, Hidalgo County, Texas. Ancestry.com, 2012.

"Kenny, Roy C." Funeral Notice. September 12, 1939.

"Kenny, Roy C." Social Security Death Index. Ancestry.com, 2008.

"Kenny, Roy C." US, Social Security Applications and Claims Index, 1936–2007. Ancestry.com, 2015.

"Kenny, Roy C." US, World War II Army Enlistment Records, 1938–1946. Ancestry.com, 2005.

"Kenny, Roy C." Texas, Find A Grave Index, 1836–2011. Ancestry.com, 2012.

"Kenny, Roy Clifton." Standard Certificate of Death. Bureau of Vital Statistics, Texas Department of Health.

"Kenny, Roy Clifton." US, Social Security Applications and Claims Index, 1936–2007, Ancestry.com, 2015.

"Kenny, Roy S., to Pamela Lynn." Nevada Marriage Index, 1956–2005. Ancestry.com, 2007.

"Kenny, Roy Scott." Nevada, Death Index, 1980–2012. Ancestry.com, 2013.

"Kenny, Roy Scott." Texas Birth Index, 1903–1997. Ancestry.com, 2005.

"Kenny, Roy Scott." US, Social Security Applications and Claims Index, 1936–2007. Ancestry.com, 2015.

"Kinney, Edward." Texas Birth Certificates, 1903–1932. Ancestry.com, 2013.

"Kinney, Roy Clifton." US World War I Draft Registration Cards, 1917–1918. Ancestry.com, 2005.

"Lorenz, Anyce J., to Edward J. Lorenz." Ohio Marriage Index, 1970, 1972–2007. Ancestry.com, 2010.

"Lorenz, Anyce J." US Public Records Index, vol. I. Ancestry.com, 2010.

"Lorenz, Anyce Jeanette 'Jenny.'" Obituary. Greater Cincinnati Tristate Obituaries. United States Obituary Collection. Ancestry.com, 2006.

"Lorenz, Anyce U." Ohio Divorce Abstracts, 1962–1963, 1973–2007. Ancestry.com, 2010.

"Lorenz, Edward." Obituary. *Cincinnati Enquirer*, January 15, 2012. Ancestry.com.

Lorenz, Jeanette and Ed. Discussion with Mary Jo Kenny. Cincinnati, Ohio. Summer 1994.

Lorenz, Jeanette. Letter to Mary Jo Kenny. December 1995.

"Lorenz, Kenny Charles." Obituary. *Cincinnati Enquirer*, November 16, 2010. Ancestry.com.

"Mass, Karen Marie (Kenny)." Minnesota Birth Index, 1935–1995. Ancestry.com, 2004.

"Roberts, Mabel." US, Social Security Applications and Claims Index, 1936–2007. Ancestry.com, 2015.

"Tarwater, Nell J." US, Social Security Applications and Claims Index, 1936–2007. Ancestry.com, 2015.

Eunice Kenny and D. M. Russell

Bennett, Carmen Taylor. "Richards, Mrs. R. R." In *Cottle County, My Dear*. Floydada, TX: Blanco Offset Printing, 1979.

Bennett, Carmen Taylor. "Richards, T. J. (Jr.)." In *Cottle County, My Dear*. Floydada, TX: Blanco Offset Printing, 1979.

Bennett, Carmen Taylor. "Richards, W. Q." In *Cottle County, My Dear*. Floydada, TX: Blanco Offset Printing, 1979.

Bennett, Carmen Taylor. "The History of Music in Cottle County." In *Our Roots Grow Deep: A History Of Cottle County*. Floydada, TX: Blanco Offset Printing, 1970.

"Corrections and Additions." Individual notes made by attendees of the Russell–Kenny Reunion, Morgan Mill, Texas, July 2017.

Harris, David. "Thompson recalls the glory days of Aggie Athletes." *The Battalion*. Texas A&M University, 2009.

"Kenny, Eunice L." US, Social Security Applications and Claims Index, 1936–2007. Ancestry.com, 2015.

"Kenny, Eunice Lucile, to D. M. Russell." Texas, Select County Marriage Index, 1837–1977. Ancestry.com, 2014.

McKnight, Barbara. Christmas letter. 2000.

McKnight, Barbara. Christmas letter. 2004.

Richards, Frances. Family Group Sheets. 1988.

"Richards, Frances R." Social Security Death Index. Ancestry.com, 2008.

"Richards, Frances Russell." US, Social Security Applications and Claims Index, 1936–2007. Ancestry.com, 2015.

Richards, M. F. Letter to Mary Jo Kenny. July 4, 1988.

"Richards, Martha Frances Russell." Texas, Find A Grave Index, 1836–2011. Ancestry.com, 2012.

"Richards, Martha Frances." US, Find A Grave Index, 1600s–Current. Ancestry.com, 2012.

"Richards, Martha." Texas Death Index, 1903–2000. Ancestry.com, 2006.

"Richards, Mineola." 1930 US Census, Cottle County, Texas, roll 2311, p. 26A, ED 1, image 1015. Ancestry.com, 2002.

"Richards, Ronald R." US Public Records Index, 1950–1993, vol. 1. Ancestry.com, 2010.

"Richards, Ronald Russell." Texas Birth Index, 1903–1997. Ancestry.com, 2005.

"Richards, T. J., Jr." US, Social Security Applications and Claims Index, 1936–2007. Ancestry.com, 2015.

"Richards, T. J., Jr." 1940 US Census, Cottle County, Texas, roll T627-4013, p. 10A, ED51-3A. Ancestry.com, 2012.

"Richards, T. J., Jr." US, Find A Grave Index, 1600s–Current. Ancestry.com, 2012.

"Richards, T. J." Social Security Death Index. Ancestry.com, 2008.

"Richards, T. J." Texas, Find A Grave Index, 1836–2011. Ancestry.com, 2012.

"Richards, T." Texas Death Index, 1903–2000. Ancestry.com, 2006.

"Richards, William Q., to Regina J. Ferguson." Texas Marriage Collection, 1814–1909 and 1966–2002. Ancestry.com, 2005.

"Richards, William Q." Texas Birth Index, 1903–1997. Ancestry.com, 2005.

"Richards, William Q." United States Obituary Collection. Ancestry.com, 2006.

"Richards, William Q." US, Find A Grave Index, 1600s–Current. Ancestry.com, 2012.

"Russell, D. M. (Dink)." A Service of Celebration. First United Methodist Church, Stephenville, Texas. January 5, 1977.

"Russell, D. M." 1920 US Census, Erath County, Texas, roll T625-1801, p. 16B, ED 5, image 125. FamilySearch Library, Salt Lake City, UT.

"Russell, D. M." 1930 US Census, Comanche County, Texas, roll 2311, p. 3A, ED 11, image 782. FamilySearch Library, Salt Lake City, UT.

"Russell, D. M." 1940 US Census, Montague County, Texas. Ancestry.com, 2012.

"Russell, D. M." Texas Death Certificates, 1903–1982. Ancestry.com, 2013.

"Russell, D. M." Texas, Find A Grave Index, 1836–2011. Ancestry.com, 2012.

"Russell, D." Social Security Death Index. Ancestry.com, 2008.

"Russell, Dink M." US, Social Security Applications and Claims Index, 1936–2007. Ancestry.com, 2015.

"Russell, Dink Mander." US World War I Draft Registration Cards, 1917–1918. Ancestry.com, 2005.

"Russell, Eli W." 1910 US Census, Erath County, Texas, Precinct 1, ED 18, sheet 10A. Ancestry.com, 2006.

Russell, Eunice. Subject of article, "Erath educator remembered." *Stephenville Empire-Tribune.*

"Russell, Eunice K." Texas Death Certificates, 1903–1982. Ancestry.com, 2013.

"Russell, Eunice K." Texas, Find A Grave Index, 1836–2011. Ancestry.com, 2012.

"Russell, Eunice Lucille." Texas Death Certificates, 1903–1982. Ancestry.com, 2013.

"Russell, Eunice Lucille." Texas, Find A Grave Index, 1836–2011. Ancestry.com, 2012.

"Russell, Eunice." Social Security Death Index. Ancestry.com, 2008.

"Russell, female." Texas Birth Certificates, 1903–1932. Ancestry.com, 2013.

"Russell, Louise." Texas Birth Certificates, 1903–1932. Ancestry.com, 2013.

"Russell, Louise." Texas Birth Index, 1903–1997. Ancestry.com, 2005.

"Russell, Treasure Louise." University of North Texas, Denton, Texas. US School Yearbooks. Ancestry.com, 2010.

Service of Christian Worship in Memoriam and Celebration of Frances Richards. United Methodist Church. Paducah, Texas. February 14, 1993.

"Stallings, John Russell." Obituary. *Dallas Morning News*, March 16, 2005.

Stallings, Louise R. Family Group Sheets. 1991.

"Stallings, Louise (Russell)." Obituary. *Austin American-Statesman*, April 9, 2000.

Stallings, Louise Russell. "The Unpolished Altar: The Place Of The Bay Psalm Book In America." Diss., Texas A&M University, 1977.

"Stallings, Louise (Russell)." Obituary Daily Times Index, 1995–2011. Ancestry.com, 2012.

"Stallings, Louise R." Social Security Death Index. Ancestry.com, 2008.

"Stallings, Louise Russell." US, Social Security Applications and Claims Index, 1936–2007. Ancestry.com, 2015.

"Stallings, Louise." US, Find A Grave Index, 1600s–Current. Ancestry.com, 2012.

Thompson, Betty Russell. Photo email attachment to Mary Jo Kenny. October 16, 2006.

Thompson, Betty. "Elizabeth Rookh (Betty) Russell." Undated essay.

Thompson, Betty. "Treasure Louise Russell." Undated essay.

Thompson, Betty. Email to Mary Jo Kenny. January 10, 2008.

Thompson, Betty. Email to Mary Jo Kenny. June 29, 2008.

Thompson, Betty. Email to Mary Jo Kenny. March 13, 2005.

Thompson, Betty. Email to Mary Jo Kenny. November 6, 2009.

Thompson, Betty. Letter to Mary Jo Kenny. July 28, 2001.

Rookh Kenny and Dan Richards

"Final Rites March 9 for Mrs. Richards." *The Paducah Post*, March 18, 1967.

"Kenny, Lalla Rookh, to D. E. Richards." *Erath County, Texas, Marriage Book P*, p. 68. Stephenville, TX: Erath County Courthouse.

"Richards, Dan C." 1920 US Census, Cottle County, Texas, Justice Precinct 1, ED 51-1, sheet 24A, line 11. FamilySearch Library, Salt Lake City, UT.

"Richards, Dan E." 1940 US Census, Cottle County, Texas, roll T627, p. 19A, ED 51.2. Ancestry.com, 2012.

"Richards, Dan." 1930 US Census, Cottle County, Texas, roll 2311, p. 24A, ED 1, image 2311. FamilySearch Library, Salt Lake City, UT.

"Richards, Daniel E." Texas Death Certificates, 1903–1982. Ancestry.com, 2013.

"Richards, Daniel E." Texas, Find A Grave Index, 1836–2011. Ancestry.com, 2012.

"Richards, Daniel E." World War I Draft Registration Cards, 1917–1918. Ancestry.com, 2005.

"Richards, Lalla." Texas Death Index, 1903–2000. Ancestry.com, 2006.

"Richards, Rookh K." Texas, Find A Grave Index, 1836–2011. Ancestry.com, 2012.

"Richards, Thomas J." 1910 US Census, Cottle County, Texas, Precinct 1, roll T624, p. 19A, ED 66. Ancestry.com, 2006.

Bennett, Carmen Taylor. "Richards, Mrs. T. J., Richards, Daniel E. Richards." In *Cottle County, My Dear*. Floydada, TX: Blanco Offset Printing, 1979.

Richards, Rookh. Letter to her mother. March 1995. In possession of Mary Jo Kenny.

Thompson, Betty Russell. Email attachment to Mary Jo Kenny. August 8, 2013.

Thompson, Betty Russell. Email to Mary Jo Kenny. March 11, 2013.

Leona Kenny and J. C. Davis

"Davis, Clarence." 1930 US Census, Erath County, Texas, Precinct 7, roll 2326, p. 6A, ED 20, image 473. FamilySearch Library, Salt Lake City, UT.

"Davis, James C." 1940 US Census, Tarrant County, Texas, roll m-t0627, p. 64A, ED 257-56. Ancestry.com, 2012.

"Davis, James Clarence." Texas Death Certificates, 1903–1982. Ancestry.com, 2013.

"Davis, James N." 1910 US Census, Erath County, Texas, Precinct 7, roll T624, p. 19A, ED 31. Ancestry.com, 2006.

"Davis, James." Social Security Death Index. Ancestry.com, 2008.

"Davis, Leona." 1949 Fort Worth, Texas, City Directory. US City Directories. Ancestry.com, 2011.

"Davis, Leona." Social Security Death Index. Ancestry.com, 2008.

"Davis, Leona." Texas Death Index, 1903–2000. Ancestry.com, 2006.

"Davis, Leona." US, Find A Grave Index, 1600s–Current. Ancestry.com, 2012.

"Davis, Peggy Ann, to Wm Clarke Kneer Jr." Texas, Select County Marriage Records, 1837–2015. Ancestry.com, 2014.

"Davis, Peggy." Texas Birth Certificates, 1903–1932. Ancestry.com, 2013.

"Kenny, Billie Leona, to J. Clarence Davis." *Erath County, Texas, Marriage Book P*, p. 21. Stephenville, TX: Erath County Courthouse.

Kneer, Nancy. Email to Mary Jo Kenny. October 7, 2008.

Kneer, Pat. Email to Mary Jo Kenny. October 9, 2008.

Kneer, Pat. Email to Mary Jo Kenny. October 17, 2008.

Kneer, Pat. Email to Mary Jo Kenny. October 20, 2008.

"Kneer, Peggy Ann." Texas Death Certificates, 1903–1982. Ancestry.com, 2013.

"Kneer, William C." 1940 US Census, Oklahoma County, Oklahoma, roll T627, p. 15A, ED 78-14. Ancestry.com, 2012.

"Kneer, William C." Social Security Death Index. Ancestry.com, 2008.

"Kneer, William Clark, to Jo Ann Steitle." Texas Marriage Collection, 1814–1909 and 1966–2002. Ancestry.com, 2005.

"Kneer, William Clarke, Jr." US, Find A Grave Index, 1600s–Current. Ancestry.com, 2012.

Thurber, Texas. "History: Some Misperceptions of Thurber." Accessed October 27, 2008. www.thurbertexas.com/history/misperceptions.html.

Jack Kenny and Ava Henry

1952 Yearbook. Eagle Pass High School, Eagle Pass, TX. Ancestry.com.

1958 Yearbook. University of Texas at Austin. Ancestry.com.

1972 Yearbook. R. L. Paschal High School, Fort Worth, TX. Ancestry.com.

1976 Yearbook. R. L. Paschal High School, Fort Worth, TX. Ancestry.com.

Azara, Sarah. "Sarah's Remarks for Joel." Funeral eulogy. McLean, VA. December 26, 1999.

Azzara, Sarah Kenny. Facebook profile. Accessed July 26, 2013.

"Brooks, Syble Darlene." Texas Birth Index, 1903–1997. Ancestry.com, 2005.

"Cadenhead, Elderidge." 1940 US Census, Wheeler County, Texas. Ancestry.com, 2012.

"Cadenhead, Peggy June." Texas Birth Index, 1903–1997. Ancestry.com, 2005.

"Henry, Larkin." 1920 US Census, Erath County, Texas, Precinct 5, ED 15, sheet 6A, January 26–27, 1920, family 104. FamilySearch Library, Salt Lake City, UT.

"Kenney, Wm C." Texas Department of Health, Standard Certificate of Death 46841, 1934.

Kenny, Anne Rosini. Email to Mary Jo Kenny. July 10, 2013.

"Kenny, Ava Edna Lorena." US, Find A Grave Index, 1600s–Current. Ancestry.com, 2012.

"Kenny, Ava Lorena." US, Social Security Applications and Claims Index, 1936–2007. Ancestry.com, 2015.

"Kenny, Carl Lynn." US, Find A Grave Index, 1600s–Current. Ancestry.com, 2012.

Kenny, Dan. "Danny's Remarks for Joel." Funeral eulogy. McLean, VA. December 26, 1999.

Kenny, Dan. Email to Mary Jo Kenny. October 9, 2013.

Kenny, David. "David's Remarks for Joel." Funeral eulogy. McLean, VA. December 26, 1999.

Kenny, David. Email to Mary Jo Kenny. February 12, 2006.

Kenny, David. Email to Mary Jo Kenny. July 17, 2008.

Kenny, David. Email to Mary Jo Kenny. July 7, 2013.

Kenny, David. Email to Mary Jo Kenny. October 26, 2008.

"Kenny, Dr. Mary J." US Public Records Index, vol. 1. Ancestry.com, 2010.

Kenny–Henry, newspaper clipping, undated, probably from *Stephenville Empire Tribune*, Stephenville, Texas.

"Kenny, Jack, to Ava Henry." Texas, Select County Marriage Index, 1837–1977. Ancestry.com, 2014.

"Kenny, Jack." 1930 US Census, Reagan County, Texas, Precinct 5, roll 2385, p. 6B, ED 6, image 415. FamilySearch Library, Salt Lake City, UT.

"Kenny, Jack." 1940 US Census, Erath County, Texas. Ancestry.com, 2012.

"Kenny, Jack." Texas Death Certificates, 1903–1982. Ancestry.com, 2013.

"Kenny, Jack." US, Find A Grave Index, 1600s–Current. Ancestry.com, 2012.

"Kenny, Joel S., to Deborah A. Kuker." New York, New York, Marriage License Indexes, 1907–2018. Ancestry.com, 2017.

"Kenny, Joel Strum." Texas Death Index, 1903–2000. Ancestry.com, 2006.

"Kenny, Joel Strum." US, Social Security Applications and Claims Index, 1936–2007. Ancestry.com, 2015.

"Kenny, Joel Strum." Virginia Birth Records, 1902–2014. Ancestry.com, 2015.

Kenny, Jon. "Jon's Remarks for Joel." Funeral eulogy. McLean, VA. December 26, 1999.

Kenny, Jonathan Matthew. Paper on personal background. 2013.

"Kenny, Mary Jo." Texas Birth Certificates, 1903–1932. Ancestry.com, 2013.

"Kenny, Raymond L., and Syble D." Texas Divorce Index, 1968–2011. Ancestry.com, 2005.

"Kenny, Raymond L., to Peggy J. Cadenhead." Texas Marriage Collection, 1814–1909 and 1966–2001. Ancestry.com, 2005.

"Kenny, Raymond Lee, to Syble Darlene Brooks." Texas, Select County Marriage Records, 1837–2015. Ancestry.com, 2014.

Kenny, Raymond. Letter to Mary Jo Kenny. April 4, 2013.

Kenny, Robert. Letter to Mary Jo Kenny. Postmarked London. January 14, 1958.

Kenny, Robert. Letter to Mr. and Mrs. Jack Kenny. Postmarked London. October 10, 1957.

Kenny, Robert. Letter to Mr. and Mrs. Jack Kenny. Postmarked London. November 13, 1957.

Kenny, Robert. Letter to Mr. and Mrs. Jack Kenny. Postmarked London. January 17, 1958.

Kenny, Robert. Letter to Mr. and Mrs. Jack Kenny. Postmarked London. February 11, 1958.

Kenny, Robert. Letter to Mr. and Mrs. Jack Kenny. Postmarked London. February 22, 1958.

Kenny, Robert. Manuscript editing notes. 2018.

"Kenny, Robert W., and Shirley S." UK, Incoming Passenger Lists, 1878 –1960. Ancestry.com, 2008.

"Kenny, Robert Wayne, to Shirley Elise Strum." Texas, Select County Marriage Records, 1837–2015. Ancestry.com, 2014.

"Kenny, Syble D." US, Social Security Death Index, 1935–2014. Ancestry.com, 2008.

"Kenny." Texas Birth Index, 1903–1997. Ancestry.com, 2005.

Porter, Marion S. "Jack Kenny is Named Outstanding Farmer." *Stephenville Empire-Tribune*, May 11, 1956.

Swann, Phil. "In Model Rocketry, Safety Comes First!" *Science World*, May 3, 1979.

Weathers, Sue Kenny. Letter to Mary Jo Kenny. July 6, 2013.

Weathers, Sue Kenny. Manuscript editing notes. 2018.

Willis, Sara. Email to Mary Jo Kenny. January 16, 2006.

Maurine Kenny and Byron Davis

Blocker, Dana A. Letter to Mrs. Byron Davis. April 10, 1984.

Davis, Byron. Biographical data, undated, including retirement in 1968. Typed copy in papers of Maurine Kenny Davis, in possession of Sue Weathers, Dallas, Texas.

Davis, Byron. Letters to Miss Maurine Kenny. November 17, 1929, and May 7, 1930.

"Davis, Byron." 1940 US Census, Grayson County, Texas. Ancestry.com, 2012.

"Davis, Byron." Social Security Death Index. Ancestry.com, 2008.

"Davis, Byron." US, Department of Veterans Affairs BIRLS Death File, 1850. Ancestry.com, 2011.

"Davis, James F." 1910 US Census, Collin County, Texas. Ancestry.com, 2006.

"Davis, Maurine." US, Find A Grave Index, 1600s–current. Ancestry.com, 2012.

"Ex-Sherman schools superintendent dies." *Sherman Democrat*, April 1984.

"Golf Cart Given Retiring Educator." *Sherman Democrat*, May 9, 1968.

Kenny, Maurine. *A Story of My Life*. Essay prepared for unnamed course. Tarleton College, Stephenville, TX, 1924.

"Kenny, Maurine." Vocational Home Economics Teacher's Certificate of Approval. The State Board for Vocational Education, State of Texas, May 28, 1930.

"Kenny, Miss Mary Maurine." Teachers Permanent Special Certificate. The Department of Education, State of Texas, January 6, 1930.

"Kenny, Miss Maurine." Teachers Permanent Certificate. The Department of Education, State of Texas, May 29, 1929.

"Marriage of Maurine Kenny and Byron Solemnized." Undated newspaper clipping, probably from *Stephenville Empire-Tribune*, Stephenville, TX. In scrapbook of Fannie Clark Kenny.

"Violet Fanciers Receive Awards." *Sherman Democrat*, April 6, 1976.

Weathers, Sue Kenny. Letter to Mary Jo Kenny. 2013.

Weathers, Sue Kenny. Manuscript editing notes. 2018.

Florence Belle Kenny
(4 Feb 1866–31 Dec 1947)

Born in Tennessee Colony, Anderson County, Texas, Florence was thirteen when the family moved to Erath County. She had no more than one additional year of school before reaching the highest grade offered by the Berlin Hall (later renamed Hannibal) school. She continued her education informally, and her granddaughter Fern described her as an avid reader who was well informed on many topics. Like her sisters, Florence was small in stature.

On August 5, 1885, Florence married Henry Thornton (9 Sep 1865–29 Sep 1930) in Berlin Hall, Erath County, Texas, with J. C. Freeman, MG, officiating. Henry was the son of Daniel Robert Thornton and Mary Anna Garland, one of the first settlers in northern Erath County. When the Thorntons first settled in the area in 1857, their nearest neighbors were eighteen miles away in Stephenville. They moved back to Anderson County during the Civil War. Daniel enlisted in the Thirteenth Regimental Calvary in 1862 and served in the Confederate army. He was captured and held at Camp Douglas, Chicago, until he was exchanged. After the Civil War, Daniel, Mary Anna, and their children returned to Erath County, where Henry was born.

Soon after their marriage, Florence and Henry moved to Reeves County, Texas, which had recently been opened to settlement after the removal of the Apache Indians and the building of a railroad through the area. They were probably accompanied on this trip by Florence's brother Will, who spent some time as a cowboy at a ranch in the Davis Mountains about this time. When they arrived in Reeves County, the town of Pecos had a three-room school, a post office, and 150 residents. The area grew rapidly, with Pecos expanding to 1,247 residents in the next five years. After about a decade in the Reeves County area, the birth of three children, and the death of one, Florence and Henry returned to Erath County, where both of their families lived. The 1900 census shows them in the Hannibal area operating a farm adjacent to the farm of William and Jackie Thornton, Henry's brother and Florence's sister. In addition to their own children, sixteen-year-old William Kay, possibly a family friend, was boarding with them and attending school. By 1910, they had moved closer to Stephenville but were still engaged in farming. Their children living at home in 1900 were Allyne, Tom, Minnie, Vera, and Wylie.

The 1920 census shows Florence and Henry living in Stephenville and sharing a dwelling with Tom and Allyne Bridges and their young son. Undoubtedly Florence was a help to Allyne in coping with the death of two young sons over the previous few years. Only Minnie of Florence and Henry's children was at home, but Odie and Vera lived nearby in Stephenville. Henry was listed as city marshal, but during the past decade, he had also worked as city clerk in Stephenville. In 1920, they moved to Breckenridge, Texas, where Henry became a member of the police force and was elected sheriff in 1924. He was reelected as sheriff in 1926 and 1928; he had a reputation for honesty and sincerity and was well respected by other law enforcement officers. Residence facilities were provided for the sheriff in the building housing the jail. While Henry was sheriff, Florence cooked for staff and detainees in the jail. Henry was unable to complete his third term because he developed cancer. His declining health caused him to resign as sheriff in the fall of 1929. The 1930 census shows the family in Breckenridge, on Walker Street. In addition to Florence, Henry's brother Tump and Florence's sister Kate Kenny Clark were in the household. The latter two were probably there to help care for the ailing Henry. Henry died in a hospital in McKinney, Texas. Funeral services were held at the Breckenridge First Methodist Church, where he and Florence were members. The burial was in Breckenridge Cemetery. Henry was a member of a Masonic lodge, as indicated by an emblem on his grave marker.

After Henry's death, Florence lived with her son Odie and daughter Vera in Fort Worth, Texas. The 1940 census shows her in Odie's home. Florence died in Fort Worth at age eighty-one. Funeral services were held at the Harveson-Cole Chapel, and she was buried in Breckenridge Cemetery.

Descendants of Florence Belle Kenny and Henry Thornton

Clytie C. Thornton
(27 Mar 1886–22 May 1886)

Clytie was born, died, and was buried in Reeves County, Texas.

Odie Thurman Thornton
(2 Nov 1888–19 Feb 1956)

Odie Thornton was born in Reeves County, Texas, but most of his early school years were at Hannibal. The move to the Stephenville area provided additional educational opportunities. He and Clara May Gibson (27 Apr 1890–Apr 1936) were married on September 22, 1909. Clara was the daughter of Marcus and Lula Gibson of Hamilton County, Texas. The 1910 census shows Odie and Clara living in Precinct 7 of Erath County and engaged in farming. Living with them was sixty-eight-year-old Marjory Roby, identified as a grandmother. In addition to farming, family tradition indicated that Odie taught school before working with the US Post Office. On June 5, 1917, Odie registered for the World War I draft in Stephenville, Texas. At that time, he worked for the US Post Office and had a wife and two children. He was described as short and slender, with gray eyes and black hair.

By 1920, he, Clara, and their children—Willie, Wayne, and Ruth—were living on Tarleton Street in Stephenville. Odie was working as a rural mail carrier. By 1922, they had moved to Fort Worth, as shown by the 1922 Fort Worth City Directory. The 1930 census shows them living in Tarrant County, Texas, with Odie working as a special clerk in the US Post Office. Their three children were at home, and Odie's sister Vera was also living with them. Over the next few years, Clara developed cervical cancer, and Vera helped care for Clara and the family, especially Ruth, who was a teenager. After cancer surgery, Clara died in 1936 in Fort Worth, Tarrant County, Texas. By 1940, Odie had continued working in the downtown Fort Worth post office. Vera and Florence were living with Odie on Gambrell Street in Fort Worth. According to Odie's granddaughter Ruth Ann, the Gambrell Street house, located across the street from the Gambrell Street Baptist Church, was a three-bedroom brick-trimmed frame house. The 1940 census shows the house with a value of $1,800.

Odie retired after thirty-seven years at the post office. His coworkers awarded him a radio and an electric razor in a retirement ceremony at the post office. After retirement, Odie doted on his grandchildren, who called him "Pop," and on his black Scottish terrier named Troubles. Ruth remembers him as quiet, wearing glasses, and bald on top with a fringe of white hair. He usually had a pipe or cigar, and his clothes carried a perpetual odor of tobacco smoke. After Florence's death in 1947, Vera continued to live with her brother until Odie's death in 1956. He died in Fort Worth from a stroke and was buried in Greenwood Cemetery in Fort Worth.

- **Willie Hansel Thornton (5 Sep 1910–11 Sep 1983):** Bill, as he was known, was born in Erath County, Texas. At nineteen, he was working as an office boy for the Nash Hardware Store in Fort Worth. Bill met his future wife, Mary Pauline Marlow (9 Jan 1918–28 Oct 1998), through actually bumping into her while both were walking in front of the Baptist church across the street from Bill's home. Pauline was studying vocal music at the nearby Southwestern Baptist Theological Seminary. They were married on October 19, 1939, at the Bellmead, Texas, home of her parents, Fred L. Marlow and Nina May Shroyer. In 1940 Bill and Pauline were living in a rented facility on Gambrell Street in Fort Worth. Virginia Smith, a bookstore employee, was a lodger.

  Bill continued working for the Nash store, except for his time in the US Army during World War II. He worked initially as a toy-and-cookware salesman, then as a sales manager until the store closed. His army service was as a clerk typist stationed at various bases in the United States, mostly on the East Coast. When he returned home after discharge, he was a stranger engendering suspicion in his young daughter Ruth, who had seen only photographs of her father. The family lived with Bill's father, Odie, after the war until they could acquire their own home in a very competitive housing market. Their first house, purchased while still under construction, was on Frazier Street in a development of two blocks of similar brick homes within a community of smaller frame houses. The new homes were not only larger but better in many respects than most of the surrounding homes. However, the kitchens were small, and the lack of central heating and air-conditioning made installing floor furnaces and swamp-type window air conditioners a priority for comfort within the first few years in the house.

Bill's work for Nash had required extensive travel. He was frequently away from home during the time his children were young. After the Nash store closed around 1962, Bill was a sales representative for a Houston firm that sold water hoses and fireplace fixtures. While working for Nash, he drove a company car, and only after he left that job did the family buy their first car, purchased from Bill's brother, Wayne.

Bill's daughter Ruth Ann indicated that Bill had black hair but fair skin that sunburned easily. She described him as thoughtful, kind, and religious. He was always polite, somewhat formal, and very strict on etiquette. Bill enjoyed telling jokes and outdoor cooking, especially hamburgers. In the summer the hamburgers were usually accompanied by Pauline's homemade peach ice cream. Bill and Pauline were members of the Gambrell Street Baptist Church, and Bill was a member of a Masonic lodge. Pauline worked as a salesclerk in a Stripling and Cox department store. She sang in the church choir and taught Sunday school. Bill died from a stroke in Dallas, Texas. Pauline survived him fifteen years; she died in Fort Worth, Texas. Both were buried in Greenwood Memorial Park in Fort Worth.

- **Ruth Ann Thornton (8 May 1943–):** Ruth Ann was born in Fort Worth, Tarrant County, Texas. She was always called Ruth Ann within the family to distinguish her from her aunt Ruth. As a child Ruth Ann was small for her age and had difficulty meeting her father's standards for proper sitting behavior at the dining table. His enforcement of these standards with swats of his belt caused considerable resentment. After completing elementary school, Ruth Ann attended Rosemont Junior High School, where one of her father's church friends was principal. She would have preferred the school her friends were attending.

On May 30, 1957, Ruth Ann married Wayne Odell Rosenthal (20 Nov 1939–). When she and Wayne approached her parents with their intent to marry, she expected strong objections because they were so young. Instead, they were told only to wait until they finished the school year. Ruth Ann and Wayne are the parents of three children, Karen, Kellie, and Doug. They have six grandchildren and three great-grandchildren. They lived in Alvarado and Fort Worth, Texas. Ruth Ann earned an associate in arts from Tarrant County Junior College, a BS in biology from the University of Texas at Arlington, and an MS in biology from Texas Christian University. She worked at Johnson & Johnson and at Alcon Laboratories as a pharmaceutical microbiologist. She is the author of numerous papers and presentations on pharmaceuticals. A number of her papers reported research on contact lens solutions and eye lubricants. Her interest in pharmaceuticals for the eye may have been influenced by her experience of having a severe oil gland cyst under her eye, which required surgery when she was an early teenager.

- **Karen Anne Rosenthal (18 Nov 1960–):** Karen was born and grew up in Tarrant County, Texas. She married Edward C. Clendennen on June 13, 1981, in Tarrant County, Texas. The marriage ended in divorce. Her second marriage was to Jim Murry. Her and Edward's daughter is Crystal Anne Clendennen (16 Dec 1981–).

- **Kellie Jean Rosenthal (17 Feb 1962–):** Kellie was born in Dallas, Texas. She married Wesley Don Hayley on December 8, 1979, in Tarrant County, Texas. They were divorced on August 7, 1986. Kellie married Roger A. Griffin on June 4, 1988, in Tarrant County, Texas, a marriage that ended in a divorce granted February 8, 1994. Kellie then married Larry R. Bushwar on June 26, 1998, in Parker County, Texas; the marriage ended in divorce.

  The children of Kellie and Wesley are Joanna Denise (20 Jul 1980–), Wesley Don (17 Jan 1982–), and David Allen (17 Sep 1983–).

- **Douglas Wayne Rosenthal (6 Mar 1963–):** Born in Tarrant County, Texas, Douglas married Rhonda Little on September 16, 1989, in Dallas, Texas. Their children, Meridith Kay (4 Feb 1992–) and Lauren Nicole (19 Mar 1995–), were both born in Tarrant County, Texas.

- **Pamela Gail Thornton (9 Feb 1948–):** Pamela Gail married Gary Don Ogburn (15 Aug 1948–) on March 27, 1968. Gary Don made a career of the air force, and the family lived in a number of places, including Fort Worth, Louisiana, Hawaii, and Montana. Pamela enjoyed being a homemaker and a great cook. After her marriage to Gary ended in divorce in 1995 in Harris County, she worked in several positions, including as an administrative assistant for the UNT Health Science Center. Pamela and Pat McKinley were married on November 3, 2001, in Tarrant County, Texas. They reside in Plano, Texas.

  - **Gail Lynn Ogburn (21 Jul 1971–):** Gail was born in Harris County, Texas. She married Paul D. Weber on March 9, 1991, in Tarrant County, Texas. Paul is a career member of the US Air Force, while Lynn is a full-time homemaker and mother and part-time website designer.

  - **Amy J. Ogburn (16 Jul 1977–):** Amy married John D. Shamburger on March 16, 2001, in Tarrant County, Texas.

  - **Willie Hansel Thornton Jr. (7 Mar 1956–):** Hansel, or Hans, was born in Tarrant County, Texas. He married Karen Quarles on July 8, 1989, in

Tarrant County, Texas. Hans and Karen lived at 4725 Darla Drive and on Trevino Lane in Fort Worth. Hans sells oil machinery tools internationally. Their children are Andrew Hansel and Dwight Henry.

- **Wayne Preston Thornton (26 Aug 1914–16 Apr 2002):** Born in Stephenville, Erath County, Texas, Wayne was living at 1513 Gambrell Street in Fort Worth, Texas, in 1936 when he applied for Social Security. He worked for Frank Kent Motor Company of 1101 W. Seventh Street in Fort Worth. Wayne married Alice Lavinia Cushing (9 Jan 1920–15 Mar 2003) in McLennan County, Texas. Alice was the daughter of J. B. Cushing and Effie Crawford. Wayne continued to work for the Frank Kent Motor Company for a number of years and especially enjoyed selling Cadillac cars. He served in the armed forces in World War II, attaining the rank of first lieutenant. He permanently injured his hands while in service. His injuries required an extended hospital stay at the end of the war. After his hospital stay, Wayne, Alice, and their infant, Mike, moved into the house next door to Bill and Pauline on Frazier Street in Fort Worth. Wayne returned to work for Frank Kent Motor Company, which relocated to the north side of Fort Worth, near the stockyards. After several years in Fort Worth, they moved to California, where Alice's family lived. Wayne died in Lake Havasu City, Mohave County, Arizona; Alice died in California the next year.

    - **Wayne Michael Thornton (16 Mar 1944–):** Born in Tarrant County, Texas, Wayne spent most of his life in California.

    - **Jon David Thornton (5 Jun 1949–5 Sep 1992):** Though he was born in Tarrant County, Texas, Jon David primarily lived in California. He died in Orange County, California.

- **Mary Ruth Thornton (17 Apr 1918–17 May 2003):** Ruth was born in Erath County, Texas. She was an early teenager when her mother was stricken with cancer. Her aunt Vera assumed much of her care. Ruth made a strong impression on her niece Ruth Ann. In her memoirs, Ruth Ann wrote:

    My aunt Ruth had a big influence on my life and was a role model for me. While my mom and dad had no college degree, Ruth had a master's degree in English. She was a schoolteacher and taught reading in a special education program. She was intelligent and took a genuine interest in me. She always made me feel like an intelligent and an important person.

    Ruth married Lawson Hubert Pritchett Jr., who served as a chaplain in the US Army. Lawson was born in Waco, Texas. His mother died when he was about two, and he grew up in the homes of various relatives. Ruth and Lawson moved to Colorado and are shown in a census in Colorado Springs in 1955. For a number of years, they lived in Denver, Colorado, where Ruth was a teacher specializing in reading. Records from 1981 and 1993 show them living in Northglenn, Colorado. Ruth developed severe osteoporosis and died from its complications in Denver. Lawson survived her only a few months, until February 2, 2004. Both were buried in Fort Logan National Cemetery, Section 21. They had two children, Diane and Nancy.

Henry Clayton Thornton
(24 Sep 1890–17 May 1968)

Born in Pecos, Reeves County, Henry Clayton Thornton, known as Clay, was young when the family moved back to Erath County. He attended schools in Erath County and married Lester Lee Sechrist (24 May 1891–11 Mar 1964), daughter of William Lindsay Sechrist and Ella Frances Davis, on January 12, 1909. Lester Lee was born in Santo, Palo Pinto County, Texas. The 1910 census shows Clay, Lester, and their infant, Lindsay, living in the Hannibal community, adjacent to Lester's parents, and engaged in farming. When Clay registered for the World War I draft in 1917, the family was living in Lubbock, Texas. He was working as a janitor for Lubbock County. His dependents were a wife and three children. He described himself as short, with a medium build, gray eyes, and black hair. A noted disability was an infection in one eye. The family has not been located on the 1920 census, but the youngest son, Melvin Lee, is listed as born in 1920 in Terry County, Texas.

The 1930 census shows the family in Littlefield, Lamb County, Texas, operating a café. The café was started, probably in the early 1920s, as a hamburger place on Main Street. Later it was expanded to a café with varied offerings. The café became known for its chicken-fried steak, and many people considered it to be the best place to eat in Littlefield. The café was a family operation with many family members working there. Lester made the bread and desserts, and the 1930 census shows Lindsay working as a waiter. Clay's brother Wylie is shown as a cook in a café on the 1930 census, and it is likely he worked in Clay's café. By 1940, Clay had sold the café to his son Lindsay, who converted it into a cafeteria. Clay worked as a newspaper agent and operated a domino hall adjacent to the cafeteria. Locals gathered to play dominoes, trade stories, and discuss politics and current events. On Sundays, when the domino hall was closed, the grandchildren were allowed to play in the domino hall. Lester continued to make bread and desserts for the cafeteria until a fall and broken leg made that impossible. She died in Littlefield from a blood clot resulting from the broken leg and was buried in Littlefield Memorial Park. Clay died four years later at the home of his son Melvin, in San Antonio, Texas.

- **Lawrence Lindsay Thornton (25 Dec 1909–6 Dec 2004):** Lindsay was known as "Brother" in the family. He was born in Hannibal, Erath County, Texas, but the family left there when he was a young child. He graduated from Littlefield High School. He and Winifred Cleo Johnston (29 Jan 1913–26 Sep 2006) were married on February

17, 1932, in Clovis, New Mexico. Winifred was born in Chriesman, Burleson County, Texas. She and her mother are shown on the 1920 and 1930 censuses in the home of her stepfather, William H. Willis, in Littlefield. She attended Littlefield High School, where she was an outstanding tennis player. Lindsay worked with his father in the Littlefield café, starting as a waiter and gradually assuming greater responsibilities until he purchased the café and converted it into the Thornton Cafeteria. Winifred worked as a cashier for the cafeteria. They operated the cafeteria for thirty-eight years.

Lindsay was noted for his interest in Western lore and his ability to tell Western stories. His niece Linda Gayle compared him to J. Frank Dobie in his Western storytelling abilities. He also developed an impressive arrowhead collection. After retiring and selling the cafeteria in the 1980s, Lindsay and Winifred moved to Eagle Lake. They spent several summers at Fun Valley Resort in Colorado. Lindsay worked as head chef and Winifred as hostess for the resort. Their winters were spent in McAllen, Texas. Later, they moved to Granbury, Texas, where their older daughter lived. They were members of the Methodist church there. Lindsay died in Granbury at age ninety-four. Winifred survived him, as did their daughter Joan, her husband, their six grandchildren, and their eight great-grandchildren. Winifred died in Granbury two years later.

- **Fern Joan Thornton (5 Feb 1933–15 Mar 2013):** Joan was born in Littlefield, Lamb County, Texas. She married John Paul Jones (27 Apr 1928–11 Aug 2007) on March 27, 1952, in Lubbock, Texas. John, a native of Booneville, Arkansas, and Joan were both educators. In 1977 she was teaching in Anton, Texas, and John was superintendent of the Anton schools. They later moved to Granbury, Texas, where they were living in 2004.

  - **Randall Paul Jones (9 Apr 1953–):** Randy was born in El Paso, Texas. He married Cheryl Lee Childers on August 27, 1977, in Lubbock, Texas. Their son, Anthony Paul, was born on July 28, 1981, in Lubbock, Texas. They were divorced on September 24, 1985.

  - **Michelle Ann Jones (30 Nov 1955–):** Michelle was born in Hale County, Texas. She married Dean W. Blaine on June 16, 1979, in Lubbock, Texas.

  - **Rex Lindsay Jones (18 Nov 1958–):** Like his sister, Rex was born in Hale County, Texas.

- **Sharon Jean Thornton (25 Jan 1941–6 May 1999):** Sharon was born in Littlefield, Texas. She married Ernest Leroy Scott in 1962. The marriage ended in divorce, granted August 21, 1970. She married Joe Don Beavers, a native of Littlefield, Texas, in 1975. They were divorced on September 2, 1980, in Swisher County, Texas. She married Michael D. Clinton on April 25, 1986, but the marriage ended in divorce in 1988. Both the marriage and divorce were in Swisher

County. Sharon died in Lufkin, Angelina County, Texas, and was buried in Lufkin.

- **Tami Sue Scott (2 Oct 1963–):** Tami Sue was born in Lubbock, Texas. She married Michael Dylan Sandlin on June 27, 1981, in Lubbock, Texas.

    - **Michael Dylan (13 Mar 1994–).**

- **Lindsay Paul Scott (22 Jan 1966–):** Lindsay Paul was born in Lubbock, Texas. He married Susan E. Hughes on June 24, 2000, in Angelina County, Texas.

- **Joe Dee Beavers (22 Sep 1975–):** Joe Dee was born in Littlefield, Texas. He married Kristen R. Parker on October 18, 2008, in Potter County, Texas.

- **Artie Thomas Beavers (8 Aug 1977–):** Born in Lamb County, Texas, Artie lived in Amarillo and Happy, Texas.

- **Olena Fern Thornton (8 Sep 1912–25 Aug 2005):** Fern was born in Stephenville, Erath County, Texas. She married Emil Harold Timian (9 Dec 1909–10 Jan 1991) on March 3, 1935, in Clovis, New Mexico. Emil was born in Dresden, North Dakota, and died in Galveston, Texas. Lubbock, Texas, was home for Fern and Emil for forty-three years. Fern was a civilian employee of Reese Air Force Base, and Emil worked in several departments of the city of Lubbock. Both were charter members of the Redeemer Lutheran Church of Lubbock. Upon retirement, they moved to Texas City, then to Jamaica Beach on Galveston Island. After Emil's death in 1991, Fern moved first to Edgewood Retirement in Galveston and later to the Terrace in Sugar Land, Texas. Fern enjoyed playing bridge and was active in a number of community organizations as well as church activities. She played a major role in organizing the 1977 Thornton reunion. When deteriorating health restricted her activities, she moved to the Vosswood Nursing Center in Houston, Texas. It was there that she died, just two weeks before her ninety-third birthday. Both of her daughters and her oldest granddaughter were with her at her death. She was buried in Lubbock Cemetery, with her grandsons serving as pallbearers.

    - **Linda Gale Timian (27 Jan 1940–):** Linda Gale was born in Littlefield, Texas. She married Rev. Melvin Glyn Herring (7 Jan 1933–14 May 2011) in Lubbock, Texas. Melvin was born to Tullie Herring and Clara Lambert. A Lutheran minister, Melvin served in churches in Texas and California for over fifty years. Melvin died in Houston, Texas. Linda survived him and lives in Houston.

        - **Leigh Gayle Herring (15 Aug 1962–):** Leigh Gayle was born in Lamesa, Dawson County, Texas. She married Craig H. Novelli on April 4, 1987, in Galveston, Texas. They lived in Longview, Dickinson, and Webster, Texas. The marriage ended in divorce. Leigh married Carlo Carreon on May 13, 2000, in Harris County, Texas. They reside in the Woodlands, Texas, with their children, Megan, Emily, Elizabeth, and Christian.

- **Mark Glyn Herring (4 Dec 1964–):** Mark was born in Lamesa, Dawson County, Texas. He married Sheila B. Froelick on March 31, 1990, in Collin County, Texas. They were divorced in 1994 in Nueces, Texas. He and his second wife, Jacqueline, live in Modesto, California, with their children, Andrew and Alicia.

- **Sarah Beth Herring (5 Sep 1969–):** Sarah Beth was born in Pampa, Gray County, Texas. She married Mark Alan Claburn on July 18, 1998, in Dallas, Texas. Mark was born on January 7, 1969, in Ward County, Texas, to Charles Claburn and Ruby Joyce Torrans. Mark and Sarah live in Mansfield, Texas, with their children, Jacob and Kathleen.

- **Rachel Ruth Herring (14 Jan 1972–):** Rachel was born in Pampa, Gray County, Texas. She married John S. Brownlee on May 22, 1999, in Dallas, Texas. They live in Lucas, Texas, with their children, Alexandra and Allison.

- **Janice Karen Timian (18 Feb 1943–):** A native of El Paso, Texas, Janice married Dale Roger Stohlman (30 Mar 1942–) on August 1, 1964, in Lubbock, Texas. Dale was born in Harris County, Texas, to Wallace Dale Stohlman and Clara Irene Wiede. Janice and Dale have lived in Galveston, Jamacia Beach, and Houston, Texas.

  - **Kevin Dale Stohlman (22 Aug 1966–):** Born in Dallas, Texas, Kevin Dale has lived in Galveston and Houston, Texas.

  - **Tony Andrew Stohlman (1 Oct 1968–):** Tony was born in Ponca City, Oklahoma. He; his wife, Theresa; and their son, Taylor, live in League City, California.

- **Ernest Dean Thornton (14 Jun 1915–3 Jan 1985):** Dean was born in Stephenville, Erath County, Texas. He married Claire Marie Mask (13 Jan 1915–21 Jul 2001) on April 29, 1938, in Archer City, Texas. Claire Marie was born in Whitt, Parker County, Texas. Her parents were William Thomas Mask and Virginia Allene McClendon. Dean and Claire lived in Littlefield, Texas, through 1935, but by 1940 they were living in a rented house on West Pearl Street in Odessa, Ector County, Texas. Dean was working as a bookkeeper for a trucking company. The 1960 Midland, Texas, City Directory lists Dean Thornton and Marie E., with Dean working as an accountant for Blount Drilling

Company. Dean died in Denison, Grayson County, Texas. Claire Marie died sixteen years later in Austin, Texas.

- **Terrance Dean "Terry" Thornton (11 Oct 1940–):** Terry was born in Littlefield, Texas. He married Sandra Cecille Nobles (22 Dec 1943–) on August 15, 1964, in Austin, Texas, Sandra's birthplace and home. They were divorced in 1987 in Williamson County, Texas.

  - **Stephen Lance Thornton (11 Dec 1966–):** Stephen was born in Dallas, Texas. He married Laura Denise Neighbors (22 Apr 1970–) on April 7, 2001, in Travis County, Texas. Laura was born in Fannin County, Texas, to Frank Ewing Neighbors Jr. and Linda Sue Henin.

  - **Michael Trey Thornton (23 Dec 1969–):** Austin, Texas, was Michael's birthplace and the location of his marriage to Angela P. Goldsby on February 21, 1998.

  - **Christopher Chad Thornton (5 Nov 1973–):** Christopher was born in Austin, Texas. He married Shelly R. Cox on February 14, 2001, in Travis County, Texas.

- **Monte Randall Thornton (27 Aug 1947–24 Feb 1991):** Monte was born in Velasco, Brazoria County, Texas. He married Lora Jane Ellard (12 Nov 1954–) in Travis County, Texas. Lora Jane was born in Dallas, Texas, to John Ernest Ellard and Betty Lou West. Monte Randall died in Austin, Travis County, Texas, at age forty-three. His and Lora Jane's children, Cory Randall (27 Oct 1984–) and Ginny Marie (1 Apr 1988), were both born in Travis County.

- **Linnie Bea Thornton (27 Jun 1917–28 Jan 2016):** A native of Lubbock, Texas, Linnie married Robert Pierce "Bob" Alguire (3 Mar 1917–9 Apr 1993) on July 19, 1936, in Clovis, New Mexico. Bob, son of George Burton Alguire and Bessie Tye, was born in Chickasha, Oklahoma. They lived in Littlefield, Texas, the first few years of their marriage. By 1940 they had moved to Oklahoma—the census shows them living in Oklahoma City, with Robert working as a salesman in a retail store. The Oklahoma City Directory identifies the store as the John A. Brown Co. They later lived in Winnsboro and Dallas, Texas. Both Bob and Linnie died in Dallas, Texas.

  - **Robert Thornton Alguire (5 Aug 1937–6 Jun 2015):** Robert was born in Littlefield, Texas. He married Michell Kay Wintersmith (May 1939–) on April 3, 1958, in Duncan, Oklahoma. Born in Oklahoma City, Oklahoma, Michell graduated from Saint Mary's Hall, Faribault, Minnesota, and attended the University of Oklahoma. Robert graduated from the University of Oklahoma in 1960 with a bachelor's degree in engineering and a commission as second lieutenant in the US Army. His service included three years in Germany. At the end of his enlistment, he returned to the University of Oklahoma, where he earned MS and PhD degrees. He became a member of the engineering faculty at the University of Arkansas at Fayetteville. Robert died in Fayetteville, Arkansas.

- **Christopher Kay Alguire (12 May 1961–):** Born in Stuttgart, Germany, Christopher attended the University of Texas at Austin. He was living in Austin at the time of his father's death.

- **James Robert Alguire (9 Nov 1962–):** James was born in Augsburg, Germany.

- **Ann Courtney Alguire (23 Feb 1965–):** Ann was born in Norman, Oklahoma. Ann married Thomas Weaver.

- **Gwynne Alguire:** Gwynne married Patrick Darden. They lived in Athens, Georgia.

- **Richard Keith Alguire (4 Nov 1939–):** Born in Littlefield, Texas, Richard graduated from Yale University and studied law at the University of Texas. He worked as comptroller for Jitco Company in Rockville, Maryland. Richard married Carolyn Barrie Teague on December 28, 1963, in Fort Worth, Texas. They lived in Germantown, Maryland; Hopewell, New York; and Arlington and Dallas, Texas. Richard and Carolyn were divorced in 1990 in Tarrant County, Texas.

  - **Richard Keith Alguire Jr. (5 Sep 1966–):** Richard was born in Dallas, Texas.

  - **Katherine Elizabeth Alguire (25 Apr 1969–):** Katherine was born in Austin, Texas.

  - **Timothy Thornton Alguire (16 Jul 1974–):** Timothy was born in Bethesda, Maryland. He married Elaine A. Hosek in Tarrant County, Texas, on November 6, 1999.

- **Judith Kay Alguire (16 Sep 1941–):** Born in Oklahoma City, Oklahoma, Judith attended the University of Oklahoma and Abilene Christian College. Judith married James McDonald Williams (22 Jul 1940–) on September 4, 1960, in Roswell, Chaves County, New Mexico. James was born in Roswell, New Mexico. He graduated from George Washington Law School, where he was editor of the *Law Review* his senior year. He became a partner in Trammell Crow Company in Dallas, Texas.

  - **Bryce Alguire Williams (4 Dec 1963–):** Bryce was born in Fairfax, Virginia. He married Leigh C. Canning (19 Dec 1965–) in McLennan

County, Texas, on May 30, 1987. Leigh was born in McLennan County to Lawrence Carroll Canning and Rebecca Alice Dawson. Their children, Dawson McDonald (7 Dec 1991–) and Brennon Thornton (7 Aug 1994–), were born in Dallas, Texas.

- **Brandon McDonald Williams (22 May 1967–):** Born in Dallas, Texas, Brandon graduated from Highland Park High School and Pepperdine University. He joined the US Navy and became an officer in the US Navy Submarine Force. On September 26, 1992, Brandon married Stephanie Paige McRee in the New Post Chapel, Fort Sill, Oklahoma. Stephanie is the daughter of Colonel and Mrs. Marshall McRee.

- **Russ Thornton Williams (5 Aug 1970–):** Russ was born in Dallas, Texas. On August 7, 1993, he and Carrie E. Brewington (28 Feb 1971–) were married at Walnut Street Church of Christ in Texarkana, Bowie County, Texas. Carol was born in Bowie County to Robert Michael Brewington and Margaret Gayle Reed. She graduated from Abilene Christian University with a degree in biology. Russ studied international business at Abilene Christian University.

- **Victor Tye Williams (28 Feb 1972–):** Victor was born in Dallas, Texas.

- **Susannah Elaine Williams (14 Feb 1975–):** Susannah was born in Dallas, Texas. She married Brandon L. Hoag on May 13, 1995, in Taylor, Texas.

- **Monte Louise Thornton (8 Feb 1920–9 Sep 1986):** Louise was born in Lubbock, Texas, which was also the location of her wedding to John Wesley Wilson (28 Aug 1917–7 Aug 1964) on February 27, 1940. John was born in Mingus, Texas, to John Wesley Wilson Jr. and Dotsy May Rogers. The 1940 census shows John and Louise living in Lubbock, Texas. Neither are listed with an occupation; Louise was listed as living in Artesia, New Mexico, in 1935, while John lived in Wink, Winkler County, Texas. Lubbock City Directories show John working as a photographer for the *Avalanche-Journal*. John enlisted in the air corps on February 22, 1943. Louise and their two children made a trip to Germany in 1955, returning from Bremerhaven, Germany, on the *General Alexander M. Patch*. John died at the Veterans Administration Hospital in Big Springs, Texas, from acute pneumonia after gastric surgery for an ulcer. Louise survived him twenty-two years. Lubbock City Directories show her working as a draftsman.

  - **Lyleon Jan Wilson (15 May 1941–):** Lyleon was born in Littlefield, Texas. She married Bobby Neal Vasek on May 13, 1961. Bobby Neal (1939–29 Jul 1985) was born in Jones County, Texas, to Jim Vasek and Bertha Lammert. Bobby was the author of the book *Speaking in Tongues–Psychologically Considered*, which was published in 1973 by Concordia Theological Seminary of Springfield, Illinois. Bobby Neal died in Potter County, Texas. Lyleon lived in Irvine, California, and Austin and Lubbock, Texas.

- **Michal Denise Vasek (4 Apr 1962–):** Michal was born in San Antonio, Bexar County, Texas. She married Roscoe A. White on May 29, 1982, in Lamar, Texas. They were divorced on February 24, 2005, in Lubbock, Texas. Michal has lived in Lubbock and Midland, Texas. Their children were Meghan Gwyneth (16 May 1985–), Ashley Lauren (7 Jan 1989–), and Ryann Courtney (9 Apr 1990–).

- **Laurel Lee Vasek (30 Dec 1969–):** Laurel lived in Lubbock, Texas, and Corona and Santa Barbara, California. She married Greig Griffin.

- **Andrew James Vasek (13 Oct 1974–):** Public records show Andrew living in Austin and Lubbock, Texas.

- **Christopher Neal Vasek (13 Oct 1974–):** Public records show Christopher living in Austin, Texas.

- **Daniel Clay Vasek (8 Oct 1976–):** Daniel lived in Austin, Denton, and Round Rock, Texas. He married Abigail S. Staples on May 23, 2009, in Hays County, Texas.

- **Jon Wesley Wilson (13 May 1942–1 Jun 1988):** Jon was born in Littlefield, Texas. He entered the US Marine Corps on July 25, 1961. He earned the rank of private first class. Jon married Sharon K. Hedden on December 27, 1963. They resided in Houston, Texas, where Jon died. He was buried in Houston National Cemetery, Section K.

  - **Charles Hedden Wilson (5 Mar 1967–):** Charles was born in Oklahoma City, Oklahoma. He married Amber K. Knowles on October 9, 1998, in Harris County, Texas.

  - **Christina Louise Wilson (23 Sep 1971–):** Christina was born in Harris County, Texas. She married Anton M. Mawhood in Harris County, Texas, on May 30, 1991. Both of their children, Ashton Morgan (24 Feb 1990–) and Keaton Ross (15 Jul 1993–), were born in Harris County. Christina and Anton resided in Houston until their divorce in 2008 in Harris County.

- **Melvin Lee Thornton (28 Jun 1922–24 Dec 1985):** Melvin Lee was born in Brownfield, Terry County, Texas. He obtained a bachelor's degree at Texas Tech University and graduated from the University of Texas Medical School in Galveston. He did his medical internship in Denver, Colorado. While in Colorado, he learned to ski and enjoyed skiing vacations. Melvin married Marguerite Geraldine Straughan (27 Dec 1926–) on September 27, 1947, in San Antonio, Texas. Marguerite was born in Bexar County, Texas, to Dwight F. Straughan and Margaret Haye. Melvin established a medical practice in San Antonio. He died in San Antonio.

- **Cyndea Marie "Cindy" Thornton (12 Oct 1949–):** Cindy attended the University of Texas at Austin. On August 12, 1972, Cindy married Robert Stewart "Bobby" Peacock (31 Aug 1948–) at Saint Peter Catholic Church of San Antonio, Texas. Bobby was born in San Antonio, Texas, to Joseph Alsup Peacock and Dorothy Menefee. Their children—Robert Stewart Jr. (8 Mar 1978–), Cyndea Lynn (8 Oct 1979–), and Catherine Heye (20 Sep 1982–)— were born in San Antonio.

- **Marguerite Heye "Margo" Thornton (13 Feb 1951–):** Margo married Gary W. Harrod (7 May 1949–) on October 2, 1971, in San Antonio, Texas. Their daughter, Brittany Lee Harrod, was born on November 4, 1975.

- **Mark Lee Thornton (8 Jan 1954–):** Mark attended Alamo Heights High School in San Antonio. After graduation, he had the opportunity to spend a summer in MalaMala Game Reserve in South Africa, assisting rangers with road construction. He attended the University of Texas at Austin, where he was a member of the Phi Gamma Delta fraternity and completed medical studies at the University of Texas Medical School at Galveston. He established a medical practice in San Antonio, where he works in internal medicine, cardiovascular diseases, family practice, and sports medicine. On August 1, 1992, Mark married Caroline Elizabeth Archer in San Antonio. Their children, both born in San Antonio, are Taylor Clay (26 Jan 1993–) and Claudia Elizabeth (20 Dec 1994–).

- **Melanie Louise Thornton (23 Apr 1957–):** Melanie was born in San Antonio, Texas. She married David Johnson Frazier on February 14, 1981, in Harris County, Texas.

    - **Travis Evans Frazier (2 Jun 1984–):** Travis was born in Harris County, Texas. He married Sarah R. Heep on December 3, 2011, in Harris County, Texas.

    - **Brent Thornton Frazier (22 Oct 1985–):** Brent was born in Harris County, Texas.

- **Geraldine Felice Thornton (18 Jan 1959–):** Born in San Antonio, Texas, Felice attended Alamo Heights High School, where she was a cheerleader, a member of the student council, and active in several other groups. She was a 1980 graduate of the University of Texas at Austin. While at the University of Texas, she was an officer of the Kappa Alpha Theta sorority. On March 2, 1981, Felice married John Dow Crocker in Dallas, Texas.

- **John Dow Crocker Jr. (23 Apr 1985–):** John was born in San Antonio, Texas.

- **Amy Clay Thornton (19 Sep 1964–):** Born in San Antonio, Texas, Amy attended Alamo Heights High School, where she was a varsity cheerleader, a member of the student council, and a member of American Field Service and Las Amigas organizations. On May 27, 1989, Amy married James P. Hinson in Harris County, Texas.

  - **Elizabeth Greer Hinson (4 Jun 1993–):** Elizabeth was born in Harris County, Texas.

Annah Allyne Thornton (6 Jun 1892–31 Jul 1972)

Allyne was born in Pecos, Reeves County, Texas. She grew up and attended school in Erath County. Allyne married Thomas M. "Tom" Bridges (27 Nov 1885–26 Apr 1967) on October 8, 1913. Tom Bridges was a pharmacist in Stephenville, Texas. They made their home in Stephenville, where they are shown in the 1920 census sharing a dwelling with Allyne's parents, Henry and Florence Thornton, and her sister Minnie. Tom was working in a drugstore, and Allyne was caring for Philip, the survivor of their first three sons. Tom and Allyne may have moved to Breckenridge with Henry and Florence; family oral history indicated that they shared a Breckenridge home with her parents for a period of time.

By 1930, they lived in Mineral Wells, Palo Pinto County, Texas. Tom was working as a drugstore manager, and another son, Alban, had been added to the family. As the economic depression deepened, many people could no longer afford their medications. Tom found that he was unable to turn away sick people, especially sick children, because they could not pay for medicine. He provided such medication without charge, absorbing the cost himself. As a result of his generosity, he lost the drugstore and found work as a pharmacist in Fort Worth until he could save enough money to establish a new store. By 1940, they had returned to Stephenville, and Tom established a drugstore on the east side of the square in Stephenville. The 1940 census shows them living on West Tarleton Street, with both Philip and Alban enumerated in the household. Tom was a highly respected pharmacist in Stephenville, and Allyne was active in civic organizations. Tom Bridges died in Stephenville, and Allyne died in Fort Worth, Texas, from a heart attack. Both were buried in Stephenville.

- **Tom Thornton Bridges (23 Feb 1915–8 Oct 1919):** Born in Stephenville, Erath County, Texas, Tom died there from diphtheria at four years, seven months, and twelve days.

- **Philip Bridges (2 Dec 1916–21 Feb 1985):** Philip was born in Stephenville, Erath County, Texas. He enlisted in the warrant officers branch of the US Army on February 11, 1941, and served the duration of the war. His enlistment description was sixty-six inches in height and 114 pounds in weight. After the war, he completed four years of college and became an accountant and auditor. Philip married Dorothy Ruth Juren (6 May 1923–). Dorothy was born in Ranger, Eastland County, Texas, to Richard August Juren and Matilda Rose Marek. Philip and Dorothy made their home in Fort Worth, Texas, where Philip worked for Acme Brick as an accountant. Philip died in Fort Worth.

  - **Richard Thomas Bridges (31 May 1947–):** Richard was born in Tarrant County, Texas.

- **Garland Bridges (2 Dec 1916–19 Jun 1918):** Garland, twin to Philip, was born in Stephenville, Erath County, Texas. He died there from whooping cough at one year, seven months, and seventeen days.

- **Alban Kit Bridges (5 Oct 1921–31 Oct 1990):** Born in Stephenville, Texas, Alban attended school in Mineral Wells and Fort Worth before graduating from Stephenville High School. He enlisted in the US Army on June 22, 1943, in Abilene, Texas, after completing four years of college. His enlistment was for the duration of the war plus six months. He married Deretta Fern "Rita" Walker (14 May 1928–) in Stephenville in 1948. Rita was born in Stephenville to Charles A. Walker and Willie Emma Stone. Rita graduated from Stephenville High School in 1945. Alban and Rita moved to Fort Worth, Texas, where he worked as a mechanical engineer with the Fort Worth District Corps of Engineers. He retired in 1989. Alban died in Fort Worth. Rita survived him and continues to live in Fort Worth.

  - **Alban Kit Bridges Jr. (24 May 1952–):** Born in Tom Green County, Texas, Kit attended public schools in Fort Worth. He received a bachelor of music from Texas Christian University and both a master of music and a PhD in music from Northwestern University. He lives in Evanston, Illinois, where he teaches at DePaul University School of Music. Among the courses he teaches are Vocal Literature, Advanced Techniques of Musical Stage, and History of Opera. He also is a sought-after accompanist in the Chicago area and has performed in recital series at a variety of venues. Dr. Bridges had his Chicago debut at Orchestra Hall in 1993.

- **Susan Kathleen Bridges (12 Jun 1956–):** Born in Fort Worth, Texas, Susan attended public schools in Fort Worth. She works as a materials buyer at Lockheed Martin in Fort Worth.

- **Laura Elizabeth Bridges (29 Nov 1960–):** Laura was born in Fort Worth, Texas. She married John Willis Carson on January 7, 1883, in Tarrant County, Texas. They live in Stephenville, Texas, where Willis is a mechanic for General Motors and Laura is a full-time homemaker.

  - **Sydney Carson (1992–):** Sydney studied at North Texas State University.

  - **Jamie Carson (1994–):** Jamie joined her sister as a student at North Texas State University.

Robert Thomas Thornton
(10 Mar 1894–20 Sep 1932)

Robert Thomas, usually called Tom, was born in the Hannibal community (then Berlin Hall). He married Rita Allie Sechrist (18 Oct 1894–10 Aug 1983) on November 17, 1911. Rita was the daughter of William and Ella Sechrist and a sister of Lester Lee Sechrist, the wife of Tom's brother Henry Clay Thornton. The Sechrist family is shown on the 1900 census of Erath County, Texas. Tom and Rita were living in Lubbock, Texas, when he registered for the World War I draft. He was working as a teamster for the Redford Company. His dependents were a wife and three children. He described himself as medium build with blue eyes and dark-brown hair. By 1930, the family was still living in Lubbock, on Thirty-Fourth Street. The family had expanded to five children, and Tom was working in a wholesale grocery warehouse. Tom died from general peritonitis in Lubbock at age thirty-eight. He was buried in Littlefield, Texas. Rita survived him more than fifty years. She married Ed Hall (19 Aug 1887–17 Mar 1982), and they lived in Weatherford, Texas. The 1940 census shows Rita Allie and Ed Hall in Parker County, Texas. Her occupation was salesperson in a novelty shop. She was living in the same house in 1935. Rita died in Parker County, Texas, and was buried by Ed Hall in Weatherford.

- **Bill Garland Thornton (20 Nov 1912–6 Dec 1984):** Bill was born in Erath County, Texas. He was not yet twenty when his father died. He married Evelyn Perry on September 18, 1937, probably in Texas. It is not known when the move to California was made, but their daughter, Patricia Ann "Patty," was born in Monterey, California, on June 25, 1939. Bill and Evelyn are shown on city directories for San Jose, California, in

1949, 1954, and 1960. Bill's occupation is listed as driver. They were living in San Jose at the time of the Thornton reunion in 1977. Bill died in San Jose, Santa Clara County, California.

- **Berta Marie Thornton (12 Jan 1915–5 May 1986):** Berta was born in Stephenville, Erath County, Texas. She married Alton T. Smith on October 26, 1946. They made their home in Garden Grove and Walnut Creek, Contra Costa County, California. She died in Solano County, California. Their daughter is Rita Suzette (29 Jul 1948–).

- **Edna Earl Thornton (4 Oct 1916–31 Jul 1995):** Edna Earl was born in Lubbock, Texas. In 1940, Edna was working as a beautician in Alpine, Texas. She married Murray John Williams on January 19, 1942. Edna died in Alvord, Wise County, Texas. Their children are Michael Thomas (22 Jan 1943–) and Jeanne Marie (29 Jul 1946–).

- **Dorothy Lucille Thornton (27 Nov 1918–24 Jun 2002):** Dorothy Lucille was born in Lubbock, Texas. She married Thurman Womack (6 Apr 1919–16 Jan 2004) on April 4, 1935, probably in Wise County, Texas. She and Thurman are shown on the 1940 Wise County census with ten-month-old Gary. Both Dorothy and Thurman died in Wise County, Texas.

  - **James Gary Womack (17 Jun 1939–12 Dec 1969):** Gary was born in Parker County, Texas. He married Peggy Garrett (25 Aug 1941–) in 1956. Peggy, the daughter of Luther Winford Garrett and Nanie Gertrude Morton, was born in Wise County. Gary died in Tarrant County, Texas. Their children are Gary Wayne (31 Dec 1957–) and Kelli Dean (20 Nov 1961–).

  - **Sammy Drew Womack (25 Jul 1943–):** Sam, as he is known, was born in Wise County, Texas. He married Delores McClung on July 24, 1964. The marriage ended in a divorce granted July 2, 1982. Sam's second marriage was to Elease K. Williams on February 6, 1987. He lives near Bridgeport, Wise County. His and Delores's son is Sean Neil (27 Dec 1966–).

- **Robert Thomas Thornton Jr. (12 Aug 1921–29 Nov 1988):** Tom was born in Lubbock, Texas. He married Kathryn Louise "Kathy" Rogers (9 Feb 1920–) on March 20, 1948. Kathy was born in Corsicana, Navarro County, Texas, to Irvin W. Rogers and Verla Ellington. Tom enlisted in the US Air Force on September 18, 1940. He was discharged on October 9, 1945. He and Kathy lived in Arlington and Fort Worth, Texas.

  - **Patrick Allen Thornton (18 Dec 1950–):** Patrick was born in Dallas County, Texas. He has lived in Virginia.

  - **Beth Ann Thornton (11 Jan 1953–):** Beth Ann was born in Wise County, Texas. She married Charles L. Hawkins on April 6, 1973, in Tarrant County, Texas.

- **Barbara Lynn Thornton (12 Sep 1954–):** Barbara was born in Parker County, Texas.

- **Andrea Thornton (15 Jan 1956–):** Andrea was born in Parker County, Texas.

Minnie Lee Thornton
(25 Mar 1896–Dec 1936)

Minnie was born in Hannibal (then Berlin Hall), Erath County, Texas. She was living with her parents in Stephenville, Texas, at the time of the 1920 census. In 1920 or 1921, Minnie married Thad Ator (1897–13 Apr 1957). Thad was born in Odessa, Ector County, Texas. They lived in Andalusia, Alabama, and Stephenville, Fort Worth, Breckenridge, and San Antonio, Texas. The 1930 census shows them living in Andalusia, Covington County, Alabama, where, according to the census, Thad worked as an auditor. Their children at that time were Austin Thad, eight; Lewis S., seven; Vera, four; Robert D., two; and Marjorie, three months. Minnie died in San Antonio, Texas, from meningitis three days after the birth of her seventh child. The 1940 census shows the five younger children living with Thad's parents in San Antonio, Bexar County, Texas. Thad died in Odessa, Ector County, Texas.

- **Austin Thad Ator (ca. 1921–5 Dec 1990):** Austin was born in Stephenville, Texas. He married Anna Lee Austin in Howard County, Texas.

- **Lewis Shannon Ator (22 Nov 1922–28 Dec 1988):** Lewis was born in Stephenville, Erath County, Texas. He married Irene Marie Pravo, and they had three children. He died in Brownwood, Brown County, Texas.

- **Vera Frances Ator (26 Mar 1926–ca. 1930):** Vera was born in Fort Worth, Tarrant County, Texas. She died before the 1930 census was taken and was buried in Andalusia, Alabama.

- **Robert Duncan Ator (26 Nov 1927–13 Sep 2005):** Robert Duncan was born in Fort Worth, Tarrant County, Texas. He married Doris Joan Lankford on February 26, 1948. They had one child. Robert Duncan worked as a telephone engineer in Brownwood, Texas.

- **Marjorie Ann Ator (1930–):** Ann was born in 1930 in Andalusia, Alabama. She married Fred Herndon Matthews. They had five children.

- **Henry Baxter Ator (6 Nov 1932–30 Nov 2015):** Henry was born in Andalusia, Alabama. He married Gloria Gene Mayfield on January 21, 1961. Their children were

Janette, married name Anderson; Regina, who married Morad Kasiri; and Diane, who married Mark McGee.

- **Minton Keith Ator (12 Dec 1936–12 Mar 1984):** Minton was born in San Antonio, Texas. His mother died soon after his birth, and he was raised by his grandparents and a sister of his father. Minton died of a heart attack in Tarrant County, Texas.

Vera Fern Thornton
(8 Jun 1896–25 Jan 1978)

Vera was born in Erath County, Texas. She married Mack Welch on May 30, 1917, and they were living in Stephenville in 1920. She and Mack divorced, and she moved to Fort Worth. The 1930 census shows Vera as a widow living in the home of her brother, O. T. Thornton, in Tarrant County, Texas. By 1940, both Vera and her mother, Florence, were in the home of Odie Thornton. She continued to live with her brother until his death, then lived in her own home. She worked for the Continental Bank in Fort Worth. Her niece Ruth described Vera as always being perfectly groomed, with never a hair out of place. She and her cousin Leona Kenny Davis kept in close touch, occasionally attending events in Hannibal and Stephenville together. Vera fell into a bathtub filled with water and drowned in her home in Fort Worth, Texas. She was eighty-two.

Wylie Garland Thornton
(Sep 1901–15 Sep 1956)

Wylie Garland Thornton was born in Stephenville, Erath County, Texas. The family lived near Stephenville, so he probably attended Stephenville public schools. The 1920 census shows him living with his brother Tom and family in Lubbock, Texas. He was working as a laborer for a wholesale garage. He married Flora Blakeley (7 Jun 1909–5 Jul 1994) on January 15, 1927. Flora, called Jude, was born in Rule, Haskell County, Texas. Her parents were Dozier Hillard and May C. "Molley" Blakeley. The Blakeley family is found on the 1910 and 1920 censuses in Haskell County, Texas. By 1930, Wylie and Flora were living in Littlefield, Texas, where Wylie worked as a cook in a café, probably the café owned by his brother Clay. They are shown on the 1932 Fort Worth City Directory, where Wylie is listed as a clerk for a Leonard Brothers department store. His son, Garland, reported that his father worked in Leonard's soda fountain department during the Depression years. By 1940, they were again in Littlefield, on East Sixth Street. The 1940 census indicates that they were living in the same place in 1935. Wylie was listed as a partner in the café, and their son, Garland, had been added to the family. At age fifty-five, Wylie died from a heart attack in Littlefield, Lamb County, Texas. He was buried in Littlefield Cemetery. Flora continued living in Littlefield, where she worked in several positions before becoming a dispatcher for the Lamb County Sheriff's Office, a position she held until retirement. She died in Cook County, Texas. Her last residence for Social Security was Denton County.

- **Wylie Garland Thornton Jr. (19 Nov 1934–):** Garland was born in Littlefield, and he attended Littlefield schools. He graduated in the Texas Tech University class of 1957. On July 12, 1957, Wylie Garland and Luanne McNeill were married at Bowman Memorial Chapel in Lubbock, Texas. Luanne (5 Nov 1935–) was born in McLennan County, Texas. Her parents were Edwin Booth McNeill and Maud Rivers Hearon. The 1940 census of Temple, Bell County, Texas, shows four-year-old Luanne with her parents, Edwin B. and Maude McNeill, ages forty-three and thirty-six respectively, and sister Joan, age eleven. Luanne also attended Texas Tech University. She and her parents were living in Lubbock at the time of her marriage. Garland and Luanne lived in Arlington and Denton, Texas. Garland worked in several small banks before affiliating with GNB Bancshares Inc. of Gainesville, Texas. He retired in 1999 as executive director of this bank. Luanne taught elementary school for several years before accepting a position with the Texas Employment Commission, a position she held until retirement.

  - **Nancy Anne Thornton (15 Feb 1964–):** Nancy was born in Lubbock, Texas. She graduated from Denison High School and the University of North Texas. Nancy works for the Olmsted-Kirk Paper Company of Dallas, Texas, as a specification sales representative. She and her husband, Kim Warner, live in Bowie, Texas, where she is a member of the Main Street Bowie Board of Directors.

  - **Susan Jean Thornton (23 Jun 1966–):** Susan married Lawrence M. Nolan on March 22, 1986, in Travis County, Texas. They were divorced in 1992. Susan lives in Fort Worth, Texas, and works for the Muscular Dystrophy Association.

SOURCES

"1924 and 1926 County Office Holders." Copy provided by Freda Mitchell of Swenson Memorial Museum of Stephens County, Breckenridge, Texas.

Author unknown. "The Hardships of a Mother of the Pioneer Days of Texas." Copied from newspaper (unspecified), by Mrs. B. H. Tapp, July 1960. Thornton Family Reunion, Hannibal, Texas, 1977. Copy provided by Alban Bridges.

Breckenridge Cemetery. Guinn Kelley Section. Copy provided by Freda Mitchell of Swenson Memorial Museum of Stephens County, Breckenridge, Texas.

Bridges, Rita Walker. Telephone conversation with Mary Jo Kenny. March 5, 2014.

Davis, Leona Kenny. Untitled paper prepared around 1968. In possession of Mary Jo Kenny.

"Henry C. Thornton and Florence Kenny." Family Bible, family record pages. Papers available at Thornton Family Reunion, Hannibal, Texas, 1977. Copies supplied by Alban Bridges.

Hannibal Cemetery (2312 County Rd. 111, Stephenville, TX). Florence Thornton gravestone.

Hannibal Cemetery (2312 County Rd. 111, Stephenville, TX). Henry Thornton gravestone.

"History of Reeves County." Reeves County Gen Website.

"Kenney, Wm." 1870 US Census, Anderson County, Texas, PO Palestine, line 9. FamilySearch Library, Salt Lake City, UT.

"Kenny, W. C." 1880 US Census, Erath County, Texas, family 196, June 18, 1880. FHLC #1255302, FamilySearch Library, Salt Lake City, UT.

"Kenny, William C." Obituary. *Stephenville Empire-Tribune*, August 1936.

Thornton, Garland. Email to Mary Jo Kenny. April 14, 2014.

"Thornton H. C." Obituary. *The Breckenridge American*, September 28, 1930. Microfilm, Swenson Memorial Museum of Stephens County. Transcribed copy provided by Freda Mitchell.

"Thornton, D. R." 1880 US Census, Erath County, Texas. Ancestry.com.

"Thornton, Florence." Fort Worth, Texas, City Directory, 1942. Ancestry.com.

"Thornton, H. C." 1920 US Census, Erath County, Texas, Stephenville. Ancestry.com.

"Thornton, Henry C." 1900 US Census, Erath County, Texas. Ancestry.com.

"Thornton, Henry." 1930 US Census, Stephens County, Texas. Ancestry.com.

"Thornton, Mrs. Henry C." Obituary. *Breckenridge American*, January 1, 1948. Microfilm, Swenson Memorial Museum of Stephens County. Transcribed copy provided by Freda Mitchell.

"Thornton, O. T." 1940 US Census, Tarrant County, Texas, Fort Worth, p. 61b, ED 257-199. FamilySearch Library, Salt Lake City, UT.

Timian, Fern. Letter to Mary Ann. In papers available at Thornton Family Reunion, Hannibal, Texas, 1977. Copies supplied by Alban Bridges.

Smith, Mary Anna Thornton. "A Brief History and Genealogy of Daniel Robert Thornton, 1833–1911 and Mary Anna Garland 1837–1906." FHLC #1318372, item 11, FamilySearch Library, Salt Lake City, UT.

Smith, Mary T. "Marianna Garland." Copied from unnamed newspaper, probably *Stephenville Empire-Tribune*. Available at Thornton Family Reunion, Hannibal, Texas, 1977. Copy supplied by Alban Bridges.

Odie Thurman Thornton and Clara Gibson

"Clendennen, Crystal Anne." Texas Birth Index. Ancestry.com.

"Clendennen, Edward C., and Karen Clendennen." Texas Divorce Index. Ancestry.com.

"Cushing, Levenia." Standard Certificate of Birth. Texas Birth Certificates, 1903–1932. Ancestry.com.

"Griffin, Roger A., and Kellie Griffin." Texas Divorce Index. Ancestry.com.

"Hayley, David Allen." Texas Birth Index. Ancestry.com.

"Hayley, David Allen." Texas Marriage Index. Ancestry.com.

"Hayley, Don, and Kellie Haley." Texas Divorce Index. Ancestry.com.

"Hayley, Joanna Denise." Texas Birth Index. Ancestry.com.

"Hayley, Joanna Denise." Texas Marriage Index. Ancestry.com.

"Hayley, Wesley Don, Jr." Texas Birth Index. Ancestry.com.

"Marlow, Fred L." 1930 US Census, McLennan County, Texas.

"O. T. Thornton Ends 37 Years at Post office, Plans Travel." *Fort Worth Star-Telegram*, unknown date. Clipping supplied by Hansel Thornton.

"Ogburn, Amy J." Texas Birth Index. Ancestry.com.

"Ogburn, Amy J." Texas Marriage Index. Ancestry.com.

"Ogburn, Gail Lynn." Texas Birth Index. Ancestry.com.

"Ogburn, Gail Lynn." Texas Marriage Index. Ancestry.com.

"Pritchett, Lawson." US Public Records, vol. 1. Ancestry.com.

"Pritchett, Mary." US, Social Security Death Index, 1935–Current. Ancestry.com.

Rosenthal, Ruth A. "Research Profile on Biomed Experts." Email to Mary Jo Kenny. February 7, 2014.

Rosenthal, Ruth Ann Thornton. *Memoirs of a Determined Woman, Ruth Ann Thornton Rosenthal.* April 22, 2010. Excerpts provided by the author in a letter to Mary Jo Kenny.

Rosenthal, Ruth Ann Thornton. "Synopsis of Related Thornton Family: July 5, 2006." Email to Mary Jo Kenny.

Rosenthal, Ruth Ann Thornton. Letter to Mary Jo Kenny. July 23, 2006.

Rosenthal, Ruth Ann Thornton. Email to Mary Jo Kenny. February 12, 2014.

"Rosenthal, Douglas Wayne." Texas Birth Index. Ancestry.com.

"Rosenthal, Douglas Wayne." Texas Marriage Index. Ancestry.com.

"Rosenthal, Karen Anne." Texas Birth Index. Ancestry.com.

"Rosenthal, Karen Anne." Texas Marriage Index. Ancestry.com.

"Rosenthal, Kellie Jean." Texas Birth Index. Ancestry.com.

"Rosenthal, Kellie Jean." Texas Marriage Index. Ancestry.com.

"Rosenthal, Lauren Nicole." Texas Birth Index. Ancestry.com.

"Rosenthal, Meridith Kay." Texas Birth Index. Ancestry.com.

"Thornton, Andrew Hansel." Texas Birth Index. Ancestry.com.

"Thornton, Clara May." Certificate of Death. Texas Department of Health, Bureau of Vital Statistics.

"Thornton, Dwight Henry." Texas Birth Index. Ancestry.com.

"Thornton, Jon David." California Death Index, 1940–1997. Ancestry.com.

"Thornton, Jon David." Social Security Death Index. Ancestry.com.

"Thornton, Jon David." Texas Birth Index. Ancestry.com.

"Thornton, Mary Pauline." Obituary. Unidentified newspaper. October 1996. Copy provided by Pamela Thornton McKinley.

"Thornton, Mary Ruth." Texas Birth Index, 1903–1932. Ancestry.com.

"Thornton, O. T." 1920 US Census, Erath County, Texas, Stephenville, family 288, June 16, 1920. Ancestry.com.

"Thornton, O. T." 1930 US Census, Tarrant County, Texas, Fort Worth, family 95, April 17, 1930. Ancestry.com.

"Thornton, O. T." 1940 US Census, Tarrant County, Texas, Fort Worth, p. 61b, ED 257-199. Ancestry.com.

"Thornton, Odie T." 1910 US Census, Erath County, Texas, Precinct 7, family 98, April 1910. Ancestry.com.

"Thornton, Odie T." Certificate of Death. Texas Department of Health, Bureau of Vital Statistics.

"Thornton, Odie T." Fort Worth, Texas, City Directory, 1942. Ancestry.com.

"Thornton, Odie Thurman." World War I draft registration form, Erath County, Texas, June 5, 1917.

"Thornton, Pamela Gail." Texas Birth Index. Ancestry.com.

"Thornton, Wayne Michael." Texas Birth Index. Ancestry.com.

"Thornton, Wayne Preston." Application for Account Number, US Social Security Act, November 25, 1936.

"Thornton, Wayne Preston." Social Security Death Index. Ancestry.com.

"Thornton, Wayne Preston." Texas Birth Index. Ancestry.com.

"Thornton, Willie H." Obituary. Unidentified newspaper, September 1983. Copy of clipping provided by Pamela Thornton McKinley.

"Thornton, Willie Hansel." Texas Birth Index. Ancestry.com.

"Thornton, Willie Hansel." Texas Marriage Index. Ancestry.com.

"Thornton, Willie." 1940 US Census, Tarrant County, Texas, p. 5B, ED 257-148. Ancestry.com.

Timian, Fern. Letter to Mary Ann. Undated, available at Thornton Family Reunion, Hannibal, Texas, 1977. Copy provided by Alban Bridges.

US Veterans Gravesites, ca. 1776–2006. Ancestry.com.

Weber, Lynn Ogburn. Email to Mary Jo Kenny. February 10, 2014.

Weber, Lynn Ogburn. Email to Mary Jo Kenny. November 1913.

Henry Clayton Thornton and Lester Lee Sechrist

"Alguire, Katherine Elizabeth." Texas Birth Index, 1903–1997. Ancestry.com.

"Alguire, Linnie Bea." US, Find A Grave Index, 1600s–Current. Ancestry.com.

"Alguire, Linnie." United States Obituary Collection. Ancestry.com.

"Alguire, R. K." US Public Records Index, vol. 1. Ancestry.com.

"Alguire, Richard K." Texas Divorce Index, 1968–2011. Ancestry.com.

"Alguire, Richard Keith, Jr." Texas Birth Index, 1903–1997. Ancestry.com.

"Alguire, Richard Keith." Texas Birth Index, 1903–1997. Ancestry.com.

"Alguire, Robert Thornton." US, Find A Grave Index, 1600s–Current. Ancestry.com.

"Alguire, Robert." US, Cemetery and Funeral Home Collection, 1847–2018. Ancestry.com.

"Alguire, Timothy T." Texas Marriage Collection, 1966–2011. Ancestry.com.

"Alguire, Timothy T." US Public Records Index, vol. 1. Ancestry.com.

"Brandon M. Williams." US Public Records Index, vol. 1. Ancestry.com.

"Brewington, Carrie Elizabeth." Texas Birth Index, 1903–1997. Ancestry.com.

"Canning, Leigh Carol." Texas Birth Index, 1903–1997. Ancestry.com.

"Claburn, Mark Alan." Texas Birth Index, 1903–1997. Ancestry.com.

"Crocker, John Dow, Jr." Texas Birth Index, 1903–2011. Ancestry.com.

"Frazier, Brent Thornton." Texas Birth Index, 1903–2011. Ancestry.com.

"Frazier, Travis E." Texas Marriage Collection, 1966–2011. Ancestry.com.

"Frazier, Travis Evans." Texas Birth Index, 1903–2011. Ancestry.com.

"Harrod, Brittany Lee." Texas Birth Index, 1903–2011. Ancestry.com.

"Herring, Leigh Gale." Texas Birth Index, 1903–1997. Ancestry.com.

"Herring, Leigh Gale." Texas Marriage Collection, 1966–2011. Ancestry.com.

"Herring, Leigh." Texas Marriage Collection, 1966–2011. Ancestry.com.

"Herring, Mark G." Texas Divorce Index, 1968–2011. Ancestry.com.

"Herring, Mark G." Texas Marriage Collection, 1966–2011. Ancestry.com.

"Herring, Mark Glyn." Texas Birth Index, 1903–1997. Ancestry.com.

"Herring, Rachel R." Texas Marriage Collection, 1966–2011. Ancestry.com.

"Herring, Rachel Ruth." Texas Birth Index, 1903–1997. Ancestry.com.

"Herring, Sarah B." Texas Marriage Collection, 1966–2011. Ancestry.com.

"Herring, Sarah Beth." Texas Birth Index, 1903–1997. Ancestry.com.

"Hinson, Elizabeth Greer." Texas Birth Index, 1903–2011. Ancestry.com.

"Mask, Claire Marie." Texas Birth Certificates, 1903–1932. Ancestry.com.

"Mask, Willie T." 1930 US Population Census, Young County, Texas, p. 2B, ED 0014, image 424. Ancestry.com.

"Mawhood, Ashton Morgan." Texas Birth Index, 1903–1997. Ancestry.com.

"Mawhood, Ashton." Texas Marriage Collection, 1966–2011. Ancestry.com.

"Mawhood, Christina L." US Public Records Index, vol. 1. Ancestry.com.

"Mawhood, Christina." Texas Divorce Index. Ancestry.com.

"Mawhood, Keaton Ross." Texas Birth Index, 1903–1997. Ancestry.com.

"Novelli, Elizabeth Leigh." Texas Birth Index, 1903–1997. Ancestry.com.

"Novelli, Emily Hughes." Texas Birth Index, 1903–1997. Ancestry.com.

"Novelli, Leigh G." US Public Records Index, vol. 1. Ancestry.com.

"Peacock, Catherine Heye." Texas Birth Index, 1903–2011. Ancestry.com.

"Peacock, Cyndea Lynn." Texas Birth Index, 1903–2011. Ancestry.com.

"Peacock, Robert Stewart, Jr." Texas Birth Index, 1903–2011. Ancestry.com.

"Peacock, Robert Stewart." Texas Birth Index, 1903–2011. Ancestry.com.

"Rogers, Katherine Louise." Texas Birth Certificates, 1903–1932. Ancestry.com.

"Sechrist, W. L." 1900 US Census, Palo Pinto County, Texas. Ancestry.com.

"Stohlman, Dale Roger." Texas Birth Index, 1903–1997. Ancestry.com.

"Stohlman, Kevin D." US Public Records Index, vol. 1. Ancestry.com.

"Stohlman, Kevin Dale." Texas Birth Index, 1903–1997. Ancestry.com.

"Straughan, Margaret Geraldine." Texas Birth Certificates, 1903–1932. Ancestry.com.

"Straughan, Margaret Geraldine." Texas Birth Index, 1903–1997. Ancestry.com.

"Thornton, Amy Clay." Texas Birth Index, 1903–2011. Ancestry.com.

"Thornton, Amy Clay." Texas Marriage Collection, 1966–2011. Ancestry.com.

"Thornton, Andrea." Texas Birth Index, 1903–1997. Ancestry.com.

"Thornton, Barbara Lynn." Texas Birth Index, 1903–1997. Ancestry.com.

"Thornton, Beth Ann." Texas Birth Index, 1903–1997. Ancestry.com.

"Thornton, Beth Ann." Texas Marriage Collection, 1966–2011. Ancestry.com.

"Thornton, Claudia Elizabeth." Texas Birth Index. Ancestry.com.

"Thornton, Clayton." 1910 US Census, Erath County, Texas, Justice Precinct 7. Ancestry.com.

"Thornton, Cyndea M." Texas Marriage Collection, 1966–2011. Ancestry.com.

"Thornton, Dean." 1940 US Population Census, Ector County, Texas, Odessa, p. 2A, ED 68–7B. Ancestry.com.

"Thornton, Dean." 1960 City Directory, Midland, Texas. Ancestry.com.

"Thornton, Dean." US Public Records Index, vol. 2. Ancestry.com.

"Thornton, Ernest D." Social Security Death Index. Ancestry.com.

"Thornton, Ernest Dean." Texas Birth Certificates, 1903–1932. Ancestry.com.

"Thornton, Geraldine Felice." Texas Birth Index, 1903–2011. Ancestry.com.

"Thornton, Geraldine Felice." Texas Marriage Collection, 1966–2011. Ancestry.com.

"Thornton, H. C." 1940 US Census, Lamb County, Texas, Littlefield. Ancestry.com.

"Thornton, Henry C." 1930 US Census, Lamb County, Texas, Littlefield. Ancestry.com.

"Thornton, Henry C." Texas Death Index, 1903–2000. Ancestry.com.

"Thornton, Henry Clay." Texas, Find A Grave Index, 1761–2012. Ancestry.com.

"Thornton, Henry Clayton." US World War I Draft Registration Cards, 1917–1918. Ancestry.com.

"Thornton, Lester Lee." Texas Death Certificates. Ancestry.com.

"Thornton, Lester." Texas Death Index, 1903–2000. Ancestry.com.

"Thornton, Lester." US, Social Security Death Index. Ancestry.com.

"Thornton, Linnie Bea." Texas Birth Certificates, 1903–1932. Ancestry.com.

"Thornton, Marguerite H." Texas Marriage Collection, 1966–2011. Ancestry.com.

"Thornton, Mark Lee." Texas Marriage Collection, 1966–2011. Ancestry.com.

"Thornton, Melanie L." Texas Marriage Collection, 1966–2011. Ancestry.com.

"Thornton, Melanie Louise." Texas Birth Index, 1903–2011. Ancestry.com.

"Thornton, Melvin L." Texas Death Index. Ancestry.com.

"Thornton, Melvin Lee." Social Security Death Index. Ancestry.com.

"Thornton, Melvin Lee." Texas Birth Certificates, 1903–1932. Ancestry.com.

"Thornton, Monte Louise." Texas Birth Certificates, 1903–1932. Ancestry.com.

"Thornton, Monte R." Texas Death Index, 1903–2000. Ancestry.com.

"Thornton, Monte R." Texas Marriage Collection, 1966–2011. Ancestry.com.

"Thornton, Monte R." US Public Records Index, vol. 2. Ancestry.com.

"Thornton, Monte Randall." Texas Birth Index, 1903–1979. Ancestry.com.

"Thornton, Monte Randall." Texas Birth Index, 1903–1997. Ancestry.com.

"Thornton, Olena Fern." Texas Birth Certificates, 1903–1932. Ancestry.com.

"Thornton, Patrick Allen." Texas Birth Index, 1903–1997. Ancestry.com.

"Thornton, R. T., Jr." Texas Birth Certificates, 1903–1932. Ancestry.com.

"Thornton, Taylor Clay." Texas Birth Index, 1903–2011. Ancestry.com.

"Thornton, Terrance D." Texas Divorce Index, 1968–2002. Ancestry.com.

"Thornton, Tom." 1920 US Census, Lubbock County, Texas. Ancestry.com.

"Thornton, Tom." 1930 US Census, Lubbock County, Texas. Ancestry.com

"Timian, Emil." 1940 US Population Census, Lamb County, Texas, Littlefield. Ancestry.com.

"Timian, Emil." 1952 City Directory, Lubbock, Texas. Ancestry.com.

"Timian, Emil." Texas Death Index, 1903–2000. Ancestry.com.

"Timian, Fern." Obituary. *Houston Chronicle*, August 31, 2005.

"Timian, Fern." US, Social Security Death Index, 1935–Current. Ancestry.com.

Timian, Fern Thornton, to Mary Anna. March 1977. Letter in papers for the Thornton Family Reunion, Huckaby, Texas, 1977. Copy supplied by Alban Bridges.

"Timian, Janice Karen." Texas Birth Index, 1903–1997. Ancestry.com.

"Timian, Linda Gale." Texas Birth Index, 1903–1997. Ancestry.com.

Vasek, Bobby Neal. "Speaking in Tongues, Psychologically Considered." Dissertation, Concordia Theological Seminary, Springfield, IL, 1973.

"Vasek, Bobby Neal." Texas Birth Index, 1903–1997. Ancestry.com.

"Vasek, Bobby." Texas Death Index, 1903–2000. Ancestry.com.

"Vasek, Michal D." Texas Marriage Collection, 1966–2011. Ancestry.com.

"Vasek, Michal Denise." Texas Birth Index, 1903–1997. Ancestry.com.

"White, Ashley Lauren." Texas Birth Index, 1903–1997. Ancestry.com.

"White, Meghan G." Texas Marriage Collection, 1966–2011. Ancestry.com.

"White, Meghan Gwyneth." Texas Birth Index, 1903–1997. Ancestry.com.

"White, Michal D." Texas Divorce Index, 1968–2011. Ancestry.com.

"White, Michal D." US Public Records Index, vol. 1. Ancestry.com.

"White, Ryann Courtney." Texas Birth Index, 1903–1997. Ancestry.com.

"Williams, Brandon McDonald." *Park Cities People*, October 1, 1992. US Newspaper Archives.

"Williams, Brandon McDonald." Texas Birth Index, 1903–1997. Ancestry.com.

"Williams, Brennon Thornton." Texas Birth Index, 1903–1997. Ancestry.com.

"Williams, Bryce A." Texas Marriage Collection, 1966–2011. Ancestry.com.

"Williams, Dawson McDonald." Texas Birth Index, 1903–1997. Ancestry.com.

"Williams, Russ T." Texas Marriage Collection, 1966–2011. Ancestry.com.

"Williams, Russ T." US Public Records Index, vol. 1. Ancestry.com.

"Williams, Russ Thornton." *Park Cities People*, August 26, 2004. US Newspaper Archives.

"Williams, Russ Thornton." Texas Birth Index, 1903–1997. Ancestry.com.

"Williams, Susan E." Texas Marriage Collection, 1966–2011. Ancestry.com.

"Williams, Susan Elaine." Texas Birth Index, 1903–1997. Ancestry.com.

"Williams, Victor T." US Public Records Index, vol. 1. Ancestry.com.

"Williams, Victor Tye." Texas Birth Index, 1903–1997. Ancestry.com.

"Wilson, Christina L." Texas Marriage Collection, 1966–2011. Ancestry.com.

"Wilson, Christina Louise." Texas Birth Index, 1903–1997. Ancestry.com.

"Wilson, John W." 1940 US Census, Lubbock County, Texas, p. 9B, Precinct 1, ED 152-6B, line 57. Ancestry.com.

"Wilson, John W." 1958 Lubbock, Texas, City Directory. Ancestry.com.

"Wilson, John W." Texas Death Certificates, 1903–1982. Ancestry.com.

"Wilson, John W." World War II Enlistment Records, 1938–1946. Ancestry.com.

"Wilson, Jon W." US, Social Security Death Index, 1935–Current. Ancestry.com.

"Wilson, Jon Wesley III." US Veterans Gravesites, ca. 1775–2006. Ancestry.com.

"Wilson, Jon Wesley." Texas Birth Index, 1903–1997. Ancestry.com.

"Wilson, Lyleon J." 1960 Lubbock, Texas, City Directory. Ancestry.com.

"Wilson, Lyleon Jan." Texas Birth Index, 1902–1997. Ancestry.com.

"Wilson, Monte L." 1960 Lubbock, Texas, City Directory. Ancestry.com.

"Wilson, Monte L." New York Passenger Lists, 1820–1957. Ancestry.com.

"Wilson, Monte." Texas Death Index, 1903–2000. Ancestry.com.

"Wilson, Monte." US, Social Security Death Index, 1938–Current. Ancestry.com.

Allyne Thornton and Tom Bridges

"Bridges, Alban Kit, Jr." Texas Birth Index, 1903–2011. Ancestry.com.

"Bridges, Alban Kit." Texas Birth Certificates, 1903–1932. Ancestry.com.

"Bridges, Alban Kit." Texas Birth Index, 1903–1987. Ancestry.com.

"Bridges, Alban." 1993 Fort Worth, Texas, City Directory. Ancestry.com.

Bridges, Alban. Correspondence with Mary Jo Kenny.

"Bridges, Alban." United States Obituary Collection. Ancestry.com.

"Bridges, Alban." US Public Records Index, vol. 1. Ancestry.com.

"Bridges, Alban." US, Social Security Death Index, 1935–Current. Ancestry.com.

"Bridges, Alban." US, World War II Army Enlistment Records, 1938–1946. Ancestry.com.

"Bridges, Alban." Texas, Find A Grave Index, 1961–2011. Ancestry.com.

"Bridges, Anna Allyne." Texas Death Certificates, 1903–1982. Ancestry.com.

"Bridges, Anna Allyne." Texas Death Index, 1903–2000. Ancestry.com.

"Bridges, Laura Elizabeth." Texas Birth Index, 1903–2011. Ancestry.com.

"Bridges, Philip." Texas Death Index, 1903–2000. Ancestry.com.

"Bridges, Philip." US, Social Security Death Index, 1938–Current. Ancestry.com.

"Bridges, Philip." US, World War II Army Enlistment Records, 1938–1946. Ancestry.com.

"Bridges, Richard Thomas." Texas Birth Index, 1903–1987. Ancestry.com.

Bridges, Rita. Telephone conversation with Mary Jo Kenny. March 3, 2014.

"Bridges, Susan Kathleen." Texas Birth Index, 1903–2011. Ancestry.com.

"Bridges, Tom." 1920 US Census, Erath County, Texas, Stephenville. Ancestry.com.

"Bridges, Tom." 1930 US Census, Palo Pinto County, Texas, Mineral Wells. Ancestry.com.

"Bridges, Tom." 1940 US Census, Erath County, Texas. Ancestry.com.

"Bridges, Tom." Texas Death Certificates, 1903–1982. Ancestry.com.

"Bridges, Tom." Texas Death Index, 1903–2000. Ancestry.com.

"Bridges, Tom." US, Social Security Death Index, 1935–Current. Ancestry.com.

"Juren, Dorothy Ruth." Texas Birth Certificates, 1903–1932. Ancestry.com.

"Walker, Charlie A." 1930 US Census, Erath County, Texas, Stephenville, p. 48, ED 4, image 151. Ancestry.com.

"Walker, Charly A." 1940 US Census, Erath County, Texas, Stephenville, p. 84, ED 72-1. Ancestry.com.

"Walker, Deretta Fern." Texas Birth Index, 1903–2011. Ancestry.com.

Robert Thomas Thornton and Rita Allie Sechriest

"Thornton, Robert T." Texas, Find A Grave Index, 1761–2012. Ancestry.com.

"Thornton, Robert Thomas." Texas Death Certificates, 1903–1982. Ancestry.com.

"Thornton, Robert Thomas." US World War l Draft Registration Cards, 1917–1918. Ancestry.com.

"Thornton, Robert." Texas Death Index, 1903–2000. Ancestry.com.

"Thornton, Tom." 1920 US Census, Lubbock County, Texas. Ancestry.com.

"Thornton, Tom." 1930 US Census, Lubbock County, Texas. Ancestry.com.

Minnie Lee Thornton and Thad Ator

"Ator, Thad." 1927 Fort Worth, Texas, City Directory. Ancestry.com.

"Ator, Julius B." 1940 US Census, Bexar County, Texas, San Antonio, sheet 4B, ED 259-3. Ancestry.com.

"Ator, Minnie L." Texas Death Certificates, 1903–1982. Ancestry.com.

"Ator, Minnie L." Texas Death Index, 1903–1982. Ancestry.com.

"Ator, Robert D." US, Social Security Death Index, 1935–Current. Ancestry.com.

"Ator, Robert D." US Veterans Gravesites, ca. 1775–2008. Ancestry.com.

"Ator, Robert Duncan." Texas Birth Certificates, 1903–1932. Ancestry.com.

"Ator, Robert Duncan." Texas Birth Index, 1903–1997. Ancestry.com.

"Ator, Thad." 1930 US Population Census, Covington County, Alabama, Andalusia. Ancestry.com.

"Ator, Thad." Texas Death Index, 1903–1982. Ancestry.com.

Davis, Leona Kenny. Letter to Mary Anna. March 17, 1977. Available in the Thornton Family Reunion Papers, Hannibal, TX, May 3, 1977.

Vera Thornton

Rosenthal, Ruth Thornton. Letters to Mary Jo Kenny. July 5, 2006, and July 23, 2006.

"Thornton, O. T." 1930 US Census, Tarrant County, Texas, Fort Worth. Ancestry.com.

"Thornton, O. T." 1940 US Census, Tarrant County, Texas, Fort Worth. Ancestry.com.

"Welch, Mack." 1920 US Census, Erath County, Texas, Stephenville. Ancestry.com.

Wylie Garland Thornton and Flora Blakley

"Blakely, Dozier H." 1910 US Census, Haskell County, Texas, Precinct 5, ED 0117. Ancestry.com.

"Blakely, Hillard." 1920 US Census, Haskell County, Texas, Precinct 5, ED 137. Ancestry.com.

"McNeill, Edwin B." 1940 US Census, Bell County, Texas, Temple, p. 14A, ED 14-21. Ancestry.com.

"McNeill, Luanne." Texas Birth Index, 1903–1997. Ancestry.com.

"Nolan, Susan T." Texas Divorce Index, 1968–2011. Ancestry.com.

"Thornton, Flora." US, Social Security Death Index, 1935–Current. Ancestry.com.

"Thornton, Flora." Texas Death Index, 1903–2000. Ancestry.com.

Thornton, Garland. Email to Mary Jo Kenny. April 14, 2014.

"Thornton, Nancy Anne." Texas Birth Index, 1903–1997. Ancestry.com.

"Thornton, Susan J." Texas Marriage Index, 1966–2002. Ancestry.com.

"Thornton, Tom." 1920 US Census, Lubbock County, Texas. Ancestry.com.

"Thornton, Wylie G." 1930 US Census, Lamb County, Texas, Littlefield. Ancestry.com.

"Thornton, Wylie G." 1940 US Census, Lamb County, Texas, Littlefield. Ancestry.com.

"Thornton, Wylie Garland." Texas Death Certificates, 1903–1982. Ancestry.com.

"Thornton, Wylie." 1932 Fort Worth, Texas, City Directory. Ancestry.com.

"Thornton, Wylie." Garland, Texas, Death Index, 1903– 2000. Ancestry.com.

"Thornton, Wylie." Texas, Find A Grave Index, 1961–2012. Ancestry.com.

Kathryn Judson "Kate" Kenny
(7 Aug 1869–10 Feb 1948)

Kate Kenny was born in Tennessee Colony, Anderson County, Texas. Her first few years of school were in Tennessee Colony, but at the age of ten, she moved with her family to Erath County, where she attended the school in Hannibal (then called Berlin Hall).

After completing the seventh-grade education provided by the Hannibal school, Kate obtained a teaching credential. She taught in various Erath County rural schools. Around 1908, Kate married Charles Graham Clark (27 Dec 1857–9 Aug 1940), a widower. Charles, a native of Stephenville, Texas, had five grown children as well as two young sons still at home. The 1910 census shows Charles, Kate, and her stepsons Elvis (thirteen) and Kyle (seven) on a farm in Erath County, Precinct 5. They were enumerated adjacent to Wilburn W. Clark; his wife, Pearl; and his brother Claude J. Wilburn and Claude were sons of Charles Clark.

In 1914, Charles, Kate, and Charles's son Kyle moved to Young, Gila County, Arizona. Young is located in Pleasant Valley, bordered by a scenic mountain area described in Zane Grey novels and other Western novels. Pine and aspen forests and abundant wild game were found in the mountains in the early twentieth century. Lower elevations held more widely spaced trees and a variety of desert shrubs and plants. It was also the location of the "Pleasant Valley War," a feud between the Tewksburys and Grahams, which started over stolen cattle and eventually involved almost all the area residents. The five-year-long feud, which resulted in nineteen deaths, had been over for more than two decades when the Clark family arrived, but it was still an important part of local lore.

The 1920 census shows Charles, Kate, and Kyle R. Clark operating a stock farm in the Young Precinct of Gila County, Arizona. Claude and Elvis also moved west, but they apparently did not arrive in Young County until several years after their father, Kate, and Kyle.

The census taken in the summer of 1930 finds Kate in Breckenridge, Texas, at the home of her sister Florence. Florence's husband, Henry Thornton, was gravely ill with cancer at that time. It is probable that Kate—as well as Henry's brother Tamp, also in the household—was there to help care for Henry.

By 1930, Claude and Elvis, with their families, had joined Charles, Kate, and Kyle in Gila County, Arizona. Charles is enumerated in Gila County adjacent to Claude J. Clark. Charles was operating the stock farm, and Claude was the proprietor of a general store. Claude's family consisted of his wife, Leona, and their children, Claude T., Wayne L., Edith H., and Neil. Kyle Clark, a contract truck driver, was enumerated with his wife, Etta, and daughters, Lois, Bonnie, and Berna. Elvis Clark, also a proprietor of a general merchandise store; his wife, Mary E.; and their children, Juanita, Charles, Lora, and Wanda, were enumerated in Gila County.

In 1937, Charles and Kate moved from Young to Globe, Arizona. In the 1940 census, Charles is enumerated in the home of his son Claude in Young, Arizona, on April 2, 1940. The information for Kate on April 17–18 in Globe, Arizona, lists her as a widow, even though records show the death of Charles Clark occurred in August of that year. According to the census, Kate was living alone at 178 Edgar Street, which she rented for nine dollars a month. It further indicates that she had a seventh-grade education. Kate continued to live in Globe until her death in 1948. She died in the Gila County Hospital after a two-week illness. Her death certificate indicates the cause of death as chronic heart disease and senility. Elvis Clark provided information for the death certificate. She was buried in Globe Cemetery. Kate was seventy-nine years old. At the time of her death, her stepsons Claude and Kyle were also living in Globe, while Elvis continued to reside in Young. D. M. Peterson, pastor of the First Christian Church, officiated at a memorial service for Kate on February 13, 1948, at the Globe Memorial Chapel. Survivors mentioned in her obituary were her sister Jackie May Thornton; her stepsons Claude J. Clark, Kyle Clark, and Elvis Clark; her nephew Sam Tracey (should be Kersey); and her niece Adelia Sprague.

Stepchildren of Kathryn Judson "Kate" Kenny

Claude James Clark
(17 Mar 1890–1 Apr 1961)

Claude, about eighteen years old when Kate joined the family, was living with his brother Welburn Clark and Welburn's wife, Pearl, in Erath County, Texas, in 1910. They were living adjacent to Charles and Kate, and Claude had his own blacksmith shop. Claude registered for the World War I draft in Colfax County, New Mexico. In 1920 Claude, Elvis, their wives, and Elvis's daughter Juanita shared a home in Socorro County, New Mexico. Both men were working as farm laborers. Around 1925, Claude and his family moved to Gila County, Arizona. In 1948, Claude and his family were living in Globe, Arizona. The children of Claude and Leona were Claude (ca. 1921–), Wayne (ca. 1925–), Edith (ca. 1927–), Nell (ca. 1929–), Dale (ca. 1931–), and Elbert (ca. 1934–).

Elvis Lee Clark
(15 Apr 1897–Mar 1984)

Elvis was living with his father and Kate in Erath County, Texas, in 1910. They were enumerated adjacent to Welburn Clark; Welburn's wife, Pearl; and Elvis's brother Claude. Elvis apparently stayed with his brother Claude when his father, Kate, and Kyle moved to Arizona in 1914. By 1920 he was in Socorro County, New Mexico, with his wife, Mary, and daughter Juanita. They shared a dwelling with his brother Claude and Claude's wife, Leona. In 1930 they were living in Gila County, Arizona. Elvis was proprietor of a general merchandise store. Elvis died in March of 1984; his last residence was listed as Globe, Gila County, Arizona. Young, Arizona, was the family's home in 1948. Elvis and Mary's children are Juanita (ca. 1919–), Charles (ca. 1921–), Lora (ca. 1923–), and Wanda (ca. 1925–).

Rybert (Rupert) Kyle Clark
(29 Aug 1902–25 Nov 1953)

Kyle was living with his father and Kate in Erath County, Texas, in 1910. By 1920, seventeen-year-old Kyle was with Charles and Kate in Young, Gila County, Arizona. The 1930 census of Globe, Gila County, Arizona, lists Kyle as a truck driver and contractor. His wife, Etta, was born around 1904. The 1940 census shows the family living in Globe, Arizona, with Kyle working as a tractor operator and contractor. Kyle and Etta's children are Lois (ca. 1925–), Bonnie (ca. 1927–), and Verna Kyle (1930–).

SOURCES

"Clark, Charles C." 1930 US Census, Gila County, AZ, Young, ED 4-53, p. 39, dwelling 34, family 35, April 5, 1930. Ancestry.com.

"Clark, Charles." 1910 US Census, Erath County, TX, Justice Precinct 5, ED 28, Sup. Dist. 12, sheet 15a, p. 272, dwelling 38, family 38, June 15, 1920. FamilySearch Library, Salt Lake City, UT.

"Clark, Charles." 1920 US Census, Gila County, AZ, Young, ED 55, p. 272, dwelling 36, family 38, January 1920. FHLC #1820047, FamilySearch Library, Salt Lake City, UT.

"Clark, Claude J." 1920 US Census, Socorro County, NM, Precinct 34, Sup. Dist. 2, ED 162, household 44, families 44 and 45. Ancestry.com.

"Clark, Claude J." 1930 US Census, Gila County, AZ, Young, ED 4-53, p. 39, dwelling 35, family 36, April 5, 1930. Ancestry.com.

"Clark, Claude James, Sr." Find A Grave Index, 1600s–Current. Ancestry.com.

"Clark, Claude James." World War I draft registration card. Ancestry.com.

"Clark, Claude." 1940 US Census, Gila County, AZ, Globe City, ED 4-1, sheet 1A, line 17, family 7, April 2, 1940. Ancestry.com.

"Clark, Elvis Lee." Find A Grave Index, 1600s–Current. Ancestry.com.

"Clark, Elvis Lee." World War I draft registration card. Ancestry.com.

"Clark, Elvis." 1930 US Census, Gila County, AZ, Young, ED 4-53, p. 38, dwelling 10, family 10, April 2, 1930. Ancestry.com.

"Clark, Elvis." 1940 US Census, Gila County, AZ, Young, ED 4-15, sheet 1B, line 67, family 22, April 20, 1940. Ancestry.com.

"Clark, Elvis." Social Security Death Index. Ancestry.com.

"Clark, Kate." 1940 US Census, Gila County, AZ, Globe City, ED 4-7, sheet 9B, line 78, dwelling 178, April 17–18, 1940. Ancestry.com.

"Clark, Kyle." 1930 US Census, Gila County, AZ, Precinct 7, ED 4-22, p. 376, dwelling 36, family 38, April 8, 1930. Ancestry.com.

"Clark, Mrs. K. J." Obituary. *Phoenix Globe*, February 12, 1948, p. 6. Microfilm, Arizona State Library.

"Clark, R. K." 1940 US Census, Gila County, AZ, Globe City, ED 4-5, sheet 8A, line 17, family 27, April 12, 1940. Ancestry.com.

"Clark, Rupert Kyle." Find A Grave Index, 1600s–Current. Ancestry.com.

"Kenny, W. C." 1880 US Census, Erath County, TX. FamilySearch Library, Salt Lake City, UT.

"Thornton, Henry C." 1930 US Census, Stephens County, TX, Justice Precinct 4, ED 120-6, sheet 11B, line 81, dwelling 231, family 243, April 17, 1930. FamilySearch Library, Salt Lake City, UT.

Workers of the Writer's Program of the Work Projects Administration, comps. *The WPA Guide to 1930s Arizona*, pp. 455-461. The University of Arizona Press, 1989. FamilySearch Library, Salt Lake City, UT.

Jackie May Kenny
(29 Dec 1871–6 Jul 1956)

Jackie May Kenny was born in Tennessee Colony, Anderson County, Texas, the youngest child of William Curry and Eliza Jane Colwell Kenny. She moved with the family to Erath County and appears on the 1880 census. She attended school at Hannibal (then called Berlin Hall), Erath County, Texas. On July 31, 1888, Rev. John Lawson officiated at the marriage of Jackie May to William Luther Thornton (11 Dec 1866–29 Mar 1928). William was a brother of Henry Thornton, the husband of Jackie's sister Florence. William was born in Erath County, Texas. He is also shown on the 1880 census in the Hannibal area with his parents, doing farmwork at age thirteen. Jackie and William resided in the Hannibal community during the first several years of their marriage. The 1900 census shows William, Jackie, and their children on a farm adjacent to that of Henry and Florence.

William and Jackie had three children: Minnie Orena, called Orena by the family; Clive; and Daniel Raymond. The second child—Clive, born in 1896—lived less than two years.

The 1910 census shows William and Jackie still farming in the Hannibal area. Both children were living at home, and Orena was teaching in high school.

By 1920, Jackie and William had moved to Desdemona, Eastland County, where they were operating a hotel and rooming house. Within the next few years, they moved to Breckenridge, Texas, where Henry and Florence resided. William died in Breckenridge and was buried in Breckenridge Cemetery. His headstone indicates membership in a Masonic lodge.

In 1930, Jackie was living with her daughter, Orena; son-in-law, Prince Kinsey; and granddaughter Alleyne in Breckenridge, Texas. At that time Prince was the manager of a department store, and Orena worked as a department store salesperson. When Orena and Prince moved to Sherman, Texas, Jackie made the move with them and continued to make her home with them. She was a member of the First Baptist Church of Sherman and a member of Sherman Eastern Star Chapter 183. She died at her home at 720 South Travis Street, Sherman. She was survived by two children, three grandchildren, and six great-grandchildren. Funeral services were at the Kiker Funeral Home in Breckenridge, and burial was beside her husband in Breckenridge Cemetery.

Descendants of Jackie May and William Thornton

Minnie Orena Thornton
(23 Sep 1891–9 Nov 1969)

Orena was born in Erath County, Texas. At nineteen, she had obtained a teaching certificate and was living with her parents and teaching high school. She and Prince (20 Jan 1892–28 Aug 1960) were married in Erath County, Texas, on June 25, 1913. Prince's parents were Taylor P. Kinsey and Mary Kaiser of Hamilton County, Texas. Prince and Orena lived in Oklahoma, where their daughter was born in 1915. In 1917, when Prince registered for the World War I draft, they were living in Lorenzo, Crosby County, Texas. In the draft document, Prince identified his occupation as clerk and his description as tall and slender, with gray eyes and dark-brown hair. By 1930, they lived in Breckenridge, where Prince managed a department store. They moved to Sherman, Texas, after 1930, and this continued to be their home. Prince died in Sherman from a heart attack in 1960. His death certificate indicates that before retirement, he had been manager of the Sherman JCPenney store. Orena survived him nine years; she died in Sherman from cerebral thrombosis. Both she and Prince were buried in Sherman.

- **Eunice Alleyne Kinsey (20 Apr 1915–5 Oct 1983):** Born in Oklahoma, Alleyne attended school in Breckenridge and Sherman. She married Daniel Henry Poole (31 Dec 1914–12 Apr 1981) in Sherman. Dan's parents were Flora and Daniel H. Poole Sr. of Sherman. The 1940 census shows an Allyne and Dan Pool residing on South Crocker Street in Sherman. Dan worked as assistant superintendent for a cotton mill. Dan and Alleyne were living in Durham, North Carolina, at the time of their deaths.
  - **Princess Poole (7 Aug 1946–):** Princess was born in Tarrant County, Texas. She married Ted Jones.

Clive Thornton
(16 Sep 1896–25 Jan 1898)

Clive was born and died in Erath County, Texas, and was buried in Hannibal Cemetery. According to family oral history, as related by Leona Kenny Davis, the day of his death was one of those warm, sunny days sometimes seen in Texas winters. A group of children was playing in a meadow in the warm sunshine when someone accidentally turned over a beehive. All the children were stung, but the toddler Clive either had more stings, was too small to survive the number of stings, or was more sensitive to beestings. He died because of the beestings.

Daniel Raymond Thornton
(19 Mar 1898–10 Aug 1963)

Daniel was born in Erath County, Texas. He married Rhoda Lewis (6 Feb 1899–Dec 1984) on December 26, 1917, in Howard County, Texas. Soon after their marriage they moved to Miami, Gila County, Arizona, where they were living in September 1918, when Daniel registered for the World War I draft. At that time, he was working as a smelter and described himself as tall and slender with brown eyes and dark hair. The 1920 census shows Raymond and Rhoda Thornton living in Miami, Arizona, where he worked as a salesman in a dry goods store. Living with them was Freda Backman, a teacher in the local public school. It is not known whether Daniel's aunt Kate Kenny Clark, who lived in Gila County, influenced their move to that area.

Daniel and Rhoda returned to Texas, where their second son, William, was born in 1923. They moved to Meridian, Mississippi, before 1935. The 1940 census indicates they had been living in the same house since 1935 and that Daniel worked as a manager of a department store. They owned their home on Twenty-Third Street in Meridian. Daniel died in Meridian, Mississippi, in 1963. Rhoda remained in Meridian until her death twenty-one years later.

- **Daniel Raymond Thornton Jr. (15 Apr 1920–11 Sep 1991):** Born in Miami, Arizona, Dan spent most of his life in Meridian, Mississippi. The 1940 census shows him in his parents' home in Meridian. Dan attended Tulane University, where he completed a medical degree before establishing a practice in Meridian. Dan married June Augusta O'Donald (16 Nov 1922–21 Aug 2003) around 1945. Dan and June lived in Arizona and Louisiana before settling in Meridian, Mississippi, around 1950. Both resided in Meridian until their deaths.

  - **Sharon Lee Thornton (24 Dec 1947–):** Sharon was born in New Orleans, Louisiana. She married John R. Coffee on April 4, 1970.

  - **Daniel Raymond Thornton III (1 Mar 1951–):** Daniel was born in Meridian, Mississippi.

- **William Lewis Thornton (21 Oct 1923–31 Mar 1996):** Born in Bexar County, Texas, William attended school in Meridian, Mississippi, and is shown on the 1940 census as a sixteen-year-old student. He married Mae Carroll Harrison on June 14, 1945. They lived in Dallas, Texas, before returning to Meridian around 1950. Both he and Mae died in Meridian. The Mae Carroll Thornton Scholarship was established at the Meridian Community College to be given to a student who is both a mother and a student in a health-care field.

- **Carroll Hodges Thornton (11 Nov 1947–):** Carroll was born in Dallas, Texas. She attended the University of Mississippi and has worked in Washington, DC.

- **Rhoda Gayle Thornton (25 Oct 1949–):** Born in Dallas, Texas, Rhoda attended school in Meridian, Mississippi, and the University of Mississippi, with a major in home economics. While a student at the university, she was named 1970 Maid of Cotton in a ceremony in Memphis, Tennessee. One of her first duties as Maid of Cotton was to attend the Cotton Bowl football game. Rhoda married Joel Callahan. They live in Meridian, Mississippi.

- **William Lewis Thornton Jr. (11 Sep 1954–):** Bill was born in Meridian, Mississippi. He attended Meridian schools and received a degree in construction engineering from Mississippi State University. He also studied at Tulane University and received a degree in business administration from the University of Dallas. Bill has lived in Euless, Texas; Arlington, Virginia; and Meridian, Mississippi. He works as construction coordinator for Paul Broadhead Associates of Meridian, Mississippi. He and his wife, Sheridan Virden, have two children, Katherine and Matthew.

- **Lee Kinsey Thornton (14 Feb 1963–):** Lee was born in Meridian, Mississippi. He graduated from Meridian High School with a full academic college scholarship. After undergraduate studies at Millsaps College and the University of Mississippi, he spent a year teaching biology at Millsaps College. He graduated, top of his class, from Tulane University School of Medicine with an MD and master's degrees in public health and tropical medicine. From New Orleans, Dr. Thornton went to Denver, Colorado, for an internship in community medicine at the University of Colorado Hospitals.

Lee was accepted in the training program for general surgery at the University of Texas Southwestern Medical Center at Parkland Hospital in Dallas, Texas. While in Dallas, he met Michelle Ham. The two were married on June 22, 1996, in Dallas.

After becoming certified in general surgery, Lee accepted a position for plastic surgery training at Emory University in Atlanta. After completing his training, he worked with Places Plastic Surgery Center in Atlanta.

With their growing family, Lee and Michelle decided to move back to his hometown of Meridian. He established Meridian Plastic Surgery, the first plastic surgery unit in the area. He specializes in cosmetic and reconstructive surgery.

Lee and Michelle live on a farm outside of Meridian with their children—Kinsey, twins Hannah and Madi, and Lachlan.

SOURCES

Breckenridge Cemetery (1301 E. Elliott St., Breckenridge, TX). W. L. Thornton headstone.

Breckenridge Cemetery Records. Copy supplied by Frida Mitchell, Swenson Memorial Museum of Stephens County.

Davis, Leona Kenny. Family stories related to Mary Jo Kenny. Summer 1984.

Davis, Leona Kenny. Untitled paper prepared around 1970.

Erath County Marriage Record, 1869–1891. Erath County Genealogical Society, 1980.

"Kenny, W. C." 1880 US Census, Erath County, Texas. FamilySearch Library, Salt Lake City, UT.

"Kinsey, Orena." Texas Death Index, 1902–2000. Ancestry.com.

"Kinsey, Orena." Texas, Find A Grave Index, 1961–2012. Ancestry.com.

"Kinsey, Prince." 1930 Sherman City Directory. Ancestry.com.

"Kinsey, Prince." 1930 US Census, Stephens County, Texas, Breckenridge, sheet 4A, ED 215, line 24. Ancestry.com.

"Kinsey, Prince." 1940 US Population Census, Grayson County, Texas. Ancestry.com.

"Kinsey, Prince." Texas Death Index, 1903–2000. Ancestry.com.

"Kinsey, Prince." Texas, Find A Grave Index, 1961–2012. Ancestry.com.

"Kinsey, Prince." World War I Draft Registration. Ancestry.com.

"Kinsey, Tayler P." 1910 US Census, Tarrant County, Texas, Fort Worth. Ancestry.com.

"Lee K. Thornton, MD." Meridian Plastic Surgery. Accessed September 20, 2023. http://www.meridianplasticsurgery.com/contents/about/our-staff.

"Lee Thornton, MD." The Plastic Surgery Channel. Accessed September 20, 2023. http://www.theplasticsurgerychannel.com/doctors/lee-thornton.

"Poole, Alleyne." North Carolina Death Indexes, 1908–2004. Ancestry.com.

"Poole, Alleyne." US, Social Security Death Index, 1935–Current. Ancestry.com.

"Poole, Dan H." 1940 US Census, Grayson County, Texas, Sherman. Ancestry.com.

"Poole, Daniel H." 1920 US Census, Grayson County, Texas, Sherman. Ancestry.com.

"Poole, Daniel H." 1930 US Census, Grayson County, Texas, Sherman, ward 3, ED 91-6, sheet 5B, line 92. Ancestry.com.

"Poole, Princess." Texas Birth Index, 1903–1997, Tarrant County. Ancestry.com.

Rhonda Gayle Thornton. "1970 Maid of Cotton" *The Tuscaloosa News.* Google News Archive Search. Thornton Reunion Papers, 1977. Copies supplied by Alban Bridges.

"Thornton, Carroll Hodges." Texas Birth Index, 1903–1997. Ancestry.com.

"Thornton, D. R." 1880 US Census, Erath County, Texas, FamilySearch Library, Salt Lake City, UT.

"Thornton, Daniel R. Jr." US, Social Security Death Index, 1935–Current. Ancestry.com.

"Thornton, Daniel R." 1920 US Census, Gila County, Arizona, Miami, ward 2, ED 50, sheet 18A, p. 207. FHLC#1820047, FamilySearch Library, Salt Lake City, UT.

"Thornton, Daniel R." 1940 US Census, Lauderdale County, Mississippi, Meridian, ED 38-7, sheet 5A, line 40. Ancestry.com.

"Thornton, Daniel R." US, Social Security Death Index, 1935–Current. Ancestry.com.

"Thornton, Daniel Raymond, Jr." 1958 Meridian City Directory. US City Directories, 1821–1989. Ancestry.com.

"Thornton, Daniel Raymond." US World War I Draft Registration Cards, 1917–1919. Ancestry.com.

"Thornton, Gayle." Texas Birth Index, 1903–1997. Ancestry.com.

"Thornton, Jackie M." Texas Death Index, 1903–2000. Ancestry.com.

"Thornton, Jackie May." Texas Death Index, 1903–2000. Ancestry.com.

"Thornton, Jackie." 1930 Sherman City Directory. Ancestry.com.

"Thornton, Lee Kinsey." Texas Marriage Collection, 1966–2000. Ancestry.com.

"Thornton, Mrs. Jackie." Obituary. *Sherman Democrat*, July 8, 1956.

"Thornton, Daniel Raymond, Jr." *1941 Jambalaya: Tulane University Yearbook*, p. 249. Ancestry.com.

"Thornton, W. L." 1900 US Census, Erath County, Texas, Precinct 7, ED 77, sheet 3, line 63. FHLC #1241632, FamilySearch Library, Salt Lake City, UT.

"Thornton, W. L." 1910 US Census, Erath County, Texas, Precinct 7, ED 20, sheet 7A, line 1. FamilySearch Library, Salt Lake City, UT.

"Thornton, W. L." 1920 US Census, Eastland County, Texas, Precinct 8, p. 14B, line 52. FamilySearch Library, Salt Lake City, UT.

"Thornton, William L." Texas Death Index, 1903–2000. Ancestry.com.

"Thornton, William L." US, Social Security Death Index, 1935–Current. Ancestry.com.

"Thornton, William Lewis." Intelius. Accessed September 20, 2023. http://www.intelius.com/people/William-Thornton/0c439rvdqcp.

"Thornton, William Lewis." Texas Birth Index, 1903–1997, Bexar County, Texas. Ancestry.com.

CHAPTER 3:
Kenny Family Background

Little information on William Curry Kenny's family background was passed down in the family. Census records indicate that he was born in South Carolina and that his son James Polk Kenny was born in Louisiana. William's tombstone provided a birth date of April 2, 1809. His grandchildren remembered their father, Will Kenny, corresponding with "Aunt Meg" Hayes, who was principal of Opelousas Female Academy in Opelousas, Louisiana. The assumption was that "Aunt Meg" was a sister of William's.

"Aunt Meg" was Margaret M. Hayes. The centennial edition of the Opelousas newspaper gave a short history of the school and its importance to the community. In addition to being a boarding school for girls, it accepted day students from the community, both boys and girls. The school had a very good reputation, and it was noted that many important citizens of the community attended. Little background was given on Margaret Hayes.

Perrin's *Bibliography of Important Individuals* gave a short biography of Margaret Hayes, indicating that she had been born Margaret White in Franklin, Tennessee. This led to a search of data in Williamson County, Tennessee. A marriage bond for Benjamin R. White and Elizabeth Kenny (spelled Kinny) for August 5, 1822, with Benjamin White and Thomas Thompson as bondsmen, was on file with the Williamson County records. The family was followed through the 1830 and 1840 censuses of Williamson County. By 1850, the family had moved to Franklin County, Tennessee, and their youngest child was listed as Margaret.

Records from Saint Landry Parish, Louisiana, show the marriage of "Margarete" White to James G. Hayes on November 10, 1868. The family is shown on the 1870 census, at which time they were operating a hotel in Opelousas. James G. and Margaret are listed with an infant Delia, Ida, Clarence, and Joseph. The latter three were James's children from a previous marriage. Also in the household were B. R. White, seventy, a carpenter, born in North Carolina, and Eliza, sixty-five, born in South Carolina. This provided strong evidence that Margaret Hayes was the daughter of Benjamin R. and Elizabeth Kenny White. Further evidence was provided when James died in

1871. Probate papers indicate that Margaret's father, Benjamin R. White, was appointed to represent the interests of Margaret's then unborn child. Delia apparently had not survived.

With Margaret Hayes established as the daughter of Benjamin R. White and Elizabeth Kenny, it seemed probable that Elizabeth was the sister of William Curry Kenny. This led to an examination of all Kenny names on available early records of Williamson County, Tennessee. Relatively few were found. Tax records showed that Daniel Kenny paid poll taxes in 1801, 1802, 1803, 1804, 1805, 1806, and 1807, but not in subsequent years. William Kenny paid poll taxes and taxes on land: 100 acres in 1808 and 1809, 120 acres in 1818, and 90 acres on the east bank of South Harpeth River in 1811 and 1812. He does not appear on the 1813 tax rolls but is listed on the 1815, 1816, 1818, and 1819 rolls for 90, 98, or 92 acres of land. James Kenny appears on the 1811 tax lists with 40 acres of land listed as on South Harpeth in 1811, and on Bedford Creek in 1813. James Kenny is listed on the 1814 tax list. Beginning in 1820, no Kenny names appear on the tax lists through 1830. David and Thomas Kinsey appear and are listed as Kinny in 1821 but as Kinsey in other listings. Although both William and James paid taxes on land, neither are listed in the grantor-grantee indexes for the county from 1800 through 1830.

Assuming the accuracy of William Curry Kenny's birth on April 2, 1809, in South Carolina, both Daniel and William Kenny could be eliminated as his father, since both were in Williamson County by 1808. The next records for James Kenny were probate records filed with an inventory on January 3, 1816, with Mary Kenny and Jonathan Stepleton as executors. John Edgar, Samuel Williams, and Samuel McMillen were instructed by the same court to set aside provisions for the widow and orphans of James Kenny. Also in the probate records was a statement of the provisions having been set aside. There is no indication of the names, or even the number of children.

The next group of records examined was the marriage records. Records for the following marriages were found from 1800 through 1853:

Nancy Kinny and John Reeves, June 30, 1809

Polly Kenney and George Wade, September 9, 1817

Sarah Kinney and Archibald Ponder, November 26, 1817

Eliza Kinny and Benjamin R. White, August 5, 1822

Peggy Kinney and Abraham Greer, August 13, 1825

Jane Kenney and Edward Long, December 14, 1828

John Kenny and Jane Douglass, December 13, 1833

William C. Kenny and Elizabeth Oldham, September 4, 1838

It was thought that Nancy Kinny was likely the daughter of William or Daniel Kenny, both of whom were in Williamson County in 1809. An examination of the original records for Sarah Kinney and Archibald Ponder at the Williamson County archives shows that, although indexed as Kinney, Sarah's name was actually Kinsey. This left six names for further investigation.

The George Wade family is listed on the 1820 Williamson County census with the following composition: three males under ten, one male over forty-five, two females under ten, one female between ten and sixteen, one female between sixteen and twenty-six, and one female between twenty-six and forty-five. This was obviously not a young couple who married in 1817, and since Polly was a common nickname for Mary, this led to the speculation that Mary, James Kenny's widow, married George Wade.

Probate papers for Moses and Elizabeth Oldham indicate that William C. and Elizabeth Oldham Kenny had moved to Louisiana, where Elizabeth died in 1840. Benjamin White filed papers on William C. Kenny's behalf and mentioned communication from William C. Kenny's sister, Isabella Hedrick. William C. Kenny is found on the 1840 census of Caldwell Parish, Louisiana. There is also a G. C. Hedrick.

Information necessary to establish James and Mary Kenny as William C. Kenny's parents and to identify his siblings came when an email from Stacy McAdams indicated that William C. Kenny of Erath County, Texas, was mentioned in the succession papers of Henry R. Wade in West Carroll Parish, Louisiana. W. H. Hedrick, nephew of the deceased, filed a listing of the brothers and sisters of half-blood and the brothers and sister of full blood of Henry Wade. Half siblings of Henry Wade on the Kenny side were established as Elizabeth White, Margaret Greer, William Curry Kenny, Isabella Hedrick, and Jane Long. John Kenny—who married Jane Douglass in Williamson County, Tennessee, in 1833—may also have been a son in this family. No additional information has been found on him, and he is not mentioned in the Henry R. Wade probate papers. If he was a member of this family, he had died without leaving children, or he had completely lost contact with the family by the time of the probate.

Alexander Kenny
(ca. 1734–ca. 1797)

James Kenny's parents were Alexander and Margaret Kenny, who were granted land in Craven County, South Carolina. The grant was one of several grants signed by the governor on May 13, 1768. Since most of the grants issued by South Carolina to Irish immigrants were to new immigrants from Protestant Ireland, it is likely that Alexander and Margaret immigrated from Ulster. Internet sources give an immigration date of 1765. Land records identify Alexander, age thirty-four; Margaret, age thirty-six; Agnes, age eight; and Isabella, age four. Alexander Kenny's will—written in 1795 and probated in Chester County, South Carolina, in 1797—lists his wife, Margaret; sons, William and James; daughters, Ann and Isabella; and grandson Alexander. The will identifies his home as a plantation on Rocky Creek, Chester County, South Carolina, and that he owned land in the Waxhaw Settlement. The text of Alexander Kenny's will is given in

Appendix B. The only other documents found referencing Alexander Kenny is a notice of his serving on a grand jury in Chester County and a 1790 census listing for Alex McKenna, which included two males over sixteen years of age and one female over sixteen. Since there was no listing for Alexander Kenny, it seems likely that the tabulator got the name wrong. Margaret's maiden name is unknown, and the only references to her other than Alexander's will are her signatures for release of dower rights when James and William sold lands inherited from Alexander. A paper attributed to Orena Thornton, a granddaughter of William Curry Kenny, suggests that Margaret's name may have been Pollock and that her father was James Pollock of Ireland. This paper has many errors and can only be used as a clue for research. The text of Orena's paper is given in Appendix C.

- **Agnes Ann Kenny (ca. 1753–ca. 18--):** It is assumed that the Agnes listed on the land records and the Ann noted in Alexander's will are the same person. She would have been born around 1753, probably in Ireland. Nothing is known of her marriage. That she received no property and only a book in her father's will suggests that she had been given property earlier, probably at the time of her marriage, or that she was partially disinherited by her father. If Agnes and Ann are two different individuals, Agnes was probably no longer living when Alexander made out his will in 1795.

- **Isabella Kenny (ca. 1757–ca. 18--):** Isabella was probably born in Ireland. With her brother William, Isabella inherited the land in the Waxhaw Settlement. When the land was sold on August 29, 1801, Jonathan Emanuel Steeples joined William Kenny in the sales. It is probable that Jonathan Emanuel Steeples was Isabella Kenny's husband. No other information is known about Isabella.

- **William Kenny (11 Oct 1768–ca. 1833):** William, son of Alexander Kenny, was born in Waxhaw Settlement, according to his Revolutionary War pension application. The 1800 census of Chester County, South Carolina, shows William Kenny as head of a household of three males under ten, one male between ten and sixteen, one male between twenty-six and forty-five, two females under ten, and one female between twenty-six and forty-five. Lyleas Kenny, wife of William Kenny, signed a dower release in January 1802 for land sold by William Kenny to Samuel Walker and another on November 20, 1800, for additional property sold to Samuel Walker. It is likely that the grandson Alexander mentioned in Alexander's will was the ten-to-sixteen-year-old male on the 1800 census. This may be the same Alexander Kenny living in Lincoln County, Tennessee, in 1820, 1830, and 1840, though only the name, approximate age, and place connect them. Since only one grandson was mentioned in the will, it is assumed that the three younger males on the 1800 census were born after the will was written in 1795.

    William Kenny is listed on the property tax rolls of Williamson County, Tennessee, from 1809 to 1814 and from 1815 to 1819. Upon leaving Tennessee, he moved to Morgan County, Alabama, where he resided when applying for a Revolutionary War pension on November 22, 1832. In his application he explained how he entered into the Revolutionary War. In August of 1780, a group of soldiers from General Gates's army stopped by his father's house in Waxhaw Settlement, demanding information on the road to North Carolina. William went with them to show them the way, but when he returned home, he learned that the Loyalists in the area were angry with him for his help in the revolution. Hearing that they were making threats against him, he decided that his best course of action was to join the revolutionary troops. He made his way to George Dunlap's company of Sumter's brigade, a company in which his father had been serving for some time.

A death date for William Kenny would have been after June 1833, when he filed an amended pension application. The pension was granted.

Children of William Kenny have not been identified. The 1800 census of Chester County, South Carolina, shows six children—four males and two females. Nancy Kenny—who married John Reeves on June 30, 1809, in Williamson County, Tennessee, during which time William Kenny paid taxes on land and presumably lived in the county—may have been his daughter. She also could have been the daughter of Daniel Kenny, a Williamson County taxpayer for that year.

Margaret Kenny—who married Anthony Livingston in Morgan County, Alabama, in 1815—was likely a daughter or granddaughter of William Kenny, as determined by DNA analysis through Ancestry.com. The analysis shows a fourth-cousin relationship between a descendant of Margaret and descendants of William Curry Kenny. Margaret could have been named for William's mother. Other Kenny names are found in Morgan and adjoining counties who may be descendants of William Kenny, but the relationships have not been established.

- **James Kenny (ca. 1775–1815):** James is assumed to have been younger than William, but no documents examined give direct or indirect evidence of his birth date. It is assumed that James is the second male in the household of Alex McKenna in the Chester County 1790 census—if this census is the enumeration of Alexander Kenny. A listing for James Kenny (or Kanny) in the 1800 Chester County census shows a household of two males between twenty-six and forty-five, one male over forty-five, and one female between sixteen and twenty-six. James and Mary could be in the age categories, but no data gives a hint on the identity of the other two males, if this is the enumeration for James Kenny.

  An estimated birth date of about 1775 is assigned to James; his birth was likely in Waxhaw Settlement, Lancaster County, South Carolina. From Alexander's will, it appears that James was living on his parents' plantation and oversaw the livestock in 1795.

  That James's wife was Mary is verified by Mary Kenny signing a dower release when James sold land in Chester County. James and Mary were married around 1800, probably in South Carolina but possibly in nearby North Carolina. All their children except Isabella and Jane list South Carolina as a birthplace. This coincides with their coming to Tennessee around 1810 and paying taxes on land in 1811. Family tradition holds that James Kenny fought in the War of 1812 and was in the Battle of New Orleans. Records indicate that James Kenny was a member of William Metcalf's regiment, which participated in the Battle of New Orleans under Major General William Carroll. James Kenny's death in 1815 would be consistent with family tradition that he died of wounds received or of illness soon after the Battle of New Orleans. Probate records of Williamson County, Tennessee, for January 1816 show that James's wife, Mary, and Jonathan Stepleton were executors of the estate. Mary retained all the inventoried goods except one gun. Among the inventoried items were twelve books, a number higher than typical of frontier homes.

Mary "Polly" Kenny's background has not been established. A paper found in the papers of Ray Kersey and attributed to Orena Thornton, a granddaughter of William Curry Kenny, was undated but reported to have been written in 1907. This paper indicates that Mary was Mary Pollock and that her father was a brother to the father of President James K. Polk. Both claims could not be accurate, since the Polk family had changed from Pollock when they immigrated to America, several generations before James K. Polk. The fact that William Curry Kenny named his oldest son James Polk Kenny supports a Polk connection and suggests that he may have named his son for both of his parents. No documented connections have been made with Mary and a brother of Samuel Polk (1772–1827), father of President Polk, or with a brother of Ezekiel Polk (7 Dec 1747–31 Aug 1824), President Polk's grandfather. A search of internet sources for the Polk family has not provided decisive data to confirm or refute the Polk name for Mary. The full text of Orena's paper is given in Appendix D. Since the possibility that Mary's maiden name could be Polk was introduced, several family trees on the internet have listed Charles Polk and his wife, Margaret Baxter, of Mecklenburg County, North Carolina, as the parents of Mary Kenny. The fact that Lancaster County, South Carolina, is adjacent to Mecklenburg County shows proximity of the two families, but the 1790 census of Mecklenburg County gives only one female in the Charles Polk family, suggesting no daughters at that date. Mary probably would have been born well before 1790.

The fact that Jonathan Stepleton was co-executor of James Kenny's estate suggests a possible kinship. Available information on Jonathan Stepleton, including census and land and tax records, has been examined, but no relationship was revealed. Several of Mary's children were given middle names that could be surnames and therefore possible maiden names of Mary, but none have been identified as such. These include Elizabeth "Eliza" Morehouse Kenny, William Curry Kenny, Lawrence Thompson Wade, James Taylor Wade, and Mary Flemming Wade.

On September 9, 1817, Mary Kenny and George Wade obtained a marriage license in Williamson County, Tennessee. Her name is listed as Polly Kinney or Kenney, but subsequent evidence shows that the record was for the widow of James Kenny. The George Wade family had also moved from Chester County, South Carolina, to Williamson County, Tennessee, and the two families may have been longtime friends. The 1820 and 1830 censuses show the George Wade family in Williamson County. After 1830, probably around 1832, they moved to Claiborne County, Mississippi, where Mary's daughter Jane and some of George's children were living. They probably followed the Natchez Trace, though other routes were available by that time. The Kenny property in Tennessee was near the northern part of the Natchez Trace, and their destination near Fort Royal is near the southern section of the trace. It was in Claiborne County, Mississippi, that Mary Kenny Wade died in 1838. George survived her and is shown in the 1850 census with his daughter in Louisiana.

Descendants of James and Mary Kenny

Margaret Ann "Peggy" Kenny
(ca. 1803–ca. 1860)

Margaret was born in South Carolina. She married Abraham Greer in Williamson County, Tennessee, on August 3, 1825. The family resided in Tennessee for a few years, then moved to Illinois. Their two youngest sons were born in Gallatin County, Illinois. The 1830 census of Gallatin County shows the Abraham Greer family with three males under five years of age. A memoir by James Greer, son of Francis Marion Greer, indicated that the family returned to Tennessee around 1834, then moved to Mississippi, and finally ended up in Louisiana. An 1840 census of Claiborne County, Mississippi, shows an Abram Greer family consisting of parents ages thirty to forty and seven children. If this is Margaret's family, three additional sons and a daughter were born by 1840, and Abraham and the four younger children died before 1850—or the younger children were not their children. The ages would be appropriate for Abraham, Margaret, and the three older sons, but by 1850 there was only Margaret and three sons. An alternate possibility is Abraham died in Illinois and Margaret and her three sons moved near her family. This would be consistent with the account of James A. Greer that the family moved from Illinois to Tennessee when F. M. Greer was age four, then to Mississippi and Louisiana when he was eighteen. The 1850 census shows Margaret as head of household in Morehouse Parish, Louisiana, with her sons William and Francis Marion. All three of the sons served in the Confederate forces during the Civil War, but only Francis Marion returned after the war. Although both William and Francis Marion are found on the 1860 census of Morehouse Parish, Margaret is not. It seems probable that she died before 1860. Probate papers for her half brother Henry R. Wade list her but indicate that she was deceased by 1886. No records were given for her descendants other than a statement that she had grandchildren living in Mississippi.

- **William Marshall Greer (ca. 1826–ca. 1864):** William Marshall was born in Tennessee, probably Williamson County. In 1850, at age twenty-four, he was living in his mother's household in Morehouse Parish, Louisiana, engaged in farming. He married Margaret E. Wilson (ca. 1825–ca. 1882), a widow, around 1857, probably in Morehouse Parish. Margaret was born in Georgia. The family is shown on the 1860 census of Morehouse Parish. In addition to William and Margaret, there are A. K. Greer, age one; J. M. (James Monroe) Wilson, age twelve; S. F. Wilson, age nine; W. E. (William) Wilson, age six; J. E. (Josephine E.) Wilson, age four; and Dafney Beale, age sixty-six. Though relationships were not identified, it seems probable that Dafney Beale was Margaret's mother. William and Margaret's three children—Abraham, George, and Ada—were born between 1858 and 1863. William was a private in Company C, Twenty-Eighth Louisiana Infantry during the Civil War. He enlisted on May 13, 1862, and was last listed on the company muster roll in July–August 1863. Exact date of his death has not been established, but the story handed down in the family was that he fought in the Civil War and never came home. He was presumed dead. After William's death, Margaret married Henry Bailey, who died in 1869. Margaret is shown in the 1870 census of Richland Parish, Girard, Louisiana, as Margaret Bailey, head of a household including William Wilson, sixteen; Josephine Wilson, fourteen; Abraham Greer, eleven; George Greer, nine; and "Aden" Greer, seven. They were operating a farm. The adjacent listing is for James Wilson, twenty-two, and his wife, Mary, who were apparently helping with the farm. On November 6, 1882, Margaret Bailey, widow of Henry Bailey, with son George A. Greer and daughters Ada D. Greer and Josephine Wilson Hunter, sold forty acres of land in Richland Parish. Margaret's death date is unknown. No grave marker is found for Margaret in Greer Cemetery, but hers could be one of several graves marked only with a fieldstone.

  - **Abraham K. Greer (ca. 1859–unknown):** Born in Morehouse Parish, Louisiana, Abraham is seen on the 1870 census of Richland Parish, but no additional records have been found for him. Since he is not listed on the 1882 property sale, he may not have survived to that date.

  - **George Andrew Greer (15 Jun 1860–29 Jan 1914):** The George Andrew Greer possessing land in the same area of Richland Parish as shown for Margaret Bailey in 1870 is assumed to be the son of William Marshall and Margaret Greer, though no direct evidence has been found. George's sons William and Marshal may have been named for his father. His birth date is consistent with census data for the age of George, son of William Marshall and Margaret. The US Find a Grave site lists George Andrew Greer's parents as Patrick Henry Greer and Josephine Cumpton of Mississippi. This notation appears to be an error. The

1860 census shows the Patrick Greer family in Claiborne County, Mississippi, with a two-month-old son, George. The 1870 census of this family lists his name as George P. Greer. George P. Greer, born in Mississippi, can be found on censuses for 1880, 1900, 1910, 1920, and 1930 in Mississippi, Oklahoma, and Colorado. Census data for George Andrew Greer gives Louisiana as his birthplace.

George Andrew Greer married Blanche Delaware Smoot (12 Jul 1862–9 Feb 1926) in Monroe, Louisiana, on August 19, 1882. They operated a farm in Richland Parish, Louisiana. George was buried in Greer Cemetery in Richland Parish. Blanche survived him and is shown on the 1920 census in the home of her son Hezzie. The children of George and Blanche Greer were William Hezekiah "Hezzie" (24 Oct 1883–29 Mar 1959), Honor Andrew (10 Jan 1887–21 Sep 1978), Billy Julery (10 Jan 1887–10 Jan 1887), Pony Marshall (24 Jan 1888–12 May 1973), Pearl Elizabeth (4 Mar 1890–14 May 1969), Josephine (27 Nov 1893–Apr 1987), and George Harrison (17 Feb 1896–2 Oct 1978).

- **Ada Greer (ca. 1863–unknown):** Ada married Joseph W. Thornsberry on May 4, 1896, in Rayville, Louisiana. In 1898 Joseph applied for an invalid pension for his service in the Civil War. They are shown on the 1900 Richland Parish census. Joseph died on May 3, 1901, and Ada applied for a Civil War pension for their son, Joseph M. Before 1910, Ada married a man with the last name of Shaw. The 1910 census shows Ada Shaw as head of household with her son, Joseph Thornsberry. The 1920 and 1930 censuses show Ada Shaw, age fifty-five and sixty-five, respectively, as a patient in the Louisiana State Hospital for the Insane in Pineville, Louisiana. Ada Shaw died on June 22, 1937, in Rapides Parish, Louisiana. It is not clear whether this is Ada Greer. No other Louisiana 1920 or 1930 census listings have been found for Ada Greer Shaw. Ada and Joseph's children were Joseph M. (26 Sep 1896–1955) and an infant who was born and died before 1900.

- **James Asa Greer (ca. 1828–20 Aug 1864):** James Asa was probably the child of Margaret and Abraham Greer, named after both of his grandfathers. Few references have been found for him. The 1850 census shows James Greer, twenty-one, born in Illinois, adjacent to the Samuel Wiggins family and working as an overseer. Samuel Wiggins was married to Mary Fleming Wade, half sister of Margaret Kenny Greer. Morehouse Parish deed records show James A. Greer as witness to deeds. James A. Greer is listed as a corporal in the Tenth Tennessee Cavalry during the Civil War. James A. Greer is listed as one of the Morehouse Parish soldiers killed during the Civil War, having died on August 20, 1864.

- **Francis Marion Greer (30 Mar 1830–24 Aug 1873):** Born in Gallatin County, Illinois, Francis Marion moved to Tennessee with his parents at age four, then to Mississippi and Louisiana at age eighteen. He is shown on the 1850 census in his mother's home in Morehouse Parish, Louisiana, working as a farmer. Francis Marion married Sarah Melvina Harthcock (1826–1905) in 1856 in Morehouse Parish, Louisiana. Sarah, a widow, had three children, G. W., John, and Martha Hicks. Francis Marion Greer served in the Civil War. He was captured at Vicksburg, Mississippi, on July 4, 1863. After the war, he returned to Rayville, Morehouse Parish, Louisiana, where he operated a farm until his death about nine years later. After his death, his widow and her sons tried to maintain the farm, but they found it difficult. G. W. and John Hicks had moved on, and the older Greer sons were inexperienced. The land was swampy and prone to flooding. James Allen, the youngest child, wrote of his terror of the snakes that escaped the floodwater by moving to the higher ground where the house was located. After a few years of this effort, the family moved to Warren County, Mississippi, where the hills prevented invasion of floods from the Mississippi. By the fall of 1878, Sarah had sold the farm in Louisiana and purchased an eighty-acre farm in Yazoo County, Mississippi. This location was near some of her relatives and her older son, James Hicks.

In the fall of 1883, Sarah and her oldest son, John Hicks, became interested in the reports of friends about opportunities in Texas. On January 17, 1884, Sarah, John Hicks, and their two families boarded a train for a two-day journey to Mexia, Limestone County, Texas. Two of Sarah Hicks's children did not make the journey. G. W. Hicks returned to Rayville, Louisiana, where he died in 1910. Martha Hicks died in 1881 and was buried in Ebenezer, Mississippi. Mexia was the family headquarters for about ten years. After a few months living in a rented house in Mexia, Sarah bought a farm in the Shiloh community. She lived on the farm until 1894. Hugh Durst, husband of Sarah's daughter Mae, died, leaving Mae and her children without support. Both Sarah and Mae moved to Haskell County, where Sarah's oldest son, Thomas Abraham Greer, had established a farm. They made their home with "Abe" except for a short period when Sarah and Mae ran a boardinghouse in Hubbard City to enable Mae's children to attend school. There was no school in Abe's section of Haskell County. Sarah died in Haskell County on February 23, 1903, of typhoid fever.

- **Thomas Abraham "Abe" Greer (16 Dec 1857–8 Jun 1926):** Abe was born in Morehouse Parish, Louisiana. He never married but was very supportive of his extended family members. In 1889 Abraham moved to Haskell County, where his half brother John Hicks had settled. He established a farm in Haskell County, Texas, near where the town of Rochester would later become established. His mother and sister soon joined his household, and the Durst children considered his home their own. Census records show various family members in his household. Abe died in Haskell County.

- **Francis Marion "Frank" Greer Jr. (15 Feb 1859–26 Nov 1941):** Frank never married. He is shown in the household of his brother James in 1910. Frank headed a Haskell County household shared with his brother William in 1920 and 1930. The 1940 census shows him as a patient in the Wichita State Hospital, with dementia. He died there the following year from a heart attack.

- **William Jefferson Greer (30 Apr 1861–7 Feb 1940):** William Jefferson was unmarried. He is shown in the household of his brother James A. Greer in 1910 and in a household headed by Frank Greer in 1920 and 1930. Like his brother Frank, he died in the Wichita State Hospital.

- **Rebecca Mae Ann Greer (31 Mar 1866–26 Jun 1904):** Mae was born in Morehouse Parish, Louisiana. On October 4, 1886, in Limestone County, Texas, she married Hugh Pickens Durst (16 Sep 1869–11 Jan 1894), a native of Mexia, Limestone County, Texas. Hugh died in Waco, Texas. After Hugh died, Mae and her children moved to Haskell County, where they made their home with her brother Abraham. Her mother, Sarah, made the move with them. In 1896, Mae and Sarah moved to Hubbard City so the Durst children could attend school. By 1900, a school had been established near Abe's place in Haskell County. Mae, Sarah, and the children moved back to his place. About that time, Mae married Jack Ellett. In 1903 and 1904, there was an epidemic of typhoid fever in the area. Both Mae and Sarah died from its effects. The children of Rebecca Mae Ann Greer were Eugene Maurice Durst (4 Jul 1887–12 Dec 1960), Alma Lee Durst (19 Nov 1888–12 Feb 1976), Katie Gertrude Durst (25 Jan 1890–25 Dec 1960), and Edgar Evans Ellett (15 Feb 1901–4 Jul 1980).

- **James Allen Greer (18 Feb 1868–26 Mar 1961):** James was born in Morehouse Parish, Louisiana. His early years were spent in various Mississippi schools, often lasting only three months of the year. At age sixteen, he took a job working on a small farm outside of Mexia, Texas. Realizing that he lacked interest and an aptitude for farming, he obtained a position with the Mexia newspaper. He was a successful newspaper man; his career included owning and editing newspapers in Mexia, Thornton, Hubbard, Stamford, Rochester, and Gustine. While pursuing his newspaper career, he obtained a degree from Metropolitan Business School in Dallas, Texas.

James's first marriage was to Maude Johnson (1878–1931). The marriage ended in divorce, and James was given custody of their son, Allen. James was interested in music; he sang with church and community groups and organized and participated in local bands. A member of the Methodist Church, he frequently led church choirs.

A second marriage in 1909 was to Willie Rose Shaw (1888–1978). James Allen returned to the Rochester area after his brother Abraham died in 1926 to assist his other two brothers. He lived in Haskell County for a number of years until his own health declined and he entered a care facility near Dallas. He died from heart failure in Irving, Dallas County, Texas. He was ninety-three years old. Children of James Allen Greer were James Allen Jr. (24 Jun 1900–14 Feb 1968), Marion Luther (11 Sep 1910–14 Jul 1986), Sarah Olive (20 Oct 1912–18 Sep 2008), Paul Franklin "Frank" (24 Nov 1914–26 Nov 1991), Thomas Henry (24 Jul 1916–15 Jan 2010), and Ina Ruth (19 May 1919–1 Dec 2009).

Elizabeth "Eliza" Morehouse Kenny (17 Mar 1805–7 Sep 1878)

Elizabeth Kenny and Benjamin R. White (15 Jan 1800–13 Dec 1873) were married on August 5, 1822, in Williamson County, Tennessee. Their growing family are enumerated in the 1830 and 1840 censuses of Williamson County. All their children were born in Williamson County, but by 1850 they were in Franklin County, Tennessee. In 1870, Benjamin and Eliza were residing in Opelousas, Louisiana, in the hotel run by their youngest daughter, Margaret, and her husband, James Hayes. As a carpenter, Benjamin probably helped with the maintenance of the hotel. A second 1870 census listing for Benjamin and Eliza White shows them living independently with two construction workers. After James Hayes's death, Benjamin was named guardian for Margaret's unborn child. Both Eliza and Benjamin died in Saint Landry Parish, Louisiana, and are buried in the Opelousas cemetery.

- **Mary Ann White (25 Oct 1823–31 Dec 1891):** Mary Ann was born in Williamson County, Tennessee. She married John Stone Davis (27 Mar 1815–27 Mar 1885), a Methodist minister, on February 28, 1841, in Williamson County, Tennessee. John was born in Giles County, Tennessee, to John and Mill Davis. They lived in several different communities, as John served in several Methodist circuits. Both taught school in some of the communities. They are enumerated with the Benjamin White family in the 1850 census of Franklin County, Tennessee. By 1860, they were in DeKalb County, Tennessee, and by the 1870 census, they were in Caldwell Parish, Louisiana. They moved to Opelousas, Louisiana, where both Mary Ann and John died.
  - **Robert Andrew Davis (24 Aug 1842–9 Mar 1926):** Robert married Elizabeth Ann "Lizzie" Day (13 Oct 1850–19 Feb 1918). They lived in Tensas and Bienville Parishes, Louisiana. Robert was a Methodist circuit rider preacher serving in both Tennessee and Louisiana conferences and was a Confederate Civil War soldier. He died in New Orleans, Louisiana. Their children were Augusta "Gussie" (1881–1936), Louise May (1 Aug 1884–13 Mar 1948), Emma (17 Dec 1885–17 Aug 1964), and Robert Bell (15 Dec 1889–30 Jul 1980).

- **Catharine Fountain Ella Davis (4 Oct 1844–11 Oct 1915):** Ella married Carter Harrison Bradley (1842–1927) in Caldwell Parish, Louisiana, on July 10, 1872. They are shown on the 1880 census of Saint Martin Parish, Louisiana, with daughter Mary E. By 1900, they were in New Orleans with their daughter Eugenia, born January 1880. Ella was listed as the mother of one living child. Also enumerated with them were fourteen-year-old Emma and ten-year-old Robert L. Davis, listed as niece and nephew. In 1910, Carter, Ella, and Eugenia were boarders in the home of Florence Dixon in New Orleans. Ella died in Lafayette, Louisiana. Her daughter, Mary Elizabeth Eugenia (31 Jan 1880–10 Aug 1961), married Thomas T. McFadden.

- **Mary Ann "Molly" Davis (May 1856–unknown):** Mary Ann is shown in the household of John Stone Davis as four years old in the 1860 census and fourteen years old in the 1870 census. Mary Ann Davis (May 1862–Mar 1923) married Alonzo Clement Skyles (1863–1944) on July 3, 1888, in Saint Landry Parish, Louisiana. The discrepancy in birth dates makes it unlikely that she is the daughter of Mary Ann White and John Stone Davis.

- **John White Davis (20 Jan 1859–5 Mar 1899):** John married Gypsie Eason Holyland (1867–1947) on September 14, 1885, in New Orleans, Louisiana. John was a Methodist circuit rider preacher. He died in Vermilion Parish, Louisiana. Gypsie and the children are shown on the 1900 census in Acadia Parish, Louisiana. They moved to California, where Gypsie married H. L. Halsell on November 12, 1905. Gypsie died in San Benito County, California. John and Gypsie's children were Hazel Lloyd (1890–1965), Duncan Kavanaugh (1890–1965), Lucille (25 May 1892–Jan 1972), and John Frederick (26 Mar 1896–9 Jul 1958).

- **Joseph Ellis White (28 Nov 1825–11 Jun 1867):** In 1844, Joseph Ellis became a Methodist circuit rider preacher in Tennessee. He served in several circuits in the Tennessee and Arkansas conferences from 1844 to 1867. He was widely respected in the church. Joseph Ellis White and Mary Elizabeth Gregory (28 Jul 1833–13 May 1907) were married on May 13, 1852. Mary Elizabeth Gregory was born in Chowan County, North Carolina, to William and Winnefred Gregory. Joseph was presiding elder of the Tuscumbia District in 1860. Joseph Ellis died in Coopers Wells, Mississippi. After his death, Mary Elizabeth and the children moved to Louisiana. Mary Elizabeth died at the home of her daughter Kate Lyons in Crowley, Acadia Parish, Louisiana.

  - **Walter Augustus White (Feb 1853–17 Jul 1917):** Born in Alabama, Walter spent most of his adult life in Abbeville, Vermilion Parish, Louisiana. An attorney, he served as parish attorney and district attorney. He was on the board of directors of the first Abbeville Building and Loan Association and was a land developer. He was instrumental in the building of a bridge over the Vermilion

River to the town of Abbeville. Walter and Mary Ella Lyons (23 Jul 1863–14 Aug 1945) were married in 1878 in Vermilion Parish, Louisiana. Mary Ella was born in Vermilion Parish, Louisiana, to Aborn Lyons and Elizabeth Ann Reeves. The 1900 Vermilion Parish census indicates that Mary Ella was the mother of eight children, five of whom were living. Walter was survived by four children. In 1904, the family moved to Covington, Louisiana, where they lived over a decade before he died. The 1930 census of Washington Parish, Louisiana, shows Mary Ella in the home of her daughter Joyce Miller. The 1940 census shows her in the home of her daughter Winnie Anderson, also in Washington Parish. She died in Bogalusa, Washington Parish. Walter and Mary Ella's children were Maggie Mae (25 Jan 1882–15 Jan 1888), Malcum Henry (May 1884–24 Sep 1907), Lawrence Augustus (4 Feb 1886–15 Apr 1966), Winnie (16 Sep 1889–13 Oct 1984), Ernest Burton (16 Jan 1892–20 Nov 1971), and Joyce (8 Aug 1896–Nov 1973).

- **William Benjamin White (4 Mar 1857–14 Jun 1927):** William was born in Rutherford County, Tennessee. He practiced law in Abbeville, Vermilion Parish, Louisiana. He participated in a number of civic and community activities, including the town council. He served as district attorney in Lake Charles. He and Jeanette Morris (19 Dec 1891–16 Dec 1937) were married on February 16, 1887, in Saint Landry Parish, Louisiana. They were members of the Methodist Church, and Jeanette was a founding member of the Abbeville Women's Club and promoted the establishment of a library in Abbeville. William died in Lake Charles, Louisiana. Jeanette is shown on the 1930 census in the home of her son Willie in New Orleans. William and Jeanette's children were Fleta Helen (5 Jun 1888–13 Mar 1902), Lloyd C. (25 May 1890–2 Jan 1918), Emily Jeanette (10 May 1993–2 May 1909), Willie Charlton (2 Dec 1894–7 May 1959), Leroy (Dec 1896–unknown), and William B. Jr. (1900–ca. 1945).

- **Kate White (1860–1940):** Kate was born in Alabama. She taught school before her marriage to Benjamin Franklin Lyons (1851–23 Oct 1915). They lived in Crowley, Acadia Parish, Louisiana. The 1900 census shows Kate as the mother of three children, two of whom were living. The 1920 and 1930 censuses show her in the household of her son Willie. Kate and Benjamin's children were William Augustus "Willie" (25 Nov 1881–14 May 1960), Lester Harry (30 Oct 1886–1 May 1919), and Julia (ca. 1890–ca. 1900).

- **Mary Jo White (24 Sep 1867–22 Apr 1937):** Mary Jo was born in Saint Francis County, Arkansas. She married James Edgar White (Oct 1870–11 Feb 1938) on September 7, 1892, in Abbeville, Louisiana. They are shown on the 1900 census in Vermilion Parish, Louisiana, where James was working as a carpenter. The 1910, 1920, and 1930 censuses show them in Crowley, Louisiana, with James working as an insurance agent. Both Mary Jo and James were buried in Crowley, Louisiana. Their children were Robert Dee (15 Sep 1893–29 Jun 1950), Guy Leonard (Oct 1895–1975), an infant son (2 Aug 1897–27 Sep 1897), and James Roy (21 Jan 1907–6 Dec 1985).

- **Benjamin Franklin White (3 Sep 1827–6 Jan 1904):** Benjamin served with the First Regiment of the Tennessee Volunteers in the war with Mexico and was captain of a heavy artillery battery during the Civil War. He became a licensed Methodist preacher in 1852. He served in both Tennessee and Louisiana conferences in capacities that included circuit rider, city pastor, presiding elder, deacon, and bishop. Benjamin married Sally Malone Wynn (5 Oct 1834–9 May 1871) on October 27, 1863. They had two children. He married Carrie Brashear Allen (1845–1880) on May 27, 1873. A third marriage was to Emma Anderson Glenn. He died in Alexandria, Rapides Parish, Louisiana.

  - **Horace Henry White (7 Feb 1864–13 Oct 1948):** Horace was an attorney, a judge, an educator, and a lay leader in a Methodist church. He lived in Alexandria, Rapides Parish, Louisiana. He obtained baccalaureate and law degrees from Vanderbilt University. He was the author of a widely used book on Louisiana law. In addition to serving several years on the school board, he was a member of a Masonic lodge and an Odd Fellows lodge. Horace and Fannie Blythe (12 Jan 1868–3 Mar 1953) were married on December 27, 1887. She was a member of the Daughters of the American Revolution and an active member and Sunday school teacher in a Methodist church. Their children were Richard Franklin (2 Nov 1888–11 Aug 1935), Ellen Blythe (11 Aug 1890–Jul 1972), Willie Wynn (6 Jul 1892–12 Aug 1968), Horace Manly (21 Oct 1894–31 Jul 1966), Julia B. (3 Nov 1897–3 Feb 1977), Arial Culver (16 Feb 1900–8 Apr 1963), Manie H. (ca. 1903–unknown), Robert McLin (25 Oct 1904–3 Sep 1961), and Fannie (12 Dec 1907–29 Oct 1989).

  - **Julia White (18 Oct 1865–25 Aug 1882):** Julia married Thomas Abner Holloman (1852–1950). They lived in Yazoo County, Mississippi. Their son was Thomas Wynn (4 Oct 1880–27 Oct 1968).

  - **William A. White (20 Apr 1874–25 Dec 1943):** William is shown as a five-year-old on the 1880 census.

  - **Sally Wynn White (1876–1953):** Sally married Neal Davidson (1878–1957). Their daughter, Carolyn, was born around 1912 in Texas. Sally and Neal were buried in Pineville, Rapides Parish, Louisiana.

  - **Walter A. White (1900–before 1904):** He is shown on the 1900 census as a one-month-old infant.

- **Eliza Jane White (29 Jan 1830–ca. 1890):** Eliza Jane and Alex Levy (ca. 1826–before 1880) were married on February 19, 1848, in Davidson County, Tennessee. The 1850 census of Davidson County shows them in Nashville. Their daughter Mary E. was one year old. Also listed in the household were Eliza Jane's brothers Thomas and James, both of whom were working as carpenters. Eliza Jane is recorded in the 1880 census of Saint Landry Parish, Louisiana, as a teacher in the Opelousas school headed by her sister Margaret.

  - **Mary E. "Mollie" Levy (ca. 1849–after 1910):** Mary married Arthur F. Clark (1847–before 1900) on January 20, 1875, in Saint Landry Parish, Louisiana. They are shown on a farm in Vermilion Parish, Louisiana, in the 1880 census. Their children were Arthur and Howard. Mary E. and her children are listed as boarders on the farm of James Folley in Vermilion Parish, Louisiana, in the 1900 census. By 1910, she and four sons were in the household headed by Anthony L. Carmouche, husband of her daughter Eliza J. The children of Mollie and Arthur were Arthur L. (4 Mar 1876–11 Apr 1951), Howard Franklin (12 Jun 1878–4 Jul 1959), Eliza Jane (Jun 1881–Apr 1937), James B. (1883–28 Mar 1931), Walter Andrew (10 Apr 1885–18 May 1946), and Mortimer (25 Aug 1887–19 Jul 1948).

  - **Sarah Tennessee "Tennie" Levy (ca. 1852–unknown):** Sarah married W. A. Reed on June 16, 1888, in Saint Landry Parish, Louisiana.

  - **James Henry Levy (dates unknown):** James died young.

- **Thomas Beeman White (Feb 1832–7 Oct 1899):** Born in Franklin, Tennessee, Thomas is shown in the 1860 census in Nashville, Tennessee, working as a carpenter. He became a circuit rider Methodist preacher in Tennessee at age twenty. He later transferred to Louisiana and spent thirteen years in Oregon and Pueblo, Colorado. In 1888, he returned to Louisiana. He was known in the church for his knowledge of the Bible. Thomas married Victoria Elizabeth Scales (21 Jun 1837–8 Jan 1920) on December 22, 1855. He died in Lincoln Parish, Louisiana.

  - **Minnie Mildred White (8 Jan 1857–13 Oct 1915):** Minnie was born in Ruston, Louisiana. She married Benjamin Lee Arnold (29 Oct 1839–30 Jan 1892) on April 25, 1877, in Albany, Oregon. They lived in Corvallis, Oregon. They are shown on the 1880 census with two-year-old son Herman.

  - **Lelia White (12 Jul 1863–29 May 1951):** Lelia married Carville H. Carson (1 Jul 1860–5 Jun 1914). They lived in Ruston, Louisiana, and Macon, Georgia. Their son was Carville H. Jr. (19 Oct 1897–24 Sep 1963).

  - **Stuart Lyons White (8 Mar 1871–13 Apr 1948):** Stuart married Mary Crenshaw (Oct 1866–22 Oct 1900). A second marriage was to Emma Theus

(21 Dec 1880–5 Dec 1964). Stuart served in the US Army Medical Corps in 1918. He was a physician in Ruston, Lincoln Parish, Louisiana. Their children were Louise (1900–unknown), married name Rawlins, and Thomas B. (6 Oct 1906–2 May 1971).

- **James Megathorn White (23 Mar 1834–23 Mar 1894):** James followed his father's occupation as a carpenter. He and Fannie Guidry (5 Mar 1843–25 Aug 1904) were married on March 14, 1867. They made their home in Opelousas, Saint Landry Parish, Louisiana, where both died and were buried.

  - **Fannie Lou White (12 Jun 1868–23 Dec 1937):** Fannie married Eugene James Chachere (ca. 1865–before 1900) on September 16, 1888. They lived in Opelousas, Louisiana. Fannie and her son are shown living with her mother in the 1900 census. Fannie and Eugene's son was Eugene James Jr. (18 Nov 1892–13 Jul 1960).

  - **Benjamin Rousseau White (5 Oct 1869–3 Jul 1935):** Ben and his first wife, Frances Alberta "Berta" Pharr (21 Aug 1870–29 Nov 1923), lived in Crowley, Louisiana, where he was a representative of the New York Life Insurance Company. They were members of a Methodist church, and he was a member of a Masonic lodge. After Berta's death, Ben married Linda Hamilton Smith (7 Feb 1884–27 Feb 1962), widow of Thomas Smith. The children of Benjamin and Berta were James Albertas (16 Jun 1893–18 May 1953), Frances Amelia (16 Jul 1894–29 Jun 1976), Eunice Dee (9 Aug 1896–15 Jun 1987), Frank Roger (8 Mar 1902–22 May 1957), Percy Pharr (1 May 1903–27 Dec 1968), Mary Maude (14 Aug 1905–8 May 1975), and Benjamin Rousseau Jr. (ca. 1910–26 Apr 1972).

  - **James Guidry White (29 Nov 1870–4 Nov 1871).**

  - **Henry Guy White (26 Feb 1871–25 May 1873).**

  - **Charles Percy White (24 Jun 1873–2 Mar 1915):** Born in Opelousas, Louisiana, Charles spent the fifteen years before his death in Chicago, Illinois. He was married but had no children.

  - **Mary Maude White (21 Nov 1874–16 Jul 1952):** Mary Maude married Louis Beaurepair Chachere (3 Feb 1867–5 Sep 1913) on June 12, 1894. They lived in Crowley, Louisiana. Their children were Louis Bennie (15 Jun 1895–6 Nov 1961), Theodore White (9 Aug 1896–18 Oct 1968), Homer Dewey (25 May 1898–24 May 1947), Ida Dee (3 Nov 1899–unknown), Fannie Zula (21 Dec 1901–24 Mar 1991), Robert Russell (10 Sep 1903–18 Mar 1954), Harold Raymond (8 Jun 1905–28 Oct 1947), Lucille Mae (23 Jan 1908–unknown),

Charles Danie (25 May 1910–5 May 1945), and Harry Alvin (12 Jul 1912–3 Jul 1981).

- **Maggie D. White (21 Aug 1876–19 Aug 1940):** Maggie married David Crawley Rose (1880–1972) on July 12, 1906. They lived in Opelousas, Louisiana. The 1910 census shows them with an infant son less than a month old. Their children were David Crowley (15 Apr 1910–Oct 1983) and Benjamin Algeron (20 Sep 1912–8 May 1979).

- **Alice Eliza White (6 Feb 1878–4 Jul 1879).**

- **Minnie Anna White (17 Jan 1880–30 Nov 1881).**

- **William Dee Hardeman White (31 Aug 1836–24 Feb 1898):** William was born in Franklin, Williamson County, Tennessee. He received a medical degree from Nashville University (now Vanderbilt). He established a medical practice in Abbeville, Louisiana. In 1862, William married Lucinda Reeves Lyons (15 Nov 1845–Apr 1918) on December 24 in Vermilion Parish, Louisiana. He served in the Confederacy during the Civil War and returned to his medical practice in Abbeville after the war. A member of the Methodist Church and a Masonic lodge, he served as the first worshipful master of the local lodge. He was one of the organizers of the Vermilion Medical Society and served as parish coroner for fourteen years. His wife, Lucinda, was one of the local nurses attending to the sick, often in their homes. He died in Abbeville, Vermilion Parish, Louisiana.

  - **Lyman White (22 Oct 1864–1864).**

  - **Willie B. White (22 Oct 1864–21 Aug 1868).**

  - **Joseph White (10 Nov 1866–26 Nov 1870).**

  - **Maggie L. White (23 Nov 1868–27 Nov 1870).**

  - **James Edgar White (Oct 1870–12 Feb 1938):** James Edgar married Mary Jo White (24 Sep 1867–22 Apr 1937), the daughter of Joseph Ellis White and Mary Elizabeth Gregory, on September 7, 1892, in Abbeville, Vermilion Parish, Louisiana. His occupation was insurance salesman. He died in an automobile-truck collision near Crowley, Louisiana. Their children were Robert Dee (15 Sep 1893–29 Jun 1950), Guy Leonard (26 Oct 1895–1975), an infant son (2 Aug 1897–27 Sep 1897), and James Roy (27 Jan 1907–6 Dec 1985).

  - **Mary Emma "Birdie" White (1 Apr 1874–3 Apr 1931):** Mary Emma attended the Opelousas school headed by her father's sister Margaret Hayes. She married James Robert Kitchell (4 Feb 1865–1 Mar 1929) on February 22, 1898. James was a teacher, a lawyer, and active in local Democratic politics. He served as alderman and mayor of Abbeville. Mary Emma was active in the local Methodist church. Their children were Isabel (6 Dec 1898–Jul 1984), Birdie (31 Jul 1900–26 Feb 1969), James Jr. (25 Jul 1902–22 Dec 1974), Louise (11 Jan 1904–Jul 1981), and Mary (29 May 1908–Feb 1982).

- **Carrie Ida White (24 Apr 1875–25 Jun 1963):** Carrie married William Oscar Pipes (Mar 1872–27 Aug 1900) on January 24, 1894. William was a newspaper editor and postmaster in Abbeville, Louisiana. The 1900 census shows the Pipes children in their parents' home as well as in the home of Carrie Ida's mother. No information has been found for Carrie after her husband's death until 1920, when she was living with her daughter Grace in Crowley, Louisiana. By 1930, Carrie had moved to Beaumont, Texas, where she lived the remainder of her life. Their children were Lucille (Oct 1894–unknown), Eugene Beall (9 Mar 1896–24 Sep 1950), and Grace Marie (16 Sep 1899–8 Nov 1972).

- **Henry Bascom White (Aug 1877–unknown):** Henry first married Ann Smith and later married Natalie Vallow, who was the mother of his children, Jimmie Walker (2 Oct 1929–) and C. T. "Tommy" (ca. 1931–).

- **Nannie R. White (1 Dec 1879–4 Sep 1884).**

- **Elizabeth Fanny White (3 Nov 1881–6 Nov 1953):** Known as Lizzy, she was a member of the faculty of Acadia College in Crowley, Louisiana, before her 1902 wedding to Walter Clifton Bier (21 Jun 1882–29 Jul 1938). Both were members of the Methodist Church. He graduated from Bowling Green Business College and was manager of Kaplan Rice Mill until ill health required hospitalization. He died from Huntington's disease. Their children were infant Bier (26 Jul 1903–26 Jul 1903), Winnie Sophie (14 Feb 1905–31 Mar 1971), Viola Dee (26 Sep 1906–Mar 1991), Walter Clifton Jr. (16 Dec 1909–14 Nov 1983), and Clyde Dalton (9 Mar 1911–26 Jun 1974).

- **Rosa Winnie White (14 Sep 1883–11 Dec 1971):** Rosa married Thomas William Rose Sampson. They lived in Orange County, Texas. Their four children were Thomas Junius (10 Feb 1915–1 Feb 1983), Anna Ella (19 Jun 1916–30 May 2007), Rosa Ruth (19 Jul 1917–27 Feb 1979), and Elizabeth (20 Nov 1920–18 Mar 2013).

- **Thomas Pasteur White (27 Jun 1885–14 Jan 1948):** Thomas married Rena Broussard (19 Nov 1889–9 Apr 1972). They lived in Crowley, Acadia Parish, Louisiana. His occupations were listed as bookkeeper, rice mill manager, and rice buyer. Their children were Sylvia E. (ca. 1912–unknown) and Rena Marie (12 Sep 1916–23 Jul 2001).

- **Walter E. White (28 Aug 1886–8 Nov 1886).**

- **John Milton White (15 Jul 1888–16 Jul 1962):** John was a physician in Port Arthur, Texas, for fifty years. He married Olive Velma Trigg (ca. 1892–10 Dec 1935) in Crowley, Louisiana. Their children were Helen (13 Oct 1913–14 Jul 1983), John Milton Jr. (26 Aug 1916–22 Jun 2001), William Dee (14 Mar 1918–19 Oct 2010), Triggs Reeves (15 Nov 1919–27 May 1990), and Joanne (9 Sep 1928–10 Aug 2015). After Olive's death, John married Chloe Dalrymple. They had one son, George H. (29 Jan 1938–22 Sep 1974).

- **Henry Octavious White (8 Jun 1840–17 Oct 1912):** Henry was born in Franklin, Tennessee. He married Elizabeth Martha Robinett (31 Oct 1846–31 Jul 1927) in 1869 in Louisiana. He became a circuit rider minister in the Methodist Church and served approximately twenty congregations in that capacity. He was known for his ability to make friends with and inspire the children in his congregations. Henry died in Richland Parish, Louisiana.

  - **Leola Belle White (12 Dec 1869–21 Jun 1958):** Leola married John Travis Nixon (6 Jul 1867–8 Feb 1909). They lived in Crowley, Louisiana. In 1900, her brother Henry and sister Daisy were enumerated with the Nixon family. By 1910, the widowed Leola was a teacher in a private school, and two daughters had been added. In 1930, she was listed as a high school teacher, and two grandchildren were living with her. Leola and John's children were Laurence Allen (30 Nov 1896–1953), Dorothy (20 May 1903–Feb 1981), and Mildred (1 Apr 1905–31 May 2003).

  - **Henry W. White (Mar 1873–31 Aug 1947):** Henry was listed as a farmer in 1900 and as a bookkeeper, owner of a cookie shop, and supervisor of building guards in subsequent censuses. Henry married Hilda Antonette Vinson. Their children were Mamie A. (5 Jul 1909–13 Feb 1990), Whitmiel Thomas (2 Feb 1911–11 Jul 1979), and Otis H. (1 Jan 1914–2 Jan 1966).

  - **Elizabeth Robinett "Nettie" White (6 Jul 1875–25 Oct 1961):** A teacher by profession, Nettie never married. In 1940, she retired and shared a home with her sister Daisy.

  - **Daisy White (8 Jun 1879–11 Feb 1954):** Daisy is shown in the home of her parents in the 1880 and 1910 censuses. She is listed as a teacher, a profession she continued. Daisy was unmarried.

- **Eugenia Mae White (19 May 1881–1 Dec 1953):** Eugenia married Ivy Albert Hearne (1884–1960). They lived in Caldwell Parish, Louisiana. Eugenia was appointed postmaster of the Riverton post office, Caldwell Parish, on July 24, 1914, and was listed as postmistress in 1920. By 1930, the family had moved to a rural area of Caldwell Parish, and Eugenia was no longer postmistress. In 1940, they were operating a farm. Their daughter was Eugenia Alberta (Bert) (9 May 1910–2 Jul 1978).

- **Marelena White (29 Jul 1887–15 Nov 1961):** The name is given as Mary Lena on the 1900 census but as Marelena in other references. Marelena is shown with sisters Nettie and Daisy in Lincoln Parish, Louisiana, in 1930. Marelena and Daisy were teachers in the public schools, while Nettie is listed as head of the household.

- **Howard White (1888–unknown):** Howard is shown in his parents' home on the 1900 and 1910 censuses. A private Howard White was listed on the army transport ship *Scandinavia* departing New York on October 20, 1918. Howard Pool White (10 May 1889–1 Jan 1965) and wife Lula May Willingham are shown on the 1930 and 1940 censuses for Baton Rouge, Louisiana. Howard Pool White registered for the World War II draft from Baton Rouge, Louisiana.

- **Margaret Isabella White (14 Nov 1843–8 Jun 1917):** Born in Franklin County, Tennessee, Margaret graduated from Soule Female College in Murfreesboro, Tennessee. She taught school until her wedding to James Gelheron Hayes (ca. 1830–1871) on November 10, 1868, in Opelousas, Louisiana. James was a widower with three children. At the time of their wedding, James was a Civil War veteran holding the position of sheriff of Saint Landry Parish. The 1870 census shows them operating a hotel in Opelousas. Their infant daughter, Delia, and Margaret's parents, Benjamin and Elizabeth White, were shown in the household. After James's death in 1871, Margaret converted the hotel into a boarding school for girls. The school gained the reputation of being one of the most outstanding schools in the area. It served not only boarding school students, but also other students, both boys and girls, from the community. The Methodist Church, of which Margaret and many of the White family were members, provided some support for the school. Margaret and James had at least two children, the infant daughter shown on the 1870 census and a son born after James's death, for whom Benjamin White was appointed guardian by the court. Neither child was listed in the 1880 census. Margaret did raise Virginia Vermel "Mel" Hayes, the daughter of her stepson, Clarence L. Hays. Some relatives thought Mel was Margaret's daughter. Mel married Dr. Frank C. Shute. Margaret died in Opelousas and was buried in the Opelousas cemetery.

William Curry Kenny
(2 Apr 1809–22 Dec 1894)

William was born in South Carolina. He married Elizabeth Oldham in 1838 in Williamson County, Tennessee. She died in 1840 in Caldwell Parish, Louisiana. William Curry Kenny is shown on the 1840 census of Caldwell Parish. The only other individual in the household, a teenage male, is probably one of his younger half brothers. A second marriage to Sarah Colvin, around 1845, produced a son, James Polk Kenny. William and his young son moved from Louisiana to Texas around 1851, presumably after the death of Sarah. He settled in Tennessee Colony, Anderson County, Texas, where he married Elizabeth Jane Colwell on July 12, 1853. Chapters 1 and 2 of this book tell the story of their family.

Isabella Kenny
(ca. 1810–26 May 1886)

Born in Williamson County, Tennessee, Isabella moved with her mother and stepfather to Claiborne County, Mississippi. There she married Gibson Clark Hedrick (ca. 1805–12 Feb 1842) on March 23, 1833. Gibson, the son of John Hedrick and Nancy Clark, was the brother of Rachel Hedrick, who married Thomas Hardin Wade, son of George Wade. Around 1837, Isabella and Gibson moved to Caldwell Parish, Louisiana. They are shown on the 1840 census with a son between the ages of five and ten and a son and daughter under five. Gibson died in 1842 in Caldwell Parish, and Isabella was executor of the estate. William Curry Kenny signed her bond for executor of the estate. Probate records show that she was delayed in filing executor papers because she had recently given birth. John H. Hedrick was appointed tutor for the four children. Isabella's second marriage was to Jonathan Hagerty on January 25, 1844. He was not shown on the 1850 census, and it is assumed that he died before that date. After his death, Isabella taught school. After the Civil War, her half brother Henry R. Wade asked her to join him in Floyd, Louisiana, to manage his household and help him with his financial records and correspondence. She did this until his death, at which time she was executor of the estate. She died in Floyd, Carroll Parish, Louisiana, before the settlement of the Henry Wade estate was completed. Her son William A. Hedrick replaced her as executor.

- **John Hedrick (1834–19 Aug 1853):** John was born in Mississippi. He is shown as an eight-year-old in his father's probate papers. He appears in his mother's household in the 1850 census. Although little information is given, it seems likely that he was the

John Hedrick who died on August 19, 1853, in New Orleans, Louisiana, as named in an obituary and a grave listing. No other records have been found for him.

- **William A. "Archie" Hedrick (18 Nov 1836–14 Jun 1904):** Born in Claiborne County, Mississippi, William was an infant when the family moved to Louisiana. William married Mary Eliza Parker (ca. 1840–31 Jun 1884) on November 28, 1865, in Carroll Parish, Louisiana. The 1870 census shows them in Floyd, Carroll Parish, Louisiana, with daughters Estell and Maggie. Archie was a dry goods clerk. He served as clerk of the district court of Carroll Parish at the time of the 1880 census, a position he still held in the 1900 census. He provided significant documents for the succession papers for Henry Wade and completed the executor's work after his mother's death. He and Mary Eliza had seven children.

  - **Estelle Isabella Hedrick (Jan 1868–Aug 1938):** Estelle was listed as a teacher on the 1900 census. On April 28, 1904, Estelle was appointed postmistress of Floyd, Louisiana. She married R. J. Hesling on October 9, 1912. His occupation was listed as sheriff in the 1920 census. Estelle's sister Maggie was living with them in the 1920 and 1930 censuses. No children were listed in either census.

  - **Margaret Parker "Maggie" Hedrick (ca. 1869–24 Mar 1936):** Maggie married Edger Calhoun Pinson (17 Oct 1869–4 Apr 1900) on April 27, 1892. Maggie and her three sons are shown adjacent to her father in the 1900 census. She is shown in the Floyd, Louisiana, home of her sister Estelle and Robert Hesling in the 1920 and 1930 censuses. The children of Maggie and Edward were Edgar Calhoun (8 Apr 1893–17 Apr 1958), Don Hedrick (12 Apr 1895–10 Aug 1959), and George Allen (24 Aug 1897–5 Aug 1971).

  - **William A. Hedrick (6 Apr 1873–26 Nov 1926):** William married Daisy Jane Hedgepeth (19 Feb 1883–12 Dec 1959) on August 5, 1909. He was listed as a farmer in the 1910 West Carroll, Louisiana, census. Margaret Estelle (12 May 1907–26 Feb 2004) was their daughter.

  - **John Charles Hedrick (16 Nov 1876–23 Aug 1883).**

  - **Martha Redman "Mattie" Hedrick (5 Jul 1879–17 Nov 1932):** Mattie married Eugene Stewart Carothers on August 15, 1899. They lived in Clay County, Mississippi, where he worked as a book company manager. By 1920 his occupation was listed as cotton buyer. Their children were Eugene Stewart Jr. (8 Oct 1900–3 Sep 1930), Margarita (9 May 1902–21 May 1984), Neva Marie (1904–1952), William H. (1907–1967), James Gibson (1909–1984), and Russell Carlisle (1913–1986).

  - **Gibson Clark Hedrick (20 Jan 1881–28 Mar 1944):** Gibson married Annie N. Thomas on December 18, 1904. He was listed as a merchant in the 1910 West

Carroll Parish, Louisiana, census. He registered for the World War I draft in Eudora, Chicot County, Arkansas. The 1940 census showed them in Fayetteville, Arkansas, where he worked as a clerk. Gibson C. (ca. 1909–unknown) was their son.

- **Hattie May Hedrick (1883–9 Feb 1970):** Hattie married William Mitchliner (10 Oct 1880–6 Aug 1967) on August 15, 1906. The 1910 census shows William, Hattie, and Hattie's sister Estele in the home of William's father in Carlsbad County, New Mexico. Later censuses show them in Oak Grove, West Carroll Parish, Louisiana. William was deputy sheriff in 1920, a farmer in 1930, and a plantation owner in 1940. Their daughter was Natalee "Nannie" (19 Jul 1916–Dec 1993).

- **Nancy Ann Hedrick (ca. 1838–):** Nancy was born in Louisiana. She married James Caldwell Weaks (1830–1924) around 1860. James was the son of George Weaks and Jane Caldwell. They lived in Ouachita and Mooresville Parishes, Louisiana.

  - **Estelle Weaks (2 May 1863–24 Oct 1950):** Estelle married William B. Reily (1887–1972) on June 29, 1886, in Ouachita Parish, Louisiana. Their children were James Weaks (1889–1970), Ethel (1893–1985), and Charlotte Ann (1896–1985). Estelle died in New Orleans, Louisiana.

  - **Kate Weaks (ca. 1866–before 1880):** Kate is shown as a four-year-old on the 1870 census but is not listed in 1880.

  - **George Weaks (22 Jun 1868–24 Jul 1943):** George married Mona Lynn Millsaps (16 Jan 1876–23 Jun 1938) on April 27, 1898, in Ouachita Parish, Louisiana. They lived in Monroe, Louisiana, where George was a merchant. The 1900 census shows they were parents of one child, no longer living. Their son was George G. Jr. (9 Jun 1914–25 Feb 1976).

  - **Jennie Belle Weaks (6 Oct 1871–7 Sep 1962):** Jennie married Harvey James Trousdale (1866–1952). Harvey and Jennie were enumerated with her parents in the 1900 census. They were in Monroe, Ouachita Parish, Louisiana, in the 1910–1940 censuses. Their children were George Weaks (7 Feb 1901–28 Sep 1981), Emily W. (1904–1959), and James Harvey Jr. (1910–1978).

  - **Bower Weaks (29 May 1876–30 Jan 1941):** Bower was unmarried and was found on census data in the home of her parents or a sibling.

  - **John Pinckney Weaks (Mar 1880–21 Jan 1950):** The 1930 census shows John working as a plumber in Chicago, Illinois. He died in Hidalgo County, Texas, and was buried in Monroe, Louisiana.

- **Gibson C. Hedrick Jr. (Dec 1841–before 1850):** Gibson was born in Caldwell Parish, Louisiana, shortly before his father's death. Records indicate that his mother delayed filing as executor of his father's estate because she had recently given birth. He apparently died before 1850, as he is not shown on the 1850 census.

Jane Kenny
(ca. 1814–12 Dec 1890)

Jane was born in Williamson County, Tennessee. She married Edward M. Long (2 Aug 1806–28 Mar 1865) in Williamson County, Tennessee, on December 14, 1828. The young couple moved to Claiborne County, Mississippi, around 1837. Since later data shows them living near Rocky Springs, it is assumed that this is the area in which they settled. Rocky Springs was a relatively new but thriving town by 1837. That year, one of the first Methodist churches in Claiborne County was built in Rocky Springs. Edward acquired land in Claiborne County in 1840, and he and Jane are shown on the 1840 census with three daughters and one son. The 1850 census shows Edward as a planter, with property valued at $4,100. Edward died in March 1865. He is probably buried in the family cemetery, where his son William is buried. The name is listed as DEM Long, and the dates are fairly consistent with other records, with a different month for the death date. The estate remained unsettled until a lawsuit by William P. Hughes in 1880 demanded a division of the land holdings. This settlement did not occur until 1887. Jane married Alexander Emerick on December 20, 1875. The 1880 census shows Jane E. Emerick as head of household with Olive Long (twenty-one), Carrie M. Morris (thirty-five), Elena L. Morris (eleven), and Lewis E. Morris (eight). She was living in Rocky Springs, Mississippi, in 1886 according to the H. R. Wade estate papers. Jane died in Claiborne County, but if she was buried in the family plot, it is in one of the unmarked graves. The cemetery has been reported to have been extensively vandalized over the years.

- **Isabella Jane Long (1830–after 1880):** Isabella was born in Tennessee. She married Daniel G. Aber on May 11, 1848, in Claiborne County, Mississippi. She and Daniel are shown on the 1850 Madison Parish, Louisiana, census with one-year-old Willie Aber, Isabella's sister Izora H. Long, and fourteen-year-old Littleton Adams. The 1860 census shows them in Morehouse Parish, Louisiana, with sons William, eleven, and Edward, four. No additional information has been found for Daniel Aber or the two boys. The 1880 lawsuit identifies Isabella's husband as A. E. Seay. They were living in Claiborne County when the lawsuit was filed. A Daniel G. Aber, age fifty-seven, died in Saline County, Missouri, in 1878, but there is no indication whether this is the Daniel G. Aber who was married to Isabella Long.

- **Izora H. Long (1833–after 1880):** Born in Tennessee, Izora was a young child when the family moved to Mississippi. She was living in Madison Parish, Louisiana, with her sister Isabella in 1850. Izora married Thomas Couch (1821–unknown) on January 4, 1855, in Carroll Parish, Louisiana. On May 1, 1860, Izora H. Couch married John W. Couch in East Carroll Parish, Louisiana. The 1860 census shows them in Franklin Parish with six children: Sarah (twelve), Bettie (ten), Emma (nine), Marian (seven), Jennie (five), and Mattie (three). The older four were probably the children of John and his first wife, Janette. Jennie and Mattie could be the children of Izora and Thomas or John and Janette. They were not shown on the 1870 or 1880 censuses. It appears that they did not survive to 1870. The 1870 census shows a child identified as G., age ten, who is not on the 1880 census. The 1880 census shows John and Izora with three children: Emma (twenty-five), Annie (fourteen), and Minnie (ten).

  - **Annie J. Couch (1866–unknown):** No information has been found beyond the 1880 census.

  - **Minnie Lou Couch (31 Jul 1868–18 Apr 1936):** Minnie married Samuel Harper Henderson (1858–1932) on October 13, 1886, in Richland Parish, Louisiana. They moved to Amarillo, Texas, where they are shown on the 1900 Potter County census with children Annie, Henry, and Sam. The 1910 census shows them in Williamson County, Texas, with sons Milburn and Samuel. Minnie is shown as a mother of four with two living. Still in Williamson County, they are shown on the 1920 census with son Sam and great-niece Jessie Scott Price, age five. By 1930, Jessie was no longer in the household. Both Samuel and Minnie died and were buried in Georgetown, Texas. Their children were Annie (2 Aug 1888–21 Sep 1969), Wilburn Henry (18 Mar 1892–5 Feb 1973), and Sam Wooten (18 Aug 1897–9 Mar 1969).

- **Mary Lou P. Long (1836–after 1880):** Mary was born in Tennessee. She married C. H. P. Ritch on December 25, 1860, in Franklin Parish, Louisiana. She was one of the defendants in the 1880 lawsuit by William P. Hughes. At that time, she was living in Tensas Parish, Louisiana, and was listed as single.

- **William C. Long (22 Aug 1838–7 Oct 1869):** Born in Claiborne County, Mississippi, William is listed with his parents in the 1850 and 1860 censuses. He married F. C. Hill. He was buried in the Long family cemetery in Claiborne County, Mississippi. Other graves in the cemetery were for the infant daughter of W. C. and E. O. Long, who died October 26, 1867; D. E. M. Long (2 Aug 1806–29 Jun 1863); and eight unmarked graves. This small cemetery is assumed to have been near the Long family home. The 1870 census of Copiah County, Mississippi, shows nineteen-year-old Frances C. Long, widow, and infant son John in the home of William K. Cheek, listed as Frances's step-father.

- **Edward Morris Long (8 Nov 1840–8 Jan 1910):** Edward was born in Claiborne County, Mississippi. He served in the Twelfth Mississippi Infantry during the Civil War. Edward married Mary Ellen Kendrick (6 Jun 1841–12 Jul 1897) around 1863. The 1870 census shows them operating a farm in Tensas Parish, Louisiana, but by 1880, they had moved to Hill County, Texas. They continued farming in Texas. After Mary Ellen's death, Edward married Alice Jones Prichett. He died in Lindsay, Garvin County, Oklahoma, while visiting his son.

  - **Edward Arastus Long (27 Oct 1864–10 Jan 1936):** Edward married Alice Forest (5 May 1870–20 Nov 1935) on December 5, 1886, in Hill County, Texas. They operated farms in Hill and Erath Counties. By 1920, Edward was listed as a farm laborer in Hill County. The 1930 census shows him in the home of his son Roy, and Alice with their son Willi. Their children were Edward Marvin (18 Jan 1894–16 Apr 1960), Roy (18 Sep 1896–24 Dec 1979), William "Willi" (13 Jan 1899–14 Oct 1980), Forest (27 Feb 1901–17 Dec 1978), Myrtle Mae (21 Jun 1903–27 Jul 1983), Weldon (1907–1969), and Lorane (28 Nov 1914–28 Apr 1991).

  - **Charles Eugene Long (28 Aug 1868–27 Jan 1930):** Charles married Lena Bowen (Oct 1872–Sep 1947) on August 23, 1891, in Hill County, Texas. They are shown in Erath County in the 1900 census with their daughter, Bertha. By 1910, they were in separate households, with Lena in Johnson County with their daughter, and Charles in Comanche County, Texas. Charles and Addie Sue Brand were married on May 13, 1916, in Van Zandt County. Charles died from pneumonia in Anderson County, Texas. Children of Charles and Lena were Bertha A. (30 Apr 1894–15 Dec 1974) and Andrew Jackson (8 Sep 1901–Feb 1986). Children of Charles and Addie were Terry Thomas (4 Jan 1918–28 Jul 1962), Allie Marie (20 Apr 1923–7 Oct 2007), and Aden Blair (20 Sep 1927–).

  - **Willi C. Long (1871–1953):** Willi married Ella McGee on September 25, 1894, in Erath County, Texas. They operated a farm near Morgan Mill, Erath County, in 1900 and 1910. In 1920, Willi was working as a laborer in Thurber, Texas. In 1930 Willi and Ella were living in Ranger, Eastland County, Texas, where he was a trucker. Willi and Ella were buried in Morgan Mill. Their children were Audie (25 Feb 1898–9 Oct 1973), Lawrence (3 Apr 1900–23 Feb 1988), Aaron (18 Dec 1901–24 Jun 1990), Buford (ca. 1904–25 Nov 1915), Lila Mae (29 Mar 1907–2 Nov 1990), and Verna (4 Mar 1909–16 Mar 2001).

  - **Harvey Austin Long (1875–1950):** Harvey and Allie Yarbro (1881–1952) were married on May 15, 1898, in Erath County, Texas. In 1900, they were farming in Erath County. By 1920, they were in Kiowa County, Oklahoma, and they were engaged in farming through 1940. Both died and were buried in Kiowa

County. Their children were Jesse Austin (17 Feb 1899–1952), Cecil T. (14 Aug 1905–May 1968), Eldon L. (13 Sep 1907–18 Jun 1947), Edith M. (ca. 1909–unknown), John (8 Dec 1910–unknown), and Millard (17 Oct 1913–23 Sep 1961).

- **Walter Long (13 Feb 1878–1960):** Walter married Lorena McGill (27 Jul 1884–1966) in Garvin, Oklahoma, on February 26, 1908. They resided in Hollis, Harmon County, Oklahoma. Walter worked as a merchant and as manager of a cotton gin.

- **George Washington Long (24 Oct 1880–Sep 1968):** George married Sallie McGee (1887–1983) on November 7, 1903, in Erath County, Texas. The 1910 census shows them with two children on a farm near Morgan Mill in Erath County. By 1920, they had moved to Kiowa County, Oklahoma, where George was described as a photographer, an occupation he continued through 1930. In 1940, Sallie was shown as a picture finisher in the photography studio. George and Sallie's children were Ovella M. (Aug 1906–Dec 1983), Fred Warren (30 Sep 1909–5 May 1956), and Alva Edison (19 Apr 1916–26 Oct 1964).

- **Miranda Carrie Long (1843–after 1880):** Miranda was born in Claiborne County, Mississippi. She married Louis P. Morris on December 20, 1866, in Claiborne County, Mississippi. In 1880, Carrie, widowed, and her two children were with her mother in Claiborne County, Mississippi.

  - **Elena L. Morris (ca. 1869–unknown).**

  - **Louis Eugene Morris (1872–1944):** Louis was born in Pike County, Mississippi. He married Winifred Irene Ferguson (1882–1942). Their children were James Elliott (1903–1994), Dorothy Ann (1905–1970), Annie Caroline (1908–1980), Winifred (1911–1988), and Louis Eugene Jr. (1918–1932).

- **Alice P. Long (1845–8 Jan 1913):** Alice was born in Claiborne County, Mississippi. She married Albert Miller. The 1900 census of Claiborne County shows A. M. and Alice Miller with daughter Rosa. It indicates that Alice was the mother of seven children, three of whom were living.

  - **Alice Belle Miller (Jan 1872–22 Nov 1915):** Alice Belle married Benjamin F. Stevens. They were living on a farm in Harrison County, Mississippi, in 1900. Their children were Benjamin Marion (31 Jan 1890–12 Jul 1964), Alta Emma (29 Apr 1894–26 Jan 1954), Alice (3 Sep 1895–8 Dec 1985), Barney Lewis (20 Mar 1898–1 Jun 1965), William Gordon (22 Mar 1901–1 Jun 1962), Ella May (12 Nov 1903–Jul 1982), Earl Thomas (22 Jun 1907–1 Mar 1986), and Rosa Belle (12 Oct 1909–24 Mar 2003).

- **William A. Miller (1877–14 Mar 1917):** William's occupation was listed as carpenter.

- **Rosa Miller (Jul 1880–unknown).**

- **Andrew Jackson Long (1847–before 1880):** Andrew was born in Claiborne County, Mississippi. Andrew J. Long is shown as enlisting in the Twenty-Fifth Infantry of the Confederate army on May 5, 1862. A. J. Long, age twenty-five and single, is shown as a farmer near Rocky Springs, Claiborne County, in the 1870 census. He was not listed in the 1880 lawsuit.

- **George Washington Long (1849–after 1910):** George was in his mother's home in Claiborne County, Louisiana, at the time of the 1870 census. George married Julia Auter (1847–19 Mar 1925), widow of Philip Toomer, on November 30, 1875. The 1900 and 1910 censuses show them in Warren County, Mississippi. George was listed as a stock salesman in 1900 and as a real estate agent in 1910.

- **Lafayette Hendon Long (1851–4 Aug 1890):** Lafayette was born in Claiborne County, Mississippi. He married Anna B. Jackson. In 1880, they were in West Carroll Parish, Louisiana, where he was a merchant. He died in West Carroll Parish, Louisiana. The story passed down in the family was that he was killed by Anna's brother. Anna continued living in West Carroll Parish until her death in 1940.

  - **Lawrence Wilbon Long (29 Jul 1878–29 Jul 1952):** Lawrence married Lillye Childress (20 Jul 1879–3 Mar 1971). In 1910 they were living in Little Rock, Arkansas. By 1920 Lawrence and Lillye were divorced. Lawrence returned to West Carroll Parish, Louisiana, and made his home with his sister Lillian. Lawrence and Lillye's son was Lawrence Wilbon Jr. (17 Mar 1902–Jul 1986).

  - **Lafayette E. Long (11 Mar 1880–29 Aug 1886).**

  - **Mabel Anna Long (22 Mar 1882–3 Sep 1957):** Mabel married Leopold Lipp (22 Jun 1873–before 1930). They were living in her mother's household in 1900. His occupation was listed as printer and editor. By 1910 they had their own household in Carroll Parish, Louisiana. The 1930 census shows the widowed Mabel as head of the household with her three sons. Mabel and her son Marion were operating the printing shop in 1940. In addition to Marion's family, five lodgers were part of the household, some of whom also worked in the printing shop. Mabel and Leopold's children were Edith (12 Dec 1902–1 Apr 1963), Lucille (12 Sep 1906–13 Aug 1986), Marvin Neal (15 Mar 1909–4 Feb 2007), Marion Trousdale (31 Jul 1912–18 Jul 1969), and Kenneth (1918–28 Jun 1937).

  - **George Wilford Long (13 Dec 1883–8 Feb 1952):** George was single and a salesman for Procter & Gamble Company in Macon, Georgia, when he registered for the World War I draft. In 1940, he was listed in the household of his sister Lillian in West Carroll Parish, Louisiana.

- **Horace Jackson Long (27 Oct 1887–5 Jul 1947):** Horace married Esta Howser (16 Jun 1888–18 Mar 1952). They made their home in West Carroll Parish, Louisiana. He worked as a retail merchant and manager of an electrical plant. Their children were Helen A. (6 Dec 1909–30 Nov 1981), George H. (8 Feb 1915–2 Oct 1953), Hazel Fay (9 Dec 1920–26 May 1987), and Edna Eleanor (24 Jul 1924–Jan 1990).

- **Lillian Long (8 Jul 1889–6 Dec 1978):** Lillian married Martin Henry "Pat" O'Connell (22 Jan 1882–2 May 1924). They were living in Oak Grove, West Carroll Parish, in 1920. Pat is listed as a lawyer. Lillian's mother, Anna, and brother Lawrence W. lived with them. In 1930, the widowed Lillian and her mother, Anna, had two boarders living with them. Brothers Lawrence and George were with her for the 1940 census.

- **Marion T. Long (27 Feb 1891–6 May 1910).**

- **Lawrence Long (1854–before 1870):** Lawrence was born in Claiborne County, Mississippi. He was shown as a six-year-old in the 1860 census but was not found in later records.

- **Olive M. Long (1856–12 Feb 1929):** Olive was born in Claiborne County, Mississippi. She married M. A. Girault on February 15, 1881, in Claiborne County. By 1900, Olive was married to Granville Ramsey, and the family was living in Ellis County, Texas. Olive was listed as the mother of five children, four of whom were living. Olive and her daughter Vivian are shown on the 1910 census in Hill County, Texas, in the home of her son William. By 1920, Olive was head of the Hill County household consisting of Olive and her ten-year-old grandson Irving James.

  - **William Earl Girault (21 Jan 1882–6 Apr 1947):** Born in Mississippi, William moved to Texas with his family prior to 1900. He established a farm in Hill County, Texas, and married Lula Pearl Mitchell (8 Sep 1893–18 Oct 1977) on January 28, 1912. The 1920, 1930, and 1940 censuses show them operating a farm in Hill County, Texas, with their growing family. Their children were William Earl (27 Oct 1912–27 Sep 2001), Olive Pearl (30 Dec 1914–2 May 2017), Mildred Argieree (14 Nov 1916–6 Jul 1994), infant son (1 Feb 1919–1 Feb 1919), Imozelle (10 Nov 1922–18 Jan 2015), and Howard (ca. 1926–).

  - **Earnest Atchison Girault (22 Sep 1884–6 Mar 1904).**

  - **Marvin A. Girault (12 Mar 1887–12 Dec 1932):** Marion married Nettie Lee Browley (5 Jan 1886–12 Aug 1966). They operated a farm in Hill County,

Texas. Their children were Malcum A. (22 May 1909–8 Feb 1993), Janette (28 Jul 1911–23 May 1995), Marvin Bryan (22 Apr 1913–31 Oct 2003), Eugene (6 Dec 1915–4 Sep 1964), Mary Lee (17 Feb 1918–22 Feb 2013), Ollie Sue (16 Jul 1922–11 Mar 2014), Roy Neal (20 Apr 1924–9 Feb 2008), and Joyce Ardene (13 Jun 1926–27 Feb 2015).

- **Jenette Girault (14 Feb 1888–21 Aug 1917):** Jenette married Gaines Lee James (16 Jun 1886–15 Sep 1945). In 1910 they lived in Murray County, Oklahoma, where Gaines was a teacher. Jenette died of cancer in Hill County, Texas. Their son was Irvin Earl (21 Feb 1907–13 Jun 1947).

- **Vivian Olive Ramsey (8 Sep 1900–14 Aug 1975):** Vivian married Andrew C. Janes (30 Nov 1885–4 Dec 1939). They were living in Dallas, Texas, in 1920. Vivian died in Fort Worth, Texas. Their children were Andrew Cornelius (21 Nov 1921–4 Jan 1971) and Johnny Granville (5 Nov 1929–13 Jun 2004).

Descendants of Mary and George Wade

Lawrence Thompson Wade (ca. 1819–21 Feb 1875)

Lawrence was born in Williamson County, Tennessee. He married Mary Jane Rife (ca. 1825–18 Aug 1888) on January 5, 1843, in Carroll Parish, Louisiana. They were living in Carroll Parish at the time of the 1850 census. He and Mary Jane had twelve children, but only four lived to adulthood. According to family stories, yellow fever was the cause of many deaths. Lawrence served as guardian to his sister's underage children after her death. The 1860 census slave schedule shows Lawrence as owner of twenty slaves, twelve males and eight females, ranging in age from fourteen to forty. In 1871, the family moved from Carroll Parish to Bolivar County, Mississippi. Lawrence Wade died in Bolivar County, Mississippi, at age fifty-six. Mary Jane maintained the household and property until her death thirteen years later.

- **William C. Wade (3 Sep 1842–16 Oct 1842).**

- **Martha Jane Wade (Oct 1843–15 Jun 1850).**

- **Mary Ruth Wade (8 Dec 1846–before 1860).**

- **Elizabeth Wade (19 Apr 1848–before 1860).**

- **Henry Lawrence Wade (11 Dec 1849–before 1860).**

- **Thomas Jefferson Wade (29 Jan 1852–before 1860).**

- **George Newt Wade (12 Apr 1854–1 Jan 1892):** George married Kate Currell (Nov 1861–26 Oct 1956) on November 10, 1880, in Mississippi. They lived in Greenville, Mississippi. After George's death, Kate continued living in Greenville until her death.

  - **Katie Florence Wade (7 Nov 1881–26 Nov 1971):** Katie married R. Edgar Walt (1871–1918) in 1903. They lived in Greenville, Washington County, Mississippi. The 1920 census shows Katie as head of the family with her three children. She married A. L. Scales around 1920, but by 1940 she was again widowed. Her children were Edgar C. Walt (1905–1925), Walter Gilliam Walt (5 Dec 1907–18 Jul 1980), Katherine Walt (20 Aug 1912–21 Jun 1924), and Alfred Leslie Scales (16 Nov 1921–5 Mar 2010).

  - **Stella Mary Wade (Feb 1884–9 Jul 1962):** Stella married Alfred Lawrence Gervin (22 Nov 1879–18 May 1850). They lived in Bolivar County, Mississippi, during the early years of their marriage. Both died in Hinds County, Mississippi. Their children were Alfred Lawrence Jr. (16 Oct 1906–16 Nov 1987), George (1 Jul 1908–Aug 1982), Louise (31 Dec 1915–11 Dec 2005), Jack Evans (26 Mar 1918–2 Nov 1968), Robert H. (6 Apr 1920–9 Jul 2003), Charles Curell (2 Dec 1922–15 Sep 1998), and Elizabeth (15 Mar 1925–5 Aug 2008).

  - **George Southerland Wade (Aug 1886–26 Nov 1918):** George died of pneumonia while serving in the US Army in France during World War I. He was buried in England.

  - **Charles Currell Wade (6 Nov 1888–6 Jun 1929).**

  - **Lawrence Thompson Wade (6 Sep 1891–12 Apr 1982):** Lawrence served with the US military during World War I. In 1920, he was living with his mother and brother Charlie and working as a clerk in a bank. The 1930 census shows him working in a lumber mill near Greenville, Mississippi. The 1940 census shows him with his wife, Rosalie, in Greenville; he continued working in the lumber mill.

- **Sammie Ella Wade (7 Mar 1856–1879):** Sammie married Percy Burrus on January 22, 1878, in Bolivar County, Mississippi.

  - **Mary Lou Burrus (ca. 1878–1967):** Mary Lou was born in Bolivar County, Mississippi. She married Banks Jennings Powell (1871–1955). They lived in Bolivar County and in Greenville, Washington County, Mississippi. Their children were Willie (1902–unknown) and Banks Jennings Jr. (20 Jul 1903–13 Aug 1967).

- **Nanie Fletcher Wade (13 Jan 1854–before 1870).**

- **James L. Wade (7 Mar 1856–before 1870).**

- **Lawrence Thompson Wade (28 Oct 1864–5 Feb 1924).**

- **Charles Walter Wade (25 Feb 1866–1912):** Charles married Martha Stacey (3 Oct 1879–Jan 1963). The 1910 census shows them in Rankin County, Mississippi, with Charles working as a levee guard. After Charles's death, Martha and Dolly moved to Greenville, Mississippi, where she worked as a dressmaker in a dry goods store. By 1920, Charles Jr. was in the US Navy, stationed in Gulfport, Mississippi, and William was with his uncle Lawrence Wade.

  - **Charles Walter Wade Jr. (19 Dec 1903–Nov 1966):** Charles married Mary Powell (1902–1969). They lived in Washington County, Mississippi. The 1930 census shows Mary and the children in the home of her uncle Ira E. Tatum, but by 1940, the family was reunited. The children of Charles and Mary were Charlotte (16 Dec 1924–3 Feb 2001), Paula (1927–), Charles Taylor (27 Dec 1929–19 Aug 2002), and Mary Jane (ca. 1934–).

  - **William Stacy Wade (28 Nov 1904–23 Feb 1973):** In 1940, William was living with his mother in Greenville, Mississippi, working as a supervisor in a private industry.

  - **Jessie May "Dolly" Wade (29 Sep 1910–17 Sep 1990):** Dolly married Stacy Ward McAdams (25 Jan 1903–Feb 1959). In 1940, they were living in Marion, Crittenden County, Arkansas, with one-year-old Stacy W. McAdams Jr.

Henry R. Wade
(ca. 1821–1886)

Born in Williamson County, Tennessee, Henry established a plantation in Carroll Parish, Louisiana. Family records indicate he was called "Uncle Bone" by nieces and nephews. The 1850 census shows him living near his brother Lawrence Wade. The 1860 census shows him providing a home for Joseph Scroggins, an orphan, with another orphan Scroggins living next door. Henry never married, and after the Civil War, he asked his half sister Isabella Haggerty to join him and maintain his household and help him with the financial records involved in freeing his slaves. She is shown with him in both the 1870 and 1880 censuses. Henry died in 1886, and Isabella was executor of the estate until her death, at which time her son William assumed the responsibility.

The records of this estate established the identities of Mary's two sets of children as well as those of George Wade's by his earlier marriage.

James Taylor Wade
(ca. 1824–ca. 1858)

James was born in Williamson County, Tennessee. He married Rebecca Fereby Mixon (1 Apr 1828–25 Sep 1896), daughter of Joel Mixon and Fereby Phillen, on November 21, 1844. Rebecca was born in Wilcox County, Alabama. The 1850 census shows James T. and Rebecca and five-year-old James in Jackson Parish, Louisiana. James was listed as a physician. The 1860 census mortality schedule for Carroll Parish, Louisiana, gives a James T. Wade—born around 1824, widowed, physician—as having died from pneumonia. If this is James Taylor Wade, he and Rebecca may have been divorced. Rebecca Gross is shown on the 1860 census of Jackson Parish, Louisiana, as head of a household consisting of Joel Gross, two; Mixon Wade, thirteen; John H. Wade, six; and Fereby Mixon, fifty-seven. Rebecca married W. S. Norris and is shown on the 1880 census of Lincoln Parish. She died in Lincoln Parish.

- **James William Wade (7 Nov 1845–6 Mar 1922):** James was born in Jackson Parish, Louisiana. He married Emma Avarette (17 Sep 1852–13 Apr 1885) on May 13, 1870, in Ouachita Parish, Louisiana. The 1870 census shows them operating a farm in Jackson Parish, Louisiana. His brother Mixon and Mixon's wife were enumerated with them. By the 1880 census, they were in Lincoln Parish, Louisiana, and three-year-old Carrie had been added to the family. James was designated by his brother Mixon to represent Mixon in matters of settling the estate of their uncle Henry Wade. James married Ella Cobb around 1890. The 1900 census shows James as head of the household with Florence, James, and Elton. Ella was not listed. James died in Lincoln Parish, Louisiana.

    - **Carrie Wade (7 Nov 1876–27 Sep 1885).**

    - **Florence E. Wade (6 Nov 1884–9 Sep 1966):** Florence was only six months old when her mother died. She married Robert Erastus Davis (12 Oct 1878–15 Sep 1972). They lived in Lincoln Parish, Louisiana, in 1920 but in Ouachita Parish in 1930. Their only child, Elexa, was born and died in 1905.

    - **James W. Wade (22 Mar 1892–15 Nov 1939):** James married Iva Mae Boyd (3 Jan 1902–24 Dec 1963) in Louisiana. Their son was James William (19 May 1927–30 Jul 2016).

- **Elton Gray Wade (14 Sep 1896–9 May 1969):** Elton was born in Choudrant, Louisiana. He and Mattie Lurline Roane (7 Oct 1901–6 Mar 1992) were married on June 16, 1921, in Lincoln Parish, Louisiana. They lived in Ouachita Parish, Louisiana, where Elton owned a paint store. Their children were Evelyn Hope (30 Apr 1923–12 Oct 2003) and Elton Gray Jr. (27 Apr 1926–1 May 2012).

- **Mixon Wade (Sep 1850–1905):** Mixon was born in Louisiana. He married Marian Elizabeth "Mittie" Newton (ca. 1853–before 1900). They lived in Lincoln Parish, Louisiana, where they operated a farm. The 1900 census shows Mixon, widowed, with five of the children.

  - **Ella "Elois" Wade (1872–15 Sep 1897):** Ella married T. C. Clark on October 1, 1895, in Lincoln Parish, Louisiana.

  - **Ira Homer Wade (Jan 1875–1905):** Ira is shown in the home of his father in 1900.

  - **Rebecca Aldora Elizabeth "Dorra" Wade (28 Oct 1877–15 Dec 1943):** Dorra was born in Indian Village, Ouachita Parish, Louisiana. She married George Harrison Emory (20 Dec 1871–unknown) in Choudrant, Lincoln Parish, Louisiana, in 1900. Dorra died in Choudrant. Their children were Wade Hampton (10 Jun 1901–17 Mar 1937), Harold Homer (2 Sep 1902–May 1980), Florine (17 Feb 1904–), Nell (6 Feb 1906–28 Jan 2004), Malcolm Harrison (23 Feb 1911–28 Feb 1966), and Dorothy Rose (21 Nov 1912–Oct 1985).

  - **Willie Wade (Jan 1880–unknown):** Willie was not listed with the family in the 1900 census. No other information was found.

  - **Minnie Laura Wade (27 Sep 1883–24 Dec 1959):** Minnie married Charles E. Stuart (22 Dec 1882–4 Dec 1945). They owned and operated a farm in Lincoln Parish, Louisiana. Their children were Mixon C. (7 Mar 1907–10 Dec 1959), Marion Anita (23 Sep 1909–30 Apr 1994), Marjorie (10 Jan 1914–17 Jan 1975), Maurice Len (8 May 1916–2 Mar 1980), and Mirdie L. (27 Jul 1919–26 Apr 1968).

  - **Malcolm Timothy Wade (Sep 1885–unknown):** Malcolm is shown as fourteen on the 1900 census. Additional information for him has not been found.

  - **Clara Belle Wade (Apr 1888–unknown):** Clara married Benjamin Good. They were in Lincoln Parish, Louisiana, in 1910 but in Buncombe County, North Carolina, in 1920 and 1930. Their children were Benjamin Franklin (9 May 1915–25 Oct 1974) and Evelyn G. (22 Mar 1921–9 Oct 2004).

- **John H. Wade (1845–unknown):** Born in Jackson Parish, Louisiana, John probably died young, since he is not mentioned in the 1886 papers of the estate of Henry R. Wade, where descendants of James Taylor Wade are identified. A John Wade, single, is shown as a laborer in the 1870 and 1880 censuses of Natchitoches Parish, Louisiana, but the ages listed, sixteen and twenty-five, are inaccurate for John H. Wade.

Mary Fleming Wade
(12 Feb 1825–24 Sep 1862)

The youngest of Mary and George's children, Mary, was born in Williamson County, Tennessee. She was a young child when the family moved to Claiborne County and only thirteen years old when her mother died. She probably took considerable responsibility for running the household for her father and brothers.

Mary married Samuel B. Wiggins on April 17, 1845, in Claiborne County, Mississippi. He had been married twice previously. His first wife, Rachel Dunham, died in 1838, less than a month after giving birth to their daughter, Henrietta. His second wife, Catherine Eldridge, and his daughter, Henrietta, both died in 1843. Samuel and Mary moved to West Carroll Parish, where Mary's brothers Lawrence Thompson and Henry R. Wade were living. By 1850 the Wiggins family had established a plantation valued at $9,000 and owned a number of slaves. They had two daughters, Laura H. and Lavena W., both born in Louisiana. Enumerated next to them was James Greer, probably the son of Mary's half sister Margaret.

By 1853, the Wiggins family had moved to Arkansas, where three more children—Mary George, Samuel Baker, and John Lawrence—were born. The 1860 census of Ashley County, Carter Township, Hamburg Post Office, shows the family as living on a farm valued at $30,000 and personal property valued at $60,000. Lavena was no longer listed in the family.

In 1859, Samuel purchased a log cabin built of native cypress and exhibiting an outstanding level of craftsmanship. The structure was listed on the National Register of Historic Places in 1984. Though it was probably used by tenant farmers rather than by the Wiggins family, the cabin served as an important example of early Ashley County architecture until it was destroyed by a fire in August 2002.

Mary Wade Wiggins died in Ashley, Arkansas, two weeks after giving birth to Henry Ricks Wiggins. She was thirty-seven years old. She was survived by three sons and one daughter. Samuel married Emma Cole in 1864. They are shown on the 1870 census of Ashley County, Arkansas, with Mary, Samuel, John, and Henry. Samuel was listed as a dry goods merchant rather than a farmer. Samuel died on October 13, 1872. Lawrence Thompson Wade petitioned the court in Bolivar County, Mississippi, for guardianship of Mary G., Sammie B., John L., and Henry R. Wiggins. The children were listed in Bolivar County, so it seems likely that they went to live with their uncle after their father's death.

- **Laura F. Wiggins (15 Jan 1847–25 Apr 1866):** Born in Louisiana, Laura is shown as three years old on the 1850 census and as fourteen years old on the 1860 census. Laura F. Wiggins married William Faulkner McCombs in 1865. She was buried in Hamburg, Ashley County, Arkansas.

- **Lavena W. Wiggins (Oct 1848–5 Jan 1855):** Lavena is shown on the 1850 census of Carroll Parish, Louisiana, but not on the 1860 census.

- **Mary George Wiggins (14 Nov 1852–17 Dec 1927):** Born in Ashley County, Arkansas, Mary George was under ten years old when her mother died. She and her brothers were placed under the guardianship of her uncle Lawrence T. Wade of Bolivar County, Mississippi. She married John Porter Benson (8 Nov 1845–10 May 1919) on September 4, 1873, in Bolivar County. John was born in Troup County, Georgia. The couple moved to Ashley County, Arkansas, where they are shown on the 1880 census sharing a home with John Porter's parents, Henry and Anne Benson. They were living near Monticello, Arkansas, in 1886. In 1900 the Benson family moved to Washington County, Mississippi, and was living in a joint household with Mary George's brother Henry R. Wiggins. Henry's wife had died earlier in the year, and it is assumed that Mary George was maintaining the household and caring for the children of both families. There was a total of seven children listed on the 1900 census: Presley R. Wiggins, eleven; Sam B. Wiggins, seven; John Wiggins, five; William H. Wiggins, two; Laura J. Benson, nineteen; Mary A. Benson, fifteen; and Lawrence P. Benson, nine. Willie Hill Benson did not make the move to Mississippi. Henry Wiggins, J. Porter Benson, and Henry Wade Benson were engaged in logging.

  By 1910, J. Porter Benson was listed as head of the family, still in Washington County, Arkansas, but Henry R. Wiggins was not in the household. In addition to Mary George, other household members were Laura, Mary A., and Lawrence Benson, as well as Presley, Sam, John, and William Wiggins. John Porter Benson died in Clover Hill, Mississippi. Mary George moved to Burbank, California, where three of her children lived; she died there.

  - **Willie Hill Benson (21 Aug 1875–28 Nov 1908):** Willie married Minor Wallace Pitts on October 24, 1893, in Ashley County, Arkansas. Minor was a physician born around 1870 in Arkansas. They moved to Luling, Texas, where Willie died. The 1910 census shows Minor Pitts and their three children with his second wife, Dora. Willie and Minor's children were Eric Baver (9 Sep 1895–unknown), Mary Erckle (1 Feb 1899–14 Nov 1974), and Dehaven (12 Nov 1902–12 Mar 1974).

- **Henry Wade Benson (18 Feb 1878–29 Jun 1930):** Henry Wade was born in Ashley County, Arkansas. He was working as a logger in Washington County, Mississippi, in 1900. He moved to California and is shown in the 1930 census as unmarried, living in the home of his sister Mary Adelle. He was listed with no employment, but he was probably ill, since he died in Burbank, California, the summer after the census was taken.

- **Laura Jo Benson (4 Oct 1880–6 Nov 1960):** Born in Ashley County, Arkansas, Laura Jo is shown on the 1930 and 1940 censuses in the California home of her sister Mary Adelle. She was not married. She died in Burbank, California.

- **Infant female Benson (12 Dec 1883–12 Feb 1884):** The infant was born and died in Ashley County, Arkansas.

- **Mary Adelle Benson (16 Apr 1885–2 Aug 1958):** Mary Adelle is found with her family on the 1900 and 1910 censuses. As an adult she listed her name as Maydelle. She was head of the household on the 1930 and 1940 censuses in Burbank, California. Her occupation was listed as stenographer in 1930 and private secretary in 1940. She died in Burbank, California.

- **Nellie Ricks Benson (6 Mar 1886–17 Jun 1892):** Nellie died in Fountain Hill, Arkansas.

- **Lawrence Porter Benson (6 Mar 1891–30 May 1956):** The 1920 census shows Lawrence in Coahoma County, Mississippi, working as a rural mail carrier. He moved to Los Angeles, California, where he married Lulu Belle Simpson (1893–1975) on June 29, 1929. The 1940 census lists his occupation as engineer. He died in Los Angeles, California. Their children were Carolyn Grant (20 Aug 1927–21 Mar 1994), Barbara Lou (24 Aug 1933–), and Lawrence Porter Jr. (25 Aug 1935–).

- **Sarah Peters Wiggins (17 May 1855–before 1860).**

- **Samuel Baker Wiggins (ca. 1856–unknown):** Samuel was born in Ashley County, Arkansas. He is shown as four on the 1860 census but as ten on the 1870 census. After his father's death, his uncle Lawrence Thompson Wade became his guardian. He was a party to the 1883–1886 succession documents for his uncle Henry R. Wade. At that time he was living in Bolivar County, Mississippi. Records have not been located for him after that date.

- **John Lawrence Wiggins (22 Jul 1859–unknown):** Born in Ashley County, John is shown as a one-year-old on the 1860 census but as eight on the 1870 census. As was true for his brother Samuel, records have not been found for him beyond the guardianship papers and succession papers of 1883–1886. He also was listed as living in Bolivar County, Mississippi.

- **Henry Ricks Wiggins (9 Sep 1862–9 Sep 1927):** Henry Ricks was born in Ashley, Arkansas. He was only a few days old when his mother died. He grew up under the guardianship of his uncle Lawrence Thompson Wade. He married Ellen Gray (17 Feb 1861–Jan 1900) on April 15, 1888, in Greenville, Mississippi. Ellen was born in Kentucky. They made their home in Bolivar County, Mississippi. Ellen died in Greenville, Mississippi, soon after the birth of their sixth child. In 1900, Henry and the children were sharing a home with his sister and her family. By 1910, only the children were in his sister's home. Henry Ricks survived Ellen twenty-seven years; he died in Brickey, Arkansas.

    - **Presley Ricks Wiggins (1889–26 Sep 1960):** Presley was born in Mississippi. He served in the armed forces of the United States during World War I. He married Ruby Park in Monroe County, Arkansas, on August 24, 1922. In 1930, he worked for the railroad. Ruby was listed as head of household on the 1940 census. Their son was Billy R. (ca. 1926–1991).

    - **Lillie George Wiggins (26 May 1891–before 1900):** Lillie was born in Bolivar County, Mississippi. She is not shown with the family in the 1900 census.

    - **Sam B. Wiggins (27 Jul 1893–unknown):** Sam was born in Cedar Point, Mississippi. He married Rena Harrington. Their daughter was Ellen Victoria (26 Sep 1920–4 Sep 2013).

    - **John Lawrence Wiggins (2 Nov 1895–Apr 1968):** John was born in Bolivar County, Mississippi. He married Laura Opal Davis (1894–1918) in Washington County, Arkansas, on September 18, 1914. Their daughter was Blanche Florine (5 Apr 1916–11 Apr 2001). A second wedding to Opha Ceil Goss (2 Aug 1893–24 Jun 1965) took place on August 2, 1920, in Webster County, Missouri. The 1940 census of Green County, Missouri, shows John and Opha with sons Clifford (4 Apr 1922–25 Oct 1944) and John H. (18 Jul 1924–25 Nov 1990).

    - **William Hoyt Wiggins (21 Oct 1897–30 Oct 1966):** William was born in Egypt Ridge, Mississippi. He was living in Faulkner, Arkansas, when he registered for the World War I draft. William and Ruby Constance Reed (18 Jan 1898–9 Oct 1979) were married on March 29, 1919, in Conway County, Arkansas. The 1940 census shows them in Memphis, Tennessee, with son Wayne W. William is listed as an engineer. William's second marriage was to Mary Elizabeth Fisher (4 Aug 1898–3 Nov 1962). William died in Memphis, Tennessee. His and Ruby's son was Wesley Wayne (10 Nov 1927–17 Nov 2015).

- **Henry Ricks Wiggins (Dec 1899–unknown):** Henry was born in Greenville, Mississippi. He is not shown on the 1900 census.

SOURCES

"Aber, D. G." 1850 US Census, Madison Parish, Louisiana, p. 754, Western division, family 296. FamilySearch Library, Salt Lake City, UT.

"Aber, D. G." 1860 US Census, Morehouse Parish, Louisiana, p. 90, ward 8, family 689. FamilySearch Library, Salt Lake City, UT.

"Aber, Daniel G." US, Find A Grave Index, 1600s–Current. Ancestry.com, 2012.

"Anderson, Albert S." 1940 US Census, Washington Parish, Louisiana. Ancestry.com, 2012.

"Anderson, Winnie." US, Find A Grave Index, 1600s–Current. Ancestry.com, 2012.

"Andrews, Emma." Texas Death Certificates, 1903–1982. Ancestry.com, 2013.

Application for Civil War pension by Ada Thornsberry on behalf of son, Joseph M. Thornsberry, January 7, 1903. Rayville Public Library, Rayville, LA.

"Appointment of Tutors for the Minor Children of Mrs. Mary E. Hedrick." Court Records, Parish of West Carroll, State of Louisiana. FamilySearch Library, Salt Lake City, UT.

"Arnold, Minnie Mildred." US, Find A Grave Index, 1600s–Current. Ancestry.com, 2012.

"Arnold, Prof. B. I." 1880 US Census, Benton County, Oregon. Ancestry.com, 2006.

"Bailey, Margaret." 1870 US Census, Richland Parish, Louisiana, p. 250, family 67. FHLC #552027, FamilySearch Library, Salt Lake City, UT.

"Bailey, Margaret." 1880 US Census, Richland Parish, Louisiana. FamilySearch Library, Salt Lake City, UT.

"Benson Laura J." California Death Index, 1940–1997. Ancestry.com, 2000.

"Benson, H. W." 1920 US Census, Coahoma County, Mississippi. Ancestry.com, 2005.

"Benson, Henry Wade." US, World War I Draft Registration Cards, 1917–1918. Ancestry.com.

"Benson, Henry." 1880 US Census, Ashley County, Arkansas. Ancestry.com, 2004.

"Benson, John P." 1900 US Census, Washington County, Mississippi. Ancestry.com, 2004.

"Benson, John P." 1910 US Census, Washington County, Mississippi. Ancestry.com, 2006.

"Benson, John Porter." Arkansas, Confederate Pension Records, 1891–1935. Ancestry.com, 2011.

"Benson, Mary G." California Death Index, 1905–1939. Ancestry.com, 2013.

"Benson, Mary." 1860 US Census, Carroll Parish, Louisiana, p. 46. Ancestry.com.

"Benson, Maydelle." 1920 US Census, Los Angeles County, California. Ancestry.com, 2002.

"Benson, Maydelle." 1940 US Census, Los Angeles County, California. Ancestry.com, 2012.

"Benson, Maydelle." California Death Index, 1940–1997. Ancestry.com, 2000.

"Benson, Willi, to M. W. Pitts." Arkansas, County Marriage Index, 1837–1957. Ancestry.com, 2011.

"Berry, Louise." Social Security Death Index. Ancestry.com, 2008.

"Berry, William." 1930 US Census, Holmes County, Mississippi. Ancestry.com, 2002.

"Bier, Charles John." Texas Death Certificates, 1903–1982. Ancestry.com, 2013.

"Bier, Clarence Ralph." North Carolina Death Certificates, 1909–1976. Ancestry.com.

"Bier, Clyde." Social Security Death Index. Ancestry.com, 2008.

"Bier, Elizabeth Fanny." US, Find A Grave Index, 1600s–Current. Ancestry.com, 2012.

"Bier, Elizabeth White." Louisiana Statewide Death Index, 1900–1949. Ancestry.com, 2002.

"Bier, W. C." 1920 US Census, Acadia Parish, Louisiana. Ancestry.com.

"Bier, Walter C." 1910 US Census, Acadia Parish, Louisiana. Ancestry.com, 2006.

"Bier, Walter C." US, Social Security Applications and Claims Index, 1936–2007. Ancestry.com, 2015.

"Bier, Walter Clifton." US, Find A Grave Index, 1600s–Current. Ancestry.com, 2012.

"Bier, Walter." Social Security Death Index. Ancestry.com, 2008.

"Bier, Wayne Ranyard." US, Find A Grave Index, 1600s–Current. Ancestry.com, 2012.

"Booth, Andrew B." *Records of Louisiana Confederate Soldiers and Louisiana Confederate Commands*, vol. III, book 1, pp. 97–98. New Orleans, LA, 1920. Morehouse Public Library, Bastrop, LA.

"Bradley, C. H." 1880 US Census, St. Martin Parish, Louisiana. Ancestry.com, 2005.

"Bradley, Carter H." Louisiana Statewide Death Index, 1900–1949. Ancestry.com, 2002.

"Bradley, Catherine Ella." US, Find A Grave Index, 1600s–Current. Ancestry.com, 2012.

"Bradley, Catter." 1900 US Census, Orleans Parish, Louisiana. Ancestry.com, 2004.

"Breazeale, Mamie Antonette." US, Find A Grave Index, 1600s–Current. Ancestry.com, 2012.

"Briggs, Dalton D." California Death Index, 1940–1997. Ancestry.com, 2000.

"Brooks, Grace." 1940 US Census, Jefferson County, Texas. Ancestry.com, 2012.

"Burroughs, Louise." Social Security Death Index. Ancestry.com, 2008.

"Burroughs, Louise." US, Find A Grave Index, 1600s–Current. Ancestry.com, 2012.

"Carothers, Eugene Stuart." Texas Death Certificates, 1903–1982. Ancestry.com, 2013.

"Carothers, Eugene Stuart." US, Find A Grave Index, 1600s–Current. Ancestry.com, 2012.

"Carothers, James Gipson." US, Find A Grave Index, 1600s–Current. Ancestry.com, 2012.

"Carothers, Marguerita." Ancestry Family Trees. Ancestry.com.

"Carothers, Martha Redmond." US, Find A Grave Index, 1600s–Current. Ancestry.com, 2012.

"Carothers, Russell Carlile." US, Social Security Death Index, 1935–2914. Ancestry.com.

"Carothers, William H." US, Find A Grave Index, 1600s–Current. Ancestry.com, 2012.

"Carouthers, Eugene S." 1910 US Census, Clay County, Mississippi. Ancestry.com, 2006.

"Carouthers, Stuart." 1900 US Census, Clay County, Mississippi. Ancestry.com, 2004.

"Carson, Carville." 1910 US Census, Lincoln Parish, Louisiana. Ancestry.com, 2006.

"Carson, Carville." 1930 US Census, Bibb County, Georgia. Ancestry.com, 2002.

Centennial Edition of *Opelousas Daily World*. Accessed at the Opelousas Public Library, Opelousas, Mississippi.

"Cheek, William K." 1870 US Census, Copiah County, Mississippi. Ancestry.com, 2003.

Chester County, South Carolina, Deed Book D, p. 393. FamilySearch Library, Salt Lake City, UT.

Chester County, South Carolina, Deed Book F, p. 104. FHLC #0023324, FamilySearch Library, Salt Lake City, UT.

Chester County, South Carolina, Deed Book I, pp. 10, 87. FHLC #0023324, FamilySearch Library, Salt Lake City, UT.

Chester County, South Carolina, Deed Book M, pp. 299–300. FHLC #0023324, FamilySearch Library, Salt Lake City, UT.

"Clark, Joe B." 1930 US Census, Washington County, Mississippi. Ancestry.com, 2002.

Collins, Anne Pickens. *A Goodly Heritage: A History of Chester County, South Carolina*. Columbia, SC: R. L. Bryan Company, 1986. FamilySearch Library, Salt Lake City, UT.

"Couch, Izora H., to John W. Couch." Louisiana Marriages, 1718–1925. Ancestry.com, 2004.

"Couch, J. W." 1880 US Census, Franklin Parish, Louisiana, p. 47, Supervisors District 3, ED 34. FamilySearch Library, Salt Lake City, UT.

"Couch, Jon W." 1860 US Census, Franklin Parish, Louisiana, Warren, p. 42, family 273. FamilySearch Library, Salt Lake City, UT.

"Couch, W. J." 1870 US Census, Franklin Parish, Louisiana. Ancestry.com, 2003.

"Crichlow, Richard B." 1920 US Census, Orleans Parish, Louisiana. Ancestry.com.

"Critchlow, Augusta." New Orleans, Louisiana, Death Records Index, 1804–1949. Ancestry.com, 2002.

"Cumpton, Josephine." US, Find A Grave Index, 1600s–Current. Ancestry.com, 2012.

Daughters of the American Revolution (New Orleans, LA). *Louisiana Tombstone Inscriptions: East and West Carroll Parishes and Some Records from Ouachita Parish*. 1957. FamilySearch Library, Salt Lake City, UT.

"Davis, Allie." US, Find A Grave Index, 1600s–Current. Ancestry.com, 2012.

"Davis, Dalton F., to George L. Briggs." Texas, Select County Marriage Records. Ancestry.com, 2014.

"Davis, Dalton." US, Social Security Applications and Claims Index, 1936–2007. Ancestry.com, 2015.

"Davis, Elizabeth Ann 'Lizzie.'" US, Find A Grave Index, 1600s–Current. Ancestry.com, 2012.

"Davis, Florence Wade." US, Social Security Applications and Claims Index, 1936–2007. Ancestry.com, 2015.

"Davis, Gipsie, to H. S. Halsel." California, County Birth, Marriage and Death Records, 1949–1980. Ancestry.com, 2017.

"Davis, Gipsie." 1900 US Census, Acadia Parish, Louisiana. Ancestry.com, 2004.

"Davis, J. S." 1870 US Census, Caldwell Parish, Louisiana. Ancestry.com, 2003.

"Davis, John S." 1860 US Census, De Kalb County, Tennessee, Alexandria, dwelling 27. Ancestry.com, 2004.

"Davis, John Stone." Obituary from the Louisiana Conference of the United Methodist Church. Ancestry.com.

"Davis, M. A., to A. C. Skiles." Louisiana Marriages, 1718–1925. Ancestry.com, 2004.

"Davis, Mary Ann White." Louisiana, Find A Grave Index, 1700–2012. Ancestry.com, 2012.

"Davis, Miss F. E., to Carter Bradley." Louisiana Marriages, 1718–1925. Ancestry.com, 2004.

"Davis, Miss May." Texas Death Certificates, 1903–1982. Ancestry.com, 2013.

"Davis, R. A., to Elizabeth A. Day." Louisiana, Compiled Marriage Records, 1815–1900. Ancestry.com.

"Davis, Rev. John Stone." US, Find A Grave Index, 1600s–Current. Ancestry.com, 2012.

"Davis, Rev. John White, to Gipsie Holyland." Louisiana Marriages, 1718–1925. Ancestry.com, 2004.

"Davis, Rev. John White." US, Find A Grave Index, 1600s–Current. Ancestry.com, 2012.

"Davis, Rev. Robert A." US, Find A Grave Index, 1600s–Current. Ancestry.com, 2012.

"Davis, Robert A." New Orleans, Louisiana, Death Records Index, 1804–1949. Ancestry.com, 2002.

"Davis, Robert Bell." US, Find A Grave Index, 1600s–Current. Ancestry.com, 2012.

"Davis, Robt A." 1900 US Census, Tensas Parish, Louisiana. Ancestry.com, 2004.

"Davis, Robt A." 1910 US Census, Bienville Parish, Louisiana. Ancestry.com, 2006.

"Dicks, Ethel." US, Find A Grave Index, 1600s–Current. Ancestry.com, 2012.

Direct Index to Deeds. Chester County, South Carolina. FHLC #0023320, FamilySearch Library, Salt Lake City, UT.

"Dixon, Florence." 1910 US Census, Orleans Parish, Louisiana. Ancestry.com, 2006.

"Dodd, Jordan." Tennessee Marriages to 1825. Ancestry.com.

"Durst, Alma, to J. L. Reid." Texas County Marriages, 1817–1965. Ancestry.com, 2016.

"Durst, Eugene M." US, Social Security Applications and Claims Index, 1936–2007. Ancestry.com, 2015.

"Durst, Eugene Maurice." US, Find A Grave Index, 1600s–Current. Ancestry.com, 2012.

"Durst, Hugh Pickens." US, Find A Grave Index, 1600s–Current. Ancestry.com, 2012.

"Durst, Maurice E." California Death Index, 1940–1997. Ancestry.com, 2000.

"Durst, Rebecca Mae." US, Find A Grave Index, 1600s–Current. Ancestry.com, 2012.

"Eliza Jane White to Alexander Levy." Tennessee State Marriages, 1780–2002. Ancestry.com, 2008.

"Ellett, Andrew J." 1900 US Census, Hill County, Texas, page 1B. Ancestry.com.

"Emerick, Jane T." 1880 US Census, Claiborne County, Mississippi, p. 565A, sheet 40. ED 67. FHLC #1254644, FamilySearch Library, Salt Lake City, UT.

"Emory, Rebecca Aldora." US, Find A Grave Index, 1600s–Current. Ancestry.com, 2012.

"Families of Williamson County, Tennessee." Old Glory Chapter DAR, Franklin, TN. FHLC #0024876, FamilySearch Library, Salt Lake City, UT.

"File, Julia." US, Find A Grave Index, 1600s–Current. Ancestry.com, 2012.

"Fuller, Pearl E." US, Find A Grave Index, 1600s–Current. Ancestry.com, 2012.

Gauntt, Marguerite, and Modelle Ballard. *When The Rails Were Laid: A History of Rochester*, pp. 283–284. Quanah, TX: Nortex Press, 1976.

"Gervin, Alfred Lawrence, Jr." US, Social Security Applications and Claims Index, 1936–2007. Ancestry.com, 2015.

"Gervin, Alfred Lawrence." US, Find A Grave Index, 1600s–Current. Ancestry.com, 2012.

"Gervin, Alfred." 1910 US Census, Bolivar County, Mississippi. Ancestry.com, 2006.

"Gervin, Alfred." 1930 US Census, Bolivar County, Mississippi. Ancestry.com, 2002.

"Gervin, Charles Curell." US, Social Security Applications and Claims Index, 1936–2007. Ancestry.com, 2015.

"Gervin, George." US, Find A Grave Index, 1600s–Current. Ancestry.com, 2012.

"Gervin, Jack Evans." US, Find A Grave Index, 1600s–Current. Ancestry.com, 2012.

"Gervin, Robert H." Social Security Death Index. Ancestry.com, 2008.

"Gervin, Stella." US, Find A Grave Index, 1600s–Current. Ancestry.com, 2012.

"Gervins, Alfred." 1920 US Census, Bolivar County, Mississippi. Ancestry.com, 2005.

Gilmore, Maude Ann, "Descendants of Benjamin Franklin White." Compiled research notes, received by Mary Jo Kenny in April 2003.

Gilmore, Maude Ann. "Descendants of Henry Octavius White." Compiled research notes, received by Mary Jo Kenny in April 2003.

Gilmore, Maude Ann. "Descendants of James Megathorn White." Compiled research notes, received by Mary Jo Kenny in April 2003.

Gilmore, Maude Ann. "Descendants of Joseph Ellis White." Compiled research notes, received by Mary Jo Kenny in April 2003.

Gilmore, Maude Ann. "Descendants of Margaret Isabella Green White." Compiled research notes, received by Mary Jo Kenny in April 2003.

Gilmore, Maude Ann. "Descendants of Mary Ann White." Compiled research notes, received by Mary Jo Kenny in April 2003.

Gilmore, Maude Ann. "Descendants of Thomas Beeman White." Compiled research notes, received by Mary Jo Kenny in April 2003.

Gilmore, Maude Ann. "Descendants of William Dee Hardeman White." Compiled research notes, received by Mary Jo Kenny, 2003.

Gilmore, Maude Ann. Email to Mary Jo Kenny. April 29, 2003.

Gilmore, Maude Ann. Email to Mary Jo Kenny. March 23, 2003.

Gilmore, Maude Ann. Email to Mary Jo Kenny. May 27, 1999.

"Greer, Abe." 1920 US Census, Haskell County, Texas. Ancestry.com, 2005.

"Greer, Abraham." 1830 US Census, White, Illinois, p. 25. FamilySearch Library, Salt Lake City, UT.

"Greer, Abraham." 1840 US Census, Claiborne County, Mississippi. FamilySearch Library, Salt Lake City, UT.

"Greer, Ada, to Joseph Thornsberry." Louisiana Marriages, 1718–1925. Ancestry.com, 2004.

"Greer, Blanche." US, Find A Grave Index, 1600s–Current. Ancestry.com, 2012.

Greer Cemetery (LA Highway 3048, Richland Parish, LA). George A. Greer grave marker.

"Greer, F. M." Civil War Prisoner of War Records, 1861–1865. Ancestry.com, 2007.

"Greer, Francis M., patient, Wichita Falls State Hospital." 1940 US Census, Wichita County, Texas. Ancestry.com, 2012.

"Greer, Francis M." Louisiana, Homestead and Cash Entry Patents, Pre 1908. Ancestry.com, 1997.

"Greer, Francis M." US Civil War Soldier Records and Profiles. Ancestry.com, 2009.

"Greer, Francis Marion, Jr." US, Find A Grave Index, 1600s–Current. Ancestry.com, 2012.

"Greer, Francis Marion." 1860 US Census, Richland Parish, Louisiana, FamilySearch Library, Salt Lake City, UT.

"Greer, Francis Marion." Texas Death Certificates, 1903–1982. Ancestry.com, 2013.

"Greer, Frank M." 1930 US Census, Haskell County, Texas. Ancestry.com, 2002.

"Greer, George A., to Mrs. Blanche Gilmore." Louisiana Compiled Marriage Records, 1851–1900. Ancestry.com.

"Greer, George A." 1900 US Census, Richland Parish, Louisiana. Ancestry.com.

"Greer, George A." 1910 US Census, Richland Parish, Louisiana, sheet 27A, ED 114, family 247. FamilySearch Library, Salt Lake City, UT.

"Greer, George." US, Department of Veterans Affairs BIRLS File, 1950–2010. Ancestry.com, 2011.

"Greer, Honor Andrew, Sr." US, Find A Grave Index, 1600s–Current. Ancestry.com, 2012.

"Greer, James A., Sr." Texas Death Certificates, 1903–1082. Ancestry.com, 2013.

"Greer, James A., Sr." US, Social Security Applications and Claims Index, 1936–2007.

"Greer, James A." 1900 US Census, Hill County, Texas, Precinct 5, vol. 59, ED 46, p. 46B, line 51. FHLC #31241645, FamilySearch Library, Salt Lake City, UT.

"Greer, James A." 1910 US Census, Jones County, Texas. Ancestry.com, 2006.

"Greer, James A." 1930 US Census, Haskell County, Texas. Ancestry.com, 2002.

"Greer, James A." Texas County Marriages, 1817–1965. Ancestry.com, 2016.

"Greer, James A." Texas, Find A Grave Index, 1836–2011. Ancestry.com, 2012.

"Greer, James." 1850 US Census, Carroll Parish, Louisiana. FamilySearch Library, Salt Lake City, UT.

"Greer, Margaret Ann." 1850 US Census, Morehouse Parish, Louisiana. FamilySearch Library, Salt Lake City, UT.

"Greer, Pony Marshall." World War I Draft Registration Cards, 1917–1918. Ancestry.com, 2005.

"Greer, Sarah M." 1880 US Census, Yazoo County, Mississippi. Ancestry.com, 2005.

"Greer, Sarah M." US, Find A Grave Index, 1600s–Current. Ancestry.com, 2012.

"Greer, T. A." Texas, Wills and Probate Records, 1833–1974. Ancestry.com, 2015.

"Greer, Thomas A." 1900 US Census, Haskell County, Texas. Ancestry.com, 2004.

"Greer, Thomas A." 1910 US Census, Haskell County, Texas, Precinct 5, sheet 11B, p. 85. FHLC #1375575, FamilySearch Library, Salt Lake City, UT.

"Greer, Thomas A." 1910 US Census, Haskell County, Texas. Ancestry.com, 2006.

"Greer, Thomas Abraham." US, Find A Grave Index, 1600s–Current. Ancestry.com, 2012.

"Greer, William Hezzie Carr." US, Find A Grave Index, 1600s–Current. Ancestry.com, 2012.

"Greer, William Jefferson." Texas Death Certificates, 1903–1982. Ancestry.com, 2013.

"Greer, William Jefferson." US, Find A Grave Index, 1600s–Current. Ancestry.com, 2012.

"Greer, Wm M." 1860 US Census, Morehouse Parish, Louisiana, p. 93, line 1. FamilySearch Library, Salt Lake City, UT.

"Greer, Frances M." 1870 US Census, Richland Parish, Louisiana. FamilySearch Library, Salt Lake City, UT.

"Greer, James A." 1940 US Census, Haskell County, Texas. Ancestry.com, 2012.

"Gross, Rebecca." 1860 US Census, Jackson Parish, Louisiana. Ancestry.com, 2004.

"Haggerty, Isabella." 1850 US Census, Jackson Parish, Louisiana. FamilySearch Library, Salt Lake City, UT.

"Hagood, Mary." US, Find A Grave Index, 1600s–Current. Ancestry.com, 2012.

"Halsel, Gipsie." California Death Index, 1940–1997. Ancestry.com, 2000.

"Hayes, James." 1870 US Census, St. Landry Parish, Louisiana, Opelousas, p. 39, dwelling 276. FamilySearch Library, Salt Lake City, UT. Ancestry.com,

"Hayes, Margaret." 1880 US Census, St. Landry Parish, Louisiana. FamilySearch Library, Salt Lake City, UT.

"Hayes, Margaret." 1900 US Census, St. Landry Parish, Louisiana, p. 223A, sheet 25, ED 52, family 513. FamilySearch Library, Salt Lake City, UT.

"Hayes, Margaret." 1910 US Census, St. Landry Parish, Louisiana. FamilySearch Library, Salt Lake City, UT.

"Hays, James G." Probate Papers. St. Landry Parish Courthouse, Opelousas, Louisiana.

"Hays, Margaret M." 1889 US Census, St. Landry Parish, Louisiana, Opelousas, p. 5, ED 45, #57. FamilySearch Library, Salt Lake City, UT.

Headley, Katy McCaleb. *Claiborne County, Mississippi: The Promised Land.* Port Gibson, MS: Claiborne County Historical Society, 1976, reprinted in 1996.

"Hearn, Eugenia Alberta." US, Find A Grave Index, 1600s–Current. Ancestry.com, 2012.

"Hearn, Eugenia Mae." US, Find A Grave Index, 1600s–Current. Ancestry.com, 2012.

"Hearn, Eugenia W." US Appointments of US Postmasters, 1832–1971.

"Hearn, I. A." 1940 US Census, Caldwell Parish, Louisiana. Ancestry.com, 2012.

"Hearn, Ivy A." 1930 US Census, Caldwell Parish, Louisiana. Ancestry.com, 2002.

"Hearn, Ivy Albert." 1920 US Census, Caldwell Parish, Louisiana. Ancestry.com, 2005.

"Hearn, Ivy Albert." US, Find A Grave Index, 1600s–Current. Ancestry.com, 2012.

"Hedric, Arch." 1920 US Census, West Carroll Parish, Louisiana. Ancestry.com, 2005.

"Hedrick, Estelle." US, Appointments of US Postmasters, 1832–1971. Ancestry.com, 2010.

"Hedrick, G. C." 1840 US Census, Caldwell Parish, Louisiana. FamilySearch Library, Salt Lake City, UT.

"Hedrick, Gibson C." Succession Papers. Caldwell Parish, Louisiana. FHLC #311882, FamilySearch Library, Salt Lake City, UT.

"Hedrick, John B." US, Find A Grave Index, 1600s–Current. Ancestry.com, 2012.

"Hedrick, John Charles." US, Find A Grave Index, 1600s–Current. Ancestry.com, 2012.

"Hedrick, W. A., to Mary E. Parker." Louisiana Marriages, 1718–1925. Ancestry.com, 2004.

"Hedrick, W. A., Sr." 1900 US Census, West Carroll Parish, Louisiana, ward 2, ED 126, p. 19B, dwelling 391. FHLC #1240586, FamilySearch Library, Salt Lake City, UT.

"Hedrick, W. A." 1880 US Census, West Carroll Parish, Louisiana, p. I, wards 1 and 2. FamilySearch Library, Salt Lake City, UT.

"Hedrick, W. A." 1910 US Census, West Carroll Parish, Louisiana. Ancestry.com, 2002.

"Hedrick, William Archibald, Sr." US, Find A Grave Index, 1600s–Current. Ancestry.com, 2012.

"Hedrick, Wm A." 1870 US Census, Carroll Parish, Louisiana, Floyd, p. 27, ward 6. FamilySearch Library, Salt Lake City, UT.

"Henry, Erkel." Social Security Death Index. Ancestry.com, 2008.

"Herring, R. J." 1920 US Census, West Carroll Parish, Louisiana. Ancestry.com, 2005.

"Herring, Rob J." 1930 US Census, West Carroll Parish, Louisiana. Ancestry.com, 2002.

"Herring." Newspapers.com Obituary Index, 1800s–Current. Ancestry.com, 2019.

"Holloman, Julia House." US, Find A Grave Index, 1600s–Current. Ancestry.com, 2012.

"Holoman, Thomas Abner." US, Find A Grave Index, 1600s–Current. Ancestry.com, 2012.

"Holoman, Thomas Wynn." US, Find A Grave Index, 1600s–Current. Ancestry.com, 2012.

"Holomon, R. A." 1880 US Census, Yazoo County, Mississippi. Ancestry.com, 2005.

"Huddleston, Loraine." US, Find A Grave Index, 1600s–Current. Ancestry.com, 2012.

Hughes, William P., v. E.M. Long et al. Chancery Court, Claiborne County, Mississippi, 1880. FHLC #1670516, FamilySearch Library, Salt Lake City, UT.

Hull, Carol J. Email to Mary Jo Kenny. February 22, 2001.

Hull, Carol J. Email to Mary Jo Kenny. February 8, 2003.

Hull, Carol J. Email to Mary Jo Kenny. July 14, 2001.

Hull, Carol J. Email to Mary Jo Kenny. March 19, 2001.

Hull, Carol J. Email to Mary Jo Kenny. March 2, 2001.

Hull, Carol J. Email to Mary Jo Kenny. March 9, 2001.

Hyde, Lillian. Email to Mary Jo Kenny. January 4, 2002.

"Jodon, Viola Blessen." US, Social Security Applications and Claims Index, 1936–2007. Ancestry.com, 2015.

"Jodon, Viola Dee Blessen." US, Find A Grave Index, 1600s–Current. Ancestry.com, 2012.

"Johnson, Manie." Texas Death Index, 1903–2000. Ancestry.com, 2006.

"Kanny, William." 1800 US Census, Chester County, South Carolina. FHLC #975.7, C168a. FamilySearch Library, Salt Lake City, UT.

Kanon, Tom. "Regimental Histories of Tennessee Units During the War of 1812." Tennessee State Library. Updated November 20, 2007.

Kenny, Alexander. Will. 1797. Chester County, South Carolina. *Will Book A*. FHLC #0023308, FamilySearch Library, Salt Lake City, UT.

"Kenny, James." 1800 US Census, Chester County, South Carolina. FamilySearch Library, Salt Lake City, UT.

Kenny, James. Probate Papers. *Will Book 2*, pp. 194, 202. County Clerk Records, Franklin, TN.

"Kenny, Jane, to Edward Long." Williamson County, Tennessee, Marriage Bonds. Williamson County Library, Historical Records, Franklin, TN.

"Kenny, William C." 1840 US Census, Caldwell Parish, Louisiana. FamilySearch Library, Salt Lake City, UT.

Kenny, William. Revolutionary War Pension Application #R.5871. Morgan County, Alabama, October 22, 1832. Amendment filed June 1833. National Archives.

"Kitchell, Birdie." US, Social Security Applications and Claims Index, 1936–2007. Ancestry.com, 2015.

"Kitchell, Isabel." Social Security Death Index. Ancestry.com, 2008.

"Kitchell, J. N." 1910 US Census, Vermilion Parish, Louisiana. Ancestry.com, 2006.

"Kitchell, James R." 1920 US Census, Vermilion Parish, Louisiana. Ancestry.com, 2005.

"Kitchell, James Robert." Louisiana Statewide Death Index, 1900–1949. Ancestry.com, 2002.

"Kitchell, James Robert." US, Find A Grave Index, 1600s–Current. Ancestry.com, 2012.

"Kitchell, Mary E." 1930 US Census, Vermilion Parish, Louisiana. Ancestry.com, 2002.

"Kitchell, Mary Emma." US, Find A Grave Index, 1600s–Current. Ancestry.com, 2012.

"Kitchell, Mary." US, Social Security Applications and Claims Index, 1936–2007. Ancestry.com, 2015.

Larned, Johney G. Letter to Mary Jo Kenny. March 6, 2005.

"Lee, Alice Gray." US, Find A Grave Index, 1600s–Current. Ancestry.com, 2012.

"Lee, Israel." 1930 US Census, Issaquena County, Mississippi. Ancestry.com, 2002.

"Levy, Alexr." 1850 US Census, Davidson County, Tennessee. Ancestry.com, 2008.

"Long, Alice." US, Find A Grave Index, 1600s–Current. Ancestry.com, 2012.

"Long, E. M., Jr." US Civil War Soldiers, 1861–1865. Ancestry.com, 2007.

"Long, E. M." 1850 US Census, Claiborne County, Mississippi, p. 60, Police District 3, Rocky Springs, family 55. FamilySearch Library, Salt Lake City, UT.

"Long, E. M." 1860 US Census, Claiborne County, Mississippi, p. 60. Police District 3, Rocky Springs. FamilySearch Library, Salt Lake City, UT.

"Long, E. M." 1870 US Census, Tensas Parish, Louisiana, p. 2, ward 1, Ashwood Lodge, family 12. FamilySearch Library, Salt Lake City, UT.

"Long, Edward A." Texas Death Certificates, 1903–1982. Ancestry.com, 2013.

"Long, Edward M." 1880 US Census, Hill County, Texas. Ancestry.com, 2005.

"Long, Edward M." US General Land Office Records. FamilySearch Library, Salt Lake City, UT.

"Long, Edward Morris, Jr." US, Find A Grave Index, 1600s–Current. Ancestry.com, 2012.

"Long, Edward." 1920 US Census, Hill County, Texas. Ancestry.com, 2005.

"Long, Edward." 1900 US Census, Hill County, Texas. Ancestry.com, 2004.

"Long, Edwin Marvin." Texas Death Certificates, 1903–1982. Ancestry.com, 2013.

"Long, Forest." Texas Death Certificates, 1903–1982. Ancestry.com, 2013.

"Long, George W." 1870 US Census, Claiborne County, Mississippi, Rocky Springs District. FHLC #552225, FamilySearch Library, Salt Lake City, UT.

"Long, Isorah, to Thomas J. Couch." Louisiana Marriages, 1718–1925. Ancestry.com, 2004.

"Long, J. W." US, Find A Grave Index, 1600s–Current. Ancestry.com, 2012.

"Long, L. K." 1880 US Census, West Carroll Parish, Louisiana, p. 2, Supervisor District 6, ED 92, wards 1 and 2. FamilySearch Library, Salt Lake City, UT.

"Long, Mrs. Jane T., to Alexander Emerick." Mississippi Marriages, 1776–1935. Ancestry.com, 2004.

"Long, Myrtle M." US, Social Security Applications and Claims Index, 1936–2007. Ancestry.com, 2015.

"Long, Roy." Texas Death Certificates, 1903–1982. Ancestry.com, 2013.

"Long, W. C., to F. C. Hill." Mississippi Marriages, 1776–1932. Ancestry.com, 2004.

"Long, William C." US, Find A Grave Index, 1600s–Current. Ancestry.com, 2012.

"Long, William." Texas Death Certificates, 1903–1982. Ancestry.com, 2013.

Lynch, Louise Gillespie. *Early Obituaries of Williamson County, Tennessee*. 1977. FHLC #1421822, item 11. FamilySearch Library, Salt Lake City, UT.

"Lyons, B. Jason." 1910 US Census, Arcadia Parish, Louisiana. Ancestry.com, 2006.

"Lyons, Benjamin." 1900 US Census, Acadia Parish, Louisiana. Ancestry.com, 2004.

"Lyons, Lester Harry." World War I Draft Registration Cards, 1917–1918. Ancestry.com, 2005.

"Lyons, William A." 1920 US Census, Acadia Parish, Louisiana. Ancestry.com, 2005.

"Lyons, William A." 1930 US Census, Acadia Parish, Louisiana. Ancestry.com, 2002.

"Lyons, William Augustus." US, Find A Grave Index, 1600s–Current. Ancestry.com, 2012.

"Mary P. Long, to C. H. P. Ritch." Louisiana Marriages, 1718–1925. Ancestry.com, 2004.

"McAdams, Dolly Wade." US, Social Security Applications and Claims Index, 1936–2007. Ancestry.com, 2015.

McAdams, Stacy. Email to Mary Jo Kenny. August 23, 2007.

McAdams, Stacy. Email to Mary Jo Kenny. August 25, 2007.

McAdams, Stacy. Email to Mary Jo Kenny. August 28, 2007.

McAdams, Stacy. Email to Mary Jo Kenny. June 1, 2008.

McAdams, Stacy. Email to Mary Jo Kenny. May 17, 2008.

"McCombs, Laura." US, Find A Grave Index, 1600s–Current. Ancestry.com, 2012.

"Memories of the Life of James A. Greer." September 20, 1952. Posted by Nick Reid to Rebecca Mae Ann Greer. Ancestry.com.

"Middleton, Jane." US, Find A Grave Index, 1600s–Current. Ancestry.com, 2012.

"Miller, Ben D." 1930 US Census, Washington Parish, Louisiana. Ancestry.com, 2002.

"Miller, Joyce." Social Security Death Index. Ancestry.com, 2008.

"Millet, Winnie." Social Security Death Index. Ancestry.com, 2008.

"Mixon, Leola." 1920 US Census, Acadia Parish, Louisiana. Ancestry.com, 2005.

Morehouse Parish Deed Book A, pp. 303–304, 307–308, 320–322, 406–408, 465–466, 479–480; *Book B*, pp. 80–81, 83–85, 267–268, 612; *Book C*, p. 442; *Book D*, p. 413. Morehouse Parish Courthouse, Bastrop, LA.

Morehouse Parish, Louisiana, Historical Records Survey. FHLC#897423, FamilySearch Library, Salt Lake City, Utah.

"Nixon, John R." 1900 US Census, Acadia Parish, Louisiana. Ancestry.com, 2004.

"Nixon, John Travis." US, Find A Grave Index, 1600s–Current. Ancestry.com, 2012.

"Nixon, Laurence." New York, New York, Death Index, 1949–1965. Ancestry.com, 2017.

"Nixon, Leola Belle." US, Find A Grave Index, 1600s–Current. Ancestry.com, 2012.

"Nixon, Leola W." 1930 US Census, Lincoln Parish, Louisiana. Ancestry.com, 2002.

"Nixon, Leola." 1910 US Census, Acadia Parish, Louisiana. Ancestry.com, 2006.

"Nolan, Mildred Eliza." US, Find A Grave Index, 1600s–Current. Ancestry.com, 2012.

"Norris, Rebecca." US, Find A Grave Index, 1600s–Current. Ancestry.com, 2012.

"Oldham, Elizabeth." Succession Papers. Williamson County Library, Historical Records, Franklin, TN.

Original Loose Papers. Williamson County Preservation of Records. Old Post Office, Franklin, TN.

Perrin, W. *Biographies of Famous People*. Accessed at the Opelousas Public Library, Opelousas, Mississippi.

"Pinson, Don Hedrick." Arizona Death Records, 1887–1960. Ancestry.com, 2016.

"Pinson, Edgar C." Texas Death Certificates, 1903–1982. Ancestry.com, 2013.

"Pinson, George A." California Death Index, 1940–1979. Ancestry.com, 2000.

"Pinson, Maggie." 1900 US Census, West Carroll Parish, Louisiana. Ancestry.com.

"Pinson, Margaret P." Louisiana Statewide Death Index, 1900–1949. Ancestry.com, 2002.

"Pinson, Margaret Parker." US, Find A Grave Index, 1600s–Current. Ancestry.com, 2012.

"Pipes, Carrie Ida." Texas Death Certificates, 1903–1982. Ancestry.com, 2013.

"Pipes, Carrie Ida." US, Social Security Applications and Claims Index, 1936–2007. Ancestry.com, 2015.

"Pipes, Eugene Beall." Texas Death Certificates, 1903–1982. Ancestry.com, 2013.

"Pipes, Grace." US, Social Security Applications and Claims Index, 1936–2007. Ancestry.com, 2015.

"Pipes, Oscar B." 1930 US Census, Jefferson County, Texas. Ancestry.com, 2002.

"Pipes, Oscar B." Texas Death Certificates, 1903–1982. Ancestry.com, 2013.

"Pipes, Oscar W." 1900 US Census, Bienville Parish, Louisiana. Ancestry.com, 2004.

"Pipes, William Oscar." US, Find A Grave Index, 1600s–Current. Ancestry.com, 2012.

"Pitts, DeHaven." Texas Death Certificates, 1903–1982. Ancestry.com, 2013.

"Pitts, Erkle." US, Social Security Applications and Claims Index, 1936–2007. Ancestry.com, 2015.

"Pitts, Minor." 1900 US Census, Fort Bend County, Texas. Ancestry.com, 2004.

"Pitts, Mrs. Willi Hill." US, Find A Grave Index, 1600s–Current. Ancestry.com, 2012.

"Powell, Banks J., Sr." 1940 US Census, Bolivar County, Mississippi. Ancestry.com, 2012.

"Powell, Banks J." 1910 US Census, Bolivar County, Mississippi. Ancestry.com, 2006.

"Powell, Banks J." 1920 US Census, Bolivar County, Mississippi. Ancestry.com, 2005.

"Powell, Banks J." 1930 US Census, Bolivar County, Mississippi. Ancestry.com, 2002.

"Powell, Banks Jennings, Jr." US, Find A Grave Index, 1600s–Current. Ancestry.com, 2012.

"Powell, Banks Jennings, Sr." US, Find A Grave Index, 1600s–Current. Ancestry.com, 2012.

"Powell, Mary Lou." US, Find A Grave Index, 1600s–Current. Ancestry.com, 2012.

Price, James Earl. *The Annals of Claiborne County, Mississippi, J&W Enterprises.* Shreveport, LA, April 1996. Harriette Person Memorial Library, Port Gibson, Mississippi.

"Ramsay, Elizabeth." Social Security Death Index. Ancestry.com, 2008.

"Rand, Ellen Blythe." US, Find A Grave Index, 1600s–Current. Ancestry.com, 2012.

"Reilly, William B." 1930 US Census, Orleans Parish, Louisiana. Ancestry.com, 2002.

"Reily, Charlotte Ann." US, Find A Grave Index, 1600s–Current. Ancestry.com, 2012.

"Reily, Estelle Weaks." US, Social Security Applications and Claims Index, 1936–2007. Ancestry.com, 2015.

"Reily, James Weaks." World War I Draft Registration Cards, 1917–1918. Ancestry.com, 2005.

"Reily, James." Social Security Death Index. Ancestry.com, 2008.

"Reily, William B." 1910 US Census, Orleans Parish, Louisiana. Ancestry.com, 2006.

"Reily, William B." 1920 US Census, Orleans Parish, Louisiana. Ancestry.com, 2005.

"Reily, William Boatner." US, Find A Grave Index, 1600s–Current. Ancestry.com, 2012.

"Reily, William." Social Security Death Index. Ancestry.com, 2008.

Richland Memories. Original Rhyme Library Restoration Society, Second Printing, 2003. West Morris, LA: Central Printer and Publisher. Morehouse Public Library, Bastrop, LA.

Richland Parish Deed Book H, p. 500. Richland Parish Courthouse, Rayville, LA.

"Rife, Mary Jane." Will, signed August 1888, filed September 1889. Photocopy of original provided by Stacy McAdams.

"Riley, W. B." 1900 US Census, Ouachita Parish, Louisiana. Ancestry.com, 2004.

Rose, E. Anette. Email to Mary Jo Kenny. March 24, 2003.

"Rostreet, Dorothy W." Social Security Death Index. Ancestry.com, 2008.

"Rusheon, Mamie White." US, Social Security Applications and Claims Index, 1936–2007. Ancestry.com, 2015.

"Sachs, Frances W." Social Security Death Index. Ancestry.com, 2008.

"Sarver, Willie." Social Security Death Index. Ancestry.com, 2008.

"Scales, Alfred Leslie." US Department of Veterans Affairs, BIRLS Death File, 1850–2010. Ancestry.com, 2011.

"Scales, Katie F. Walt." US, Find A Grave Index, 1600s–Current. Ancestry.com, 2012.

"Scales, Katie." 1940 US Census, Leflore County, Mississippi. Ancestry.com, 2012.

"Scales, Katie." Social Security Death Index. Ancestry.com, 2008.

"Shaw, Ada, patient, Central Louisiana State Hospital." 1930 US Census, Rapides Parish, Louisiana. Ancestry.com, 2006.

"Shaw, Ada, patient, Louisiana Hospital for Insane." 1920 US Census, Rapides Parish, Louisiana. Ancestry.com, 2005.

"Shaw, Ada." 1910 US Census, Richland Parish, Louisiana. Ancestry.com, 2006.

"Shaw, Ada." Louisiana, Statewide Death Index, 1819–1964. Ancestry.com, 2002.

"Smith, Anna." US, Social Security Applications and Claims Index, 1936–2007. Ancestry.com, 2015.

"Smith, Myrtle." Social Security Death Index. Ancestry.com, 2008.

"Speer, Birdie K." Social Security Death Index. Ancestry.com, 2008.

"Stacy, Martha." US, Social Security Applications and Claims Index, 1936–2007. Ancestry.com, 2015.

"Stewart, Minnie Laura." US, Find A Grave Index, 1600s–Current. Ancestry.com, 2012.

Tax Records. Williamson County, TN. FHLC #0456076, FamilySearch Library, Salt Lake City, UT.

"Thornsberry, Joseph." 1900 US Census, Richland Parish, Louisiana. Ancestry.com, 2004.

"Thornsberry, Joseph." Application for Civil War invalid pension, December 8, 1898. Rayville Public Library, Rayville, LA.

"Thornsberry, Staff Sargent Joseph Frances." Texas Death Certificates, 1903–1982. Ancestry.com, 2013.

"Trousdale, George." US Department of Veterans Affairs BIRLS Death File, 1850–2010. Ancestry.com, 2011.

"Trousdale, J. Harvey." 1940 US Census, Ouachita Parish, Louisiana. Ancestry.com, 2012.

"Trousdale, James H." 1930 US Census, Ouachita Parish, Louisiana. Ancestry.com, 2002.

"Trousdale, James Harvey, Jr." US, Find A Grave Index, 1600s–Current. Ancestry.com, 2012.

"Trousdale, James Harvey." US, Find A Grave Index, 1600s–Current. Ancestry.com, 2012.

"Trousdale, Jas H." 1920 US Census, Ouachita Parish, Louisiana. Ancestry.com, 2005.

"Trousdale, Jennie B." US, Social Security Applications and Claims Index, 1936–2007. Ancestry.com, 2015.

"Wade (Waid), J. W." 1870 US Census, Jackson Parish, Louisiana. Ancestry.com, 2003.

"Wade, Ann Elizabeth." US, Find A Grave Index, 1600s–Current. Ancestry.com, 2012.

"Wade, C. W." 1910 US Census, Rankin County, Mississippi. Ancestry.com, 2006.

"Wade, Carrie Bell." US, Find A Grave Index, 1600s–Current. Ancestry.com, 2012.

"Wade, Charles Curell." US, Find A Grave Index, 1600s–Current. Ancestry.com, 2012.

"Wade, Charles Curell." World War I Draft Registration Cards, 1917–1918. Ancestry.com, 2005.

"Wade, Charles W." 1900 US Census, Shelby County, Alabama. Ancestry.com, 2006.

"Wade, Charles W." US Civil War Pension Index: General Index to Pension Files, 1861–1934. Ancestry.com, 2000.

"Wade, Charles W." US, Find A Grave Index, 1600s–Current. Ancestry.com, 2012.

"Wade, Elton Gray." US, Find A Grave Index, 1600s–Current. Ancestry.com, 2012.

"Wade, George S." WWI, WWII, and Korean War Casualty Listings. Ancestry.com, 2005.

"Wade, George." 1820 US Census, Williamson County, Tennessee, p. 156. FHLC #0193687, FamilySearch Library, Salt Lake City, UT.

"Wade, George." 1830 US Census, Williamson County, Tennessee. FamilySearch Library, Salt Lake City, UT.

Wade, Henry R. Succession Papers, West Carroll Parish, Louisiana, 1886. FHLC #1240586, FamilySearch Library, Salt Lake City, UT.

"Wade, H. C." 1880 US Census, Carroll Parish, Louisiana, p. 413A. ED 92, image 329. FamilySearch Library, Salt Lake City, UT.

"Wade, H. R." 1880 US Census, West Carroll Parish, Louisiana. Ancestry.com, 2005.

"Wade, Henry R." 1850 US Census, Western District, Carroll Parish, Louisiana. Ancestry.com, 2009.

"Wade, Henry R." 1860 US Census, Western District, Carroll Parish, Louisiana. Ancestry.com, 2004.

"Wade, Henry R." 1870 US Census, Carroll Parish, Louisiana. FamilySearch Library, Salt Lake City, UT.

"Wade, J. W." 1920 US Census, Lincoln Parish, Louisiana. Ancestry.com, 2005.

"Wade, James T., to Rebecca F. Mixon." Louisiana Marriages, 1718–1925. Ancestry.com, 2004.

"Wade, James T." 1950 US Census, Jackson Parish, Louisiana. Ancestry.com, 2009.

"Wade, James T." US Federal Census Mortality Schedules, 1850–1885. Ancestry.com, 2010.

"Wade, James W., to Emma Averette." Louisiana Marriages, 1718–1925. Ancestry.com, 2004.

"Wade, James W., Sr." 1910 US Census, Lincoln Parish, Louisiana. Ancestry.com, 2006.

"Wade, James W." US, Find A Grave Index, 1600s–Current. Ancestry.com, 2012.

"Wade, James William." Louisiana Statewide Death Index, 1819–1964. Ancestry.com.

"Wade, James." 1880 US Census, Lincoln Parish, Louisiana. Ancestry.com, 2005.

"Wade, James." 1900 US Census, Lincoln Parish, Louisiana. Ancestry.com, 2004.

"Wade, John." 1880 US Census, Natchitoches Parish, Louisiana. Ancestry.com, 2005.

"Wade, Kate C." 1910 US Census, Washington County, Mississippi, p. 8A, ED 117, dwelling 402, family 113. FamilySearch Library, Salt Lake City, UT.

"Wade, Kate." 1900 US Census, Washington County, Mississippi, sheet 9A, ED 81, dwelling 92, family 145. FamilySearch Library, Salt Lake City, UT.

"Wade, Kate." 1920 US Census, Washington County, Mississippi. Ancestry.com.

"Wade, Kate." US, Find A Grave Index, 1600s–Current. Ancestry.com, 2012.

"Wade, L. T., owner." 1850 US Census, Slave Schedule, Carroll Parish, Louisiana. Ancestry.com.

"Wade, L. T." 1850 US Census, Western District, Carroll Parish, Louisiana. FamilySearch Library, Salt Lake City, UT.

"Wade, L. T." 1860 US Census, Issaquena County, Mississippi. Ancestry.com.

"Wade, L. T." 1870 US Census, Issaquena County, Mississippi. Ancestry.com.

"Wade, L. T." 1900 US Census, Issaquena County, Mississippi. Ancestry.com, 2006.

"Wade, Lawrence T." 1920 US Census, Issaquena County, Mississippi. Ancestry.com, 2005.

"Wade, Lawrence Thompson, to Mary Jane Rife." East Carroll Parish Marriage Records A–C. FHLC #311905, FamilySearch Library, Salt Lake City, UT.

"Wade, Lawrence Thompson, Sr." US, Find A Grave Index, 1600s–Current. Ancestry.com, 2012.

"Wade, Lawrence Thompson." US, Find A Grave Index, 1600s–Current. Ancestry.com, 2012.

"Wade, Lawrence." 1910 US Census, Issaquena County, Mississippi. Ancestry.com, 2006.

"Wade, Lawrence." 1940 US Census, Washington County, Mississippi. Ancestry.com, 2012.

"Wade, Lawrence." US Department of Veterans Affairs, BIRLS Death File, 1850–2010. Ancestry.com, 2011.

"Wade, Martha J." 1850 US Census, Carroll Parish, Louisiana, Mortality Schedule. Ancestry.com.

"Wade, Martha S." 1930 US Census, Washington County, Mississippi. Ancestry.com, 2002.

"Wade, Martha." 1940 US Census, Washington County, Mississippi. Ancestry.com, 2012.

"Wade, Mary Emma." US, Find A Grave Index, 1600s–Current. Ancestry.com, 2012.

"Wade, Mary F., to Samuel B. Wiggins." Mississippi Marriages, 1776–1935. Ancestry.com, 2004.

"Wade, Mary Jane Rife." Family record pages of Bible. Photocopy of original provided by Stacy McAdams.

"Wade, Mattie S." 1920 US Census, Washington County, Mississippi. Ancestry.com, 2005.

"Wade, Mixon, to Marion E. Newton." Arkansas County Marriages Index, 1837–1957. Ancestry.com, 2011.

"Wade, Mixon." 1880 US Census, Lincoln Parish, Louisiana. Ancestry.com, 2005.

"Wade, Mixon." 1900 US Census, Lincoln Parish, Louisiana. Ancestry.com, 2004.

"Wade, Sammie, to Percy Burrus." Mississippi Marriages, 1776–1935, Ancestry.com, 2004.

"Wade, Stella M." US, Social Security Applications and Claims Index, 1936–2007. Ancestry.com, 2015.

"Wade, Thomas J." 1860 US Census, Caldwell Parish, Louisiana, Mortality Schedule. Ancestry.com.

"Wade, William Rife." US, Find A Grave Index, 1600s–Current. Ancestry.com, 2012.

"Wade, William Stacy." US, Find A Grave Index, 1600s–Current. Ancestry.com, 2012.

"Walt, Edgar C." US, Find A Grave Index, 1600s–Current. Ancestry.com, 2012.

"Walt, Katherine." US, Find A Grave Index, 1600s–Current. Ancestry.com, 2012.

"Walt, R. E." 1910 US Census, Holmes County, Mississippi. Ancestry.com, 2006.

"Walt, R. E." US, Find A Grave Index, 1600s–Current. Ancestry.com, 2012.

"Walt, Walter Gilliam." US, Find A Grave Index, 1600s–Current. Ancestry.com, 2012.

"Walt, Latoe F." 1920 US Census, Washington County, Mississippi. Ancestry.com.

Warren, Mary Bondurant. *Citizens and Immigrants—South Carolina, 1768*. Danielsville, GA: Heritage Papers. FHLC #30633, FamilySearch Library, Salt Lake City, UT.

"Weaks, Bower." US, Social Security Applications and Claims Index, 1936–2007. Ancestry.com, 2015.

"Weaks, Bower." US, Find A Grave Index, 1600s–Current. Ancestry.com, 2012.

"Weaks, Edmonia Lynn." US, Find A Grave Index, 1600s–Current. Ancestry.com, 2012.

"Weaks, Estelle, to Wm. B. Reily." Louisiana Marriages, 1718–1925. Ancestry.com, 2004.

"Weaks, G. C." 1900 US Census, Ouachita Parish, Louisiana. Ancestry.com, 2004.

"Weaks, George G., Sr." 1940 US Census, Ouachita Parish, Louisiana. Ancestry.com, 2012.

"Weaks, George G." 1920 US Census, Ouachita Parish, Louisiana. Ancestry.com, 2005.

"Weaks, George Gibson." US, Social Security Applications and Claims Index, 1936–2007. Ancestry.com, 2015.

"Weaks, George." Social Security Death Index. Ancestry.com, 2008.

"Weaks, J. C." 1900 US Census, Ouachita Parish, Louisiana. Ancestry.com, 2004.

"Weaks, James C." 1870 US Census, Morehouse Parish, Louisiana, ward 1, Bastrop. FHLC #552016, FamilySearch Library, Salt Lake City, UT.

"Weaks, James C." 1910 US Census, Ouachita Parish, Louisiana, Ancestry.com, 2006.

"Weaks, James C." 1920 US Census, Ouachita Parish, Louisiana. Ancestry.com, 2005.

"Weaks, James Caldwell." US, Find A Grave Index, 1600s–Current. Ancestry.com, 2012.

"Weaks, Jane C." 1960 US Census, Morehouse Parish, Louisiana. Ancestry.com, 2004.

"Weaks, Jennie Bell, to Harvey J." Trousdale, Louisiana Marriages, 1718–1925. Ancestry.com, 2004.

"Weaks, John Pinckney." US, Find A Grave Index, 1600s–Current. Ancestry.com, 2012.

"Weaks, Nancy." US, Find A Grave Index, 1600s–Current. Ancestry.com, 2012.

"Weaks, Pinckney." US Register of Civil, Military and Naval Service, 1883–1959. Ancestry.com, 2014.

"Weaks." 1880 US Census, Morehouse Parish, Louisiana, Bastrop, ED 54, p. 381. FHLC #1254457, FamilySearch Library, Salt Lake City, UT.

"Weeks, George G., to Mona Lynn Millsaps." Louisiana Marriages, 1718–1925. Ancestry.com, 2004.

"Weeks, George G." 1930 US Census, Ouachita Parish, Louisiana. Ancestry.com, 2002.

"Weeks, John Pinckney." Texas Death Certificates, 1903–1982. Ancestry.com, 2013.

"White, Anna." US, Find A Grave Index, 1600s–Current. Ancestry.com, 2012.

"White, B. F., to Carrie Allen." Louisiana Marriages, 1718–1925. Ancestry.com, 2004.

"White, B. R." 1850 US Census, Williamson County, Tennessee, District 7, Franklin, Tennessee. FamilySearch Library, Salt Lake City, UT.

"White, Bascom H." 1940 US Census, Calcasieu Parish, Louisiana. Ancestry.com, 2012.

"White, Benj F." 1870 US Census, St. Landry Parish, Louisiana. Ancestry.com, 2003.

"White, Benjamin F., to Sallie M. Wynn." Alabama, Select Marriages, 1816–1942. Ancestry.com, 2014.

"White, Benjamin Franklin." US, Find A Grave Index, 1600s–Current. Ancestry.com, 2012.

"White, Benjamin R." 1830 US Census, Williamson County, Tennessee. FamilySearch Library, Salt Lake City, UT.

"White, Benjamin Rogers." US, Find A Grave Index, 1600s–Current. Ancestry.com, 2012.

"White, Benjamin, grantor." *Williamson County, Tennessee, Deed Book P*, pp. 47, 215, 339. FamilySearch Library, Salt Lake City, UT.

"White, Benjamin." 1840 US Census, Williamson County, Tennessee. FHLC #0024550, FamilySearch Library, Salt Lake City, UT.

"White, Daisy." 1940 US Census, Lincoln Parish, Louisiana. Ancestry.com, 2012.

"White, Daisy." US, Find A Grave Index, 1600s–Current. Ancestry.com, 2012.

"White, Dr. Stuart L." 1910 US Census, Lincoln Parish, Louisiana. Ancestry.com, 2006.

"White, Dr. Stuart Lyons." US, Find A Grave Index, 1600s–Current. Ancestry.com, 2012.

"White, Dr. William Dee." US, Find A Grave Index, 1600s–Current. Ancestry.com, 2012.

"White, E. Victoria." 1900 US Census, Lincoln Parish, Louisiana. Ancestry.com, 2004.

"White, Eliza Martha." US, Find A Grave Index, 1600s–Current. Ancestry.com, 2012.

"White, Eliza Mothershed Kinny." Louisiana, Find A Grave Index, 1700–2012. Ancestry.com, 2012.

"White, Eliza Robinett 'Nettie.'" US, Find A Grave Index, 1600s–Current. Ancestry.com, 2012.

"White, Ellen B." US, Social Security Applications and Claims Index, 1936–2007. Ancestry.com, 2015.

"White, Emma." US, Find A Grave Index, 1600s–Current. Ancestry.com, 2012.

"White, Ernest Burton." US, Find A Grave Index, 1600s–Current. Ancestry.com, 2012.

"White, Eugenia M." US, Social Security Applications and Claims Index, 1936–2007. Ancestry.com, 2015.

"White, Fannie Andrews." US, Find A Grave Index, 1600s–Current. Ancestry.com, 2012.

"White, Fannie." 1900 US Census, St. Landry Parish, Louisiana. Ancestry.com, 2004.

"White, Guy L." US, Find A Grave Index, 1600s–Current. Ancestry.com, 2012.

"White, Guy." US, Department of Veterans Affairs, BIRLS Death File, 1850–2010. Ancestry.com, 2011.

"White, H. O." 1910 US Census, Richland Parish, Louisiana. Ancestry.com, 2006.

"White, Helen Fleta." US, Find A Grave Index, 1600s–Current. Ancestry.com, 2012.

"White, Henry B." 1920 US Census, Calcasieu Parish, Louisiana. Ancestry.com, 2005.

"White, Henry B." 1930 US Census, Calcasieu Parish, Louisiana. Ancestry.com, 2002.

"White, Henry Bascom." Louisiana Statewide Death Index, 1900–1949. Ancestry.com, 2002.

"White, Henry Bascom." US, Find A Grave Index, 1600s–Current. Ancestry.com, 2012.

"White, Henry O., to Eliza M. Robinett." Louisiana Marriages, 1718–1925. Ancestry.com, 2004.

"White, Henry O." 1880 US Census, East Carroll Parish, Louisiana. Ancestry.com, 2005.

"White, Henry Otis." US, Find A Grave Index, 1600s–Current. Ancestry.com, 2012.

"White, Henry W." 1920 US Census, Caddo Parish, Louisiana. Ancestry.com, 2005.

"White, Henry W." 1930 US Census, Caddo Parish, Louisiana. Ancestry.com, 2002.

"White, Henry Whitmel." US, Find A Grave Index, 1600s–Current. Ancestry.com, 2012.

"White, Henry Whitmel." 1940 US Census, Caddo Parish, Louisiana. Ancestry.com, 2012.

"White, Henry." 1900 US Census, East Carroll Parish, Louisiana. Ancestry.com, 2004.

"White, Horace H., to Fannie A. Blythe." Tennessee State Marriages, 1780–2002. Ancestry.com, 2008.

"White, Horace H." 1900 US Census, Rapides Parish, Louisiana. Ancestry.com, 2004.

"White, Horace H." 1920 US Census, Rapides Parish, Louisiana. Ancestry.com, 2005.

"White, Horace H." 1930 US Census, Rapides Parish, Louisiana. Ancestry.com, 2002.

"White, Horace H." 1940 US Census, Rapides Parish, Louisiana. Ancestry.com, 2012.

"White, Horace Henry." US, Find A Grave Index, 1600s–Current. Ancestry.com, 2012.

"White, Horace Manley." US, Find A Grave Index, 1600s–Current. Ancestry.com, 2012.

"White, Horace." 1910 US Census, Rapides Parish, Louisiana. Ancestry.com, 2006.

"White, Howard P." 1930 US Census, East Baton Rouge Parish, Louisiana. Ancestry.com, 2002.

"White, Howard Pool." US, Find A Grave Index, 1600s–Current. Ancestry.com, 2012.

"White, Howard." 1940 US Census, East Baton Rouge Parish, Louisiana. Ancestry.com, 2012.

"White, Howard." Social Security Death Index. Ancestry.com, 2008.

"White, J. Milton." Texas Death Certificates, 1903–1982. Ancestry.com, 2013.

"White, James E." 1900 US Census, Vermilion Parish, Louisiana. Ancestry.com, 2004.

"White, James E." 1910 US Census, Acadia Parish, Louisiana. Ancestry.com, 2006.

"White, James E." 1920 US Census, Acadia Parish, Louisiana. Ancestry.com, 2005.

"White, James E." 1930 US Census, Acadia Parish, Louisiana. Ancestry.com, 2002.

"White, James E." Louisiana Statewide Death Index, 1900–1949. Ancestry.com, 2002.

"White, James Edgar." US, Find A Grave Index, 1600s–Current. Ancestry.com, 2012.

"White, James M., to Edmonia F. Guidry." Louisiana Marriages, 1718–1925. Ancestry.com, 2004.

"White, James M." 1889 Census, St. Landry Parish, Louisiana. Ancestry.com, 2005.

"White, James Megathorn." US, Find A Grave Index, 1600s–Current. Ancestry.com, 2012.

"White, James Roy." US, Find A Grave Index, 1600s–Current. Ancestry.com, 2012.

"White, Jas M." 1870 US Census, St. Landry Parish, Louisiana. Ancestry.com, 2003.

"White, Jeanette." US, Find A Grave Index, 1600s–Current. Ancestry.com, 2012.

"White, Joseph A." US, Find A Grave Index, 1600s–Current. Ancestry.com, 2012.

"White, Joseph E., to Mary E. Gregory." Alabama, Select Marriages, 1816–1942. Ancestry.com, 2014.

"White, Joyce." US, Social Security Applications and Claims Index, 1936–2007. Ancestry.com, 2015.

"White, Julia B., to Norman B. File." New York, New York, Marriage Certificate Index, 1866–1937. Ancestry.com, 2014.

"White, Julia House, to Thomas A. Holoman." Louisiana Marriages, 1718–1925. Ancestry.com, 2004.

"White, Lawrence Augustus." US, Find A Grave Index, 1600s–Current. Ancestry.com, 2012.

"White, Leola." US, Social Security Applications and Claims Index, 1936–2007. Ancestry.com, 2015.

"White, Lloyd Ellis." US, Find A Grave Index, 1600s–Current. Ancestry.com, 2012.

"White, Lou R." 1900 US Census, Vermilion Parish, Louisiana. Ancestry.com, 2004.

"White, Lucinda Reeves." US, Find A Grave Index, 1600s–Current. Ancestry.com, 2012.

"White, Lula Willingham." US, Social Security Applications and Claims Index, 1936–2007. Ancestry.com, 2015.

"White, Maggie L." US, Find A Grave Index, 1600s–Current. Ancestry.com, 2012.

"White, Maggie Mae." US, Find A Grave Index, 1600s–Current. Ancestry.com, 2012.

"White, Malcolm Henry." US, Find A Grave Index, 1600s–Current. Ancestry.com, 2012.

"White, Manie H." US, Social Security Applications and Claims Index, 1936–2007. Ancestry.com, 2015.

"White, Margaret M., to James H. Hayes." Marriages, St. Landry Parish, 1807–1897, 5057W, p. 97, Book D. FHLC #0870687, FamilySearch Library, Salt Lake City, UT.

"White, Margaret, to James G. Hays." St. Landry Parish Marriage Records, Parish Courthouse, Opelousas, Louisiana.

"White, Margaret." US, Find A Grave Index, 1600s–Current. Ancestry.com, 2012.

"White, Marlena." US, Social Security Applications and Claims Index, 1936–2007. Ancestry.com, 2015.

"White, Marlena." US, Find A Grave Index, 1600s–Current. Ancestry.com, 2012.

"White, Mary Ann, to John S. Davis." Tennessee Marriage Records, 1780–2002. Ancestry.com.

"White, Mary Clare." US, Find A Grave Index, 1600s–Current. Ancestry.com, 2012.

"White, Mary E." 1870 US Census, St. Landry Parish, Louisiana. Ancestry.com, 2003.

"White, Mary E." Louisiana, Statewide Death Index, 1900–1949. Ancestry.com, 2002.

"White, Mary Ella." US, Find A Grave Index, 1600s–Current. Ancestry.com, 2012.

White, Mary Emma, in application of James Robert Kitchel for membership in US Sons of the American Revolution. Membership Applications, 1889–1970. Ancestry.com, 2011.

"White, Mary J." Louisiana Statewide Death Index, 1900–1949. Ancestry.com, 2002.

"White, Mary Jo." US, Find A Grave Index, 1600s–Current. Ancestry.com, 2012.

"White, Minnie." Oregon, Biographical and Other Index Card File, 1700–1900s. Ancestry.com, 2014.

White, Mrs. Gilbert. *Abstracts of Mortgage Records, Morehouse Parish, Louisiana*, vol. II. Abraham Morehouse Chapter NSDAR. Morehouse Public Library, Bastrop, LA.

"White, Nannie R." US, Find A Grave Index, 1600s–Current. Ancestry.com, 2012.

"White, Nettie." 1930 US Census, Lincoln Parish, Louisiana. Ancestry.com, 2002.

"White, Rev. B. F." 1880 US Census, St. Mary Parish, Louisiana. Ancestry.com, 2005.

"White, Rev. Henry Octavius." US, Find A Grave Index, 1600s–Current. Ancestry.com, 2012.

"White, Rev. J. E." 1860 US Census, Giles County, Tennessee. Ancestry.com, 2004.

"White, Rev. Thomas Beeman." US, Find A Grave Index, 1600s–Current. Ancestry.com, 2012.

"White, Richard Franklin, Sr." US, Find A Grave Index, 1600s–Current. Ancestry.com, 2012.

"White, Robert Dee." Texas Death Certificates, 1903–1982. Ancestry.com, 2013.

"White, Robert McLin." US, Find A Grave Index, 1600s–Current. Ancestry.com, 2012.

"White, S. L." 1900 US Census, Lincoln Parish, Louisiana. Ancestry.com, 2004.

"White, Sallie Malone." US, Find A Grave Index, 1600s–Current. Ancestry.com, 2012.

"White, Stuart L." 1920 US Census, Lincoln Parish, Louisiana. Ancestry.com, 2005.

"White, Stuart Lyons." US, Headstone Applications for Military Veterans, 1925–1963. Ancestry.com, 2012.

"White, Stuart." New Orleans, Louisiana, Birth Records Index, 1790–1915. Ancestry.com, 2002.

"White, T. B." 1880 US Census, Linn County, Oregon. Ancestry.com, 2006.

"White, Thomas Beeman." US Sons of the American Revolution Membership Applications, 1889–1770. Ancestry.com, 2011.

"White, Thomas." Social Security Death Index. Ancestry.com, 2008.

"White, Victoria E." US, Find A Grave Index, 1600s–Current. Ancestry.com, 2012.

"White, W. A." 1880 US Census, Vermilion Parish, Louisiana. Ancestry.com, 2005.

"White, W. D." 1880 US Census, Vermilion Parish, Louisiana. Ancestry.com, 2005.

"White, Wallis." 1910 US Census, Saint Tammany Parish, Louisiana. Ancestry.com, 2006.

"White, Walter Augustus." US, Find A Grave Index, 1600s–Current. Ancestry.com, 2012.

"White, Walter." 1900 US Census, Vermilion Parish, Louisiana. Ancestry.com, 2004.

"White, Whitmel Thomas." US, Find A Grave Index, 1600s–Current. Ancestry.com, 2012.

"White, William B., to Jeanette Morris." Louisiana Marriages, 1718–1925. Ancestry.com, 2004.

"White, William B." 1900 US Census, Vermilion Parish, Louisiana. Ancestry.com, 2004

"White, William B." 1910 US Census, Vermilion Parish, Louisiana. Ancestry.com, 2006.

"White, William Benjamin." Louisiana Statewide Death Index, 1900–1949. Ancestry.com, 2002.

"White, William Benjamin." US Veterans Gravesites, ca. 1775–2006. Ancestry.com, 2006.

"White, William Benjamin." US, Find A Grave Index, 1600s–Current. Ancestry.com, 2012.

"White, William." 1870 US Census, Vermilion Parish, Louisiana. Ancestry.com, 2003.

"White, Willie B." US, Find A Grave Index, 1600s–Current. Ancestry.com, 2012.

"White, Willie Charlton." US Veterans Gravesites, ca. 1775–2006. Ancestry.com, 2006.

"White, Willie Wynn." US, Find A Grave Index, 1600s–Current. Ancestry.com, 2012.

"White, Willie." Social Security Death Index. Ancestry.com, 2008.

"White, Wm B." 1920 US Census, Calcasieu Parish, Louisiana. Ancestry.com, 2005.

"Wiggins Cabin Moved from Bayou to Crossett." *Ashley County Ledger*, January 17, 2006.

"Wiggins, Henry Ricks, to Ellen Gray." Mississippi Marriages, 1776–1935. Ancestry.com, 2004.

"Wiggins, John Lawrence." US, Find A Grave Index, 1600s–Current. Ancestry.com, 2012.

"Wiggins, Mary G., to John P. Benson." Mississippi Marriages, 1776–1935. Ancestry.com, 2004.

"Wiggins, Presley R." US, Headstone Applications for Military Veterans, 1925–1963. Ancestry.com, 2012.

"Wiggins, Rev. Sam B." US, Find A Grave Index, 1600s–Current. Ancestry.com, 2012.

"Wiggins, S. B." 1860 US Census, Ashley County, Arkansas. Ancestry.com, 2004.

"Wiggins, Samuel B." 1850 US Census. Carroll Parish, Louisiana, FamilySearch Library, Salt Lake City, UT.

"Wiggins, Samuel." 1870 US Census, Ashley County, Arkansas. Ancestry.com, 2003.

"Wiggins, William Hoyt." US, Find A Grave Index, 1600s–Current. Ancestry.com, 2012.

"Willis, Neva Marie." US, Find A Grave Index, 1600s–Current. Ancestry.com, 2012.

Williamson County Marriage Records, Book 1, 1800–1836, pp. 54, 144, 182, 262, 319, 399. Williamson County Library, Historical Records, Franklin, TN.

Williamson County Marriage Records, Book 2, 1837–1865. Williamson County Library, Historical Records, Franklin, TN.

Williamson County, Tennessee Marriage Bonds. Williamson County Library, Franklin, TN.

Williamson County, Tennessee, County Court Minutes. October 1815. County Clerk Records, Franklin, TN.

Williamson County, Tennessee, Deed Book O, p. 39. FHLC #0454108, FamilySearch Library, Salt Lake City, UT.

Williamson County, Tennessee, November 1998 Queries, in genweb.org.

Williamson County, Tennessee, Tax List, 1800–1825. County Clerk Records, Franklin, TN.

"Windham, Louise Gervin." US, Social Security Applications and Claims Index, 1936–2007. Ancestry.com, 2015.

"Wright, Emily." US, Find A Grave Index, 1600s–Current. Ancestry.com, 2012.

Yoder, Jim. Email to Mary Jo Kenny. March 26, 2002.

Yoder, Jim. Email to Mary Jo Kenny. March 3, 2002.

"Younse, Dorothy Leola." US, Find A Grave Index, 1600s–Current. Ancestry.com, 2012.

CHAPTER 4:

The Colwell Family

The earliest Colwell ancestors for which we have direct evidence are William and Mary Colwell, who came to Texas from Tennessee in 1835. Age records indicate both were born around 1775. Their backgrounds have not been established. It is probable that they were the William Colwell and Polly Curry who were married on May 19, 1806, in Murfreesboro, Rutherford County, Tennessee. Polly was a common nickname for Mary; it is likely that she was Mary Curry. John Curry signed the marriage bond, indicating the amount the groom must pay if an impediment to the marriage was found. John Curry probably was Mary's father. The 1810 census shows two John Curry households in Rutherford County. One was headed by a male between sixteen and twenty-six and the other by a male over forty-five. The older John Curry could be Mary's father, and the younger one was possibly her brother.

Evidence indicates that the parents of William Colwell were probably William Colwell Sr. and Mary Cartwright of Oglethorpe County, Georgia. Data for William and Mary of Oglethorpe indicate that they had a son named William born around 1775. William Colwell Sr. made a gift of one slave to his son William of the state of Alabama. The deed was written on April 15, 1829, and recorded on February 17, 1830. Census data on reported birthplaces for the children of William and Mary Colwell of Texas suggest they were living in Alabama from around 1816 through 1826. The 1800 census for Oglethorpe County lists both John Curry and William Colwell, each with a daughter or son of appropriate age to be Mary Curry and William Colwell. John Curry is listed in several land records, usually as witness for deeds, in Oglethorpe County from 1796 to 1805 but not after 1805. The family pattern of the John Curry on the 1800 census for Oglethorpe County closely resembles that of the John Curry family of the 1810 census of Rutherford County if one male and one female had left the family. Furthermore, DNA evidence through ancestry.com shows a likely common ancestor for descendants of William Colwell Kenny and thirteen individuals who trace their ancestry to Glenn, Peter, or Mary, children of William Colwell Sr. and Mary Cartwright. The relationship was given a very high level of confidence rating.

A possible scenario would be that both William Colwell Jr. and Mary Curry grew up in Oglethorpe County. The John Curry family moved to Rutherford County around 1805. William Colwell followed them to Rutherford County, where he and Mary were married.

If we accept the DNA evidence as indicating that the William Colwell who settled in Angelina County was the son of William Colwell Sr. and Mary Cartwright, additional family background can be cited. Published family trees of other researchers (not verified by independent research) have identified the original Colwell immigrant to America as John Colwell who arrived in 1690. His wife was Mary Black; it is not stated whether she immigrated or was born in America. Information on the generations from John Colwell to William Colwell, as reported by these researchers, and information on the children of William Colwell Sr. and Mary Cartwright is included in Appendix C.

Little is known of Mary Curry's family background. Two weddings in Rutherford County, Tennessee, were probably those of her siblings. Sarah Curry married William Hall on March 1, 1814, and James Curry married Rebecca Hoshone on June 15, 1814. Neither John Curry nor James Curry is found on the 1820 Rutherford County census. Several John and James Curry names are found on the 1920 censuses of other Tennessee counties, but none have been identified as the John and James Curry previously of Rutherford County. William Hall is listed on the 1820 Rutherford County census. Family trees have also been posted for the William Hall family. These trees identify Sarah's parents as John Curry and Margaret Adams. They indicate siblings of Sarah named Mary and James but give only birth and death dates for the siblings. The birth and death dates for the sibling Mary do not coincide with the assumed dates for Mary Colwell. Additional research is needed to determine whether Mary, wife of William Colwell, was Mary Curry and whether she was the daughter of John Curry.

William and Mary Colwell were in Georgia when their first child, Wiley, was born in 1807. It is not known how long William and Mary lived in Georgia. The birthplaces for their second and third children are unknown. They moved to Alabama, but their location in Alabama is unknown. Their daughter Allie, born in 1815, indicated Tennessee as her birth state, but the births of the next three children make it likely that Alabama was their home at their births, with no record of where their daughter Martha was born in 1825. Caroline and George, born in 1827 and 1830, gave Tennessee as their birthplaces. The family had probably moved from Alabama when the deed of gift was signed, but it is possible that the deed was written earlier and was ready for a signature, or that the father, William Sr., did not know that his son had moved to Tennessee. 1830 census data for William Caldwell, consistent with the family structure of William and Mary Colwell, is recorded in Maury County, Tennessee.

Around 1835, William and Mary moved from Tennessee to the Mexican state of Texas. The family is shown on the 1835 census by the Mexican government. The three oldest sons were not with the family at the time of the census. On September 25, 1835, William received from the Mexican government a land grant on the Atoyac River in the large Nacogdoches District. As they were settling into their new location, the Texas Revolution began, followed by the subsequent independence from Mexico. Records indicate that William and Mary's son Lemuel participated in the Texas Revolution, but it is not clear whether other family members participated. Family stories suggest they were among the settlers who followed the army as a protection against possible Indian attacks on the settlements. After Texas gained independence, William Colwell was given a larger land grant in the area that became Wise County. After a short while in the new area, they returned to Angelina County and settled near the town of Zavalla. William Colwell died in Angelina County in 1849. Mary was living with her son George in 1850. She died in Angelina County on April 13, 1854.

William and Mary Colwell had ten children: Wiley F., William, Lemuel, Allie, Matthew, Andrew, Susan, Martha, Caroline Elizabeth, and George.

Wiley F. Colwell
(1807–18 Apr 1867)

Wiley, born in the state of Georgia, had the nickname of Georgia. He moved with his parents to Alabama and Tennessee. On May 11, 1827, in Hardeman County, Tennessee, Wiley married Elizabeth Keziah "Kizzie" Hanks (31 May 1811–ca. 1875), daughter of Thomas Hanks and Sarah Hill. Kizzie was born in Maury County, Tennessee. The Wiley Colwell family is shown on the 1830 census of Hardeman County under the name of Willi Caldwell. They moved to Texas around 1835, probably with a group including the William Colwell family. Wiley filed for a Mexican land grant in September 1835 and settled in the area that would become Angelina County. Wiley was involved in many aspects of the development of Angelina County, including building roads, serving on a committee for selecting the location for the county seat, and serving on juries. In 1849 the family moved to Anderson County, where Kizzie's parents had settled. They operated a farm on Keechi Creek, five miles northwest of Palestine in Anderson County. After Wiley's death, Kizzie and her son James continued operating the farm until it was sold. On April 16, 1873, heirs of Wiley Colwell sold 148 acres of land in Anderson County. Those signing the deed were Kizzie Colwell, E. J. Kenny, and James J. Colwell of Anderson County; Frances Caddel of Denton County; W. T. Colwell of Wise County; and Mary A. Anderson of Ellis County. Kizzie died prior to the 1880 census, and her descendants report that Wiley and Kizzie are buried in Old Antioch Cemetery in Anderson County. This cemetery is on private land and not open to the public.

- **William Thomas Colwell (25 Jul 1828–1 Dec 1880):** William was born in Hardeman County, Tennessee. As a child he moved with his parents to Texas, first to Angelina County, then to Anderson County. On December 28, 1851, he married Eliza Jane Carpenter in Anderson County. In the summer of 1852, William joined some of his Hanks cousins on a trip to the California goldfields. William and Eliza's son James Calvin was born that fall. When William had not returned by 1855, Eliza Jane obtained a divorce. On June 3, 1857, Eliza Jane married Thomas G. Kimbrough.

William returned to Texas in 1874 with three young sons, William T., Robert, and Reese P. Their mother's name is not known. On October 17, 1874, William Thomas married Sarah Colvin Brown, a widow with a young daughter. Her daughter, Sarah Brown, is enumerated with the Colwell family in the 1880 census. William and Sarah had three children, Mary A., Francis B., and Hilary W. The 1880 census shows the W. T. Colwell family living in Wise County, Texas, with William's oldest son, James Calvin, living on the adjacent farm. A Wise County newspaper account of Thomas Colwell's death indicated the cause of death as "congestive chill" and described him as "a worthy citizen of Salt Creek."

- **James Calvin Colwell (8 Nov 1852–23 Sep 1915):** James was raised by his mother and stepfather, Thomas Kimbrough. He was only five when his mother remarried. He did not meet his father, William Thomas, until he was a young adult. On November 11, 1874, James Calvin married Martha "Mattie" Seagler (15 Feb 1857–9 Sep 1900), the daughter of George Seagler and Jane Holley. Except for a brief time in Wise County, James and Mattie lived in Tennessee Colony, Texas, and all their children were born there. After Mattie's death, James married Berta Bell Seigler, widow of Robert H. Hudson. They are shown on the 1910 Anderson County census with Berta's son, Perry Hudson, and a boarder, Tom Hudson, age seventy-three. Both James and Mattie are buried in Tennessee Colony Cemetery.

  - **George Richard Colwell (12 Oct 1875–23 Nov 1883).**

  - **Bula Bell Colwell (14 Feb 1878–13 Jan 1961):** Bula spent her childhood in Tennessee Colony, Texas. On January 16, 1889, she married William Franklin "Frank" Morris (15 Sep 1875–24 Nov 1944) in Anderson County. Frank, the son of Reuben J. Morris and Sallie Malissa Braly, was born in Smith County, Texas. Early in their marriage, Frank and Bula lived with his parents in Anderson County. The 1900 census shows them in the home of his parents in Palestine, with Frank employed as a schoolteacher. In 1910, Frank, Bula, and their five children, all of whom were born in Anderson County, were living in Palestine. Frank was working as a real estate abstractor. The 1920 census shows Bula as head of the family, working as a seamstress. By 1930 the family was living in Lubbock County, and Frank was again listed as the head of the family. Frank and Bula moved to San Angelo, Tom Green County, Texas, where Frank was listed as a deputy in the county tax office in the 1940 census. Frank and Bula continued residing in San Angelo until their deaths. Their children were Ned (31 May 1901–8 Apr 1958), Frank Colwell (12 Feb 1903–1 Oct 1988), Martha Inez (16 Jan 1905–27 Dec 1998), Ruth Edwin (7

Mar 1907–14 May 2002), Gladys Melissa (8 Jan 1909–28 May 1953), and Beulah Francis (2 Jun 1915–30 Aug 1999).

- **Margaret Inez Colwell (4 Dec 1882–20 Mar 1957):** Inez married John Edgar Tucker in December 1900 in Anderson County, Texas. The 1910 census shows James E. Tucker, thirty-five; Margaret I., twenty-seven; Una, seven; Hoyle, five; Mattie, four; and Russell, one, as residents of Houston County, Texas. James was working as a night watchman in a sawmill. The 1920 census of Wichita County, Texas, shows John working as a machinist. They had nineteen lodgers, but Russell is not listed. In the 1930 census, Margaret I. Tucker is listed as divorced, working as a saleswoman for a furniture store, and living in a boardinghouse. Inez died in September 1955 in Wichita Falls, Texas, from a heart attack. She was buried in Midland, Texas. Their children were Una (ca. 1903–unknown), Hoyle (ca. 1904–unknown), Billie Marguerite "Mattie" (4 Nov 1905–22 Jul 1995), and Russell (1910–before 1920).

- **Thomas Leroy Colwell (6 Apr 1885–30 Jan 1944):** Born in Anderson County, Texas, Thomas Leroy was living in Palestine when registering for the World War I draft. He was a farmer but later became a rural mail carrier. He married Edwin Link Morris (ca. 1889–18 Apr 1967) on April 21, 1913, in Anderson County. The 1930 and 1940 censuses show them living in San Angelo, Texas. Both died and were buried in San Angelo. Their children were Myrtle Inez (4 May 1914–23 Jun 2002) and Mildred Melissa (4 Oct 1916–16 Nov 1993).

- **Ellis Colwell (23 Dec 1887–3 May 1889).**

- **Elmer Colwell (23 Dec 1887–6 May 1889).**

- **Bernard Colwell (26 Mar 1898–20 Feb 1899).**

- **William Thomas Colwell Jr. (7 Feb 1865–10 Jan 1952):** William Thomas Jr. was born in Sacramento, California, to an unknown mother. He came to Texas with his father and is shown on the 1880 census of Wise County. He and Ada Thrasher (Nov 1872–29 Mar 1954) were married around 1896. The 1900 census finds them in Mangum, Greer County, Oklahoma, adjacent to the family of his brother Robert. By 1920 they were farming near Stanton, Martin County, Texas. Both William Thomas and Ada died in Stanton and were buried in Stanton's Evergreen Cemetery.

  - **William Roy Colwell (19 Jul 1897–15 Mar 1954):** Born in Jacksboro, Texas, William Roy grew up and married in Oklahoma. He and his wife,

Mabel, are shown in Grandfield, Tillman County, Oklahoma, in the 1920 census. In 1930 he was working as an automobile salesman in Stanton, Martin County, Texas. There were three children: William R., seven; Betty J.; and three-month-old Rex L. By 1940, William and Mabel were divorced. William (Billie) was with his father in Midland. William Roy died from heart failure in Stafford, Texas, and was buried in Stanton. Their children were William Roy (9 Mar 1923–18 Nov 1961), Betty Jo (ca. 1925–), and Rex Lee (5 Apr 1927–19 Sep 2004).

- **Elmer Jones Colwell (6 Feb 1900–14 Dec 1939):** Elmer was born in Mangum, Oklahoma. Elmer was living in Dallas, Texas, in 1924. He married Rose Ella Lee (1902–1979). In 1930 they were living in San Antonio, Bexar County, Texas. Elmer was working as an accountant. Elmer died in an automobile crash in Cuero, DeWitt County, Texas, at the age of thirty-nine. His residence at the time of his death was Stanton, Texas. Their son was Elmer Jack (22 Jul 1922–16 Apr 1989).

- **Jewel Colwell (ca. 1907–unknown):** Jewel married Edwin Glenn Thomas on June 20, 1928, in Dallas, Texas. Mrs. E. J. Thomas, probably Jewel, was the informant on death certificates for William Thomas and William Roy Colwell. Additional information on Jewel has not been found.

- **Robert Colwell (Nov 1867–unknown):** Robert was born in California to an unknown mother. He married Dollie Anderson (8 Sep 1872–28 Mar 1936) in Jack County, Texas, on November 12, 1889. They were living in Mangum, Greer County, Oklahoma, in 1900 and 1910, engaged in farming. By 1920 they were living in Menard, Menard County, Texas, with Robert working as a truck driver. They were divorced prior to Dollie's death in 1936. In 1940, Robert was living alone in Breckenridge, Texas.

  - **Ethel E. Colwell (5 Nov 1890–20 Apr 1985):** Ethel married Walter L. Jackson (25 Apr 1879–14 Mar 1965) on May 21, 1907, in Greer County, Oklahoma. In 1910 they were living on a farm in Greer County, Oklahoma, with their daughter, Bonnie (24 Mar 1909–Aug 1969). They were living in Seminole County, Oklahoma, in 1930, where Walter was working in a grocery store and Bonnie was a teacher. By 1940 they were in Mayes County, Oklahoma; Ethel died in Mayes County.

  - **Thomas Clyde Colwell (9 Jun 1894–10 Jul 1977):** Thomas moved to Missouri as a young man, where he married Isabelle Langley (14 Jul 1909–16 Dec 1994). They are shown in Kansas City, Missouri, on the

1930 census; he worked as a taxi driver. He died in Henry County and was buried in Benton County, Missouri.

- **Claude William Colwell (1 Dec 1895–19 Aug 1971):** Claude was living in Kansas City, Missouri, when he registered for the World War I draft. He served in France with the US Army during World War I.

- **Mary Cally Colwell (31 Oct 1899–3 May 1937):** Mary married Herman Thompson McDonald (1894–1952) on October 12, 1913, in Menard, Texas. The 1920 and 1930 censuses show them in Eastland County, Texas, where Herman was working as a mechanic. By 1930, they were in La Salle County, Texas, where Herman was a tractor driver for the state highway department. Mary died in Frio County, Texas. Their children were Pauline (3 Oct 1915–17 Jan 1999), Margaret Marie (31 Aug 1917–7 Dec 1973), Virginia (8 Oct 1920–15 Sep 2016), and Dorothy (8 Oct 1920–18 Aug 1994).

- **Lillie L. Colwell (ca. 1904–unknown):** The 1920 census shows Lillie in the home of her sister Ethel.

- **William Jennings Bryan Colwell (23 Jun 1906–Dec 1986):** Bryan married Lessie Fay Addington on April 8, 1934, in Greer County, Oklahoma. The 1940 census shows him in Wichita County, Texas, working as an insurance salesman. Other household members were his wife, Lessie, and infant son, Clyde Stephen.

- **Reese P. Colwell (ca. 1871):** Reese is shown on the 1880 census in Wise County, Texas, as a nine-year-old. No additional information has been found for him.

- **Mary A. Colwell (ca. 1876–unknown):** Mary was the first child of William Thomas and Sarah Colvin. She was four on the 1880 census.

- **Florence Belle Colwell (ca. 1878–unknown):** Florence is shown as a two-year-old on the 1880 census.

- **Hilary Walter Colwell (10 Apr 1880–30 Mar 1960):** Born in Decatur, Wise County, Texas, Hilary is listed as Neilrah in the 1880 census. Later data confirms Hilary Walter as his name. In 1901 he and Byankie Alice Gardner (1876–1960) were married in Oklahoma. The family lived in Colorado, Oklahoma, and finally in Glendale, Arizona. All their children were born in Oklahoma. Family tree records indicate that both Hilary and Byankie died in Glendale, Maricopa County, Arizona.

- **Walter Colwell (1903–Feb 1975):** In 1965 Walter and his wife, Marie, are shown in the Phoenix City Directory. He was living in Phoenix, Arizona, at the time of his death.

- **Oscar Jackson Colwell (31 May 1906–Sep 1989):** The 1930 census shows Jack Colwell; his wife, Ola; and their children, Lorine and Kenneth, in Globe, Gila County, Arizona. He was buried in Okmulgee Cemetery, Okmulgee, Oklahoma.

- **Beatrice Colwell (1909–28 Jan 1911):** Beatrice is shown as a one-year-old in the 1910 census. The grave of Beatrice Colwell, death date of January 28, 1911, in Powers County, Colorado, is probably her grave. Only the name and death date were on the gravestone.

- **Harriet C. Colwell (1913–1988):** Harriet married Marshall R. Trebilcock in Glendale, Maricopa County, Arizona, on July 2, 1934. The 1940 census shows them in Glendale with children Allen and Mary Jane.

- **Lillie Colwell (1917–unknown):** Lillie was shown as a three-year-old in the 1920 census. She was not with the family in the 1930 census.

- **Suzette Colwell (19 Dec 1919–29 Jan 1994):** Suzette married Archie Charles Guliver on April 13, 1940, in Maricopa County, Arizona. Her second marriage was to Charles Rankin on February 7, 1946, in Coos County, Oregon. She was living in Idaho at the time of her death.

- **Eliza Jane Colwell (1830–1910):** Eliza was born in Maury County, Tennessee; married William Curry Kenny in 1853 in Anderson County, Texas; and died in Erath County, Texas. She is featured in chapters 1 and 2 of this book.

- **Mary Ann Colwell (29 Feb 1832–6 Mar 1914):** Born in Hardeman County, Tennessee, Mary Ann was three years old when the family moved to Texas. On August 27, 1847, Mary Ann married John C. Anderson, a young teacher boarding in a nearby household in Angelina County. They moved with the Colwell family to Anderson County in 1849 and are shown in the 1850 census with their daughter, Margaret T., age one. By the 1860 census, Mary Ann and John C. Anderson were enumerated adjacent to W. C. and Eliza Jane Kenny. By that time, they had four children: M. T. (Margaret), eleven; A. E., female, age ten; I. J., female, age eight; and R. G. (Robert G.), age two. In 1873, at the time of the sale of her parents' property, Mary Ann and John Anderson were living in Ellis County. They moved to Young County in 1877, and John died there on April 27, 1877. In 1880 Mary Ann was listed as head of the household in Young County. Other members of the household included her son, Robert G., age twenty-two, a cattle broker; her daughters Lizzie, age thirteen, and Mattie L., eleven; and her brother James

J. Colwell, age thirty-one, a schoolteacher. In both 1900 and 1910, Mary Ann and her daughter Lizzie were enumerated in the Abilene household of her son, Robert G., and his wife, Nannie. Mary Ann died in Abilene, Texas. She was buried in Abilene Municipal Cemetery. Mary Ann was the mother of twelve children, but only six were living by 1906. The names of only seven of the children are known.

- **Margaret Jane "Maggie" Anderson (20 Sep 1848–20 Mar 1924):** Born in Angelina County, Texas, Maggie was an infant when her parents moved to Anderson County. In 1866 she married William Robert Wolverton (28 Nov 1840–9 Aug 1925), probably in Anderson County. W. R and Maggie, with children Josephine and Mary, were living in Burnham, Ellis County, Texas, during the 1870 census. The 1880 census finds them in Limestone County. They moved to Erath County in the early 1880s, where they are shown on the 1900, 1910, and 1920 censuses. They continued to live in Erath County the rest of their lives. Both are buried in Acrea Cemetery in Erath County.

  - **Josephine Jannette "Josie" Wolverton (14 Jun 1868–31 Mar 1955):** Josephine was born in Ellis County, Texas. She married Ben B. Croft on August 2, 1885, in Erath County, Texas. They are shown in the 1900 census of Erath County with their four children. Ben died later that year. In 1910 Josie is shown as head of the household. By 1920 Josie was no longer maintaining her own household but was enumerated in the home of her daughter Juanita and Juanita's husband, Will G. Knowles, in Blanket, Brown County, Texas. The 1940 census finds her in the home of her daughter Tam and Tam's husband, R. M. Barham. Josie died in Stephenville, Texas. Josie and Ben's children were Tam Lorene (ca. 1891–unknown), Clifford Ray (22 Jul 1892–6 Jan 1963), Gladys Inez (17 Aug 1894–26 Jun 1979), and Juanita (ca. 1896–7 Mar 1961).

  - **Mary Mollie Olivia Wolverton (8 Oct 1869–1907):** Born in Limestone County, Texas, she was listed as Mary in the 1870 census but as Mollie in subsequent records. Mollie married Henry Bailey Pool (1863–1935) in Erath County, Texas, around 1888. They are shown in the 1900 Erath County census with their four children. Mollie died in Fort Worth, Texas, and was buried in Oakwood Cemetery. Their children were Ruth May (23 May 1897–2 Apr 1989), Joseph Bailey (18 Jun 1900–31 Jan 1940), Vern Faye (12 Dec 1901–6 Jan 1978), and Crawford A. (18 Feb 1904–22 Dec 1986).

  - **Serena Laura Wolverton (1873–1875).**

  - **John Bird Wolverton (26 Jan 1875–3 Jul 1950):** John was born in Limestone County, Texas. He married Nellie Viola Norris (1882–6 Sep

1950) in Erath County in 1898. All their children were born in Bluff Dale, Texas. They were living in Parker County when he registered for the World War I draft. He was working as a bookkeeper. John died in Stephenville, Texas, because of cancer. He was buried in East Memorial Cemetery. Their children were Perdie Birdie (ca. 1901–unknown), Nellie Rose (20 May 1906–23 Sep 1977), Mary E. Doris (28 Feb 1908–unknown), Leola (23 Jun 1909–29 Aug 1999), and Ruby (12 Jan 1911–28 Aug 1989).

- **Jesse Claude Wolverton (15 Oct 1876–8 May 1957):** Claude was born in Limestone County, Texas. He married Eldora "Dora" Barham (Jun 1880–24 Oct 1903) on April 12, 1900, in Erath County. They are shown in the 1900 census in Thurber, Texas. Their daughter was Jewel Wolverton (ca. 1902–unknown). On October 16, 1910, Claude married Alberta Wood (7 Aug 1884–24 Oct 1959) in Erath County. Claude and Alberta operated a farm in Erath County, Texas. Their children were Robert Tull (21 Jan 1911–17 Dec 1915), Martha J. (31 Aug 1912–29 Sep 1989), Wanda Grace (10 Mar 1914–19 Mar 2003), male infant (2 Oct 1915–before 1920), Jessie Claud Jr. (15 Dec 1916–24 Mar 1945), Lois Roberta (21 Jun 1918–16 Dec 2009), Richard F. (18 Oct 1919–28 Nov 1941), Beryl Larena (1 Jul 1922–24 Dec 1996), and Cecil Wood (24 May 1924–22 Feb 2009).

- **Annie Estelle Wolverton (1878–1878).**

- **Ann E. Anderson (Oct 1850–1932):** Ann married Bird A. Shelton (Sep 1844–1932) in 1867. Bird served in the Confederate army during the Civil War. They were living in Erath County, Texas, in 1880. By 1900, the family was farming in Mangum, Oklahoma. Looney Township, Harmon County, Oklahoma, was their home in 1910. Only Arthur and Layton among their children were at home. Their son Walter; his wife, Ida; and their two daughters were enumerated on the adjacent farm.

  The 1910 census indicated that Ann was the mother of thirteen children, eight of whom were living. Ann and Bird were still in Harmon County in 1920; all their children had left home, but Ann and Bird were still adjacent to Walter and his family. Both died in Harmon County, Oklahoma.

  - **Mary Elizabeth Shelton (2 Oct 1869–28 Aug 1956):** Mary married Walter Everet Pruet (1851–1932). They lived in Norman, Cleveland County, Oklahoma. Their children were Lawrence Evert (25 Apr 1884–17 Feb 1916), Elmer Wilson (24 Apr 1886–1 May 1960), Robert Ray

(Jul 1892–1933), Arthur B. (24 Mar 1894–30 Jul 1907), Earl Dayton (20 Jan 1900–Jan 1949), and Jewel (25 Sep 1905–13 Apr 1989).

- **Walter W. Shelton (Jul 1872–1952):** Walter married Ida L. Neeley (29 Sep 1883–3 May 1953). The 1910 census of Harmon County, Oklahoma, shows Walter and his wife, Ida, on a farm with their children Verna and Edith. In 1940 Walter and Ida were divorced, and Walter was living with his daughter Verna and her husband, Jack Moore. Walter died in Russell, Greer County, Oklahoma, in 1952. Their children were Verna (8 Aug 1905–21 Sep 2000), Edith (21 Feb 1910–6 Jul 1965), and Alma Mae (2 Mar 1912–Jan 1990).

- **Artemus D. Shelton (31 Mar 1873–11 Jun 1932):** Artemus married Matilda "Mattie" Henderson (10 Jan 1876–30 Dec 1950) on December 18, 1894. They are shown on a farm in Looney Township, Harmon County, Oklahoma, in 1910 with their son, Gordon Philas (25 Sep 1895–9 Nov 1974). Artemus died in Mangum, Greer County, Oklahoma.

- **Elenor Shelton (1879–before 1900).**

- **Lena Rivers Shelton (28 Oct 1881–24 Jun 1869):** Lena married Edward Baxter McQueen (1877–1959). They are shown in the 1900 census of Indian Territory, Oklahoma, with their son, Claude (ca. 1899–1971). The 1910 census of Harmon County, Oklahoma, indicates that Lena had two children, but only one (Claude) was living. By 1940 they were living in Sherman County, Texas. Claude and Claude's daughter, Claudine, were living with them. Lena died in Amarillo, Potter County, Texas, and was buried in Stratford, Sherman County.

- **Reginald Shelton (Nov 1885–1949):** The 1910 census of Harmon County, Oklahoma, shows Reginald and his wife, Maude, with infant son Carl. Jaunita and Marylee were additions in the 1920 and 1930 censuses, respectively. Reginald's occupation was listed as Baptist minister. Their children were Thomas Carl (1908–1969), Juanita (ca. 1918–unknown), and Marylee (ca. 1926–1949).

- **Paul Hayden Shelton (5 Feb 1888–Mar 1969):** Paul and his wife, Easter Duncan (1890–1983), were operating a farm in Harmon County, Oklahoma, in 1910. By 1920 they had moved to Covington, Garfield County, Oklahoma, where Paul was postmaster. Geneva and Ila had been added to the family. By 1940 Paul and Easter had returned to Harmon County. Easter's mother, Susan Duncan, was living with them. Paul died in Lawton, Comanche County, Oklahoma. Their children were Geneva (1912–1972) and Ila Fern (1917–unknown).

- **Arthur Holt Shelton (27 Sep 1889–8 Mar 1969):** In 1920 Arthur; his wife, Fay Jackson (1895–1973); and their sons, Glen Hoshel (3 Nov 1914–17 May 1983) and Kenneth Rex (3 Aug 1919–12 May 1989), were on a farm in Harmon County, Oklahoma. Arthur and Fay's daughter, Mozelle (2 Oct 1929–13 Oct 2005), had been added to the family by 1930.

- **Layton Shelton (18 Aug 1891–1931):** Layton and Lydia Frances Shinn (ca. 1893–unknown) were married in Oklahoma County, Oklahoma, on May 2, 1914. They lived in Stillwater, Payne County, Oklahoma, in 1920. By 1930 they were in Oklahoma City.

- **Isabella Anderson (25 Jan 1853–14 Mar 1930):** Isabella married James G. Wofford (4 Jul 1848–17 Oct 1925). They made their home in Fresno, California. The 1900 census shows Isabella as mother of nine children, six of whom were living. Their children were Mary A. (ca. 1872–unknown), James Ralph (Oct 1875–6 Mar 1932), Robert Lee (8 Nov 1977–22 May 1898), Willey May (Jan 1880–unknown), Charlie R. (Sep 1881–unknown), Guy Cleveland (23 Dec 1883–8 Mar 1953), and Maggie (Jan 1889–19 May 1907).

- **Robert G. Anderson (28 Mar 1858–26 May 1936):** Born in Anderson County, Texas, Robert moved with his family to Ellis County, then Young County. In Young County he worked as a cattle broker. In 1882, Robert; his mother, Mary Ann; and his sisters Lizzie and Mattie moved to Abilene, Texas. He and Nancy Elizabeth "Nannie" Hoshall (14 Apr 1860–10 Jan 1947) were married on April 16, 1884. Robert worked for the grocery firm of Wylie and Donovan. He later set up his own grocery business and worked first with a partner, then later purchased his partner's interest. In 1904, he sold the retail and wholesale grocery business and began a semiretirement as a real estate salesman. Robert died and was buried in Abilene, Texas.

  - **Hoshall C. Anderson (21 Mar 1885–17 Mar 1956):** Hoshall was born in Abilene, Texas. He married Minnie Cora Taylor (3 Jun 1886–4 Jan 1983) around 1912. In 1920 they were living in Sweetwater, Texas, where Hoshall was doing office work for a freight company. The 1930 census shows Hoshall, Minnie, and their son Ralph in the household headed by Nannie's brother Thomas Taylor Jr. Household members also included Thomas's wife, Anna, and his and Minnie's father, Thomas Taylor Sr. Hoshall and Minnie's younger son, Jack, was not with the family. Their children were Ralph (10 Jan 1912–18 Dec 1951) and Jack (1919–unknown).

- **Robert G. Anderson Jr. (Oct 1889–28 Jul 1927):** Robert was a dentist in Wichita Falls, Texas. He married Norma Ester Matney (20 Sep 1893–15 Mar 1976). They had one son, also named Robert (26 Apr 1914–6 Jun 1990). Robert Sr. died from a diabetic coma in Wichita Falls, Texas.

- **Frank Jack Anderson (6 Sep 1891–5 Oct 1928):** Frank worked as a switchman for T&P Railroad. He died from heart failure in Big Springs, Howard County, Texas. His son, Frank, age sixteen, was listed in the 1930 household of his grandparents, Robert and Nannie Anderson.

- **Lizzie Anderson (ca. 1867–29 Apr 1929):** Lizzie was living with her brother Robert during the 1910, 1920, and 1930 censuses of Abilene, Texas.

- **Mattie Lou Anderson (31 Mar 1869–19 Nov 1889):** Mattie was listed as eleven years old in the 1880 census. She moved to Abilene, Taylor County, with other family members. It was the site of her death.

- **Cynthia C. Colwell (1834–before 1877):** Cynthia was born in Tennessee. She married W. H. Malone on September 9, 1855, in Anderson County, Texas. They have not been found on the 1850 or 1860 censuses. In July 1861, he enlisted as a private in the Twelfth Regiment, Texas Cavalry, Parson's Mounted Volunteers, Confederate States Army. J. M. Hogg was the commander. Cynthia was not listed on the sale of her father's property in 1877, and it is presumed she had died before that date and that she left no children.

- **Sarah Francis Colwell (25 Mar 1837–11 Apr 1899):** Sarah was the first child of Wiley and Kizzie Colwell born in Texas. She married John H. Lane on January 17, 1857. A private in the Confederate army, John died on July 31, 1864, and was buried in North Alton Confederate Cemetery in Alton, Illinois. Sarah Francis married Anthony Bains Caddel (1825–1890) on January 1, 1865. Anthony served in Company E, Texas Thirteenth Infantry during the Civil War. Anthony had married Ruth Wilds in 1852, but she died prior to the 1860 census. Anthony and Sarah Francis settled on a farm in Denton County. Mary and William Lane and Anthony's daughters, Martha and Adella, are shown with the family on the 1870 census. Children of both earlier marriages had left the home by the 1880 census.

- **Mary C. Lane (ca. 1857–unknown):** Mary is shown on the 1870 census of Denton County as thirteen years old. No additional information has been found.

- **William Lane (ca. 1858–unknown):** William is shown on the 1870 census as twelve years old. Several William Lanes with connection to Denton County have been found, but correct identity has not been established.

- **Eliza Jane Caddel (ca. 1867–unknown):** Eliza Jane is shown on the 1870 and 1880 censuses of Denton County.

- **Elijah D. Caddel (ca. 1869–unknown):** Elijah registered to vote in Modoc County, California, in 1892. He is shown on the 1910 census operating a farm in Modoc County, California. He was single and head of a household with farmworkers and a cook. A grave for E. D. Cadell, born February 1, 1869, and died April 5, 1937, is reported in LaCrosse, Whitman County, Washington. It has not been determined whether this is the grave of Elijah D. Caddel.

- **Cordelia (Adelia) Frances Caddel (23 Oct 1870–1951):** She is listed as Cordelia in the 1880 census but as Adelia in other records. Around 1890, she married a man with the last name of Collins, and they had one son, Prince. Her second marriage was to Charles B. Blakey (1854–1924) around 1894. They were living in Knox County, Texas, in 1900 and 1910, and in Nadine, Lea County, New Mexico, in 1920. Adelia died in 1851 in Hobbs, Lea County, New Mexico.

  - **Prince A. Collins (ca. 1891–ca. 1950):** Prince is shown with his mother and stepfather in the 1900 and 1910 censuses. He and his wife, Loula, are listed in Jack County, Texas, in the 1920 census. Prince is listed as a cattle buyer. By 1930, they were in Knowles, New Mexico, on a stock farm. A son, Prince Jr., age four, had been added to the family. Prince died before 1951. Loula is listed in the Hobbs, New Mexico, City Directory as a widow. Loula; their son, Prince; and his wife, Dorothy, are listed in the Hobbs, New Mexico, City Directories for 1951, 1955, 1957, and 1960.

  - **Yelberton Blakey (6 Jan 1896–28 Sep 1918):** Yelberton was a private in the US Army, 133 Infantry Regiment, Thirty-Fourth Infantry Division. He was buried in the American Cemetery, Suresnes, France.

  - **Charles D. Blakey (4 Dec 1897–Jul 1981):** Born in Texas, Charles spent most of his adult life in New Mexico. He married Florena George in 1934 in Eddy County, New Mexico. He and Florena are shown on the 1940 census of Lee County, New Mexico, with son Billie Burke Blakey and Florena's children, Geraldine George and Richard George.

  - **Richard Lee Blakey (26 Apr 1902–6 Nov 1946):** Richard and his wife, Norma Mae, are shown in Hobbs, New Mexico, in the 1940 census.

- **Sonora (Nora) Tyson Caddel (5 Apr 1872–4 Feb 1938):** Born in Denton County, Texas, she is listed as Sonora in the 1880 census but as Nora in subsequent documents. She and Harvey Breathitt Phythian (9 Oct 1847–27 Nov 1921) were married in 1898. They made their home in Dumas, Moore County,

Texas. Nora and her son Harvey were operating a boardinghouse in Dumas during the 1930 census. Nora died from pneumonia in Dumas and was buried in Dumas Cemetery.

- **Charles Caddel Phythian (13 Mar 1900–26 Sep 1985):** The 1940 census of Moore County, Texas, shows him as a cattle dealer with his wife, Hattie, and children, Charles, four; Dan, three; and Beverly, two. Charles died in Lamar, Prowers County, Colorado.

- **Harvey Breathitt Phythian Jr. (2 Jul 1903–11 Sep 1980):** Harvey was born in Dumas, Texas. He had been married but was divorced at the time of his death in Amarillo, Texas. His occupation was truck driver.

- **John Coke Phythian (20 Nov 1906–20 Sep 1993):** John was born in Dumas, Texas. He and his wife, Dorothy, are shown on the 1940 census in Denver, Colorado, with children Clayton, eleven, and Harvey, eleven months. John died in Adams County, Colorado.

- **Minnie Lee Caddel (1 Jun 1874–17 Feb 1945):** Minnie married William Clark Blakey (1870–1961). They are shown in Knox County, Texas, in the 1910 and 1920 censuses. By 1930 they had moved to Modoc County, California, where they appear on the 1930 and 1940 censuses. Minnie died in Santa Clara, California.

  - **Flossie Irene Blakey (10 Mar 1895–15 Jan 1985):** Flossie married Thomas Wallace Arnett on June 16, 1915, in Knox County, Texas. They are shown in Imperial County, California, in the 1920 census. A second wedding, to Harry W. Warren, took place on December 27, 1932, in Los Angeles, California. She died in Marin County, California.

  - **William Kenneth Blakey (3 Jan 1896–15 Sep 1945):** Kenneth was shown in his parents' home in the 1940 census. He died in Alameda County, California.

  - **Frank H. Blakey (28 May 1898–24 Dec 1980):** Frank enlisted in the army on June 27, 1918, and was discharged on August 31, 1919. The 1920 census of Shasta, California, shows Frank; his wife, Mary; and their daughter Royce M. By 1940 they were still in Shasta, and a second daughter, Nola, had been added to the family. Frank died in San Mateo County, California.

  - **Mary Gladys Blakey (18 Jun 1901–26 Oct 1977):** Mary is shown on the 1910 census as a nine-year-old. She married Frederick Parks Cronemiller

(5 Jul 1895–13 May 1976) in Alturas, California, in 1921. Their son was Robert Keith Cronemiller (5 Jul 1926–21 Feb 2021).

- **Josephine Blakey (ca. 1902–unknown):** Josephine is listed on the 1910 census but not on the 1920 census.

- **Rayce Blakey (26 Nov 1903–Apr 1997):** Rayce married Perry J. Ivory on January 26, 1929, in Sacramento, California. She died in Volusia County, Florida.

- **Hollice Blakey (16 Oct 1905–Jan 1981):** Hollice married Alwyn Boyd. They are shown on the 1930 census in Modoc County, California, with daughter Janeil and Hollice's parents. They were still in Modoc County in 1940. Hollice died in Klamath, Oregon.

- **Della C. Blakey (14 Jan 1908–30 Dec 1993):** Della married L. E. Williams (1901–unknown). They are shown on the 1930 census in Modoc County, California, with children Kenneth and Joy Lee. By 1940 Della was listed as divorced. She and the children were living in Sacramento, and Della was working as a mail clerk in a state office. Della died in Marin County, California.

- **Richard Coke Caddel (1 Aug 1876–2 Jul 1950):** Richard was born in Denton County, Texas. By the time of the 1910 census, Richard was working as a blacksmith in Lassen County, California. He was unmarried. He died in Napa, California.

- **Wiley Colwell (1842–1862):** On April 2, 1862, Wiley enlisted in Company B, Eighteenth Texas Infantry, Ochiltree's Regiment. During the unit's first battle, Wiley was captured on August 22. He died in the Union army prison camp in Little Rock, Arkansas, from "infection of lungs."

- **Devilla B. Colwell (ca. 1840–unknown):** Devilla is shown as a ten-year-old in the family in the 1850 census. No additional information has been found for her. She was not listed in the 1877 sale of her father's property, and it is assumed that she died before that time.

- **James J. Colwell (1849–unknown):** Born in Angelina County, James is shown with the family in the 1850 and 1860 Anderson County censuses. In 1870, he is listed with his mother in Anderson County, with his occupation being farm labor. Also in the household and assisting with the farm and housework was the family of Harry and Hannah Andrews and their three young children. The 1880 census shows James as a teacher living in the Young County household headed by his sister Mary Ann Anderson. Records for him beyond 1880 have not been found.

Lemuel Colwell
(ca. 1812–ca. 1840)

Lemuel Colwell was born in Georgia or Alabama. He was not with his parents in the 1835 census. A participant in the Texas Revolution in 1836, Lemuel served under the command of Adolphus Sterne. He was granted land in 1839 and paid taxes in 1840. The only other reference found for him was in the sale of land of William Colwell in Wise County, Texas. This indicated that he died before age twenty-one. Either the estimated birth year or the statement of death before age twenty-one must be in error.

William Colwell
(ca. 1814–2 Oct 1850)

William Colwell was not listed on the 1835 Mexican census, but he and Wiley Colwell applied for land from the Mexican government on the same September 1835 day, with each vouching for the character of the other. William married Elizabeth Bridges Rhodes (1814–1858), a widow, on March 17, 1837, in Angelina County. He and Elizabeth are shown on the 1850 census of Angelina County. His age is listed as thirty-six, he was born in Alabama, and his occupation was farmer. William died in Angelina County soon after the census date. Elizabeth Colwell's will dated November 5, 1858, and proved November 12, 1858, gave her property to her sons Peter Rhodes and Barney Rhodes.

Allie Colwell
(4 Jun 1815–8 Oct 1883)

Allie was born in Tennessee. She married Samuel Gilliland (9 Jan 1807–9 Jan 1890) soon after the family settled in Texas. The Gilliland family was probably in the same group moving from Tennessee to Texas. Sam was born in Rutherford County, Tennessee, to Eli Gilliland and Keziah Hayne. Allie and Sam were married by bond of the Mexican government on January 19, 1836. After Texas gained independence, Allie and Sam were among the first to obtain a marriage license in the newly formed Angelina County, on September 30, 1837. Allie and Sam established a farm in Angelina County, where all their children were born and where both died.

- **Samuel Blaxton Gilliland (1 Oct 1837–8 Aug 1862):** Samuel was a member of the Thirteenth Calvary of the Confederacy and died in Walnut Hill, Arkansas.

- **James Lucien Gilliland (13 Jul 1840–13 Mar 1918):** James served with the Confederate Thirteenth Cavalry, Burnett's Regiment, during the Civil War. He married Sarah M. Campbell Porter (20 Oct 1845–6 Sep 1898), a widow, around 1870. He and Sarah had nine children, all of whom were born in Angelina County. His second wedding was to Rebecca Lee on December 31, 1899. James was a farmer in Angelina County. The 1900 census shows Samuel H. Colwell, age nineteen, in the household working as a farm laborer. He is assumed to be a relative, but his identity has not been established. Allie's brother had a son named Samuel Houston Colwell, but he would have been much older than nineteen. James died in Angelina County and was buried in Boykin Cemetery.

  - **Ella Gilliland (6 Jan 1872–23 Dec 1956):** Ella married William J. Williams on February 1, 1893, in Angelina County, Texas. They lived in Zavalla, Angelina County. The 1900 census shows Ella operating a boardinghouse in Angelina County. A daughter, Ester Williams (31 May 1895–17 Jun 1988), was age five at the time.

  - **Samuel Gilliland (13 Mar 1874–17 Aug 1880):** Samuel was buried in Boykin Cemetery.

  - **James B. Gilliland (1 Jan 1877–4 May 1903):** James married Ellen Waddell on August 1, 1899, in Angelina County, Texas. Their son was Scott Roy (8 Jun 1900–28 Oct 1963). James was buried in Boykin Cemetery.

  - **William E. Gilliland (5 Feb 1879–24 Apr 1929):** William married Lillie Colwell (1884–1918) on March 11, 1917. The 1920 census shows William and his young daughter, Lillie, in Angelina County. Their daughter, Lillie Eulalia (25 Feb 1918–25 Mar 2004), married Roy Marshall.

  - **Emma Lou Gilliland (11 Jun 1881–30 Aug 1922):** Emma married James Hardy Poland on May 16, 1901, in Angelina County, Texas. Their children were Lessie Pearl (1902–1991), Lois (1903–1991), James Eli (1905–1987), Sallie Vera (1906–1964), Tannie Inez (1915–1984), and James Loyd (1919–1988).

  - **Allie M. Gilliland (Dec 1882–before 1916):** Allie married Felder C. Jones (1876–1946) on July 4, 1900, in Angelina County, Texas. They are shown on the 1910 census of Angelina County, occupation farming, with children Stella (ca. 1902–unknown), Travis (4 Apr 1903–5 Oct 1967), and Van (18 Dec 1904–Dec 1983). Felder had remarried by the time he registered for the World War I draft.

- **Lillie Eliza Gilliland (28 Feb 1885–24 Jul 1982):** Lillie married Harrison A. Dunkin (1883–1925). They operated a farm near Zavalla, Angelina County, until Harrison's death. In 1930 Lillie operated a rooming house. Their children were Jewell (1909–unknown), Grace (19 Apr 1910–20 Oct 2001), Lillian (1912–unknown), James Harrison (4 Nov 1913–2 Jan 1959), and Mary (1918–unknown).

- **Mattie D. Gilliland (1 Jan 1887–1 Sep 1888).**

- **George Regan Gilliland (17 Apr 1892–29 May 1986):** George married Myrtle Dudley (17 Nov 1896–14 Sep 1989) in Angelina County on August 31, 1913. They lived in Angelina County, where he worked as a merchant, a laborer, and a peace officer. Their children were Blanche (4 Aug 1914–14 Mar 2006), George (2 Oct 1920–6 Nov 1979), Marge (19 Dec 1921–28 Jul 2002), and William (27 Dec 1933–).

- **Manley Gilliland (29 Sep 1842–17 Nov 1842).**

- **Martha Ann Gilliland (5 Jul 1844–24 Apr 1904):** Martha married Simeon Walter Boykin (2 May 1838–27 Nov 1890) around 1864. They are shown on the 1870 census with three children and on the 1880 census with six children. On May 5, 1894, Martha married Jessie E. Ivy. The 1900 census shows Martha and Jessie with her sons James and Cue D. (listed as Ivy instead of Boykin) and Jessie's two sons. Martha is listed as mother of ten, five of whom were living in 1900. Martha lived and died in Angelina County and was buried in Boykin Cemetery.

  - **Barbara Boykin (ca. 1865–before 1880):** Barbara is shown on the 1870 census, but not on the 1880 census.

  - **Allie Mary Boykin (5 Jun 1866–9 Mar 1963):** Allie married Henry Miles Hastings (2 Nov 1865–28 Apr 1951) on December 25, 1888. They made their home in Angelina County, Texas, where they are shown on censuses of 1900 through 1940. No children were listed on any of the censuses. After Henry Miles's death, Allie continued living in Angelina County until about 1961, when she relocated to Newton County, where she died. W. E. Thomas is listed as the informant on her death certificate.

  - **James T. Boykin (27 Mar 1868–9 Jul 1934):** James married Lula Mae Townsend (1895–1971). They operated a farm in Angelina County, Texas. Their children were Willie May (1912–1978), Linnie D. (1915–2006), and James Timothy (1919–1995).

  - **William Eli Boykin (12 Sep 1870–25 Mar 1925):** William Eli and Rhoda Florence Stovall (10 Jan 1876–10 Apr 1960) were married on April 1, 1896, in Angelina County, Texas. The 1900 census shows William Eli as a teacher.

They were operating a grocery store in 1910. Their daughter was Hexie (28 Dec 1896–19 Oct 1988).

- **Leon Lemonades Boykin (ca. 1875–unknown):** Leon is shown on the 1880 census of Angelina County, but no further information has been found.

- **Cue Dallas Boykin (13 Feb 1877–27 Jul 1928):** Cue Dallas married Lollie Scarborough (1892–1985) on November 9, 1905, in Angelina County. They lived in Lufkin, Angelina County. His death certificate identifies his occupation as treasurer of Angelina County. Their son was C. D. Boykin Jr. (8 Dec 1911–Feb 1987).

- **Maude A. Boykin (1 Jun 1879–14 Mar 1962):** Maude married J. M. Thomas (1872–ca. 1915) in Angelina County on February 24, 1898. They are shown on the 1910 census with children Mel (Earl Milan, 13 Feb 1899–2 Nov 1978), Ross (1900–unknown), Clyde (12 Dec 1901–27 Feb 1942), Joseph (25 Apr 1903–Sep 1982), and William (7 Dec 1905–19 Apr 1990). In 1917, Maude married William Monroe Gilbert (1877–1943). They are shown on the 1920 and 1930 censuses with Maude's son William Thomas. At her death, her married name was Jones.

- **Mary Keziah Gilliland (3 Dec 1846–18 Jan 1933):** Mary K. married Thomas Scott Sayers (1849–1897) on February 6, 1871. Thomas was born in Louisiana to C. J. Sayers and Sarah Thomas. The 1880 census of Angelina County shows a T. S. Sayers as a merchant. They had ten children, seven of whom were living in 1900. The 1900 census shows the widowed Mary K. living in Lufkin with six of her children. She and her son Lewis were listed as farmers, and her daughter Claudia was a teacher. Mary K. continued to live in the Lufkin area with her daughter Claudia. Mary K. was known in the community for her ability to accurately remember historical facts, events, names, and dates. She died in Angelina County and was buried in Walker Cemetery.

  - **Allie Devilla Sayers (21 Nov 1871–28 Sep 1892):** Allie married John F. Renfro (1866–1952) on January 11, 1892.

  - **Sarah Claudia Sayers (12 Feb 1872–Apr 1969):** Claudia taught in the Lufkin area public schools. She lived with her mother until Mary K.'s death. She continued to teach and live in Lufkin. She was buried in Walker Cemetery.

  - **Lewis Carey Sayers (15 Feb 1875–15 Jan 1933):** Lewis married Pearl Lilly Russell (1886–1946) in 1904. They operated a farm in Angelina County. Their children were Samuel Scott (23 Aug 1905–9 Oct 1991), Lewis C. (4 Oct 1910–3 May 1991), Fannie M. (1913–1932), and Charlie Ruth (25 Jun 1926–). Lewis was buried in Huntington Cemetery.

- **Thomas Scott Sayers (3 Aug 1876–13 Sep 1894):** Thomas was buried in Walker Cemetery, Angelina County.

- **Mary Josephine "Josie" Sayers (19 Dec 1878–31 Aug 1958):** Josie married Martin M. Feagin (1874–1955) on September 8, 1897, in Angelina County. They lived in Lufkin, Fort Worth, and Livingston, Texas. Their children were Ruth (1898–1992) and Melvin Martin (1904–1996). Josie died in Livingston, Polk County, Texas. She was buried in Glendale Cemetery in Lufkin, Texas.

- **Mattie Pearl Sayers (1 Jan 1880–30 Jan 1961):** Mattie married Willie Clayte Binnion (1871–1956) in 1903. They lived in Lufkin, Angelina County. Clayte worked in the post office and retired as postmaster. Their children were Jack Scanlon (1904–1972), Mary Emma (1910–1973), Willie Clayte (1912–1994), and Cavett Sayers (1918–1959).

- **Ellen Inez Sayers (5 Nov 1882–12 Aug 1974):** Inez married C. Dee Kinnard (1875–1938) in Angelina County, Texas, on June 17, 1906. By 1910 they had moved to Houston, Harris County, Texas, where they resided through 1930 and where Inez lived in 1940. Inez worked as a social worker for the welfare department. She died in Lufkin, Angelina County, at the age of ninety-one.

- **Rose Ella Sayers (8 Dec 1884–17 Dec 1968):** Rose was born in Homer, Angelina County. She married Sidney Sampson Moss (1882–1937) on November 15, 1908. The 1920 census shows them in Nacogdoches County, Texas, with children Joe (Joseph Sidney, 1911–1979), Pauline (1912–1989), Francis Louise (1915–1995), and Bonnie (1918–1994). In 1930 Rose was head of the household in Lufkin, Angelina County. Neither Sidney nor Joe was in the household. Rose was working as a retail salesperson. Rose died in Lufkin, Angelina County, and was buried in Walker Cemetery.

- **Louisa Sayers (Feb 1885–8 Aug 1886):** Louisa is buried in Boykin Cemetery, Angelina County.

- **Samuel Regan Sayers (17 Dec 1887–15 Jan 1956):** Sam married Clyde Philen (1890–1961) on March 20, 1912, in Angelina County. They lived in Fort Worth, Texas, where Sam had a law practice. Their children were Reagan S. (1914–1969) and Scott (1929–1968).

- **William Eli Gilliland (7 Feb 1849–1 Oct 1920):** Eli was born in the Old Popher community of Angelina County. He married Henrietta Arkansas Spier (15 Dec 1854–3 Feb 1929) on February 14, 1871. Henrietta was shown on the 1900 census as born in Kansas and as a mother of five children, all of whom were living. Eli was a farmer in

Angelina County and a member of a Masonic lodge. Eli and Henrietta were buried in Huntington Cemetery.

- **Eva Gilliland (15 Sep 1878–10 Jun 1962):** Eva married James Ellis Sharp (1869–1929) on September 25, 1897. They lived in Newton County, Texas. James and Eva were both teachers at the time of their marriage. By 1920 they lived in Wichita Falls, Texas, where James was in the insurance business. After James's death, Eva became a real estate agent. Their children were Burford (1898–1963), Harold (1901–1982), Annie Laura (1903–1989), and Mary Beth (1910–1939).

- **Burke Gilliland (29 Jul 1882–20 Nov 1943):** Burke married Ella Peavey (1886–1937). In 1910 they were operating a farm in Angelina County, which they continued operating through 1930. Burke and Ella were buried in Huntington Cemetery. Their children were Elymae (1906–1969), Sallie Ruth (1908–1979), Martha Devilla (1910–1980), Samuel (5 Mar 1913–1968), Sophie (14 Aug 1915–2003), and Florene (1919–1996).

- **Sam Henry Gilliland (23 Dec 1885–21 Oct 1933):** Sam and his wife, Sophia Starken, were living in Liberty County, Texas, in 1918, when he registered for the World War I draft. He was working as a store manager. The 1930 census shows them in Lufkin, Texas, with sons William (1915–1991) and James (1921–unknown) and eight boarders. Sam was described as an invalid; his death certificate indicated debilitating arthritis. He was buried in Huntington Cemetery.

- **Martha Devilla Gilliland (26 Dec 1889–10 Feb 1971):** Devilla married Jim Walker (1884–1962). They lived in Lufkin, Angelina County.

- **James Blaxton Gilliland (22 Jun 1892–19 Jul 1924):** Blaxton was single and living with his parents in Angelina County at the time of the 1920 census.

- **Wiley Gilliland (14 Feb 1850–14 Jan 1851).**

- **Devilla Caroline Gilliland (27 Apr 1853–3 Feb 1897):** Devilla married William James Townsend (27 Feb 1850–18 Jan 1916) on July 4, 1872. The 1880 census of Angelina County lists William as a merchant in Homer. Devilla was buried in Walker Cemetery, Angelina County.

  - **Samuel Henry Townsend (25 Oct 1873–2 Jan 1942):** Samuel married Willie Tilden Leach (1876–1900) in November 1897. Samuel died in Lufkin, Angelina County. Their daughters were Ina Mae (1898–1989) and Rosalie (1900–unknown), both born in Lufkin, Texas. His second wedding, to Susan Prestridge (1880–1923), took place on May 18, 1902. Their children were Ruth (1903–1973), Sam Henry (1908–1997), James Warner (1910–1997), and Allen

Prestridge (1913–2001). Jo Ann (1929–) was the daughter of Samuel's third marriage, to Maude Cummings (1892–1966). Samuel was a lawyer in Angelina County, Texas.

- **William James Townsend (28 Aug 1875–25 Nov 1956):** The 1910 census shows William as a lawyer with wife Zoe (Zoe Wilson, 1881–1928) in Lufkin, Texas. In 1918, when he registered for the World War I draft, and in the 1920 census, William and Zoe were living in Austin, Texas, where he was working as assistant attorney general for Texas. William returned to Angelina County, where he was listed as widowed in the 1930 census. William and Joyce Clark (1901–1988) were married in 1940. He died in Lufkin, Angelina County, and was buried in Walker Cemetery.

- **George Eli Townsend (31 Mar 1877–21 Apr 1929):** George Eli was born in Homer, Angelina County. He married Mary Lee Simmons (1885–1929) on February 4, 1902, in Tyler, Smith County, Texas. He was a farmer in Angelina County. He was buried in Glendale Cemetery, Lufkin, Texas.

  Their children were Paul Monarch (1902–1961), Zoe Mary (1910–2005), George William (1911–1935), Jane Elizabeth (1917–1977), Jessie Calvin (1919–1947), and Rebecca Marie (1921–1994).

Matthew Colwell
(26 Jun 1819–13 Jun 1899)

Born in Alabama, Matthew Colwell moved with his family first to Tennessee and then to Texas. He married Caroline Worden (ca. 1830–ca. 1856) on September 22, 1846, with a license recorded on page one of Angelina County Marriage Records Book One. Caroline was born in New York, but little else is known about her. They are shown on the 1850 census with children Mary and John. Their third child, Wiley, was born in 1856. Matthew married Martha Wallace (26 Mar 1838–11 Feb 1916) on October 14, 1857, in Anderson County, Texas. Martha was born in Augusta, Alabama, to Joseph Wallace and Priscilla Edwards. Matthew was a farmer in Angelina County. He and Martha had nine children. Matthew died in Angelina County and was buried in Cochran Cemetery, Ora, Angelina County. Martha is shown on the 1900 census with her daughter Sallie and Sallie's husband, Alfred Wigley. Martha died in Zavalla, Angelina County, and was also buried in Cochran Cemetery.

- **Mary Jane Colwell (27 Jan 1848–10 Feb 1902):** On November 1, 1866, Mary Jane married Clark McNeal (15 Jan 1841–8 Jan 1871). Clark was a Confederate veteran who had enlisted in 1864. In the 1870 census, Mary Jane and her daughter, Martha, are enumerated in Mary Jane's father's household. Clark is found in the home of William and Larise Manning. Clark died on January 8, 1871, and was buried in Zavalla, Angelina County. Mary Jane, listed as a widow, is shown in the 1880 census with her ten-year-old daughter, Martha. They are listed adjacent to the listings for Matthew Colwell.

  - **Martha "Mattie" McNeal (6 Sep 1869–23 Aug 1950):** Martha married William O. Harrison (ca. 1865–before 1920). In 1920 Martha was the head of a household including two widowed daughters and one son. Martha was living with her daughter Alma and son-in-law Clarence Anthony in Tyler, Smith County, Texas, in 1930. She died in Tyler. Mattie and William's children were Edna (1896–after 1940), Alma M. (17 Jan 1900–24 May 1962), and James Barron (26 Jul 1904–5 Nov 1950).

- **John M. Colwell (27 Oct 1849–10 Apr 1939):** After his mother's death, John lived with his aunt Allie Gilliland part of the time, but he is listed in his father's family in both the 1860 and 1870 censuses. His first wedding, to Miranda (1857–1875), was in 1872. Their daughter was Ella. John and Anna Betty McGauhey were married on September 19, 1876, in Angelina County. John was a farmer and stockman all his life. He and Anna had thirteen children. John died from influenza in Zavalla and was buried in Zavalla Cemetery, Angelina County.

  - **Ella Colwell (ca. 1874–unknown):** Ella is shown as a six-year-old on the 1980 census. Ella married Thomas A. McBride on January 12, 1896, in Angelina County, Texas. They are shown on an Angelina County farm in the 1900 census.

  - **Charles Ewing "Charlie" Colwell (9 Dec 1877–19 Jun 1947):** Charles's occupation was merchant in 1918, when he registered for the World War I draft, but farmer on the 1920 and 1930 censuses. Charlie married Lessie Emma Wilson (24 Oct 1897–6 Aug 1981). They made their home in Angelina County. Their children were Robbie Jean (1918–2003), Helen (1919–2008), Betty Joe (1922–unknown), Ruby Maxine (1923–1995), Nina Ruth (1927–unknown), Charles Ray (1925–), Barbara Ann (1933–), David (1936–2014), and Doris (1937–).

  - **Mary Jane "Mollie" Colwell (May 1879–1905):** Mary Jane married J. M. Burns on December 22, 1897. They were shown operating a farm in Angelina County, Texas, in 1900. Their children were Hazel (Oct 1898–unknown), C. B. (23 Oct 1902–Jan 1977), and Eunice (4 Dec 1904–26 Feb 1993).

  - **Laura Anna Colwell (12 Jan 1881–12 Jul 1942):** Laura was born in the Popher Creek community, Angelina County. She married Noah Gibson (8 Dec 1877–8

Dec 1960) on November 26, 1899, in Angelina County. Census data show him as a salesman, garage operator, and farmer. Laura died in Zavalla, Angelina County. Their children were Bethel (ca. 1902–unknown), Verba (3 Oct 1904–24 Feb 1959), Glea (9 Dec 1909–6 Mar 2002), Gentra (3 Jul 1912–23 Sep 1935), and Ruth (29 Jun 1923–25 Sep 2010).

- **Jack Colwell (3 Aug 1882–21 Dec 1974):** Jack was a farmer in Angelina County, Texas. He married Ida Jones (28 Feb 1886–18 Feb 1908). Their daughter was Winnie (20 Jan 1907–1912). Jack's second marriage was to Oda Shofner (9 Dec 1893–6 Dec 1975). Their children were Johnnie (12 Dec 1910–30 May 1883), Anna Beth (6 Oct 1917–10 Apr 1986), Robert J. (12 Jan 1920–24 Nov 2000), Harrell (1 Jan 1922–17 May 2013), and Clyde (19 Feb 1929–11 Dec 1941).

- **Lillie Colwell (6 Mar 1884–26 Feb 1918):** Lillie married William Eli Gilliland (5 Feb 1879–23 Apr 1929) on March 11, 1917. Their daughter was Lillie Eulalia (25 Feb 1918–25 Mar 2004).

- **Rosa Emma Colwell (28 Jun 1886–20 Feb 1936):** Rosa married Elmer Gibson (25 Jul 1883–15 Feb 1977). They lived near Zavalla in Angelina County, Texas. Their children were Theron Tommy (21 Jul 1910–5 May 1986), John Rasmus (27 Jul 1912–8 May 1976), Donald (19 Nov 1914–30 Dec 2009), Abbie (4 Aug 1917–23 Nov 1994), Olivette (17 May 1920–18 May 1995), Delbert Wayne (18 Sep 1922–27 Dec 1991), Serilla (10 Jun 1925–3 May 1985), and Glyn (6 Sep 1927–4 Nov 2013).

- **William Samuel Colwell (3 Feb 1888–14 Apr 1984):** Samuel married Avie Hopson (22 Mar 1889–19 Nov 1971). Their children were John Stacy (1 Jan 1913–24 Oct 1969), Eula V. (6 Jan 1916–22 May 1993), and William Fletcher (30 Jul 1919–18 Sep 1996).

- **Thomas Matthew Colwell (5 Nov 1889–14 Jan 1927):** Thomas married Lenora Mae Fuller (20 May 1894–6 Jul 1971). They lived on a farm in Angelina County, Texas. Their children were Blanche (3 Apr 1913–21 May 2003), Wilma (23 Aug 1914–4 Jul 1964), May Delle (30 Nov 1916–11 Sep 2002), and Kenneth (10 Jan 1924–16 Sep 1989).

- **I. D. Colwell (3 Jan 1892–29 Nov 1963):** I. D. married Mary Virginia Hawkins (12 Dec 1897–1 Nov 1967). They operated a farm in Angelina County, Texas. Their children were Coy (5 Dec 1914–22 Jan 1984), Clara Loreen (4 Jul 1916–28 Mar 2003), John Durward (8 Feb 1918–4 Sep 2005), and Florence Ercelle (22 Jun 1920–5 Jan 2005).

- **Addie Velma Colwell (25 Jul 1895–24 Aug 1988):** Velma married Charles Liles (13 Oct 1895–3 Aug 1918) on September 21, 1913, in Angelina County, Texas. Their children were Linell (7 Aug 1914–26 Jul 1991), Hazel (4 Mar 1916–31 May 2003), and Dillen (5 Aug 1918–12 Feb 1991). Velma's second marriage was to William Calaway Jones (18 Feb 1881–17 Jan 1956). Their children were Imogene (20 Jul 1921–25 Jun 2007) and Willie Velma (13 Jun 1924–1 Nov 2005).

- **James Elton Colwell (2 Mar 1998–20 Aug 1978):** James married Nora Mott (26 Dec 1900–12 Sep 1995). Their daughter was Jimmie L. (2 Jan 1920–3 Dec 2016).

- **Vara Colwell (28 Dec 1902–4 Dec 1981):** Vara married Cornelius Cary Walker (25 Dec 1900–24 Jan 1966). Their children were Mozelle (20 Nov 1920–3 Jul 2002) and Hyral Berwyn (15 Nov 1923–22 Aug 2012). Vara's second marriage was to Jessie Barge (27 Sep 1890–27 Mar 1976).

- **George Washington Colwell (17 May 1905–23 May 1975):** George was born in Zavalla, Angelina County. He married Marguerite Minton (1908–1991). The 1940 census shows them in Jasper County, Texas, with a two-year-old daughter, Frances Sue (1937–2015).

- **Wiley Colwell (6 Jun 1856–5 Dec 1928):** Wiley married Rachel Ann Jackson (11 Feb 1861–Dec 1928) around 1879. Rachel was born in Alabama. They are shown with their infant son James on the 1880 census of Angelina County. They lived near the community of Zavalla. Censuses for 1900, 1910, and 1920 show them operating farms in Nacogdoches and then San Augustine Counties. Wiley and Rachel died within a week of one another. Both were buried in Cochran Cemetery.

  - **James Matthew Colwell (9 Mar 1880–28 Dec 1959):** James married Martha Robertson "Mattie" James. He registered for the World War I draft from San Augustine County, Texas. He noted that he had part of a foot missing and that he worked in farming. He died in San Jacinto County, Texas.

  - **George Kenion Colwell (30 Jun 1882–16 Nov 1958):** George married Mary Beckie Spinks (26 May 1891–19 Jun 1972). They lived in Broaddus, San Augustine County, Texas, where all their children were born. George died in Woodville, Tyler County, Texas, and Mary Beckie died in Houston, Texas. Their children were George Kenion (12 Nov 1909–16 Nov 1958), Olga Mae (3 Jan 1912–unknown), Annie Bell Colwell (15 Jan 1915–unknown), Orpha Elnora (15 Dec 1917–unknown), Charlsie L. (ca. 1919–unknown), Myrtie O. (ca. 1923–unknown), Iris J. (ca. 1926–unknown), and James Raymond (26 Dec 1933–unknown).

- **John Thomas Colwell (12 Feb 1886–19 Apr 1928):** John was born in Chireno, Nacogdoches County, Texas. John Thomas married Ollie Rae (1896–unknown). He died in Woodville, Tyler County, Texas. Their children were Holly (25 Oct 1913–19 Apr 1928), Rassie (19 Jun 1915–16 Nov 1984), Katy B. (24 Feb 1919–13 Jul 2009), and Charlcie (9 Sep 1927–6 Sep 2005).

- **Mary Bell Colwell (30 Aug 1888–15 Jul 1956):** Mary was born in Chireno, Nacogdoches County. She married John Tillman Patterson (23 Nov 1887–17 Jul 1938) in 1909. Their children were Mary Lee (2 Sep 1914–18 Sep 1978), Katie Belle (14 Nov 1917–14 Oct 1976), Wiley E. (1 Mar 1920–22 Jan 1989), Leroy (ca. 1926–), and Charlsey M. (ca. 1928–).

- **Denton Kelly Colwell (28 Jul 1892–24 May 1917):** Denton was born in Chireno, Nacogdoches County. He is shown in the home of his parents in the 1910 census. Denton died in Angelina County.

- **Margaret Caroline Colwell (2 Jul 1898–4 Apr 1974):** Margaret was born in Chireno, Nacogdoches County. She married D. O. Mott (9 Nov 1880–unknown) in 1919. She died in Lufkin, Texas. Their children were Joel (25 Nov 1921–6 Jun 1965), Jesse (ca. 1932–), and Wiley (30 Mar 1934–).

- **Caroline Colwell (26 Aug 1859–20 Mar 1943):** Caroline married James Kelly Lovelady on September 10, 1882, in Angelina County. The 1900 census indicates that Caroline was the mother of no children, but the 1910 census lists her as mother of seven children, three of whom were living in 1910. No children are listed on the 1900 or 1910 censuses.

- **Priscilla Francis Colwell (3 Jan 1861–28 Apr 1954):** Priscilla was born in Zavalla, Angelina County, Texas. Priscilla married Joseph Logan Pickard (8 Sep 1853–29 Mar 1918) on December 20, 1882. The 1900 and 1910 censuses show them operating a farm in Angelina County. After Joseph's death, Priscilla and her son Oscar operated the Angelina County farm as shown in the 1920 and 1930 censuses. Her sons Jerome and Arthur operated nearby farms. Priscilla died in Lufkin, Texas.

  - **Jerome Bonaparte Pickard (Dec 1883–30 Apr 1969):** Jerome married Laura Dearmond (ca. 1888–before 1920) on December 28, 1904, in Angelina County, Texas. They operated a farm. Their children were Hessie W. (11 Apr 1907–2 Mar 1991), Eula Mae (30 Apr 1909–11 Aug 1968), and Paul (16 Dec 1912–12 Aug 1985). A second marriage was to Millie Matilda Roberts (29 Aug 1894–22 May 1990). Their children were Burl Darwin (19 Jul 1921–17 Sep 2013), Johnie Marvin (6 Oct 1922–7 Jun 1989), and Joe (17 Oct 1926–).

- **William Mathew Pickard (15 Jul 1886–15 Nov 1964):** William married Nina Hering (18 Jun 1880–16 Jul 1978). They lived in San Augustine, where William was a depot agent for the railroad and in Dallas and Hockley Counties, where he did farmwork. Their children were Joseph Herring (22 Jun 1910–16 Oct 1982), Conway Ferrell (29 May 1913–26 May 2003), Willie Edward (25 Mar 1919–3 Mar 2016), and Kenneth Glendale (8 Mar 1923–24 Nov 1929).

- **Codella "Della" Pickard (16 Dec 1888–27 Sep 1976):** Della was born in Zavalla, Angelina County, Texas. She married Ordie Cleveland Stuart (6 Nov 1884–19 Feb 1964) on October 20, 1915, in Nacogdoches, Texas. Ordie was born in Butler County, Alabama. They lived in Angelina County, Texas. Ordie worked in the logging and lumber industries. Their children were Ordie Boyce (31 Aug 1917–27 Sep 1970) and Sarah Frances (16 Apr 1924–22 Sep 2006).

- **Arthur Bertis Pickard (12 Sep 1893–25 Feb 1929):** Arthur and his wife, Eva Mott (12 Jan 1895–4 Apr 1980), are shown farming in Angelina County in the 1920 and 1930 censuses. Priscilla and Oscar were on the adjoining farm. Their children are Arthur Vernon (8 Jun 1914–2 Oct 1970) and Robert Doyle (3 Jul 1919–4 Nov 1957).

- **Oscar Pickard (15 Jan 1895–30 Oct 1968):** Oscar is shown operating a farm with his mother in the 1920, 1930, and 1940 censuses. He was not married.

- **Eliza Jane Colwell (6 Dec 1862–5 Aug 1899):** Eliza married David Archibald Cochran (12 Dec 1861–26 Oct 1931) on October 25, 1885, in Angelina County, Texas. Her gravestone gives the death date of August 5, 1899, but the 1900 census lists her as a household member.

  - **Densil (Denzil) C. Cochran (13 Feb 1890–16 Jun 1959):** Densil was born in Angelina County, Texas. He registered for the World War I draft as a cowboy for the Metzel Cattle Company in Lakeview, Beaverhead County, Montana. He served in the US Navy during World War I. He is shown in the Angelina County household of his father in the 1920 census but returned to Montana, where he married Laura Beatrice Masolo on September 5, 1937. He was buried in Mountain View Cemetery in Dillon, Montana.

  - **William Scott Cochran (29 Jan 1892–2 Dec 1974):** Scott married Eureka Texas Ellis (14 Feb 1898–10 Jun 1991) on February 17, 1914, in Angelina County, Texas. They operated a farm in Angelina County. Their children were Eugene Dee (18 Feb 1915–4 Apr 1998), Felix Prentis (22 Jan 1916–26 Sep 1995), Ora Lu (29 Oct 1918–24 Mar 2014), infant son (5 Apr 1921–5 Jul 1921), Eliza M. (3 May 1923–3 May 2008), Talmadge C. (19 Aug 1925–25 Jun 1973), Martha

Elizabeth (10 Sep 1927–1 Jul 1972), Rebecca Sue (24 Dec 1934–1 Apr 2005), and William Bertice (15 Feb 1937–25 May 2005).

- **Stella Cochran (23 Jan 1894–4 Dec 1989):** Stella married Joseph Edward Shofner (26 May 1884–30 May 1966). They lived in Angelina County, Texas, where Joseph worked on the railroad and later farmed. Their children were Robert E. (18 Jun 1903–5 Apr 1986), Louis B. (28 Sep 1905–31 Jul 1991), Minnie Lee (23 Jan 1912–26 Apr 1974), Muriel F. (27 Jun 1914–Aug 1984), and Nan Leah (9 Oct 1926–Jun 1995).

- **William Joseph "Billy" Colwell (3 Oct 1865–19 Mar 1943):** Billy was a farmer in Angelina County. He married Luella Parker (3 Sep 1972–13 Jul 1947) on January 26, 1888, in Angelina County, Texas. Their son was Layfette Bassett. Billy and Luella were divorced. Billy married Katherine "Catie" Stanley (3 Aug 1874–27 Jan 1907) on September 10, 1893. Their children were Gertrude, Mertie Ellie, and Matthew Hollis. His third marriage was to Alice Lenora Coleman (17 Oct 1878–28 Mar 1941). Their daughter was Lois. Billy was buried in Cochran Cemetery.

  - **Layfette Bassett Colwell (5 May 1889–6 Feb 1964):** Layfette remained with his mother after his parents' divorce. They are shown operating a farm in Angelina County, Texas, in the 1920 census. He continued farming through the 1940 census. He and Artie Windsor (7 Apr 1890–29 Nov 1962) were married in Angelina County on January 11, 1914. Their children were Annie May (1 Nov 1914–16 May 2006), Jessie Lafayette (7 Apr 1917–14 Jan 2003), Lois (27 Aug 1919–21 Jul 2010), and Thomas Jefferson (26 Feb 1922–23 Apr 2010).

  - **Gertrude "Gertie" Colwell (13 Jun 1894–13 Apr 1982):** Gertrude married Henry Floyd Wells (22 Feb 1868–11 Jul 1959). They lived in Liberty County, Texas, where he worked as a farmer and in the oil fields as a pumper. Their children were Matthew Hollis (14 Feb 1915–27 Oct 1985), Annie May (7 Jun 1917–1 Dec 1986), and Billie Joe (24 Feb 1930–27 Feb 2011).

  - **Myrtle "Myrtie" Colwell (6 Dec 1895–30 Aug 1980):** Myrtie married Jonathan Cicero Cleveland in Angelina County, Texas, on February 2, 1915. He worked in the logging industry in 1920, but by 1940 they had bought and operated a farm. Their children were Thomas William (5 Jan 1916–11 Oct 2003), Katy May (1917–1919), Lois Esther (4 Jul 1919–12 Jun 1973), Robert (13 Sep 1921–23 Dec 1997), Mary Elizabeth (7 May 1926–27 Aug 2008), and Tenney Laverne (7 Sep 1929–).

  - **Ellie Colwell (25 Oct 1898–Jun 1989):** Ellie married Cyrus J. Ivy (13 Jul 1881–14 Aug 1970) on December 27, 1917, in Angelina County, Texas. Her son was Gaylon Colwell (24 Mar 1914–17 Jan 1976).

- **Matthew Hollis Colwell (20 Oct 1900–12 Dec 1987):** Matthew married Minnie P. Stuart (25 Mar 1896–17 Sep 1977). They operated a farm in Angelina County, Texas. Their children were Willie Estelle (25 Dec 1919–31 May 2015), Hazel Barnett (9 Apr 1922–21 May 1980), Ellie Lucille (17 Aug 1924–15 Feb 2010), Mertie Mozelle (7 Mar 1927–6 Jul 2002), Nela Mae (17 May 1931–23 Aug 1979), and William James (22 Nov 1933–1 Jun 1981).

- **Lois Colwell (11 Jan 1910–21 Jun 1984):** Lois married Rosier Ezell Davis (1900–1976). They are shown on the 1940 census of San Augustine County, Texas, with two children. Cemetery records indicate they had an infant son who was born and died in 1939. Their other children were Billy Jack (5 Nov 1931–26 Aug 2013) and Sue Nell (11 Oct 1935–).

- **James Colwell (2 Feb 1868–8 Oct 1899):** James was listed as one in the 1870 census. He lived and died in Zavalla, Angelina County, Texas.

- **Martha Ann "Annie" Colwell (1 Apr 1871–17 Feb 1965):** Martha married George J. Harvey (18 Apr 1866–15 Aug 1951) on September 6, 1888. The 1910 census lists Margaret Ann as the mother of nine children, eight of whom were living. They lived in Angelina, Austin, Stephens, and Parker Counties. Both Mary Ann and George were buried in Parker County.

  - **Seth Alvin Harvey (22 Feb 1891–17 Mar 1969):** Seth married Iva Jo Ray (14 Apr 1891–13 Apr 1981) in Angelina County, Texas, on January 1, 1914. He worked for the railroad, in farming, and for the government. Their children were Grady (31 Dec 1914–5 Mar 2010) and Maybelle (21 Feb 1919–2 May 2010).

  - **Jessie Curtice Harvey (Feb 1892–unknown):** He is listed as Jessie on the 1900 census and as Curtice on the 1910 and 1920 censuses. Additional information has not been located.

  - **Samuel Bullitt Harvey (9 Jul 1894–28 May 1984):** Samuel was born in Huntington, Angelina County, Texas. He served as a member of the US Army in France during World War I. He married Chappie Faulker. In 1942, he was stationed at Naval Air Station in Corpus Christi, Texas. Margurite Harvey of Corpus Christi was listed as the contact person. He died in Los Angeles, California.

  - **George Reginald Harvey (15 Apr 1897–unknown):** Reginald married Annis Belle Harrelson (14 Jul 1907–20 Oct 1995). They were living at the Columbian Carbon Company Camp in Gray County, Texas, at the time of the 1940 census. Their sons were Lloyd Raymond (3 Jan 1927–14 Oct 2007) and T. J. (18 Jun 1934–).

- **Roy Mathew Harvey (15 Jul 1899–1 Jan 1961):** Roy was born in Angelina County, Texas. He is shown in Stephens County, Texas, in the 1930 census and in Gray County in 1940. His wife, Inez Herrington (10 May 1902–23 Aug 1956), was also a native of Angelina County, Texas. Their children were Anne Maurine (22 May 1922–25 May 2011) and Roy Edward (27 Feb 1925–).

- **Ruby Harvey (ca. 1901–unknown):** Ruby is shown as a nine-year-old in the 1910 census. No additional information has been provided.

- **Eula Mae Harvey (24 Apr 1903–13 Oct 1999):** Eula married Lonnie W. Dobbs (1906–1980). They lived in Parker and Palo Pinto Counties, Texas. Their son, Wayne Harold (1 Aug 1935–), lived in Mineral Wells, Texas.

- **Abbie Harvey (ca. 1906–unknown):** Abbie was living with her parents in Stephens County, Texas, at the time of the 1930 census.

- **Sarah "Sallie" Colwell (26 Mar 1874–30 Jun 1957):** Sarah was born in Angelina County, Texas. She married Alfred John Wigley (18 Mar 1868–24 Dec 1940) on September 28, 1893. They are shown in the 1900 census in the household headed by her mother, Martha, operating the farm. By 1910, they were in Lufkin, Texas, where he was a shipping clerk for a grocery company. The 1920 and 1930 censuses show them in Shelby County. Sarah died in Rusk County, Texas.

  - **Charles William Wigley (2 Jul 1898–28 Oct 1955):** Charles married Janice Spencer (22 Mar 1908–29 Jun 2002) in Smith County, Texas, on July 7, 1928. Charles worked as a salesman for a milling company.

- **Alabama "Allie" Colwell (3 Sep 1876–8 Jun 1970):** Allie married William Henry Cassels (1872–1905) on November 14, 1895. The 1900 census shows them on a farm in Angelina County, Texas, with one child, Robert. Otis and Edward were the next additions to the family. Allie married Fred Dearmond on May 20, 1906, in Angelina County. The 1910 census shows them on an Angelina County farm.

  - **Robert Lee Cassels (24 Sep 1896–8 Jun 1961):** Robert served with the US Armed Forces in France during World War I. He and his wife, Mary Odelle McGee (5 Apr 1905–Jun 1983), are shown on the 1940 census in Wood County, Texas, with children Charles (ca. 1931–) and Annie Sue (ca. 1935–).

  - **Odis Charlie Cassels (20 Nov 1900–4 Sep 1987):** Odis married Myrtle Leah Barge (7 Nov 1912–2 Dec 2004). The 1940 census shows their children as Jackie Charline (22 Jan 1933–) and Henry Wayne (31 Aug 1937–19 Nov 2013).

- **Edward Henry Cassels (4 Nov 1904–Jul 1968):** Edward married Jimmie Stewart (22 Dec 1911–2 Oct 1938). His second marriage was to Mamie Lee Russell (8 Apr 1903–6 Dec 1998).

- **Sammie Bassett Dearmond (31 Oct 1907–10 May 1996):** Sammie lived in Henderson, Rusk County, Texas. He married Lutie Corinne Magrill (19 Nov 1912–3 Feb 2007).

- **Lemond Browder Dearmond (8 Jun 1913–16 May 1991):** Lemond married Opal Anthony (9 Nov 1918–7 Jul 2003). They are shown on the Nacogdoches County, Texas, census with children Patsy Deloris (6 Mar 1936–11 Apr 2012) and Jerry Leemon (26 Jul 1938–22 Mar 2006).

- **Samuel "Sam" Colwell (12 Sep 1880–14 Jan 1965):** Sam was living in Huntington, Angelina County, Texas, when he registered for the World War I draft. He married Mary Elizabeth Smith (4 Apr 1895–14 Mar 1968) on April 7, 1912. Census data shows him working on the railroad. He died in Lufkin, Angelina County.

  - **Martha O. Colwell (19 Feb 1915–8 Jun 1992):** Martha was born in Lufkin, Angelina County, Texas. She married Truman Holder. They were living in Hill County, Texas, in 1940 with daughter Renna Jean, age six.

  - **Matthew H. Colwell (13 Jan 1917–12 Jan 1976):** Matthew served in the US military from October 30, 1940, to November 27, 1943.

  - **Lessie Mae Colwell (1 Jan 1919–26 Sep 1995):** Lessie was married to Clark Brookshire (ca. 1921–19 Sep 1974). They are shown in Angelina County, Texas, on the 1940 census. She married Leland R. Henley on February 20, 1976, in Angelina County.

  - **Annie Colwell (27 Jan 1920–3 Dec 1985):** Annie married Virgil Clarence Summers (25 Mar 1902–10 Apr 1981). They lived in Colorado City and other Texas areas, but both were buried in Lufkin, Angelina County, Texas.

  - **Woodson Samuel Colwell (25 Aug 1924–28 Feb 1972):** Woodson served in the US Army Infantry during World War II. After the war, he went to Elon College, Alamance County, North Carolina. He married Violet Beatrice Childress (20 Jul 1923–30 Jul 2005).

Andrew Jackson Colwell
(3 May 1822–10 Jan 1902)

Born in Alabama, Jackson Colwell grew up and married in Angelina County, Texas. Most of his adult life was spent in Tarrant and Dallas Counties. He and Nancy Harriet Hughes (30 Jun 1834–9 Aug 1923) were married on June 7, 1850, in Angelina County. Nancy was born in Louisiana. They were living in Tarrant County at the time of the 1870 census. In 1879 Jackson bought 319 acres of land in the Hackberry community of Dallas County. Jackson died on January 10, 1902, in Dallas County. He was buried in Keenan Cemetery of Farmers Branch, Texas. After Jackson's death, Nancy moved to Long Beach, California, where she died and was buried. The Dallas County land remained in the Colwell family for 103 years and was home to six generations. In 1982, the land was sold to the Las Colinas Corporation for a business and industrial complex.

- **Wiley Colwell (21 Sep 1850–2 Oct 1850).**

- **Mary Jane Colwell (Nov 1852–before 1870).**

- **Martha Colwell (8 Mar 1855–before 1876):** Martha is shown on the 1870 census but died before age twenty-one.

- **Robert J. Colwell (1857–before 1870).**

- **Melvina Melinda Colwell (Oct 1858–11 Jan 1911):** Melvina married John Carothers (22 Jan 1850–10 Dec 1892). They are shown in Tarrant County, Texas, in 1880. The 1910 census in Wise County, Texas, shows Melvina as head of a household including her mother, Nancy, and son Wiley. Both John and Melvina are buried in Boonville, Wise County.

  - **Nancy V. Carathers (ca. 1876–unknown):** Nancy is shown as a four-year-old in the 1880 census.

  - **William Andrew Jackson Carathers (21 Dec 1878–27 Oct 1959):** The 1900 census of Chickasaw Nation, Indian Territory, shows a William A. Carothers, age twenty-one, working as a blacksmith. By 1920, he; his wife, Mary Parry (13 Apr 1891–14 Sep 1947); and their son Thomas were in San Francisco, California. Both the 1930 and 1940 censuses show the family in Oakland, Alameda County, California. Their children were Thomas David (20 Feb 1912–8 Dec 1964) and Wilbert (ca. 1927–).

  - **John Lee Carathers (14 Aug 1881–23 Aug 1957):** John Lee married Julia Mae Dunn (23 Oct 1882–3 Apr 1951). They operated a farm in Floyd County, Texas. Both John Lee and Julia died and were buried in Amarillo, Potter County,

Texas. Their children were William David (31 Oct 1906–13 Jan 1971), Elmer D. (14 Oct 1908–3 Sep 1994), Nora Marie (24 Apr 1910–Jan 1994), Minnie L. (ca. 1913–unknown), Johnnie (8 Dec 1915–31 Jan 1979), and Walter Gerald (7 May 1921–16 Sep 2005).

- **Wiley Remie Carathers (13 Oct 1884–18 Jan 1949):** Wiley married Bessie Colwell (27 Aug 1896–11 Sep 1979). They lived in Dallas, Texas. Wiley worked for the city of Dallas in 1920, at the Ford plant in 1930, and in his own business in 1940. His death certificate lists him as a retired gasoline station operator. The children of Wiley and Bessie were Catharine (ca. 1916–unknown), John Andrew (26 Sep 1918–25 Jun 1976), Warren Harding (11 Jan 1922–8 Dec 1995), and Bessie M. (8 Jan 1925–).

- **James Thomas Colwell (20 Mar 1861–7 Apr 1939):** James Thomas married Lucy E. Stanley (29 Aug 1867–4 Nov 1889). They had no children. The 1900 census shows James in his parents' Dallas home. He did not remarry, and he continued to work in agriculture in Dallas County.

- **Ara Bell Colwell (5 Jul 1863–14 Mar 1943):** Ara Bell married Gustave Toussant Ferguson (28 Aug 1861–11 Feb 1934) around 1890. They were divorced. The 1920 census shows Bell and her daughter, Melissa, in Oklahoma City. Bell was working as a nurse and Melissa as a stenographer. The 1940 census shows Bell living alone in Glendale, California.

  - **Kathryn Melissa Ferguson (15 Sep 1891–7 Jun 1949):** Melissa married Raymond Cales (1896–). They lived in Riverside and San Bernardino, California. Melissa's mother, Belle, was living with them in 1930. Their son was Paul Raymond (4 Mar 1924–).

- **John Colwell (29 Jun 1865–26 Aug 1939):** John married Allie Leonard (14 Jan 1877–11 Apr 1951) in Texas. John and Allie are shown on a farm in Custer, Montana, in 1910. They had lived in Texas, Oklahoma, and New Mexico and finally settled in Montana. Allie was appointed as postmaster of Ragus Post Office, Powder River, Montana, on March 20, 1926. John died in Powder River, Montana, and Allie died in Lawrence, South Dakota.

  - **Mabel Colwell (6 Nov 1903–12 Nov 1975):** Mabel married Edward Tekautz (1903–19 Jun 1964) on May 10, 1933. The marriage ended in divorce. Mabel married Roy Kelsey (ca. 1901–unknown). Her third marriage was to Charles Burlison (20 Dec 1891–14 Mar 1971).

  - **Irene Jane Colwell (5 Feb 1910–4 Jun 1972):** In 1930 Irene was a student in the Montana State School for Deaf and Blind in Jefferson, Montana. Irene married

Reinhold Roy Roebuck (17 Jan 1896–3 Oct 1951) on June 3, 1935, in Powder River County, Montana. They made their home in South Dakota. He worked for the Chicago and Northwestern Railroad. Irene died in South Dakota.

- **Wiley W. Colwell (24 Apr 1868–8 Jun 1945):** Few records have been found for Wiley beyond the 1870 and 1880 censuses, the California Death Index, and cemetery records, which show his death and burial in Stanislaus County, California.

- **Andrew Jackson Colwell Jr. (9 Apr 1871–16 Jun 1942):** Andrew Jackson married Catherine Dick (27 Sep 1872–26 May 1943). The 1900 census shows them engaged in farming in Dallas County, Texas. Catherine was listed as the mother of three children, two of whom were living. By 1910, Charles was listed as a policeman.

  - **Charles Jackson Colwell (14 Oct 1888–19 Oct 1972):** Charles married Belle Ward (25 Apr 1892–10 Jan 1990). In 1920 and 1930, they owned and operated a farm in Dallas County, Texas. Their children were Remie Jackson (13 Sep 1911–15 Aug 1969), Mabel (7 Mar 1913–13 May 2000), Ruby (24 Oct 1914–12 May 2007), Charles (10 May 1918–14 May 1991), Joe Walter (13 Dec 1919–20 Jan 2014), Gilbert (6 Jun 1922–7 Jun 2013), William Robert "Billie" (27 Jul 1926–6 Apr 1976), and Martha Ruth (14 Oct 1927–).

  - **Bessie Colwell (27 Aug 1896–11 Sep 1979):** Bessie married Wylie Remie Carathers (13 Oct 1884–18 Jan 1949). He was a gasoline station operator in Dallas County, Texas. Their children were Catherine (23 Sep 1915–18 Jul 2018), John Andrew (26 Sep 1918–25 Jun 1976), Warren Harding (11 Jan 1922–8 Dec 1995), and Bessie M. (8 Jan 1925–).

- **Dora Ophelia Colwell (23 Feb 1973–28 Oct 1910):** Dora married Earl S. Aulsbrook (9 Mar 1868–18 Jan 1923) around 1890. The 1910 census shows Dora as head of the household, with her children. Her death was later that year.

  - **Charlie Jackson Aulsbrook (1 Aug 1891–18 Oct 1980):** Charlie married Mary Elizabeth Morrison (13 Jul 1890–2 Apr 1953). They lived in Dallas, Texas. His second wedding, to Jessie May Sargent, was on November 3, 1956.

  - **Daniel Colmen Aulsbrook (8 Jan 1894–30 Dec 1956):** Daniel registered for the World War I draft as single and employed as a convict at the Imperial State Farm. He is shown in the 1922 Dallas City Directory as working in his brother Stanley's Dixie Vulcanizing Company. He was living in Tyler, Texas, when he registered for the World War II draft.

  - **Stanley Edward Aulsbrook (12 Sep 1896–21 Dec 1957):** Stanley married Mary Ledbetter (18 Apr 1901–13 Nov 1973). In 1930 they were living in Wichita Falls, Texas, where he was the owner of a tire shop. By 1940 he and

Mary had divorced. He and their son, Stanley Jr., were in Dallas, where Stanley was working as a salesman. Stanley died in Sulphur Springs, Hopkins County, Texas. Their children were Dorothy E. (28 Nov 1919–18 Feb 1963), Rosemary (3 Jul 1921–27 Feb 1998), and Stanley Edward Jr. (13 Oct 1930–12 Jun 1992).

- **Josephine "Josie" Aulsbrook (9 Mar 1899–25 May 1971):** The 1920 Dallas County census shows Josephine and her sister Eugenia living in a Dallas boardinghouse. Both were working as stenographers for insurance companies. She married James V. Eastman. They were living in Dallas at the time of the 1940 census.

- **Eugenia "Gene" Aulsbrook (10 Sep 1901–26 Oct 1981):** The 1920 census shows Gene with her sister Josephine in a Dallas boardinghouse, working as a stenographer for an insurance company. Gene married Andrew Aitken. The 1930 census shows them in Dallas, Texas, with eight-year-old daughter Gloria.

- **Grace Harriett Aulsbrook (26 Aug 1903–19 Mar 2001):** Grace married William Lowery Minor (1901–1959). Her last residence for Social Security was Mesquite, Dallas County, Texas.

- **Joan Margaret Colwell (3 Jul 1875–19 Mar 1952):** Joan Margaret married Perry Murt Frailia (23 Feb 1874–1 Nov 1900). In 1900, Joan, Perry, and sons Harry and Henry were in Pecos County, Texas, where Perry worked on a ranch. The 1910 census lists Joan as the mother of four children, three of whom were living. Perry was murdered, according to family records. Joan's second marriage was to Ausber Monroe Scarborough (23 Mar 1873–5 Jun 1927). The 1930 census, though, shows Joan and husband E. N. Hukill with grandson Harry Frailia, age eleven. By 1940, Joan Hukill was head of a household with Ray C. Lane, Myrtle Lane, Joan Melton, and Billy Jo Dehn. She is listed as Joan Crocker on her death certificate.

  - **Jack Harry Frailia (17 Nov 1895–10 Mar 1966):** Jack married Annie Cornelia Atkinson (27 Feb 1907–20 Jan 1970). They lived in Fort Worth, Texas. Their children were Nathaniel Murt (1930–), Billy Jack (1932–), and Thomas Warren (1934–).

  - **Warren Henry Frailia (10 Sep 1898–1 May 1950):** Warren served in the engineering unit of the US Army during World War I. The 1930 census shows Warren and his first wife, Marie (Julia Marie Alexander, 4 Jun 1902–22 Nov 1968), in Fort Worth, Texas, where he was working as a fireman. They were divorced before 1940; Warren and his second wife, Ella Carter, lived in Fort Worth. Children of Warren and Marie were Warren Pat (23 Aug 1920–6 Aug 1985) and Betty Marie (27 Feb 1926–26 Mar 2004).

- **Myrtle Ophelia Fralia (29 Oct 1900–12 Jul 1980):** Myrtle married J. C. Melton (ca. 1893–unknown). They are shown on the 1920 census of Tarrant County, Texas. By 1930, Myrtle was in Houston, Texas, with husband William Dehn and daughters Joanne and Billy Jo. The 1940 census shows Myrtle, husband Ray C. Lane, and daughters Joanne Melton (1922–) and Billy Jo Dehn (1924–) in the Fort Worth, Texas, home of her mother, Joan Hukill.

Susan Colwell
(22 Sep 1823–9 Jan 1904)

Susan Colwell was born in Tennessee or Alabama; both states are listed on various census records. She married Zachariah Johnson on November 11, 1838, in Nacogdoches, Texas. Zachariah Johnson paid taxes for 1838 in Nacogdoches County, but records for him beyond that date have not been found. In the 1850 census Susan was in the home of Enoch Needham in Angelina County. They were enumerated on the same page as her brother Matthew and her sister Caroline Stovall. By 1860, Susan was listed as head of the household, with son Enoch and daughter Nancy. Her six-year-old son, Francis, was enumerated with the Anderson family, apparently living adjacent to Susan. Susan moved to Fayette County, Texas, before 1870. She is shown in the 1870 census as head of a household that included Enoch and Francis Needham, Mary Faris, and Mary Neering. The latter two were granddaughters. Susan retained the name of Susan Johnson until the 1880 census, where she is listed as Susan Needham, with her son Frank Needham and the two granddaughters. There is no record of a marriage for Susan and Enoch Needham. Susan died on January 9, 1904, and was buried in Cheatham Cemetery, Sheridan, Colorado County, Texas.

- **Mary "Polly" Johnson (ca. 1844–ca. 1867):** Mary is shown on the 1850 census of Angelina County. On March 15, 1860, she married James M. Alexander in Angelina County. The 1860 census shows the couple in Homer, Angelina County, Texas. With the onset of the Civil War, James enlisted in the Confederate army. He died during his service. Mary married Edward W. Faris on January 4, 1866. Mary died soon after the birth of their daughter, also named Mary.

  - **Mary Faris (ca. 1867–22 Apr 1930):** Mary lived with her grandmother Susan in Fayette County, where she is shown on the 1870 and 1880 censuses. She married William Curtis (1848–29 Feb 1914) on December 18, 1888, in Colorado County, Texas. They are shown in the 1900 census of Colorado County, Texas. No children were listed. Mary married Francis Albert Sevier (1 Dec 1842–1 Apr 1924) on December 17, 1914. Mary committed suicide by hanging.

- **Enoch Johnson Needham (29 Oct 1849–27 Mar 1930):** Enoch was born in Angelina County, Texas. He was listed as Enoch Johnson in the 1850 and 1860 censuses. Enoch used the name Enoch Needham after moving to Fayette County. He was married three times. His first marriage, to Lenor Roberson Taylor, beginning on March 7, 1870, ended in divorce, with Lenor having custody of the two children, Oscar and Mary. His second wedding, to Virginia Quick, occurred around 1875. He and Virginia are shown on the 1880 census with two children, Green C. and Hilrey, and on the 1900 census with ten children. By 1910, the household consisted of Enoch, Virginia, daughter Dora, son Marion, daughter-in-law Mertier, and Marion and Mertier's two children. Enoch and Virginia were divorced around 1915. He married Minnie Johnson. The 1920 census lists Enoch, sixty-six; Minnie, twenty-three; and three Johnson children. Virginia was enumerated with her son Enoch and his family in the 1930 census. Enoch died in Fayette County, Texas, from pneumonia.

  - **Oscar Needham (14 Feb 1871–15 Apr 1953):** Born in Fayette County, Texas, Oscar was living in Fort Worth, Texas, by 1940. Oscar married Henrietta Little on May 27, 1891, in Williamson County, Texas. Their children were Josephine Beatrice (3 Feb 1892–12 Feb 1976), Mamie (Feb 1894–unknown), Albert (Sep 1895–before 1910), Ollie Elmer (14 Oct 1897–Feb 1970), Arthur Wilmer (29 Apr 1899–25 Apr 1935), and Viola (ca. 1904–unknown).

  - **Mary Needham (23 Jun 1873–23 Sep 1946).**

  - **Benjamin Greene Cox (1875–1904):** Benjamin was Virginia's son by a previous marriage. He was raised by Virginia and Enoch.

  - **Hilrey (Hilsie) Needham (2 Jul 1878–4 Sep 1943):** Hilrey married Lenora Norma "Nora" Hart (18 Jun 1882–31 Dec 1955) on 28 November 1900 in Fayette County, Texas. They lived in Bastrop and Austin, Texas. Their son was Jesse J. (1904–after 1930).

  - **Edward Needham (29 Mar 1881–4 Mar 1952):** Ed married Ida Richardson (16 Sep 1877–31 Dec 1948). In 1910 they operated a farm in Fayette County, Texas. Their children were Leroy (9 Nov 1908–22 May 1977) and Everett Wade (12 Jun 1911–12 Mar 1971).

  - **Samuel Needham (23 Dec 1883–4 Mar 1953):** Samuel married Francis O. Hatch (11 May 1881–4 Jul 1965). They lived in Fayette County, Texas. Their children were Ora E. (22 Aug 1902–15 Oct 1986) and Ernest Green (14 Aug 1905–29 Nov 1979).

  - **Beulah Needham (23 Jan 1885–28 Jun 1928):** Beulah married Albert Hart (11 Jan 1879–29 May 1934) on February 11, 1903, in Fayette County, Texas. Their children were Lester (15 Apr 1904–2 Mar 1991), Elzie Evin (8 Aug 1905–5 Jan

1984), George (1908–before 1920), Marie (21 Sep 1917–9 Mar 1993), Clarence (25 Jan 1919–17 Sep 1938), and Estelle (23 Jan 1923–26 Oct 2003).

- **Marion Needham (10 Jun 1887–21 Nov 1947):** Marion married Marrian McMulllin (3 Aug 1891–7 Dec 1974) on May 7, 1911, in Fayette County, Texas. The 1930 census shows them in Travis County, Texas. Their children were Wilma (1 Jan 1914–11 Jun 1979), Cecil Marion (30 May 1915–22 May 1993), Ida (22 Mar 1917–4 Nov 2012), Mary Eva (7 Mar 1919–13 Sep 2001), and Kenneth (8 Jul 1920–20 May 2002).

- **Lulu Needham (Feb 1889–unknown):** Lulu is shown as an eleven-year-old in the 1900 census, but no additional records have been found.

- **Cordie Needham (12 Feb 1891–18 Aug 1989):** Cordie married Marvin Fried (18 Nov 1892–28 Sep 1957). They lived in San Antonio, Texas. Their children were Marvin (24 Sep 1912–4 Dec 1992) and Myrtle (22 Jan 1914–23 Jan 1970).

- **Enoch Needham (18 Mar 1893–30 Apr 1970):** Enoch married Bessie Bigley (5 Oct 1898–22 Jun 1982). They lived in Fayette County, Texas. Their children were Edward Earl (6 Apr 1914–19 Feb 2009) and Lexie Estell (10 Jul 1918–2 May 1989).

- **Dora Needham (13 Aug 1896–9 Jun 1980):** Dora married Plez Raymer (28 May 1891–Feb 1975). The 1930 census shows them in San Antonio, Texas, with their son, Victor William (16 Mar 1920–23 Feb 2005). By 1940 they were divorced, both still in San Antonio.

- **Rabey Ray Needham (6 Mar 1900–9 Aug 1967):** Rabey married Blanche McMullen (1898–unknown) on September 11, 1918, in Fayette County, Texas. The 1920 census shows them on a farm in Fayette County, Texas. Rabey's World War II draft card indicates his 1940 residence as Houston, Texas. His and Blanche's daughter was Mildred Blanche (14 Jun 1919–27 Feb 1996).

- **Nancy Jane Needham (1850–1870):** Nancy was born in Angelina County, Texas. She married George W. Neering on March 1, 1866, in Angelina County. She died in 1870, leaving a young daughter.

  - **Mary Corine Neering (18 Feb 1867–3 Nov 1937):** Mary is shown living with her grandmother Susan in both the 1870 and 1880 censuses. Mary married William King Henderson (1864–1910) around 1885. Though she was born in Angelina County, Mary lived most of her life and died in Fayette County, Texas. Her children were Nancy (1886–1983), Pearl Mae (1890–1957), George Franklin (17 Jun 1896–23 Dec 1962), Rosa Lee (1900–1995), John Henry (1902–1973), Cody Mitchell (1903–1978), and William King Jr. (1910–unknown).

- **Francis "Frank" Needham (18 Jan 1855–20 Aug 1943):** Born in Angelina County, Francis Needham is listed in the 1860 census in the household of the parents of James Alexander, the husband of Francis's sister Mary. Francis was with his mother in Fayette County in 1870. The 1880 census shows him as head of the household with his mother, listed as Susana Needham, and his nieces. By this time, he was using the name Frank rather than Francis. On November 15, 1882, Frank Needham and Susan E. Henderson (1860–1904) were married. Frank and Susan had three children: Ida, Lee, and Susan. Susan Henderson Needham died the same year Frank's mother died. The only census showing the Frank Needham family was the 1900 census, which showed Frank, forty-six; Susan, forty; Ida, fourteen; Susan, eleven; and Susan's mother, Lucy Henderson, seventy-six. Lee was not listed on the census. Frank and Susan were operating a farm near Sublime, Lavaca County, Texas. In 1910 Frank was in the home of his daughter Ida and son-in-law Mark Seiver. Before the 1920 census, he relocated to the home of his daughter Susan and her husband, Elijah Gilcrease. It was in their home that Frank was found on the 1930 and 1940 censuses. Frank died in Colorado County and was buried in Cheatham Cemetery, Sheldon, Colorado County, Texas.

  - **Ida Needham (26 Sep 1883–31 Dec 1923):** Ida was probably born in Sublime, Lavaca County, Texas. She married Marcus Jodie "Mark" Sevier on February 6, 1899, in DeWitt County, Texas. Census data show the family on a farm in Colorado County in 1910 and 1920. Ida died in Sheridan, Colorado County, Texas, and was buried in Cheatham Cemetery.

    Their children were Allie Mae (14 Dec 1899–29 May 1976), Frederick "Fred" (6 Feb 1902–2 Nov 1989), Susan Grace (21 Oct 1904–13 Jul 1990), and Walter A. (21 Dec 1906–31 Dec 1929).

  - **Lee Needham (17 May 1886–22 Nov 1978):** Lee was born in Colorado County, Texas. He was living in Sheridan, Colorado County, when he registered for the World War I draft. Lee and Mamie Brown were married and made their home in Hallettsville, Lavaca County, Texas. The 1930 census shows Lee and four-year-old Oscar, but Mamie is not listed. The 1940 census shows Mamie Needham with daughters Marie and Kathline and son Monroe, but Lee and Oscar were not part of the household. The obituary for Lee and Mamie's daughter Marie lists Oscar Needham, Monroe Koehne, Cathrine Koehne, Harvey Koehne, and Charles Koehne as siblings of Marie. In 1950, Lee and Oscar were building contractors in Lavaca County, Texas. Lee's last Social Security address was Hallettsville. He died in Victoria, Texas, and was buried in Cheatham Cemetery, Sheridan, Texas. Their children were Oscar Lee (24 Apr 1925–3 Mar 2011), Marie (5 Sep 1928–1 Jun 2013), and Catherine (21 Sep 1930–).

- **Susan Needham (1889–1973):** Susan married Elige Gilcrease (3 May 1878–22 Dec 1941) in Lavaca County, Texas, on April 5, 1908. His name was spelled Elijah on some censuses, but Elige was the most frequent spelling on records. The family lived in Lavaca and Colorado Counties, Texas. Susan's father, Frank Needham, was living with them in 1920 and 1930. Their children were Elmer (25 Dec 1909–16 Jul 1982), Earl (17 Feb 1912–22 Apr 1999), Gertrude (1913–unknown), William Gregory (24 Oct 1916–20 Mar 1974), Harry Douglas (12 Jan 1924–19 Aug 2004), and Eugene (10 Oct 1927–9 Jul 2006).

Martha Colwell
(ca. 1825–ca. 1840)

Martha Colwell was shown as ten years old in the 1835 Mexican census. Family records indicate that she died in Jasper County, Texas. Wise County land records indicate that Martha died before the age of twenty-one, unmarried.

Caroline Elizabeth Colwell
(22 Sep 1827–7 Sep 1911)

Caroline Elizabeth Colwell was born in Tennessee. She and John McDonald Stovall (2 Sep 1822–11 Jul 1866) were married on August 22, 1844, in Angelina County. They are shown in the 1850 and 1860 censuses on a farm near Homer in Angelina County. John Stovall served in the Confederate army during the Civil War. He was murdered on July 11, 1866, near Homer. He was shot from an ambush as he and Caroline were returning home from a trip into Homer. Caroline married Thomas Surlock, a Methodist minister. She is listed as Mrs. Lizzie with the four Stovall children in the 1870 Angelina County census. By 1880, Caroline Stovall is the head of the household, with children Lizzie and William. Her occupation was listed as farmer. In 1900, she was living with her son Frank and his four children. She was apparently managing the household and caring for the children after the death of Frank's wife. Caroline died in Diboll, Angelina County, Texas, and was buried in Prairie Grove Cemetery.

- **Mary Lucinda Stovall (15 Apr 1846–25 Sep 1925):** Mary Lucinda married William Jackson Jones (1839–1866) around 1864. They had one child, Beulah Corine. Mary's second wedding was to James Chishum (ca. 1840–before 1900) on December 23, 1868.

The 1880 Angelina County census shows James, Mary Lucinda, and her daughter, Beulah. In 1900 Lucinda was shown in the home of her daughter. She is listed as widowed. The 1910 census shows her in the home of her grandson Claude Smith, his wife, and their infant son. The family is listed adjacent to Claude's parents. Mary Lucinda died in Lufkin, Angelina County.

- **Beulah Corine Jones (2 Oct 1865–19 Jun 1954):** Corine married James Monroe Smith (2 Jan 1858–31 May 1930) on December 23, 1880, in Angelina County. In 1910 and 1920 they lived in Lufkin, Angelina County, where he operated a livery stable. Corine continued living in Lufkin until her death. Their children were Claude Monson (16 Nov 1882–17 Oct 1918), Beulah (29 Feb 1884–18 Jul 1904), Bill Jones (12 Jul 1888–12 Oct 1938), Willie Lee (16 Dec 1892–1 Jan 1989), Noble (25 Jul 1895–Jul 1981), and Gordie (8 Dec 1899–10 Oct 1953).

- **Sarah A. Stovall (7 Dec 1848–3 Aug 1849):** Sarah was born in Angelina County. She was buried in Prairie Grove Cemetery.

- **George Cary Stovall (1851–1917):** George married Martha Smith (23 Oct 1854–4 Jul 1928) on February 28, 1972, in Angelina County, Texas. They are shown on the 1880 census on an Angelina County farm. They continued as farmers through the 1910 census. They were the parents of six children, but only two were living in 1900.

  - **Rhoda F. Stovall (10 Jan 1876–10 Apr 1960):** Rhoda married William Eli Boykin (12 Sep 1872–25 Mar 1925) on April 1, 1896, in Angelina County. They owned and operated a grocery store. Their daughter was Hexie (28 Dec 1896–19 Oct 1988).

  - **Edwin Hobby Stovall (21 Jun 1880–28 Apr 1954):** Edwin married Elizabeth E. Curtis. They lived in Houston, Harris County, Texas. The marriage ended in divorce, and their daughters lived with their mother and stepfather in 1930. Edwin died in Galveston, Texas. Their children were Gladys Adair (27 Mar 1911–19 Oct 1979), Mary Elizabeth (10 Oct 1912–7 Oct 2003), and Doris Louise (17 Dec 1914–9 Feb 1992).

- **John C. Stovall (17 Jan 1852–14 Oct 1854).**

- **Eliza F. Stovall (20 Aug 1855–7 Jan 1857):** Eliza was buried in Prairie Grove Cemetery.

- **James Thomas Stovall (19 Nov 1857–Mar 1944):** James married Nancy Jane Warner (11 Feb 1861–25 Dec 1957). They were dairy farmers in Angelina County, Texas. The 1900 census shows them as the parents of seven children, six of whom were living. By 1910 another three children had been born, but of the three, only Ruth was still living.

- **James Thomas Stovall (4 Jan 1886–6 Jul 1872):** James married Johnie Tucker (23 Sep 1886–15 Jun 1926) on February 26, 1905, in Angelina County, Texas. In 1910, they lived in Lufkin, Texas, where James worked for a wholesale grocery company. The 1923 Dallas City Directory shows them in that city. By 1942, James had moved to Calcasieu Parish, Louisiana, where he remained until his death. Their daughter was Nancy (ca. 1908–unknown).

- **Vida E. Stovall (8 Feb 1888–22 Dec 1982):** Vida married Robert L. Kirby (19 Feb 1885–3 Feb 1943) on November 17, 1907, in Angelina County, Texas. They lived in Jackson County, Oklahoma, in 1919 and in San Augustine County, Texas, in 1920. By 1930, they were living in Texarkana, Arkansas, where Robert was in the automobile industry and Vida was a hospital dietician. Both Robert and Vida were buried in Texarkana, Texas. Their children were Margie (16 Dec 1910–18 Mar 1995), Robert Little (17 Nov 1913–26 Apr 1993), and Nancy Jo (6 Oct 1917–Jun 1979).

- **Bessie Caroline Stovall (25 Sep 1890–28 Jun 1985):** Bessie married Ernest Webster Rutland (17 Mar 1886–30 Sep 1928). They lived in Angelina County, Texas. Their children were Jane (17 Oct 1916–28 Apr 2000) and Ernest (4 Nov 1925–18 Dec 2018).

- **Elby J. Stovall (25 Nov 1892–26 Jan 1976):** In 1930 Elby was living with his parents and working as a clerk in a gasoline station. In 1940 he was working on a farm in Angelina County. His death certificate indicated work in surveying.

- **Jewell J. Stovall (9 Mar 1895–5 Jul 1986):** Jewell married Frank Porter Sadler (13 May 1892–27 Jan 1992). They lived in Houston, Harris County, Texas, and in Fort Worth, Tarrant County, Texas. Jewell died in Angelina County.

- **Sam Jones Stovall (13 Dec 1898–2 Sep 1984):** Sam married Myrtle Irene Courtney (28 May 1899–24 May 1995). They lived in Lufkin, Angelina County, Texas, where they operated a tailor shop in 1930, but he was listed as a deputy sheriff in 1940. Their son was Sam Jones Jr. (4 Oct 1934–6 May 1992).

- **Ruth Stovall (1 May 1902–16 Dec 1998):** Ruth married Leslie Tatum (2 Nov 1896–10 Dec 1952). They lived in Angelina County, Texas, where Leslie worked as traffic manager in a foundry. In 1940, Ruth's parents and brother Elby were living with Ruth and Leslie. Their children were Thomas Franklin (17 Jul 1927–27 Aug 2015) and Joseph Leslie (17 Nov 1929–23 Jan 2014).

- **Nancy Melvina Stovall (Mar 1860–18 Jan 1946):** Nancy married Perry Welch (24 Jan 1851–Dec 1923) on January 14, 1876, in Cherokee County, Texas. In 1900, they were operating a farm in Angelina County, Texas. Nancy was listed as the mother of nine children, eight of whom were living. By 1910 they were living in Montgomery County, Texas, where Perry was listed as a carpenter. Both Perry and Nancy died and were buried in Montgomery County, Texas.

- **Fredrick Welch (ca. 1876–before 1900):** Fredrick is shown as a four-year-old on the 1880 census.

- **Clark Lafayette Dennom Welch (29 Jul 1879–7 Oct 1955):** Clark married Alice Anderson (31 Dec 1886–5 Aug 1973) in 1907 in Robertson, Texas. They are shown in the 1910 census of Liberty County, Texas, where Clark was a contractor for railroad ties. By 1920 they were in Harris County, Texas, and Clark was managing a sawmill. The 1930 and 1940 censuses show them in Rusk, Cherokee County, Texas. Clark died in Cherokee County and was buried in Liberty County. Their daughter was Crystal Rose (3 Sep 1908–5 Sep 1988).

- **Allie N. Welch (19 Aug 1881–13 Sep 1968):** Allie married Allen B. Kemp (5 Sep 1881–5 Apr 1946) in Angelina County, Texas, on June 22, 1907. They lived in Hardin, Liberty, and Montgomery Counties, Texas.

- **Ray R. Welch (20 Jun 1884–12 Jan 1943):** Ray married Devilla Ivy (22 Jun 1881–22 Jan 1947) on April 11, 1905, in Angelina County, Texas. They lived in Montgomery County, Texas. Their children were Clarkie Dell (17 Jul 1909–26 Dec 1996), Paul Cecil (2 Mar 1912–5 Feb 1982), Lucille (17 Jul 1913–31 Aug 1955), and Ray (19 Jul 1916–15 Nov 1995).

- **Timothy Collins Welch (20 Feb 1887–6 Dec 1966):** Timothy married Vashtie Walters (1885–1934) on December 25, 1912, in Harris County, Texas. They lived in Montgomery and Harris Counties, Texas. Their children were Samuel (7 Dec 1913–24 Feb 1980), Homer Dell (21 Sep 1916–18 Apr 2002), Helen (18 May 1920–Jan 1992), and Levy Perry (29 Oct 1923–15 Jul 1990).

- **Samuel Burch Welch (12 Sep 1889–27 Apr 1957):** Sam was single and living in the Montgomery County home of his parents in the 1920 census. By 1930 Sam and his mother were in the home. The 1940 census shows Sam as head of the household, which included his mother. Sam worked in the lumber industry.

- **Sadie A. Welch (16 Sep 1892–18 May 1975):** Sadie married Taylor Alvin Ford (26 Aug 1893–29 Nov 1953) in 1917 in Polk County, Texas. They were in Montgomery County, Texas, in 1920 and 1930. Taylor is listed as county constable in the 1930 census. Sadie was living in Houston, Harris County, Texas, at the time of her death. Sadie and Taylor's children were James (8 Mar 1918–28 Aug 2005), Geneva (19 Dec 1918–13 Sep 2008), Maurice Beverly (23 Mar 1923–18 Mar 2006), and Elton Gene (22 May 1928–25 May 1985).

- **Cecil Monroe Welch (1895–1969):** Cecil and Blanche Overton (29 May 1898–13 Apr 1950) were married prior to 1917. Cecil was working in an oil field in Liberty County, Texas, when he registered for the World War I draft. They lived in Jim Hogg County in 1930 and Webb County in 1940. Both Blanche and Cecil died in Webb County. Their children were Lex (11 Apr 1918–23 Jul 2003) and Virginia (6 Feb 1920–9 Feb 2019).

- **Hazel Welch (16 Jul 1899–13 Dec 1989):** Hazel married Ed James Burrow (1895–27 Oct 1940) on September 9, 1915, in Montgomery County, Texas. Their children were Edith (3 Oct 1916–13 Jun 2005) and Beatrice (5 Jan 1922–10 Jan 2008).

- **Elizabeth Victoria "Lizzie" Stovall (1 Jul 1863–1 Mar 1933):** Lizzie married Albion Brown Russell (12 Mar 1854–23 Nov 1936). They operated a farm in Angelina County, Texas. The 1900 census shows Lizzie as the mother of seven children, six of whom were living. An additional child, Albion, was born in 1904.

  - **Beulah Russell (15 May 1881–5 Feb 1916):** Beulah married David J. Cochran (1868–1910) on March 3, 1901, in Angelina County, Texas. The 1910 census shows Beulah and her two children in her parents' home. Her second marriage was to Frank Jones (ca. 1887–unknown). Beulah and David's children were Exie (31 Aug 1902–26 Aug 1986) and Stetson (31 Jan 1904–18 Feb 1978).

  - **Ida Russell (Sep 1882–25 Aug 1952):** Ida married Charles Fletcher McClure (22 Jan 1873–25 Aug 1956) in Angelina County, Texas. In the 1910 census, they and three children were shown in the home of Ida's parents. By 1920 they were operating a produce farm in Tyler County, Texas. Their children were Nobie (4 Jan 1902–1 Nov 1984), Brown (18 Jun 1905–21 Oct 1918), Flora (7 Nov 1909–31 May 1981), Doyle (15 Apr 1910–8 Jul 1985), Baine (11 Dec 1912–22 Mar 1935), Cleo (1914–3 Nov 1934), Ruby (24 Sep 1915–22 Mar 1985), Gay (3 Dec 1918–2 Jun 1997), Ruth (9 Oct 1921–7 Jan 1989), Willie Mae (May 1923–1 Mar 2009), and Thomas (9 Apr 1927–26 Sep 2009).

  - **Corine M. Russell (16 Nov 1884–4 May 1909):** Corine married William Martin Jones (1879–1954) on September 7, 1902, in Angelina County, Texas. Their son was William Martin (15 Jul 1902–14 Dec 1972).

  - **Callie N. Russell (26 Oct 1886–20 Oct 1918):** Callie married William C. Jones (19 Feb 1881–17 Jan 1956). They operated a farm in Angelina County, Texas. Their daughter was Mary Lucille (7 Dec 1908–11 Jul 1992).

  - **Brown Wood Russell (14 Sep 1889–3 Jan 1962):** B. W. married Sarah Margaret Collins (15 Mar 1893–31 Jan 1989). The 1930 census shows them in Lufkin,

Angelina County, Texas, operating a butcher shop. They were listed as owners of a meat market.

- **Nolia Chip Russell (3 May 1891–after 1940):** Nolia Chip married Ira John Hill (22 Feb 1888–14 Feb 1937) on July 23, 1914, in Angelina County, Texas. The 1930 census shows them living in separate boardinghouses in Lufkin, Angelina County, Texas. In 1940, Nolia was living in Orange County, Texas, working as a seamstress.

- **Albion Russell (3 May 1902–Apr 1992):** Albion married Jean Turner (29 Oct 1911–26 Oct 1997). They were operating a farm in Angelina County, Texas, in 1940.

- **William Franklin Stovall (21 Aug 1865–13 Nov 1935):** William operated a farm in Angelina County, Texas. He married Molly Thompson (1867–1893) in Angelina County, Texas, on October 4, 1883. Their children were Levy William, Virginia Victoria, Mollie, and Sam. His second marriage was to Alex Lula Jordan (ca. 1878–before 1900). Gussie was their child. The 1900 census shows William's mother living with him and his four living children. William and Sarah Young (9 Feb 1878–21 May 1916) were married on September 11, 1904. Their children were Ollie, George, Nobie, William Jodie, John Wesley, and Ester Bell. His wedding to Anna Johnson (ca. 1899–unknown) was before 1920. Caroline, Dale, and Mary Nannie were their children.
  - **Levy William Stovall (18 Aug 1884–31 Jan 1957):** Levy married Agusta Welch (23 Dec 1888–18 Nov 1961). They are shown in the 1910 census in Angelina County, Texas, operating a farm. They were divorced around 1921. The children of Levy and Augusta were Joseph Preston (9 Sep 1910–30 Jun 1934), Archie Paul (22 Jan 1913–2 Apr 1987), Thelma Jewell (4 Jan 1917–3 May 2004), and Myrl (23 Sep 1920–7 Jan 1990). Levy married Jewel Cloyd on October 2, 1926, in Harris County, Texas. The 1940 census shows Levy in the home of his sister Virginia in Angelina County, Texas.
  - **Virginia Victoria Stovall (May 1888–7 Mar 1972):** Virginia married Mitchel Thompson (1883–1933) in 1902 in Nacogdoches, Texas. They lived in Angelina County, Texas. Their children were Houston (28 Sep 1903–12 Feb 1997), Bulah (25 Aug 1905–22 Sep 1980), Azalee (ca. 1908–30 Mar 1918), William Hershel (19 Feb 1811–14 Mar 1957), Hobby Doris (30 Sep 1912–21 Feb 1978), and Evelyn (20 Apr 1916–15 Dec 1974).
  - **Mollie Stovall (Jan 1890–1938):** Mollie married John Thomas Johnson (24 May 1894–11 Mar 1976). The 1920 and 1930 censuses show them operating a farm in Angelina County, Texas. Their children were Opal (17 Apr 1913–26 May 1950), John Marcos (1 May 1922–4 Jul 1966), Alterby Ethby (ca. 1916–unknown),

Kester Denman (4 Mar 1924–31 Jul 1936), John Thomas (20 Jan 1929–23 Mar 1929), and Marjorie Jane (31 Jan 1929–23 Mar 1929).

- **Sam J. Stovall (1893–unknown):** Sam is not listed with the family in the 1900 census.

- **Gussie Lee Stovall (31 Dec 1897–23 Jun 1989):** Gussie married Floyd Benjamin Wright (18 Aug 1864–13 Aug 1967) in 1912. They owned a farm in Angelina County, Texas. Their children were Radford Franklin (21 Feb 1914–29 Aug 1962), Rachel (4 Jan 1917–14 Apr 1992), Gordie Lee (11 Apr 1922–29 Apr 1928), and William Rutland (10 May 1926–21 Nov 2008).

- **Ollie Victoria Stovall (17 Aug 1905–31 Jan 1977):** Ollie married Jimmie Lee White (31 Aug 1899–21 Sep 1959). In 1930 and 1940 they lived in Cherokee County, Texas, but they returned to Angelina County, Texas, after World War II. Their children, as shown in the 1940 census, were Jimmie Lee (24 Feb 1926–25 Dec 1972), William Henry (7 Mar 1928–1 Sep 2008), John Stovall (14 Jul 1931–18 Oct 2010), Charles Franklin (7 Jun 1934–2 Jul 2001), Ollie Kendall (5 Apr 1937–10 Jul 2008), and Herman Lewis (12 Aug 1938–2 May 2010).

- **George Stuart Stovall (5 Oct 1906–4 Apr 1973):** A lifelong resident of Angelina County, Texas, George worked in a sawmill. His wife was Mary Elizabeth Mosley (14 Jan 1908–24 Oct 1970).

- **Nobie Estelle Stovall (8 Jan 1908–17 Jan 1977):** Nobie married Floyd Frazor Frankens (29 Mar 1904–16 Jul 1988). Records indicate at least three children: Sarah Etta (19 Dec 1929–27 Mar 2007), Ruth (18 Sep 1932–13 May 1934), and Gilbert Lee (7 Nov 1934–16 Jan 1980).

- **William Jodie Stovall (1 Nov 1910–25 Jun 1988):** William Jodie served in the US military from March 7, 1944, to March 29, 1945.

- **John Wesley "Johnnie" Stovall (1 May 1912–21 Jun 2001):** John married Zanie Jane Mosley (1919–1978). They were living in Angelina County, Texas, in 1940.

- **Ester Bell Stovall (10 Oct 1914–8 Dec 1996):** Ester Bell is not shown with the family in the 1920 census but is in the 1930 census. Ester Bell married Orva Havard (1912–unknown). They are shown in the 1940 census in Angelina County, Texas, with four-year-old son K. C.

- **Caroline Stovall (28 Nov 1923–12 Dec 2006):** Caroline was born in Angelina County, Texas. She married Vollie Lee Lockhart (15 Nov 1921–24 May 2013). Caroline died in Houston, Texas.

- **R. Dale Stovall (16 Jul 1925–12 Aug 2001):** Dale married Wilma Ruth Fielden (1 Jul 1923–16 Sep 2011).

- **Mary Nannie Stovall (30 Oct 1926–29 Jun 2008):** Mary Nan married Adrian Marion VanCourt (21 Feb 1902–15 May 1974). They lived in Houston, Texas.

George Colwell
(7 Feb 1830–19 Mar 1859)

Born in Tennessee, George W. Colwell was a young child on the trip to Texas. His was the life of a frontier child without access to formal education. The 1850 census shows him as a farmer, with his mother, Mary, as the other household member. On January 27, 1852, George and Sarah Cochran (ca. 1838–June 3, 1881) were married in Angelina County. Sarah was born in Tennessee to Joshua Butler Cochran and Sarah McNeal. Only seven years after their marriage, George died, leaving Sarah with three young children. George was buried in the old Homer Cemetery in Angelina County. Sarah married Doby B. Stevens. They had two children, Jane and Charles. The 1870 census shows the three Colwell children; their mother, Sarah Stevens; and their half sister, Jane, enumerated in the household of Sarah's brother Joshua Cochran and his wife. Sarah died in Angelina County.

- **Mary Catherine Ann Colwell (1854–after 1930):** Mary was born in Angelina County. She married John Nicholas Thompson (10 Aug 1844–21 Jan 1925) around 1879. John was born in San Augustine County, Texas, to Henry Sewall Thompson and Margaret F. Matthews. John and Mary are shown in the 1880 census on a farm in Precinct 3 of Angelina County. By the 1900 census, the household had expanded to include their widowed daughter, Sarah, and her children. By the 1920 census, John was no longer farming but was postmaster of the local post office. The 1930 census shows Mary and her daughter Sarah in the household headed by Mary's grandson Seigle Scroggins.

  - **Sarah Margaret Thompson (23 Oct 1877–23 Jun 1948):** On September 24, 1893, Sarah married Robert Phillip Scroggins (5 Jan 1859–18 Mar 1900) in Angelina County, Texas. Robert was born in Sumpter, Trinity County, Texas. He died in Homer, Texas, and was buried in Homer Cemetery. Sarah and her five children moved into the home of her parents, where the children grew up and Sarah continued to live after the death of her father. Sarah died in Harris County after thyroid surgery. She was buried in Homer Cemetery. The children were Seigle Earl (30 May 1894–24 Feb 1984), Robert Webster (1895–28 Jan 1928), Mary Margaret "Mae" (22 Oct 1896–10 Aug 1984), Gordon P. (19 Dec 1897–9 Sep 1978), and Leah Catharine (5 Jan 1900–1992).

- **George Henry Thompson (10 Jan 1880–before 1900):** George was not with his parents on the 1900 census, and no additional records have been found. The 1910 census indicates that Mary Thompson was the mother of only one living child.

- **Alvin Thompson (17 May 1881–before 1910):** Like his brother, no census or other records have been found for him.

- **Samuel Houston Colwell (ca. 1857–unknown):** Samuel was the only son of George Colwell and Sarah Cochran. Sam is on the 1870 census with his mother and sisters. He is not with the family in the 1880 census, and no further record of him has been found.

- **Sarah Caldonie Colwell (1859–26 May 1931):** Caldonie is shown with her mother in the 1870 and 1880 censuses of Angelina County. She married Charles Bentley Smith (1855–before 1910) on December 21, 1890, in Angelina County. The 1900 census shows them in Center, Shelby County, Texas. By 1910, Caldonie, now listed as Donie Smith, was a widow heading the household with her three children. They were living in Timpson, Shelby County. The 1920 census of Timpson shows Donie and her daughter Verna as roomers in the home of W. S. Nelson and adjacent to Donie's daughter Vesta and Vesta's husband, Clyde Haden. Donie's son, Victor A. Smith, was in the Haden household. Donie was living with Clyde and Vesta Haden in 1930. Donie died from chronic bronchitis.

  - **Vesta Smith (16 Dec 1893–27 Feb 1968):** Vesta married Clyde Haden. Their last name is given as Huglin in the 1920 census but Haden on subsequent records. Clyde was a pharmacist working in a drugstore. No children were listed in the 1920, 1930, or 1940 censuses. Vesta died in Henderson, Rusk County, from a heart attack. Clyde survived her less than two years; he died on November 10, 1969. Both were buried in Memorial Gardens, Henderson, Texas.

  - **Victor Augustine Smith (24 Sep 1895–22 Apr 1940):** Victor and Lois Lucille Langhome were married around 1923. He was a lawyer in Henderson, Rusk County, Texas, when he died suddenly from a heart attack at age forty-four. The 1940 census of Henderson shows Lucille with Vesta (29 Sep 1924–23 Aug 1992) and Victor Augustas Jr. (27 Sep 1931–22 Oct 1956).

  - **Verna Kate Smith (26 Apr 1899–18 Aug 1977):** Born in Timpson, Texas, Verna was shown with her mother in the 1920 census. The 1930 census shows Verna teaching in the public schools of Jefferson, Texas. She was boarding with the Luther T. Dill family. Around 1939, Verna moved to Kilgore, Gregg County, Texas. In Kilgore she worked at Kilgore College and as a county tax assessor and collector. Verna died from a stroke.

SOURCES

"Anderson, Ann, to Bird Allen Shelton." US and International Marriage Records, 1560 to 1900. Ancestry.com.

"Anderson, Bob." 1900 US Census, Taylor County, Texas. Ancestry.com.

"Anderson, John C." 1860 US Census, Anderson County, Texas. LDS FamilySearch Library, Salt Lake City, UT.

"Anderson, M. V., to Wylie, J. J." Texas Marriage Collection, 1814–1909 and 1966–2002. Ancestry.com.

"Anderson, Margaret Jane, to Robert W. Wolverton." US and International Marriage Records, 1560 to 1900. Ancestry.com.

"Anderson, Mary A." 1880 US Census, Young County, Texas. LDS FamilySearch Library, Salt Lake City, UT.

"Anderson, Mary A." Texas, Find A Grave Index. Ancestry.com.

"Anderson, Mattie Lou." US, Find A Grave Index, 1600s–Current. Ancestry.com.

"Anderson, Miss Lizzie." Texas Death Certificates, 1903–1982. Ancestry.com.

"Anderson, Robert G." 1910 US Census, Mitchell County, Texas. Ancestry.com.

"Anderson, Robert G." Texas Death Certificates, 1903–1982.

"Anderson, Robt G." 1920 US Census, Mitchell County, Texas. Ancestry.com.

"Anderson, Thomas Isabel, to Jas G. Wofford." Texas, Select County Marriage Records, 1837–2015. Ancestry.com.

Angelina County Marriage Records, vol. 1 and vol. 2. LDS FamilySearch Library, Salt Lake City, UT.

Angelina County Will Book 1. LDS FamilySearch Library, Salt Lake City, UT.

Angelina Historical Survey Committee. *Land of the Little Angel: A History of Angelina County, Texas.* Edited by Bob Bowman. Lufkin, TX: Lufkin Printing Co., 1976. LDS FamilySearch Library, Salt Lake City, UT.

"Ashbrook, Dora." 1910 US Census, Dallas County, Texas. Ancestry.com.

"Aulsbrook, Dora." US, Find A Grave Index, 1600s–Current. Ancestry.com.

"Boykins, Siemon W." 1880 US Census, Angelina County, Texas. Ancestry.com.

"Boykins, Siemon." 1870 US Census, Angelina County, Texas. Ancestry.com.

"Caddel, A. B." 1880 US Census, Denton County, Texas. Ancestry.com.

"Caddell, Sarah F." US, Find A Grave Index, 1600s–Current. Ancestry.com.

"Caddle, Anthony." 1870 US Census, Denton County, Texas. Ancestry.com.

"Caldwell, A. J." 1870 US Census, Tarrant County, Texas. Ancestry.com.

Caldwell, Jack L. *A Personal Glimpse of My Line of Caldwells.* Macon, GA: FamilySearch, April 8, 1981. LDS FamilySearch Library, Salt Lake City, UT.

"Caldwell, Kizzie." 1870 US Census, Anderson County, Texas. LDS FamilySearch Library, Salt Lake City, UT.

"Caldwell, Sallie, to Alfred J. Wigley." Texas Marriage Collection, 1814–1909 and 1966–2002. Ancestry.com.

"Caldwell, Sarah." 1860 US Census, Angelina County, Texas. Ancestry.com.

"Cales, Melissa." California Death Index, 1940–1997. Ancestry.com.

Canterbury, Ruth Morris. "Colwell Family." In *Pioneer Families of Anderson County Prior to 1900*. Anderson County Genealogical Society. Anderson County Public Library, Palestine, Texas.

Canterbury, Ruth Morris. Letter to Mary Jo Kenny. October 7, 1987.

"Canterbury, Ruth." Social Security Death Index. Ancestry.com.

"Carothers, Melvina." 1910 US Census, Wise County, Texas. Ancestry.com.

"Cassels, Allie, to Fred Dearmond." Texas, Select County Marriage Index, 1837–1977. Ancestry.com.

"Chisum, J. M." 1880 US Census, Angelina County, Texas. Ancestry.com.

"Chisum, Mrs. Lucinda." Texas, US, Death Certificates, 1903–1982. Ancestry.com.

"Cochran, David." 1900 US Census, Angelina County, Texas. Ancestry.com.

"Cochran, Eliza Jane." US, Find A Grave Index, 1600s–Current. Ancestry.com.

"Colwell, A. J., to Nancy H. Hughes." Texas, Select County Marriage Index, 1837–1977. Ancestry.com.

"Colwell, A. J." Texas, Find A Grave Index, 1836–2011. Ancestry.com.

"Colwell, Ada." US, Find A Grave Index, 1600s–Current. Ancestry.com.

"Colwell, Allie, to Henry Cassels." Texas Marriage Collection, 1814–1909 and 1966–2002. Ancestry.com.

"Colwell, Allie, to Samuel Gilliland." Texas, US, Marriage Index, 1824–2017. Ancestry.com.

"Colwell, Andrew J." 1900 US Census, Dallas County, Texas. Ancestry.com.

"Colwell, Andrew Jackson, Jr." 1900 US Census, Dallas County, Texas. Ancestry.com.

"Colwell, Andrew Jackson." Texas Death Certificates, 1903–1982. Ancestry.com.

"Colwell, Annie, to G. J. Harvey." Texas Marriage Collection, 1814–1909 and 1966–2002. Ancestry.com.

"Colwell, Bernard." US, Find A Grave Index, 1600s–Current. Ancestry.com.

"Colwell, Bula, to W. F. Morris." Texas, US Select County Marriage Records, 1873–1965. Ancestry.com.

"Colwell, Caledonia, to C. B. Smith." Texas, US, Marriage Index, 1824–2019. Ancestry.com.

"Colwell, Caroline, to J. K. Lovelady." Texas Marriage Collection, 1814–1909 and 1966–2002. Ancestry.com.

"Colwell, Caroline, to John Stovall." Texas Marriage Collection, 1814–1909 and 1966–2002. Ancestry.com.

"Colwell, Edwin." US, Find A Grave Index, 1600s–Current. Ancestry.com.

"Colwell, Eliza Jane, to D. A. Cochran." Texas Marriage Collection, 1814–1909 and 1966–2002. Ancestry.com.

"Colwell, Ellis and Elmer." US, Find A Grave Index, 1600s–Current. Ancestry.com.

"Colwell, Elmer J." 1930 US Census, Bexar County, Texas. Ancestry.com.

"Colwell, Elmer Jones." Texas Death Certificates, 1903–1982. Ancestry.com.

"Colwell, Elmer." US, Department of Veterans Affairs BIRLS Death File, 1830–2010. Ancestry.com.

"Colwell, George Richard." US, Find A Grave Index, 1600s–Current. Ancestry.com.

"Colwell, George W., to Sarah Cochran." Texas, Select County Marriage Index, 1837–1977. Ancestry.com.

"Colwell, Hilary." 1910 US Census, Baca County, Colorado. Ancestry.com.

"Colwell, Hilary." 1920 US Census, Atoka County, Oklahoma. Ancestry.com.

"Colwell, I. C., to W. H. Malone." Texas Marriage Index, 1837–1965. Ancestry.com.

"Colwell, Jackson." 1880 US Census, Dallas County, Texas. Ancestry.com.

"Colwell, James C." 1880 US Census, Wise County, Texas. Ancestry.com.

"Colwell, James C." 1900 US Census, Anderson County, Texas. FamilySearch Library, Salt Lake City, UT.

"Colwell, James C." 1910 US Census, Anderson County, Texas, Precinct 5, District 21. LDS FamilySearch Library, Salt Lake City, UT.

"Colwell, James Calvin." US, Find A Grave Index, 1600s–Current. Ancestry.com.

"Colwell, James T." Texas Death Certificates, 1903–1982. Ancestry.com.

"Colwell, Jewell, to Edwin Glenn Thomas." Texas Select Marriage Records, 1837–2015. Ancestry.com.

"Colwell, John C." 1920 US Census, Custer County, Montana. Ancestry.com.

"Colwell, John M." 1880 US Census, Angelina County, Texas. Ancestry.com.

"Colwell, John M." 1900 US Census, Angelina County, Texas. Ancestry.com.

"Colwell, John." Texas Death Certificates, 1903–1982. Ancestry.com.

"Colwell, Keziah, et al., grantors." *Anderson County Deed Book P*, p. 799. Palestine, TX: Office of the County Clerk.

"Colwell, Mary Ann, to John C. Anderson." Texas Marriage Collection, 1814–1909 and 1966–2002. Ancestry.com.

"Colwell, Mary Jane, to Clark W. McNeal." Texas Marriage Collection, 1814–1909 and 1966–2002. Ancestry.com.

"Colwell, Matthew, to Caroline Worden." Texas Select County Marriage Index, 1837–1977. Ancestry.com.

"Colwell, Matthew, to Martha F. Wallace." Texas Select County Marriage Index, 1837–1977. Ancestry.com.

"Colwell, Matthew." 1850 US Census, Angelina County, Texas. Ancestry.com.

"Colwell, Matthew." 1860 US Census, Angelina County, Texas. Ancestry.com.

"Colwell, Matthew." 1870 US Census, Angelina County, Texas. Ancestry.com.

"Colwell, Matthew." 1880 US Census, Angelina County, Texas. Ancestry.com.

"Colwell, Matthew." Texas, Find A Grave Index, 1836–2011. Ancestry.com.

"Colwell, Melvina." Texas Death Certificates, 1903–1982. Ancestry.com.

"Colwell, Priscilla Francis, to J. L. Pickard." Texas, Select County Marriage Index, 1837–1977. Ancestry.com.

"Colwell, Rex." US, Department of Veterans Affairs BIRLS Death File, 1830–2010. Ancestry.com.

"Colwell, Robert L." 1910 US Census, Mangum County, Oklahoma. Ancestry.com.

"Colwell, Robert Lee." US, Find A Grave Index, 1600s–Current. Ancestry.com.

"Colwell, Robert, to Dollie Anderson." Texas Marriage Collection, 1814–1909 and 1966–2002. Ancestry.com.

"Colwell, Sam, to Lizzie Smith." Texas, Select County Marriage Index, 1837–1977. Ancestry.com.

"Colwell, Sam." 1930 US Census, Angelina County, Texas. Ancestry.com.

"Colwell, Sam." Texas Death Certificates, 1903–1982. Ancestry.com.

"Colwell, Sarah F., to John H. Lane" Texas, Select County Marriage Records, 1837–2015. Ancestry.com.

"Colwell, Susan, to Zachariah Johnson." Texas Marriage Collection, 1814–1909 and 1966–2002. Ancestry.com.

"Colwell, T. L., to Eddie Link Morris." Texas, Select County Marriage Index, 1937–1977. Ancestry.com.

"Colwell, Thomas L." 1940 US Census, Tom Green County, Texas. Ancestry.com.

"Colwell, Thomas L." Texas, US Death Certificates, 1903–1982. Ancestry.com.

"Colwell, Thomas Leroy." 1930 US Census, Tom Green County, Texas. Ancestry.com.

"Colwell, Thomas." 1880 US Census, Wise County, Texas. LDS FamilySearch Library, Salt Lake City, UT.

"Colwell, Thomas." Obituary. *Paradise Messenger*, December 3, 1880. LDS FamilySearch Library, Salt Lake City, UT.

"Colwell, W. J., to Catie Stanley." Texas, Select County Marriage Index, 1837–1977. Ancestry.com.

"Colwell, W. J., to Luella Parker." Texas, Select County Marriage Index, 1837–1977. Ancestry.com.

"Colwell, W. J., to Nora Stanley." Texas, Select County Marriage Index, 1837–1977. Ancestry.com.

"Colwell, W. R., to Mabell Corn." Texas, US, County Marriage Records, 1817–1965. Ancestry.com.

"Colwell, W. T., to Ada Thrasher." Texas, US, County Marriage Records, 1817–1965. Ancestry.com.

"Colwell, Wiley F." US, Civil War Soldiers, 1861–1865. Ancestry.com.

"Colwell, Wiley." 1800 US Census, Angelina County, Texas. Ancestry.com.

"Colwell, Wiley." 1850 US Census, Anderson County, Texas. LDS FamilySearch Library, Salt Lake City, UT,

"Colwell, Wiley." 1860 US Census, Anderson County, Texas. LDS FamilySearch Library, Salt Lake City, UT.

"Colwell, Wiley." 1900 US Census, Angelina County, Texas. Ancestry.com.

"Colwell, Wiley." Texas Death Certificates, 1903–1982. Ancestry.com.

"Colwell, Wiley." US, Find A Grave Index, 1600s–Current. Ancestry.com.

"Colwell, William J." 1910 US Census, Angelina County, Texas. Ancestry.com.

"Colwell, William Joseph." US, Find A Grave Index, 1600s–Current. Ancestry.com.

"Colwell, William R." 1930 US Census, Martin County, Texas. Ancestry.com.

"Colwell, William R." 1940 Census, Midland County, Texas. Ancestry.com.

"Colwell, William Roy." Texas Death Certificates, 1903–1982. Ancestry.com.

"Colwell, William Roy." US, Find A Grave Index, 1600s–Current. Ancestry.com.

"Colwell, William T." 1900 US Census, Greer County, Oklahoma. Ancestry.com.

"Colwell, William Thomas." Texas Death Certificates, 1903–1982. Ancestry.com.

"Colwell, William, to Polly Curry." Tennessee Marriage Records. LDS FamilySearch Library, Salt Lake City, UT.

"Colwell, William." 1800 US Census, Oglethorpe County, Georgia. LDS FamilySearch Library, Salt Lake City, UT.

"Colwell, William." 1850 US Census, Angelina County, Texas. Ancestry.com.

"Colwell, William." 1910 US Census, Martin County, Texas. Ancestry.com.

"Curry, John." 1800 US Census, Oglethorpe County, Georgia. LDS FamilySearch Library, Salt Lake City, UT.

"Curry, John." 1810 US Census, Rutherford County, Tennessee. LDS FamilySearch Library, Salt Lake City, UT.

"Dandridge, Myrtle Inez." US, Social Security Applications and Claims Index, 1936–2007. Ancestry.com.

"Davis, Gladys." US, Find A Grave Index, 1600s–Current. Ancestry.com.

"Dearmond, Alabama." US, Find A Grave Index, 1600s–Current. Ancestry.com.

"Dearmond, Fred." 1910 US Census, Angelina County, Texas. Ancestry.com.

DNA matches for Mary Jo Kenny. Ancestry.com.

Dunn, Sara Stuart. Letter to Mary Jo Kenny. March 20, 1998.

"Farmer, Michal Martin." *Oglethorpe County, Georgia, Deed Books F–J*, 1809–1820. Published by Michal Martin Farmer with a grant from the R. J. Taylor Jr. Foundation, Dallas, Texas. LDS FamilySearch Library, Salt Lake City, UT.

"Ferguson, Arabelle." US, Find A Grave Index, 1600s–Current. Ancestry.com.

"Ferguson, Belle." 1930 US Census, San Bernardino County, California. Ancestry.com.

Fisher, Marjorie Hood. *Tennesseans Before 1880*. Frontier Press, 1996. LDS FamilySearch Library, Salt Lake City, UT.

"Fralia, Murt." 1900 Census, Dallas County, Texas. Ancestry.com.

"Gilcrease, Elge." 1920 US Census, Lavaca County, Texas. Ancestry.com.

"Gilliland, Alley." US, Find A Grave Index, 1836–2011. Ancestry.com.

"Gilliland, D. C., to W. J. Townsend." Texas Marriage Collection, 1814–1909 and 1966–2002. Ancestry.com.

"Gilliland, Eli." 1900 US Census, Angelina County, Texas. Ancestry.com.

"Gilliland, James." 1870 US Census, Angelina County, Texas. Ancestry.com.

"Gilliland, James." 1880 US Census, Angelina County, Texas. Ancestry.com.

"Gilliland, James." 1890 US Census, Angelina County, Texas. Ancestry.com.

"Gilliland, James." US, Confederate Pensions, 1884–1958. Ancestry.com.

"Gilliland, Mary K., to Thomas S. Sayers." Texas, Select County Marriage Index, 1837–1977. Ancestry.com.

"Gilliland, Sam." 1870 US Census, Angelina County, Texas. Ancestry.com.

"Gilliland, Samuel Blaxton." US, Confederate Soldiers Compiled Service Records, 1861–1865. Ancestry.com.

"Gilliland, Samuel." 1860 US Census, Angelina County, Texas. Ancestry.com.

"Gilliland, Samuel." 1880 US Census, Angelina County, Texas. Ancestry.com.

"Gilliland, William Eli, to Henrietta K. Spier." Texas Marriage Collection, 1814–1909 and 1966–2002. Ancestry.com.

"Gilliland, William Eli." US, Find A Grave Index, 1600s–Current. Ancestry.com.

Goodspeed, Edgar J. *The Goodspeed Histories of Fayette and Hardeman Counties of Tennessee*. 1887. Reprint, Columbia, TN: Woodward and Stinson Printing Co., 1973. FHLC #0924074, item 2, LDS FamilySearch Library, Salt Lake City, UT.

"Haden, Vesta Smith." Texas, US, Death Certificates, 1903–1982. Ancestry.com.

"Harvey, George J." 1910 US Census, Angelina County, Texas. Ancestry.com.

"Harvey, George." 1900 US Census, Angelina County, Texas. Ancestry.com.

"Harvey, Martha Ann." Texas Death Certificates, 1903–1982. Ancestry.com.

History of Angelina County. Lufkin Genealogical and Historical Society, Lufkin, Texas, 1992. LDS FamilySearch Library, Salt Lake City, UT.

"Hood, Billie Margaret Tucker." US, Social Security Applications and Claims Index, 1936–2007. Ancestry.com.

"Ingmire, Frances T." Oglethorpe County, Georgia, Marriage Records, 1795–1852. LDS FamilySearch Library, Salt Lake City, UT.

"Ivy, Martha Ann." US, Find A Grave Index, 1600s–Current. Ancestry.com.

"John Colwell to Allie Leonar." Montana, County Marriage Records, 1865–1993. Ancestry.com.

"John Colwell." US, Find A Grave Index, 1600s–Current. Ancestry.com.

"Johnson, Susanna." 1860 US Census, Angelina County, Texas. Ancestry.com.

"Johnson, Susanna." 1870 US Census, Fayette County, Texas. Ancestry.com.

"Jones, Bill." Texas, US, Death Certificates, 1903–1982. Ancestry.com.

"Lane, J. H." 1860 US Census, Anderson County, Texas. Ancestry.com.

"Lane, John H." US Civil War Prisoner of War Records, 1861–1864. Ancestry.com.

"Lee, Rose." US, Social Security Applications and Claims Index, 1936–2007. Ancestry.com.

"Lovelady, Mrs. Caroline." Death Certificates, 1903–1982. Ancestry.com.

"Malone, W. H." Texas, Muster Roll Index Cards, 1837–1900. Ancestry.com.

Marriage Records, Hardeman County, Tennessee, 1823–1861, item 64. FHLC #1750734, LDS FamilySearch Library, Salt Lake City, UT.

"McNiel, Clark." Texas Death Certificates, 1903–1982. Ancestry.com.

"McNiel, Mary Jane." US, Find A Grave Index, 1600s–Current. Ancestry.com.

Medford, Gail, et al. "Angelina County, Texas, Cemetery Records, vol. 1." Lufkin, TX: Lufkin Genealogical and Historical Society, 1986. LDS FamilySearch Library, Salt Lake City, UT.

"Morris, Bula." Texas, US, Death Certificates, 1903–1982. Ancestry.com.

"Morris, Bulah." 1920 US Census, Anderson County, Texas. Ancestry.com.

"Morris, Frank Colwell." US, Find A Grave Index, 1600s–Current. Ancestry.com.

"Morris, Gladys Melissa, to Alvis O Davis." Texas County Marriages, 1817–1965. Ancestry.com.

"Morris, Inez, to Myles Wooten." Texas, US, Select County Marriage Records, 1837–1965. Ancestry.com.

"Morris, Ned." Virginia, US, Death Records, 1912–2014. Ancestry.com.

"Morris, Rubin." 1900 US Census, Anderson County, Texas. Ancestry.com.

"Morris, Ruth, to Edwin Canterbury." Oklahoma County Marriages, 1890–1995. Ancestry.com.

"Morris, W. F." 1910 US Census, Anderson County, Texas. Ancestry.com.

"Needham (Nedone), Frank." 1900 US Census, Colorado County, Texas. Ancestry.com.

"Needham, Enoch, to Lenor Taylor." Texas Marriage Collection, 1814–1909 and 1966–2002. Ancestry.com.

"Needham, Enoch." 1850 US Census, Angelina County, Texas. Ancestry.com.

"Needham, Enoch." 1880 US Census, Fayette County, Texas. Ancestry.com.

"Needham, Enoch." 1900 US Census, Fayette County, Texas. Ancestry.com.

"Needham, Enoch." 1920 US Census, Fayette County, Texas. Ancestry.com.

"Needham, Enoch." US, Find A Grave Index, 1600s–Current. Ancestry.com.

"Needham, Frank." 1880 US Census, Fayette County, Texas. Ancestry.com.

"Needham, Frank." 1910 US Census, Colorado County, Texas. Ancestry.com.

"Needham, Frank." US, Find A Grave Index, 1600s–Current. Ancestry.com.

"Needham, Nancy J., to G. W. Nerren." Texas, US Select County Marriage Index, 1837–1985. Ancestry.com.

"Needham, Nancy Jane." Texas Death Certificates, 1903–1982. Ancestry.com.

"Needham, Susana." Texas, Find A Grave Index, 1836–2011. Ancestry.com.

"Niederauer, Mildred Melissa." US, Find A Grave Index, 1600s–Current. Ancestry.com.

Paddock, B. B., John C. Anderson, and Robert G. Anderson. *History and Biographical Record of North West Texas*, vol. 11, pp. 565–566. Chicago, IL: Lewis Publishing Co., 1906. LDS FamilySearch Library, Salt Lake City, UT.

"Pickard, Joseph L." 1900 US Census, Angelina County, Texas. Ancestry.com.

"Pickard, Priscilla." US, Find A Grave Index, 1600s–Current. Ancestry.com.

"Rainey, Mrs. Frances Morris." US, Social Security Applications and Claims Index, 1936–2007. Ancestry.com.

"Russell, Alvin B." Texas, US, Death Certificates, 1903–1982. Ancestry.com.

"Russell, Alvin." 1900 US Census, Angelina County, Texas. Ancestry.com.

"Russell, Alvin." 1910 US Census, Angelina County, Texas. Ancestry.com.

"Russell, Elizabeth Victoria." US, Find A Grave Index, 1600s–Current. Ancestry.com.

"Sayers, Mary K." 1900 US Census, Angelina County, Texas. Ancestry.com.

"Sayers, Mary K." Texas, US, Death Certificates, 1903. Ancestry.com.

"Sayers, T. S." 1880 US Census, Angelina County, Texas. Ancestry.com.

"Scurlock, Thomas." 1870 US Census, Angelina County, Texas. Ancestry.com.

Seagler, Martha Matilda. "Heritage Consulting: The Millennium File." FamilySearch Library, Salt Lake City, UT.

"Sevier, Mrs. Mary." Texas, US, Death Certificates, 1903–1982. Ancestry.com.

"Shelton, Ann E." US, Find A Grave Index, 1600s–Current. Ancestry.com.

"Shelton, Bird." 1900 US Census, Greer County, Oklahoma. Ancestry.com.

Sistler, Byron, and Barbara Sistler. *Early Middle Tennessee Marriages*, vol. 1. Nashville, TN: Byron Sistler & Associates, 1988. LDS FamilySearch Library, Salt Lake City, UT.

"Smith, C. B." 1900 US Census, Shelby County, Texas. Ancestry.com.

"Smith, Caledonia." US, Find A Grave Index, 1600s–Current. Ancestry.com.

"Stovall, Caroline Elizabeth." US, Find A Grave Index, 1600s–Current. Ancestry.com.

Stovall, Caroline. "Statement on heirs of William Colwell, owner of land certificate no. 2674/2775 in Wise County." Given to W. J. Townsend, Notary Public, in Angelina County, Texas, October 12, 1858. Wise County, Texas, Court Records. LDS FamilySearch Library, Salt Lake City, UT.

"Stovall, Caroline." 1880 US Census, Angelina County, Texas. Ancestry.com.

"Stovall, Eliza F." US, Find A Grave Index, 1600s–Current. Ancestry.com.

"Stovall, Frank, to Sallie Pilley." Texas, Select County Marriage Index. Ancestry.com.

"Stovall, Frank W." 1900 US Census, Angelina County, Texas. Ancestry.com.

"Stovall, George Gary." US, Find A Grave Index, 1600s–Current. Ancestry.com.

"Stovall, George, to Martha Smith." Texas Marriage Collection, 1814–1909 and 1966–2002. Ancestry.com.

"Stovall, George." 1880 US Census, Angelina County, Texas. Ancestry.com.

"Stovall, George." 1900 US Census, Angelina County, Texas. Ancestry.com.

"Stovall, James T." US, Social Security Applications and Claims Index, 1936–2007. Ancestry.com.

"Stovall, James Thomas." US, Find A Grave Index, 1600s–Current. Ancestry.com.

"Stovall, John Colwell." US, Find A Grave Index, 1600s–Current. Ancestry.com.

"Stovall, John M." 1860 US Census, Angelina County, Texas. Ancestry.com.

"Stovall, John N." 1850 US Census, Angelina County, Texas. Ancestry.com.

"Stovall, Mollie." US, Find A Grave Index, 1600s-Current. Ancestry.com.

"Stovall, Nancy M., to P. M. Welch." Texas Marriage Collection, 1814–1909 and 1966–2002. Ancestry.com.

"Stovall, Sarah A." US, Find A Grave Index, 1600s–Current. Ancestry.com.

"Stovall, Thomas J." 1910 US Census, Angelina County, Texas. Ancestry.com.

"Stovall, Tom." 1900 US Census, Angelina County, Texas. Ancestry.com.

"Stovall, W. F., to M. S. Thompson." Texas Marriage Collection, 1814–1909 and 1966–2002. Ancestry.com.

"Stovall, William Frank." 1910 US Census, Angelina County, Texas. Ancestry.com.

"Stovall, William Frank." 1920 US Census, Angelina County, Texas. Ancestry.com.

"Stovall, William Frank." US, Find A Grave Index, 1600s–Current. Ancestry.com.

Texas, US, Compiled Census and Census Substitute Index, 1820–1890. Ancestry.com.

"Thompson, John N." 1880 US Census, Angelina County, Texas. Ancestry.com.

"Thompson, John N." 1900 US Census, Angelina County, Texas. Ancestry.com.

"Thompson, Mary." US, Find A Grave Index, 1600s–Current. Ancestry.com.

"Thompson, Mrs. Mary." Texas, US, Death Certificates, 1903–1982. Ancestry.com.

"Townsend, Devilla C." Texas, Find A Grave Index, 1836–2011. Ancestry.com.

"Townsend, William." 1880 US Census, Angelina County, Texas. Ancestry.com.

"Tucker, Inez Margaret." Texas Death Certificates, 1903–1982. Ancestry.com.

"Tucker, J. E." 1920 US Census, Wichita County, Texas. Ancestry.com.

"Tucker, James E." 1910 US Census, Harris County, Texas. Ancestry.com.

"Tucker, James E." US, Find A Grave Index, 1600s–Current. Ancestry.com.

"Welch, Nancy Mellvina." US, Find A Grave Index, 1600s–Current. Ancestry.com.

"Welch, Perry M." 1880 US Census, Angelina County, Texas. Ancestry.com.

"Welch, Perry M." 1900 US Census, Angelina County, Texas. Ancestry.com.

"Welch, Sam." 1940 US Census, Montgomery County, Texas. Ancestry.com.

White, Gifford. "The 1840 Census of the Republic of Texas." *The Pemberton Press*, Austin, TX, 1966. LDS FamilySearch Library, Salt Lake City, UT.

Whitley, Edythe Rucker. *Marriages of Rutherford County, Tennessee, 1804–1874*. Baltimore, MD: Genealogical Publishing Co., 1981. LDS FamilySearch Library, Salt Lake City, UT.

"Wigley, Alfred." 1910 US Census, Angelina County, Texas. Ancestry.com.

"Wigley, Sarah Geneva." Texas Death Certificates, 1903–1982. Ancestry.com.

"Wilie, Verna." 1900 US Census, Taylor County, Texas. Ancestry.com.

"William Colwell Deeds of Gifts." *Monroe County, Georgia, Deed Book C.* Dated April 15, 1829; registered February 16–17, 1830. FHLC #0164137, LDS FamilySearch Library, Salt Lake City, UT.

"Wofford, J. G." 1880 US Census, Erath County, Texas. Ancestry.com.

"Wofford, James." 1900 US Census, Fresno County, California. Ancestry.com.

"Wofford, Thomas Isabelle." US, Find A Grave Index, 1600s–Current. Ancestry.com.

"Wolverton, Margaret Jane." Texas Death Index, 1903–2000. Ancestry.com.

"Wolverton, Robert W." 1880 US Census, Limestone County, Texas. Ancestry.com.

"Wooten, Inez." Social Security Death Index. Ancestry.com.

"Wylie, M. V." 1910 US Census, Taylor County, Texas. Ancestry.com.

"Wylie, Mary V." 1930 US Census, Taylor County, Texas. Ancestry.com.

"Wylie, Mary V." 1940 US Census, Taylor County, Texas. Ancestry.com.

"Wylie, Mary Varina." Texas Death Certificates, 1903–1982. Ancestry.com.

"Wylie, Mrs. M. V." 1920 US Census, Taylor County, Texas. Ancestry.com.

Sources for those for whom only birth and dates are given were one or more of the following:

Death Certificates, US Find A Grave Index, or Social Security Death Index.

APPENDIX A

During and after the Civil War, descendants of Thomas Hanks in Anderson County, Texas, believed that the mother of Abraham Lincoln was Thomas's cousin Nancy. Family members' memories and records indicated that Thomas's uncle Abraham had a daughter named Nancy. Both of her parents died while she was young, and she lived with relatives. This was widely discussed within the Hanks family, and children were warned to keep the story in the family to avoid ire of many neighbors who strongly disliked Lincoln. This story was repeated verbally and occasionally in writing in several branches of the family through the early years of the twentieth century. This is the only thing that can be said with certainty about a family relationship to Abraham Lincoln.

A search for the parents of Nancy Hanks resulted in at least four possibilities:

- Lucy Hanks and an unknown father

- Lucy Shipley and James Hanks

- Joseph Hanks and Nancy (Ann) Shipley

- Abraham Hanks and Sarah Harper

Two books by Adin Baber support the claim indicating that the parents of Nancy Hanks were Abraham Hanks and Sarah Harper. This is the claim that supports the Anderson County Hanks family beliefs. Baber claims twelve years of research, during which he examined records for seven Nancy Hanks born in the 1780s and living in Kentucky at the time of the Lincoln–Hanks marriage. Marriage records eliminated four, and three were researched. Family records and the books by Baber indicate that Abraham Hanks and Moses Hanks were sons of Luke Hanks and his wife, Elizabeth. Nancy Hanks was the sixth of the nine children of Abraham Hanks and Sarah Harper. Moses Hanks and Agatha Dodson had eleven children, of which Thomas was sixth. Abraham and Sarah died in 1793 and 1792 respectively, leaving Nancy an orphan before age ten. Baber concluded that after her parents' deaths, Nancy lived with her aunt, the wife of Richard Berry. A relationship between Nancy Hanks and the Berry family is well documented. Richard Berry signed the marriage bond of Nancy Hanks and Thomas Lincoln as her guardian. Reports indicate that Nancy was living in the Berry home at the time of the wedding and that the ceremony was in the Berry home. Baber also noted that Nancy's daughter was named Sarah. Although Baber's conclusions seem very plausible, they are not the most widely reported identity of Nancy Hanks Lincoln's parents. The most frequently cited listing is of Lucy Hanks and an unknown father.

SOURCES

Baber, Adin. *Nancy Hanks of Undistinguished Families.* Kansas, IL: privately published by the author, 1960. LDS FamilySearch Library, Salt Lake City, UT.

Baber, Adin. *Nancy Hanks: The Distinguished Mother of a President.* Kansas, IL: privately published by the author, 1963. LDS FamilySearch Library, Salt Lake City, UT.

Johnson, Gladys Hanks. *Our Hanks Family.* Privately published by the author, 1965. Copy in possession of Mary Jo Kenny.

Paper attributed to Orena Thornton, see Appendix C.

APPENDIX B

Will of Alexander Kenny, dated September 15, 1795, recorded on September 20, 1797.

(An attempt was made to keep wording spelling and format as close to the original as I could.)

In the name of God Amen   State of S Carolina

I Alexander Kenny of Rockey creek Chester county S Carnler being very sick and weak but yet in perfect mind and memory Thanks be to God for the same calling to mind the mortallety of my body knowing that (not legible) appointed for all men once to die do make and ordain this my last will and testament that is to say primerlarlly and first of all I give and recommend my soul into the hands of Almighty God who gave it of my body I recommend to the earth to be burried in Descent Christian burial at the Discreation of my Executors nothing but at the general resuurection shall receive the same again by the mighty power of God And as touching such worldly estates as Wherewith it hath pleased god to bless me with in this world I give devise and dispose of the same in the following manner and form Viz. First I give and bequath to my son James Kenny all my Plantation that I now live on and likewise all my Plantation tools Likewise I give and bequath to my son William Kenny and deaughtor Isabella Kenny all my Plantation Joint equal shares alike in Waxaw Settlement Likewise I allow William Kenny at my son James's his choice of one grey horse or one black mare Likewise I Give and bequeath to Alexander McElwagon one colt to be at my son Jas chosing Likewise I allow Jas my large house Bible and for to purchase a Bible for Alexander Kenny gran son when he kneeds it Likewise I allow my son William Kenny my confessions at large of Boston's four fold state to Isabella Willison's mediations to my deaughter Ann Likewise all my body cloathes to my son William Kenny Likewise I allow all my cattle horses sheep and hogs and household furniture to be equally divided Share and Share between my Wife and my son James and deaughter Isabella and if any dispute arises in dividing to call David McCallor and John McDill to settle their disputes Likewise I allow my dear and loving wife Margaret Kenny full and free posession of my dwelling house during life or widowhood and to be maintained by son James sufficiently Likewise I constitute make and ordain my loving wife Margaret Kenny my supream Executrix likewise my sons William and James Kenny assistant executory and I do hereby utterly disallow revock and disannut all and every other former testimony wills legacies bequasts and Aeuctors by me in any wise before name will ds or bequathed ratifying and confirming this and no other to be my last will and testiment In witness whereas I have hereunto set my hand and seal this fifteenth day of Septr in the year of our Lord one thousand seven hundred and ninety five. Interlined before signed in the thirteenth part (at my son James

Alexander Kenny (seal)

Signed Seald & Delivered by the said

Alexander Kenny as his last will &

testament in the presence of us

David McCalla . Margaret Nixon   Recorded 20th Sept 1797

Garde Jmison

APPENDIX C

Paper on the background of William Curry Kenny, undated and not signed but attributed to Orena Thornton, granddaughter of William Curry Kenny. Original in the papers of Clarence Ray Kersey. Copy provided by Sandra McGeorge.

Grandma Kenny was of Scotch-Irish descent. Her father, Mr. Colwell being Scotch and her mother English. Her grandmother's nephew, A. P. Hill, was a Confederate General during the Civil War. Her grandfather Hanks was a first cousin to Abraham Lincoln's mother, Nancy Hanks, all being raised in South Carolina.

Grandma was born in Murry County, Tennessee, August 1st, 1830. Her father moved to Texas during the winter of 1835 and 1836, landed in St. Augustine County, lived there a few years and moved to Angekina County where she lived until she was 17 or 18 years of age. She moved then to Anderson County where she was married to Grandpa.

Grandpa Kenny was of Scotch-Irish extraction, his grandfather being born and reared in Scotland and the name there was McKenny, but there being a split in rekigion, some being Catholic and others Protestant, when his grandparents legt Scotland, they left the Mc there.

Grandpa's father was born in Scotland, but reared and married in Ireland. His wife was Mary Pollock and of a prominent Irish family, related to James K. Polk, the name Pollock being called Polk in America. James K. Polk's father was a brother to the father of my great-grandmother and was James Pollock, gentleman of Ireland.

Grandpa was born in Charleston, South Carolina, April 2, 1809. His father was killed in New Orleans during the war of 1812. His mother then moved to Knoxville, Tenn. There he grew up and was educated. He married Miss Emily Oldham who lived only three months.

He studied medicine and received his diploma at New Orleans. He moved from Knoxville to Jackson, Mississippi about the time of the Mexican War. He joined the army and was made captain of the Mississippi Rifles, fought in the battles of Palo Alto, Monterrey and others under General Taylor. After the war he moved to Louisiana and married Mrs. Elizabeth Calvin. Two children were born to them.

In 1850 they came to Anderson County, Texas. His wife died in 1851 and he married Grandmother in 1853, lived and almost raised a large family there. In 1874 he moved to Erath County.

(As written by Orena Thornton).

369

APPENDIX D

Family Background of William Colwell of Oglethorpe County, Georgia

The original Colwell immigrant was John Colwell. His wife was Mary Black. It is not indicated whether she was an immigrant or native born.

Their son Edward (ca. 1690–unknown) married Tabitha Hill. The children of Edward and Tabitha were as follows:

- **Mary (1717–unknown):** Mary married William Pettypool.

- **Sarah (1720–unknown):** Sarah married Stephen Pettypool.

- **Anna Covill (1720–1799):** Anna married Valentine Brown.

- **John (22 Jan 1724–4 Feb 1762):** John married Sarah Wilkinson in Virginia. They lived in Edgecombe County, North Carolina. They had four children:
    - **Mary (ca. 1752–unknown).**

    - **Sarah Wilkinson (ca. 1754–unknown).**

    - **William (3 Dec 1757–ca. 1830):** William married Mary Cartwright (ca. 1754–ca. 1800).

    - **John (11 Oct 1761–28 Oct 1839):** John married Elizabeth Spell.

William Colwell Sr., listed as William Barnes Colwell in several family histories, was born in Edgecombe County, North Carolina. He was only four years old when his father died, and he had several guardians appointed for him until he reached adulthood. He married Mary Cartwright around 1778 in Edgecombe County. They moved to Oglethorpe County, Georgia, before 1790. William and Mary had ten children. After Mary's death around 1800, William married Sarah Hornbuckle (1776–1810); they had one son, Richard Hornbuckle Colwell (1805–1868). After Sarah's death, William and Anna Stubblefield were married on November 17, 1818. William signed deeds of gifts to Anna, his children, and two grandchildren on April 14, 1829, in Monroe County, Georgia. These were filed on February 17, 1830; it is assumed his death was near the filing date. Anna survived him.

Children and Grandchildren of William Barnes Colwell and Mary Cartwright

- **Mary "Polly" Colwell (1780–1850):** Mary married David Davis in Oglethorpe County, Georgia, on September 25, 1802. Their children include David (1810–unknown), Martha (1813–unknown), Joseph Hopsom (1818–25 Aug 1878), and John H. (unknown dates).

- **Edward Colwell (1784–before Apr 1829):** Edward married Mary "Polly" Paine on September 22, 1812, in Greene County, Georgia. Edward died before April 1829. Edward's children were listed but not named in their grandfather's deeds of gift.

- **William Colwell (1785–1849):** William married Mary Curry.

- **Mathew Colwell (1787–unknown):** Mathew was living in Pike County, Georgia, when the 1829 deed of gift was written.

- **Glenn Colwell (1789–1863):** Glenn married Sarah "Sally" Moore on August 18, 1820. Their children include Martha Jane (23 Jul 1822–20 Oct 1904), William C. (ca. 1823–10 Sep 1863), John M. (ca. 1827–unknown), Mary E. (ca. 1829–unknown), Glenn O. (ca. 1831–4 May 1864), Robert B. (20 Aug 1834–29 Jan 1909), Sarah A. (2 Mar 1837–14 Jun 1909), Susan J. (ca. 1839–unknown), James B. (ca. 1842–unknown), and Henry (1844–8 Mar 1864).

- **Peter Colwell (1790–1849):** Peter married Sarah Corry or Curry (1792– - 1825). His second wedding was to Elmira Johnson on November 11, 1829, in Morgan County, Georgia. Peter's The children of Peter and Sarah were Robert (ca. 1812–unknown), William Barnes (15 Mar (1817–20 Mar 1900 - 1800), James Matthew (ca. 1819– 1815 - 1888), and twin daughters (ca. 1823–ca. 1830), -1829/30), and George Warren (20 Mar (1825–23 May - 1902), Glenn, David, Matthew, Peter, Nancy, and Martha.). A second marriage was to Elmira Johnson on November 11, 1828, in Morgan County, Georgia. One family story indicates that their stepmother (Elmira) persuaded a slave to drown the young twin girls with the promise of her freedom. The slave was hanged. Elmira was not reported to authorities, and she remained Peter's wife. The children of Peter and Elmira were Glen, David, Peter, Nancy, and Martha.

- **Susan Colwell (1791–unknown):** Susan married William Stephenson.

- **Dorthea Colwell (1795–1930):** Dorthea married Fail Paine in Oglethorpe County, Georgia, on January 4, 1813. Their children include Adeline (ca. 1814–unknown), Emily (1815–unknown), John M. (ca. 1817–unknown), William (1822–1902), Martha (1824–unknown), Almira (1827–unknown), Mary (1828–unknown), James (1830–unknown), Safrona (1833–unknown), and Sarah Caroline (1837–unknown).

- **Elizabeth Colwell (1797–1830):** Elizabeth married Abner Paine in Oglethorpe County, Georgia, on January 14, 1813. Her second marriage was to Jacob Woolbright prior to 1829.

- **Sarah Colwell (1802–1860):** Sarah married Wateman Blackman. They were living in Morgan County, Georgia, in 1830. Their children include Willis (ca. 1831–unknown), Gibsen (ca. 1836–unknown), James (ca. 1837–unknown), John (ca. 1838–unknown), Josiah (Joseph) (ca. 1841–unknown), Mary (ca. 1843–unknown), and Francis (Frank) (ca. 1846–unknown).

- **Richard Hornbuckle Colwell (8 Jan 1805–22 Sep 1865):** Richard married Harriet Louisa Waller. Their children were John Richard (1833–unknown), Sarah Emily (1834–unknown), James B. (1836–unknown), Martha (1838–unknown), Algeann (1842–unknown), Poker Dallas (1844–unknown), and Harriet (1847–unknown).

An interesting notation is found in the Oglethorpe County deed records. Dated October 10, 1800, Nathaniel Willis of Wilkes County indicates an agreement with William Caldwell of Oglethorpe County that Willis would make no charges of any kind for the maintenance of Caldwell's infant daughter called Kitty if Willis was allowed to keep the child, then in his care. The record was filed August 7, 1815. If this reference is to William Colwell (the spelling of the name is not always consistent), it would suggest that Mary Cartwright died in 1800, at or soon after Kitty's birth. In the nineteenth century, survival of a young infant whose mother died depended on care from a lactating female. The Willis family probably filled that role. Records show that Carolyn "Kitty" Willis, born January 7, 1800, in Oglethorpe County, Georgia, married Edward David Jones on May 10, 1819, in Maury County, Tennessee, and died there on January 10, 1859. This record suggests that Carolyn "Kitty" was the tenth child of William Colwell and Mary Cartwright. If this is true, Sarah, listed as the tenth child, born in 1802, would be the daughter of William and Sarah Hornbuckle rather than William and Mary Cartwright,.

SOURCES

Caldwell, Jack L. *A Personal Glimpse of My Line of Caldwells.* Macon, GA: FamilySearch, April 8, 1981. LDS FamilySearch Library, Salt Lake City, UT.

"The Colwells/Caldwells of the American South." Ancestry World Tree Project. Ancestry.com. Accessed February 15, 2004.

"William Colwell Deeds of Gifts." *Monroe County, Georgia, Deed Book C.* Dated April 15, 1829; registered February 16–17, 1830. FHLC #0164137, LDS FamilySearch Library, Salt Lake City, UT.

Caldwell, Lynn. Email to Mary Jo Kenny. April 23, 2008.

Made in the USA
Columbia, SC
20 July 2024

6033bb5a-f393-448b-b515-f8183a5a5698R01